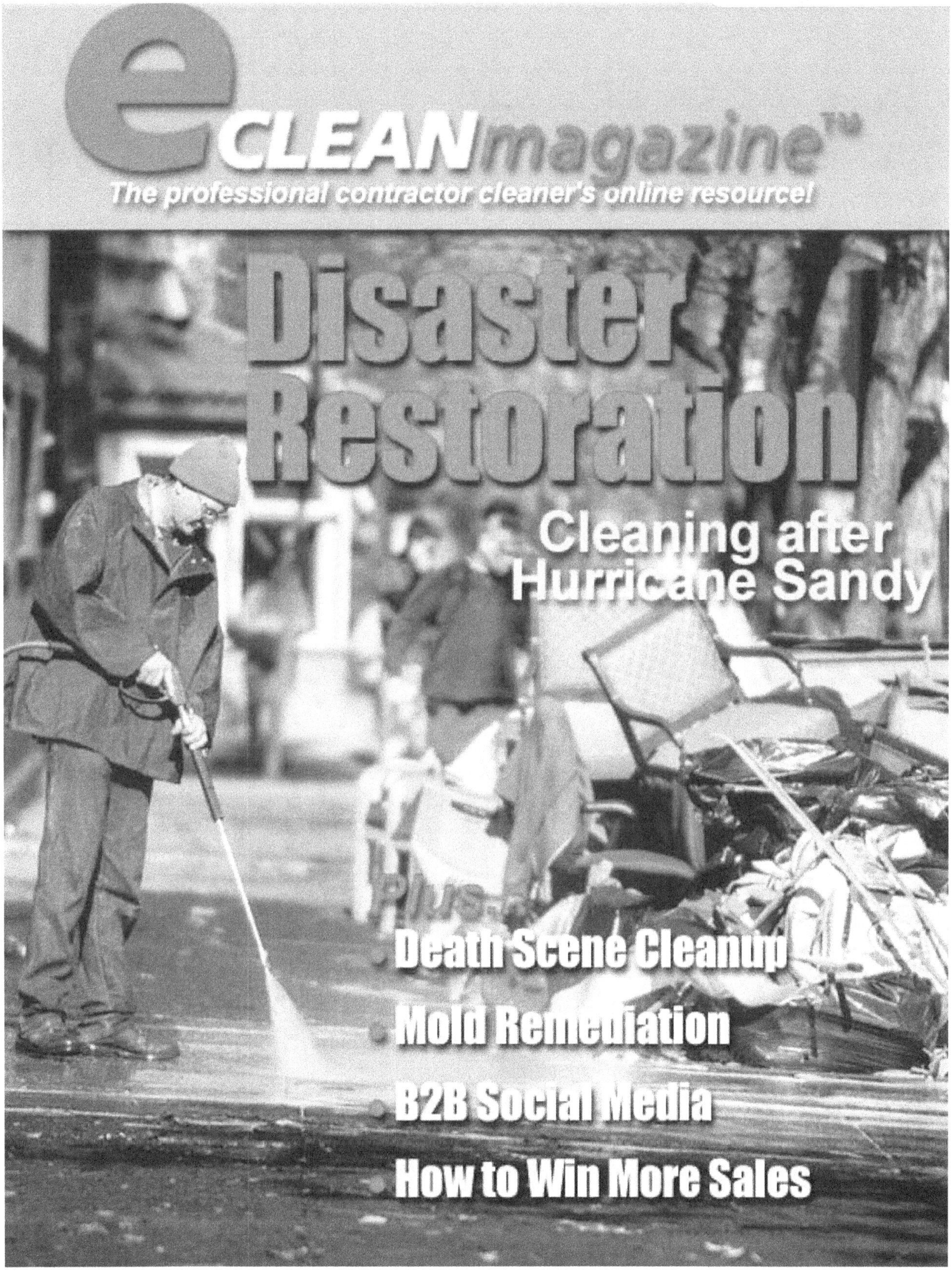

eCLEANmagazine™
The professional contractor cleaner's online resource!

Disaster Restoration
Cleaning after Hurricane Sandy

Plus...

- Death Scene Cleanup
- Mold Remediation
- B2B Social Media
- How to Win More Sales

 # 1.800.433.2113

Disaster Recovery

Quick Links - Pressure Washers - Surface Cleaners - Chemicals & Detergents - Cleaning Supplies - Parts & Accessories - Pumps & Repair Kits - Training Materials

DNB-1430 Degreaser (*)
A liquid cleaner formulated for cleaning heavy equipment, concrete, and vinyl. It combines emulsifiers, solvents and high alkalies to penetrate grease, and soil. 1 kit makes 55 gallons. Click Here

Canvas and Vinyl Super Awning Cleaner
A specially formulated blend of active deep cleaning agents to give the maintenance professional a powerful tool to remove even the most deeply embedded soils. Click Here

D-Vandal Graffiti Remover
A fast-acting penetrating semi-gel that removes paints, inks (including ball point pen), permanent markers, crayons, caulking, urethane sealants and more off most surfaces. This product eliminates tedious scrubbing to remove stubborn stains on surfaces by simply wiping with a soft cloth or using an all-purpose sprayer. Click Here

R-202 Concrete Cleaner
Cleans heavy grease and scuff marks from unpainted concrete and other alkaline water safe hard surfaces. Click Here

Adhesive Spray
An adhesive spray formulated for permanently applying fabric or paper products to a flat or slightly contoured surface. Click Here

Oil Absorbing Filters
- absorbs petroleum based fluids such as diesel fuel, engine oil, gasoline and transmission fluids but repels water.
- Made with a double skin, this boom won't tear or shed its filler. Absorbs up to 20 times its own weight in oil
- Strong skin
- Light weight
- Squeeze them out for repeated use.
Click Here

Vacu-Boom
The Vacu-Boom is a hollow, flexible tube five inches in diameter that is placed directly on a hard surface to form a downslope side dam or to completely encircle the wash or containment area. During use, the boom is connected by a vacuum hose to the portable wet vacuum recovery unit.
Click Here

BE-6000EXD 6000 W Diesel Generator
- Forced Air-Cooled, 4-Stroke Diesel Engine
- Max Output: 10HP @ 3600 RPM
- 6000 Watt Max Output
- AC Voltage 120/240V
- Fuel Tank Capacity 16L
- Continuous Operating Hours: 10.5 @ 50% Load, 8.5 @ 100% Load
- CSA Approved
Click Here

The Vacuum Sludge Filtering Systems
- The Vacuum Sludge Filtering System vacuums up wash water with an included 50 foot vacuum hose and runs it through a 200 micron dirt/sander filter. Then an automatic sump pump discharges the wash water through an included 30 foot, 1½ inch, hose to the sanitary sewer

There are two models available
- The VSF-55 (230 CFM, 110" static pressure, 55 gal. tank, 9.6 Amp sump pump, Two 13 Amp Vacuum motors @ 120V per vac motor, operational range 50 ft. with vaccum recovery concrete cleaner)
- The VSF-55-XL (270 CFM, 83" static pressure, 55 gal. tank, 9.6 Amp sump pump @ 120V & 13.5 Amp vacuum motor @ 230V, operational range 130 ft. with vacuum recovery concrete cleaner

Click Here

Wash Pit Sump Pump
An extreemely cost effective method for collecting your wash water before it enters the waters of the state.
- 7" diameter
- 115 volt
- 5 amps
- 8 ft cord
- garden hose discharge
- sump wash pit to 1/8 inch.

The Multi Tech Hydrocarbon and Silt Separator Pod System
The MuliTech™ Hydrocarbon & Silt Separator Pods are part of a complete system to prepare wash water for Sanitary Sewer Discharge in accordance with the EPA's Model Cosmetic Cleaning Ordinance. It is designed to be a modular system so that cosmetic power washing operators can augment their present equipment or purchase a complete kit. The first pod on the left is the Sludge Buster. This pod filters sludge down to 800 Microns, and injects air into the waste stream to aid in hydrocarbon separation and interception in pod 3. The second pod from the left is the Silt Buster. This pod filters silt smaller than 800 Microns down to 200 microns, and injects air into the waste stream to aid in Hydrocarbon Separation and interception in POD 3. The third pod is the Hydrocarbon Separator. It removes oil, grease and hydrocarbons. Pod Four is the Finishing Pod. It prepares your water for a recycling system so that it can be used again.

www.eCleanMag.com

IN THIS ISSUE:

14

THE DISASTER RESTORATION ISSUE

5 Surviving Sandy: Cleaning the Hurricane's Aftermath

10 Abrasive Blasting for Mold Remediation, by Nick Graomicko and Ethan Ward, InterNACHI

14 Death and Accident Cleanup: Helping Families in Their Time of Need

ADDITIONAL FEATURES

13 How to Win More Sales from Your Quotes (and Proposals), by Stuart Ayling

14 How Do You Measure Success? 2013 IWCA Conference & Trade Show, Feb. 13 - 16, by Mandie Bannworth

16 Sheila Smeltzer: A+ Pro Window Cleaning

20 Marketing to Commercial Clients Using Social Media, by Dick Wagner Disaster Restoration Consulting

16

21 Where You Park Makes a Difference, by Tom Grandy

29 The Anatomy of a Restroom, by Rick Meehan, Marko Janitorial Supply

29 Keeping Cool: Tips for Storing Pressure Washers in Winter, by Paul Horsley

COVER PHOTO
Used with permission by Damon Dahlen, AOL Huffington Post

---

eClean Magazine is published monthly

Publisher: Paul Horsley, paul@ecleanmag.com
Editor: Allison Hester, allison@ecleanmag.com

eClean Magazine
Box 262, 16 Midlake Blvd S.E.
Calgary, Alberta
Canada T2X2X7
www.eCleanMag.com

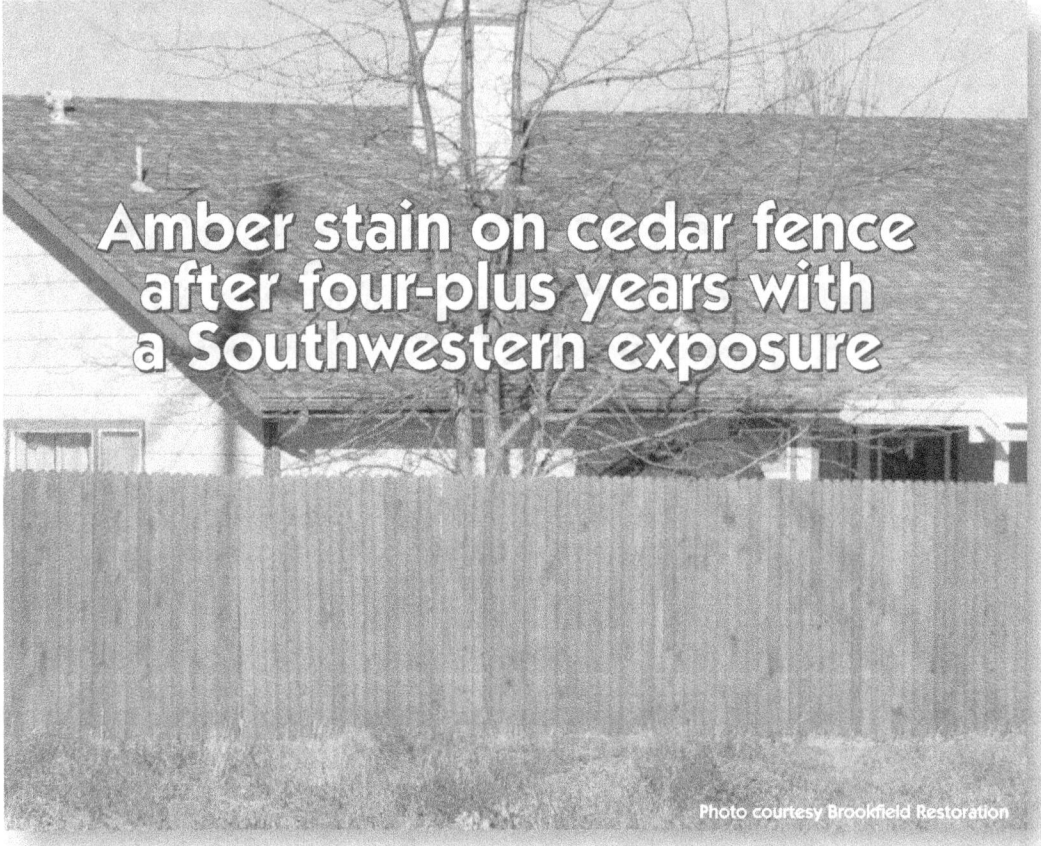

Surviving Sandy

Cleaning the Hurricane's Aftermath

by Allison Hester, Editor

Hoboken, NJ, Oct. 31, 2012: Man standing on the flooded street is talking to someone left in the building, ambulance car in the background

"Words can't even begin to describe the devastation," said Jim VanHandel of Innovative Pressure Cleaning.

"Imagine houses floating together and ending up in a pile. Not just a half dozen or so, but whole communities. Some areas are just totally destroyed. It's going to take years for them to recover."

From those with a few fallen limbs to those who lost everything, members of the cleaning industry have been impacted by the worst hurricane the East Coast has ever seen. And the cleaning industry has been instrumental in picking up the pieces – literally – in what will inevitably be a long, wearisome cleanup process.

Sandy's Wrath

Adam Griffin, owner of Island-Shine and Mobile Truck Washing in Long Island, NY, decided to stay home the night Hurricane Sandy was coming, as did most of the neighbors around him. "We've had scares before with other hurricanes where we were told to evacuate – then nothing major happened," he explained. "We all expected something to happen, but nothing big. It wasn't until that evening when we knew this one was different. We could feel it in the air."

The "difference" of this storm was huge for Griffin, who lost two homes, two cars, his work truck, and all of his pressure washing equipment. His entire hometown of Breezy Point – including his parents' home – was completely under water. "At my parent's house, they had six-foot swells going under the house," he explained. "A neighbor had water up to his second floor. We had other neighbors whose houses were on one block before the storm, but they moved two blocks over by the time it had passed."

New Jersey: People waiting in line to get gas after Hurricane Sandy

A number of homes in his area also burned, including the local fire station. "You'd see cars underwater that were on fire," he added. "It was surreal."

Once the storm passed, Griffin and his neighbors tried to survey the damage. There was no power, no heat, no water, no cellular service and no gas. In the meantime, people were pulling everything from the basements and first floors out of the homes and piling it in their front yards. "You couldn't even see the houses because there was so much debris."

Although his home suffered damage and he was without power for weeks, Griffin was one of the lucky ones in his area. His block soon became known as "the refugee block," as people who did not fair so well ended up living with Griffin and his neighbors. At one point, Griffin had 16 family members living with them. They also regularly had neighbors coming by to take showers and get a hot meal.

For others, such as Michael Pontillo of New Jersey Softwashing in Westwood, New Jersey, the aftermath was not as bad, but he still was without power for nine days. "No one was going to work. Schools were cancelled. Power was out to hundreds of thousands. A lot of businesses closed. It was a state of emergency."

Chris Lambrinides of Window Cleaning

Resource was also without power and unable to help his customers for several days. "We lost about two weeks of work, too," he adds. "Many of our staff couldn't make it into work, but we didn't have much work anyway. Everything was shut down. Clients were without power and the last thing on their mind was having their windows cleaned," he explained. He did, however, go out and help many of his customers remove gutters, clean siding and so on.

A fleet washing customer who lost a number of their trucks in the storm contacted Griffin. "They asked if I wanted to make a few bucks by helping drive some trucks in from other parts of the country," he explained. "I needed the money, but my family needed me more so I had to turn it down."

The Cleanup

As FEMA moved in and people began trying to put their homes and their lives back together, the need for cleaning contractors – for any contractors, really – was huge. For instance, FEMA contacted VanHandel because they needed contractors with pickup trucks to haul fuel to the generators that were being used to run the cell towers until the power came back on. So for two weeks, Innovative Power Wash's crew's sole job was hauling gas to the cell towers and to the first responders, 20 hours a day, for which they got paid an hourly rate. "It wasn't that much, but we didn't care," he added. "We just wanted to help."

As seen on the news, gas was unavailable in the area for over two weeks. Lines backed up for miles as cars waited to fill up their tanks as well as gas cans for running generators. Fights broke out at the gas stations and police and military had to be brought in. Looting began to take place. Generators were frequently stolen and cars were broken into for their gas.

Lambrinides went so far as to make one of his employee's sole responsibility to drive two hours away to Pennsylvania to fill up his trucks and fuel tanks, return to New Jersey, then do it again.

Ed Thompson of Thompson Roof Cleaning, who experienced near total loss of his vacation properties in the Barrier Island, Mantoloking,

New York: Debris and broken fence near flooded and damaged house after Hurricane Sandy on Manhattan Beach on November 8, 2012, Brooklyn, NY

NJ (see sidebar and video), started blogging promos for emergency roof tarping the day before the storm started. "Within six hours, our blog post made it to Google's front page and we received our first call at midnight," he explained. "We dove right in."

"The immediate need that we saw was helping people make the best out of what they had left," adds Michael Pontillo of New Jersey Soft Washing in Westwood, NJ, who was without power for nine days himself. People came out of the woodwork seeking contractors. Making the living space in their house usable. Pumping out water. Removing damaged contents. Contacting insurance agents.

http://www.youtube.com/watch?v=gC_HWzneN8c&feature=player_embedded

This video was made by Ed Thompson of Thompson Roof Cleaning and Pressure Washing shortly after Hurricane Sandy hit his vacation home.

eClean Magazine

Flooded car removal. Shutting off utilities to prevent a problem if the power came back on. Helping out the neighbors or the elderly lady on the street."

Within a couple of weeks, VanHandel was contacted by Servpro to help with pressure washing projects in the badly damaged Long Beach Island area. "They didn't have any power or water, so we had to go out and buy trailers and water tanks so we could haul our own water in," he added.

Because of looting on the island, VanHandel and his crew had to stop at check points where they had to actually leave their licenses and registration. They got their paperwork back on the way out after the authorities checked their vehicles for any stolen goods.

VanHandel started out by cleaning the mud from the floors of a number of fire departments. "Then we started helping the people out," he added. "They would see us working and come ask if we could clean and sanitize their basements."

Griffin, who again has been in the middle of the worst areas, has had to make do with a "Home Depot special" after losing his quality Hydro Tek machines in the storm. The problem he is still finding with cleaning and sanitizing is that the tides roll in each day and the moisture issues start all over again.

"It's like the movie *Ground Hog's Day*," he laughed. "One day just leads to the next, and you know you'll have to just figure it out later."

Seeing the Bright Side

As much of the northeast is getting cleaned up and back to normal, there are people impacted by the storm without power or without homes. VanHandel said early on he saw colonies of people in tents, with nowhere else to go. Griffin's father-in-law did not get power on until December 12. Some areas may not get power again for months, and many homes will never be restored.

Yet despite the surrealness of the experience, there have been some good things to come out of Sandy. "You saw a sense of community that was unmatched," explains Pontillo.

Griffin agreed, saying that it is that

sense of community that has made the storm's aftermath manageable. "I've learned that there are still good people in the world," he adds. "There have been lots of groups – the American Red Cross, Habitat for Humanity, the Army and Marines, church groups and more – that have come out to help us, mostly from the goodness of their hearts." He laughed, adding that he never imagined he'd be waiting in line all day for the Red Cross to give him a meal. "It gives you a real sense of what's important."

He adds, too, that once the power came back on and he was able to check his email, he saw that several industry members had sent him notes to let him know they were thinking about him. "That made me feel good," he adds.

All those involved with the cleanup agreed that the work was not about the money as much as it was helping others. "Some people can pay and wait for insurance checks. Some can't pay so you wait for insurance. The money is ok, but not like residential power washing wages," said Pontillo. "I find it very rewarding to know that we helped someone take a big step at getting back on their feet and helping them move on in the healing process."

New York City: In the aftermath of Hurricane Sandy a utility company work crew and truck seen in a water extracting operation from underground flooded electrical and communication spaces in the Lower Manhattan Financial District.

Abrasive Blasting for Mold Remediation

by Nick Gromicko and Ethan Ward, International Association of Certified Home Inspectors (InterNACHI), www.NACHI.org

Health concerns related to the growth of mold in the home have been featured heavily in the news. Problems ranging from itchy eyes, coughing and sneezing to serious allergic reactions, asthma attacks, and even the possibility of permanent lung damage can all be caused by mold, which can be found growing in the home, given the right conditions.

All that is needed for mold to grow is moisture, oxygen, a food source, and a surface to grow on. Mold spores are commonly found naturally in the air. If spores land on a wet or damp spot indoors and begin growing, they will lead to problems. Molds produce allergens, irritants and, in some cases, potentially toxic substances called mycotoxins. Inhaling or touching mold or mold spores may cause allergic reactions in sensitive individuals. Allergic responses include hay fever-type symptoms, such as sneezing, runny nose, red eyes, and skin rash (dermatitis).

Allergic reactions to mold are common. They can be immediate or delayed. Molds can also trigger asthma attacks in people with asthma who are allergic to mold. In addition, mold exposure can irritate the eyes, skin, nose, throat and lungs of both mold-allergic and non-allergic people.

As more is understood about the health issues related to mold growth in interior environments, new methods for mold assessment and remediation are being put into practice. Mold assessment and mold remediation are techniques used in occupational health. Mold assessment is the process of identifying the location and extent of the mold hazard in a structure. Mold remediation is the process of cleanup and/or removal of mold from an indoor environment. Mold remediation is usually conducted by a company with experience in construction, demolition, cleaning, airborne-particle containment-control, and the use of special equipment to protect workers and building occupants from contaminated or irritating dust and organic debris. A new method that is gaining traction in this area is abrasive blasting.

Abrasive Blasting

The first step in combating mold growth is not to allow for an environment that is conducive to its growth in the first place. Controlling moisture and assuring that standing water from leaks or floods is eliminated

are the most important places to start. If mold growth has already begun, the mold must be removed completely, and any affected surfaces must be cleaned or repaired. Traditional methods for remediation have been slow and tedious, often involving copious amounts of hand-scrubbing and sanding. Abrasive blasting is a new technique that is proving to be less tedious and time-consuming, while maintaining a high level of effectiveness.

Abrasive blasting is a process for cleaning or finishing objects by using an air-blast or centrifugal wheel that throws abrasive particles against the surface of the work pieces. Sand, dry ice and corncobs are just some of the different types of media used in blasting. For the purposes of mold remediation, sodium bicarbonate (baking soda) and dry ice are the media commonly used.

Benefits of Abrasive Blasting

Abrasive (or "media") blasting provides some distinct advantages over traditional techniques of mold remediation. In addition to eliminating much of the tedious labor involved in scrubbing and sanding by hand, abrasive blasting is extremely useful for cleaning irregular and hard-to-reach surfaces. Surfaces that have cross-bracing or bridging can be cleaned more easily, as well as areas such as the bottom of a deck, where nails may be protruding. Areas that are difficult to access, such as attics and crawlspaces, can also be cleaned more easily with abrasive blasting than by traditional methods. The time saved is also an advantage, and the typical timeframe for completion of a mold remediation project can often be greatly reduced by utilizing abrasive blasting.

Soda-Blasting

Soda-blasting is a type of abrasive blasting that utilizes sodium bicarbonate as the medium propelled by compressed air. One of the earliest and most widely publicized uses of soda-blasting was on the restoration of the Statue of Liberty. In May of 1982, President Ronald Reagan appointed Lee Iacocca to head up a private-sector effort for the project. Fundraising began for the $87 million restoration under a public-private partnership between the National

Park Service and The Statue of Liberty-Ellis Island Foundation, Inc. After extensive work that included the use of soda-blasting, the restored monument re-opened to the public on July 5, 1986, during Liberty Weekend, which celebrated the statue's centennial.

The baking soda used in soda-blasting is soft but angular, appearing knife-like under a microscope. The crystals are manufactured in state-of-the-art facilities to ensure that the right size and shape are consistently produced. Baking soda is water-soluble, with a pH near neutral. Baking-soda abrasive blasting effectively removes mold while minimizing damage to the underlying surface (i.e., wood, PVC, modern wiring, ductwork, etc.). When using the proper equipment setup (correct nozzles, media regulators, hoses, etc.) and technique (proper air flow, pressure, angle of attack, etc.), the process allows for fast and efficient removal of mold, with a minimum of damage, waste and cleanup. By using a soda blaster with the correct-size nozzle, the amount of baking soda used is minimized. Minimal baking soda means better visibility while working, and less cleanup afterward.

Dry-Ice Blasting

Dry ice is solidified carbon dioxide that, at -78.5° C and ambient pressure, changes directly into a gas as it absorbs heat. Dry ice pellets are made by taking liquid carbon dioxide (CO_2) from a pressurized storage tank and expanding it at ambient pressure to produce snow. The snow is then compressed through a die to make hard pellets. The pellets are readily available from most dry ice suppliers nationwide. For dry-ice blasting, the standard size used is 1/8-inch, high-density dry ice pellets.

The dry-ice blasting process includes three phases, the first of which is energy transfer. Energy transfer works when dry ice pellets are propelled out of the blasting gun at supersonic speed and impact the surface. The energy transfer helps to knock mold off the surface being cleaned, with little or no damage.

The freezing effect of the dry ice pellets hitting the mold creates the second phase, which is micro-thermal shock, caused by the dry ice's temperature of -79° C, between the mold and the contaminated surface. This phase isn't as much a factor in the removal of mold as it is for removing resins, oils, waxes, food particles, and other contaminants and debris. For these types of substances, the thermal shock causes cracking and delaminating of the contaminant, furthering the elimination process.

The final phase is gas pressure, which happens when the dry ice pellets explode on impact. As the pellets warm, they convert to CO_2 gas, generating a volume expansion of 400 to 800 times. The rapid gas expansion underneath the mold forces it off the surface.

HEPA Vacuuming

A HEPA vacuum is a vacuum cleaner with a high-efficiency particulate air (or HEPA) filter through which the contaminated air flows. HEPA filters, as defined by the U.S. Department of Energy's standard adopted by most American industries, remove at least 99.97% of airborne particles that are as small as 0.3 micrometers (μm) in diameter. HEPA vacuuming is necessary in conjunction with blasting for complete mold removal.

While abrasive blasting with either baking soda or dry ice is an effective technique, remediation will not be complete until HEPA filtering or vacuuming has been done. Abrasive blasting removes mold from contaminated surfaces, but it also causes the mold spores to become airborne again. The spores can cover the ground and the surfaces that have already been cleaned. So, the mold spores need to be removed by HEPA filters. Additionally, while some remediation companies claim that there will be no blasting media to remove after cleaning, especially with the dry-ice method, there will be at least a small amount of visible debris left by the blasting that must be removed before HEPA vacuuming can occur. HEPA vacuuming removes all invisible contaminants from surfaces and the surrounding air. When HEPA vacuuming is completed, samples at the previously contaminated areas should be re-tested to ensure that no mold or mold spores remain.

Abrasive blasting using dry ice or baking soda, combined with HEPA-filter vacuuming, is an effective method for mold remediation. InterNACHI inspectors who offer ancillary mold inspection services should be aware of the benefits and applications of this technique adapted for remediating mold in home.

Southside Equipment Inc.
Pressure Washers, Generators, Chemicals
www.Pressurewasherky.us
502-231-6506   888-243-6506

Panel Bright brushless truck wash
Big Red powdered truck wash
Aluma Bright HD brightener
Super Crete Relief safe concrete remover
Super Spray Wax superior water beading
F102 polished aluminum cleaner

How to Win More Sales From Your Quotes (and Proposals).

by Stuart Ayling

You've discussed the situation with your prospect. You have the information you need. Now it's time to prepare your quote or proposal.

You spend time writing-up and reviewing your quote, being sure to address the key requirements discussed with your prospect. You've invested time, effort and money in getting to this point.

What do you do next? How do you communicate your quote to maximize sales?

Practices you should avoid:

- Sending the quote by email, because you don't have time to talk with the prospect.
- Not calling to see if the prospect has received or reviewed the quote.
- Believing the prospect will read (and fully understand) the quote.

Let's face it… in many cases the prospect will have additional questions about the quote, or may need to have some aspects explained to them so they can clearly understand how you will provide your product or service. But they are busy too and may say they don't want any further contact.

Prospects will skip to the price.

However, if you don't explain your recommendation to the client, they will usually go straight to the price and skip the main contents.

Plus, most times once the prospect has your quote they will be reluctant to meet with you again because they will feel as though they now have all the information they need. It is extra difficult to get them to schedule time with you.

The danger here is that you are the expert in what you provide. If you don't explain your quote you cannot expect your prospect to have the same degree of insight as you do about how you will deliver the outcome.

Tips for success:

So here are some tips to ensure your prospect fully appreciates how you are proposing to help them.

(1) In your quote include a section on "Our Understanding of Your Requirements." In this section you re-state the key points identified during your discussion with the prospect. Be sure to include details so they prospect knows you understand exactly what they need.

(2) Position the section on your price within the quote after you have explained the benefits or outcomes. Do not place the price as the very last item or section. (Typically pricing is on the last page and people flick over to the last page looking for it.)

(3) During your sales discussion let your prospect know you will require a separate time to discuss the recommendations included in the quote. If possible, set an appointment for the quote discussion before you prepare the quote. Your objective is to get a commitment from the client to discuss the quote.

(4) Take the quote to your prospect and deliver it in person at the agreed meeting. At this meeting take your prospect through the quote section by section. Don't just hand over the quote and wait for questions.

Your objectives in using this approach are to:

- Remain in control of the information flow;
- Ensure your prospect does fully understand what you propose; and
- Establish yourself as a true professional by helping the prospect with their decision.

Emailing the quote and not following up because you are "too busy" is a wasted opportunity. Instead, be proactive and win more sales.

Stuart Ayling is Chief Sales Strategist at Marketing Nous. He specializes in sales improvement initiatives for companies that sell services or technical products. For additional resources visit the online library and sign up for the free newsletter at www.marketingnous.com.au.

by Mandie Bannworth

"I figured out years ago that I always pick up enough information for my business at conventions to more than cover the cost of attending. I have attended the IWCA convention seven times, for example, and always came home and made significant improvements. If any business owner is deciding whether or not to attend the next meeting, remember that staying ahead of the curve in the service business means knowing more than the next guy. This is one of the best places to get that kind of information." - Pete Marentay, Sun Brite Supply

How do you measure success?
2013 IWCA Convention & Trade Show
Feb 13-16, 2013

Professionals in the contract cleaning business not only need to know the most efficient methods for performing their specialty services, but also understand how to be a marketing guru, a web designer and a savvy business manager. With the evolution of technology, the success of a business is based on more than just the skill of employees and customer service; it's now contingent on the entire package that is delivered to the client and prospective client base.

Entrepreneurs are continually expanding their repertoire through various methods. However, the most successful owners know that capitalizing on resources and the knowledge gained from networking with industry peers can often be what turns a fledgling business into a profitable career. That is why the International Window Cleaning Association's (IWCA) Annual Convention & Trade Show, Feb. 13-16, 2013 in St. Pete Beach, Fla. is the premier industry event for those who dream of building something great.

Lynne Fiscelli, Pane View Window Cleaning LLC, first learned about the IWCA event while researching methods to improve her Michigan window cleaning business.

"My husband and I attended the IWCA Convention & Trade Show in 2012, and it was time and money well invested." Fiscelli added, "The absolute most valuable part of the event was the face-to-face networking with other business owners who have taken their business where we want to take ours."

Following the convention, Fiscelli reported that she integrated many of the techniques she learned at the convention into her day-to-day business which resulted in her company's most profitable year to date.

While many business owners use the convention to learn from others how to add on services to their businesses, there are many in other areas of the contract cleaning industry that have decided to expand their businesses by adding on window cleaning services. Gabor Viczko, Nevada Professional Inc., has been in the carpet cleaning business for more than 14 years, servicing commercial and residential properties. Viczko found that after hiring several employees, it was becoming difficult to make decent profits since his overhead increased substantially. After talking to others in the industry, he decided to look into expanding his services.

"I was advised by a friend that I should expand my service to include window cleaning, as it would be VERY easy to market this service to my current clientele," Viczko said. He added that his first initiation into the business was the IWCA convention. "I attended my first IWCA Annual Convention in 2004 and became educated in the window cleaning business. I was able to network with dozens of other companies who shared with me countless ideas on how to start up my new window cleaning venture. The IWCA has been an instrumental part in my company's success and the annual convention continues to be a terrific resource for me to continue to grow and improve my company."

To this day, 40 percent of Viczko's business is generated from window cleaning and his net profits are at least double from what they were a decade ago.

The 2013 IWCA Convention & Trade Show brings contract-cleaning professionals from around the world to share ideas, network and help make businesses better. Sheila Smeltzer, A+ Pro Window Cleaning, inherited her window cleaning business and realized that she knew nothing about field work and operations. (See Sheila's profile on page 20.) She found the answers she needed by attending her first IWCA convention as a scholarship winner in 2007. She was nervous to attend the first convention, not only because she was a woman, but also because she was so new to the knowledge base of the industry. Her fears were soon allayed when other professionals welcomed her into their inner circles.

"There were key individuals that took me under their wings at that first convention who are still influential colleagues and great friends today," Smeltzer said. "I am hooked on the annual convention for the innovation and professionalism it brings to my company, especially during the winter slow down. When I look at the success I inherited from attending IWCA conventions over the years, I realize the investment was priceless."

Additionally, IWCA dedicates part of the convention to its trade show, which showcases the top products and services in the market. When professionals are looking for a solution for their business needs, the IWCA Annual Convention & Trade Show is the place to be. With the right tools and services, a company can take its business to the next level by being able to work more efficiently, incorporating add-on services and utilizing new products to help make tough projects a little easier.

This year's event offers one of the best educational programs to date. Attendees can choose to attend the full convention or just a day or two. There is something guaranteed to fit everyone's budget and need. The knowledge and contacts gained from attending the convention will benefit contract cleaning professionals for years to come.

For a full list of session descriptions, more information and to register for the event, please visit the IWCA website at www.iwca.org or contact IWCA Headquarters at info@iwca.org or at 1-800-875-4922. Specific information can be found on these pages:
- Schedule of Events
- Session Descriptions
- What's the Cost?
- Register Now

About the IWCA

The International Window Cleaning Association (IWCA), a non-profit trade 501(c)(6), is committed to raising the standards of professionalism within the window cleaning industry. The IWCA represents all facets of the window cleaning industry, from high-rise to route work, residential to industrial. Through its various programs, the IWCA promotes safety, training and a highly professional, responsible image of the window cleaning professional. The IWCA delivers at least three regional safety training programs a year at various locations throughout the country. These programs cover all aspects of window cleaning safety and equipment use. The IWCA is also the secretariat for the IWCA I 14.1 Window Cleaning Safety Standard. For more information, call 1-800-875-4922 or visit them at www.iwca.org.

Women's Work

Sheila Smeltzer

Written by Allison Hester,
Sponsored by the National Cleaning Expo and
Pressure Washing Insitute.

Sheila Smeltzer, owner of A+ Pro Window Cleaning in Holden Beach, NC, believes that being a woman in the window cleaning industry has clear advantages.

"When a woman starts speaking technically, people listen," she explains. "When a woman bids a job, there is a certain level of trust. When a woman shows up to actually clean their property, there is a level of comfort." And as a woman, Smeltzer has taken the once-failing company she married into and turned it into an industry powerhouse, with over 1,000 customers.

"Ski Bum" turned CEO

A mid-western girl from just west of Chicago, Smeltzer and a friend "high tailed it to Colorado" three days after high school graduation. There she attended Colorado State University and ultimately became a ski – "well, actually snowboard" – bum for about six years in the mid 1990s.

"I look back on these years and realize the jobs I had there groomed me for being successful in my company today," she said. These jobs included sales at a high-end men's clothing retailer, a laborer at Summit Landscaping, and a dog sled/snowmobile tour guide at Good Times Adventure Tours in Breckenridge, Colorado. "The hands-on style of catering to my customers' needs, along with sales to mostly high-end clientele, have played a huge role in my ability to build relationships with my customers, sell the jobs, and facilitate the work promised."

In 1999, Smeltzer moved to NC with her new husband, who had been in the window cleaning

industry for 15 years. She explained that while she could not save her struggling marriage, she did save her failing business. In 2006, Smeltzer incorporated and became one-hundred-percent owner of A+ Pro Window Cleaning, Inc.

"The work was grueling," as just she and her one surviving employee operated from a single black Toyota Tacoma "loaded with two pressure washers, stacked with ladders and equipment, humping it every day trying to earn back the patronage of over 100 customers."

Today, A+ Pro is made of professional window cleaners who offer a number of complimentary services such as pressure washing, gutter cleaning, high or specialized interior cleaning, vinyl enclosures, glass restoration, concrete sealing, deck restoration, hurricane storm panel manipulation, and even a few janitorial accounts.

And, A+ Pro is comprised mostly of women.

The A+ Pro Team

A+ Pro Window Cleaning currently has a payroll of seven, including Smeltzer, five of whom are women. "I know a lot of readers are thinking that we are unable to do technical types of work and that we probably stick to the interior. Not true," she added.

Finding women who are physically capable of doing the work has been the greatest breakthrough for A+ Pro. "Amanda and Heather are window cleaning experts in facilitation and strategy of a job," she adds. Both women handle everything below 28 feet "without complaint" and have the ability to find the "most creative and efficient ways to get the work done. They take execution of jobs seriously."

While Sheila prefers the hands-on fieldwork, she spends most of her time these days managing everything. She still hits the field at a customer's request and in their peak Spring, post-pollen season. "I am fortunate to have staff that allows me to nurture organization and customer relations." Glass restoration and scratch removal are the most challenging aspects of A+ Pro's work, she adds, because of the need to know and understand about different glass surfaces, chemicals and reactants. "I love making surfaces shine. I have always held comfort in knowing that if all went bust, I would survive and could ultimately single-handedly manage all operations in my company and keep my kids clothed and in school."

The two men on staff handle most of the 32-feet and higher jobs, gutter cleaning and pressure washing. The men are also trained to do interior work, such as windows and chandeliers "with detail." Smeltzer adds that A+ Pro's diverse staff allows her "to place the perfect crew to each job's needs."

And her customers seem to love working with her team of women. "If you asked my customers which crew they would prefer to clean their windows, hands down they prefer the women. From interior work to accessing high clerestory windows outside, they always comment about it being done by a woman! "

Finding Staff

Smeltzer has always been an athlete, a factor that she says helps her do her job. About five years ago, she joined her local parks and recreation's softball league, which is where she found several of her staff members.

"Players would occasionally ask if I was hiring, and although I was leery of bringing teammates on, I realized that I already knew their families, temperament, dedication, timeliness, and work ethic from playing ball with them, not to mention they had physical capabilities to facilitate our work," she adds. Four out of seven A+ Pro employees are ball players, so she chose to sponsor a team. "The experience has opened numerous networking opportunities, as well as promoting teamwork and camaraderie into my company."

Smeltzer recognizes that while her staff consists mostly of women, it is certainly not a job for everyone. Her advice to any woman looking to enter the industry is to "get a realistic view" by attending either the quarterly high-rise or residential IWCA (International Window Cleaning Association) safety training seminars. "The seminar will give them a clear understanding of the challenges that will be experienced in the field and also how to safely address and maneuver their challenge."

Smeltzer attended her first safety training in Nashville, Tennessee, at the 2008 IWCA convention. "I apply these OSHA safety standards in every employee training and every move I make on a job. If a woman is able to ascertain this component of the industry, she will dominate."

IWCA involvement hasn't stopped with training for Smeltzer, however, as she is in the final season of her three-year Board term. She also serves on their glass education committee and residential council. She is also a member of her local chamber of commerce, and is or has been a member of the Power Washers of North America (PWNA), Master Window Cleaners of North America (MwoNA), and the Association of United Window Cleaners (AUWC).

"From my first IWCA convention and serving on the Board of Directors, to National Cleaning Expos, and even smaller networking events regionally and locally, I have always found that the folks in our industry are business minded, active, creative, and professional," she adds. "The relationships built are priceless. Communicating with professionals around the country who are doing the same as I am every day makes me feel like I am part of a greater community that I tend to forget about in the everyday grind. This is why attending these events keeps us innovative as business owners."

Putting Customers First

While Smeltzer is proud of her staff, her company and her industry, it is A+ Pro's customers that she holds dearest. "Many of my customers are now longtime friends," she says. "I am grateful for their trusting in my service, as a woman, and holding the key to my success. I could have never unlocked the door without these customers!"

And it's customer satisfaction that makes her job worthwhile. She loves following up with her customers to ask them how her crew performed for them. "Their reply is something like 'They did an excellent job and they were very professional,'" she concludes. "Wow! I love that conversation! I also love the relationships that I have built with my customers over the years. I love that I have grown to feel more like their peer and not their laborer."

Fall Deals on Hot Water Pressure Washers

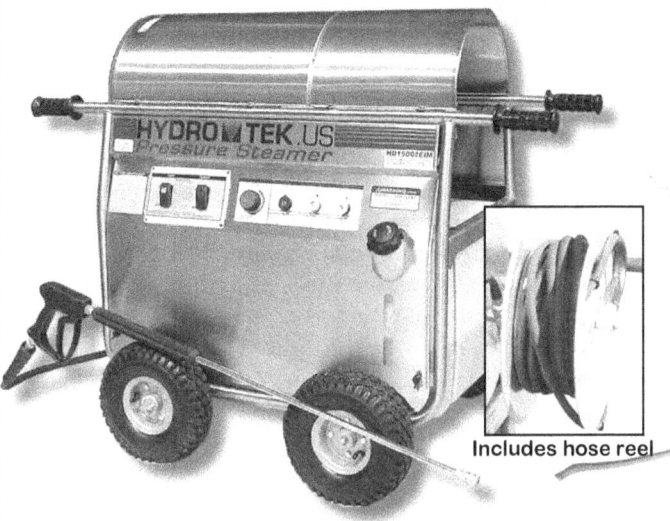

Hot Water Power Washer

- 2500 psi, 3.8 gpm
- 230v, 1ph motor - Diesel heated
- Adjustable temperature, up to 250°F
- Full pressure soap injection
- Rustproof stainless frame and panels
- Wheel kit
- Stainless hose reel

$3595
Save over $2100

Includes hose reel

Promotion ends December 31

Hot Water Mobile Wash Skid

- 3500 psi, 3.5 gpm
- Twin cylinder gas engine - Diesel heated
- Adjustable temperature, up to 250°F
- Steel Pro-Tect-It frame
- Rustproof stainless panels
- 13" 4-wheel kit included

$3995
Save over $2600

Available at your local Hydro Tek distributor thru 12/31/12. Ask for the Harvest Special. Includes free freight to distributor location in the continental U.S. Call 800-27-HYDRO or visit www.hydrotek.us to find a distributor near you.

HYDRO TEK.US

Marketing To Commercial Clients Using Social Media

by Dick Wagner, www.AskDickWagener.com Disaster Restoration Consulting

If your cleaning company targets commercials accounts, i.e., a business-to-business (B2B) company, this social media strategy is critical you your business success!

You can readily reach out to your hundreds (or thousands) of business customers more often and effectively with social media than using any other tool currently available The key is to provide information they want to hear. It won't work if you try to approach B2B social media just like a business-to-consumer company does. They are an entirely different type of customer and require a completely different action plan.

For a business-to-consumer (B2C) company, it's all about how many followers (friends, circles, connections) you have and how much activity you get. For a B2B company, it's not about quantity; it's about quality - does your social media directly drive business results?

Business-to-Business (B2B) companies will often use social media to give potential customers an idea of "who, what, when, why, where and even the how" of doing business with them. Commercial prospects and clients like this interaction and information, especially when it's presented in a non-selling format.

The difference with social media is that it's more about the conversations and the community. B2B companies have to balance both building a community and directing it toward a sale. To do this, you should implement the following social media strategies, donating about 33% to each one:
- Advertising, marketing, promotions, deals
- News, events, happenings (in your business or industry)
- Relevant content (preferably with interactive conversations) about legitimate topics for your audience. You can certainly "steer" the conversation toward your products and services, but it needs to be very subtle and limited. Your conversations should involve and engage your "community." The instant it appears to be a commercial, you've gone too far in the conversation.

Blogs are a great place to post "white papers" and other technical notices and articles. They will draw the attention of those that are truly interested, and you'll be surprised at how many views you get. The more relevant and useful posts you have, and the more you interact with those who do read and comment on your posts, the stronger the following and the more trust you will build with your readers and followers. If they aren't reading it, you likely aren't posting info that is interesting, helpful or useful. If your company does not have a blog yet, then you are already seriously behind in marketing B2B in our new world of SM.

According to comScore, social networking has reached 94.7 percent of users age 55 and older, representing a 12 percent jump between July 2010 and October 2011. During that same period, the use of email for this group rose merely one percent, while email usage among every other age category fell by more than 30 percent, peaking with a 42 percent drop among users age 15 to 24. (This group spends the largest amount of time on social networks, at an average of 8.6 hours per month).

The quality of the relationships you create are far more important than the number of followers or likes that you have. It's rarely about how many followers you have; it's almost always about interacting with interested participants that can affect your business positively while bringing value in advance to them.

Dick Wagner has served the disaster restoration industry for over 16 years, providing disaster recovery services to both regional and national clients. Wagner brings expertise in Structural Drying, Environmental Inspection, Remediation, and Fire and Smoke Restoration. He also brings extensive experience in Personal Contents Inventory and Replacement Cost Pricing for the Insurance Claims Industry.

Where You Park Makes a Difference

By Tom Grandy

I have a quick question for you: Does the customer really care where you park your vehicle? The answer is a resounding yes!

Here are just a few reasons why from the customer's perspective and from your company's perspective.

- Parking in the driveway – That's no big deal, right? Well it might be from the customer's standpoint. What if one of the members of the family wants to leave while you are still working? Now they have to ask you to move the truck. That just caused lost time (and increased expense to the customer, if you are still on time and material pricing). Not only that, but now the customer is a bit irritated that you are in the way and a bit embarrassed that they have to come to you and ask you to move the vehicle. Both strain customer relations.

- Does your vehicle leak fluids? – Do you want someone else's vehicle leaking oil on your driveway? The homeowner doesn't appreciate it either. Parking in the street helps, but here's a better solution. Carry a pack of cardboard with you to the service location. When you get out of the vehicle place the cardboard under your vehicle in the area where it leaks. If you do that, and the customer sees you doing it, that earns brownie points. The customer is thinking, "If the tech cares about dripping oil on my driveway or the street, surely he will care about my home and equipment as well."

- Marketing – There is no better marketing and/or advertising than word of mouth. How many times has a neighbor seen your truck at their neighbor's home and then called your company for service? The neighbor may be thinking, "If ABC Company is doing work for my friend, Bill, they must do great work. I will call ABC Company next time I need work done." Your vehicle is a moving billboard.

Now let's take a quiz. Would more people see your vehicle parked: A.) in the driveway, B.) next to the house, or C.) on the street in front of the house? Answer: C.) in front of the house.

- Don't kill the customer's grass – Now that we are parking in the street, remember one more thing. Don't pull too far off the street and, therefore, onto the customer's grass. Parking in the street is the best place to be, but killing your customer's grass wipes away all the benefits of parking in the street!

- Beware of where you walk – It's the first call of the day. You did a great job of parking in front of the customer's home without being on the grass. Since it's early morning, the grass is still damp. PLEASE use the driveway and/or sidewalk to get to the customer's front door. Don't walk through the yard and track all that wet grass into the customer's home. Yes, that does sound a bit ridiculous, doesn't it? It did to me ... until the plumbing tech did exactly what I just described! Think before you walk.

These are just a few things to think about as you arrive at the customer's home. They may not seem like a big deal to you, but they are in the eyes of the customer and they are the ones that will make to decision whether to use your company again ... or not!

This article was brought to you by Grandy & Associates. If you are serious about running a profitable business please check out their website at www.GrandyAssociates.com, call them at 800-432-7963, or email to TomGrandy@GrandyAssociates.com. "We teach contractors to run profitable businesses!"

Death and Accident Cleanup
Helping Families in Their Time of Need

by Allison Hester

Last week, the world watched in horror as every parent's worst nightmare came true, as a gunman murdered young children in their classrooms. As families and communities try to make sense of this tragedy, they cling to the hope of someday resuming some sense of normalcy. And the cleaning industry is a key, yet unseen player in the efforts to make that hope a reality.

Death – whether from natural, accidental or malicious circumstances – is messy. When families lose loved ones, the last thing they want to deal with is figuring out how to clean up afterward. This is what led David O'Brien to start Rapid Responders 10 years ago.

O'Brien, who at the time worked transporting bodies for a crematory, recalled a particularly brutal transport call. When the grieving family asked the first responders who would clean up the mess, the responders "shrugged their shoulders."

This led O'Brient to research the situation. begin researching the options for families. What he found was that not only was there a large need for death and accident cleanup, there were strict, and often confusing laws about disposing of bodily fluids. Yet families were generally left to figure it out for themselves.

The need for cleanup services was great, and has only gotten bigger. Tighter regulations have prohibited practices that were once deemed acceptable, such as firefighters cleaning outside accident scenes and washing the bodily fluids down the sewer.

"First responders had to start calling people like us to come out, decontaminate it, remove it and simultaneously capture the water so it doesn't go into the waterways. It has to be reclaimed," he said.

There is a great need for death accident cleanup services, and for those who can handle it, there is money to be made. In fact, there is such a need for these cleaning specialists, O'Brien is working to put unemployed and disable individuals back to work. "Why make $25 to $50 an hour when you can make $250 to $1,000 an hour?" he asked.

"The Worst of the Worst of the Worst"

Eight years ago, O'Brien opened the CTS Decontamination Training Academy in Las Vegas, which combines web-based training, followed by two "strenuous, vigorous eight-hour days" of on-site training in Las Vegas. The two-day onsite training is done in an actual house that is made to look like a death scene. There, students are fitted for respirators, then must decontaminate, clean, remove and dispose of all the remnants of the scene, bringing it back to its preexisting condition.

"We put blood splatter everywhere – ceilings, doors, walls, floors – put live and kicking, juicy maggots crawling," said O'Brien. "The nice thing about the hands-on training is we make it as real as possible. So if someone cannot handle the training, they won't be able to handle the real thing." And the real thing involves "the worst of the worst of the worst" imaginable.

Safety is a key issue that is focused on throughout the training. "We train on the OSHA safety standards, ladders, extension cords, hand tools, cutting tools, heat stress – it's all about safety, and a lot of it are things people don't normally consider," O'Brien added.

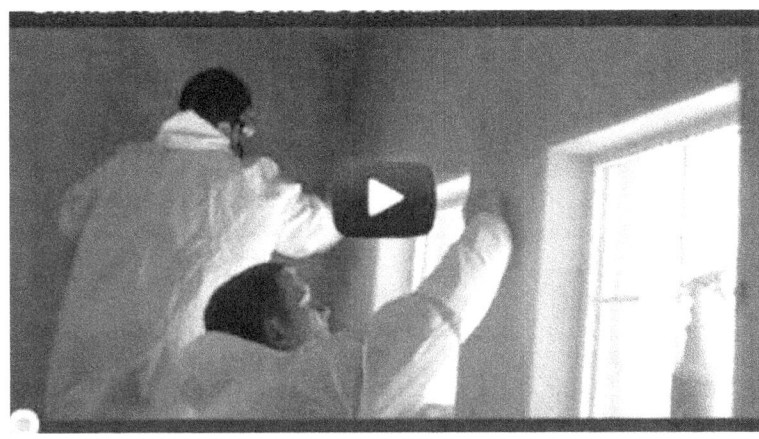

Additionally, students are taught about marketing their services, including O'Brien's "unconventional" marketing techniques that are proprietary and "very effective."

Following the hands-on training, students take a final exam. If they pass, they receive their certification. If they fail, they can retake the training and exam at a later date.

Not for Everyone

While the money is "very good," this is obviously not an industry for everyone. To be successful in this industry, you've got to possess several characteristics:

1. The Stomach: Contractors entering this field obviously need to be able to stomach blood and other bodily fluids, maggots, decomposition and indescribable stenches. They also have to be able to work wearing respirators and full protective suits.

2. The Schedule: Death and accident cleanup is a 24/7 business. "We're just like the first responders," said O'Brien. "We get a call and we are there in 20 minutes or less, weather and traffic permitting." So if you are not able or willing to handle such a schedule, this is not the industry for you.

3. The Equipment: While death and accident cleanup is about much more than just pressure washing, the correct pressure washing system is imperative to ensure that bodily fluids do not go down the drain. They also have to be powerful enough to remove baked on blood and other fluids from hot concrete, then have reclaim capabilities. O'Brien said that he refers his students to Jerry McMillen of Cleaning System Specialists for his instant capture reclaim systems.

4. The Persistence and Diligence: While this field pays well, getting paid can be complicated. In fact, O'Brien stressed that billing is the most difficult part of this industry. "We are dealing with insurance companies and they don't want to pay. We deal with municipalities who call us out to clean up, but when it's time to get paid they say that the City has no money," he added.

5. The Psyche: More than the ability to endure the blood itself, O'Brien stressed that you have to be able to handle the story behind the blood. "You're dealing with a lot of tragedies on a daily basis, and it takes a toll on you psychologically," he stressed. "It gets to me at times. The psychological aspects of this job are horrific."

6. The Heart: "If you're in it just for the money, then don't bother," O'Brien stressed. "When we do it, we do it because we want to help individuals during the worst moment of their life. It's not our job to tell them they have to pay up front or we won't come. It's our job to assure them that we are on our way and it will be ok."

If you believe you have what it takes to enter this industry and are interested in learning more about CTS Decontamination Training Academy, visit their website at www.cts-decon-training-academy.com.

Anatomy of a Restroom

by Rick Meehan, Vice President of Marko Janitorial Supply, www.MarkoInc.com

Whether you call them restrooms, bathrooms, loos, dunnies, or other endearments, one thing's for sure, these personal spaces are the most germ-ridden of all places. (Oh look, I'm a poet and didn't know it.)

Here's an axiom: cleaning professionals that do a great job of sanitizing restrooms not only ensure future repeat business, but perform sheer poetry when it comes to facility cleanliness. Nothing dampens a first impression faster in a home or business than an unpleasant aroma drifting from the W.C. Remember, cleanliness is next to Godliness, and disagreeable odors must be eliminated to ensure a sense of wholesomeness. Goodness gracious, I'm waxing philosophical too.

If you are a cleaning professional assigned the task of making a restroom sparkle, then you are the key to your company's future business from that client. Of all the maintenance chores, this is the most dreaded and hated. Why? Well, not only is it in many cases a nasty job, but it takes a special person to ignore the stigma associated with cleaning commodes and other restroom fixtures. It takes an attitude adjustment, that's what!

To quote actor Will Smith from *Men in Black*, "First off, you chose me…so you recognize the skills." Will's character was pointing out that he deserved respect for his talents. Anyone who performs a superior job in the wonderful world of restroom maintenance should be venerated, praised, admired, and rewarded.

A cleaning firm that can consistently perform superior work in this key area ensures a customer's gratitude. Of course, there are always those folks that can never be satisfied. In the grand scheme of continued business, that client type should probably be let go in favor of doing a better job for others who recognize the skills. That's where the profit will be. Therefore, it is imperative to instruct cleaning staff on the proper methods of cleaning restrooms. Don't allow shoddy cleaning procedures to take a bite out of your profitability.

Before we talk about these procedures, let's identify surfaces that harbor germs in all restrooms and bathrooms. Here is a list including various material types to be expected, whether in a home or commercial facility:

- **Doors:** doorknobs, door panels
- **Walls:** splash areas around sinks, commodes, and urinals
- **Floors:** vinyl, ceramic tile, stone, concrete, composite, and wood
- **Ceilings:** ductwork and vents
- **Sinks:** porcelain, chrome, brass, copper, fiberglass, plastic
- **Dispensers:** towels, toilet tissue, hand soap, hygiene units, seat covers
- **Mirrors:** includes all glass
- **Trash Cans:** inside, outside, lids, and sanitary napkin disposal units
- **Fixtures:** commodes, urinals, and bidets
- **Showers:** ceramic tile, vinyl, porcelain, stone, plastic, fiberglass
- **Tubs:** ceramic tile, porcelain, plastic, fiberglass
- **Matting:** carpet, vinyl, polyester
- **Baby Changing Stations:** plastic
- **Deodorant systems and dispensers:** solid, liquid, gel, and aerosol
- **Grout:** found in various places in a restroom, wherever a water seal is needed

While not every facility has all of the above components, it is a sure bet that a cleaning company must go prepared for all of these situations. Thankfully, the materials required will work in nearly all cases. If a cleaning company has the proper equipment and chemicals for handling the restroom, at least that means they have nearly everything they need for the rest of the facility too. The bathroom requires the most intense use of cleaning products and labor; thus, efficient procedures reduce overall costs.

When dealing with a bathroom, no matter the size or location, the following procedure will obtain a high level of cleanliness – with a conscientious person behind the elbow grease. Train your restroom people well.

CLEANERS REQUIRED:

1. **All Purpose Disinfectant:** A professional quality neutral cleaner, deodorizer, and disinfectant all-in-one. These come in a variety of deodorants, but contain basically the same active disinfectant. The active ingredient is quaternary ammonium chloride, commonly called quat.

2. **Non-Acid, Mild Acid, Acid Porcelain Cleaner:** Porcelain should always be cleaned with a non-acid product, which has not always been the case in the past. Porcelain can stain and be the devil to clean. Once an acid is used, it becomes likely that from that point, acid will always have to be used on that fixture to get it clean. Rule of thumb: use the weakest product that will get the job done to avoid further damage to the porcelain.

3. **Pumice Sticks:** These handy little tools will not scratch porcelain. They are perfect for removing the toughest stains, even rust, from old or new porcelain fixtures.

4. **Foaming Germicidal Cleaner Aerosol:** Although aerosols are more expensive for the same basic chemicals as liquids, sometimes the speed factor outweighs the extra expense. Labor hours are more costly than cleaners.

5. **Hospital Disinfectant Spray:** Using the same reasons as above, these products are fast drying, quick to permeate, and eliminate odors in hard-to-reach places.

6. **Glass and Plexi-glass Cleaner:** There is a choice between liquid and aerosol here. My personal preference is liquid glass cleaner in restrooms because liquids are less expensive. Avoid ammonia based cleaners here mainly because ammonia can cause damage to Plexi-glass and plastic surfaces along the nature of permanent fogging.

7. **Enzyme-based Deodorant-Digestant:** These products usually contain a pleasant deodorant, but that's not why we need them – it's the enzymes. Organic matter, from feces, to urine, to bacteria, cause odors in restrooms. These enzymes break down the odor-causing bacteria just as they do in a septic system.

8. **Graffiti Remover:** This is an indispensable aerosol product for the removal of inks, dyes, lipstick, markers, glues, and other damaging materials from restroom stalls and fixtures.

9. **Household Bleach:** CAUTION. AVOID USING BLEACH AND BLEACH-BASED CLEANERS EXCEPT WHEN ABSOLUTELY NECESSARY. Bleach damages many surfaces, tracks easily where it doesn't belong, is unhealthy to breathe, and isn't very compatible around other chemicals, especially

ammonia. However, sometimes it is needed to remove stains in latex grout where the grout has been damaged by mildew.

10. **Household Ammonia:** DON'T USE, PERIOD.

11. **Solid, Liquid or Aerosol Deodorizer:** These are optional; however, nothing pleases a customer more than a pleasant experience when visiting the restroom. I highly recommend a deodorant system (more on this later).

EQUIPMENT REQUIRED:

1. **Microfiber Flat Mop System: While not necessarily efficient in large areas, flat mops** are great for most restrooms. The exceptions might run to football stadiums or airports where fifty-stall restrooms are not uncommon. Flat mops offer a simple solution to a thorny problem. Mops contaminate chemicals and harbor germs themselves. Flat mops are easily changed, never dipped in cleaning solution after initially saturated, outlast regular mops, and are easily laundered. Put simply, they perform well for disinfection processes where cross-contamination of materials is a problem.

2. **Microfiber Cloths or Disposable Wipers:** I am a proponent of microfiber. The material  outlasts standard terry towel rags and other forms of cellulose wipers. Microfiber cloths are launder-able innumerable times. This means in the long run they are less expensive to use.

3. **Toilet Bowl and Urinal Brushes: Wrapped-wire bowl and urina**l brushes with  extensions, commercial grade, offer the strength of bristle needed to actually clean most commodes, urinals, and bidets, without having to use harsh acid-based cleaners.

4. **Trigger Sprayer or Small Pump Sprayers:** Disinfectant and other liquid cleaners should be pre-diluted in these handy little devices. Sprayers offer exceptional control over the amount of chemicals and liquids applied to a restroom. These are major cost-saving tools.

5. **Stick Broom and Lobby Dust Pan:** This equipment is the fastest way to remove heavier debris like wadded paper and dust bunnies from a restroom floor.  They may not always be necessary

6. **Janitor Cart or Dolly (OPTIONAL):** Depending on the size of the facility, a cart may be necessary in order to carry all of the accoutrements needed to clean a restroom. Never allow  the cleaning staff to do the Janitor's Shuffle, from car to job and back again. This takes too much time away from the cleaning effort. Time is money. Determine the best way to get all of the required cleaners, tools, tissues, towels, etc. to the location as efficiently as possible.

7. **Supply Refillables (Add-On Sales):** Don't lose the opportunity to add on to the

---

Let us put our expert knowledge of **legendary Landa equipment** to work for your cleaning needs.

Specializing in Power washing equipment sales, service and custom manufacturing

(403) 771-7774

www.HydraEquipment.com

HYDRA EQUIPMENT LTD.

cleaning contract by offering, at an extra charge of course, to refill all restroom dispensers. Hand soap, towels, toilet tissue, trash bags, deodorant refills, urinal floor mats – these and other common usage items offer extra profit points.

8. **Gloves and Goggles:** Every cleaning chemical used has some form of safety gear requirement. Refer to your Material Safety Data Sheets for further information. In general, always wear protective gloves! I like latex commercial grade disposable gloves that can easily be removed and thrown away between jobs. This reduces contamination risks to people, places, and things.

9. **Stepladder:** A handy tool in case overhead work such as vent cleaning must be done.

10. **Acrylic Extension Duster:** This tool  makes short work of spider webs, dust on vents, ceiling lights, and other restroom furnishings that may not like to be cleaned with water-based chemicals. Always clean the duster after use by swishing out in pre-diluted leftover disinfectant and hanging to dry.

11. **Large Cellulous Sponge:** Invaluable for swiping areas that cannot withstand lots of water.

12. **Hand-held Scrub Brush:** Useful around fixtures where soap scum and other buildup may be an issue.

13. **Scrubbing Machine (Optional):** Depending on the size of your job, assistive machinery may speed up your process. A good example is when it becomes necessary to detail the grout lines on a ceramic tile floor.

14. **Deck Scrub Brush on a Handle:** This  tool is usually needed in tile restrooms where grout lines can be a problem. If the job is too small for a scrubbing machine, then a deck brush can still take care of the situation.

THE RESTROOM CLEANING PROCEDURE

Throughout the entire procedure listed here it is assumed that the cleaning person will be using these basic products for most tasks: a sprayer of pre-diluted cleaner-deodorizer-disinfectant and a microfiber system including cloths, mops, and bucket unless otherwise noted.

Prerequisites

• Follow instructions on cleaning chemicals and make sure they are prepared for use in sprayers or other containers.

• Make sure all necessary cleaning equipment is handy (loaded caddies, carts, etc.).

• Remove all trash cans and any other furnishings (if possible) from the area to be disinfected.

• Empty all soiled materials from mounted trash cans, sanitary napkin disposal units, and floor model receptacles. (If the area is large, it is more efficient to empty refuse into a nearby janitor cart hopper or rolling trash receptacle.)

• Dispose of all expended urinal and toilet floor mats, urinal screens, deodorant canisters, hanging commode blocks, etc.

• Sweep any heavy debris from the floor with a stick broom and lobby dust pan.

• Remove dispenser towels, toilet tissue, facial wipes, deodorants, seat covers, etc., to prevent them from becoming wet and unusable. They will be replaced once disinfection is near completion.

STEP ONE – ABOVE THE WAIST OR THEREABOUT

• If any ceiling work is needed, such as removing dust and mildew from vent fan covers, swishing away spider webs, cleaning light fixtures or other high objects, do this now. TIP: Spider webs are easily removed with an inexpensive extension acrylic duster.

• If fingerprints or smudges need to be cleaned from walls or doors, now is the time. However, we will disinfect the door knobs as we leave.

• If graffiti is present, use the aerosol graffiti remover now.

• Depending on the wall surface type, lightly apply disinfectant to counters, sinks, urinals and commodes inside and out, and wall splash areas around those fixtures. Allow disinfectant to soak a minimum of five minutes in order to kill germs. If walls are made of sheetrock or another permeable material, wipe splash areas to remove excess moisture. Alternatively, use a sponge or wiper to gently scrub the walls in the splash zones. DO NOT SKIP THIS STEP because of inconvenience, as walls are easily damaged by acidic urine. Walls also become odor sources.

• After the required "dwell" or "soak" time listed on the disinfectant label has passed, wipe away the excess. This is the time to scrub problem areas such as around the hand soap dispensers, swish out the toilets and urinals.

• Finish cleaning all surfaces above the knee, paying particular attention to the facings of dispensers.

STEP TWO – MOVING ON DOWN

• Using the sprayer, apply disinfecting solution to the floor. If the microfiber flat mop goes dry during mopping, simply spray down more solution. (Please note that we are not restoring tile and grout here, only cleaning thoroughly. Restoration will be for another article.)

• After the required dwell time has been reached, use the pre-moistened microfiber pads according to manufacturer instructions to mop the floor. These systems are designed to be "touch-free" if used properly, which is safer for the user and reduces the chance of cross-contamination of chemicals, equipment, and

MICROFIBER FLAT MOP SYSTEM SAVINGS

Microfiber flat mops are the most durable mopping products on the market. So what's the big deal? It's a touch-less system. That means you don't have to mess with the contaminated mop with your hands. It also means that your clean mops are never mixed with your dirty ones. When it comes to sanitization, a regular string mop or dust mop won't come anywhere close to matching the ease of use and versatility of a microfiber flat mop. There's only one drawback: flat mop systems are only efficient in moderate to small areas. Clean rooms, hospital rooms, doctor's offices, and multi-stall restrooms are great examples of spots to use microfiber flat mop systems.

Microfiber, the material used to create quality flat mops, is made from polyester fibers which are split during production to produce voids in each strand. This makes the fiber soft, tough for scrubbing, and porous so it will hold dust, dirt, and liquids without releasing until the mop is washed under running water or in a laundry. Microfiber mops leave no lint either, nor do they fall apart, even after uncounted washes. The components of a flat mop system are:

• Microfiber flat mop heads
• Frame
• Handle, either extension-style or straight
• Dual bucket with strainer (cleaning solution, dirty mop disposal)

BENEFITS OF MICROFIBER FLAT MOP SYSTEMS:

1. Handles with the ease of a dust mop.
2. Works great in tight places.
3. Prevents cross-contamination.
4. Hands don't touch used mop heads: touch-less.
5. Extremely portable.
6. Economizes on expensive chemicals.
7. Fast cleaning without back strain.
8. No need to lug gallons of water.
9. Fits on a janitor cart for mobility.
10. More thorough than either dust mop or wet mop.
11. Indefinitely washable.
12. Can be used on walls, floors, and ceilings.
13. Low water use means floors dry faster.
14. Quick changeover to fresh mop head.
15. Most systems can double as a super floor finish application method.

Using Ben Franklin's favorite decision-making process, the pros outweigh cons; therefore, don't hesitate to get a set of these babies to immediately save money in cleaning chemicals and labor costs. They're fast and reliable.

even rooms. (See sidebar tip on how these systems are designed to work.)

• Remember to change out dirty flat mops as needed. Be sure to use clean pads, rags, and wipers too. A three-stall restroom with two urinals and two sinks, given an industrial situation where grease is present can require up to five flat mops. Carry the number of flat mops that will complete the task without having to waste time washing them out on the fly.

• Work toward the exit door.

• If odors are an issue, as soon as the floor cleaning is completed, grab the sprayer of Enzyme-based Deodorant-Digestant. Pump several squirts of Enzymes into the toilet and close the lid. Spray the inside of the urinals thoroughly. Lightly apply Enzymes to splash areas on the walls and floors. (If the walls are sheetrock or other surface harmed by excess water, use a sponge or wiper instead.)

• Refill all paper product, hand soap, deodorant, seat cover, and hygiene dispensers, and install fresh trash bags to mounted trash cans. Add all accessories like floor protective mats and urinal screens. Restore furnishings to original positions.

• Clean the inside and outside of all floor model trash cans. Replace the trash bags in the cans. Restore trash cans to original positions. If restroom odors are an issue, apply a few squirts of Enzyme-based Deodorant-Digenstant to the INSIDE of the trash bag liner.

• Remove all cleaning materials that may still be in area back to the carrier or cart.

• As the final task, clean the doorknobs. Close the door. Why? This indicates that the restroom has been sanitized. The next person in begins the process of re-contamination. Move on to the next area to be cleaned.

STEP THREE – CLEANUP OF EQUIPMENT USED

• This is very simple. Cleaning equipment must be sanitized before the next job.

• Use the left over disinfectant to spray down the cart, buckets, tools, in short, every piece of cleaning equipment.

• Allow the proper dwell time. Rinse the cleaning equipment.

• Wash the microfiber flat mops and rags in disinfectant either by hand or with a machine. DO NOT USE BLEACH!

• Store equipment in a clean facility. What good is sanitized cleaning equipment if it is re-contaminated by a dirty janitor closet?

Is it necessary to perform all these tasks in every situation? Emphatically yes! Remember, germs know no limits except that of disinfection, and germs cause illness as well as unpleasant odors. Don't skimp in the restrooms as this is where your cleaning company can be broken.

We've talked a lot about procedures. It all boils down to one thing: proper restroom cleaning is an art backed by scientific fact.

Fact #1: germs create issues concerning health.

Fact #2: most restrooms are never fully disinfected which puts visitors at risk.

Fact #3: cleaning staff in general dread the task of sanitizing these very human spaces because they get negative remarks – which can usually be resolved by giving them proper training.

Fact #4: customers complain about unclean restrooms constantly and quite faithfully tell their friends about the terrible job the janitorial service has done.

And Fact #5: when a restroom, or whatever you want to call it, is properly cleaned to poetic perfection, you don't have to philosophize on the wholesomeness it exudes. It just is – clean. Cleanliness makes the Higher Power happy. Keep those W.C.'s sparkling to keep your customers enthralled with your inspired labor.

Advantages of Hiring Pressure Washing Services for Train

by Paul Horsley, Publisher

Pressure washing for trains has dramatically changed the way people think about rail car cleaning. For the first 100 years or so of train history, cars were washed in a pull-through building that modern thinkers would probably associate with a car wash. Today, however, engineers can rely on pressure washer services to keep trains in tip-top shape – regardless of whether there's an open washing bay nearby.

Pressure washing for trains includes cleaning the exterior, engine, carriage, wheels and even the interior, depending on the type of train. (The interior of box cars may be pressure washed, but passenger trains will require gentler cleaning approaches.) Graffiti may also be removed. Many pressure washing services also include a degreasing solution to prevent future grime buildup. A pressure washing approach to rail car cleaning has many advantages, including:

1. COST SAVINGS. Many rail managers have chosen to switch from in-house cleaning to outsourced pressure washing services to save money. Specialization typically improves job performance, and pressure washing for trains is no exception. Because pressure washing is all they do, many pressure washer services can undercut traditional employment costs. By hiring out cleaning duties, management can save money on employment taxes, benefits and other labor costs.

2. QUICKER TRAIN TURNAROUNDS. A whole unit train includes 125 cars, equating to an incredibly large surface area that must be cleaned. Many rail yards aim to clean a one-unit train quickly. However, because they specialize solely in pressure washer services, professional pressure washing experts can usually complete the enormous task of washing a train in just a few days. This means more rail time and less downtime – bringing even more cost savings and profit.

3. MOBILE CLEANING OPPORTUNITIES. Trains are often cleaned only when they need repairs or maintenance. This is a shame, since a clean train not only improves employee morale, it also improves the public's perception of the train industry. Finally, a clean train is usually a faster train, since all that dirt and grime adds unnecessary weight to the whole unit. However, time and equipment constraints limit how often trains can be cleaned in wash bays.

When it's not possible to run a train through the bay wash, pressure washing services can step in. Pressure washing for trains requires certain equipment, including lifts to reach the top of the train as well as a waste management system. Assuming you select a prepared rail car cleaning partner who has equipment that is ready to go, you should be able to achieve mobile train cleaning, even if there's not a wash bay nearby. With more frequent washing, your trains will be more appealing overall.

4. EFFECTIVE GRAFFITI REMOVAL AND PREVENTION. Graffiti is an eyesore that just grows larger and uglier with time. As soon as one tag appears on a train, others are sure to follow. Fortunately, pressure washing for trains can include graffiti removal and prevention. Anti-graffiti solutions can even prevent future tags from appearing.

5. EARTH-FRIENDLY TRAIN CLEANING. Some pressure washing services are dedicated to environmentally conscious operations. Such forward-thinking organizations capture their wastewater, since the water coming off of dirty trains is usually quite polluted with engine chemicals, road dust and more. Wastewater from cleaning trains can taint local watersheds if not collected. Green pressure washing companies also use earth-friendly cleaning solutions to wash trains.

From saving money to saving the earth, there are many advantages to cleaning trains through outsourced pressure washing. One last benefit: Many pressure washing services are also capable of painting trains, so you can take care of even more maintenance tasks at a time.

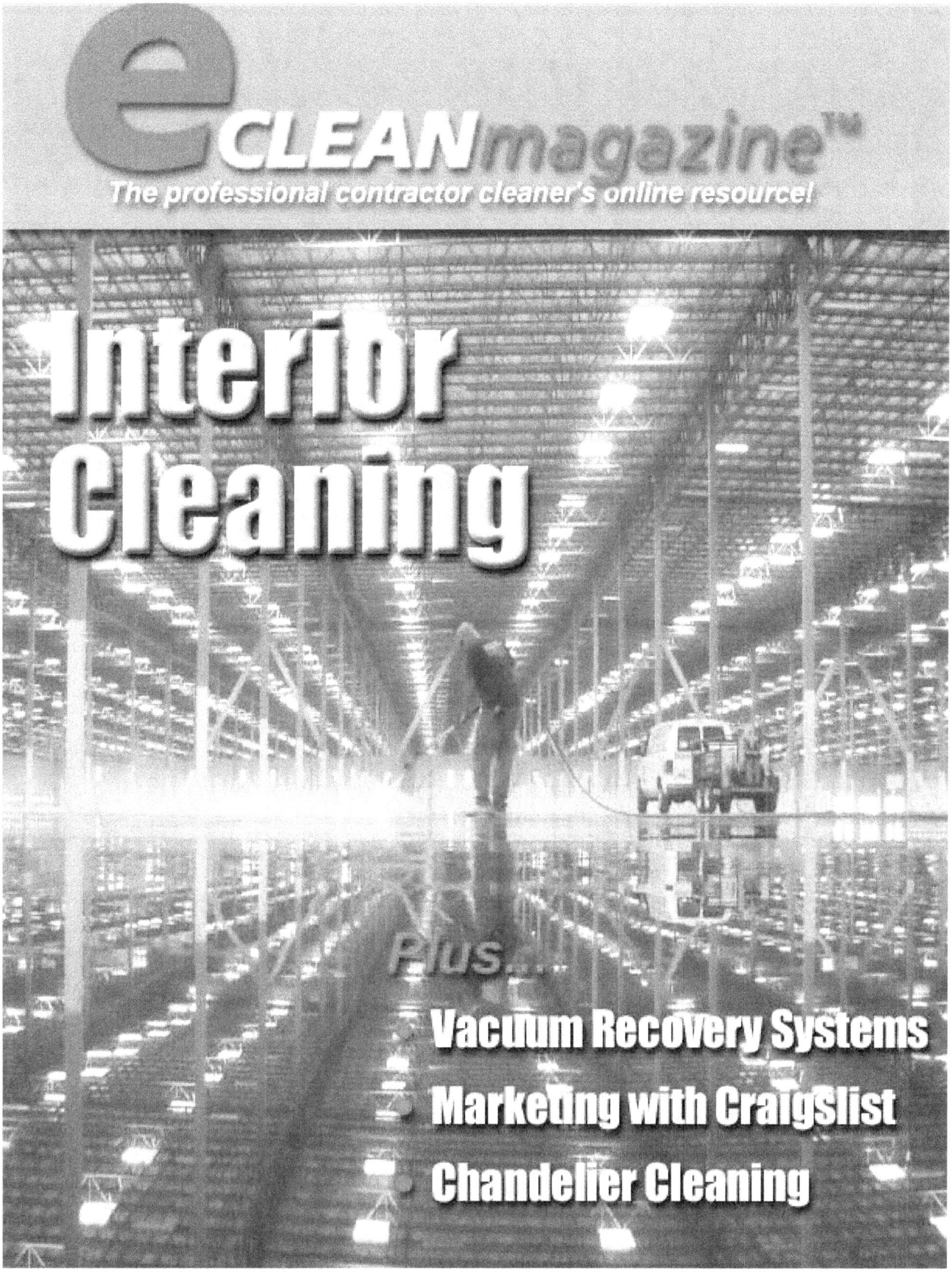

eCLEAN magazine™
The professional contractor cleaner's online resource!

Interior Cleaning

Plus...

Vacuum Recovery Systems
Marketing with Craigslist
Chandelier Cleaning

1.800.433.2113

Carpet Cleaning

Quick Links - Pressure Washers - Surface Cleaners - Chemicals & Detergents - Cleaning Supplies - Parts & Accessories - Pumps & Repair Kits - Training Materials

Rotovac 360i Carpet, Tile & Grout Cleaning Machine
An excellent tool for carpet cleaning and tile and grout cleaning in one effortless, self-propelled motion. The Rotovac 360i has a Patent Pending Rotary Extraction Power Head that utilizes rotary vacuum heads to thoroughly deep clean carpet with hundreds of multi-directional cleaning passes. The 360i weighs only 39 lbs and is extremely easy to use as it operates in a self propelled side to side motion. Simply put, it cleans better with less effort.

The Rotovac 360i is air flow calibrated to work with any portable or truck mount extractor that uses a standard 12" wide cleaning wand. Give your business a boost and your back a break by hooking up the 360i to your existing portable or truck mount. It utilizes rotating vacuum heads to thoroughly deep clean carpet with hundreds of multi-directional cleaning passes. The new and improved carpet cleaning head is equiped with 3 stainless steel shoes and three spray jets to create less overspray, more agitation and quicker dry times.

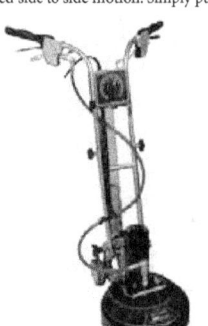

Click Here

Rotovac Wide-Track Carpet Cleaning Machine
The cleaning heads spin at an adjustable 0 to over 200 RPM. The Wide Track operates like a lawn mower and cleans equally in both directions up and back. Designed for use with any truck mount or dual 3 stage portable, the Wide Track delivers all the power of your extractor while requiring only one man to operate. The WideTrack is airflow calibrated and high pressure plumbed to operate with everything from small 3 stage carpet cleaning extractors to the largest, most powerful truck mount systems.

Click Here

Viking PDS-21 Carpet Restoration Air Mover
- 2600 LPM - 92 CFM Air Flow
- 2-Stage Tangential By-Pass Motor
- 115V AC
- 1200 Watts
- 2-position Rocker Switch with Moisture Guard and Light
- 9 AMP
- 106 Inches Vacuum
- 21 Air Nozzles
- Thermal Protection Switch with Auto Reset
- 25-Foot Cord Length
- 3/8" ID X 1/2" Tubing - (200 ft supplied)
- Rotomolded Polyethylene Housing
- Suitable for Stacking
- 19 lbs.
- 20.5" X 16.7" X 18.5" in (H x W x D)

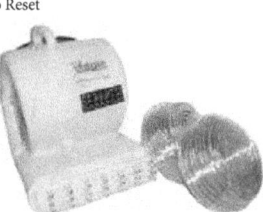

Click Here

Rotovac DHX Carpet Cleaning Machine
The Rotovac DHX thoroughly deep cleans and restores heavily soiled carpet conditions. Matted traffic lanes and stubborn stains can now be deep cleaned and restored with minimal operator effort. The Rotovac DHX takes the backbreaking "wand fatigue" labor out of carpet cleaning. Dual high torque motors along with a comfortable ergonomically designed dual grip handle team up to make the DHX extremely easy to operate and maneuver.

The DHX is equipped with a variable head speed control dial which allows the operator to customize the head speed from 0 to 250 RPM This feature allows the DHX to adapt to a wide variety of carpet from direct commercial glue downs to plush installed over pad residential carpeting. Glue down carpet may require a slower head speed for smooth operation and maximum recovery while installed over pad plush carpeting may need a faster head speed for best results.

The Rotovac works with any truck mount or portable carpet cleaning machine. It is airflow calibrated and high pressure plumbed to operate with everything from small carpet cleaning extractors to the largest, most powerful truck mount systems.

Click Here

Villa 1000 OdorFree Ozone Generator Odor Remover
With the OdorFree, there is no need to saturate the indoors with strong fragrances. Simply close off the area to be treated and let the OdorFree do its work. With the turn of a dial, it attacks odors at their source and leaves your cleaning space smelling fresh and clean. It generates O3, or ozone, which disburses into the space to be treated.
- Up to 4,000 Square Feet Coverage
- Timer: 1 - 12 hrs + continuous hold setting
- 100 CFM Fan
- 110 Volts
- 1800 Mg/Hr Output
- 3 Plates
- 7.5"H 9"W 12.5"D
- 9.75 lbs

Click Here

Sonin 4-in-1 Stud, Moisture, Metal & Voltage Detector
Do it all with this innovative 4-in-1 Meter & Detector. It detects moisture percentages 8%- 22% and finds if potentially damaging excess moisture is present; locates and traces water leaks; detects wood and metal studs, beams, and joists; and detects nails in wood up to 2" deep - all in a fast, accurate and easy to read LED display.

Click Here

Grandi Groom Carpet Brush
The Grandi Groomer is a versatile tool that can be used for agitation of soiled traffic lanes and loosening embedded dirt. It's also deal for agitating pre-spray into the carpet and excellent for working protector into the carpet. The carpet will look like new when finished with Grandi Groom after cleaning!

Click Here

In This Issue:

Interior Cleaning

35 Pressure Washing Indoors

40 Vacuum Recovery Systems, by Steel Eagle

48 Why I Use What I Use: The Unger SpeedClean Indoor Window Cleaning Kit

54 Chandelier Cleaning, by Keith S. Campbell, Acu-Bright Chandelier Services

Additional Features

41 Staying Committed to Your Business Plan, by Carlos Gonzales, New Look Power Wash

42 PWNA Announces 2013 Certification Schedule

44 Power Washers of North America: What it Means to be a Member, by Paul Horsley

46 Hydro Tek: Big Enough to Deliver, Small Enough to Care

51 Marketing Your Company On A Budget? Get Free Advertising On Craigslist!, by Henry Bockman, Contractor's Foundation

56 Floor Finishing Mythologies, Part 1, by Rick Meehan, Marko Janitorial Supply

46

54

Cover Photo
Courtesy of James Lewis, Underpressure Powerwashers, Inc., www.UnderpressureInc.com

---

eClean Magazine is published monthly

Publisher: Paul Horsley, paul@ecleanmag.com
Editor: Allison Hester, allison@ecleanmag.com

eClean Magazine
Box 262, 16 Midlake Blvd S.E.
Calgary, Alberta
Canada T2X2X7
www.eCleanMag.com

Photo courtesy of Extreme Clean Pressure Washing, www.ExtremeCleanPressureWash.com

Pressure Washing Indoors

by Allison Hester

James Lewis, Underpressure Powerwashers, Inc., is no stranger to taking on unusual projects both indoors and out. Living in Oak Hills, California, near the heart of Hollywood, Lewis has been called to clean up a number of television sets, like the Top Gear warehouse project shown on this month's cover. (See sidebar to learn more about his unique project.) But he does a number of "normal" interior projects as well, such as warehouses, auto garage and transmission shop floors, mechanics' bays at the big box stores, as well as restaurant kitchens and dining room floors.

"I know a lot of guys in the cleaning industry who won't take their work inside. It's too intimidating," he said. "However, if they would take the task on, they'd probably find it's easier than they expect...and it will open doors for all kinds of new projects."

Pressure washing indoors does present some unique challenges, but it also can be quite lucrative, particularly since many contractors don't offer these services. The keys are to choose jobs wisely, invest in proper equipment, utilize smart cleaning practices, and price to make a profit.

Here are some specifics to consider when cleaning inside:

Can the job be done safely? The first thing Lewis looks at when considering an interior job is how hard it will be to clean the area without causing damage. "We get some pretty crazy requests, and those we will turn down," he explained.

"But if it is a fairly straightforward project, we're not afraid to tackle it."

One of the biggest obstacles to cleaning inside is working around electrical outlets, wiring and lighting, because obviously water and electricity do not mix. Jobs that require cleaning ceilings and walls, in particular, call for extra precautions.

"When asked to clean the ceiling of a warehouse, we use a lift and cover all the lights with plastic, then tape everything up watertight and cut off the power," explained Matthew Pate of Extreme Clean Pressure Washing in Johnson City, Tennessee, who has experience doing several warehouse cleanings, tile and grout cleanings for commercial properties, walk-in coolers as well as some commercial garages. "We will then perform the cleaning using large lights that we run off our generator or extension cords to another section where the power is still on. We wait until the next day or so to remove the protective covers on all the light fixtures, switches, outlets and any other item that we might have covered, then fine clean those areas by hand."

However, even with these types of precautions, problems can arise. This was something Lewis learned the hard way when cleaning a Vertec garbage transfer station. Despite covering all electrical outlets, etc., water somehow, somewhere got into the electrical system and shut the plant down. Lewis had to "make the embarrassing phone call in the middle of the night" to let the plant manager know what had happened, then pay for an electrician to make an emergency call – on a holiday, no less. "They (the client) weren't happy, but they got over it because we did a great job...and we still managed to make a profit." Lewis has since cleaned that station again, but avoided the area where he believes the electrical problem originated.

However, electricity is not the only problem inside jobs can present. Ideally, the facility managers will have any products or machines covered or moved prior to the cleaning, but if not, contractors need to take precautions.

Then there are the unique situations. For example, Daniel Simmons of Pressure Washing America, LLC, in Houston, Tex., was recently hired to clean a refrigerated warehouse where the refrigerant used contained ammonia, so no

bleach could touch it.

For Lewis, an enclosed parking garage at an upscale shopping mall presented an unexpected problem when the water from the floor they were cleaning leaked through tiny cracks and poured onto the expensive cars parked below. Situations like these require some extra know-how in order to effectively complete the job. They may also require extra safety equipment – such as respirators – due to chemical fumes inside.

Speaking of fumes, there's the issue of carbon monoxide. Many contractors run their equipment outside, using long hoses to reach the interior. However, some jobs and contractors work better by bringing the equipment indoors, which can be dangerous if not handled properly. It can also cause problems with carbon monoxide metering devices.

Lewis said that prior to cleaning the enclosed parking garage, a friend warned him that a lot of garages have carbon monoxide metering devices. "If too much carbon monoxide is in the air, they will kick on fans. Green is ok. Yellow kicks off the fans. Red kicks off fans and alarms, which also notifies emergency services," he explained. "So we make sure the alarms are off, because we are going to make some carbon monoxide. The fans still work. We are also trained to recognize how to sense if the carbon monixide is causing problems and if so, we'll shut down the rigs." He also makes sure there is plenty of ventilation any time his equipment runs indoors.

How much time is allotted for cleaning? One of the biggest issues that interior jobs present is that of time constraints. For instance, with the refrigerated warehouse job, Simmons not only had a massive 860-linear foot, four story building to clean, he had a short window to do it in. "The warehouse is open almost 24 hours a day, every day. The only time it's closed is between 10 p.m. Saturday to 8 a.m. Sunday. So that was when we had to go out there," he explained. The maintenance manager, fortunately, recognized the challenges and told Simmons to put a four-man crew together and get as much done as possible. "I'm glad we charged by the hour rather than the square foot. That saved us a lot of stress."

Pate, too, mentioned that "how long of a time frame we are allowed to be on property to perform our cleaning services" plays a big role in how he prices a job.

However, there are also instances where the work can be done quickly. For instance, Underpressure offers kitchen exhaust cleaning and has started washing the kitchens and dining areas in some of their restaurants. "We can clean the kitchen floors in 15 minutes," said Lewis. "They look great when we're done, it pays well, and the clients are thrilled."

How clean is "clean?" For the refrigerated warehouse, Simmons' client recognized that the walls were covered in a quarter-inch of black "gunk" that was going to be very difficult to remove – particularly given some of the job's limitations. For instance, the internal temperature for the warehouse was only 38 degrees, causing the chemicals to react slower than they would in warmer conditions. And as mentioned earlier, cleaning products

had to not conflict with the ammonia in the refrigerant. In this case, the client wanted them to just do what they could.

Lewis' garbage transfer station job required removing layers of dust and grime from the building's ceilings and walls, which were so thickly covered that the outside light could not shine in. However, the client had no concerns about where the water went because the floors were simply covered with huge piles of garbage that would eventually be taken to a landfill.

What equipment is needed? One of the biggest issues to consider when cleaning inside a building is what to do with the water. While it won't take care of 100 percent of the water, one of the most popular options is to use a surface cleaner with a vacuum recovery system. (See the article on page 10 to learn more about these types of systems.)

Lewis, for instance, was "so impressed with Hydro Tek's Hydro Loop system that all our trailers are equipped with that system. When they upgraded the machine, we upgraded what we had to keep up with their technology, and they get better and better and better."

Pate, on the other hand, has two hot water machines, and a complete Sirocco reclaim system that reclaims all the wastewater as they are cleaning. "If you don't have a recovery machine, doing a large warehouse is not impossible to perform; however, you will have to check to make sure the drains in the floor are not clogged, or some higher than others causing other parts of the warehouse to flood," he added.

Getting the water off the floor is a big issue, and if reclaim equipment is not being used, it's important to know how to get the water from point A to point B despite obstacles. "When discharging down the drain, be sure to contact your local wasterwater department first to get the wastewater requirements that must be performed before discharge," warns Pate.

There are also areas, such as corners and around small obstacles, where you may have to clean without a surface cleaner, and it's important to note those and prepare ahead of time. Floor scrubbers are a nice addition, whether you purchase, rent, or possibly borrow from the facility being cleaned.

For reaching high areas, lifts are generally a must. The facility may have them on site and allow you to use them. However, you still may

Before and after photos of grocers supply warehouse. Photo courtesy of Pressure Washing America, LLC.

have to come up with other solutions, such as extension wands.

How much to charge? Pate says you should consider all of the following before pricing an interior job:
- How long we have to clean
- The size of the area to be cleaned
- What has to be removed in order to clean
- Walls cleaned? Ceilings cleaned?
- What is stored in the facility
- Obstacles that may cause issues
- Chemicals used
- Fuel Prices
- Labor

Finally, look for extra opportunities while you are there. For example, Pate's most difficult interior job required cleaning over 300,000 square feet to prepare for a coating to be applied. "They needed us to remove tire marks, but these were silicone and very thick. We were able to remove most of the tire markings. The coatings contractors were very pleased when they came in to inspect." Since that time, Pate has been working closely with David Phillips of Southern Stain and Seal to learn the process of floor coatings "since we left a large amount of money on the table by just cleaning and not sealing."

Again, Lewis encourages contractors to consider taking on interior cleaning. "Don't be afraid. Understand you're going to produce some water – that's just part of it. Get a vacuum recovery system to get it. Cover your bases. It will get you a lot more work in the long run."

eClean Magazine

About the Photo Cover

Jim Lewis received a phone call asking if he cleaned warehouse interiors. He was then asked to show up at a certain address for what he believed was going to be a 500x100 foot warehouse. When he arrived, he realized the facility was much larger, but the customer only needed a portion cleaned.

Upon entering the facility, the customer asked him to be very quiet because they were filing. It turned out to be the TV show *Top Gear*, a program where they compare different vehicles. In this particular episode, Tanner Foust – the famous race car and stunt car driver – was testing four exotic cars – "some that weren't even on the market yet" – to compare their acceleration and braking capabilities inside the warehouse.

"The mess we had to clean up was the gunk they put on the floor near the braking area to make sure they didn't go through the wall," he explained. "It was corn syrup. They really stuck to it. But they tracked it everywhere. So we did the 500 feet section, about 200 feet wide. rinsed with hot water, and vacuumed out of the warehouse.

Vacuum Recovery Systems

by Steel Eagle, www.SteelEagle.com

One of the major advantages of having a setup that allows for recovery of waste water is the opportunity to bid high paying jobs you may not be otherwise able to. Anytime you are able to have the equipment that allows you to tell a client "yes we can" – and deliver – the better!

Similarly, while you may have substantial competition in your area for more standard cleaning jobs, having a clean and capture recovery system will open you up above the crowd.

Also, now more than any other time in our history, customers are looking for environmentally-friendly solutions for their cleaning needs. Not only are there new federal, state and local laws, folks are just getting more eco-minded.

Usually there are a couple of scenarios that require wash water to be captured:

The local community or state codes mandate that wastewater from pressure washing must be recovered and treated before being dumped down the sanitary sewer.

The facility or area being cleaned does not have floor drains for the wastewater to go down.

If your client falls into one of these categories there are some things to consider.

What is the distance of the water recovery in feet? How far will your cleaning tool be from the vac unit?

What is the size of the cleaning tool: 11", 16", 24", etc.?

Once you have addressed these questions you can make a more informed decision of your needs. For example, if you want to run a 16" clean-and-capture tool 100 feet from the vac unit, then you need a much smaller setup than if you want to run a 16" clean-and-capture 600 feet from the vac.

Of course, the larger and further away the variables, the more expensive the setup will be due to needing higher CFM's (Cubic Feet per Minute), bigger engines and blowers to create the suction you will need.

There are several components that make up a vacuum recovery system:

The pressure washer itself, usually a hot water 4-5 gpm unit that is capable of 3000 to 4000 psi

The vacuum unit, commonly ranging in size from 16 to 38 hp, providing CFM ratings from 250 to 475. These vacuums are capable of retrieving from up to 600 feet depending on the tool size and number of operators.

The primary separation tank. This is where solids are separated from fluids.

The clean and capture tool. There are the different sized surface cleaners that connect to the vacuum. They are available in 11" to 24" diameters and some are made with handheld accessories, allowing for vertical wall usage.

The vacuum hose. Hoses must be 1.5"-2" and are available in 50' and 100' lengths. They are connected with hose barb connectors to attain the desired full length.

Accessories like vac hose reels and high-pressure hose reels are needed.

Take the time to discuss the particular cleaning situations you will most likely be presented with, with your salesperson. They can recommend the perfect system utilizing the correct complement of tools for the job.

Whether you are doing smaller interior office spaces or kitchens, or larger industrial/manufacturing facilities, Steel Eagle has a system that will do the job with ease and speed.

Steel Eagle was founded in 1993 to innovate new and dynamic pressure washing accessories. We are a customer driven company providing world class products for commercial and industrial cleaning and storage applications. To learn more, visit our website at www.SteelEagle.com

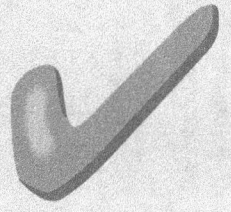

Staying Committed to Your Business Plan

by Carlos Gonzalez, New Look Power Wash, www.NewLookPowerWash.com

Starting a business is easy. Anyone can start one. Keeping motivated and committed is what sustains it and keeps you ahead of the pack. It can be tough to do, especially when things are not going so well. Following are some tips to help you in your quest to keep committed:

1. Set realistic and measurable goals. Without doing this first step, there is really no reason to continue. If you want to create a business that's there for the long haul, make sure you know exactly what you want to do and how soon you expect to do it.

2. Keep your goals in mind. Remind yourself what you want to accomplish. Don't let the mundane daily tasks keep you from your vision. You might find it helpful to write down these goals and put them in a place where you'll see them on a consistent basis.

3. Be flexible. The best business plans are the ones that are adaptable to a changing marketplace. Make sure your goals and methods can easily be changed if conditions call for it. Most of all, you must be willing to change. Don't forcibly squeeze yourself into a one-size-fits-all hat when there may be other options if you keep your eyes open.

4. Stay persistent The flexibility mentioned previously is important, but so is a level of persistence. Don't be so quick to bail on a method if it doesn't produce immediate results. Some marketing techniques, such as search engine optimization, can take months before seeing the fruits of your labor. Stick with these types of techniques until you are positive it will never be of benefit to your vision.

5. Keep it interesting and fun. Try to make your pursuits an enjoyable task. You probably started a business with the idea of being your own boss. This should be a motivating factor as you move forward. Even if it is slow to grow, at least you are not answering to anyone but your customers.

6. Surround yourself with supportive people. It's much easier to stay committed to something if you have a good circle of people on your side, whether they are investors, friends, family, or even customers. Remember that most people that are critical of your business likely work for someone else, and thus have no right to do so.

7. Do not be afraid to ask for help. Most people get into a small business thinking they can do it all themselves. This is extremely difficult, if not impossible. Starting a business is a huge undertaking and it's normal to require help. Doing it on your own might seem like it would be more rewarding, but not if it takes too much time to make it successful.

8. Review your accomplishments. If you are having a bad day or feeling like you are not getting anywhere, look back at all you've done since getting started. Write it down. By the time you are finished you will probably be surprised at all you have done. Keep this list handy and keep updating it with new accomplishments. Eventually all this work will probably lead to more profits.

9. Expand your horizons. Try to find ways to enhance your current products or services. Look at your competitors to find out what they are doing differently. Always be expanding your mind and your business will likely follow suit. This type of effort can also keep things more exciting.

10. Most importantly, stay positive. A positive attitude goes farther than you think and can be a great help in keeping you motivated. This goes for bothyour business and your personal life. Treat each disappointment as an opportunity to learn and grow in order to do it beter the next time.

Carlos Gonzales is the owner of New Look Powerwash, a high pressure cleaning company that provides services in California. To learn more, visit their website at www.NewLookPowerWash.com.

PWNA Announces 2013 Certification Schedule

by Allison Hester

For over 20 years, the Power Washers of North America (PWNA) has helped educate thousands of pressure washing contractors on how to clean the right way, and how to be successful in their businesses.

Two years ago, PWNA expanded their educational assistance even more by developing and implementing six new certification programs – in addition to their kitchen exhaust cleaning course – in house washing, roof cleaning, flat work, fleet washing, wood restoration, and environmental washing. Since that time, the PWNA has certified over 220 contractors in these various areas of expertise, and has announced a full schedule of certification classes for 2013. (See schedule on page 13.)

Why Certification?

With its long track record for quality educational seminars, roundtables and trade shows, why did the PWNA decide to add certification programs into their educational mix? And why should power-washing contractors want to be certified by the PWNA?

To answer these questions, I interviewed five of the PWNA board members who helped develop the association's certification programs, and who currently teach the six certification courses. Here's what I learned.

1. PWNA Certification Ensures Contractors are Up-to-Date on Techniques, Technology and Regulations.

Most of the PWNA certification courses were developed by a team of contractors with several years of experience in their fields. The purpose for this is to ensure that multiple perspectives are given during the course.

"PWNA recognizes that there is more than one way to do something, so we try to teach the basic, across-the-board techniques," said Charlie Arnold of Arnold Powerwash in Lewes, Delaware, who teaches the Roof Cleaning and Flat Surface Cleaning certification classes. "For example, there are several philosophies about the best method to clean a roof. I touch on two of the most popular methods, then encourage the class members to decide which method is best for them."

Additionally, certification courses allow individuals to learn about things they might never have otherwise thought of, explained Dan Galvin of East Coast Power Washing, Inc., who teaches the House Washing course. "Most contractors just think about throwing some chemicals on a house and washing them off. We look at the behind-the-scenes elements of the house washing process."

Paul Horsley of Scotts Pressure Wash, who teaches the Fleet Washing course, added that there is value for everyone to become certified. "Certification has obvious advantages for those who are new to the industry or who are new to a certain type of cleaning, but we can all benefit. We can all learn things, even if we've been in business for several years. I had been running a pressure washing business for 25 years when I joined the PWNA, and I learned a lot at the first meeting I attended. It was one of the smartest business moves I've ever made."

Finally, the courses can help contractors learn about the latest equipment options, as well as determine which types of equipment they need – or, in some cases, don't need.

"Most contractors wait until after the environmental course to purchase equipment so they will know what is required by law and won't invest in more than what's necessary," added Robert Hinderliter, who teaches the environmental certification course. "We also never promote the purchase of expensive reclaim equipment."

2. PWNA Certification Helps Contractors Set Themselves Apart Professionally

Credibility is one of the biggest advantages of certifications, and being certified by the industry's longest-standing, best known organization, in particular, looks good to customers. While customers may not know what the PWNA is, they can appreciate that it has been in existence for over 20 years.

"PWNA certification establishes a level of authority with contractors and lends professionalism to their company's image by demonstrating their commitment to continuous improvement," explained Wood Restoration Course Instructor John Nearon, Director of Operations for Exterior Wood Restoration, Inc., in Indiana, and founder of the Timber Ox product line. "This is important in separating you from the pack in the eyes of your clients."

Galvin reiterated this point, adding that PWNA certification "shows customers you're getting educated by a reputable, well established organization. You're keeping up on the industry, and you're in it for the long haul. It gives them peace of mind knowing you're not

---

2013 PWNA Certification Schedule

Fleet Washing Certification
March 21, Calgary, AB
Cost: $249 members/$449* non-members
Fee includes at one-year PWNA membership

House Washing Certification
March 8-9 at the ACR Products Round Table, Eaton, PA, Cost: $150

Roof Cleaning Certification
March 8-9 at the ACR Products Round Table, Eaton, PA, Cost: $150

Wood Restoration Certfication,
March 23, Cicero, Indiana, Cost: $395 members, $595 non-members

Environmental Certification,
Ft. Worth, Texas
March 15   June 14
Sept. 20   Nov. 15
Cost: $150, Participants must register for this course at least 14 days prior to the event

Kitchen Exhaust Cleaning,
Ft. Worth, Texas
Feb. 4-8   Mar. 4-8   April 8-12
May 6-10   June 3-7   July 8-12
Aug. 5-9   Sept. 9-13   Oct. 7-11
Nov. 4-8   Dec. 2-6

ACR PRODUCTS, INC.

ROUNDTABLE 2013

NON-REFUNDABLE PREPAID $55.00 ENTRANCE FEE

MARCH 8TH + 9TH 2013

START: 8:00 AM–?? BOTH DAYS CATERED BREAKFAST AND LUNCH

acrroundtable.com
acrproductsinc.com – acrpws.com

PWNA House Washing & Roof Cleaning Certification Classes Available

just throwing chemicals up on their house and dashing away with their cash." He also points out that many PWNA certified contractors can currently claim they are the only one certified in their community, giving them a distinct marketing advantage over their competitors.

3. PWNA Certification Strengthens Contractors' Authority with Regulators

The PWNA was founded in 1992 because wastewater regulators let Robert Hinderliter know they could not talk with him as an individual company owner, but could as a representative of a national trade association. "At that time, the industry was dominated by small businesses that could barely survive," he explained, "yet they were being required to purchase expensive wastewater recycling equipment.

Through the development of the PWNA, contractors were able to change the industry

Power Washers of North America:
What it Means to be a Member
by Paul Horsley, Publisher

Not all power washers are created equal. A truly effective power wash company will have not only the right equipment but a vast body of expertise gained from hands-on experience. Finding quality power washing professionals can be tricky, however – especially for companies or individuals who aren't sure what to look for in a reliable power wash company.

One easy hallmark to look for when vetting power washing companies is membership in the Power Washers of North America. A power wash company that belongs to the PWNA will go out of its way to make sure its power washers do an outstanding job, because that's what it means to belong to an organization that's committed to high standards. If a power washing contractor has membership in the PWNA, here are three things you can tell about them:

1. They take the environment seriously. Power washers in the PWNA take a pledge to comply with local environmental regulations, from collecting and responsibly disposing of wastewater to using biodegradable cleaners. But many don't stop there; members often go above and beyond to minimize their industry's impact on the environment.

2. They follow industry best practices for power washing. The PWNA provides a set of standards and best management practices (BMP'S) for power washing companies, which makes them more efficient and effective.

3. They're committed to education. Certification and ongoing education is an important component of the PWNA. The organization offers many classes and resources for power washers, including certifications such as house washing, fleet washing and wood restoration. Members stay up to date on the latest pressure washing technologies and have a firm grasp on how to apply them. In a nutshell, choosing a power washing contractor who belongs to the PWNA is one of the most reliable ways to ensure you hire a professional, reputable company for your pressure washing needs.

eClean Magazine   www.eCleanMag.com

requirements – which had previously been based off of the coin-op carwash and liquid waste hauler industries. "The result of the PWNA's effort is that expensive recycling equipment was no longer needed. I showed contractors how they could comply for a few hundred dollars – not thousands – and I gave out enough information that the average contractor could build his own equipment."

The fact is that "regulators look at a national organization differently than they do an individual company," explained Horsley. "It's also true that being certified by an organization that's been around for 20 years holds more weight with regulators than certifications from a private entity or a startup group."

4. Keeping Contractors Updated on the Newest Trends and Regulations

Because technologies and regulations change, PWNA members must recertify – i.e., retake the test, not the course – every two years to help ensure members can continue to demonstrate ongoing proficiency and professionalism

"More importantly though, we all need to re-freshen our skill sets occasionally. Recertifications reintroduce a level of clarity and focus to our respective disciplines, whatever our cleaning specialty may be," concluded Nearon. "Recertification also helps us, as an organization, establish and maintain the highest professional standards, which is vital to our mission at the PWNA."

Several PWNA certification courses will be offered in March, at October's Annual Meeting and Convention, and at other times throughout the year (see the PWNA calendar on page 13). To learn more about PWNA and their certification programs, visit their website at www.PWNA.org or email info@pwna.org.

PWNA Vendor Profile

Big Enough to Deliver, Small Enough to Care

Written by Allison Hester,
Sponsored by Power Washers of North America

2012 PWNA Convention's Hydro Tek skid giveaway winner Charles Puglusi (third from left) of Absolute Fleet Wash, Riverhead, New York. Also shown are Hydro Tek Regional Managers Bob Gruetzmacher (left) and Marv Gerdes (right), with ACR Products owner Tom Vogel.

Since 1999, Hydro Tek has supported the Power Washers of North America as a vendor, helping sponsor events and exhibiting and demonstrating their equipment, and recently giving away skid units at the annual conventions. (See sidebar.) "We like the PWNA and support them because it's for the end user – the contractor who is out there using the equipment every day," explained Hydro Tek Marketing Director Casey Meelker. "The PWNA provides these contractors with education and a brotherhood of sorts to talk about ideas and solve problems together. We really support that."

And PWNA members love Hydro Tek as well. "When we go to PWNA shows, we get the opportunity to meet so many people who own Hydro Tek," Meelker added. "They really like the equipment."

That is largely because Hydro Tek's equipment is designed with the contractor in mind – stainless steel, high quality components, and built from contractor feedback. "The main reason we support PWNA is that we know the equipment we build stands up and it helps the contractor who is using it every day. They need something that's dependable because they can't afford a breakdown. Our equipment stands up to that test."

The Hydro Tek Philosophy

It's a principle that Founder and President John Koen has implemented since starting Hydro Tek back in 1985. Koen had worked part time for a high-pressure pumping systems company, but felt there was a better way to design and make pressure washers. He started the company and was responsible for all aspects of the company: engineering, manufacturing, marketing and sales. The company began to grow – primarily in southern California at first, but later spread to distributors across America. Today, Hydro Tek equipment is sold and used around the world.

Koen's philosophy from day one was this: if you focus on quality and reliability from the very beginning, you will develop equipment that lasts longer than the competition's, help the end users do their jobs better, and build customer satisfaction.

And it's a philosophy he still practices today.

"John (Koen) is still very involved with the business, coming in every day and staying involved in our day-to-day operations to ensure our company's growth," Meelker explained. "I think that's important to a lot of our customers. It's nice for end users to know the owner is still very interested in helping people."

Hydro Tek also now employs around 60 staff members, each one of whom has a share in the company's success. Meelker added, "That really plays into peer accountability, helping us reduce waste and maximize accountability."

Several Hydro Tek team members get together for a monthly meeting to discuss how

In 2008, Hydro Tek moved into its 40,000-square-foot, state-of-the-art facility.

www.eCleanMag.com

to improve current products or improve what it already designed. "We get ideas directly from our customers," Meelker said. "If they call in with an idea or suggestion, we put them on an idea board, then discuss the ideas at our meetings."

The team also takes every customer very seriously, according to Meelker. "If someone has an issue or a problem, we want to take care of that right away. John has instilled this into us because he wants to make sure every customer is satisfied."

These types of concepts helped Hydro Tek achieve its ISO 9001: 2008 world-class quality certification in 2011, which is required by many foreign markets to ensure quality. "It's not an easy thing to do. We are audited every year by an independent agency to make sure we're handling everything correctly, measuring customer satisfaction, and meeting other certification requirements," Meelker explained.

Constant and Continuous Improvement

Another of the Hydro Tek team's guiding principles is constant and continuous improvement. One way they achieve this is to have a team of professional contractors, such as Jim Lewis of Underpressure Powerwashers, Inc. (see this month's cover story), test equipment prototypes prior to releasing it on the market.

"These contractors take our products out on a few jobs to let us know what works, what doesn't work, what needs to be tweaked, and how we can make it better," Meelker explained. "It's the best way to get honest feedback. So by the time it hits the market, it's already been used by contractors and adjusted based on their feedback."

Taking all these things into consideration, Hydro Tek has recently introduced two new surface cleaners onto the market. "Our surface cleaners have always been very popular with the contractors. You can clean concrete at least 10 times faster with a surface cleaner than with a wand," said Meelker.

At the end of 2012, Hydro Tek did a "complete redesign" of their surface cleaners, applying contractor feedback into the changes. For one, there had been a splash coming out the bottom that was hitting the areas along the side and getting the operator wet. "We took that feedback and added a brush along the back so there's no backsplash," Meelker added.

They also redesigned the three-in-one contractor

Hydro Tek demonstrations at the 2012 PWNA Annual Convention

Twister, a surface cleaner with a water broom spray bar that could be used for rinsing and for gum removal. At the recommendation of contractors, the new version has an edging nozzle to help users when they have to clean alongside walls. "We added this feature, changed the look of it, and were able to get it out without increasing the price."

The other surface cleaner Hydro Tek redesigned for 2013 is the vacuum surface cleaner, which used to have an 18-inch cleaning path. "We have a new piece of equipment that we're able to use to roll the vacuum tube. This has resulted in much better pickup, and we're able to produce a 24" cleaning path," Meelker explained. "It picks up a lot better and cleans more surface area, so it allows the contractor to clean much faster. Also, picking up the water at the same time allows the contractor to be more environmentally responsible and not putting contaminated water down the storm drain."

Environmental responsibility is something that Hydro Tek knows well. Being a California-based manufacturing facility has some unique challenges, as regulatory standards are stricter than in most parts of the country. However, it has allowed Hydro Tek to stay on top of pressure washing regulations. "We are usually at least a year or so ahead of the rest of the country," when it comes to compliance. "There are a lot of hurdles to overcome, but we try to be part of the solution."

To learn more about Hydro Tek and its products, please visit their website at www.HydroTek.us.

Why I Use What I Use

The Unger SpeedClean Indoor Window Cleaning Kit

an Interview with John Lee, John Lee Window Cleaning
by Allison Hester

For years, the traditional way of cleaning interior windows has been to wipe with a window mop then squeegee the water off. However, even "after years and years, no matter how good you are, it's almost impossible to not drip water," explained John Lee of John Lee Window Cleaning in Knoxville, Tenn. "That's where the challenge is – not dripping water on things that should not get wet," he explained, adding "I've done that so I know."

And Lee should know. He has been cleaning windows professionally since 1982, and does interior cleaning for around 70 percent of his clients, which includes residential, commercial and mid-rise cleaning projects.

At last year's International Window Cleaning (IWCA) convention and trade show, Unger introduced their SpeedClean Window Kit, designed for "drip-free interior cleaning." (Unger actually sent one to Lee prior to the meeting, and he helped test the product for them.)

The kit includes:
- A 1 Quart Sprayer on a Belt
- An 8" Aluminum Pad Holder
- Three 8" Microfiber Washing Pads
- Three 8" Microfiber Polishing Pads
- 1 HiFlo Thread Adapter
- 1 OptiLoc 3-section, 6 foot Telescopic Pole

(Note that each of these items can also be purchased individually.)

Lee's Findings

As with anything new, there was a learning curve – primarily on using the pads. As mentioned, the kit comes with two types of pads – a washing pad and a polishing pad. The washing pad is a longer micro-fiber pad than the polishing pad. "Because the wash pad has longer fibers, it has more carbon fibers

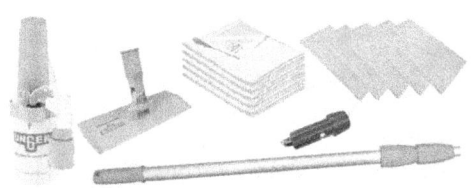

touching the surface of the glass, so you get better cleaning. The micro-fiber pulls the dirt from the surface, traps the dirt into the pad, and pulls it down into the bottom of the fibers. Then you can throw it in the washing machine to clean it."

The polishing pad, which is designed to polish out the glass, uses a much shorter fiber and is "quite a bit slicker," according to Lee. The original plan was for window cleaners to take a spray bottle with water in it, spray a little on the polishing pad, then rub the windows down. "The problem I found was that the polishing pad had so much friction on the glass that it was very difficult to slide," Lee explained. "The washing pad, on the other hand, was much smoother on the glass and had a much better glide. So I actually found that the washing pad, for me, was easier to use."

However, Lee found that too much water on the washing pad caused streaks. "There's been a learning curve to find the exact right amount of moisture to put on the washing pad so you can clean the windows but have it dry clear," he adds.

Lee also tested mixing water with Ecover, a brand of cleaner derived from plants. "Ecover uses plant enzymes to break down minerals and dirt on the glass. Through experimentation, I found the perfect mixture of pure water and Ecover to be able to clean the window and also have it dry clear," he explained. He carries the pre-mixed water/Ecover solution with him. "Unger sells a really nice spray bottle that connects to your belt so you can keep it there until you're ready to spray it on the pad."

One argument people have had about trying the indoor kit is that it won't clean dirty windows as well as the mop/squeegee method. "But actually, the traditional mop is a microfiber pad just like the indoor kit pad is," he adds. For really dirty windows, Lee says he has found that by submerging the pad in the water/Ecover solution, then ringing it out as dry possible, pretreating all the windows, then doing it a second time, he gets as good of results as he would have using a standard method.

However, in most instances, Lee says that the dry pads without any kind of spray are all that's necessary.

Lee also mentioned that he's found he doesn't personally use the HiFlo Thread Adapter because the Unger kit "screws right into the Unger pole."

Jeff Graveline with Unger explained the adapter's purpose. "This adapter has a special thread, referred to as Euro-Thread (we call it HiFlo Thread Adapter), and is common with water fed pole accessories. We use this adapter to screw into the aluminum pad holder, and the adapter fits into the end of Unger Aluminum poles," he said. "The reason we use the Euro thread is that the pad holder was designed to be used with waterfed poles. But John uses our regular ergo locking cone adapter to screw into the pad holder – which is an ACME thread (like the end of a common broom handle). Although the two threads are different, each will work with the pad holder."

Easier on the Body

A second argument people have about using an indoor kit is that it takes longer to finish the work. Lee admits that may be minimally true, but "because of my age and arthritis, I'm finding the indoor kit is much easier on my body," he points out. The kit has an aluminum pad holder that swivels 360 degrees so it's easier to reach low spots, "whereas if you're using traditional

method, you have to bend down to get the bottom half. With the kit, I can stand up and get the bottom half without having to bend."

So in the long run, at least for Lee, the value of the indoor kit being easier on his joints far outweighs any small amounts of time that might be lost by taking a little longer to clean. "It's basically the same argument that we face with people who still climb ladders as opposed to using the waterfed pole," Lee added. "There's a learning curve involved. It's taken me this long to perfect it, but once you get through the learning curve, it's easier and just as fast. Just like the waterfed pole is safer than ladders, the indoor kit is safer when it comes to preventing damage to your client's belongings."

It's important to note that other companies have their own versions of Unger's indoor cleaning kit, each with their own unique designs and gadgets. For Lee, it ultimately comes down to the pad. "That's the most important element. I think Unger has done a super job at creating the right pads."

2013 IWCA Convention & Trade Show
Feb 13-16, 2013 • St. Pete Beach, Florida

WHY YOU SHOULD ATTEND THE 2013 IWCA CONVENTION & TRADESHOW

- Meet face-to-face with more than 400 window cleaners from around the globe.
- Get step-by-step demonstrations of window cleaning tools by the industry's top manufacturers on the trade show floor.
- Help your business grow by attending educational sessions.
- Learn from industry leaders how to survive economic challenges.
- Get hands-on safety training all in one place.
- Enjoy a week away from the office at a beautiful beach front resort.

"2012 was the first time we attended the IWCA Conference, and I have to say it was time and money that was well invested. The conference was inspiring, educational, and motivating."

— LYNNE FISCELLI

"Hands down the most beneficial part of the entire convention were the networking opportunities with fellow business owners, from small to large companies."

— COBY POWELL

"At the recommendation of a fellow window cleaner I attended my first convention 7 years ago and haven't missed one since. We have gone from 5 window cleaners to over 25 window cleaners and owe much of that success to the investment in attending and getting involved in the IWCA years ago."

— MATT PIERCE

REGISTER TODAY AT WWW.IWCA.ORG
FOR MORE INFORMATION, CALL 1.800.875.4922

Marketing Your Company On A Budget?
Get Free Advertising On Craigslist!

by Henry Bockman, Contractor's Foundation

If you're just starting a new business, or even if your an established company, it takes constant promotion to keep a steady flow of new clients and jobs coming in.

Here is a quick overview on how you can use Craigslist as one resource for new clients.

How Craigslist Works

With over 50 million visitors a year, Craigslist can be a very effective tool for bringing targeted leads to your website. Craigslist allows you to place a post in nine major categories in more than 500 cities in 50 countries around the world. All postings are free, except certain postings in some major cities (even then, the cost to post is well below market average).

Craigslist is an open market for every combination of business you can think of. This includes business to business, business to consumer, consumer to consumer and even consumer to business.

Craigslist's "Tricks of the Trade" for Advertisers

Craigslist has a basic "no-frills" look. Your ad should mimic that overall look and feel. How? Just by keeping it simple and unlike some other, more content controlled websites, Craigslist users have absolute freedom to post ads with little limit to what one can say (which is refreshing in a society dominated by corporations).

It's very important to create an advertisement that is equivalent in quality to one that would be used in any other marketing medium. With that said, in order to get the most out of your Craigslist efforts (or any type of advertising for that matter), you need to keep several things in mind:

1. Make sure your spelling, punctuation and grammar are spot on.
2. Keep the posting simple. Don't ramble on unnecessarily (don't put extra fluff content).
3. Make sure the posting is up to date (if you had a special offer, did it expire? If so take down the posting).
4. If you have a website, make sure to include the link within the ad posting.
5. Stay on top of your phone and email to ensure a quick reply to any inquiry.

One thing you need to keep in mind when posting is the words you use in the post. As with any major search engine (Google, Bing, Yahoo), search terms and phrases are important. If used correctly, they can be effective marketing tools.

From a marketing perspective, it's vital to get the most out of the terms directly associated with its posting and/or website. For example, a business advertising "Commercial Cleaning Services" would want to make sure to include the following terms in its ad in order to produce the highest number of "relevant" responses: cleaning company, janitorial, janitorial service and office cleaning, to name a few.

Now, where do we advertise our cleaning business? The placement of your Craigslist listing is a rather important decision. There are nine main categories (and roughly 169 sub-categories) in every location. Craigslist is generally a very regional-based marketing outlet, so we will discuss placement with that in mind. With that said, pick the metro closest to your target area.

Next up is picking a category. Category placement is an important part of finding the right customer. Some categories may attract more attention, but may also be more competitive. You'll notice that some of the main categories feature sub-categories that are quite similar to others.

For our purposes we will be choosing the "services" category. The sub-category will be "skilled trade." Craigslist allows you to post ads for services here. People who visit this

more attention, but may also be posting is the words you use in the post. As with any major search engine (Google, Bing, Yahoo), search terms and phrases are important. If used correctly, they can be effective marketing tools.

For our purposes we will be choosing the "services" category. The sub-category will be "skilled trade." Craigslist allows you to post ads for services here. People who visit this area are actively looking to purchase specific services. I would recommend this category for commercial cleaning services. (For house cleaning services, you would probably want to post to the "household" sub-category.)

Now let's build an ad to market your commercial cleaning service. The following commercial cleaning advertisement portrays several elements that indicate a well thought out and effective Craigslist ad:

Let's break down what we did with this posting.
- The title was simple, "Affordable Commercial Cleaning Services" summed up our service.
- I created a little "separation" from all the other ads by adding the triple asterisks (***) on each side of the title.
- I made sure to include the benefits of our service (free quotes, the fact that we are bonded, etc...)
- Brief mention of what we offer (dusting, vacuuming and trash removal).
- Our website.
- Phone number.
- The simple design (copy is organized, aligned, and error free).

.***Affordable Commercial Cleaning Services***

Do you have an office that needs to be cleaned regularly? Choosing a quality office cleaning service can be a very stressful undertaking. With so many office cleaning companies to choose from, it can be very difficult to weed through all the less than reputable office cleaning / janitorial companies that are out there. YOUR NAME Cleaning Service set out to change all that.

Our company's mission is to provide the best cleaning services found anywhere in YOUR STATE OR COUNTY. We maintain a loyal customer base that includes not only many smaller commercial clients, but many large corporate and municipal customers as well. Benefits of our service include:
Free No Obligation Quotes
Security of a Fully Bonded Company
100% Satisfaction Guarantee On All Services
Peace of Mind by Dealing with a Fully Insured Company

We will work hard to craft a plan that meets your needs without breaking your budget.

Though the needs of each customer are different, the basic cleaning service includes the following:
Dusting
Vacuuming
Trash removal
Break room cleaning
Bathroom cleaning and disinfecting
Sweeping and mopping of hard surface floors

Whether you need a "highly detailed" or "just the basics" service plan, we can deliver where others have failed. We would love to have you as our next "satisfied customer." Contact us at 555-555-5555 for a free no obligation quote. Check us out on the web: http://www.your-website-here.

I fit in several variations of "commercial cleaning" (janitorial, office cleaning, cleaning companies, etc). This can help ensure the ad shows up when the searcher types in different search phrases that also convey the same meaning as "commercial cleaning" (some people like to call our services "janitorial, office cleaning and cleaning service" to name a few).

We could have gone a little further and added a special offer for the first three callers (20% off the first month for example). The point is we got our point across without going overboard.

Now what you need to do is track the response of this particular ad. This means how many people called, and how many turned into customers.

You will want to constantly test different posting to see what works best. Sometimes a simple tweak here or there can result in considerable improvement (or decrease) in ad's effectiveness.

If you start out testing from day one, you will be an expert after six months to a year, so make sure to track the ads consistently. As long as your service is professional and meets (and hopefully exceeds) the customer's expectations, there is no limit to the positive buzz that will channel through the various discussion forums available on Craigslist. Word of your business may even appear on the "Best of Craigslist" (postings that are nominated by craigslist readers) at some point.

At the end of the day, customers want the facts about your business. Include the pertinent information related to your cleaning service (like we did in the example ad). Feel free to use the example ad as a template for your first ad.

To summarize, your commercial cleaning Craigslist ad should allow who you are to show through (what you and your company represent). Your ad should also express a level of professionalism consistent with how you want your cleaning service viewed.

Get A 50 Page Guide With Tips And Techniques To Marketing Your Companies Services To Fifty Million Visitors On Craigslist! Click Here: For Your Copy Of "The Contractors Guide To Marketing On Craigslist"

Henry Bockman is a Navy Veteran that served with an F-14 Squadron on the USS America as an Aviation Ordinance man that specialized in Explosives and weapons. After leaving the military he started a home maintenance company in Maryland called Henry's Housework. Since 1989 Henry Bockman has dedicated himself to learning everything he can about marketing, web site development and Internet Marketing Systems.

Bockman currently resides in Maryland with his wife of over 20 years and two teenagers. He operates 5 companies, 2 contracting companies; Henry's Housework Inc, Commercial Restorations, a marketing company called Extreme Marketing Solutions which specializes in SEO, Social Media Marketing, online marketing, and lead generation. Contractors Foundation, which is a training company that provides power washing training, marketing and business success classes to help companies start up and succeed in any type of service based business, He also runs two On-line companies and several internet directories.

Chandelier Cleaning

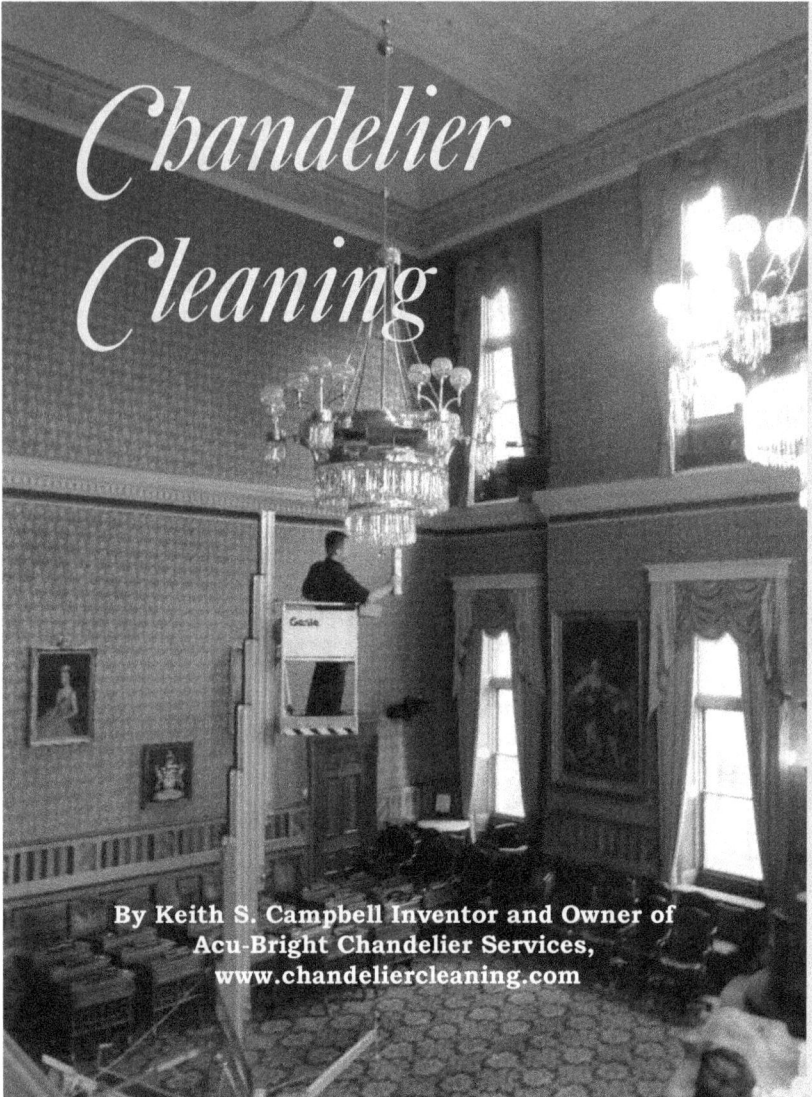

By Keith S. Campbell Inventor and Owner of
Acu-Bright Chandelier Services,
www.chandeliercleaning.com

Chandelier cleaning is a daunting task for home and business owners, as it presents a unique set of challenges with no easy in-house solutions. Chandeliers are often difficult to reach, fragile, complicated to disassemble (see diagram) and they have electrical components that must be handled with care.

In addition to these obstacles, chandeliers are generally very valuable and proper maintenance deems that they be serviced annually, or in some locations more frequently. That's why chandelier cleaning is a popular add-on service for window and other cleaning contractors.

But what are the options for safely caring for a chandelier and keeping it sparkling at all times?

Before reviewing the options, just a word of caution regarding chandelier spray cleaning products. These cleaners claim to be an easy and safe method for cleaning chandeliers but they, in fact, cause significant damage and make subsequent cleanings more difficult. Use of these cleaners can actually void the manufacturer's warranty (and yes, they will test the damaged area for chemicals). In short, chandelier spray cleaning products, no matter how they are marketed, should ***never*** be used on a fixture.

There are really only three options available to properly clean chandeliers. Following is a review of each method.

Option A:

The most commonly used method is hand cleaning. This option is often believed to be the least expensive because it can be done in-house, but it is so labor intensive that there are no actual savings. Proper hand cleaning involves the following steps:

• Documentation of crystal parts before removing (pictures are helpful)
• Removal of each crystal (ladders or scaffolding may be needed depending on height)
• Washing in hot water with a couple of drops of dish detergent
• Rinsing in de-ionized hot water
• Placing on a soft cloth to dry (hand drying with a microfiber cloth will be necessary to eliminate remaining spots)
• Reinstalling cleaned crystals (wear cotton gloves to avoid fingerprints)
• Clamping wires holding crystals for safety (be careful not to stretch pins on swags as this weakens them)
• Aligning crystals

An average size chandelier can contain thousands of crystal parts so allow extra time to properly clean by hand.

(Note: Be sure not to turn the chandelier during cleaning as this can cause an electrical short or in the worst case a fall from the ceiling.)

Option B:

There are a few small companies that will disassemble and hand clean chandeliers. When choosing such a company, we recommend customers make sure the contractors:

• Are fully insured.

• Do not use chemicals or chemical sprays.

• Have at least 10 years experience in the field.

• Have a large enough crew to complete the job in a reasonable amount of time, especially if the chandelier is in a frequently-used area.

• Agree that they are responsible for breakage and dropped crystal.

Option C:

The final option is the use of chandelier cleaning technologies using sound waves and a patented atomizer system. The benefits of these methods are:

• These chemical-free systems do not harm any portion of the chandelier.

• All chandelier styles are cleaned at least 85 percent faster than the hand-cleaning method.

• This touchless system eliminates breakage of crystal resulting from repeated handling of pieces.

• This touchless system eliminates stretching of pins resulting from excessive handling of pieces.

• The advanced equipment accesses areas that fingers cannot reach.

• The efficiency of the system makes it the most cost effective method.

• The efficiency of the system also makes it

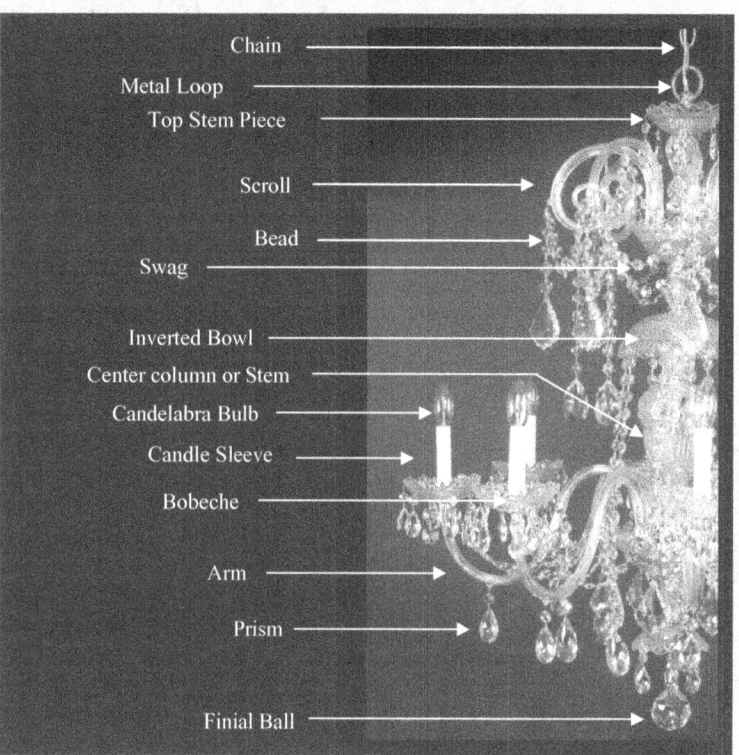

the least disruptive to customers.

Whichever method you choose, the end result will be a dazzling chandelier.

Keith Campbell is the only person in the world who designs equipment to clean chandeliers. His inventions have revolutionized the way chandeliers are serviced and his chemical free systems are ensuring the preservation of valuable and historical chandeliers across the country and in Canada.

Floor Finishing Mythology, Part 1

by Rick Meehan, Vice President of Marko Janitorial Supply,
www.MarkoInc.com

One of the great quests in the contract cleaning world is to properly apply coatings to floors so clients are dazzled by perfection to the point they become repeat customers. The mythos surrounding the process is that most cleaning professionals know how to achieve this level of excellence, while in reality they don't!

The prevailing attitude from the pros is they've seen it all, done it all, and know it all. As a supplier of floor finishing products, I get this lackadaisical attitude regularly. No offense intended to hardworking contractors – I'm just simply stating a fact. For many contractors this brashness results in declining profits.

Here's another fact: the cleaning realm evolves over time. Advances in technology tend to render prior methods obsolete, or at the least, antiquated. It takes continual updating of product knowledge and procedures to remain a floor finishing legend. Therefore, it is imperative that cleaning professionals humble themselves to the idea that they should seek the latest information prior to tackling every floor-finishing job!

Just because a cleaning pro has applied coatings successfully in the past does not mean that the same pro can do it again in the future. Experience is outweighed by advances in product engineering. Case in point: I have personally witnessed better floor finishing jobs performed by rank amateurs than by professional floor care specialists simply because the amateurs are careful to follow the latest methods and instructions. Amateurs tend to be more conscientious because they "feel the pain" directly. Applying floor coatings is physically draining, mentally tiring, and a sizable monetary investment.

Beautiful floors bespeak cleanliness. That's why floor care is a lucrative business. Unfortunately, much floor work can be a waste of time and money, either for the customer, or contractor, or both, due to procedural deficiencies. Before tackling a floor coating job, know these things:

TYPE of floor to be coated.
COATING recommended by flooring manufacturer or other authority.
AMOUNT of square footage to be coated.
PROCEDURE for applying the particular coating.
TOOLS needed for applying the coating most efficiently.
LABOR broken down by hours, people, and wages to completion.
TOTAL COST of all products and labor required.

Each item above represents a volume of information. How a contractor assimilates and handles the data affects profits. I recommend study, training, and practice.

Type of Floor Coating

Floor coatings fall into two major categories: water-based or solvent-based (oil-based). Water-based products include standard acrylic floor finishes, more commonly and incorrectly referred to as waxes, water-based polyurethanes, and latex paints. Solvent-based finishes include polyurethanes, epoxy paints, true natural waxes, and cure-seal concrete products. Each of these floor finish types requires a different set of rules and tools for preparation, removal, and application.

Another myth about floor coatings is the main reason for using them: they improve the appeal of floors – everyone wants a shine, you know. While partially true, I contend that protecting floors from damages due to wear, tear, and aging are the main reasons for using coatings. This is especially true when it comes to resilient floor types (man-made materials like vinyl).

My own showroom floor here at Marko Janitorial Supply was installed in 1971, an Armstrong Brand "no wax" rolled vinyl. This floor was designed to last up to eight years. By applying a quality acrylic finish despite the "no wax" claim, keeping it clean, buffing the surface occasionally, it still looks fabulous! This is the type of performance a floor specialist would want to sell and provide with every job. It's not about the shine; it's about curb appeal and cost control! Without protecting our floors, we would have spent approximately $30K replacing them at least three times during the 42 year period.

Materials and labor for stripping and waxing once every four years only cost us around $3200. Four years between stripping can be achieved by applying the proper acrylic finish for the floor situation, general damp mopping as needed, and buffing every month with a high-speed machine. Since acrylic floor finishes are the most important category of coatings due to shine and protection properties, considering that they may be applied to almost all floor types, and especially since they may also be used to protect other floor coatings, I will expound on them for the duration of this article. If a contractor can become expert at applying and maintaining acrylic finishes, laying all other types should be a piece of cake, naturally. Yes, I'm just being waggish.

Acrylic floor finishes, being water-based, are the simplest to apply, the easiest to remove, the shiniest, the best protectant; in short, the perfect choice for most resilient floors (manmade). Even some stone, ceramic tile, concrete, and aggregates can benefit from acrylic finishes depending on the particular situation.

The rule of thumb is this: if the floor material itself allows moisture to permeate freely between the substrate and the surface, it is unlikely that a resilient floor acrylic coating should be used.

Most acrylics seal the floor so water gets trapped underneath. This can cause major issues, both with the look of the finish and with the floor material. Loosening of glue, grout, discoloration of finish, mildew buildup under finish – these are among the problems that can be experienced if an acrylic finish is incorrectly applied to the wrong floor type.

There are synthetic coatings made today that specifically allow moisture to "breathe" from the floor. Usually this type of finish is applied to ceramic tile, stone, and concrete – but not necessarily. Remember the rule above. Make sure to identify the flooring material and match the coating to that material. As long as the floor doesn't need to breathe, acrylic floor finishes may be used.

Since acrylic finishes are strippable with standard high pH (13-14) caustic-based

strippers, and since most other types of coatings can withstand this stout stripping agent (not all), then acrylics can be applied to protect and improve the appearance of other coating types. Examples of compatible surfaces that would benefit: epoxy paints, moisture-cured polyurethane, polyurethane undercoats.

Another rule to keep in mind is that the tougher finish is always the first applied to the surface; the softer finish is always the last. Thus, a standard resilient floor can have an under-coat "permanent sealer" applied (although no longer recommended), followed by multiple coats of acrylic. What should be noted about all this is how important it is to know your finishes and procedures. Find a competent floor finish supplier. Utilize their expertise concerning compatibilities and procedures. Know exactly what you are doing before starting a job.

More to come next month. Visit www.MarkoInc.com to learn more.

Survey Results
Industry Trade Assocuations

Earlier this month, eClean Magazine surveyed readers about their thoughts on industry trade associations. Despite several industry websites requesting their fans to participate in the survey, the number of responses was significantly lower than our past surveys. While we could come up with various theories as to why, they would just be guesses.

So let's look at what we do know.

Of those individuals who answered the survey, 78% had been in business at least six years, with 63% of those having been in business 10 or more years.

Of those who answered the survey, 68% were currently members of a cleaning industry trade association. The Window Cleaning Resource Association (WCRA) had the highest showing, followed by the Power Washers of North America (PWNA), with the United Association of Mobile Cleaning Contractors (UAMCC) rounding out the top three. (Keep in mind that some associations have industry bulletin boards, and the survey was promoted on those.)

Here's the part that could be of value: what industry members want from an association. Each topic could receive a score between 1 and 4. Here are the results, from most important to least important:

1. Education/Training   (Score 3.5)
2. Networking with Peers   (Score 3.3)
3. Discounts from Vendors   (Score 3.0)
4. Marketing Materials, etc.   (Score 2.9)
5. Industry Advocacy/Support   (Score 2.8)
6. Association Publications   (Score 2.7)
7. Certification Programs   (Score 2.6)

Finally, those who answered the survey but were not members of an association listed that they did not see the value in them as their top reason for not joining (45%), followed by the answer that they just had not thought much about joining one (27%).

eCLEANmagazine™
The professional contractor cleaner's online resource!

Preparing for the Busy Season

Equipment
Education
Marketing

POWERWASH.COM™
SUPPLIES CHEMICALS TRAINING
1.800.433.2113
2513 Warfield St. Fort Worth, TX 76106

Shop Online 24 Hours a Day

BE READY FOR ANYTHING!   We have EVERYTHING you need!

Quick Links - Pressure Washers - Surface Cleaners - Chemicals & Detergents - Cleaning Supplies - Parts & Accessories - Pumps & Repair Kits - Training Materials

Add Soft Wash to Your Services!

Soft Washing is a low entry cost, high profit potential business. It is a perfect addition to any power washing business. Soft Wash machines spray chemical at low pressure to remove mold, mildew, algae, moss & airborne contaminants from Stucco, Dryvit, Vinyl, Aluminum, EIFS, Brick, roofs and more!

 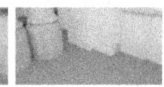

Soft Wash 5850 Kit
This kit includes 1 Delavan PowerFLO 5850-101E Pump, 4 5/8" PVC Hose Barbs with 1/2" MPT, 3 HZCP-8 #8 Hose Reel Clamps, 1 JA-8000 Soft Wash Gun, 1 PVC Soft Wash Wand, Qucick Coupler Plugs and Sockets, 4 V-Jet Nozzles, Clear Vinyl Tubing, 1 Mesh Filter Screen, 1 Roll of Teflon Tape

Mustang
Just install a battery, drop the pick up tube into your chemical tank, & you are ready for business!
- 12 volt, 7 GPM, 80 PSI, Flojet diaphragm pump with a maximum temperature of 160 F.
- Water tight battery box
- 10"x16" aircraft grade aluminum frame
- pneumatic tires
- ½" x 24" PVC Wand
- VJ-0080B Brass Nozzle
- ¾" x 150' Rubber Garden Hose
- Clear Vinyl Tubing with a mesh filter screen.

Colt
- 12 volt, 100 PSI diaphragm pump with a max temp of 140°F.
- JA-8000 Soft Wash Gun
- 1/2"x 24" PVC Wand
- ¼" stainless steel quick coupler socket
- 4 ¼" stainless steel quick coupler plugs
- Four V-Jet Nozzles 0°, 15°, 25°, 40°
- 162 feet of 5/8" poly braid hose
- 50 mesh filter screen

Some insurance companies cancel policies because of dirty roofs! Check out this news story reported by KJRHTV out of Tulsa, Oklahoma!
Click Here

Stock up & SAVE BIG on chemicals

Fresh Wash
Original   Lemon

When added to a bleach based cleaning solution Fresh Wash augments cleaning results by:
1. Allowing surface tension to be broken on the cleaning surface
2. Allowing bleaching reaction to happen at a lower overall bleach concentration
3. Allowing cleaning products to dwell longer
4. It also includes rinsing agents that help fight hard water spotting, and a masking scent

Landscape Fortifier
Developed to reverse the negative impact that caustics, sodium hypochlorite and sodium hydroxide based chemicals have on and around landscaping.

PM for Bleach
A buffering soap that can be used to reduce the damaging effects of caustic cleaners containing bleach or sodium hydroxide. PM for Bleach also includes an ingredient that adds a layer of protection for the next day's work.
This product is non-hazardous

Briggs & Stratton / Honda Engine Parts
- Briggs & Stratton Air Filters
- Briggs & Stratton Pre Air Filters
- A/C Air Filter, Honda HP
- Honda Pre Air filter for 20 HP engine
- Honda Air Filter for 20 Hp Engine
- Briggs & Stratton Spark Plugs
- Alternator, 15 or 20 Amp
- Briggs & Stratton Oil Filter
- Honda Oil Filter
- Briggs & Stratton Fuel Filter
- Briggs & Stratton Muflers
- Honda Muflers

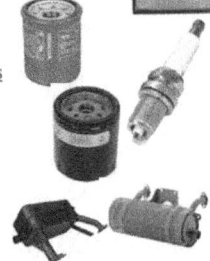

Burner Tune Up & Repair Parts
- Beckett Burner Drive Coupling
- Wayne Burner Drive Coupling
- Racor Fuel Water Separator
- Beckett Burner Fan
- Wayne Burner Fan
- Fuel Nozzles
- Burner Motors
- Transformers

www.eCleanMag.com

IN THIS ISSUE:

63 WHY Are You Buying WHAT You're Buying?

66 5 Ways to Work Smarter, Not Harder, by Larry Miller, Larry Miller, Inc.

69 PWNA Vendor Profile: Armstrong Clark

71 Three PWNA Certification Courses Offered in March

72 Why I Joined the PWNA, by Guy Triger, Puma Power Wash

75 New Products

76 How to Get the Most from Your Past Customers, by Linda Chambers, Soap Warehouse

78 Classifieds

79 2013 Pressure Washing Seminar, Mar. 13-16, Albany, NY

82 Do You Need a Hot Water Machine? by Aaladin Industries

85 Are You Ready to Spring into Action? by Tony Evans, A New View Window Cleaning

86 Floor Finishing Mythologies, Part 2, by Rick Meehan, Marko Janitorial Supply

89 Staying Ahead of the Curve, by Jason Wellman, KECSuppies.com

91 Get Listed! by Henry Bockman, Contractor's Foundation

93 Benefits of Spring Cleaning with Commercial Power Washing, by Paul Horsley

94 Snapshots of the 2013 IWCA Convention & Trade Show

COVER PHOTO
Window cleaning contractors were preparing for the busy season by comparing waterfed poles at the IWCA Convention and Trade Show, photo courtesy of Mark Reinhart

eClean Magazine is published monthly

Publisher: Paul Horsley, paul@ecleanmag.com
Editor: Allison Hester, allison@ecleanmag.com

eClean Magazine
Box 262, 16 Midlake Blvd S.E.
Calgary, Alberta
Canada T2X2X7

www.eCleanMag.com

EnviroSpec
Your Authority on High-Pressure Cleaning

| 18 HP Vanguard |
| TS-2021 |
| 5.6 @ 3500 |
| $3995.00 |

visit us at www.envirospec.com

When you arrive at our web site 'click on' Articles.

- PRESSURE WASHERS FOR DUMMIES
- PRESSURE WASHING FOR DUMMIES

OUR START:
- THE ENVIROSPEC STORY

GIVING BACK:
- SHRINERS CHILDREN'S HOSPITAL - TAMPA, FL
- SUZIE'S FRIENDS ANIMAL SANCTUARY
- THE BRODY YOUNG STORY
- THE WASHIN' WARRIOR STORY

BUSINESS:
- ADVERTISE YOUR BUSINESS BY DIRECT MAIL
- BUSINESS 101: IT'S ALL ABOUT THE CUSTOMER
- IMPROVING YOURSELF & YOUR PROFESSION
- SOCIAL MEDIA-THE BEST MONEY YOU'LL NEVER SPEND

CHEMICAL ARTICLES:
- PROBLEM/SOLUTION TRUCK WASHING
- RINSING - WHERE YOUR PROFITS ARE LOST!
- THE MAGIC OF SUPERFLO POLYMER

EQUIPMENT ARTICLES:
- ETHANOL - IS YOUR ENGINE RUNNING TERRIBLE?
- PRESSURE WASHER RECOMMENDATIONS

PUMP ARTICLES:
- SETTING UP A PUMP CORRECTLY
- PUMP RECOMMENDATIONS
- THE RIGHT HORSEPOWER FOR YOUR PUMP
- TIRED OF REBUILDING YOUR PUMP

SCHOOLS AVAILABLE:
- HOUSE WASH SCHOOLS

TECHNICAL ARTICLES:
- SETTING UP A BURNER DIAGNOSTIC CENTER
- K7 UNLOADERS - A LOVE/HATE RELATIONSHI
- CHOOSING A PRESSURE HOSE
- FREQUENT PUMP REBUILDS - WHY?
- HEATERS - VERTICAL VS. HORIZONTAL
- UNLOADERS, ALL YOU WILL EVER NEED TO KNOW!
- WATER TANK - HOW TO SET-UP

TOOLS YOU MUST HAVE & WHY!
- GLASS DAMAGE REPAIR PRODUCTS

WASHING ARTICLES:
- 10 EASY STEPS TO RUN-OFF CUSTOMERS
- FLEET OWNERS BEWARE!
- HOUSE WASHING
- WASHING THE BIG RIGS

NEW NEW NEW NEW **2013**

Our newest House Wash is just in time for the 'kick-off' of
HOUSE WASH SEASON

Each year in the 'off-season' we work on bringing something new to the contract cleaning industry that we hope will make their job easier and more profitable.

This year was no different. For the past several months our application engineers have been working diligently to produce a product that will meet many of the concerns that contractors brought to our attention over the last season. Concerns like mold, mildew, exhaust carbons containing lead have always been a major concern of the contractors and homeowners alike.

This year you can put a lot more 'kick in your step' with this new product. **MoJo** produces a high alkali bed that attacks all of these concerns and yet is gentle on the surface.

First introduced in the 70's the
TS-2021
is still a popular pump and here is a...
VERY POPULAR PRICE!
$422.00

More Contractors visit ENVIROSPEC.COM than all other industry web sites. To the left is why!

WHY Are You Buying WHAT You're Buying?

by Allison Hester

As you get ready for the busy season, are you going to purchase equipment? If so, choose your distributor wisely.

In interviewing a handful of reputable pressure washing and window cleaning equipment distributors – and please note that this is only a sampling of those who are out there – a common thread quickly became apparent. A reputable distributor does much, much more than simply sell whatever equipment is going to make them the most profit. They help contractors become successful.

In fact, distributors spend hours upon hours educating customers, and they ask questions – LOTS of questions.

Question 1: What Do You Plan to Clean?

When someone calls looking to get into the pressure washing or window cleaning industry, the first thing each of these distributors ask is what the contractor plans to clean. Very often, the potential contractor has no idea.

That's one of the reasons many distributors have developed educational resources – online bulletin boards, article libraries, Facebook groups, and even print magazines. All of these are designed to help the veterans and newcomers alike get their questions answered so that they can be more successful.

"If someone calls us up and has no idea what they want to do, the first thing I say is check out our forum," explained Alex Lambrinides of Window Cleaning Resource (WCR). "I try to direct them there because a lot of their questions are basic industry knowledge that they can easily find answers to on the forum."

"The first thing I ask is 'what's your business model? Are you doing commercial work? Are you doing residential?' And the list goes on and on," added Paul Kassander of PowerWashStore.com. "I don't want to sell someone a $6000 hot water skid when he can get by with a $1400 cold water unit."

That seemed to be a common theme among reputable distributors. They weren't out to just make a quick buck. They wanted to make long-term customers who will be successful and hopefully provide repeat business.

"Contractors overkill everything when it comes to buying the equipment they need," said John Allison of Envirospec. "Just because manufacturers produce an eight gpm, 4500 psi hot water machine doesn't mean that's what you should buy. In many cases, hot water is only needed if you aren't using the right chemicals." (There are situations where hot water is necessary. See "Do You Need a Hot Water Machine" on page 24 for more on this topic.) Allison added that with the right chemicals, "you can get into a high-quality entry-level machine for less than $1500 and be right there with the big boys."

PowerWash.com's Michael Hinderliter mentioned another important consideration is where you live. "If you're in a big city, you can choose to specialize in a certain type of cleaning. That's why living in the Dallas/Ft. Worth area, I've been able to focus on fleet washing and kitchen exhaust cleaning," he explained. "If you're in a more rural area, you really need to have holding tank, hot water, high-volume, and good pressure because you're having to cover a broad spectrum of cleaning in order to stay in business."

A good option for new window cleaners, on the other hand, are the starter kits for both residential and

TOP: Window cleaning contractors test water fed poles during the outdoor demonstrations at February's IWCA Convention and Trade Show.

BOTTOM: Contractors test new equipment during the PWNA outdoor demontrations last October.

commercial cleaning, such as the ones that WCR sells. Some of these kits are put together by manufacturers, while WCR puts others together themselves. "We put a lot of thought into these kits to really give new window cleaners what we feel will best benefit them," Lambrinides said. "However, we can customize one for you as well if, after your research, there something you feel is missing"

Question 2: What Is Your Budget?

For reputable distributors, this question is not asked so they can get you for every penny you've got. It's to help them prioritize where you should spend your money to get the most from your budget.

"Otherwise, I just spent all your money on equipment and three months later it's on Craigslist," Kassander explained. "I like to leave people with as much money in their pocket as I can so they can operate the business. I think a lot of people don't understand that even if you're doing well, it's probably a six-month process before you start bringing in enough revenue in to start paying yourself anything above covering your expenses."

Also, Kassander points out, some contractors have different priorities when it comes to getting their equipment set up. Some have larger monetary budgets but little time, so they want a turnkey system. Others may have more time than money. "That helps us determine where they can save money, such as having them pick up a water tank at their local farm supply place rather than through us," he added.

Another consideration is that a contractor doesn't have the budget for a hot water machine now, but hopes to get one in the not-too-distant future. "Then we know we have to get them a certain type of equipment so they can add hot water heater later without having to add a generator," Kassander said. "If we know the direction of where they want to go with their long-range planning, we can put something together that helps them achieve that goal."

The same premise holds true for window cleaners as well. "For instance, if an upstart individual does not have much cash to get started, we will provide him with a proposal for equipment that will get the job done but not exhaust his funds all at once," explained Dwight Rowe of J.Racenstein, a window cleaning supply house that has provided equipment to contractors for over 100 years.

"On the other hand, sometimes businesses look to add window cleaning to their existing services. In that scenario, perhaps a more elaborate offering could be proposed including water fed poles and a reverse osmosis/de-ionization processing unit."

Finally, the same general principles hold true for buying chemicals as well. "We definitely encourage the contractor who wants to get his pricing (on chemicals) down to buy higher quantity if he can afford it and has the storage space. There's less shipping and handling involved so you save money," said Hinderliter. "If you can get away from having to ship UPS and use a large quantity shipping company, you can save quite a bit."

Question 3: Are You Ready to Upgrade?

Contractors who have been in the business for awhile and are ready to upgrade typically have a general idea of what they are needing.

"Contractors looking to upgrade usually want more reliability and durability," said Hinderliter. "We encourage them to buy better quality equipment that's going last. If you buy this cheap, it's going to break down and you're going to lose time and money."

"The most expensive way to go into the mobile wash business is cheap," stressed Allison. "Talk with others about which parts they like. Don't necessarily talk just to your local distributor because they're may just try to sell you whatever the special the week is. Talk to other contractors and talk to people like us. I'll tell you what works and what doesn't; if anyone knows, we know."

That said, even if you think you know what you want, a quality distributor may have other ideas worth considering. "You may have a certain type of equipment in mind, but we may know of something else that we believe will work better in your situation," said Kassander. "And because I've been a contractor for 20 years and have done a lot of different types of cleaning, I try to offer suggestions on how to achieve the results you want in a way you may not have yet considered."

A Final Note

As mentioned, distributors spend many hours on the phone talking with contractors, trying to help them make smart equipment choices. Look for a distributor who is willing to listen and help.

"This time of year we get lots of calls from guys researching the industry. It's not unusual for them to call us from five to 15 times," said Lambrinides. "They're trying to figure out what they need to get started. These are the guys we can sell the right equipment to because we know that they're doing their research."

On that same line, however, respect these distributors' time. Sadly, it's not uncommon for contractors to spend hours getting help from a distributor, only to then go and buy from someone else who had the same product for a few dollars less. "We always encourage contractors to buy from whoever has helped them get the answers they needed, whether it's us or someone else," said Hinderliter.

Remember, as Kassander concluded, you're not just buying equipment from these distributors. "Because prices really are not that much different, when it comes down to it, the only thing a distributor has to offer over another distributor is their experience and their service."

eClean Magazine

5 ways to work Smarter, not Harder

by Larry Miller, owner of Larry Miller, Inc., and IWCA Board Member

The International Window Cleaning Association (IWCA) encourages members to share stories about what they've learned in the business – good and bad. The more we learn, the better we can do our work and keep our business growing. One thing I've learned, sometimes the hard way, is that it can be a real "pane" for window cleaning professionals to try to do everything themselves. Here are five tips you could use to step up your window cleaning business.

1. Spend Less Time Running Around Doing Estimates

Picture yourself being freed up from all that hectic driving around or time on the phone you may still be doing to provide residential window cleaning estimates. Think what better things you could do with all those hours and money you spend on gas. That's something I was talking about at the last IWCA Convention when I ran into Curt Kempton. Turns out that Curt has a way to make giving and getting window cleaning estimates a whole lot simpler, thanks to technology.

ResponsiBid is a product designed to help residential customers (prospective and current) use an online form to prepare an estimate. It only takes two to five minutes to fill out the form and submit it. They get an automatically calculated basic estimate promptly. If it costs too much for their budget, they walk away which is also a simple way to prequalify leads. Find an online form service and for a monthly service fee you can focus more on what you do best, window cleaning.

2. Don't Get Stuck in an Office

Phone call overload? Who's fielding all those calls? Service companies like exec-u-sist provide people that answer your phones to bring all that into line for you. Find a U.S. based phone service that can answer phones, make appointments and help you stay in contact when you're on the road. Having such a "virtual office" can pay off in countless ways.

For instance, if somebody calls with a question about an estimate, the service company can get you on the phone in a conference call so you can provide attention directly to your customers promptly. It frees you up from unnecessary interruptions and distractions when you're on the job.

3. Stop Trying to Play "Tech Geek"

You know how to clean all kinds of windows but if you're like me, probably not Microsoft Windows! That's why it's smart to find a professional IT guy to help keep your website and computer running smoothly and up to date. I count on Charles Dean, founder of Science & Technology Solutions, Inc.

Now I can even get all the information I need to keep things running right from my cell phone. It's like having all the resources in the office, on my phone. So I can see online estimates by email wherever I am. That keeps us all coordinated and communicating "on the same page." Having an IT professional on call can help take your window cleaning business to a whole new level.

4. Be Prepared for "Breaking" News

Homeowners may be unaware of small cracks or chips in windows or a ripped screen. When we first get to a home, we do a visual walk-around inspection before we start work. We may spot damage then and call the homeowner right away to report and see how they want to handle it. We work with a local, reputable repair company called American Screen and Glass in Sterling.

Choose a company that can provide a free online estimate to your customers promptly and schedule an appointment to pick up the screens and/or do repairs right on the property. When they're pleased with results, they'll recommend that company to their friends and neighbors and that's a good reflection on you.

5. Leave Basic Paperwork to a Professional

Accounting, bookkeeping and tax preparation are a necessary part of doing business. But personally, I'd rather be out meeting people and sharing business leads. Paperwork can be demanding. Your time is more valuable speaking with prospective customers and business partners. Find a reliable professional and/or firm to take care of that work and focus on your networking.

Outsourcing, as I've described here, is becoming more and more popular as a way to grow your business while keeping payroll and overhead costs affordable. Once you've made those contacts, you can find and share business referrals with them, too.

Larry Millir is the owner of Larry Miller, Inc., in Ashburn, Virginia, and a member of the BOD for the IWCA. To learn more about the International Window Cleaning Association,

PWNA Vendor Profile

ARMSTRONG-CLARK COMPANY

Jake Clark of the Armstrong-Clark Company

by Allison Hester

Jake Clark worked seven years as a coatings contractor, helping teach guys around the country how to clean and preserve wood shake roofs. And for seven years he walked along wooden shake roofs, scratching his head, trying to figure out a better process.

Clark came from a paint and coatings background, a career that goes back five generations in his family, with ties to the Civil War era. In the painting industry, which was where he had worked since 1974, the available products were dry sealers that were applied to dry wood.

It didn't make sense.

"Wood deteriorates because it dries out, cracks and curls," he explained. "It seemed like common sense. If you're hands are dry and chapped, you put a non-drying conditioner on it. Not a drying coat. The same holds true with wood."

Clark was getting his roof coating materials from Jim Armstrong, and was actually buying about 95 percent of Armstrong's production. This, and the desire to return to his coatings manufacturing background, led him to join with his supplier and create the Armstrong Clark company in 1989. "I used what I had learned from both manufacturing and contracting experience to create a sealer that would actually give wood the treatment it needed."

The result was a different kind of product – one that incorporated non-drying oils that separated from the dry parts of the formula (e.g., linseed oil, fungicide, water repellents and pigments). This allowed the non-drying components to seep into the wood while the dry components sealed the wood at the surface, locking out water.

Entering a New Industry

For several years, Armstrong-Clark sold most of their products to paint stores, and mostly on the West Coast.

Then Alan Broom, a wood restoration contractor in Birmingham, Alabama, happened upon the Armstrong Clark website. Broom bought some product, tried it, liked it, then wrote about the stain on some of the industry bulletin boards. He found that essentially no one had heard of Armstrong Clark, and they were leery of what they felt might be another "fly by night" company – even though in truth, the manufacturer has been around for 24 years.

"To be honest, I'd never heard of the pressure washing/wood restoration industry before either," Clark added. "Oh, I knew there were a handful of contractors that did this kind of work, but I had no idea how large the market really was."

So, Clark set up a program to help interested contractors eliminate their risk by sending out free four-ounce sample cans of each product in each color. "We let them brush those out, pick the one color they liked the best, then sent them a free five-gallon pail," he explained.

The program was extremely successful. "It seemed like a common sense offer to me, but it had bigger dividends than I ever imagined," Clark added. In fact, today about 30 percent of Armstrong-Clark's business comes from the pressure washing industry.

Since that time, Armstrong Clark has become a leader in wood sealers for the pressure washing/wood restoration industry, and Clark has made many great friendships along the way. "I really like this industry," he adds. "It's a great bunch of hard-working people who are dedicated to their craft."

National Growth

A large contractor, Steve James, asked to open a physical and cyber store called the Stain Shop. Other distributors, such as ACR Products, The Sealer Store, and PowerWash.com, have also come on board.

Having distributors greatly helped Armstrong Clark get their products into the contractors' hands faster. "Not having to ship from California has helped out a lot, and it's been a wonderful experience getting to know the wood restoration guys."

However, perhaps his favorite way of getting to know the "wood restoration guys" has been through his involvement with the Power Washers of North America (PWNA) where he has been a member and sponsor since 2008. "It's been very exciting to meet these guys and become great friends with them at the PWNA conventions," he said. "It's exciting to see them take the wood certification classes. I love getting to talk with people who know about wood restoration. That's why I'm a major sponsor for the PWNA, other national organizations and round tables."

In 2010, Armstrong was given the Robert Hinderliter Award for Excellence by the PWNA.

Continued Growth

While Armstrong Clark has some new products in development, the company's biggest change for 2013 will be moving to a new, much larger facility. Clark assures his customers there will be no interruption of service during the moving process, but adds that he's holding off on some new product campaigns until he can give them his full attention.

"We really enjoy our affiliation with the PWNA," Clark concludes, "and we know we never would have gotten as far as we have – to a place where we need a new, larger facility – if it wasn't for their support."

To learn more about the Armstrong Clark Company, visit their website at www.ArmClark.com.

Three PWNA Certification Programs Offered in March

by Allison Hester

In March, the Power Washers of North America (PWNA) will be offering three opportunities for certification (in addition to the montly kitchen exhaust cleaning school) – in fleet washing, wood restoration and environmental cleaning.

Last month, eClean Magazine looked into the benefits of PWNA certification by talking to those who developed and teach the courses. (You can read the article here.)

But if you're wondering if the everyday contractor has found that certification really makes a difference in their business, the answer is a resounding "YES!"

"Since joining the PWNA and becoming certified in flatwork, house washing and roof cleaning, our company has more than doubled its sales," said Mark Forbach of Green Thumb Professional Services. "Being able to educate the customer and show them we are trained and certified has made a significant impact on our business."

Guy Triger of Puma Pressure Washing in San Francisco has also seen phenomenal results since becoming certified in fleet washing and environmental cleaning last October. "When I go to do an estimate and show the potential client my certification, they are immediately impressed," he explained. "They usually have no idea that there are organizations, training and certification programs available for power washing. More often than not, I am hired on the spot!"

So as you're preparing for the busy season, consider participating in one of these three courses offered next month to get a jumpstart on your marketing and sales for the year.

Environmental Certification Course, Ft. Worth, Texas

"Best Management Practices (BMPs) are changing from year to year, and contractors will have to learn new ways of doing business," explained Robert Hinderliter, who teaches the PWNA

2013 PWNA Certification Schedule

Fleet Washing Certification
March 21, Calgary, AB
Cost: $249 members/$449* non-members
Fee includes at one-year PWNA membership

Wood Restoration Certfication,
March 23, Cicero, Indiana, Cost: $395 members, $595 non-members

Environmental Certification,
Ft. Worth, Texas
March 15   June 14
Sept. 20   Nov. 15
Cost: $150, Participants must register for this course at least 14 days prior to the event

Kitchen Exhaust Cleaning Certification,
Ft. Worth, Texas
Feb. 4-8   Mar. 4-8   April 8-12
May 6-10   June 3-7   July 8-12
Aug. 5-9   Sept. 9-13   Oct. 7-11
Nov. 4-8   Dec. 2-6

Robert Hinderliter

Environmental Certification Course. "Contractors are generally afraid of the Clean Water Act and what it may require. We teach what is actually happening in the field, based on a 'Public Comment Period' with 40 regulators and 100 contract cleaners who arrived at a consensus that was good for the environment, the municipalities, the contractor, and the public."

The course was developed and is taught by Hinderliter, who founded the PWNA 20 years ago because of environmental pressures for the power washing industry, and who has since taught thousands of contractors and hundreds of regulators. "My courses have been reviewed by more regulators than any other course," he added.

And contractors with environmental certification are finding they have a definite advantage over their competition. For instance, Triger – who lives in the highly-regulated San Francisco area – has learned to work closely with his area's regulators, and as a result is getting quite a bit of business, despite only being in the industry a few months.

John Tornabene, owner of Clean County Powerwashing in Long Island, NY, took the environmental certification course last October as well, primarily to help him land more

Why I'm a Member of the PWNA

by Guy Triger, Puma Power Wash, San Fancisco
www.facebook.com/PumaPowerWash

There are many reasons one becomes an entrepreneur. I am sure every business owner has a unique story to tell about how it all started. For me, personally, it was always for two reasons: first, to improve other people's lives with my products and services and, second, to challenge myself by setting unrealistic goals and finding ways to reach them.

When I decided to establish Puma Power Wash, my pressure wash company based in San Francisco, I knew I could change people's lives by providing an excellent cleaning service in the commercial and residential sectors. First, I started research online, and I discovered the complexity of the pressure washer industry. One needs to have the knowledge, abilities, and resources to be successful. When I found out about Power Washers of North America (PWNA), I called the website's number and had a long conversation with Jackie Gavett, executive director of PWNA, I am glad I made this call. Jackie provided me with excellent information and answers to my hundreds of questions. Right then, I decided to join PWNA and even register for the upcoming convention in Florida. Jackie helped me choose the classes to fit a newcomer in the pressure wash industry.

parking garage cleaning jobs.

"Some of the parking garage bids specifically laid out that they wanted their drains to be protected. They also did not want wash water runoff to leave the premises," he explained. "In the PWNA Environmental Certification Course, I learned how to berm storm drains, then how to collect wash water to filter out the sludge so that it can then be dumped in a designated area assigned by the garage facility manager. I learned about oil socks and where to place them in different situations, such as by a storm drain or in a drum while vacuuming up your wash water in your filtering process. Also I learned that in some instances you can have your wash water go into a landscaped area when that's considered an acceptable practice." Since becoming certified, Tornabene has since won several new parking garage contracts because he had this knowledge and the certification to back it up.

The cost of the environmental course is $150 and participants must register for this course at least 14 days prior to the event.

Fleet Washing Certification, March 21, Calgary, Alberta

Ross Welhelms of West Coast Fleet Wash attended last year's Fleet Washing Certification Course in Calgary, Alberta, and gave it "five stars!" He continued, "What a great experience! I'm leaving with key lessons, insider tips, and true inspiration. The value I got out of this program is easily worth 10 times the amount it cost!"

The fleet washing course is led by eClean's very own Paul Horsley, owner of Scotts Pressure Wash, who has more than 35 years industry experience and is the mastermind behind one of Canada's most successful power

---

The convention in Florida was a great learning experience for me. I had the opportunity to meet people, attend classes, and learn from the most expert leaders in the pressure wash industry. The classes about environmental issues, led by Robert and Michael Hinderliter, were eye opening. The course by Paul Horsley about fleet washing was spectacular. During the breaks, I had the privilege to meet members from different states, who provided me with great advice. One of the best suggestions was to find my customer base before purchasing the pressure wash machine.

When I returned to San Francisco, I had a long list of notes taken during classes and my conversations with PWNA members. By implementing those strategies, I was able to build a steady customer base in a very short time. When prospective customers call me for an estimate, I always show them my certifications from PWNA, and their next question is, "When can you start?" The PWNA provides such an amazing support group; whenever I have a question about cleaning procedures or choosing the right detergents, all I do is send a picture of the area that needs cleaning to Larry Hinckley, senior technical advisor at Powerwash.com, and he will advise me about the best cleaning steps. I am so impressed with the professionalism of Powerwash.com that I have registered for the five-day mobile power school held in Fort Worth, Texas.

Joining the PWNA was the best business decision I ever made. It helped me start Puma Power Wash successfully. As Richard Branson, founder of the Virgin Group, says, "Business is like a picture: You have to get all the little nuances right to create the perfect picture or the perfect company." Join the PWNA—it will help you get all the nuances right from the start, and you will have a support group that does not exist in other industries.

Paul Horsley

wash companies. Horsley has a staff of over 40 employees and a fleet of more than 23 mobile units that specialize in fleet washing, commercial and flat surface pressure washing, and rail car cleaning.

Because fleet washing is one of the most tightly regulated cleaning markets, the fleet washing course not only cover the in's and out's of how to efficiently wash fleets, but covers a lot of environmental-related topics as well.

The cost for this certification course is $249 for members, $449 for non-members (cost includes a one-year PWNA membership).

March 23, Wood Restoration Certification, Cicero, Indiana

The PWNA Wood Restoration certification course was created by a panel of contractors from across the U.S. and Canada who have spent years in the wood restoration industry. The course is taught by John Nearon – who helped write the curriculum – and who has been in the wood restoration field for many years operating Exterior Wood Restoration, Inc. Nearon specializes in almost all types of outdoor wood structures, from the cleaning and restoration of cedar shake roof systems, to decks, fences and log homes.

"John (Nearon) is an absolute scholar about wood restoration," said Mike Palubiak of Perfect Power Wash in Akron, Ohio, who took the wood certification course at last October's PWNA convention. "I don't think you could find someone better to put that course on and help put the curriculum together."

Palubiak, who has been in the industry for 13 years and has done a lot of wood restoration projects, added that he gained a number of valuable insights through the course that have changed how he approaches customers. "The course was very scientific, which was extremely valuable from a sales standpoint," he explained. "Since becoming certified in wood restoration, my staff and I can speak to a customer on a whole different level so that they feel confident that we know what we are doing, which definitely gives us an edge over our competitors."

Future Courses

While obtaining PWNA certification prior to your busy season will give you a definite edge, if you are unable to take a certification course in March, don't fret. Each of these courses – along with several others – will be offered again at the PWNA Annual Convention, October 17-19, in Orlando, Florida. Some certification courses will also be offered again at other times during the year. Check with the PWNA or the eClean events page to keep up with these dates.

To learn more about the PWNA or its certification programs, visit their website at www.PWNA.org, or contact Jackie at info@pwna.org.

New Products

New Automated Window Cleaning System is Ideal for Washing Mid-Height Buildings

The new Sky Pro® Window Cleaning System is a technological breakthrough in automated window and building washing equipment, providing a safe and inexpensive way to clean windows, frames and exteriors of buildings. The brand new model, Sky Pro Mini™, is a smaller version of the Sky Pro® Window Cleaning System that is portable, lightweight (weighing just over 100 pounds), and ideal for cleaning windows on mid-height buildings. A two-person operation can safely, quickly and profitably clean not only windows, but an entire building. It is much safer and easier to use than manual window cleaning equipment.

The Sky Pro Mini™ is made of lightweight aluminum so it will not rust or corrode. It folds down for easy transport, easily fitting into the back of a pickup truck. It has removable transport wheels for easy and fast maneuvering, and is easy to set up and ready to work in minutes.

The Sky Pro Mini's 40-inch self-cleaning quick-change brush cleans all surfaces gently and effectively. The brush uses finger foam technology that keeps grit and dirt from becoming embedded in the brush. The dual motor design maintains brush torque and speed to assure an even cleaning motion. The unit cleans an entire building at a variable speed up to 30 linear feet per minute, translating to 25,000 square feet per day. It uses less than half a gallon of de-ionized or reverse osmosis water per minute and leaves a spot-free clean without chemicals.

A special lithium-ion battery delivers 8 hours of operation to power the Sky Pro Mini. Two batteries are included along with a quick charger. The unit features an emergency stop button, 12-volt wireless remote to start and stop the brush rotations, and quick on- and off-connections.

Architects, building owners, window washing companies, building management or maintenance companies should seriously consider investing in one of the many Sky Pro System models. Most models will pay for themselves in less than a year. Sky Pro eliminates the danger associated with manual window washing and reduces labor and insurance costs.

"Sky Pro is one of the most ingenious pieces of equipment to be made available to building owners, managers, and cleaning companies. It has reduced our cost of window cleaning services by approximately 50k per year. We have also been able to reduce our liability exposure by not having "bodies" over the side of the building," stated Robert Thomson, Manager – Cassidy Turley Commercial Real Estate Services.

For more information, visit www.skypro.com or contact Kari Francois at kfrancois@skypro.com or 1-800-699-0251.

Promote YOUR New Product in eClean Magazine!

email Allison Hester
allison@ecleanmag.com
to learn how

To see more new products, go to
www.eCleanMag.com/Products

How to Get the Most from Your Past Customers

by Linda Chambers, Soap Warehouse, www.SoapWarehouse.biz

For many of you cleaning season is getting ready to start next month, but are you really ready?

You have probably already thought about getting your equipment in shape and buying supplies for the start up. You may have plans for marketing to new customers. But have you also planned for how you're going to keep and manage your current customers?

In our website blog posts, I have touched on the importance of existing customers before, but this topic is so important I will do so again here as a refresher for some and maybe give even new things to think about for others.

- Selling to past customers only requires about 20 percent of the amount of time and effort that it takes to gain new prospects. That means getting jobs from current customers saves four times the cost of marketing old versus new.

- A business, no matter how successful, will lose about 15 to 20 percent of its customer base year to year by no fault of the business.

- A satisfied customer may only tell one to three close friends they liked your service, but an unhappy customer will tell at least 10 people they know.

- Referrals from happy customers usually only come in the initial 24 to 48 hours after service is completed, unless motivated to do so.

- The national average of unsolicited word of mouth referrals is two percent of your customer base. That means with 300 customers, you should get at least six new customers from the existing ones.

Here are some steps to plan and use your current satisfied customers to bring you much more new business than the 20 percent you will more than likely lose, or the two percent you'll gain if you do nothing at all.

Go back over your jobs from last year. Make an index card for each one with who and where they were, when the work was done, what type of work they received, how long it took, how much they paid versus how much it cost you, and any other factors you deem important.

Armed with this information you can build a skeleton job schedule for this year to then work to make it permanent, filling in the gaps. These can also help you divide up the jobs between crews if you have them, keeping them in the same geographical area during work days.

Get out your rough calendar for the season and place the cards of the current customers where you think they might fall this year, if at all. You may have a job that you did that you know will not be repeated this year. But that customer may have a different need this year or be able to refer you other work. Place them in a separate pile as you fill in your calendar.

Start with repeat contract work as to when they most likely will be. For example a fleet you wash twice a month on Sunday afternoons, a commercial restaurant you clean once a quarter on a Wednesday night, an apartment complex you spend four days cleaning in May. Make a card for each visit. These are contracts you most likely already have signed, sealed and delivered as guaranteed work. Now let's work on the maybes.

Example 1: You cleaned Mr. Miller's house and pool area for the first time last June. He called at the last minute because they where going to have a summer pool party, he got your name just from seeing your rig around the neighborhood earlier that year, he paid top dollar for the fast service and was very happy with the results. Place his customer card somewhere in May.

Make a list by month noting to call, mail or email him a reminder about summer and pool season and if he books early he will get the best time and maybe also make a special offer. Remember do not discount services; offer added value first instead, like free patio furniture cleaning with the pool deck cleaning. This is also the time to mention your referral program, how he can participate and what benefits he can get. (To learn more about referral programs, see the article in the Fall 2011 issue of *PCC/eClean Magazine*.) For example give us names and numbers of four friends and if someone books before your cleaning you will save $50, or if after his cleaning they get a $25 gift card. This promotes your customer to think about getting the work done earlier (better for you) plus already thinking about getting the word out about your service to save him some money (even better for you).

Example 2: Next customer card is an elderly lady who has had her house washed every spring for the last four years. She always sends you two or three referrals each year. Put her card down in the time she is used to getting the service. Be sure to contact her and discuss the timing of her cleaning, to thank her for her past referrals, to let her know what the current benefits are this year for helping you again with referrals. You might want to give her an added bonus for being such a loyal customer, like a free air conditioner coil cleaning. You will already be at the house and this service will not take more than 15 to 20 minutes to perform at a very minimal cost to you.

Plan this year as you are gaining satisfied customers to ask for testimonials along with the referrals at the completion of the service. If you can, get them on video; if not, try for a photo and at least the written testimonial. These you should post as soon as possible to your Facebook business page, and added to your web site along with the date to show repeat visitors to your site that you are continually having satisfied customers. That in itself will get you new business with no need of having to pay out referral fees.

Now back to the cards in the pile you did not place in your calendar. For instance the fellow that answered a direct mail campaign for soft roof washing late last year at a special price and you know that it has only been 6 months and his roof is still going to be clean and not need service. He is the customer that you can market a different service to early this year. Hopefully you noted during that job other jobs you could do for him. Like the fact that he has a large back deck that could be washed or stripped and stained or a weathered fence around his back yard. His drive way and sidewalk were really dirty last Fall that you even gave him a quote on, but he did not want anything but the deal on the soft wash. He would be one to send a special offer card to along with the referral pre-service incentives to save him money on a job this spring or summer. You already know that deals motivate him so capitalize on that.

Work to try and pre-plan and place 60 to 80 percent of the customers you already have for this coming season before it starts. This way you can budget and plan your other expenses and profits around it, besides family time and industry events. For instance if you already know you will be doing more wood restoration and cleaning this summer than last year you can take that Wood Restoration Certification class, order your supplies to take advantage of a vendor sale or to get the best bulk price and lower shipping cost. You may be able to see you have a weak work gap of weeks that need to be filled late in the summer and can plan a marketing campaign well in advance so you will not hit a slow spot. Leave a few mornings, afternoons or one day a week open each week to fill in with reschedules due to weather, customer changes and new business.

I am not saying to slow down or stop working hard to gain new business throughout the season, but with better management of your existing customers you will be able to more easily fill openings at a lower cost and hopefully increase the amount of business and profit you make this coming year.

Linda Chambers is Brand & Sales Manager at Soap Warehouse where she has worked since 2007. Linda enjoys writing articles for industry publications, blogs and social media. She also travels for the company exhibiting at trade shows and events. Visit the company's website at www.SoapWarehouse.biz.

Classifieds: Products and Services

www.SkyPro.com
Automated window cleaning systems. A safe way to clean windows, frames and exterior of high rise buildings. Call 800-699-0251 or 651-967-9031.

www.PowerWash.com
Mobile power wash equipment, schools, training, videos, environmental supplies & maintenance services. Call for a free catalog, 800-433-2113.

www.PWNA.org
Power Washers of North America. For certification or membership information, visit our website, email info@pwna.org, or call 800-393-7962.

To Advertise in our New Classifieds Section

Contact Allison Hester
allison@ecleanmag.com

The Pressure Washing Seminar 2013
March 13-16, Albany, New York

EClean Magazine is proud to be a sponsor for one of the industry's most popular and talked about events, the Pressure Washing Seminar, March 13 through 16 in Albany, New York.

This will be the third such seminar put on by Matt Johnson and Jack Kramer of Contractor Education Services, which has been hosting roundtables and other educational venues since 2006. This year's theme is "Learn to Earn, the Dollars and Sense," and will include a power-packed program for both new and established pressure washing businesses.

The Pre-Seminars

If you are relatively new to the industry, you will not want to miss the two-day pre-seminar, a comprehensive power washing and wood restoration course that combines in-class and on-the-job training. The course will include information on chemicals and detergent use and application, equipment, bidding, marketing, as well as house washing, roof cleaning, wood restoration and commercial cleaning.

"From newbies, to novice contract cleaners, to the veteran contractor with many years' experience – all come away from the class with an increased knowledge that is applicable to increase profits, increase speed and ensure success in this industry," said Kramer.

Mike Morin of Maine Power Wash Pros said he had never even touched a pressure washer before attending last year's pre-seminar, but afterward gained the knowledge needed to go out and have a "very successful" first year. "Matt and Jack's help did not stop after the seminar was over," Morin stressed. "I have called them on several occasions with questions and they have always been happy to help us." When asked if he will be attending this year's event, Morin responded, "Definitely!"

On Thursday, pre-seminar attendees have a choice between two courses.

The first, due to requests by past attendees, is a pre-seminar focusing exclusively on wood restoration. This course will provide education on how to add wood restoration services, teaching participants the correct methods to ensure a quality product and maximum profits. This course will examine the various types of wood, detergents needed for stripping and brightening wood, the restoration process from start to finish, as well as how to profitably bid wood projects.

"This is the wood restoration class that will make you money. It is the perfect class to learn not only the art of wood restoration,

but the science behind the detergents and the process that provides excellent results and maximum profit. The second Thursday option is a brand-new class for the Contractor Education Services venue. The Maintenance, Troubleshooting and Repair Class, led by Sam Jackson, Hydro Tek's Senior Service Technical Advisor and Educator, will teach contractors how to keep their equipment up and running. The course will cover electrical issues, burner maintenance and repair, troubleshooting and general service.

"This is the class that saves you money and makes you money," said Johnson. "Come learn to troubleshoot and repair your equipment, saving you costly repairs. Minimal downtime means more work done, which means more money in your pocket."

The Main Event

The Pressure Washing Seminar officially kicks off Thursday night with a welcoming reception. "Kick back in the pool courtyard after your trek to Albany and enjoy a cold one on tap with hot appetizers, dips and snacks," said Johnson. "It will be a great start to networking for your 2013 Seminar." It will also be a time for participants to connect with the event's vendors and sponsors. (Be sure to stop by the eClean booth to say hello!)

The Seminar begins on Friday, with a full morning filled with top-notch, state-of-the-art presentations. These will include:

General Session: Disaster Response and The Aftermath of Super Storm Sandy, led by Matt Johnson and Tom DeFranesco

"Dominating Your Residential Market," by Thad Eckhoff, Pressure Washing Resource Association (PWRA)

"Upselling Exterior Window Cleaning Using a Water Fed Pole," by Steve Blythe, J. Racenstein Company

Following a barbecue lunch, the afternoon will feature outdoor demonstrations by several participating vendors.

Then Friday evening, it's the pressure washer power hour, an informal, old fashion round table where participants can "ask questions and get them answered," said Kramer.

Additionally, for those who want to venture out, the hotel area is surrounded by a number of "great restaurants," according to Johnson, and the hotel offers a complimentary shuttle to and from dinner locations so participants don't have to drive.

Education continues bright and early Saturday morning, following a continental breakfast, with a general session by a certified Quickbooks trainer. The rest of the morning will be separated into different tracks, with potential topics including roof washing, specialty wood restoration, informatics, decorative & protective coatings, house washing, water reclamation and recovery, website SEO, and what BMPs mean to you.

"You will be able to select classes to attend, and we will be repeating some of the sessions to make sure you get to many of the topics that interest you," explained Johnson.

The Seminar will close out Saturday afternoon with a feast, complete with a wide variety of food and desserts. "No one will leave hungry!" added Johnson.

Following lunch will be the drawings and giveaways, and participants must be present to win. The grand prize – a Trailer / Truck Bed Mounted Self-Contained Filtration, courtesy of Hydro Tek.

To learn more about the event or to register, visit The Pressure Washing Seminar site at www.PWSeminar.com.

Grand Prize Giveaway

The Hydro Tek RZV vacuum recovery and filtration system provides 7 stages of filtration with up to 12gpm continuous five micron processing of wastewater where soaps and other chemicals are not used.

The system is the choice of professional cleaners to protect the environment, conserve water, and comply with EPA storm drain requirements. (For use with cold water or hot water up to 200°F)

Information Taken from Hydrotek's Website

Pressure Washer Special

$5,995
save over $3,595
Tanks A Lot Promotion

Gas Powered, Diesel Heated
3000psi, 4.8gpm
Adjustable temperature up to 250°F
479cc Vanguard twin cylinder engine
Belt drive pump

Includes:
- 200 gallon tank skid
- Rustproof stainless inlet AND high pressure hose reels, plus 100' inlet hose

Hydro Tek mobile wash skid
model# SS30005VS / T185TW

Or FREE Wheel Kit
with purchase of the SS30005VS alone

Conveniently slides in (and out of) a full size truckbed and most flatbed or enclosed trailers. Skid, water tank and hose reels are plumbed and securely mounted to a steel powder coated tank skid. Saves time and hassle, just tighten bolts and go.

HYDRO TEK.US

Contact us for a Distributor Near You:
WWW.HYDROTEK.US   (800) 274-9376   Brilliant Design, Tough on Grime

Limited time offer. Free freight to distributor location within the continental US. Price does not include sales tax or battery. Available through a participating distributor near you. Ask your distributor for the Tanks A Lot Special or free wheel kit. Call Hydro Tek for a distributor near you. Not to be combined with any other offers, programs, or discounts.

Do You Need a Hot Water Machine?

by Aaladin Industries, www.Aaladin.com

Spring is around the corner, and with it, the time for a myriad of cleaning projects. No matter what industry you're in, your equipment is the motor that drives your profits. All varieties of industrial cleaning are demanding -- you must be able to produce results in a variety of situations. We know that's complicated and we've listened to you and your peers to create pressure washers geared to your personal needs.

The first thing to do is assess those needs. What specific surfaces will you be cleaning? Is your current equipment capable and efficient? Have you thought about different solutions that could save time and money? While pondering these questions, consider how a hot water pressure washer could address your situation.

Do You Need HOT Water?

Cold water pressure washers are in every big box store, and you're probably wondering why you need to get a hot water machine. There are a number of reasons why this could be the solution for you:

1. Environmental. Cold water pressure washers often require harsh chemicals in order to clean effectively. Hot water cleans so much better that for many applications, nothing else is needed. For particularly stubborn cleaning, an environmentally-friendly soap can be used. Hot water is a good choice.

2. Oil. It's in the air because of vehicles driving down your street. It sticks to everything. Dirt sticks to it. If your hands were dirty and greasy, would you try to clean them with cold water? You use hot soapy water for a reason – it works. The majority of your cleaning probably involves cutting oil and grease, so hot water just makes sense.

Once you have decided that a hot water pressure washer is a good idea, the next step is to narrow down which specific type you need. This can be a challenge due to so many options available. Let's take a look at some of them:

Will it need to move? Will the pressure washer be permanently installed in a wash bay or building? If the answer is yes, you will need to look at a stationary washer. When looking at stationary washers, be sure to ask about venting/stacking costs (there are high efficiency units available that will vent through CPVC as opposed to expensive traditional stacking).

Will it need to be mobile (mounted on a trailer or moved around a job site on skids)? If your washer will be trailer- or skid-mounted, look at a self-contained unit capable of running without an external power source.

Do you need to move your washer by hand? Will your work require your washer to be in many different places? If so, you will want a portable pressure washer.

One of the most important things to consider when choosing a portable washer is safety. Let's face it -- when you add water to any surface (especially with soap), it makes it slick. Choosing a pressure washer with swivel wheels helps diminish the possibility of falls with heavy equipment. Most pressure washers with fixed wheels require the operator to lift one set of wheels to make a turn, increasing the probability of slipping and falling.

Make sure the portable unit has flat free tires as well. Flat tires tend to take the portability out of a portable unit and cause expensive downtime.

Don't forget to also be aware of power and fuel access where you will be using the portable unit.

How much power do you need?

Pressure washer "power" is gauged in two ways - PSI (pounds of pressure per square inch) and GPM (gallons of water released per minute). Both are important, but paying close attention to GPM is a critical thing.

Paying attention to flow (GPM) is an important factor when deciding on the right pressure washer for your application. The higher the GPM, the larger the droplets are that are making contact to the surface of what you are cleaning.

Think about it like this –- if you were to throw a handful of sand against a window or a handful of rocks, which would have the greater effect? The larger the droplets of water that are making contact with the surface the better and more efficiently they clean. Combine a high PSI machine with a high flow rate and you get a machine with quite a punch!

What kind of fuel will you want to use?

Pumps and burners are driven by different fuel sources. Which you pick depends on your specific application.

Pumps are commonly either driven by electric motors or gas/diesel engines. Which of these you choose commonly depends on whether or not the machine is stationary, mobile or portable, and if there is an electrical power source available.

Burners are fired with vaporized liquefied petroleum (LP), natural gas (NG), or diesel oil. Each fuel source has its own advantages and disadvantages. If you are stationary or have the capability to plumb for LP or NG, they are the most cost effective and clean burning. If portability is the biggest factor, diesel oil is the way to go. Completely electric models for clean environments are available as well.

How much will you be running the unit?

No matter how much you will be running your washer, something else you should consider is a model that is higher efficiency than others. Purchasing a pressure washer that utilizes the most advanced high efficiency technology will save money over traditional models (on average between 35 to 38 percent). Obviously, the more hours you run the machine per year, the more money you will save and therefore put towards increasing your bottom line.

Another advantage to a higher efficiency unit is the reduced carbon footprint, allowing you to feel good about "keeping it green" and making it easier to comply with local and state code.

When operating a pressure washer, also consider a unit that includes a clutch drive feature. When the gun is not engaged, there will be no wear to the pump, allowing it to perform longer under the toughest conditions. This effectively extends the life of your washer, resulting in less downtime and increased profits.

Some other things to consider:

Fueling a machine frequently takes time and energy away from the work at hand. Choosing a high efficiency machine will save the obvious fuel costs. Keep in mind it will also require less frequent fueling, saving labor costs and getting the job done quicker and more efficiently.

Finally, when shopping, look for the value in the pressure washer you are buying. Is it made from the highest quality components? Is it built here in the US by skilled craftsmen? Has the manufacturer paid close attention to detail in every aspect? Is there a knowledgeable service support system available? Make sure you can answer yes to all of these questions before signing on the dotted line.

AaLadin Cleaning Systems offers pressure washers to fit any situation. We do this because we understand you aren't the same as every other contractor out there. You have created a place in your market that demands specific solutions. We pride ourselves on being the innovator of numerous pressure washer features.

We are also proud to be the ONLY pressure washer manufacturer to offer a High Efficiency Line of equipment. Our Eco-Green Line is available in several different models to fit your needs. Please go to www.aaladin.com or visit your local AaLadin distributor to learn how our products can save you time and money.

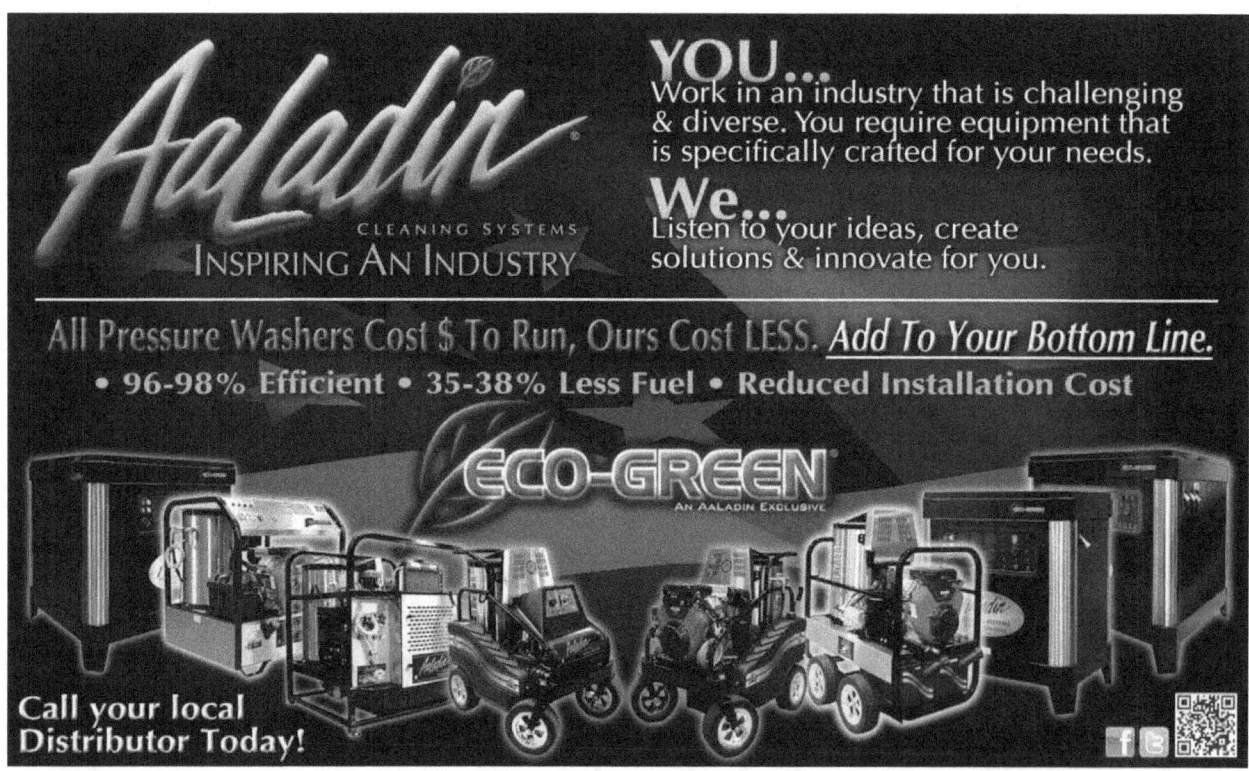

Are You Ready to SPRING into Action?

by Tony Evans, A New View Window Cleaning, windowcleaningschool.blogspot.com

It's that time of year again, and no, I'm not talking about taxes or even baseball. It's almost spring and that means great weather and for those of us in the window cleaning industry the ever popular spring cleaning rush. But there are some important questions we should ask ourselves before that time arrives.

Are You Ready – *Physically?*

Most of us experience a slowdown (if not complete stop) in our work pace thru the winter months and to go from zero to full speed ahead can be difficult and dangerous. If we haven't been very active, I suggest a good regiment of exercise with weights and cardio. A simple routine of walking a couple miles each day and some small free weights will keep you from pulling a muscle, or worse, as you get into high speed production in your business. Also, taking a few more breaks in the first couple of weeks can help you avoid over-stressing yourself and causing downtime from preventable injuries.

Also there will be those things that are unique to a few like allergies. Do we have the medication we need to deal with our particular Achilles heel? I should mention that with the blooming of flowers and trees come those flying hypodermic needles – bees, hornets, and wasps. If you are allergic, have you taken the proper precautions in case of stings? Just as a reminder, if you use what is called an epipen (Epinephrine injector) for those reactions, they have an expiration date so make sure you've checked that.

Are You Ready – *Mentally?*

The amount of scheduling and new clients in the spring can be very demanding on us mentally. We can minimize this by making sure our systems to handle this influx are up and running properly and pre-scheduling as much as possible. Of course, no matter how much you prepare in advance it will get hectic. Taking a break is vital. I know, I can hear you now: "I can't take a break! I'm too busy." I'm not suggesting a long break, but a few minutes away when things are overwhelming can keep you focused and prevent frustration from leaking through to a client or potential client. Remember, we are selling ourselves as much as our service. People don't want to deal with angry contractors.

Are You Ready – *Equipment Check?*

One of the most important things we have to ask ourselves is do we have the tools necessary to do the work at hand? Some order their spring supplies during the previous fall. If you aren't one of them, have you checked your shop and work vehicles to make sure they are stocked and ready to go? It's not just embarrassing and inconvenient to get to a job and find you are out of soap or squeegee rubbers, it's downtime that you don't want in your busiest season.

Also, do you have the shop in order and the work vehicle maintenance done? It might seem like an oversimplification, but those are the things that are often overlooked in our race to get going again.

Are You Ready – *Intangibles?*

There is no way for one article to cover all the things you need to be ready for in the busy times. But if you think back to previous Springs, you may come up with a list of issues you could have handled better and make this the year they don't happen again.

Are You Ready To SPRING Into Action?

No doubt some of this has been simply a list of things you already do. It might even seem like common sense for most business owners. Hopefully, however, we have made you think about an area or two where you can tweak your processes and get even better this spring.

Tony Evans and his wife own and operate A New View Window Cleaning, which offers window cleaning, house washing, roof cleaning, and scratched glass restoration. Evans also enjoys helping new window cleaners learn the value of good tools and techniques. To learn more, visit thewindowcleaningschool.blogspot.com.

Floor Finishing Mythology, Part 2

by Rick Meehan, Vice President of Marko Janitorial Supply, www.MarkoInc.com

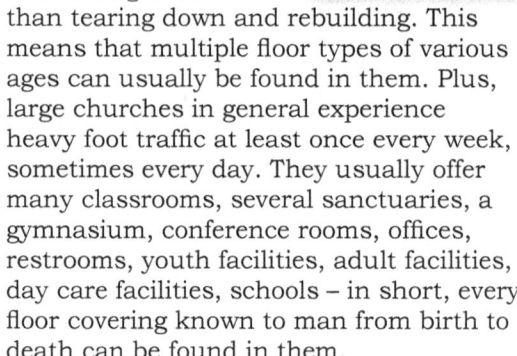

Last month in *eClean*, we began dispelling the myths about floor finishing. As a quick review, we discussed the need to understand the following before tacking a floor coating job:

1. TYPE of floor to be coated.

2. COATING recommended by flooring manufacturer or other authority.

3. AMOUNT of square footage to be coated.

4. PROCEDURE for applying the particular coating.

5. TOOLS needed for applying the coating most efficiently.

6. LABOR broken down by hours, people, and wages to completion.

7. TOTAL COST of all products and labor required.

Let's continue where we left off...

Quality of acrylic finishes is of major importance when determining job costs, but more importantly, quality directly affects customer satisfaction. If a customer's floor isn't shiny enough, scratches easily, in short, looks bad, do you think they're going to hire you again? Resolving the quality issue is easy enough; however, selling quality is perhaps the most important factor in customer satisfaction. Help the customer afford the level of floor finish that is required for their particular situation.

As a perfect example, which may be applied to almost any other client, let's discuss large, established church floors. Grand old churches are notorious for adding on and remodeling rather than tearing down and rebuilding. This means that multiple floor types of various ages can usually be found in them. Plus, large churches in general experience heavy foot traffic at least once every week, sometimes every day. They usually offer many classrooms, several sanctuaries, a gymnasium, conference rooms, offices, restrooms, youth facilities, adult facilities, day care facilities, schools – in short, every floor covering known to man from birth to death can be found in them.

Floor maintenance is a huge headache, especially in those gyms. So, what type or types of acrylic finishes should be offered to help them maintain a high appearance, withstand the traffic, save the most money on stripping and refinishing in the long run? The answer lies in understanding details about acrylic finishes.

Metal interlocked acrylic polymer floor finishes, the most common coating used on resilient floors today, would be excellent choices for big old churches. Factors to consider when choosing the finish are:

• **Coverage** – usually ranges from 1000 to 2500 square feet per gallon.

• **Drying Time** – usually ranges from 20 to 40 minutes per coat depending on weather conditions. Rain means much longer drying time; sun means much shorter of course.

• **Freeze/Thaw Stability** – it is best not

to allow acrylics to freeze, period.

• **Gloss Rating (ASTM D 1455-87 Testing Standard)** – the higher the number the greater the light reflect-ability, or shine. A finish rated 75-90 is considered brilliant. This is an actual test, not a subjective choice.

• **Heel Mark Resistance** – Subjective by manufacturer ranging from good to excellent. In general, more expensive acrylics have a better resistance due to higher quality ingredients.

• **Leveling** – Most acrylics are termed "self-leveling" which means they will spread evenly and flatten even if bubbling occurs during initial application.

This is another subjective rating that ranges from good to excellent.

• **pH** – Most acrylics will fall between 8 – 9 on this scale. This has nothing to do with longevity, simply a tech spec for the material safety data sheet.

• **Recoat** – The ability of the finish to be recoated without stripping original finish first. This is subjective, but in general, no problems occur from recoating the exact same product on itself.

• **Shelf Life** – This is an estimate of how long a sealed container of unused finish can remain in storage before it goes bad. Acrylic finishes will rot like milk. Fresh product smells slightly sweet with a touch of ammonia, while old product smells distinctly bad! Never apply finish that smells rotten.

• **Specific Gravity** – This refers to the density of the liquid versus the density of water. With water rated at 1.0, the higher the rating, the thicker the product. Thickness makes a difference for self-leveling and spread-ability. Acrylics fall within 1.01 – 1.04.

• **Percent Solids** – Of all the features in an acrylic coating, the solids content, which refers to the amount of acrylic in water, is perhaps the most important quality-defining feature. Solids content in acrylics range from 10% to 35%. If quality products are being considered, a higher solid content usually means a better finish.

Since a wide variety of acrylics are available, it takes a thorough understanding of these features to choose the right finish for the job. In the case of large churches that plan to administer to the congregation forever, the approach is to choose a finish that will withstand the volume of traffic, last the longest under those conditions, and can be easily maintained over the long run. The biggest expense the church (or any client) will incur is the stripping and re-waxing of the floors. The longer the finish lasts, the less money invested.

To save a large church (or any client) the most money while making a good profit on the application and maintenance of the floor finish requires a plan. As a contractor, the plan is synonymous with long-term profits. With a church, every member is a potential client. If these clients are happy with the look of their floors, they will tell

everyone they know about it; likewise the opposite. I usually recommend selling the highest quality finish to large churches for this reason.

The best type of finish I have found rates a high gloss, heel mark resistance, and 33 percent solids content. There are many good brands to choose from in this category. With high solids content, a good quality finish will be very resistant to even extreme gym floor use. My company sells one that remains on gym floors for several years without the need to strip while still looking fresh. Of course, proper maintenance must occur. That aspect should be part of the contractor's sales plan too.

An add-on sale is to return with high-speed buffing equipment to polish those expensive acrylic floors as needed. This ongoing cost is still far lower than starting over from scratch. Churches like that because their funds are limited by congregational giving. With proper sales techniques, any contractor can use these arguments to convince other types of customers of the benefits of applying quality floor finishes, plus returning for maintenance polishing. Over the long haul, both client and contractor benefit – the perfect sale!

A final aspect to choosing the right finish is the ability of the finish to be used on multiple floor types. Generally, the same water-based gym floor rated acrylic finish can be used on every other resilient floor in those large churches, so why sell multiple coating types to the same customer? Remember this: the more complicated you make the issue, the lower your profits. Too many factors increase the chances of making errors.

Every floor coating requires knowledge, experience, and training. If you have a quality professional finish that works great in high-traffic situations, then what's more costly, training for many types of finish applications or training for one?

I contend that choosing a limited group of floor finish products that work well in a large variety of situations is the least expensive cost to the contractor and insures better performance for the customer. Specializing in those few finishes insures fewer complaints and greater repeat business. While most floor finishing jobs are relatively easy to perform, choosing the proper finish for each situation requires dispelling the myths by acquiring detailed product knowledge coupled with practice, practice, practice. Any cleaning agency may become a legendary floor maintenance company if care is taken to aggressively understand the world of coatings rather than assuming they know it all.

Rick Meehan is the Vice President of Marko Janitorial Supply, which has been selling a full range of janitorial products since 1968. To learn more about their

---

Let us put our expert knowledge of **legendary Landa equipment** to work for your cleaning needs.

Specializing in Power washing equipment sales, service and custom manufacturing

(403) 771-7774

www.HydraEquipment.com

HYDRA

Kitchen Exhaust Cleaning

Staying ahead of the curve

by Jason Wellman, KEC Supplies, www.kecsupplies.com

As a service provider to other facilities, your company is tested on a daily basis. What steps can you make to stay out in front of your competition?

The pressure washing industry as a whole has evolved into a full service industry. Your customers are looking for problem solvers as well as cost effective solutions. I will be talking about a few ways you can improve your company's image as well as boost your sales. Not all of these suggestions may fit your business model and feel free to pick and choose what relates to you.

Grease Management: Facilities are now being pushed by the EPA, health inspectors, and local fire marshals to change the way their facility operates. Acceptable practices have been changed every year, sometimes even more often. Your company can take advantage of these changes as well as help save your clients money by offering services that will lessen the amount of exposure, utility costs, and labor costs your clients are being forced to pay by simply doing things the hard way.

In the past, outsourcing has been looked upon as a bad thing by some workers of larger corporations. However, in our industry, outsourcing is the way of the future to keep costs down for facilities, as well as limiting your customers' exposure. Here are a few services that will save your customers thousands each year while making your company harder to replace:

Grease Filter Exchange has the potential to lower the facility's grease disposal by up to 70 percent! This same service will save, on average, up to five percent of your clients' labor costs, as well as hundreds of dollars in chemical, water, sewage, and electric expenses. The potential savings is thousands a year for your customer.

Rooftop Grease Containment: while not a new service and often looked upon by your clients as an expensive solution to rooftop grease collection – has been proven to save clients significant money. Many studies over several years show that the amount your client will spend to replace a roof in a five-, 10- or even 20-year time frame will be significantly more than a simple grease containment product that will only cost a few hundred dollars each year to maintain. There have been many products to enter the market as well as ideas on how to collect, retain, or redirect the grease flow. The one thing to keep in mind when deciding what products to offer your customer is what system will work most effectively for the situation your customer is having. What this means is a four-sided system may not be the best thing to install on a pizza oven fan.

Grease Dumpster Containment Solutions: finding a good solution is key to this problem that plagues most facilities. Dumpster pads, for years, are the part of the restaurant that is kept out of sight, out of mind until it is too late. By then, the facility is being forced by the

Before and after dumpster pad cleaning courtesy of Carlos Gonzales, New Look Power Wash, www.NewLookPowerWash.com

landlord or, even worse, an official, to clean the mess up.

Anyone who has been pressure washing for some time now knows that cleaning up a grease spill on a dumpster pad is not an easy process, and could end up costing the facility hundreds if not thousands to do properly. Simple solutions like the LaneGuard from Omni Containment Solutions will save your customers significan money each year in cleanup and fines!

Updating your services: Simple yet effective tools will allow your company to not only offer more to your clients, but also increase your professional image.

Picture program: using services like DropBox will allow you to store and share pictures with your clients the moment services have been performed. DropBox also allows you to create separate sharing folders as well as special access for your employees and management staff to view, add, or delete photos from the folders. There are many programs out there similar to DropBox; choose the one that works best with your systems.

Smart Phones/Tablets: these allow your employees and management staff to better communicate and share information about job information, pictures, and service reports. There are hundreds of apps on the market that will make your life that much easier. Afraid of employees breaking the devise? OtterBox makes the case you need to ensure the life span of your devises. Make it a work-only devise that employees must sign out before service and turn in afterward.

800 numbers: these are not a thing of the past anymore considering the offerings that cloud services now offer. Companies like AT&T, Grasshopper, and many more offer a cloud service that your customers can call into and enter the extension they wish to speak to, then the call will be forwarded to either a land line or a cell phone. The services are typically one flat monthly fee and you do not have to pay the tolls of the incoming calls. Well worth the upgrade.

Contract programs: SignNow and others are a great add on to limit the amount of paperwork that you have to keep on hand to fill out CASR or service contracts. SignNow is an annual-fee service that will pay for itself in paper alone. This program allows your customers to sign contracts on your smart phone or tablet, as well as email a copy to your customer for signing.

The most important thing to keep in mind with the upcoming years of business is how you will remain the best option for your customers to call. Simple add ons like this will give you a shoe in, but ultimately will depend on your company's ability to adapt to change. Never be satisfied, and always look for better ways to show your customers you care.

Jason Wellman is the owner of KECSupplies. com, a FilterShine USA Company.

See page 34 to learn how to receive this guide for free.

Get Listed!
Create a Steady Flow of Traffic to Your Website from Those Looking for Your Services, Part 1

by Henry Bockman, Contractor's Foundation

More and more small businesses today are using online directories to their benefit. If you run a small business then the odds are you spend a great deal of your time thinking about your marketing plan. Online directories can be a great addition to your current small business marketing strategy. Online directories can help your small business expand its website traffic, increase the likelihood that your website will be found by interested viewers and increase your bottom line. If you haven't taken a look at online directories and considered how your small business could use them to increase its market presence- then now is the time to start!

What Are Online Directories?

There are many different types of online directories available on the Internet. Each of these online directories serves a specific purpose and can be used by your small business in specific ways.

An online directory is a website submission service that allows your small business' website to be added to a specific category where it can be searched for by interested viewers. These searchable online directories allow their viewers to search for websites and businesses that they find interesting or that they want to learn more about. Listing your small business on an online directory increases your website's visibility on the web and helps to create inbound links to your business's website.

Online directories make it easy for people to find what they are looking for. These directories can be accessed from just about anywhere that has an internet connection. This means that people could find your business's website from their home, office or even while traveling.

Every website that is submitted to an online directory is placed in a specific category. These categories can range in how they are organized. Some are organized by business-related categories, some are organized according to personal preferences and others are organized by subject. Each category consists of several websites relating to a specific topic. Each website listing features the name of the website, a direct link to the website and a short description of the website. Interested Internet viewers will be able to browse through the various categories in the directory and locate websites like yours that they may be interested in viewing.

Essentially, online directories make it easier for random viewers to find your business's website.

How Do Online Directories Work?

The concept of online directories is actually a pretty simple one. Online directories are very similar to the Yellow Pages in the real world, only these listings are only online. (Actually Yellow Pages.com is an online directory.) A directory is just a listing place for a number of websites. Any type of website you can think of could be listed in an online directory. Some online directories are huge and cover every topic that someone could create a website for, while others are very small and specific to a specific niche.

Let's use an example. Say you are a model airplane enthusiast and you want to find some websites that cater to your specific interest. You could look through a huge online directory such as Yahoo's online website directory and find several dozen websites that are related to model airplanes. Or you could look for an online directory that is niche-specific, which means that the entire online directory would be based on hobbies such as model airplanes.

With a niche-specific directory you may find even more websites that are based on your specific interest than what you could find on the larger directories.

Since online directories are organized by categories, finding websites that relate to a specific interest such as model airplanes is very easy.

You could find information and websites about model airplanes in your local region too if you use a regional-specific online directory. So if you live in Phoenix you could find websites that relate to both model airplanes and the

Phoenix area. Online directories will direct you to websites that you want to find. All you have to do is perform a search in the online directory for a specific topic or browse through the various categories until you find the type of websites you are looking for.

When you perform a search you will be given a list of all of the websites that relate to your search term. You will be presented with a number of links to these websites and each link will have a short description of what you are likely to find on the website. You can read the descriptions and choose to click on the website that best suits you.

There are many different types of websites that you could find under a specific topic as well. For example, if you search several online directories for information relating to model airplanes you may find websites that are about building model airplanes, flying model airplanes, creating historically accurate model planes, tips and instructions about how to fly model planes, websites that sell model airplanes and charters and associations that you could join regarding model airplanes. These are just a few of the examples you could find using an online directory.

There are simply too many topics to list them all here.

You can see how anyone can use an online directory to find websites relating to things that interest them. As a small business owner you can see how people who could be potential customers of yours are using online directories too. Now that you understand how online directories work it is time to see how they can work for your business.

Next issue we will look into How Online Directories can help your small business, as well as listing best practices and where to list your business.

In the meantime, you can get our guide for free! Normally I sell this information with a step-by-step guide and a list of over 250 other directory sites for $29.99, but since you are an *EClean Magazine* Reader, You Can Get A Free Copy! Just click the link below and **use Coupon Code: ECleanMag** for your discount!

http://contractorsfoundation.com/product-category/business-marketing-guides-service-companies/

Please Leave A Review On This Article And The Guide Here: http://contractorsfoundation.com/shop/get-listed-create-a-steady-stream-of-customers-to-your-web-site/

After leaving the military, Henry Bockman started a home maintenance company in Maryland called Henry's Housework. Since 1989 Henry Bockman has dedicated himself to learning everything he can about marketing, web site development and Internet Marketing Systems.

Bockman currently resides in Maryland with his wife of over 20 years and two teenagers. He operates 5 companies, 2contracting companies; Henry's Housework Inc, Commercial Restorations, a marketing company called Extreme Marketing Solutions which specializes in SEO, Social Media Marketing, online marketing, and lead generation.

Contractors Foundation, which is a training company that provides power washing training, marketing and business success classes to help companies start up and succeed in any type of service based business, He also runs two Online companies and several internet directories.

Benefits of Spring Cleaning with Commercial Power Washing

by Paul Horsley, Publisher

After a winter of rain, snow and winds, it's a simple matter to revive the appearance of your business with the help of a commercial power washing service. When your commercial building needs a facelift, you don't have to plan a remodel. One of the best ways to perk up the exterior of a building is to simply make it look clean. Pull the weeds, trim the hedges and call a commercial power washing service to beautify the property. By doing so, you can reap the following rewards:

Motivate employees. When employees feel negatively about their place of work, they will feel less motivated to perform well, less connected to the work environment and less eager to keep up productivity. And the outside of the building can be as important a part of the environment as what goes on indoors. It takes only one staff member to gripe about a building's dirty appearance to bring the rest of the team down. Help your employees feel proud about their place of employment, and this pride will translate into improved retention, teamwork and productivity.

Attract more customers. When it comes to free enterprise, beauty isn't in the eye of the beholder; it's in the eye of the consumer. According to the book *Contemporary Marketing 2011*, customers are attracted to ideal "atmospheric" conditions, which refers partly to the physical characteristics that attract customers. Consumers often consider clean-looking, well-kept commercial buildings as places that will satisfy their shopping needs. Part of being a business owner is satisfying customer wants and needs, and satisfaction can come with something as simple as making a building look cared for with the help of professional power washing services.

Increase your bottom line. Up to 70 percent of consumers make their purchasing decisions after walking through the front door of the store. Getting a prospect through the front door is one of the biggest challenges when you own a business. When your building sparkles, there is a better chance you'll see an increase in foot traffic. Once a customer is inside, you have achieved the hardest part of making a sale.

Reduce risks. Keeping the area around your commercial building clean with the help of a commercial power washing company can help reduce the number of employee and customer accidents. Mud, built-up dirt, leaves, grease and other fluids can make your building's exterior a danger zone. They can also make your building seem less welcoming overall.

Wastewater Recovery. When you hire professional power washing services to help beautify your commercial property, the wastewater has to go somewhere. In some areas, it is against the law for wastewater created by pressure washing (or even water from a hose) to go down any storm drains. The reason for this is to help protect wildlife from toxins that may enter the water, such as car oil from a parking lot. Avoid a hefty fine and hire a commercial pressure washing professional who has the proper certifications and permits to clean your building's exterior and handle the wastewater responsibly.

Scheduling Concerns. Springtime in many regions comes with nighttime temperatures that are sometimes below freezing. Professional power washing services often clean the exteriors of commercial buildings after hours so your customers are not inconvenienced. If the forecast calls for freezing temperatures on the night of your scheduled pressure washing service, you may need to be flexible and reschedule the cleaning for another time.

Using a commercial property cleaning service is an effective way to freshen up the look of your property, attract new customers and increase your sales. Now that you know that enhancing the outside of your commercial building is so simple, there is no excuse to put your spring cleaning off any longer.

Snapshots from the IWCA Convention and Trade Show
by Allison Hester

In February, I joined alongside over 400 window cleaning contractors and vendors in St. Pete Beach, Florida, for the International Window Cleaning Association's (IWCA) Annual Trade Show and Convention. Additionally, over 90 contractors will be working more safely this year due to completing IWCA's safety training course.

While there, participants learned ways to successfully and safely run their businesses through training, a wide variety of educational opportunities, networking, and leading industry vendor exhibits.

I personally took home several valuable insights that I will be sharing with *eClean* readers over the next several months. I also want to say a special thank you to the IWCA Board of Directors who went out of their way to make me feel welcome and appreciated.

Finally, a special congratulations to Medley Winner Marcus Bauman, and Speed Winner Justin Russell

Next year's event – which will celebrate IWCA's 25th Anniversary – has already been scheduled. Mark your calendar for February 12-15 in Memphis, Tennessee, so mark your calendars.

To learn more about the IWCA, visit their website at www.IWCA.org.

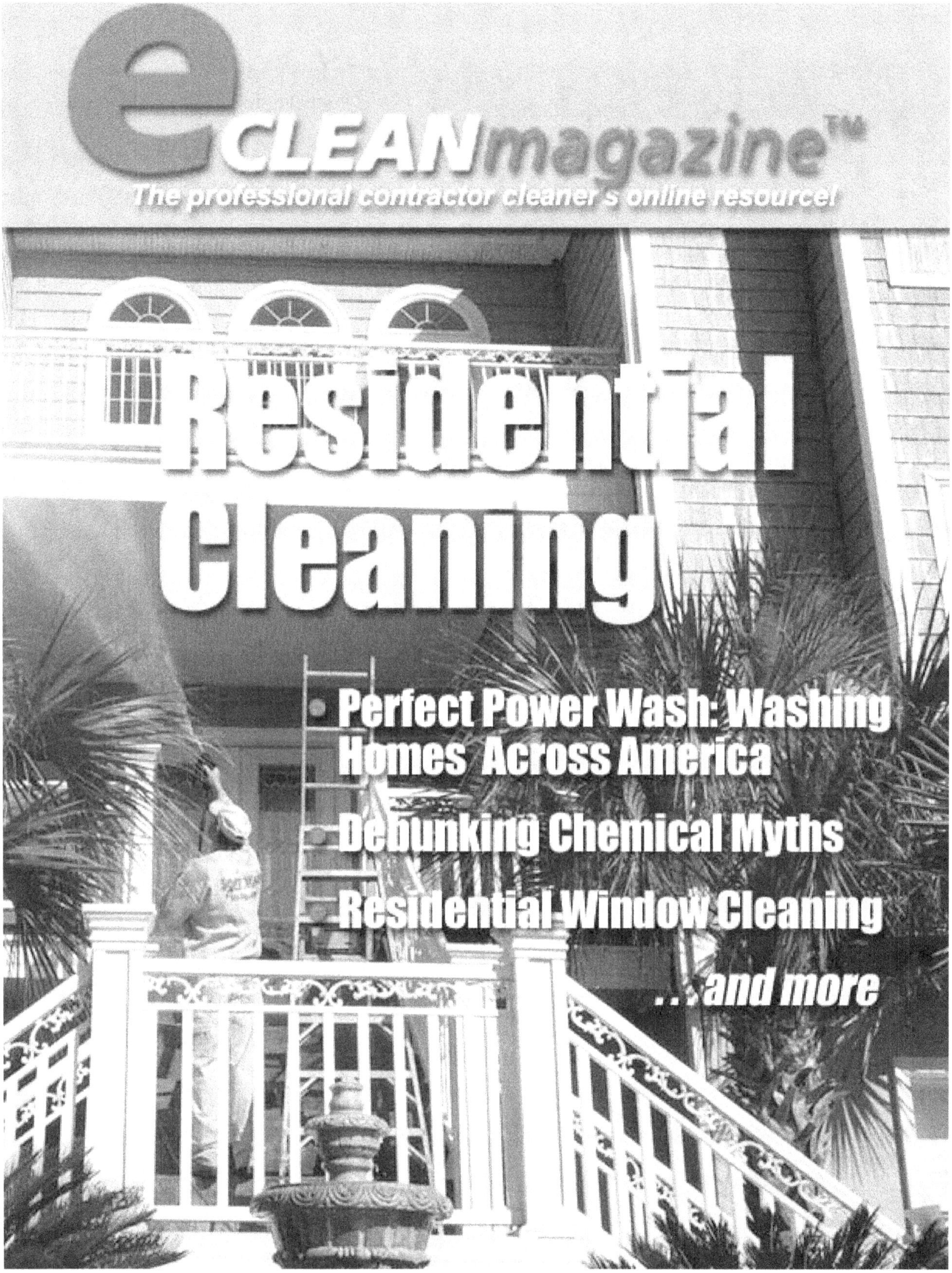

eCLEANmagazine™
The professional contractor cleaner's online resource!

Residential Cleaning

- **Perfect Power Wash: Washing Homes Across America**
- **Debunking Chemical Myths**
- **Residential Window Cleaning**
- **…and more**

PowerWash.com
SUPPLIES CHEMICALS TRAINING

1.800.433.2113
2513 Warfield St. Fort Worth, TX 76106

Shop Online 24 Hours a Day

We provide the products you NEED with helpful service you Deserve!

Quick Links - Pressure Washers - Surface Cleaners - Chemicals & Detergents - Cleaning Supplies - Parts & Accessories - Pumps & Repair Kits - Training Materials

DSR-49 Deck Restorer
DSR-49 Disodium Peroxydicarbonate removes mildew stains and dirt while restoring a natural and bright look to vertical and horizontal grayed and weathered wood surfaces. Ideal for wood preparation prior to water sealer application.

V-505 Butyl All Purpose Cleaner
Perfect for cleaning blood, animal fats and protein from any hard surface that water and alkaline will not harm. Use it on pans, kettles, mixing tubs, molds, smoke-house equipment, work tables, cutting boards, knives, saws, mixers, choppers, trucks, and poultry equipment.

DELTA-60™ Heavy Grease Remover (*)
Contractors first choice for grease spot removal. Just apply Delta 60 to a dry grease spot and pressure wash off. Watch years of deep stains disappear! It restores drive-thru and entrance pads to look like new! The oils come out as solids leaving the concrete as clean as possible.

R-202 Concrete Cleaner
Cleans heavy grease, oil and scuff marks from unpainted concrete and other alkaline water safe hard surfaces. USDA authorized for use in meat plants.

R-1400 Super Foaming Booster
Designed for enhancing detergent performance by increasing dwell time on vertical surfaces. This unique PowerWash.com exclusive surfactant system boosts the cleaning performance of acid or alkaline based cleaning compounds in foamers.

RP-3500 Window Cleaner Concentrate
This non-streaking cleaner leaves glass with reflective finishes and a film-free sparkling appearance. 1 gallon of concentrate makes 10 gallons of cleaner.

Stainless Steel Airless Foamer Kit
This kit is ideal for applying stronger or more aggressive chemicals. It includes metering tips for accurately setting the chemical dilution ratio, a quick connect fitting, tubing, and a strainer. Two foam nozzles are also included - a fan pattern for quick coverage close up and a zero degree for distance. - up to 30 feet! 1000 PSI minimum needed for operation.

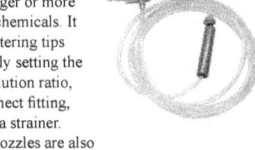

Combo Airless Foamer/Sprayer Kit
Designed for pressure washers NOT equipped with a downstream chemical injector. This kit features venturi injector that connects to the discharge of the pump and a foam wand that connects to a trigger gun. Two foam nozzles are also included - a fan pattern for quick coverage close up and a zero degree for distance. - up to 30 feet! Max.Temp: 180 F

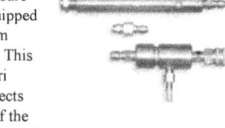

General Pump Multireg Nozzle
Perfect when high and low pressures are needed and also when switching between a solid or a flat spray pattern. Select between high or low pressure with a push-pull action. Adjust for straight to fan jet by turning the nozzle.
- Maximum Pressure: 3000 PSI
- 5.5 Max GPM
- Max Temperature: 140 F
- Inlet Port: 1/4-19 BSP-F

Specify GPM, and Pressure when ordering

5535 Belt Drive Washer
PowerWash.com Standard Equipment

PW	Others	
✓	☐	50" High Pressure Hose
✓	☐	36" Insulated Wand w/QC for Nozzles
✓	☐	Trigger Gun
✓	☐	4 Color Coded, quick coupled nozzles
✓	☐	Extra 1/4" & 3/8" O-Rings
✓	☐	6 Gal. Gas Tank
✓	☐	Down Stream Injector

Dare to Compare!

Features
50 mesh inlet filter
Low oil shutdown

Specifications
3,500 PSI at 5.5 GPM
Honda 20 HP, 4 Stroke, Electric Start Motor, with a Separate 6 Gal. Gas Tank
General, Belt Drive Pump
Low Pressure Chemical injection
Mobile Mount

16' Tandem Axle Trailer Package
- One Pressure Washer of your choice
- 6.5' x 16' double axle trailer with electric brakes and 2" ball hitch
- One 525 Gallon Water Tank & one 35 gallon chemical tank,
- Two High Pressure Hose Reels
- 150' of High Pressure Hose & 110' of fill water hose,
- One Trigger Gun, 36" wand, and 79" wand with quick couplers
- 0, 15, 25, & 40 degree nozzles
- High side injector kit for acid.

Please note: Price shown is for unit with an RK-40 power washer. Please call 800-433-2113 for specific quote on a unit with a different model power washer.

In This Issue:

The Residential Cleaning Issue

99

99 Perfect Power Wash, Akron, Ohio: Cleaning Houses Across America

107 Window Cleaning FAQs: Residential vs. Commercial, by Larry Miller, Larry Miller, Inc. Window Cleaning Svc.

114 Residential Cleaning with Surface Spinners, by Steel Eagle

109 Spray and Pray, by Dan Galvin, Owner of East Coast Power Washing

112 Pressure Washing & Spring Cleaning: How to Avoid Damaging Your Home or Business, by Paul Horsley

Additional Features

112

102 Debunking Chemical Myths, by Pete Marentay, Sun Brite Supply

105 Thank You Larry Hinckley

109 Understanding the PWNA's BMPs

112 PWNA Vendor Profile: EDI Distributors

115 How Do Online Directories Benefit Small Businesses? (Pt. 2), by Henry Bockman, Contractor's Foundation

118 Snapshots of the 2013 Pressure Washing Seminar

122 PWRA Explodes Across America...and Beyond! by Thad Eckhoff, Pressure Washing Resource Association

124 Let Go to Grow!, by George Hedley

126 To Be or not: Should a Janitorial Contract Include Disposables?, by Rick Meehan, Marko Janitorial Supply

Cover Photo
Courtesy of Gary Odum, Carolina Soft Wash, LLC, www.CarolinaSoftwash.com

---

eClean Magazine is published monthly

Publisher: Paul Horsley, paul@ecleanmag.com
Editor: Allison Hester, allison@ecleanmag.com
Sales: Jenna Horsley, jenna@ecleanmag.com

eClean Magazine
Box 262, 16 Midlake Blvd S.E.
Calgary, Alberta
Canada T2X2X7
www.eCleanMag.com

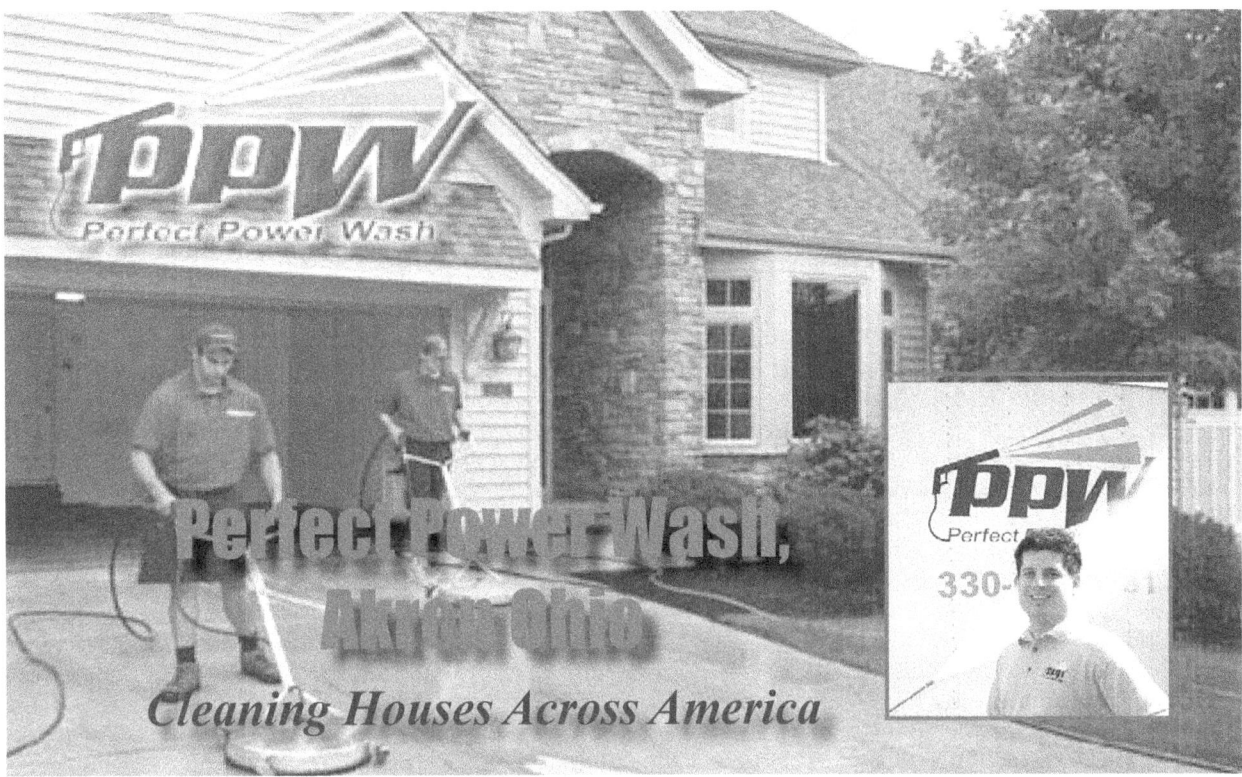

Perfect Power Wash, Akron Ohio
Cleaning Houses Across America

Upon high school graduation, Mike Palubiak came up with a list of five potential summer jobs that might help him pay for college. The one he chose was pressure washing – an industry he had never been involved in before, but that seemed like a good way to make money. So while other teenagers were flipping burgers or sacking groceries, Palubiak was "passing out a bunch of flyers" and washing houses.

Thirteen years later, Palubiak is still washing houses, only today it's as the owner of Perfect Power Wash in Akron, Ohio, a multi-million dollar residential pressure washing business that employs around 30 technicians and office staff, and is getting requests for residential cleaning nationwide.

From Business School to Business Success

The Fall of his freshman year of college at Kent State University, Palubiak began working toward his business management degree. "It was interesting to sit in a college course and be able to apply it directly to my company. I wasn't just going to school, I was starting a business, and for that reason the degree had a ton of value."

In the summer, he and a few of his fraternity brothers would clean houses, roofs and decks. In the fall and spring, he would take classes in marketing, accounting, and business management.

"By the time I finished school, I had a nice little business started." In fact, Palubiak was faced with a choice: continue in the pressure

> Participating "doesn't cost you anything. We're just sending you work. If the schedule works for you, get it done and we'll send you a check."

washing services industry – something he really never intended to do – or look for a new industry. He decided to stick with pressure washing.

"That's when I really started ramping up, buying equipment and hiring a professional team." He also trained under a couple of mentors, and ramped up his research into proper cleaning techniques.

Success in Residential

"Residential cleaning was a natural market for us," Palubiak stated. "There are a lot of nice homes and neighborhoods in our area, so that's where we started." While theydoes do some commercial cleaning – such as four "very large" college campuses in his community – the majority of their work comes from homeowners – houses, low-pressure roof washing, gutter cleaning, flatwork and deck cleaning.

And he likes it that way. "It's nice that we're not dependent on that one enormous commercial account that we're petrified we might lose," he explained. "Residential can be very rewarding when it's done correctly."

And Perfect Power Wash certainly does it correctly. From trained and certified technicians, to top-notch vehicles and "the best equipment money can buy," to a "beautiful, professionally designed website," and a fully-staffed office and sales center, Perfect Power Wash's business screams of professionalism. That is likely why they do a lot of work for homeowner associations, property management companies and insurance companies not only in their immediate area, but who request to work with them across the country.

The Subcontractor Program

"The reason the subcontractor program started is because our customers who were really happy with our services have asked if we can do work for them in other areas of the country," Palubiak explained. So he faced a choice: turn down work requests or find reputable cleaning professionals who could help him. Being the entrepreneur that he is, Palubiak has chosen to find help.

"If you're in the pressure washing field, have insurance, workers comp, the correct equipment, and follow some guidelines on what needs to be done and are willing to make sure the customer is happy, there could be an opportunity here for you," he explained. "A lot of guys working with us now love it because they're not having to do a lot of marketing or cold calling. They prefer to wash rather than sell, and we have the support staff to make that happen."

Essentially, Perfect Power Wash is building a subcontractor network so that when job requests come in from other areas of the country – either from the property management and insurance companies they already serve, or from customers who find their website – Perfect Power Wash can fulfill the work. They email their network of area contractors when jobs come up, and if the approved contractors can meet the customer's schedule, they do the job. Perfect Power Wash handles the rest.

"It's been a great thing for me – percentage wise and value wise – opening new doors and opportunities for my business," explained Ken Ramsey of Ramsey's Property Maintenance in Syracuse, New York, who has been working with Perfect Power Wash for two years now. "Everything has been smooth sailing and I'm definitely happy to be involved. I'm very appreciative for the opportunity the subcontractor program has given me."

And that's the point behind the program, according to Palubiak. "We see an opportunity to help other people in the pressure washing field who want to make more money. We have a lot of companies who are doing that right now and it's working well for them."

Palubiak also emphasized that participating "doesn't cost you anything. We're just sending you work. If the schedule works for you, get it done and we'll send you a check."

To learn more about Perfect Power Wash's subcontractor program, visit their website: perfectpowerwash.net/how-to-make-more-money-power-washing.html.

Pressure Washer Special

$5,995
save over $3,595
Tanks A Lot Promotion

Gas Powered, Diesel Heated
3000psi, 4.8gpm
Adjustable temperature up to 250°F
479cc Vanguard twin cylinder engine
Belt drive pump

Includes:
- 200 gallon tank skid
- Rustproof stainless inlet AND high pressure hose reels, plus 100' inlet hose

*Hydro Tek mobile wash skid
model# SS30005VS / T185TW*

Or FREE Wheel Kit
with purchase of the SS30005VS alone

Conveniently slides in (and out of) a full size truckbed and most flatbed or enclosed trailers. Skid, water tank and hose reels are plumbed and securely mounted to a steel powder coated tank skid. Saves time and hassle, just tighten bolts and go.

HYDRO TEK.US

CONTACT US FOR A DISTRIBUTOR NEAR YOU:

WWW.HYDROTEK.US   (800) 274-9376   BRILLIANT DESIGN, TOUGH ON GRIME

Limited time offer. Free freight to distributor location within the continental US. Price does not include sales tax or battery. Available through a participating distributor near you. Ask your distributor for the Tanks A Lot Special or free wheel kit. Call Hydro Tek for a distributor near you. Not to be combined with any other offers, programs, or discounts.

Debunking Chemical Myths

By Pete Marentay,
Sun Brite Supply,
www.SunBriteSupply.com

There are a few urban legends in our cleaning trade that I think deserve some air time. They center on the chemistry we use and have become increasingly dependent upon for our profitability.

Myth #1: Everything in the world can be cleaned by throwing a little bleach on it.

Myth #2: All you need is a handful of soda beads to make the best cleaner for the job.

Myth #3: Prepared cleaners (products designed by chemists to target certain cleaning challenges) are too expensive to use and therefore cut into a contractor's necessary profitability.

My Perspective

Of course my opinion on all of these things is somewhat biased. My company is a leading seller of prepared cleaners to the industry. The reason I have promoted cleaners over the years goes back to my days as a contractor and my experience using all sorts of cleaners, which is the reason I wanted to start this discussion among contractors here.

Like most contractors, what I was on the lookout for in those days was the one single cleaner I could carry on my truck that would handle everything I would encounter. I soon learned just how naïve this was, but not before trying everything I could lay my hands on locally. In fact, probably 90 percent of the cleaners I tried just plain didn't work on anything very well.

I later figured out that products the general public could buy would never accomplish much. Too many lawyers were involved in deciding what was safe enough to sell to Do-It-Yourselfers. When McDonalds was sued because the coffee was hot I realized that I could never find the power I wanted in a cleaner that just anybody could buy.

From there I turned to a few different suppliers who specialized in chemical products for contractors. One sold predominantly powders, and the other sold liquids. I found concentrated power in each, although the powders gave me fits because they didn't dissolve well in the cold water I had available. What I really discovered was the variety of cleaning products available and how they applied to the variety of jobs that I was doing. Suddenly I regretted all those wasted hours playing dots in chemistry class just waiting for the clock to move. The chemistry of cleaning fascinated me and I set out to learn whatever I could.

Since our company specialized in cleaning and sealing decks and fences, we were actually "soft washing" (cleaning with chemistry and minimal pressure) long before this term became the latest buzzword. Chemistry played a huge role in our ability to do the work and turn a profit. Alkalines, acids, surfactants and all of the possible variations became more important every day.

When we started the supply division of Sun Brite, we started it with wood cleaners that we had developed in conjunction with a local manufacturer. These were the cleaners we found worked better than anything we were able to buy elsewhere because we were concentrating on our specialty. We used these cleaners every day, and that gave us the confidence to offer them to others. Our jobs went faster and we made more money on those jobs with these cleaners. It was a slam dunk.

The popular cleaning method for decks at the time was to throw a little bleach at the wood (maybe with a little dish soap mixed in, or maybe not). Sound familiar? So right off the bat, Sun Brite was bucking the popular methods by promoting cleaners with specific strengths with specific surfactants made to leave the wood in the best possible condition. The cost to use these cleaners was comparable to using a homemade bleach mix (under $1 per gallon), but the results were visibly and microscopically better. We didn't steal the color out of the wood and we didn't spend anywhere near as much time to rinse out the suds that dish soap left in the wood. In addition, we told our customers that we were more professional because we used "specially prepared wood cleaners" and that let us charge more for our work. At the end of the day, my company made more money per job than anybody else we compared notes with – which leads us back to the myths.

Myth 1: Just Throw Bleach on It

I have to admit to all of you that bleach has its place in any arsenal of cleaners. There is no better mold killer for the money that I know of. I use it whenever I am up against mold. It works for the mold on roofs and it takes the mildew off my lawn furniture in the spring.

Bleach alone is not a cleaner, however. It is the action element in a bleach-based cleaner when you add a surfactant. Bleach mixes are not a one-size-fits-all solution, but they do have their place.

So why do so many contractors use bleach or a bleach mix as their cleaner of choice? The answer has several layers, but it starts with the urban myths I started with today and ends on the convenience factor. You can buy bleach anywhere. It is easy to find. You don't have to plan three days ahead for your needs as you would if you were buying a prepared cleaner from a supplier who is not local to you, either.

So what is wrong with using bleach? There are three major problems with bleach:

It is not stable. It breaks down in heat and sun over time. Bleach that is 12.5 percent on Monday can easily be 11 percent on Friday if it isn't properly protected. That means you use a different quantity on Monday than you do on Friday. That is a difficult thing to guess at.

It is not as effective as a cleaner as sodium hydroxide, for example. Just looking at the pH factor, the rating of bleach is 12.6 while the rating of sodium hydroxide is 13.5. Not only does this mean that sodium hydroxide is stronger, it means that every time you add

bleach to your cleaner you are likely weakening that cleaner instead of strengthening that cleaner.

It is not always an appropriate combination for the surfactant or detergent you mix with it. Dish soap is created to wash dishes, not wood or concrete or your newborn baby's hair. We buy special no-tears shampoo for a child's hair because we want to protect that skin, that surface. We should adopt the same approach for every surface we want to clean, because that makes us more professional – to our employees and to our customers.

Now you can see bleach the way I do, as a necessary biocide agent but not as the world's best cleaner. Bleach is not a bad thing, but it is unpredictable and over-used and does not add to our image as an industry because of how it has been misused by people who didn't take the time to learn about the chemical.

Myth 2: Just Throw on Some Soda Beads

We should take a look at 'soda beads' next. For those who don't know, this is sodium hydroxide in its most usable form. You can create cleaners with it that are extremely effective and low cost. Soda beads are harder to find and buy than bleach, but they are stable and predictable and work very well against grease and oil. You can make an effective cleaner for driveways with it, for example.

I think that creating deck strippers with them is possible, but the lack of availability of good surfactants for wood makes this a shaky proposition for serious wood restoration contractors. The only reason ever expressed to me for making your own deck stripper with soda beads is the end cost of the product. No one has ever made the case that they can make a better deck stripper, just a cheaper one. Considering that we sell deck strippers today that cost less than $1.50 per gallon, this is not a really strong argument.

The important thing to understand about using soda beads is that sodium hydroxide is not always the best choice for a cleaner. If you are cleaning around a fast food outlet, for example, potassium hydroxide is a much faster and more effective chemical cleaner. It attacks animal fats far better than sodium hydroxide. It's better for cleaning hoods in restaurants, too. When you are cleaning those black stripes off of gutter surfaces and stucco, a solvent cleaner using d-limonene or butyl is a far better choice than sodium hydroxide.

So I will be the first to say that using soda beads can work on some jobs, particularly if you are able to lay your hands on the right surfactant for the job you need. I must also say at the same time that soda beads are not the best answer for all cases.

Myth 3: Prepared Chemicals are a Waste of Money

One final point – those folks (myself included) who develop and sell you cleaners are not the enemy. Quite the opposite, actually. If not for the guys in the white lab coats, we would be in the dark ages of cleaning. Most cleaners sold today are extremely powerful and cost effective.

Using homemade cleaners can work, but they have their limits. As I said earlier, we buy special shampoo for our children, special soap for the dishwasher and washing machine, and special soap to get our greasy hands clean after working on the truck engine.

I think we add to the image of the industry by using professional products created exactly for the job. When you do, it would be great if you bought your cleaner from my company. In the end, however, using a prepared cleaner from any distributor is arguably better than using a home-made concoction. I used this approach to make more money as a cleaning contractor, and you can too.

Pete Marentay is the owner of Sun Brite Supply in Lawrenceville, Ga, and an instructor for Contractor's Foundation. To learn more, visit his company's website at www.SunBriteSupply.com.

ROOF SNOT

THE choice of professional roof cleaning contractors for controlling runoff & maximizing dwell time on ugly black roof stains.

Visit www.RoofSnot.com for more information. Available exclusively through Southside Equipment, Inc., www.PressureWasherKY.com

Thank You Larry Hinckley

Reprinted with Permission of PowerWash.com (edited for space)

Larry Hinckley has spent his career working to improve the power washing industry. His designs have helped to make power washers safer and more efficient, his articles have been published in many respected journals, and his seminars have become required training in a lot of companies. Larry is never too busy to answer a question or demonstrate a concept. He believes that business is about people and knowledge. "Anyone who intends to be successful in this industry has to keep learning. In business, you never stand still. There's no treading water."

Larry's power washing career started with a casual conversation in 1984. At the time, he was working 18-hour days for a bottling company in Houston. His son-in-law remarked, "I have trouble finding people who are willing to work eight hours a day. I wish I had a person like you." Larry jokingly responded, "Don't make any offers you can't back up!"

One thing led to another, and Larry came to work for Rahsco Manufacturing in August 1984. Soon Larry became recognized for his ability to think on his feet and solve problems quickly.

Over the last 29 years, Larry has been a Field Service Technician, Shop Foreman, Production Manager, Salesman, Purchasing Manager, Senior Technical Advisor, Instructor, Technical Writer, Bulletin board administrator, and General Manager. When asked why he decided to stay, he replied, "It's a constant challenge. It's never, ever, boring!"

Larry also gets great satisfaction from helping the industry grow. "When I first came into it, there was nobody you could get information from because there was no Internet, no cell phones. If you were getting ready to do a job and you needed information, the only way you could get that information was to know somebody, call that person and talk to them on the telephone. So, I guess if I do have any great accomplishments, it would be that I have been able to help so many people through the years."

Larry's advice:

1. "Seek education. Do not come in unadvised. There's so much information available to you today that you can save yourself a fortune." And education is not for newcomers only. "You never know so much that you don't need to learn something else. Anything that is going to add to your bottom line is obviously worth the doing."

2. "Don't purchase equipment without knowing what you need for what you are going to do."

3. "Don't just choose one thing that you want to do and say that's all I'm going to do. Diversify. Be flexible. That way if one sector of the industry begins to slow down, you can move very comfortably into another sector."

Larry is ready for his next chapter. "I'll soon be 70 and I'm realistic enough to know that no one lives forever. I'd like to do more of the things I enjoy that I have so little time to do now. I'd like to spend time with my family, in my flower beds, in my yard, and cooking. I love to cook! And I am considering writing a book. It would be a technical manual. Somebody needs to compile a reference book."

Larry plans to remain active on the Internet after his retirement. "I've made too many friends out there to just walk away. It's kind of comforting to share personal experiences with many of those friends. I have people I've known for 20 to 25 years. I get to say good morning to them every day and I like that."

To Larry: You always made time to mentor anyone who sought your help. Your dedication to serving and educating your fellow man has enriched everyone who has had the privilege of knowing you. Your influence will continue to ripple through this industry long into the future. Thank you!

You can view Michael Hinderliter's final interview with Larry at http://www.youtube.com/watch?v=Oplo03Xr2OU&feature=youtu.be

WINDOW CLEANING FAQs: Residential vs. Commercial

by Larry Miller, owner of Larry Miller, Inc. Window Cleaning Services and IWCA Board Member

Photo courtesy of Rick Kadletz, Mid Missouri Window Cleaning Co. LLC, Moberly, Missouri, www.mmwindowcleaning.com

I cleaned commercial properties for almost 20 years before I got into residential. I switched over about 12 years ago. It has been one of the best moves I ever made in my company, and meant less stress in my life. There are many reasons that you may feel "at home" with residential window cleaning.

Q: What are the benefits of residential window cleaning vs. commercial?

You get paid faster. With typical commercial window cleaning contracts, you have to wait 30 to 60 to 90 days for payment. Another benefit is that you don't have "all your squeegees in one bucket." With commercial, you could have 20 chain stores on your commercial window cleaning schedule that represent a major source of your profits. You think you're doing fine until some national contractor shows up and makes them an offer they can't refuse.

You have many more individual customers with whom you can develop personal relationships. If there's a disagreement with one of those customers, you can walk away if you feel that's best. It's different in commercial. If somebody's not happy, even if it's not your fault, you could risk losing a much larger percent of your business.

You have more opportunity to use a wider range of professional window cleaning skills. Plus you could do add-on services like gutter cleaning and power washing and make more money.

Q: What kinds of things are important to know when taking on residential jobs?

You always have to be neat whether you're working indoors or outdoors. Wearing booties indoors to help protect the carpets is a sign of respect for residential customers. Remember to take the booties off when you're using a ladder.

Having good communication with your individual residential customers is key for your success, repeat business and referrals.

There are so many different kinds of windows! That's obvious to someone who's been doing residential window cleaning for a while. But if you're just starting residential, it's impossible to know all the "ins and outs." Especially when you're working on high windows where you have different ways to maneuver and safety is an issue. You have to teach members of your team.

That's why it's important to go out and observe your teams at work. You can see what they're doing and help turn it into a learning experience when they need help. It's good to have a member "on call" for residential. So they can answer questions and help members of your team through a task.

Q: What are some of the things that you've done that have gotten the best response from residential customers?

When people get their home's windows professionally cleaned for the first time, they can't believe the difference. They personally experience the value of cleaning windows. Their neighbors do, too. When they come over for a party everybody says, "Who did this?" "How come your house looks different?" After that experience, residential customers swear they're going to get those windows cleaned every six months.

Realtors know prospects can really see the difference, when the windows are clean. They say homeowners should have had this done before putting their property on the market.

Q: What are some safety issues unique to residential work?

Hardwood floors and tile floors are very slippery when you're using a ladder. Putting a mat under the ladder helps stabilize it. When you're working high up on the ladder, take your time and don't rush.

Watch out for drips. If you're cleaning a skylight, use a product like Dirtex® to wet a chamois or microfiber cloth so dirt doesn't drip onto the carpet or floor like it could using a squeegee.

Moving expensive furniture can be an issue. Always make sure the residential customers move their own valuables whenever possible to avoid damage and liabilities.

Safety's the number one thing when you're doing residential. If you can't do it, don't do it. It's better to leave the window dirty than to risk somebody getting hurt.

Q: Are there any techniques or strategies that make residential jobs easier or more efficient to complete?

Set up a team with two or three people so the work goes efficiently. You could have one guy pull out the screens, another one start cleaning the inside and maybe a third outside. With that systematic team approach, the work gets much more smoothly, efficiently. It's also a lot easier than working by yourself. Residential customers like seeing that teamwork, too. That provides a high level of customer satisfaction.

Schedule residential customers geographically – with homes that are in the same neighborhood where possible. That saves time (and gasoline) on travel expenses. When you have good signage on your trucks, neighbors driving by can jot down your name and phone number. That's inexpensive marketing that gets results.

Larry Miller is the owner of Larry Miller, Inc., and a director for the International Window Cleaning Association (IWCA). The IWCA is a non-profit trade 501(c)(6) association committed to raising the standards of professionalism within the window cleaning industry. The IWCA represents all facets of the window cleaning industry, from high rise to route work, residential to industrial. Through its various programs, the IWCA promotes safety, training and a highly professional, responsible image of the window cleaning professional. For more information, call 1-800-875-4922 or visit them at www.iwca.org

Understading the PWNA's BMPs

by Allison Hester, Editor

In the early 1990s, the pressure washing industry was "in turmoil." The Environmental Protection Agency (EPA) was largely requiring pressure washing contractors to use some sort of expensive wastewater recycling equipment, and it was putting them out of business. Contractors in the Miami and San Francisco areas stopped power washing altogether for a short time, and the trend was going to spread – unless someone did something to change it.

Robert Hinderliter, who at the time owned the Delco Cleaning Systems of Ft. Worth (which is now PowerWash.com), disagreed with the EPA's costly requirements, believing instead that the easier it was for contractors to conform to regulations, the more likely they would be to comply with the Clean Water Act.

"This radical thinking was not widely accepted by our industry at the time," he explained.

Hinderliter did not have the finances to fight the regulators in court, and even more, it was a political problem. "I was not a political person." But he knew he needed to do something, so he contacted his local AHJ (Authority Having Jurisdiction), who took Hinderliter under his wing and taught him the in's and out's of the regulatory community.

The Clean Water Act states that "no person shall throw, drain, or otherwise discharge, cause or allow separate storm sewer system (a.k.a. "MS4") any pollutants or waters containing any pollutants, other than storm water."

However, Hinderliter soon learned that the Clean Water Act was "basically interpreted by everyone's economic revenue stream and that our industry was being controlled by the coin-op carwash association and the liquid waste haulers."

He also learned that individuals held little authority when it came to working with regulators; they wanted to deal with an industry trade association. "I tried to get the equipment manufacturers to open up their association to everyone, but they would not do it."

So in April 1992, Hinderliter used his company's newsletter to announce he was wanting to form a contract cleaning trade association – which became the Power Washers of North America (PWNA) – to fulfill the needed trade association role for contract cleaners. It took a few years, but eventually regulatory agencies began to listen.

Hinderliter arranged a compliance conference that was attended by 40 environmental regulators – national, state and local – and 100 contract cleaners. "There was a lot of discussion among everyone, AHJ to AHJ and contractors to AHJs. The Feds, State, and Locals decided what each would be responsible for and basic structure and BMPs (Best Management Practices).

Hinderliter and the PWNA fought hard for some aspects of these BMPs – such as raising the defining temperature of "hot water" to 110 degrees from the initial description, which was essentially "anything hotter than tap water" as the municipalities initially called for.

The end result was a set of BMPs establishing that the ordinance should be "reasonable, rational, and logical." The Model Ordinance is just that, a model for the municipalities to follow, not a requirement. Ultimately, each municipality has the right to create their own regulations.

Additionally, these BMPs are for regular

maintenance cleaning, not for the purpose of cleaning hazardous materials. Another important note is that if your discharge does not reach the waters of the United States, there are no requirements by the Clean Water Act.

While the PWNA guidelines list specific BMPs for a wide variety of cleaning applications some basic elements are consistent. These are as follows:

Always Preclean

This means before any power washing begins, contractors should collect debris (dirt, sand, leaves, twigs, etc.) by sweeping with a broom, using a leaf blower or vacuuming and disposing into a trash receptacle. The gathered debris should never go to a sanitary sewer or storm drain. Finally, any oil and grease spots should be pretreated with an oil absorbent clay (such as kitty litter) and then thrown away in a trash receptacle.

Always filter wash water before discharging to the sewer

For debris, this may mean running through a 20 mesh (or smaller) screen. A 20 mesh screen is about the equivalent of a pair of pantyhose. Hydrocarbons (grease/oil) need to be run through an oil absorbent filter/oil sock or an oil/water separator such as an oil absorbent boom, sand trap, grease trap, clarifier, recycling system, etc. After filtering the water, there should be no oil sheen (i.e., multi-colored water) visible.

Sanitary sewer is the PWNA's first choice for disposal in most situations. Because studies found that "the amount of wastewater delivered to the sanitary sewer was insignificant compared to the total amount of wastewater the POTWs are handling," the PWNA made this their first choice for most types of disposals. Some cities require a license to discharge to the sanitary sewer; others do not. Start with your local Public Works Department to find out whether a permit is required. (They may direct you to another department).

Additionally, discharge must be in compliance with local regulations and limits, which varies by municipality. Use a pH test to ensure the pH of wash water is between 5.0 and 12.0 and below 150F; solids - less than 250 mg/L, petroleum -less than 250 mg/L. Finally, filter "using the best available method of convenience that removes the largest amount of contaminants." The best available methods of convenience may be a sand trap, grit trap, grease trap or clarifier, or it may require discharging to some sort of sink, toilet, indoor floor drain, or sanitary sewer clean-out stub.

Discharging to a landscaped area is the PWNA's second choice.

As mentioned before, it is true that if your wastewater discharge does not reach the waters of the United States, there are no requirements by the Clean Water Act. The PWNA considers discharging to a landscaped area an acceptable choice if guidelines (below) are followed, although sanitary sewers remains the preferred method. "If you discharge pollutants long enough to the same landscaped area, you're going to contaminate the soil, and potentially make it hazardous," Hinderliter explained. "The sanitary sewer is the best place because that goes to the City municipality, and they have an NPDES permit to discharge to the waters of the United States."

First, it's important to note that on-property washwater discharge can only occur on the property where the washwater is generated. To discharge to landscaped areas, you should first obtain the property owner's permission and ensure that the discharge volume is small enough to soak into the ground without running into the property. Limit your discharge to 1,000 gallons per acre, per month. Discharge only at the property where the wash water was generated. Do not discharge repeatedly to the same area because doing so can contaminate the soil and groundwater, damage plants and cause other problematic conditions. Ensure the pH of the wash water is between 6.0 and 9.0.

The third preferred method is to recycle wash water then discharge to the sanitary sewer.

"Recycling really should be avoided if at all possible, as this concentrates the waste," Hinderliter explained. In other words, recycling wash water has the effect of concentrating the contaminants and pollutants, and the POTW (Publically Owned Treatment Works) usually won't accept concentrated wastewater. In fact, if recycled long enough, it can become hazardous waste, which requires contractors to have a hazardous waste haulers permit. If the water is recycled and collected for reuse, all discharge locations need to be reported to the Sanitary Sewer Department in advance, and should be tested annually and reported to the Sanitary Sewer Department as required.

Discharging to storm drains is not recommended, but there are times it may be allowed.

Washing with cold water (less than 110 degrees F) without use of chemicals is considered no worse than a "rain event" and may be discharged to the storm drains if the surface cleaned has no oil, grease, or similar contaminants. In some cases, hot water without chemicals may be allowed to the storm drain if the AHJ preauthorizes the cleaning.

"Anything that physically, chemically or biologically changes the water is considered a pollutant," explained Clifford M. Lawson, P.E., Supervisor of the Permits Branch for the Bureau of Water Pollution Control, Nevada Division of the EPA, who recently spoke at the Gamble Garage Cleaning Event in Las Vegas. "Elevating the temperature means you're creating pollution."

"High Pressure Power Washing with hot water or chemicals dislodges more contaminates than a rain event and cannot be treated the same. The dislodged items need to be collected before being washed into the MS4 (storm sewer), which is not designed for the increased load. The extra dislodged items will increase the TSS and turbidity of the water and impair living organisms. Chemicals are nutrients and when added to the MS4, they unset the natural habitat," said Hinderliter.

Robert Hinderliter (second from left) joins with members of the State of Nevada's Dept. of Conservation & Natural Resources, Division of Enviromental Protection Agency, following Clifford M. Lawson (middle), P.E.'s talk during last week's 2013 Gamble Garage Cleaning Event. Also shown: John Tornabene (left), Jim Gamble (second from right) and Nigel Griffith (right).

The Impact

The result of the PWNA's Model Ordinance in 1995 was that expensive recycling equipment was no longer needed. "I showed contractors how they could comply for a few hundred dollars, not thousands," Hinderliter explained. In fact, the PWNA's BMPs provided plans "that everyone with any talent could copy," publishing remediation basics so contractors could build their own systems if they so chose. All of this information has always been free. "I only get orders for wastewater equipment from contractors who determine they have more money to buy the equipment premade than time to build it themselves."

The PWNA's BMPs are available online at pwna.org/water_reclaimer.php#updatedbmp. The PWNA also is offering its environmental certification course several times throughout the year (visit www.ecleanmag.com/events for dates), as well as at its annual convention, October 17 through 19, in Orlando. To learn more, go to www.PWNA.org.

PWNA Vendor Profile

EDI Distributors

by Allison Hester, Editor

Skip Markowitz of EDI Distributors in Cherry Hill, New Jersey, has witnessed numerous changes in the pressure washing industry over the past (almost) 40 years. But one thing that hasn't changed is EDI's support for the Power Washer's of North America (PWNA).

"I joined the PWNA, almost at inception, initially as an opportunity to generate additional sales," said Skip. "Since that time, we have found the annual conventions to be the best opportunity to see existing customers face-to-face, many whom we have never before met in person."

While Skip said he enjoys greeting existing customers with whom he has developed long-lasting friendships, "we enjoy the opportunity to work with some newer members to answer their questions about the industry," he explained. "Of course, these conventions also offer the best venue to show off new products as well as meet new prospects.

EDI was also honored to be selected as "PWNA Vendor of the Year" in 2009.

FROM SHIPS TO FLEETS ...AND BEYOND

After graduating from the University of Pennsylvania on a Navy ROTC scholarship and with a degree in Electrical Engineering, Skip spent almost five years engineering sea duty on destroyers. When it was time to "move on and try civilian life," he remained in the Navy Reserve, retiring as a Captain.

With a degree in Electrical Engineering, but little knowledge of the products developed over the previous five years, he started a civilian career with several large companies in their manufacturing engineering divisions. When the opportunity presented, Skip joined a four man start-up company and was "charged with developing a line of reliable cold water pressure washers, electric and gas engine, to accurately dispense two-step chemical cleaners."

After the equipment and sales strategy was developed and successfully marketed in the Philadelphia metro area, the company decided to advertise to expand and market the products nationally, but without any local area distributors.

"I recall a particular sale of a complete package, equipment and chemicals, to a mail carrier in West Memphis, Arkansas. After a few great weeks of clean trucks, the equipment failed. So, I got on a plane to Memphis and was met by an irate customer with a pig in the back of his truck," he laughed. Skip fixed the equipment, but quickly learned the importance of a distributor network.

Over the next 25 years, the group became the industry's dominant manufacturer of two-step, cold water vehicle cleaning chemicals and equipment. Unfortunately, however, environmental and other considerations forced the closure of this business. "But it was a great ride!" he said. "It is interesting to note that some of our original equipment is still in operation today and that two-step or twin-chem vehicle washing is having resurgence, although it will likely never reach the level it was at in the 1980s."

With his company closed and no suppliers for their products, many distributors Skip had known over the years reached out to him for parts support. "As I knew all of our suppliers, it was a natural for me to fill that void."

So Skip started EDI Distributors almost 20 years ago. EDI stocked and still stocks most parts for two-step equipment, which was manufactured and still in use since 1972.

More Than Two-Step

Over the years, EDI has evolved and its support for the two-step industry has become less important. "Our business has since grown to become a supplier of high pressure pumps and product support for the power washing industry," Skip added. Changing technology has also impacted the way that EDI can sell products, which are now offered through its website as well as via telephone, local walk-in contractors, "and to the customer base we have built over the years."

Over the last three years, there has been a further business shift and now EDI exports high pressure pumps internationally to over 10 countries.

"From the very beginning, we have always strived to present a professional image and now sell to several Fortune 500 companies. But we have never varied from our core value of providing prompt service, serious technical support, at competitive prices to all customers, regardless of size," Skip concluded. "When we get a call or request for a quote, we work with any prospect to source even the smallest o-ring or seal for a pump until they are satisfied. We are serious about customer service."

To learn more, visit their website at www.EDIdistributors.com.

GAIN THE SUPPORT OF THE ORIGINAL POWER WASHING TRADE ORGANIZATION

JOIN THE EXPERIENCE...

Since 1992 the PWNA has represented contractors in the Power Washing industry. We stand for all power washers: fleet washing, concrete cleaning, kitchen exhaust, wood restoration, as well as everything in between. The PWNA provides quality education and certification to power wash contractors along with conventions, networking opportunities, and a clear voice for our industry.

Visit **www.pwna.org** for more info on becoming a member.

POWER WASHERS OF NORTH AMERICA
PH 800-393-7962 | FX 651-213-0369 | WWW.PWNA.ORG

VISIT US ON

Residential Cleaning with Surface Spinners

by Steel Eagle, www.SteelEagle.com

Residential cleaning is challenging as there are many different kinds of surfaces to clean. Depending on what you are cleaning (metal, concrete, tile, etc.), you need different amounts of power to get the job done without damaging the surface. You also want to have a quick and efficient tool that minimizes the hours it takes to complete the job safely – that's where a surface spinner comes in.

Control of the Pressure and Flow:

Gallons per minute (GPM) and pressure rating (PSI) are both critical to know before trying to clean any other surfaces. For example, 5 GPM at 3000 PSI might be appropriate for concrete at a close distance but it may damage softer surfaces. Knowing this information will allow you to use the correct setup for your cleaning application.

Spinners commonly come assembled from the factory designed to clean concrete and asphalt for sidewalks and parking garages – not softer surfaces.

So What Do You Do?

The spray nozzles can be changed or sized to ensure proper flow and pressure from your pressure washer. The larger the nozzle, the lower the pressure. You can also change the angle of the nozzle (the wider the angle, the less aggressive). Nozzles commonly come in 15°, 25° and 40°. Make sure the spinner you are using has the correct nozzles for the surface you are cleaning.

All situations are unique but here are some starting points:

15°: The most aggressive, suited for the hardest surfaces like metal and concrete.

25°: Moderately aggressive, suited for intermediate surfaces.

40°: The least aggressive, used for softer surfaces.

When cleaning a tile or brick surface with grout, pay particular attention to the hardness of the grout and start with a less aggressive nozzle.

If you plan to use the same spinner on several different surfaces, you might want to consider a spinner with adjustable spray bars. By controlling the pressure based on raising or lowering the adjustable bars, this surface cleaner will allow you to do many jobs that require different pressures without changing or resizing your tips. The farther the tips are from the surface being cleaned, the more fanned out or wider the spray pattern will be, effectively lowering the pressure and preventing damage to softer surfaces. You can go from cleaning sidewalks and driveways to cleaning softer surfaces by simply raising or lowering the adjustable setting on the surface cleaner.

The exclusive adjustable version of the 30" Steel Eagle Surface Cleaner will allow you to raise or lower the position of the spray bars to provide you the ability to clean different surface types. After determining the proper setting to use for your application, start off by cleaning a very small area and checking to ensure no damage is being done. If there is damage, then you will need to reduce the pressure while keeping the volume of water - so you can raise the adjustable surface cleaner as necessary.

Final Thoughts:

When cleaning any surface with a lance, it is almost impossible to get a professional, consistent cleaning pattern. Surface spinners not only clean faster but the end result is a cleaner, better looking surface without random streaking.

Finally, when cleaning any surface, err on the side of caution. You can always increase the pressure to clean faster. Always begin cleaning on an area that is less prominent in case of damage. If you are using the adjustable spinner, you will want to start at the highest setting to prevent any possible damage.

We understand your time is important and you need the correct product for your application. Take a minute to discuss your particular cleaning situations with your Steel Eagle sales person. They can recommend the perfect system utilizing the correct spinner and nozzles for the job. Whether you are doing concrete, wood or a variety of surfaces, Steel Eagle has a system that will do the job with ease and speed.

To learn more about Steel Eagle and our products, visit www.SteelEagle.com.

How Do Online Directories Benefit Small Businesses? Part 2

By Henry Bockman, Contractor's Foundation

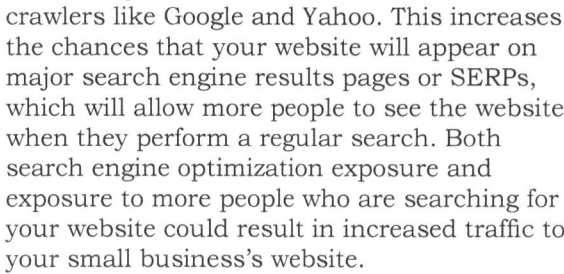

There are many benefits associated with listing your small business in an online directory. This article lists some of these many benefits. Remember, the more online directories you can list your business in, the more benefits you will reap.

Exposure. Exposure is important for all business marketing strategies. After all, the more people who are exposed to your business, the more people are likely to utilize your business's services. If online viewers aren't able to see your website or even know that it exists, then they probably aren't going to purchase your products or services.

Listing your business's website in online directories helps your website to gain exposure. Thousands of people use online directories everyday to find things they are interested in. These are people who are actively searching for websites that are directly related to your products or services. They are already looking – all you have to do is make it easy to find you. Online directories will expose your business to more online viewers, which could increase traffic to your website, leading to our second benefit.

Increased Traffic. There are several ways that online directories can help you increase the amount of traffic your website receives. For starters, the more exposure your website has, the more people are likely to visit it.

But online directories offer more than just exposure from potential viewers. They also offer exposure to the various major search engine crawlers like Google and Yahoo. This increases the chances that your website will appear on major search engine results pages or SERPs, which will allow more people to see the website when they perform a regular search. Both search engine optimization exposure and exposure to more people who are searching for your website could result in increased traffic to your small business's website.

Cheap Advertising. As a small business owner, you already understand the importance of advertising. You know that it helps customers to find your business and recognize your name and brand.

You probably have little room in your budget for more advertising right at this moment. That is one of the major benefits of listing your business's website in an online directory. Online directories are inexpensive to join and they offer a lot of exposure for the price.

Some online directories will allow you to list your business for free, while others will charge a minimal fee. Either way, you are getting a lot of exposure for less money than you would spend on a TV or radio advertisement.

Professional Appearance. You want everything about your business to look professional in the eyes of your customers. A professional appearance enhances your status and makes customers more likely to patronize your business. Online directories help you to look like a professional business.

When an online consumer sees your business listing in an online directory they will consider your business to be an authority on the subject and a professional place to do business. Unlike a search that is performed on a major search engine like Google where there is little difference between the legitimate websites relating to a topic and the less-than-useful websites, online directories are mostly legitimate websites. Online consumers are more likely to trust what they see on online directories.

SEO Benefits. Online directories offer several search engine optimization or SEO benefits as well. First off, these online directories offer you more inbound links. When an online viewer sees your website link in an online directory, they will be able to click on it and be instantly redirected to your website. This is a great way to increase traffic. It is a great way to improve your status in the eyes of search engine crawlers too. The more backlinks that a search engine crawler can find, the more relevant they will rank your website. This is especially true of authoritative online directories. Being linked to a major online directory, such as Google Places, will give your website more relevancy in the eyes of Google's search engine crawlers. This will result in a higher page ranking on the SERP.

As you know, a higher search engine result page rank you get, the more people are going to click on your website link.

Increased Revenue. When more people are able to find your website, it increases the chances that they will visit your website. When people visit your website, they are more likely to purchase your goods or services. This means that online directories can help you increase your revenue stream. Online directories are good for your bottom line.

Increased Brand Recognition and Customer Interaction. When an online viewer locates your website though an online directory, they are more likely to remember your business's name and directly interact with it. Online directories can help your business stand out to customers as well. Overall, listing your small business in an online directory will help you to create a more comprehensive and effective online presence.

Listing your small business's website with several online directories will help more people find your website, whether they are specifically searching for it or if they are just browsing around. In addition to gaining exposure, online directories will provide major SEO benefits, which will help your website get found by search engines. Increased exposure and higher search engine rankings will result in more traffic to your website, which will result in higher revenue.

There are many different types of online directories, from large global directories to small, niche and location-specific ones. Some examples of other types of online directories can include reciprocal link directories, free directories, paid, directories, Business 2 Business directories, theme-related directories, small business directories and many, many more.

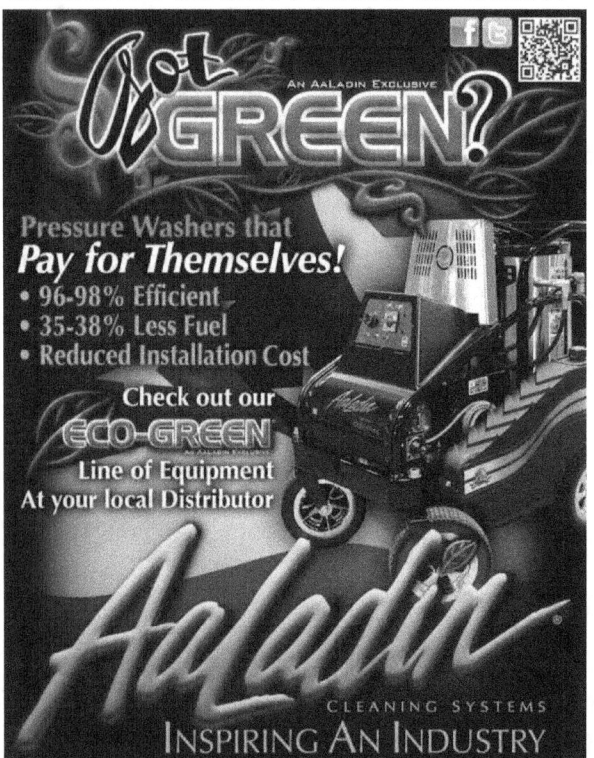

Why You Should Consider Listing Your Small Business in an Online Directory

Apart from the concept that online directories will increase the amount of exposure your website gets and help with your SEO strategies, they are also a very effective way to directly target potential customers. Online directories make it easy for online users to find something they want.

According to a study performed by Burke, 8 out of 10 people will use a print or online directory to find companies or products they are looking for. The same study also suggested that 8 out of 10 people who use these directories to locate a business do so with the intent to purchase a product or service from them. This is a very effective form of targeted advertising. The customer already needs or wants your product or service and you can directly target them by listing your website in an online directory.

Another reason why you should consider listing your small business has to do with your Return On Investment or ROI. Since the potential benefits of getting increased website traffic are great when compared to how much you will have to spend to list your website in an online directory, you can see a great return on your investment in the form of increased revenue. You also want to keep your brand and your company name in the minds of consumers at all times, which is something else that an online directory can help with.

In next month's *eClean*, we will finish this article series by talking about which online directories you should use for your small business.

After leaving the military, Henry Bockman started a home maintenance company in Maryland called Henry's Housework. Since 1989 Henry Bockman has dedicated himself to learning everything he can about marketing, web site development and Internet Marketing Systems.

Bockman currently resides in Maryland with his wife of over 20 years and two teenagers. He operates 5 companies, 2contracting companies; Henry's Housework Inc, Commercial Restorations, a marketing company called Extreme Marketing Solutions which specializes in SEO, Social Media Marketing, online marketing, and lead generation.

Contractors Foundation, which is a training company that provides power washing training, marketing and business success classes to help companies start up and succeed in any type of service based business, He also runs two On-line companies and several internet directories.

Normally I sell this information with a step by step guide and a list of over 250 other directory sites for $29.99, but since you are an EClean Magazine Reader, You Can Get A Free Copy! Just click the link below and use Coupon Code: ECleanMag for your discount!

http://contractorsfoundation.com/product-category/business-marketing-guides-service-companies/

Please Leave A Review On This Article And The Guide Here: http://contractorsfoundation.com/shop/get-listed-create-a-steady-stream-of-customers-to-your-web-site/

Snapshots from the 2013 Pressure Washing Seminar in Albany

by Allison Hester, Editor

From March 14 through 17, I joined with around 120 contract cleaners and vendors in Albany, New York, for the 2013 Pressure Washing Seminar, sponsored by Matt Norman and Jack Evans of Contractor Education Services.

There they experienced education-packed days filled with seminars, presentations, demonstrations, exhibits and networking.

"I can't say I liked any one thing best," said John Suberbielle of It's So Clean in Austin, Texas, who attended all four days of the event. "I was looking for information about starting a pressure washing business so everything I heard from the hosts and presenters, from vendors and from talking shop with the other attendees was all 'grist for the mill.'"

Ed Burgess of ELB Power Washing Services in Norton, Massachusetts, also attended all four days. "I found the pre-seminar classes helpful as well as speaking with the vendors," he said. "Just as important was the networking. I learned a few things by picking some brains and made several new friends."

The networking opportunities also stood out for Andy Reinsel of A2Z Pressure Washing, LLC, in Pittsburgh, Pennsylvania – a self-proclaimed "newbie" to the industry – who arrived at the Thursday evening get together. "I gained a lot of information that will be helpful in my new venture, but I would have to say that the networking was my favorite. I met a lot of great people and a few really stood out," he explained. "Tom Vogel (ACR Products) and Barry Riddell (Cyclone Pressure Washing), in particular, flooded my brain with tons of information and direction based off their many years in the industry."

Michael Albaladejo with Thunder Wash Pressure Washing "liked all the new information I learned to help me do my job better, like how to clean roofs in a whole new way," he explained. "I learned a lot of new tactics to apply while working."

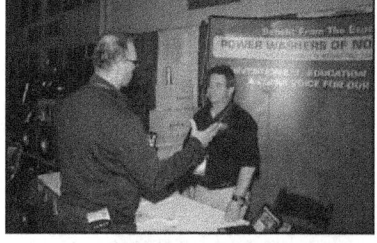

Each contractor interviewed agreed that the event was well worth attending, and that the knowledge and connections gained will help them grow their businesses. "I plan on attending more events like this if the future," added Reinsel. "They are a wealth of knowledge that a newbie or veteran can't afford to miss!"

Burgess agreed, concluding that "Jack and Matt did great!"

Classifieds: Products & Services

www.SkyPro.com

Automated window cleaning systems. A safe way to clean windows, frames and exterior of high rise buildings. Call 800-699-0251 or 651-967-9031.

www.PowerWash.com

Mobile power wash equipment, schools, training, videos, environmental supplies & maintenance services. Call for a free catalog, 800-433-2113.

www.PWNA.org

Power Washers of North America. For certification or membership information, visit our website, email info@pwna.org, or call 800-393-7962.

To Advertise in our New Classifieds Section
Contact Allison Hester
allison@ecleanmag.com

eClean Magazine

SPRAY and Pray

by Dan Galvin, owner of East Coast Power Washing and Founder of SuccessInPowerWashing.com

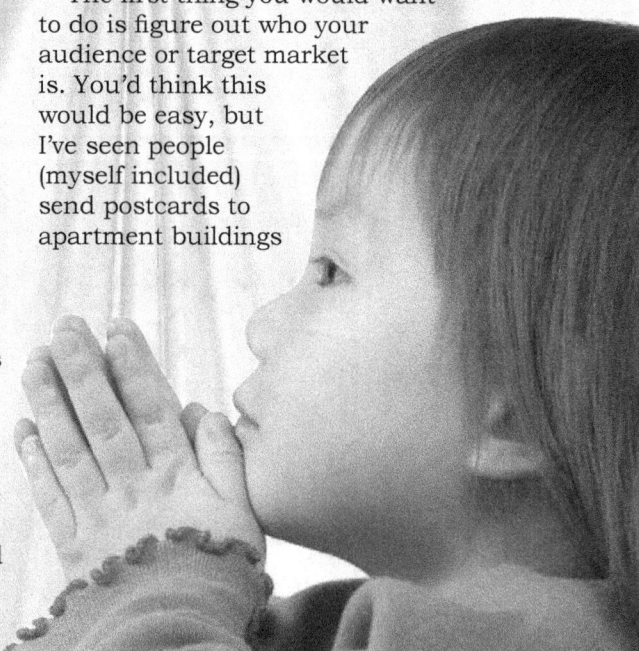

Have you ever sent out a postcard or brochure about your power washing business and got no sales from it? Well you're not alone!

A lot of power washing business owners do what I call "spray and pray." In other words, they buy 5000 postcards cheap, then send them out to anyone and everyone they can find an address for, praying that someone calls. They have no strategic plan and no clue who their target market is. Theit approach is that their power washing service could really help just about everyone. But here is something to think about: if you have everybody for a prospect I can guarantee you will have nobody for a client!

Ok, yes, I know about this all too well. Why? Because I was a sprayer and prayer for years. It got to the point that it was so expensive and frustrating that I said "forget it! This stupid marketing stuff just doesn't work" and I stopped sending out postcards.

What I didn't realize was that I was running a hit or miss type of marketing, which is probably the most costly marketing out there. I had absolutely no plan whatsoever when it came to my marketing. I would go buy some stamps and send some postcards out. That was my plan. I had no clue who my target market was and it was killing my business.

The Need for Niche

Power washing is a niche business, but there are niches within this niche of a business. You have residential and commercial/industrial and you can even break it down more. On the residential side you have house washing, roof washing, deck cleaning, driveways, walkways – the list can go on and on. The commercial side is even larger: fleet washing, flat surface cleaning, hood cleaning, large building cleaning, mine equipment cleaning, rail car cleaning, boat and ship cleaning, and so on. The more narrowly you define your market the easier and less expensive it will be to fill your business with new clients.

For the sake of this article, we are going to use house washing as our target market.

The first thing you would want to do is figure out who your audience or target market is. You'd think this would be easy, but I've seen people (myself included) send postcards to apartment buildings or areas of town that typically aren't going to have their homes washed. Not only did these people not want my service, many did not need it.

Now we know that our target market is homeowners, but what type of homes are you looking for? Are you only looking to do vinyl or are you a wood guy? Large homes or small homes? The more you can narrow it down, the easier it is to define which niche you want to be in and the less expensive your marketing cost will be per customer.

Getting Your Target's Attention

Now that you know who your target market is, how do you get their attention? Here are some examples:

"Attention Homeowners" (General): This would be a general attention getter, and good if you an area in mind and you know what the homes are like.

"Attention Lion Estate Residents:" (Narrower): This one is really cool for developments. This gets the prospect to look at the postcard because it's narrowed down to their development. Where I live, I'm really lucky to have one development with 800 homes and just down the street have another development with 400 homes. I develop postcards for those specific developments and they work fantastic.

"Attention Homeowners with a wooden deck:" This is a general attention getter to homeowners but your narrowed it down with a specific niche -- deck restoration. If you just want to restore decks this is a great method.

"Attention Lion Estate Residents with a Wooden Deck:" (narrow with a niche): That's even more specific because you are targeting one particular area and you're looking for a specialized niche to do in that area.

Making your marketing material as specific as you can helps get your target market's attention. Think of it like you are writing a personal ad for a specific type of client you want to work with. Once you have their attention, structure a message that resonates with them because you know who they are. Your response will increase and the cost of each client will decrease. And that's awesome!

Dan Galvin is the owner of East Coast Power Washing and the founder of SuccessInPowerWashing.com. He also teaches the PWNA's House Washing Certification Course and the House Washing School.

Pressure Washing Resource Association Explodes across North America ...and Beyond!

by Thad Eckhoff, Co-Founder of the PWRA and Owner of Apex Services

As the PWRA nears its one-year anniversary, membership is growing rapidly (over 120 members as of March 25, including two non-continental international members joining in March). Contractors are lining up to jumpstart their spring marketing and take their business to the next level.

Three new sponsors have also joined the team: Bob Williamson of Pressure Tek, Jake Clark of Armstrong Clark, and Peirce Flitchett of Ready Seal. There are more sponsor opportunities open so watch for new announcements.

The Pressure Washing Resource Association (PWRA) – founded by Thad Eckhoff, owner of Apex Services, and Chris Lambrinides, owner of Window Cleaning Resource.com – is a for-profit group that aims to provide practical and profitable business and marketing benefits that will help individual contractors increase their bottom lines.

The PWRA is not an organization. It's not about politics. It's not about charity. It's not about larger industry-related issues. It's about helping honest, hardworking individual contractors make money so they can support their families...and the benefits begin as soon as they sign up.

So what are these benefits?

Tested and proven marketing materials. These include postcards, door hangers, proposal packets, email templates, mailings, business forms, and more.

The Pressure Washing Resource forum. In its first year, the Pressure Washing Resource forum (www.pressurewashingresource.com) has grown to around 7,500 users and has built a solid reputation as a business-oriented, drama-free zone where contractors can feel free to talk about their businesses and whatever else is on their minds. The main forum is free to join. You don't even have to create a log-in, as the forum boasts a one-of-a-kind custom-coded feature which allows users to participate directly with their Facebook account and have their comments appear directly in the thread instead of in small print at the bottom of the page. The innovation keeps moving light years ahead of the rest of the pack! You can also interact with other PWRA members on our Facebook group and page, if you prefer.

One new feature that is proving to be quite popular and a lot of fun is the "Like-orometer" Forum software automatically tallies who had the most "liked" posts in the past day, week, and in forum history. Right now Tim Fields of Complete Power Wash in Hagerstown, Maryland is firmly seated as the "Most Liked Overall" poster but Len Sutton of Sea to Summit in Clemson, SC has captured the "Most Liked" for the day and the week as of this writing. Who will be on top tomorrow? Check it out and see for yourself.

The private, member-only forum provides a tight-knit community where contractors can discuss their business issues, strategies, and aggravations in an intimate environment. It's the place to freely discuss such topics as money, growth strategies, employee issues, difficult clients, and those super secret marketing campaigns that are not for public view. This is also where the RFP job leads are posted. Members have access to local, state, federal, and military requests for proposals in the United States and Canada.

The huge printing discount from Gotprint.com, which has more than paid for many contractors' memberships whether they used one of the many free PWRA templates or their own designs. Members have saved tens of thousands of dollars on printing since it became available.

The second highest savings has probably come from Ambidextrous Services' 30% discount on web design and search engine optimization work.

The newest benefit is from CLC Lodging, which provides hotel discounts- save money on those overnight work trips!

So if you're ready to move forward into the 21st century with your pressure washing business check out the Pressure Washing Resource Association. Remember, PWRA is not involved in politics and industry infighting. It doesn't presume to speak for "the industry" as a whole. The sole purpose is to put more money in its members' pockets today.

Click here to learn more or to join.

Laurie Benjamin, owner of All Aspects Maintenance Ltd., Trinidad and Tobago, is one of the PWRA's newest members. Visit www.trinicompass.com/allaspects to learn more about his business.

Let Go to GROW!

By George Hedley

Business owners need to get a huge return on their time. Every year, your company sells, creates, performs, builds, produces, or manufactures products or services. So, you don't have extra time to waste sweating all the small stuff. But you need great people who do!

When entrepreneurs start their companies, they take care of everything themselves including hiring, supervising, purchasing, marketing, selling, pricing, managing, paying bills, and doing the work. You name it, if it has to be done, they do it! Often until the wee hours of the night.

Can't find any good help?

To allow their companies to grow, many small business owners hire the best people they can find: their family and friends! Not the best idea, as it's hard to build professional companies with inexperienced people who don't respect their bosses. As they continue to gain more customers, more people are added to the staff. With more employees, they soon learn how hard it is to find anyone who'll do work exactly the way they want it done. Nobody seems to care, be accountable or accept responsibility - except the boss.

When this happens, pressure mounts and many companies have trouble keeping good people. Hire people, put them to work and then watch them leave within the year. Not a good thing for the bottom-line! Your job description changes from business owner to personnel complaint department. The business owner continues to search for answers to the people problem and look everywhere for the magic fix. Then fully frustrated, he tries a new approach: let go of daily decisions and try to delegate. But this is too uncomfortable so he takes back control again.

Look in the mirror!

So, what's holding your company back? Is it you? Perhaps you are the real problem as you continue to control everything and everybody. This poor leadership style holds people back from accepting responsibility and becoming accountable. When you make every decision, people can't and don't take on more responsibility. When you fix or solve problems for employees, they can't be accountable. When you lead every meeting, managers don't grow. When you approve every purchase, contract or strategic move, good people don't have to think or be their best.

The more you control, the less employees perform. When you solve other people's problems, they bring you more problems. But it makes you feel powerful when you control everything for everyone and wear a sign that says: "Bring me your problems."

When a customer calls with an issue, do you immediately handle it yourself and get right back to them? A better solution would be to listen and then turn your customer's concern over to a supervisor or manager.

When it's time to make a major purchase or award a large contract, do you get right in the middle of the negotiations? Instead, ask your manager to review the proposals, analyze the inclusions and exclusions, negotiate terms with the lowest responsible company, and then get your final approval.

When a supervisor asks you to call a supplier who isn't performing, do you jump in and take charge? Train your supervisors to plan ahead, use written procedures, checklists, schedules, team meetings, and manage their workflow. A simple delegation strategy is to increase the maximum spending limit for all employees. Delegate by allowing them to spend at least $1,000 or more before they have to get the boss's approval. The key is to stop making decisions for them!

eClean Magazine

Lead to grow!

Performance and getting results are the top indicators of effective leadership. No performance or results equals poor leadership. When you control the work, hold your people back, and constantly tell them what to do, you hurt your company's growth and profit potential. An effective leader's role is to inspire others to perform at higher levels and maximize results. Your job is to lead, not do. When you worry about every little detail and do the work yourself, you waste a valuable resource – YOU.

George Hedley works with contractors to build profitable growing companies. He is a professional business coach, popular speaker and best-selling author of "Get Your Business To Work!" available online at www.HardhatPresentations.com. To sign-up for his free e-newsletter, join his next webinar, be part of a BIZCOACH program, or get a $100 discount coupon for online classes at www.HardhatBizSchool.com, e-mail GH@HardhatPresentations.com

To Be or Not:
Should a Janitorial Contract Include Disposables?

by Rick Meehan, Vice President of Marko Janitorial Supply, www.MarkoInc.com

Cleaning contractors are always trying to find ways to make more money, which is of course, understandable. One of those ways involves refilling restroom disposables like paper toweling, toilet tissue, deodorizers, and hand soap.

These kinds of add-on services throw wrenches into contracts and quotes though. When it comes to pricing a janitorial contract, the more moving parts, the harder it is to ensure a profit will be made if the contract is won.

I get complaints regularly from cleaning folks that they can't seem to make any money because the customer uses a lot more paper towels and toilet tissue than expected. Likewise, I get complaints all the time from former contract cleaning customers that have decided to do it themselves because they are tired of the restroom disposables running low, trash not getting removed, or grating odors waft from the restroom. I am therefore a proponent of knowing the facts in advance to ensure a suitable profit will be made on exemplary services received. A job well done is the only way a contractor will increase profits. This is an axiom of the janitorial world.

Part of doing a good job should include producing a well-designed contractual agreement which includes compensation for add-on services. Otherwise, add-ons can sabotage a cleaning contract. What are add-ons? Any service over and above the actual labor of doing the job is an add-on, something that brings more profitability to the contract. The trick to making extra money with add-ons is to understand the processes involved with each type. The main types include specialty cleaning such as window washing or carpet spotting, and the performance of stocking restroom disposables. Add-ons must become well-oiled parts are the janitorial machinery and not broken wringers in order to turn more profits.

There are several approaches to handling add-ons in cleaning contracts, each with their own challenges and rewards. Generally, it is best for the customer to provide all towels, tissue, hand soap, plastic trash bags, and a variety of cleaning detergents. This puts the responsibility squarely with them if something goes amiss. Yet, with a bit of study and consideration, a good contract can be written that compensates the contractor for extra services performed. The customer will be happier knowing all bases are covered and no hidden costs will be forthcoming. Everything spelled out; everything above board. That's the way a janitorial contract should be written. The following scenarios each have issues that must be addressed if profits and happy clients are to be made.

SCENARIO #1: THE CUSTOMER PROVIDES ALL

Here the customer handles the purchase and stocking of all items needed for the janitorial contractor to clean the facility, including refillables. This method limits the profits to labor only, the simplest form of contract. In many cases, these items are delivered by a janitorial supply house on an "as needed" basis, or picked up by the customer from a large box store. From a cost standpoint, the customer can price around and do all the work finding items that are right for them, getting those items to the location, and keeping those items in stock for the janitorial staff. It takes no more thought on the contractor's side than figuring the number of labor hours and the cost of travel required to handle the job.

There are several down sides involved with this scenario:

There are many qualities of cleaning items available. Just because the customer buys these items does not mean that they are the correct ones for handling the job most efficiently. After all, the customer is not the cleaning expert.

The proper stocking of the janitor's closet is a low priority for most businesses, so quality and quantity suffer simply because cleaning experts are not handling the purchases. Ever try using a cleaning chemical that does not work for the job at hand?

Profitable add-ons are limited. A contractor can only charge for extra labor when performing more intense jobs like window cleaning, fine furniture polishing, or carpet spot removal. Expertise is neither required nor compensated under this contract. For contractors wishing to limit the chances of losing money, this scenario is best – or is it?

To improve profitability, tweak the contract by providing the customer with a list of exact chemicals, equipment, and refillables by brand required to do the job. Spell out the details, even down to the correct packaging of the favorite cleaner. Provide an inventory checklist, train your janitorial staff to check the stock levels regularly, keep the customer informed when items are getting low. Nothing costs more than wasted time. A cleaning person cannot perform the job without the proper equipment and materials. As part of the selling approach, the contractor must convince the customer that by using the proper products for the job, the contractor can perform with efficiency, thus reducing the customer's costs. NEVER, simply hand in a quotation for gettin' the job done! As my daddy used to say, "You're cruisin' for a bruisin'."

SCENARIO #2: THE CUSTOMER OR CONTRACTOR OR BOTH PROVIDE PART

For any of these combinations to work, the customer and the contractor must hold up their respective ends of the bargain. It is important that each party keeps a tight stock check; however, the customer handles only a portion of the items needed to clean the facility, perhaps just the refillables. These methods can get confusing because the contractor will take the blame if items are not in stock even though the customer may have overlooked items they agreed to purchase. It is in the best interests of the contractor to simply check the stock of all janitorial items and inform the customer when items on the customer's list are in arrears.

Keeping a tight tab on products needed to perform

the job is of paramount importance, even if the contract states otherwise. After all, the customer does not have to clean the facility. A contractor will save money by insuring the things they need are always on hand, no matter whom else may be responsible. Don't leave it up to the customer to make sure products are on hand when needed, even though the contract doles out responsibility to them on certain items. That's how contractors get caught – out of supplies, out of jobs, and out of profits. Make sure to include a clause that allows breaking the contract by mutual agreement, something along the lines of "with a two week written notice, either the customer or the contractor may terminate this agreement." That way, at least the contractor can flee from uncooperative customers without a major loss of face.

SCENARIO #3: THE CONTRACTOR SUPPLIES ALL

In this scenario, the contractor handles the purchase and stocking of all items needed to clean the facility, including refillables. The onus is completely on the contractor to ensure proper stocking of all items pertaining to the contract. Unfortunately, this also can cost the contractor the job if miscalculations occur in the amount of disposables. Nothing eats away the profits faster than a math error.

Here's the way it happens: the customer estimates X number of cases of towels used each month. With an increase in business, they hire new employees, which in turn raise paper usage. The contractor has to purchase more towels unexpectedly. Then, along comes a price increase. The towels cost more to boot. Practically overnight, the contractor's bottom line is eaten away.

The contractor then asks for more money; the customer refuses, citing the contract. The contractor begins to cut corners, both in the quality of disposables and chemicals, and in the number of hours on the job. Cleaning quality suffers. The contract is lost. Ill will radiates from both sides. Unfortunately, it is the contractor's reputation that suffers – not the customer's. Remember, word-of-mouth advertising is the biggest way cleaning folks get new business. Good referrals mean greater chances of landing new clients.

Although this scenario is the most complicated to pull off properly, it is also the most profitable. The tightest inventory, the best-trained cleaning staff, the most efficient methods, and the properly written agreement covering all the bases – all this requires thought and knowledge on the contractor's part. The advantages are these: the contractor knows the products will work for the job; the contractor knows the disposables will work for the job; the contractor knows the job cleanliness will be exemplary. Add-on profits range from filling dispensers to specialty cleaning, instead of just extra labor charges.

A good way to reduce the complexity of purchasing, stocking, and training involved with janitorial products is to find and utilize a reputable janitorial supply house. Even if their pricing on paper, plastics, or chemicals are not the lowest across the globe, these professionals offer the most cost-reducing factor in any cleaning contract – consistency. A janitorial contractor can feel more comfortable knowing that supplies are stocked, improved products and methods are considered, and proper staff training is provided, usually at no extra charge. A good janitorial supply company can be the greatest profit-increasing resource a contractor can have. Find one.

It boils down to this. To avoid agreement issues and improve profits, a contractor must build automatic increases into the contract, or be content to work harder for less money over time. I contend that all janitorial contracts should be designed as win-win scenarios; therefore, regardless of the type of scenario chosen for a particular customer, the only way to achieve harmony (and greater profits) is to apply THOUGHT to the process. For some contractors this may require a change in business philosophy. Consider: janitorial contracting is not about labor, and it's not about profits either. It's about a mutually beneficial process whereby the customer gets a sparkling facility and a contractor gets a living. The entire process of walking in and out of the customer's door should be designed – not left to chance. Shakespeare's Hamlet put it best. "To be or not to be, that is the question." The answer: with knowhow on your side you can be what you wish. If you want to make more money by supplying disposables to your customers, make sure you have the background knowledge coupled with a mutually beneficial

Pressure Washing & Spring Cleaning:
How to Avoid Damaging Your Home or Business

by Paul Horsley, Publisher

When it comes to spring cleaning your home or business, pressure washing is the easiest way to clean large areas efficiently. However, if you are inexperienced with home or commercial property cleaning, it would be best to consider using expert pressure washing services from a professional power washing company.

Pressure washing services offer many benefits, the primary one being the safety and expertise a professional company can offer. Safety in this sense means not only protecting yourself from physical harm but protecting your home or building from the accidental damage a pressure washer can cause. The following is a look at some of the ways inexpert pressure washing can damage your property.

HOME & BUILDING EXTERIORS

Pressure washing your home or building can cause physical damage if done improperly. For instance, cleaning mold and algae off a roof can blast off shingles and diminish roof quality if the pressure washer is turned up too high. Pressure washing with too much PSI can also damage your deck or patio finish and chip paint off your home siding. To avoid damaging your home or office, consider hiring a residential or commercial property cleaning service as a viable alternative that will save you time and energy – and potentially even money, considering the hazards. Rather than risk damaging your home and devaluing your property, have a professional with years of pressure washing experience do the job for you.

YARD & OUTSIDE AREAS

For the outside of your home or office, pressure washing also needs to be practiced safely to avoid structural damage. Your driveway or parking lot should not be power washed quickly or with too much force; rather, this job requires a careful, thorough cleaning on a low-medium setting. Misuse of a pressure washer on a high setting can degrade and wear down concrete, especially older concrete, and create flying debris and dust particles.

Likewise, if you are pressure washing your fence or deck, use low pressure and be careful not to spray carelessly; otherwise, you can damage the wood as well as nearby vegetation. Wood decks and fences can be easily scarred by careless power washing.

EQUIPMENT USE

One often overlooked area when considering whether use professional pressure washing services is the potential risks of using pressure washing equipment without proper training or experience. Depending on the type of pressure washer you are using – electric or gas powered – you run different risks. Oil fires, fluid leaks and blowing a circuit are just a few examples of possible equipment failures. And whatever you do, do not use a gas-powered pressure washer indoors, ever, as exhaust poisoning can occur. Always wear some kind of face mask, gloves and other protective gear if available. Do not aim the pressure washer at your feet or hands – on a high setting it can easily rip your skin off and cause severe bodily damage.

To avoid these safety concerns, consider using a professional power washing company instead. This is especially recommended if you need to wash your business building. A commercial property cleaning service will make sure neither your building nor your employees are hurt during the spring cleaning process.

There are many pressure washing services to choose from, but only a handful lead the pack. Do some research, and go with a professional power washing company that has high safety standards and a track record for professional expertise. For your business, make sure you go with pressure washing services that have commercial property cleaning experience. Pressure washing isn't as easy as one might think. Wielding a high-pressure water gun can be dangerous and damaging to your property and health, so make sure you know what you are doing, or call on the professionals for help.

eCLEAN magazine™
The professional contractor cleaner's online resource!

Highrise Cleaning

Plus...
- Ladder Safety
- Collecting Info on Competitors
- Inside Soap Warehouse

POWERWASH.COM™
SUPPLIES CHEMICALS TRAINING

1.800.433.2113
2513 Warfield St. Fort Worth, TX 76106

Shop Online 24 Hours a Day

We provide products you NEED with the helpful service you Deserve!

Quick Links - Pressure Washers - Surface Cleaners - Chemicals & Detergents - Cleaning Supplies - Parts & Accessories - Pumps & Repair Kits - Training Materials

DSR-49 Deck Restorer
DSR-49 Disodium Per-oxydicarbonate removes mildew stains and dirt while restoring a natural and bright look to vertical and horizontal grayed and weathered wood surfaces. Ideal for wood preparation prior to water sealer application.

D-Vandal Graffiti Remover
A fast-acting penetrating semi-gel that removes paints, inks (including ball point pen), permanent markers, crayons, caulking, urethane sealants and more off most surfaces. This product eliminates tedious scrubbing to remove stubborn stains on surfaces by simply wiping with a soft cloth or using an all-purpose sprayer.

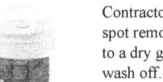

DELTA-60™ Heavy Grease Remover (*)
Contractors first choice for grease spot removal. Just apply Delta 60 to a dry grease spot and pressure wash off. Watch years of deep stains disappear! It restores drive-thru and entrance pads to look like new! The oils come out as solids leaving the concrete as clean as possible.

R-202 Concrete Cleaner
Cleans heavy grease, oil and scuff marks from unpainted concrete and other alkaline water safe hard surfaces. USDA authorized for use in meat plants.

AC-12 Fabric Awning Cleaner
Quickly removes normal dirt and grime from woven fabric materials. 1 gal. bottle = 5 gal. of solution.

AC-22 Vinyl Awning Cleaner
Quickly removes dirt from vinyl fabric materials. 1 gal. bottle = 10 gal. of cleaner.

RP-3500 Window Cleaner Concentrate
This non-streaking cleaner leaves glass with reflective finishes and a film-free sparkling appearance. 1 gallon of concentrate makes 10 gallons of cleaner.

Mosmatic 12" Graffiti Remover with Recovery Port + 1 Quart of D-VANDAL Graffiti Remover
This professional wall cleaner is specially designed for quickly removing graffiti and stubborn dirt. The recovery port allows the user to attach a vacuum system to suction the dirty water. The brush ring prevents splashing and injuries from loose pebbles. It is soft and elastic but extremely effective thanks to the thickness of the bristles.
Specifications:
- Surface Cleaning Diameter: 12"
- Pressure: 5000 PSI
- Max Temperature: 250 F
- Weight: 7.1 lbs.
- Swivel: 1xDYW
- Rotor Arm: 2x 1/8" NPTF
- Rotor Nozzles: Two (2) 1503 (15-Degree Size 3)

Whisper Pro Big Guy Platinum Series Surface Cleaner
The Whisper Wash Big Guy Surface Cleaner incorporates a signature balanced and machined spray bar with a 28" wide surface coverage area. The Big Guy's pivoting wheel design and a heavy-duty nylon brush provide for easy navigation through large areas while still containing the pressurized spray. The Platinum Series of Whisper Pro Surface Cleaners offers:
- A One-Piece Unitized Swivel Cartridge
- A One-Year Full Coverage Warranty
- 5000 PSI Max Working Pressure
- 212° F Max Working Temperature
- BONUS! This PowerWash.com EXCLUSIVE Bundle Pack also includes a FREE 5 lb. Sample Pack of R-202 Cleaner. This powerful sudsing alkaline powdered detergent is designed to clean heavy grease, oil and scuff marks from unpainted concrete and other alkaline water safe hard surfaces.

Big Guy Surface Cleaner Specifications:
- 2" Nylon Brush
- One 4" Caster
- Two (2) 10" Pneumatic Tires
- Oversized, self-lubricating twin thrust bearings
- 2000-5000 PSI Pressure Range
- Max Temperature: 212° F
- Max Flow: 4-10 GPM
- Housing Size: 28"
- Two (2) 25-Degree Size 2 Spray Tips

Personal Protective Equipment
- Wrap-Around Safety Goggles
- 12" Gauntlet PVC Safety Gloves
- Cordova Steel Toe PVC Safety Boots
- Full Brim Non-Slotted Hard Hat
- Heavyweight Apron
- Visor Assembly for Hard Hat
- Glacier Glove Stillwater Neoprene Bootie

10% OFF Orders of $100 or more!
Use Coupon Code eClean10
Cannot be combined with any other offers. Exp: 06.01.13

www.eCleanMag.com

IN THIS ISSUE:

135

135 High-Rise Cleaning: 4 Things to Consider before Taking the Plunge

138 Ladder Safety and You, by Tony Evans, A New View Window Cleaning

140 Collecting Information on Your Competitors: Discover the Do's and Don'ts of Competitive Intelligence

144 Mark Your Calendars: 2013 PWNA Convention & Trade Show, October 17-19

146 PWNA Vendor Profile: Soap Warehouse

148 Benefit from Emotional Control, by Bill Kinnard, Grandy & Associates

151 PowerWashStore.com Helps Family in Need

152 How to Prevent Accidents: Stay Alert, Stay Focused, Stay Safe, by Larry Miller, Larry Miller, Inc.

154 Stay on Your Feet (If You Can), by Rick Meehan, Marko Janitorial Supply

156 Which Online Directories Should You Use for Your Small Business? by Henry Bockman, Contractor's Foundation

144

158 What Happened in Vegas: A Recap of the 2013 Garage Cleaning Event

161 How to Build Your Brand, by Jenna Horsley

163 4 Reasons to Pressure Wash Your Building, by Paul Horsley

164 Classifieds

Cover photo courtesy of Shaun Downham, Oahu Power Wash

---

eClean Magazine is published monthly

Publisher: Paul Horsley, paul@ecleanmag.com
Editor: Allison Hester, allison@ecleanmag.com
Sales: Jenna Horsley, jenna@ecleanmag.com

eClean Magazine
Box 262, 16 Midlake Blvd S.E.
Calgary, Alberta
Canada T2X2X7
www.eCleanMag.com

In March, an Australian window cleaning company finished the three-month project of cleaning the world's tallest building, Burj Khalifa. The Dubai skyscraper (featured in *Mission Impossible 3*) stands at a whopping 2,717 feet tall, is more than 160 stories, and hosts 24,830 windows for a total of 1,292,500 square feet of glass. Can you imagine yourself cleaning that? If so, then high-rise cleaning may be something that interests you.

However, there's another important fact to consider. If you watch the headlines – and you can find them on our "Cleaning in the News Page" – you'll quickly realize that hardly a week goes by without a cleaning related accident, often leading to death.

In what is becoming an increasingly cutthroat industry, too many professional high-rise cleaning companies are cutting corners when it comes to safety. That was the subject of a 2012 award-winning news story by Trish Van Pilsum of Fox 9 News in Minnesota, where four window-cleaning deaths had occurred since 2007 – the highest number in any state. In each case, OSHA determined the accidents could have been prevented through the use of proper safety training, equipment and procedures.

High-Rise Cleaning:
4 Things to Consider before Taking the Plunge
By Allison Hester, Editor

In the news report, Van Pilsum worked with Jeff Scott, owner of Green Window Cleaning, to experience safely going "Over the Wall." Scott, who has been doing rope access work for nearly 25 years and who is on the Board of Directors for the International Window Cleaning Association (IWCA), is known for his meticulous focus on safety. So for this article, I spoke with Scott to learn what a potential high-rise cleaner needs to consider before ever "Taking the Plunge."

Left: Jeff Scott of Green Window Cleaning and reporter Trish Van Pilsum of Fox 9 News. All photos courtesy of Green Window Cleaning. Click on the photo to link to the video.

Are You Right for High-Rise Cleaning?

1. Are you willing to learn? Safety training is imperative to high-rise cleaning, and there are several places to get it. The IWCA offers classroom, hands-on and online safety training. Scott, who has taught the hands-on safety training in the past, said that the IWCA program "is a very good starting point. You can learn about the overall general information needed, but by no means will it make you ready to go off a building." You can learn more about this training at www.IWCA.org.

Next, Scott recommends getting certified through SPRAT (Society of Professional Rope Access Technicians). "SPRAT is a great place to go for their level 1 (worker) training. It's very comprehensive – much more than what a window cleaner may need – but it's something everyone who works from a rope should have. It prepares you for the situations you're going to encounter."

SPRAT has three levels of certification. Scott is currently SPRAT Level II certified and aims to get his Level III sometime in the near future. Many training companies offer SPRAT certification courses almost weekly in different parts of the country. You can learn more about SPRAT training at www.SPRAT.org.

Finally, for suspended scaffolding, there's the SAIA (Scaffold and Access Industry Association), which offers a variety of programs in different areas of the country almost weekly. To learn more, visit www.SAIA.org.

And training doesn't stop there. For instance, Scott and his crew still undergo monthly training sessions where they go over every piece of equipment and through the company handbook. Bottom line: being safe means being trained.

2. Are you willing to wait? You should never dive into high-rise cleaning. That's what leads to accidents, injuries and even deaths.

"There's nothing glamorous about putting workers' lives at risk," stressed Scott. That's

About Jeff Scott

Jeff Scott is a second generation window cleaner, who recalls going with his dad at a very young age to clean pay phone booths in Central Wisconsin. Scott was introduced to chair work in his mid-teens.

He worked for his dad's company until a little over four years ago, when his father sold his business for a handsome sum. Because there was no non-compete clause with the acquisition, Scott started his own company – Green Window Cleaning – the day after the deal closed.

"I had actually planned to switch to residential work," he explained. But when another company needed help with high-rise cleaning, he took all the money he had planned to use for marketing his residential business and instead put it into high-rise equipment.

Today, Green Window Cleaning has four employees, three trucks, and focuses on high-rise windows in Minnesota, Wisconsin and Illinois. "We cherry pick jobs where our skills are still an advantage," he explained.

Scott is Secretary of the International Window Cleaning Association (IWCA) and has taught the association's hands-on self rescue courses in the past. A big advocate of SPRAT training, Scott actually took one of the organization's first rope access training courses. That accounted for the highest structure he's ever descended from – the Hoover Dam. As for buildings, the high-rises he cleans "generally" are 300 feet high or less. He is also IRATA (International Rope Access Trade Association) Level II certified.

Today, Scott also offers safety training to companies around the country. He travels to their location to teach classroom and hands-on skills including equipment, rigging, self rescue and partner rescue. He also looks at companies' kits, practices and procedures and helps them come up with the best options.

why "the novice should never, ever try to take on high-rise cleaning unless he's worked along someone who has done it for some time."

The first step, according to Scott, is to work for someone else. "Work for a company that has a good training program already set up. Talk to their employees. Talk to the owners on their willingness to train you. Talk about retraining."

If you are already an established window cleaning business owner thinking of adding high-rise cleaning, Scott suggests hiring an experienced, well-trained crew and let them teach you the ins and outs of the business.

3. Are you willing to do it? Over the years, Scott has run across several guys who underwent training, got on the rooftop, but just couldn't go over the side. "And that's OK. It's not for everyone. Some guys also just need more time," he said. "If they're around me for a time, I can often sense if they have an aptitude for it."

However, there are also the overconfident guys "who have no respect for the dangers," Scott added. Those are the guys Scott won't allow to go over the edge until they "adjust their mentality. They often just get tired of having to wait and eventually go off and do something else."

Beyond the need to be able to endure the heights, high-rise cleaning is hard work. You must also be able to physically handle it. "I enjoy it, but it does wear on you," Scott stressed.

In addition to the physical work, there is a ton of documentation and paperwork that must be kept up with in high-rise cleaning. Without it, you – and the property owner – could be in big trouble. So in addition to physically and mentally being able to do the cleaning, you have to be organized enough (or hire someone who is) to be successful as a business owner in the high-rise cleaning industry.

4. Are you willing to pay? High-rise cleaning is expensive. You have to pay for training – and retraining – a qualified staff. You have to pay for equipment. And you have to pay for insurance. "The most expensive thing in our business is the insurance and workers compensation," Scott said. "In Wisconsin, for every dollar of payroll, we pay over 38 cents to workers comp insurance alone." And in Wisconsin, there are no split workers compensation codes. Since Scott cleans high-rises, his insurance takes the same percentage whether he's cleaning a skyscraper or a house. So he has completely stopped doing small jobs and route work. "It's far too expensive for us."

Which brings up another point. "Honestly, if you do it right, you can make good money doing residential and mid-rise buildings," Scott said. "High-rise cleaning doesn't necessarily mean more money."

So why do it?

On the surface, high-rise window cleaning is a glamorous looking job. But a lot of people go into it too quickly, and just as promptly get right back out.

However, for those who enjoy a challenge, high-rise cleaning can certainly fill that need. That's one of the things that Scott likes best about this field. "Every jobsite requires different rigging," he explained. "I especially enjoy the relationships I've built with property managers. It's fun when they come up with problems and we can create solutions."

Additionally, Scott says that the days go very fast, although they require hard work. And, when done right, there is money to be made. Even with all its added safety-related expenses, Green Window Cleaning has learned how to be very competitive because of their efficiency in cleaning. "What it boils down to is we work hard. We work efficiently, safely and by the book."

ROOF SNOT

THE choice of professional roof cleaning contractors for controlling runoff & maximizing dwell time on ugly black roof stains.

Visit www.RoofSnot.com for more information. Available exclusively through Southside Equipment, Inc., www.PressureWasherKY.com

Ladder Safety and You

by Tony Evans, a New View Window Cleaning, www.windowcleaningschool.blogspot.com

One of the most profound statements I've ever heard when it comes to ladder safety is "there are two kinds of ladder users: those who have fallen off a ladder and those who will." While you may not like the either/or scenario of that statement, it is sadly all too true. If we use ladders long enough we can find ourselves on the wrong side of an accident. But as professional cleaners, ladders are an essential part of our equipment. What can we do to minimize the risk?

Location, Location, Location!

While most of us recognize this adage as something to do with real estate, it is a vital element of ladder safety. Where we place our ladder is the most important step we take in using it safely. We need to make sure that the ground we are setting our ladder on is solid.

The ladder should also be set at a 75 degree angle. How do we know if we have it right? There are simple ways to check. To establish the angle, simply set the ladder where you need it. Now, with your arms stretched out straight, your hands should land on the rung straight in front of you, then you have the proper angle. As for the stable ground, when the ladder is set, simply stand on the bottom rung and bounce a little. If the ladder doesn't sink unevenly or deeply, then you're ready to think about climbing.

What about uneven ground or getting on a roof?

Every Ladder Needs These

I have found two ladder accessories to be invaluable when it comes to ladder safety – a standoff and the PiViT tool.

We use a Werner quick click standoff (some guys call them bullhorns) every time we set up the extension ladder. It keeps the top of the ladder away from the wall, which gives you a better angle to clean. It also gives more stability to the top of the ladder, which is especially beneficial when going from the ladder to a roof.

We also use the PiViT tool, which looks like a big black wedge. It is designed as a leg leveler as well as a plank support for interior scaffolding. Whatever you use, a leg leveler is a must for ensuring the ladder is always straight. Never climb a ladder that is leaning to one side, even if it's only by a couple of inches.

Other Concerns

If you live in an area where you may use a ladder in winter, you may run into snow or ice where you set up. If there is no other option, then make sure to clear the surface of any snow or ice before setting up your ladder. Of course, there are other options for certain types of window cleaning, like extension poles or using different techniques to clean the exterior from the inside. Another great way to reduce the risk of using ladders is to not use them. We use water fed poles as often as possible to keep ladder use to a minimum in window cleaning. Or if you are soft washing a house, can you use a longer wand or telescopic pole to get the solution to a setback dormer?

Training is Essential

One thing we also should discuss it the need for training. While climbing a ladder may not be rocket science, it is dangerous, and as with any dangerous activity, training can reduce those dangers. Most fire departments have training classes, so check with your local one to see if you can take a class.

There are networking events for cleaners around the country and some have safety courses and/or demos that you can attend. OSHA (Occupational Safety and Health Administration) has online classes (OSHA 10 and OSHA 30) that will help you with the classroom aspects of ladder safety if you take the ones for the construction industry.

To Use a Ladder or Not

Whatever you decide, no job is worth taking an unnecessary risk with a ladder. Analyze your options beforehand, apply any and all safety devices for the ladder, be willing to walk away from an unsafe scenario, and remember the only safe ladder is the one you never use!

Tony Evans and his wife own and operate A New View Window Cleaning, which offers window cleaning, house washing, roof cleaning and scratched glass restoration. Evans also enjoys helping new window cleaners learn the value of tools and techniques. To learn more, visit windowcleaningschool.blogspot.com.

Collecting Information on Your Competitors

Discover the Do's and Dont's of Competitive Intelligence.

by Marketing Scoop, Inc., www.marketingscoop.com/collecting-information.htm

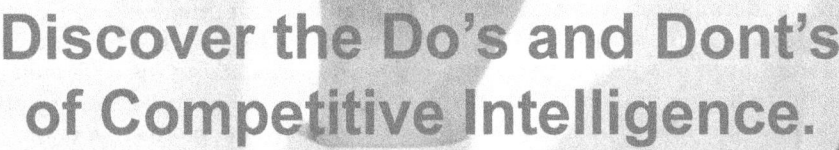

Collecting information about your competitors makes good business sense. However, you must do so in an ethical and reasonable way. Competitive intelligence from public sources, customers, and third parties can help businesses anticipate market opportunities, trends and competitive strengths and weaknesses.

These guidelines provide a step-by-step guide for acquiring the information you need without crossing the line.

1. Ask questions - If you come across or are offered competitive information and believe that it may be confidential or proprietary ask questions to find out how the information was obtained or why it was made available.

2. Be ethical - How would you or your business react if you found out that your competitors were receiving the kind of information that you acquired? If you think that a particular way of gathering competitive intelligence may be unethical, you should assume that your competitors would view it the same way.

3. If it doesn't seem right, don't do it - If you're ever in doubt as to whether a source of information or contemplated technique of gathering information is proper or legal, you should contact your manager or attorney.

4. Breaking the law has consequences - If you improperly gather or use competitive information, you can be disciplined or terminated, and you could face criminal and civil penalties. Breaking the law can also result in adverse publicity to your company. Think about how you'd feel if your actions were publicly disclosed on the front page of a newspaper.

5. Legitimate sources of competitive information include:
Public sources. You may gather information about your competitors from public sources

such as:
- Newspapers, magazines, other published articles and television programs
- Advertisements and brochures intended for public distribution
- Information freely available on the Internet and online research services
- Public filings made with governmental or regulatory authorities, such as SEC reports, patent filings and litigation records
- Analyst reports
- Industry surveys or reports
- Public presentations given by competitors at trade shows and conferences
- Freedom of Information Act (FOIA) and similar requests from governmental or regulatory agencies

Conversations with customers. Talking with customers is essential. The more you know about your customers and their businesses, the better you can meet their needs. However, you shouldn't contact customers for the purpose of obtaining confidential information about a competitor. Customers may disclose information about a competitor's products or pricing, so long as the information is not confidential.

Hiring third parties to obtain information. Sometimes companies hire third parties to help us gather competitive intelligence and information about the market for products and services. Third parties are subject to the same standards of behavior that you abide by, so you should assume that if we can't do it directly, you can't hire someone else to do it.

Third parties conducting focus groups or interviews with a competitor's suppliers or customers generally don't have to identify you as their client, so long as they identify themselves and their company. While a third party doesn't have to disclose the purpose of the focus group or interview, the third party shouldn't intentionally misrepresent the purpose.

A few of your competitors may have informed you that you cannot subscribe for their products and services. In these cases, you should not hire third parties to access the competitor's products or services. However, absent knowledge that a competitor would have barred or prohibited your access, you may engage a third party to subscribe to the product or service.

Keep in mind that your company can sometimes be legally responsible for damages or losses caused by a third party if you authorized or appear to have authorized any illegal actions. This can be the case even if you don't issue direct instructions to the third party, but know of the third party's likely conduct and "turn a blind eye."

If you engage a third party to gather competitive information, you should have the third party confirm that it is aware of, and agrees to abide by, applicable laws related to competitive intelligence.

Some types of information gathering, however, can violate the law or may be considered unethical. Some examples include:

New Hires. There are things you can and can't ask former employees of competitors.

You shouldn't ask or encourage employees who previously worked for a competitor to divulge confidential or proprietary information

about the competitor, such as specific details about a competitor's operations and intentions, including pricing, future plans and forecasts which may have been considered confidential or proprietary by a competitor.

If you previously worked for a competitor, you shouldn't disclose information about your former employer that you believe is confidential or proprietary, or bring any of this information into your office.

However, you may discuss items of a general nature with an employee who previously worked for a competitor including anything that's a matter of public record or that wasn't treated by the employer as confidential.

Misrepresenting your identity. You shouldn't misrepresent your identity in order to obtain competitive information, if the person you're seeking information from would not ordinarily give you the information if they knew your true identity. This can be considered fraud. For example:

- You shouldn't contact a competitor, posing as a customer, student, private research firm or potential vendor/supplier, to find out information.
- When providing information in order to gain access to a competitor's website, you should answer all required blanks accurately, but you don't have to fill in blanks that are not required.

Stealing information. You shouldn't attempt to acquire a competitor's confidential or proprietary information through illegal means, such as theft, spying or hacking.

You shouldn't perform any surveillance or monitoring of competitors outside of public places or engage in any form of electronic eavesdropping. However, if you're sitting on an airplane or are at an industry conference and happen to overhear a competitor discussing a confidential matter in the row ahead of you, the competitor likely has no reasonable expectation of privacy.

Giving gifts for confidential or proprietary information. In gathering competitive intelligence, you should not give entertainment, gifts, favors or gratuities to induce someone to provide you with information that's confidential or proprietary. You may, however, pay third parties for competitive intelligence that's derived from legitimate sources.

Anonymous packages containing confidential information. If you receive anonymous submissions of competitive information you shouldn't distribute or use the information.

Information marked "Confidential." etc. You shouldn't use or purchase information belonging to a competitor that is marked "confidential" or "proprietary."

Offers to access competitors' products and services. If you're offered access to a competitor's product or service by a customer, friend or other person, and you ordinarily would not be able to access the product or service on your own, you should decline the offer.

Misplaced or unattended confidential information. You shouldn't use confidential information belonging to a competitor that is accidentally misplaced or left unattended.

Dumpster diving. This is inappropriate and it may also be illegal.

Competitive bid information. You shouldn't seek or use information that you may receive about a competitor's bid if you're involved in bidding, especially on government contracts. However, you are free to use information that is disclosed by the government, publicly available or retrievable pursuant to a FOIA or other similar request.

Information offered in business pitches. If a customer offers competitive information to us during a business pitch, we should understand that the customer may owe a confidentiality obligation to our competitors who are also pitching for the business. As such, we should generally decline to receive information under these circumstances. However, if we are being told something very general or high-level, it may be appropriate for us to use this information in our bid and in our larger business strategy.

Regardless of what method you use to collect competitive intelligence, if you have any question as to the legality of your activity, err on the side of caution and chose another method!

2013 New Products Recap
Stop by your local distributor to give one a try

Updates to AZV / RZV recovery & filtration system
- Rustproof, stainless vacuum box with drain
- Lift-out basket stainer replaces bag filter
- New stringwound replaceable filters
- Same small footprint, 5-10gpm process rate

For current Specials, go to www.hydrotek.us click 'what's new'

Redesigned surface cleaners
- Octagon and square decks, giving you an angle over your competition
- Splash reducing brush on rear of deck
- Contractor Twister is now 4-in-1 tool: edger, gum spotter, water broom, surface cleaner
- Hydro Vacuum surface cleaner picks up even better with its new vacuum ring

Two Honda models added to the SS Series product line
Available as a 3500psi @ 5.5gpm or 4000psi @ 4.8gpm
Belt drive pump and PowerLight 12v burner module

All the Best Things You've Come to Expect From Us
- Wash Skids & Trailers
- Electric, Hot Washers
- Wash Accessories

Brilliant Design, Tough on Grime

Manufacturing pressure washers and wash accessories for over 25 years.
Visit website or call for a distributor near you. Distributor inquiries welcome.

www.hydrotek.us   (800) 274-9376

MARK YOUR CALENDARS
2013 PWNA Convention & Trade Show
October 17 - 19

October 17 through 19, the Power Washers of North America will host its annual convention and trade show, which will again be at the Embassy Suites in Orlando, Florida. While the venue will be the same as last year, the event itself will be featuring many added highlights this year.

Education and Certification

"We're planning to have several new classes this year, yet still offer certification courses," explained PWNA Director Jackie Gavett. Certification classes that have been confirmed as of now are the Wood Restoration, Fleet Washing, Roof Cleaning, House Washing, and Environmental Certification Classes. "We will also offer a Kitchen Exhaust Cleaning class with Daryl Mirza. However, this is not a certification class."

Back on the schedule this year is "Taking Your Business into the Millions." This invaluable panel discussion/question and answer session will be led by several PWNA members who have million-plus dollar businesses.

Another educational opportunity is the "snack and chat" round tables, which "are great for open discussion on specific topics," said Gavett. Each round table has a designated facilitator to help keep the conversation on topic. Previous convention topics have included:
- Equipment– Materials, Cleaners & Chemicals
- Flatwork, Concrete Cleaning, Commercial Svc.
- Fleet Washing
- Growing Your Business
- House Washing
- Kitchen Exhaust Cleaning
- Marketing
- Residential Services
- System & Processes
- Wood Restoration

Trade Show and Demos

The trade show floor will be open on Friday and Saturday, and the PWNA is aiming to bring in more vendors than ever. Saturday will also include outdoor equipment demos, which are always a conference favorite. PWNA has many sponsorship and exhibitor opportunities available. Interested vendors should contact the PWNA headquarters.

"We also expect to have more vendors actually lead classes this year," added Gavett. One example will be Seal n Lock's Authorized Technician/PWNA Flatwork Certification Course. "We're very much looking forward to Orlando. We've found the pressure washing industry to be a great group of guys, and they are a perfect fit for the sealing industry," explained Rich Colletti of Seal 'n Lock. "PWNA is a great outlet for us to introduce these guys to paver sealing. We've helped several pressure washing companies take their businesses into new directions with customers they were already serving."

eClean Magazine

Trade Show & Demos

Networking

Education

Networking

Another new program that the PWNA will be unveiling soon and implementing at the conference is the New Member Mentoring Program. Watch for details on this in a future issue of eClean.

There will be a cocktail reception every night, opening up more opportunities for networking. The Embassy Suites host a wonderful full breakfast buffet, as well as free snacks and drinks in the evenings. "The facilities are beautiful, affordable, and are in an area where weather should allow us to do outdoor demos," said Gavett.

So mark you calendars now because at the PWNA convention, you get it all. Certifications taught by qualified instructors. Educational courses to help you grow your business. Time to meet face-to-face with vendors and see the latest equipment and products in action. Plus, networking opportunities with some of the top power washing business owners in North America.

To learn more about the PWNA, its certification courses or the annual convention and trade show, visit their website at www.PWNA.org.

PWNA Vendor Profile

For over 20 years, Soap Warehouse has been providing members of the pressure washing industry with a wide variety of top quality cleaners. Soap Warehouse is also actively involved with a number of industry associations and sponsors a variety of events. The company first joined PWNA in 2006, and has been an active vendor member exhibiting since 2010.

Soap Warehouse was started in 1993 by Bob Belk in Norcross, Georgia. Belk passed away in 2005, and the company was purchased then relocated to its current location East of Atlanta, Georgia. However, the product formulations never changed.

Soap Warehouse's first products were primarily industrial transportation cleaners such as Brown Derby, Aluma Brite, Blue Lightning, White Lightning, Truck N Tuff, Triple Duty Aluminum Brightener, and others.

Over the years, however, the Soap Warehouse product line grew to include

Linda Chambers, who was born and raised in Florida, originally wanted to work with horses on a Brood mare farm. With that goal in mind, she attended a college in Southern Georgia and graduated with an AS degree in a Agri-Business, Agri-Science and Animal Health Technology. But after a Winter internship at Florida Downs racetrack, she realized that the life of raising horses was not the right direction, instead moving her focus to smaller animals. After graduation and getting married, "I was stuck in south Georgia with no chance of a job in my field, so I started my first business – Albany Mail Service – where I had a fast education in business, packing and shipping, which still helps today."

After moving to Atlanta, Linda landed a job as vet tech and sold her mail business. She worked up from being a tech to eventually managing the veterinary clinics where she worked. After 17 years as a tech and manager, she moved into the corporate world going to work for Merial, makers of Heartguard, Frontline, animal vaccines and pharmaceuticals. After 18 months, she was let go due to "hiring of local, cheaper contract labor" and took some time off before trying her hand at retail.

She managed and worked in a local gift shop chain for almost three years before they closed, worked for two more year as admin and HR for our local DirecTV franchise before they were sold, "which finally got me the job here at Soap Warehouse in February of 2007, six years ago."

industrial degreasers, car washes, detailing and kitchen exhaust cleaners. In 2000, the company had created and certified its own aircraft cleaner, "Top Gun," adding "another facet to covering transportation cleaning of all kinds – road, rail and air," explained Linda Chambers, Brand and Sales Manager.

Those familiar with Soap Warehouse have undoubtedly come to know Linda Chambers as the face and voice behind the company. In 2007, Linda joined on with Soap Warehouse as Operations and Sales Manager. Since that time, she has diligently worked to increase the percentage of sales of pressure washing products by supporting industry organizations. "We are members of the PWNA and UAMCC," she explained. "We support by sponsoring or exhibiting at industry conventions, NCE events, regional roundtables and training seminars."

Linda added that she tries to attend as many events in person as I can and love to meet and interact with our current and potentially new customers. Some events are outside pressure washing, such as truck shows, aircraft conventions and training seminars.

Additionally, Linda has improved Soap Warehouse's website, "with industry informational links and a great blog," she said. Linda and Soap Warehouse also sponsor two other websites, one for Top Gun and "one that is a consumer only, non-hazardous product site called ShopSoapWarehouse.com. We also have a big social media presence with three pages on Facebook, for both Soap Warehouse and Brown Derby, as well as on many Facebook industry pages."

Soap Warehouse is also on Twitter, Pinterest and "on any industry forum I have found to be a part of," said Linda. "I have been writing and publishing articles for the industry since 2009, and have continued with articles here in *eClean* and others over the years. I enjoy educating and helping the individual pressure washing contractor."

Since Linda's arrival, Soap Warehouse has also continued in growing their product line. These include:
- Exterior maintenance products like Citrus X-terior House Wash
- Non-Acid Coil Cleaner for air conditioning and heating coils
- Nature's Green, an "all green cleaner"
- Dyn-O -Coil descaler for pressure washers
- An entire line of laundry products
- Scat stain remover
- Blast Off and Shadow Away graffiti removers
- Bonzi and Hood Cling for hood cleaning
- A line of powder products in new 10 pound ratchet lid pails; and, most recently,
- HangTen, a thickened roof cleaner.

Overall, transportation cleaners still make up 80 percent of Soap Warehouse's business, with Brown Derby accounting for 50 percent of those sales, and Top Gun accounting for 20 percent. "The remaining 20 percent of our business is in the exterior pressure washing, car wash and detailing, building maintenance and now laundry items," Linda added.

Since Soap Warehouse's office has a small staff with low overhead, Linda can offer customers a personalized one-on-one buying experience with usually lower costs than their competition for similar products. "I am always happy to talk with contractors that may need help with a cleaning problem and discuss what they can buy or what they may already have on hand that can get the job done. Education, marketing and new product development is a big part of what I like to do."

1-800-762-7911   www.soapwarehouse.biz

With this ad save on your next purchase. $10 or 10% off product costs when order placed by May 30th. Stock up on this seasons needs now. Best shipping prices when you order close to 300 lbs including hazmat items.

eClean Magazine

Benefit from Emotional Control

by Bill Kinnard, Grandy & Associates

Having emotional control means having the ability to maintain a rational and objective demeanor when faced with stressful or emotional situations; a measure of self-composure in a difficult situation and the ability to act objectively, rather than impulsively or emotionally.

Why is this skill important?

A person who has good skills in the emotional control capacity is comfortable handling emotional employees or co-workers. They are able to distance themselves from the emotions involved and logically deal with the situation at hand calmly, sensibility, and compassionately.

Good emotional control involves several key factors:

1. Understanding and managing your own emotions, as well as those of other people.

2. Listening carefully to understand the wants and needs of others.

3. Analyzing situations objectively, rather than impulsively or emotionally.

4. Resolving difficult or emotional situations with specific, manageable action steps.

There are two types of emotional control: internal and external. Internal is what is going on in your mind, but may not be seen by anyone else. External emotional control is what others see in your actions. In order to be able to maintain emotional control, you have to be able to control both.

A person with a low score in this area may have difficulty separating his emotions from his actions. He may instead allow his emotions to lead his actions and, as a result, he may lose composure at critical times.

Why Do We Lose Emotional Control?

1. We spent a lot of time, effort, emotional energy into a project and it was rejected or unsuccessful for some reason.

2. Other people don't seem to value our solutions, ideas, or proposals.

3. Fatigue, stress, or anxiety.

4. Improper focus, or focusing on our own survival instead of our customer's satisfaction.

5. Personal problems carrying over to the workplace.

6. Poor management, which may make us outwardly angry or aggressive.

The end result of losing emotional control is almost always bad – from negatively affecting others' opinions of you to losing a job to losing profits, revenues, and repeat business.

Remember, your goal should be to RESPOND with carefully thought-out solutions, rather than REACTING with strong emotion.

What are Skills Associated with Emotional Control?

Someone who has mastered skills associated with Emotional Control:
- Keeps their eye on the prize
- Realizes that nothing is ever over until it's over
- Thinks clearly and strives to be at their absolute best.
- Has mastered negotiation skills
- Has good problem solving skills
- Listens well
- Understands and manages their own emotions
- Is as prepared as possible for problems or crisis situations

How do you develop your own skills in Emotional Control?

- Do not allow anyone or anything to control you. You can control you own reactions to events around you.

- Choose to respond, not just react. Don't just have a knee jerk reaction. Develop a pre-planned, thoughtful response.

- Try to remain as unemotional as you can and try to find meaningful, positive solutions to any problem before you allow your emotions to enter into the scene.

- Develop your skill set, systems, and solutions. They will defeat emotionalism every time.

- Never (ever) say anything, anywhere, anytime about anything or anybody that you will regret later.

- Once you have resolved an emotional issue, put it behind you.

- Keep careful notes in meetings related to potential problem areas that will affect you or your department. Try to make initial plans for handling those problems you deem likely to occur.

- Think ahead about decisions you know you will have to make. Start early in gathering information you need to address these decisions.

- Define the potential impact of current events or decisions at your workplace. Will these events or decisions cause problems or concerns?

- Think carefully about each problem you perceive, and try to discover what the main cause of each problem is.

• Ask managers or peers for their perceptions of current organizational events. This may enlighten you about problems you didn't know existed or help you to define a current problem better.

• Understand that both parties in any disagreement must get something they want before an agreement is feasible. Research the topic of disagreement thoroughly and think carefully about what you perceive the differing opinions to be.

• Use open-ended questions to encourage parties to express their thoughts can concerns. Not only will this help you understand others better, but it can also buy you time to master your own emotions.

• Listen carefully to all points of view to identify and understand what each party wants. It is helpful to write down on a whiteboard or easel what both parties' goals and objectives are.

• Determine what each party is willing to accept in an agreement.

• Work to understand the needs behind each request that is made. By identifying specific needs behind the issues, you can better develop alternatives that both parties can benefit from.

• Don't get into "win/lose" discussions-the ideal is to find "win/win" solutions.

• Once an issue has been resolved, state terms of the agreement deliberately and establish positive expectations of both parties.

• Don't jump too quickly to a conclusion about the best solution to each problem. List all possible solutions to the problem before you choose the best alternative.

• Gather information about the problem from any resources you have at your disposal.

• Look at each problem from different perspectives.

• When you discover a problem, recognize that you must solve the problem within an organizational system. Effects of solving the problem may be felt across your department or across the entire organization.

• When you feel you have gathered all relevant information, make sure the conclusion you draw really follow from the facts.

• Prioritize action steps towards solving the problem. Break the solution into manageable tasks and delegate them to relevant individuals or complete them in order yourself.

PowerWashStore.com Helps Family in Need

by Allison Hester, Editor

On March 17, a tragic fire broke out and destroyed a Milwaukee-area duplex, killing two 14-year-old boys. One of the deceased, Isaiha Kobow, was the son of a long-time friend of Bill Wilson, Sales and Distribution Manager for PowerWashStore.com.

"Lori (Isaiha's mother) and I grew up in the same area. Isaiha liked skateboarding and my son is a semi-pro skateboarder, so we would meet up at the skate park for her son to watch and learn," he explained.

Two younger boys were rescued from the fire, but Isaiah and his friend were consumed by the flames.

Knowing that Lori was going to need all the helps she could get, Wilson asked PowerWashStore.com Owner Paul Kassander if it would be OK to ask for donations on Pressure Washing Institute and on their Facebook page. Kassander said he would like to do more, so he donated a Whisper Wash surface cleaner to auction off to help the family.

"I talk to these contractors daily and they have sort have become like family to me over the past couple years," Wilson said. "I felt like it was the right thing to do."

The surface cleaner, which normally sells for $770, sold for $650 in the auction. Wilson raised another $450 in donations from industry members, for a total contribution of $1,100. "When I brought Lori the donation check, she was very thankful and relieved. I guess a couple of people put together donation funds in her son's name but she had yet to see a single penny from any of them," Wilson added.

According to Wilson, Lori plans to use this tragedy to inform parents about things "we don't like to think about, such as life insurance on our children," said Wilson.

"Lori has always been a great friend, good mother, and a strong woman who's seen a life that would've broken a lot of people," Wilson concluded. "The fact that she gets up in the morning after all she's been through is enough for me to want to help her. I'm very thankful to Paul's willingness to help, and to all those who chipped in to help in this horrible tragedy."

How to Prevent Accidents

Stay Alert | Stay Focused | Stay Safe

by Larry Miller, Owner of Larry Miller, Inc. and IWCA Director

The IWCA (International Window Cleaning Association) believes that "in an industry where one error can potentially be fatal, it is important that you and your staff have the most up-to-date training possible." It only takes one day for you and your team to take the hands-on IWCA Safety Training session. The opportunity for one-on-one instruction as well as classroom training are both vital to learn professional-level safety practices and procedures to help keep you safe on the job.

Another resource that's important for your safety is the OSHA/IWCA Alliance. (OSHA stands for Occupational Safety and Health Administration.) The OSHA/IWCA Alliance "was created to provide important information and tools to the window cleaning industry." OSHA has developed a web page exclusively for members of IWCA. You'll find links to products and programs you can use to help prevent accidents.

Training doesn't end in the classroom

After 20 years in the window cleaning business, I've heard all kinds of stories about unusual and unexpected things happening. And they can happen very quickly. I encourage members to share the stories you hear from other window cleaning professionals on the job so you can recognize potential problems and help avoid accidents from happening when you're out there on the job.

1) Cell phone distraction

Do you ever get interrupted by calls on your cell phone when you've just arrived at the location and you're on a tight schedule? It's tempting to leave your phone in the truck and just get to work. But what if you're still thinking about that request to reschedule the next job when you're putting up your ladder?

You get up to the roof to clean three skylights and now you're ready to climb back down. You inspect that ladder and see you forgot to secure all the locks! Now you're "up the creek without a paddle." What's worse – not only can you not climb back down the ladder...you can't call for help. Remember why? You left your cell phone in the truck.

The homeowner's not home. No neighbors are home. You could end up stuck on the roof until the homeowner returns. (Another reason to always wear protective sunscreen when you're working outdoors, even if it's just a "short" job.)

2) Just scraping by

You're indoors scraping paint off one of the windows in a warehouse. You take a quick look around. Your team is doing well, staying on schedule – but wait. Somebody new to the team is making what could be a risky move on his ladder. When you call out to warn him, the paint scraper bangs off the window frame, into your hand.

Ouch! That's only the beginning. The accident could mean you can't use that hand and can't work for two months or more. What's worse, because you own the business, you didn't think you needed workmen's comp like the rest of the team that works on a regular basis. So you end up not only with rehab but

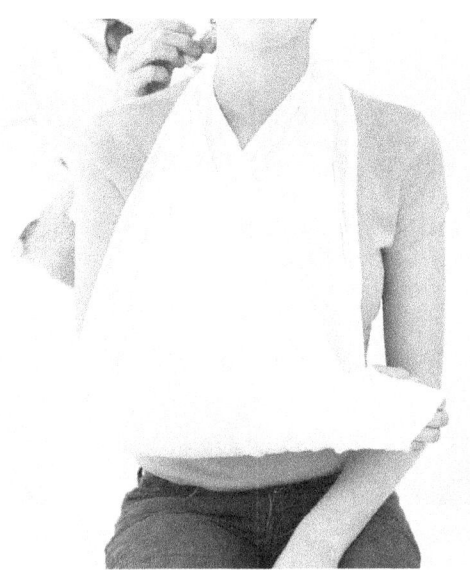

paying hundreds or thousands of dollars not covered by insurance. (Another reason why window cleaning business owners should always include themselves under workers' comp even if they only rarely work "hands on.")

3) It Takes Two to Tango

If you do have to work by yourself, at least make sure the homeowner is around. Or if it's a commercial job, make sure that there's a business representative there to answer questions or help out. And just to be sure, always let somebody on your team know where you are. Call to check in during the day from time to time with an update and report on your progress.

Instead of working alone, it's safer to have another member of your team working with you. Sometimes you need help moving something heavy out of the way, like furniture – especially if the homeowner is older or has a bad back. It's good practice to have someone who is professionally trained to hold a ladder safely or to help carry storm windows up and down stairs for washing and installation.

Say you're inside on the second floor of a home cleaning windows. You finish cleaning the last window on the inside, open it and step outside to the ledge to work on the outside. You carefully start to close the window, but you're starting to feel a little tired and thinking about taking a break. What's worse – "Click!" Oh, oh. The window suddenly locked by itself because you forgot and closed the window all the way. You're stuck outside. What would you do without somebody there who is prepared and ready to come to your rescue?

Online Safety Training Now Available

One of the fastest and most convenient ways to get up to speed on professional safety training would be to look into the online training modules that IWCA provides. It's not only for someone new on your team, but also good for a refresher course – no matter how long you've been in the window cleaning business. Learn more at www.iwca.org.

4 Steps to Ladder Safety

Falls from ladders (portable, step, straight, combination and extension) are one of the leading causes of occupational fatalities and injuries in the window cleaning industry.

• Always maintain a three-point (two hands and a foot, or two feet and a hand) contact on the ladder when climbing. Keep your body near the middle of the step and always face the ladder while climbing (see diagram).

• Ladders must be free of any slippery material on the rungs, steps or feet.

• Do not use a self-supporting ladder (e.g., step ladder) as a single ladder or in a partially closed position.

• Do not use the top step/rung of a ladder as a step/rung unless it was designed for that purpose.

For more information go online to OSHA QUICK CARD Portable Ladder Safety.

Stay on Your Feet
(If You Can)

by Rick Meehan
Vice President of Marko Janitorial Supply, www.MarkoInc.com

It sounds great to tell a customer that you'll be glad to have your cleaning crew handle overhead work, but is it really a good idea? Not without the right equipment it's not! Overhead work requires excellent liability and health insurance, and that's a fact. Step stools, ladders, boxes, crates, chairs, tables, desks – all are likely candidates for helping a crewmember to reach a high spot – and just as likely to put them out of work indefinitely if they fall. Purchase the right tools for the overhead job. It is always better to stand on your own two feet than to dangle from a ladder or perch on an object while trying to get something clean.

There are many different brands and styles of equipment designed to make overhead cleaning easier. Pressure washing systems we are all familiar with. They squirt volumes of water and detergent under high pressure; however, pressure washing is rarely able to be used inside a building. So, are we back to square one? Nowhere close; there are many tools available to keep cleaning personnel grounded.

Before we hit the tool manifest, let's remember that most overhead work involves cleanup of dust, oils, and bugs. Dust, bugs, yeah – but oils? Absolutely! If nothing else, we humans cover every surface in a room with body oil over a period of time. Just the act of opening a door to the outside brings in petroleum-based oils from motor vehicles, both from tracking via feet and wafting on the air. High places require extra cleaning efforts, thus high places rarely get cleaning attention. Grime builds up on the tops of cabinetry, window sills, door jams, ductwork, pipes, walls, and especially in high corners.

Another aspect of overhead cleaning is the cost in terms of labor hours. A cleaning contractor must include extra time in the quotation if a client needs overhead work. Too, able-bodied cleaning professionals make the job go faster. Since time is money in the cleaning industry, be extremely careful putting out quotes for overhead work or you will get burned. As a supplier of janitorial products for the last 32 years, believe me, I've heard all the tales of woe. You don't want to sink your ship under the weight of underbids, lost work time, workman's compensation claims, and liability issues from damages to a client's property while your people were on the premises.

If you've covered the bases, then here's a list of standard tools that indoor overhead cleaning requires:

Extendable Dusters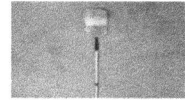

Brushes that Fit in High Corners

Extension handles for brushes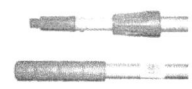

Dusters that Fit on Long Handles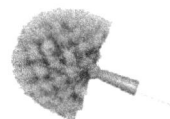

Arm extender gripper tools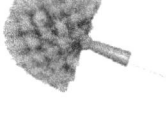

Microfiber cleaning tools designed for walls, floors, and ceilings

Dry cleaning chemical sponges

Large cellulose sponges

Microfiber clothes or cotton rags

Claw-type mop handle for gripping sponges and rags

Universal pad holders to go with extension handles

Bendable microfiber dusters that fit on extension handles

Backpack vacuum cleaners with extension tools

Fatigue is a big issue for cleaning folks working overhead. Proper tools and cleaning chemicals reduce labor. Anything that you can do to make the work easier, even if it costs more to get the proper equipment and hire people able to handle the task, is better than getting someone hurt, maimed, or even killed. I once had a customer that fell off a rickety old ladder while scrubbing brick. He fell only 10 feet – to his death. Don't let this happen to you or your staff.

Speaking of falls, if you absolutely must have cleaning folks on stools and ladders, buy only the best professional models. These products have built-in safety features to reduce risk. Never let your people use the height-boosters at hand like a client's furniture. Always, always, always use your own approved equipment! Train your staff to make sure they utilize those safety features too.

While overhead cleaning is a profitable add-on service, spend the money for the best equipment, the sturdier personnel, good insurance, and don't try to rush the job. The old adage, "It's better to be safe than sorry," should be your policy. Only then can you confidently tell your clients that you'll be glad to get rid of the unsightly spider webs and other high-jinx that plagues the world of overhead cleaning!

eClean Magazine

Which Online Directories Should You Use for Your Small Business?

by Henry Bockman, Contractor's Foundation, www.ContractorsFoundation.com

Even though listing your website in many online directories will improve your website's exposure and SEO ranking, it is not effective to just SPAM your website into every single online directory you can find. You will want to take some time to consider which specific online directories will give you the best ROI.

The best option is to find a great combination of directories to join. If you run a small business the best place to start may be with a local directory. This is because most people will search for businesses in their area they can patronize. Local market and niche-specific online directories can offer extremely targeted advertisements to potential local customers.

After your business is listed in these directories you can take a look at the larger and potentially more expensive general-interest directories. You will probably want to consider listing with the top 10 online directories, as these will be used by a lot of people and will offer higher relevancy and authority in the eyes of search engines.

Google Places and Google Maps are large general-interest directories that you will want to list your small business in. If your website sells tangible goods you may also want to consider listing it in comparison shopping websites and product listings directories. Studies show that 42 percent of consumers will look at a comparison shopping website before they decide to purchase a specific product.

The best way to figure out which specific online directories your small business should be listed in is to start with your competitors. Take a look at your local and niche-specific options and figure out if your competition is already listed. If they are, you need to be listed too. If they are not listed, you may want to list your website as a way to beat them to the punch. In some situations it may not make sense for you to have a listing in a specific online directory, even if your competitors are listed in it. Your goal should be to be listed in every relevant and niche-specific directory you can find as well as many of the major directories, but no so many directories that you appear SPAMMY.

In addition to listing your website in online directories, you also need to maintain these listings. It is important for your online directory listings to be up to date and accurate, or else you could just be wasting your time. If your directory information seems out of date, your customers will probably look elsewhere.

It will probably take some time to see the results of listing your small business's website in so many online directories, but eventually you will see results. The best way to find the perfect combination of online directory listings for your business is to use some sort of tracking or analytics system. You will want to be able to see how many people clicked on your website links from within the directory and if your website has shown increased traffic since then. You will want to stop wasting your time with online directories that are not producing results and increase the time and effort you spend on online directories that are productive.

Best Practices for Listing Your Small Business in Online Directories

Now that you understand why your small business should be listed in online directories and have started locating the directories that you want to be listed in, you are ready to begin creating your business listings for submissions. Here are some tips and best practices for listing your small business in online directories:

• Start by choosing local directories and directories that are niche-specific. So if you own a model airplane hobby shop in Phoenix, make sure you find a local Phoenix business directory and a directory that is related to model airplanes. If you can find a model airplane hobby directory for the Phoenix area, you are all set.

• After the local directories start searching for larger and more generalized directories. Pick directories that get a lot of traffic and that are listed highly on major search engines like Google. A higher search engine ranking means that the directory will be considered as both authoritative and relevant in the eyes of search engines, making any links you get through these directories more valuable to your SEO strategy.

• Include all of the relevant information regarding your small business in your websites directory description. This should include your business's name, location, telephone number, contact information and possibly reviews, business hours and anything else that is relevant. Add in photos, maps or other interactive features if the directory lets you.

• Try to keep your information consistent across all of your online directory listings. This will help your website to retain its credibility in the eyes of search engines and will assist with your SERP rankings.

• Try to make your business stand out by offering an explanation of your business or any specific message the customer should know in your description.

• Keep all of your information up to date. This may mean updating all of your listings several times per month.

• Allow customers to leave positive reviews and use them in your listing if the directory allows it.

• Always be professional and consistent with your business's listings and message. This includes any information regarding your brand.

• If you sell products or services to a local market, make sure your business is listed in a local business directory. Include geo-specific keywords and information. An example would be: "Dave's Model Plane Shop" + "Phoenix."

• Optimize your website for SEO purposes and include the relevant keywords in your meta titles and listing descriptions. Keyword research is important.

Henry Bockman is the owner of Henry's Housework in Maryland and a partner in Contractor's Foundation, a training company that provides power washing training, marketing and business success classes to help companies start up and succeed in any type of service based business, He also runs two Online companies and several internet directories.

Normally I sell this information with a step by step guide and a list of over 250 other directory sites for $29.99, but since you are an EClean Magazine Reader, You Can Get A Free Copy! Just click the link below and use Coupon Code: **ECleanMag** for your discount!

http://contractorsfoundation.com/product-category/business-marketing-guides-service-companies/

Please Leave A Review On This Article And The Guide Here:

http://contractorsfoundation.com/shop/get-listed-create-a-steady-stream-of-customers-to-your-web-site/

What Happened in Vegas

A Recap of the 2013 Garage Cleaning Event

by Allison Hester, Editor

In mid-March, I joined alongside approximately 45 contractors and vendors from across the country to learn the in's and out's of parking garage cleaning from Jim Gamble, a.k.a. "The Garage Doctor," of Crystal Cleaning Company.

Day 1: In the Classroom

The event began on Tuesday morning in the hotel's meeting room. "Dodge lined the conference room with beautiful, heavy-duty trucks. They were incredibly work ready, loaded with style and comfort," said Jim Lewis of Underpressure Powerwashers, Inc. "Hydro Tek parked an awesome rig next to the trucks, making you dream of the combination of the two being yours – a perfect fit."

Tuesday was an in-the-classroom day, and kicked off with John Tornabene of Clean County Powerwashing in Long Island, NY, and Linda Ruth Tossetti (Babe Ruth's Granddaughter) speaking on following your

Photos: Above (Left to Right) Linda Ruth Tossetti, Jim Gamble (a.k.a. "The Garage Doctor") and eClean Editor Allison Hester atop the Rio Hotel in Las Vegas.

Below: Linda Ruth Tossetti and John Tornabene (right) presented Nigel Griffith of Griff's Services witth a plaque of appreciation.

Bottom of this page: Participants introduce themselves at the opening of the meeting.

Next Page: Equipment demonstrations and garage cleaning walk through photos.

dreams. Other speakers included Nigel Griffith of Griff's Services, who spoke on environmentally-safe flatwork cleaning, Robert Hinderliter who covered environmental regulation changes, and later his son Michael Hinderliter, who spoke on Nine Tips to Help Manage the Growth of Your Business.

The full-day of learning ended with a two-hour talk by Gamble, who covered the in's and out's of parking garage cleaning. His presentation included a variety of topics, from working with environmental regulators, to a side-by-side comparison of different cleaning products.

"What brought me to Vegas was the interest in learning about environmentally safe garage cleaning from someone who has had more exposure to it than anyone else I know in the industry," said Lewis. "That would be Jim Gamble."

Day Two – In the Garage

Wednesday was the most highly anticipated day, when attendees were supposed to clean an actual garage using the latest and best equipment from participating vendors. The planning had been a nightmare, as two locations backed out earlier in the month.

Then on Tuesday, the event committee members learned that the parking garage owners had failed to clear the top deck and the one directly beneath it where the cleaning was supposed to take place. Then late Tuesday afternoon, the garage owners decided Gamble needed to significantly increase the amount of insurance he was carrying. (Note that this location had already required Gamble to increase his insurance the Friday before the event began, and Gamble had scrambled to meet the changes. This time, the amount of insurance they required more than doubled and there was no time to get it done.)

So Wednesday morning, while each of the participating vendors – which included Hydro Tek, Steel Eagle and Cyclone – talked about the equipment they brought, the event committee was searching for last minute alternatives and options. Ultimately, they decided to just try to make

eClean Magazine

Photos: (Left) Steel Eagle (top) and Hydro Tek (bottom) each gave away hose reels to one lucky winner.

Right: Committee members John Tornabene, Robert Hinderliter, Jim Gamble and Nigel Griffith stand with members of Nevada's Dept. of Conservation & Natural Resources, Division of Enviromental Protection Agency, including presenter Clifford Lawson (center).

the best out of the situation, and most participants agreed it ultimately worked out fine.

The afternoon was spent on the top lot of the hotel's parking deck. Participants studied the equipment while vendors answered all their questions. (Note that Cyclone was able to run their machines.) "Some of the manufacturers brought equipment that I had no idea was on the market. I was very impressed!" said Lewis. "We didn't need a whole level of the garage cleaned to do what we needed to get done. The vendors were able to give us a longer look at the tools of the trade and a quick run through of their abilities, along with an open Q&A forum for each item on display."

"Not being able to actually clean wasn't a problem at all," said Jim Jenkins, owner of Hydroclean, which is based in Springfield, Missouri. " I thought that they did a good job recovering from that little curve ball that was thrown out there at the last minute."

After a couple of hours of networking with vendors, Gamble took the group to the deck below, where he walked the class through the garage. There he covered the cleaning process step-by-step, drawing attention to things to look for and watch out for.

That evening, I went to dinner with three contractors who had each traveled quite a ways to participate. When I asked if the event had been worth attending despite the day's setback, they quickly answered "yes." Each had come with a specific goal in mind, and each had gotten the answers they needed.

Thursday

Day three featured a special presentation, followed by a Q&A session, by Clifford M. Lawson of Nevada's Department of Conservation and Environmental Resources, Division of EPA . During the talk, Lawson explained that his role is to "protect the waters of the U.S. and State" – period. Therefore, everything implemented by his department had to keep this goal in mind.

Essentially, the take away from Lawson's talk was the contractors needed to work with their local AHJ's (Authorities Having Jurisdiction) to create acceptable best management practices (BMPs). "They (AHJs) are not the enemy. They are here to help," he explained.

Thursday officially ended early, but participants continued to network throughout the day and evening, adding to the overall value of the event.

"Everybody that I talked with was super friendly and helpful," Jenkins concluded. "As is the case with most of these types of events the networking factor is probably one of the most helpful. You learn as much at the dinner table as in the meeting room."

How to Build Your Brand

by Jenna Horsley,
eClean Magazine Sales Manager

Can you summarize at least two pillars of your company's brand identity? Before you attempt this, let's talk brand and what it means.

A brand is a personality **and a** promise.

This personality your company has projects the experience, qualities and results your customer can expect. What you put out there is what you will get; if your company projects a quality and professional identity, you will attract a customer who values and is willing to pay for the promise associated with your brand.

Who are we and what are we about?

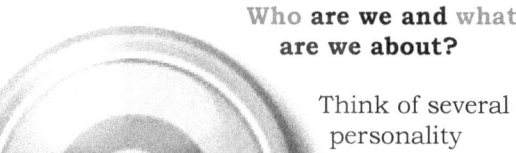

Think of several personality traits prominent to your company – e.g., reliable, quick, innovative. Be honest with yourself. If you continually lose customers or have received complaints, what does this tell you about your company? Were you too slow? Was the work not up to par? Were your employees not as professional as you would hope? This can tell you what you need to change to help you your company what you want it to be.

A survey is a great way to help uncover your existing brand image. Your customer's responses can help clarify how your company is perceived by your target market. If you do develop a survey, be prepared for the results; they may not be what you want to hear or have unexpected consequences. It's cliché, but knowledge is power and may potentially afford you the change necessary to take your company to the next level. Let this knowledge direct the development of both your company, and the brand you want to build.

Brand Positioning

Brand positioning entails knowing your demographic inside and out. This will change the brand you want to project, or assist you in refining your image. Whether it's a corporation or a homeowner, they will probably wish to use the products or services that are a reflection of, or represent them well.

While contemplating the personality of your brand, consider your prospective customer. Who do they want to invest their money in and why? What do they stand for?

While considering your customer and their needs, think of what will differentiate you from your competition. What makes your company's services worth paying for over the other marketplace forces and does your competitor say the same thing? You want to stand out.

Brand Identity

The purpose of brand identity is to organize a uniform personality for your company, product or service to achieve differentiation. To be useful, this cohesive personality must be unique, recognizable, and honest. Fulfill your promises. If you project your company as reliable, make sure your men show up on time and perform as expected. People are more willing to pay for what they can count on. Live up to your brand.

Branding is imperative to the success of what you sell. When you have branded, you have officially established yourself in the mind of your customer.

Branding builds equity. It is a long-term investment in your company. Branding is, in a sense, a legacy for your company. This is why brand is so important, and even more of a reason to begin developing your brand.

The last thing you want is your competitors defining your brand. I can assure you it won't be to your advantage. Develop your personality, your promise, and maintain it. Differentiate yourself within your niche, and further, guarantee your customers' commitment to what you sell. This is what branding will do.

Reasons to Pressure Wash Your Building's Exterior
by Paul Horsley, Publisher

For many businesses, image is everything. Yet image-boosting services such as commercial pressure washing are often overlooked, as many business owners get so caught up in daily deadlines, meetings and projects that maintaining a clean building exterior is the last thing on their minds.

Not only can hiring a power washing company help improve your image, but it can provide many other benefits for your business as well. Here are three things a visit from the local power washers can do for you:

1. Attract more customers. A clean building – both outside and in – demonstrates that you take pride in your company. Customers are more likely to trust a business that is well taken care of than one that appears dirty and neglected. Regular commercial pressure washing lets customers know that you care about your image and are careful not to tarnish it, which encourages them to go ahead and purchase your products or services.

2. Improve your building's longevity. Without the use of power washers, your building will eventually become covered with dirt, graffiti, grime and mildew – which can ultimately lead to rot. Regularly bringing in a power washing company will not only help keep your building healthy, but it will prevent dirt and stains from accumulating over time. The more often your building receives commercial pressure washing, the easier it will be to remove grime.

3. Reduce pollutants. Urban buildings pick up a lot of pollution from car exhaust and other environmental factors. Not only do these pollutants make your building appear dirty, but they create an unhealthy environment. A professional power washing company can use eco-friendly cleaning products to wash away exhaust and other pollutants from your building and parking lot.

4. Create a positive work environment. Commercial pressure washing ensures that your employees won't be greeted each day by an image of dirt and neglect. Plus, clean windows help contribute to a more pleasant work environment.

Regular pressure washing can benefit your business in surprising ways. Your employees, customers and visitors will thank you for taking the time to properly care for your building by keeping the exterior clean.

Thank you for a GREAT first year!

On April 18, 2012, we launched the first official issue of eClean Magazine. Since then, we have grown to become the contract cleaner's online resource.

We want to thank all of you – our readers, our advertisers and our supporters – for making this a fanastic first year!

We are looking forward to growing, expanding and providing professional cleaning contractors with the information they need for years and years to come!

Classifieds: Products & Services

www.PowerWash.com
Mobile power wash equipment, schools, training, videos, environmental supplies & maintenance services. Call for a free catalog, 800-433-2113.

www.SkyPro.com
Automated window cleaning systems. A safe way to clean windows, frames and exterior of high rise buildings. Call 800-699-0251 or 651-967-9031.

www.PWNA.org
Power Washers of North America. For certification or membership information, visit our website, email info@pwna.org, or call 800-393-7962.

To Advertise in our New Classifieds Section
Contact Allison Hester
allison@ecleanmag.com

eCLEAN magazine
The professional contractor cleaner's online resource!

Marine Markets

Plus

- Cleaning Products as Add-Ons
- How to Get Free Publicity
- Inside Seal 'n Lock

and more!

POWERWASH.COM
SUPPLIES CHEMICALS TRAINING

1.800.433.2113
2513 Warfield St. Fort Worth, TX 76106

Shop Online 24 Hours a Day

We provide **products** you NEED with the helpful **service** you Deserve!

Quick Links - Pressure Washers - Surface Cleaners - Chemicals & Detergents - Cleaning Supplies - Parts & Accessories - Pumps & Repair Kits - Training Materials

DSR- 49 Deck Restorer
DSR-49 Disodium Peroxydicarbonate removes mildew stains and dirt while restoring a natural and bright look to vertical and horizontal grayed and weathered wood surfaces. Ideal for wood preparation prior to water sealer application.

D-Vandal Graffiti Remover
A fast-acting penetrating semi-gel that removes paints, inks (including ball point pen), permanent markers, crayons, caulking, urethane sealants and more off most surfaces. This product eliminates tedious scrubbing to remove stubborn stains on surfaces by simply wiping with a soft cloth or using an all-purpose sprayer.

DELTA-60™ Heavy Grease Remover (*)
Contractors first choice for grease spot removal. Just apply Delta 60 to a dry grease spot and pressure wash off. Watch years of deep stains disappear! It restores drive-thru and entrance pads to look like new! The oils come out as solids leaving the concrete as clean as possible.

R-202 Concrete Cleaner
Cleans heavy grease, oil and scuff marks from unpainted concrete and other alkaline water safe hard surfaces. USDA authorized for use in meat plants.

AC-12 Fabric Awning Cleaner
Quickly removes normal dirt and grime from woven fabric materials. 1 gal. bottle = 5 gal. of solution.

AC-22 Vinyl Awning Cleaner
Quickly removes dirt from vinyl fabric materials. 1 gal. bottle = 10 gal. of cleaner.

RP-3500 Window Cleaner Concentrate
This non-streaking cleaner leaves glass with reflective finishes and a film-free sparkling appearance. 1 gallon of concentrate makes 10 gallons of cleaner.

Mosmatic 12" Graffiti Remover with Recovery Port + 1 Quart of D-VANDAL Graffiti Remover
This professional wall cleaner is specially designed for quickly removing graffiti and stubborn dirt. The recovery port allows the user to attach a vacuum system to suction the dirty water. The brush ring prevents splashing and injuries from loose pebbles. It is soft and elastic but extremely effective thanks to the thickness of the bristles.
Specifications:
- Surface Cleaning Diameter: 12"
- Pressure: 5000 PSI
- Max Temperature: 250 F
- Weight: 7.1 lbs.
- Swivel: 1xDYW
- Rotor Arm: 2x 1/8" NPTF
- Rotor Nozzles: Two (2) 1503 (15-Degree Size 3)

Whisper Pro Big Guy Platinum Series Surface Cleaner
The Whisper Wash Big Guy Surface Cleaner incorporates a signature balanced and machined spray bar with a 28" wide surface coverage area. The Big Guy's pivoting wheel design and a heavy-duty nylon brush provide for easy navigation through large areas while still containing the pressurized spray. The Platinum Series of Whisper Pro Surface Cleaners offers:
- A One-Piece Unitized Swivel Cartridge
- A One-Year Full Coverage Warranty
- 5000 PSI Max Working Pressure
- 212° F Max Working Temperature
- BONUS! This PowerWash.com EXCLUSIVE Bundle Pack also includes a FREE 5 lb. Sample Pack of R-202 Cleaner. This powerful sudsing alkaline powdered detergent is designed to clean heavy grease, oil and scuff marks from unpainted concrete and other alkaline water safe hard surfaces.

Big Guy Surface Cleaner Specifications:
- 2" Nylon Brush
- One 4" Caster
- Two (2) 10" Pneumatic Tires
- Oversized, self-lubricating twin thrust bearings
- 2000-5000 PSI Pressure Range
- Max Temperature: 212° F
- Max Flow: 4-10 GPM
- Housing Size: 28"
- Two (2) 25-Degree Size 2 Spray Tips

Personal Protective Equipment
- Wrap-Around Safety Goggles
- 12" Gauntlet PVC Safety Gloves
- Cordova Steel Toe PVC Safety Boots
- Full Brim Non-Slotted Hard Hat
- Heavyweight Apron
- Visor Assembly for Hard Hat
- Glacier Glove Stillwater Neoprene Bootie

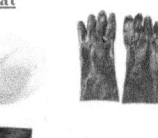

10% OFF Orders of $100 or more!
Use Coupon Code eClean10
Cannot be combined with any other offers. Exp: 06.01.13

www.eCleanMag.com   Issue 14

IN THIS ISSUE:

178

182

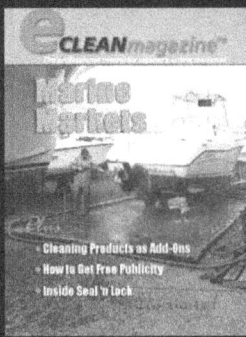

169 Water, Water Everywhere: The Marine Industry

174 Cleaning Product Add-Ons: Tom Sickel of Knight Norros Explains Why It's a Smart Idea

178 Networking: Why Bother? by Tony Evans, A New View Window Cleaning

179 3 Tips for "Streak Free" Business Networking, by Larry Miller, Larry Miller, Inc.

180 PWNA Vendor Profile: Seal 'n Lock

182 PWNA Flatwork Certification: How It's Raising One Company's Bottom Line

185 Commercial Powerwashing Equipment: Types of Trigger Guns, by Paul Horsley

186 Lessons from the Sales Rack

189 5th Annual Midwest Cleaning Event

190 Marine Cleaning Requires Smart Equipment Choices, by Steel Eagle

191 Classifieds

192 Bring in the Bounty: Spring Cleaning Exposed, by Rick Meehan

194 How to Get Free Publicity for Your Product or Service, by Michael Fleischman

196 Correct,, Don' Break: Improving Your Skills, by Bill Kinnard, Grandy & Associates

200 Play Business Like Golf, by George Hedley, Hard Hat Presentations

Cover photo courtesy of Ken Boddie, Pressure Washer Warehouse, www.PressureWasherWarehouse.net

---

eClean Magazine is published monthly

Publisher: Paul Horsley, paul@ecleanmag.com
Editor: Allison Hester, allison@ecleanmag.com
Sales: Kelly Jacobsen, kelly@ecleanmag.com

Box 262, 16 Midlake Blvd S.E.
Calgary, Alberta
Canada T2X 2X7
www.eCleanMag.com

eClean Magazine

Water, Water Everywhere

Photo courtesy of Rick Petry,
Windsor Wood Care, www.WindorWoodCare.com

One of the biggest challenges in pressure washing is ensuring that no illegal discharges of wastewater reach the U.S. and State waters. But what if you're cleaning property directly on or next to those protected waters?

That's the challenge that comes with cleaning marinas, boats, docks and other items found near the waterways. Yet, this is a huge market for pressure washers because these items need cleaning and protecting more than most. In fact, in some bodies of water, pressure washing is not just a nicety; it's the law.

by Allison Hester

Photo courtesy of Ken Boddie, Pressure Washer Warehouse, www.PressureWasherWarehouse.net

The recreational boating industry is HUGE. In 2011, the industry reported 32.3 billion in sales and service in the U.S. alone (National Marine Manufacturers Association's 2011 Recreational Boating Statistical Abstract). That same year, more than half a million new boats were sold.

That's a lot of boats to clean.

While some marinas provide their own pressure washing equipment, others hire contractors to come in and take care of the boats.

In either case, there's a common thread: washwater should not go back into the waterway. Even without the use of detergents, the wastewater is considered contaminated for several reasons. For one, the pressure washing is removing hydrocarbon buildup from the engine exhaust. But perhaps even more, the paint used in the boating industry is actually a sacrificial coating that uses anti-fouling agents including heavy metals and pesticides, and a little bit of the paint wears off during cleanings. Then, of course, there's the algae, barnacles and mussels (we'll get to those on page 7).

That means there has to be a place for the boats to be washed. Many larger marinas install expensive wash pads, but smaller marinas often can't afford that. Instead, they need to look for alternatives.

That was the situation Ken Boddie of Pressure Washer Warehouse, Hanover, Massachusetts, faced a few years ago when the "water police" starting fining area marinas for wastewater discharges. To save his business, he developed a small, portable, easy to set up wash mat called the Sea Saver System. It is basically a modified version of what was available for the fleet washing industry. The heavy-duty vinyl containment features a 4-inch berm, and is typically 20 by 30 feet, although it can be made to order.

"Small marinas could not afford to be compliant if they had to purchase a $25,000-plus in-ground system. Besides, bigger is not always better," explained Boddie. "This is a very inexpensive alternative – costing around $5,000 o $7,000 instead." The Sea Saver's Alkota ecs5000 filtrations system filters the water down to five microns, but Boddie added that a complete closed loop recycling system is not a necessity. "Some marinas just contain the wastewater, vacuum it into the 250 gallon totes and have a certified waste hauler dispose of it correctly." Water can also be evaporated, with the remains swept up and disposed.

Boddie said he does suggest using a lower gpm machine and recycling the water when possible. "The less water you use, the less you have to clean up," he explained.

A few boat washing tips:

- Make sure all hatches, etc. are closed before you start washing.

- Inspect for pre-existing damage and point any problems out before you start cleaning.

- Watch out for stickers and decals because they can come off easily.

- Don't spray water up the exhaust pipe. You can seriously damage the engine.

- Careful with the pressure! While steel boats can withstand quite a bit, Fiberglas is much more delicate.

- Use hot water to kill any unwanted mussels, etc.

Boat Washing: It's the Law
(...well, sometimes)

Around 1988, a group of tiny critters hitched a ride from Eurasia to Lake St. Clair, a small water body that connects Lake Huron and Lake Erie, where they decided to settle down and grow their families. Some grew restless, however, wanting to see more of this new world, so they stowed away on passing ships, moving on to unchartered waters.

Today these tiny invaders, known as zebra mussels, have caused quite an environmental ruckus. Don't let their size fool you. Though only about the length of a fingernail, these mollusks upset ecosystems, threaten wildlife, damage structures, cause other serious problems, and are an environmental nightmare. To make matters worse, they attach themselves – and their invisible babies – to boats and other structures and follow them to new bodies of water where they lay their millions of eggs and restart the cycle.

As if this weren't bad enough, another similar species – the Quagga mussel – decided to follow the zebra mussel's example in the early 1990s, and the cycle began again.

In the battle against these tiny yet relentless invaders, there is one primary weapon of choice – the hot water pressure washer. Three things have been found to kill these pests – hot water, preferably at least 140 F; low humidity; and time.

In many areas it is now illegal for boaters to transport zebra or quagga mussels. Boats found with evidence of the mussels may be quarantined, and boaters may be fined. Boaters MUST wash their boats before entering a new waterway. When cleaning for mussel removal, there are some primary guidelines to follow:

1. Remove the boat from the water and away from the launch ramp.
2. Scrape off any mussels you find, crush to kill them, then throw the remains away in the dumpster.
3. Wash off or remove all plants and mud.
4. Feel around the boat for rough or gritty spots. These may be microscopic mussels that are too young to be seen.
5. Wash the boat, trailer, etc., away from the waterway. Use hot water (155 F at the nozzle) then dry the boat as much as possible.
6. Drain all the water from the boat and dry everything you can (motors, bilges, lower outboard units, etc.).

Specific instructions for removing mussels from all types of watercraft can be found on various websites, such as www.DontMoveaMussel.com.

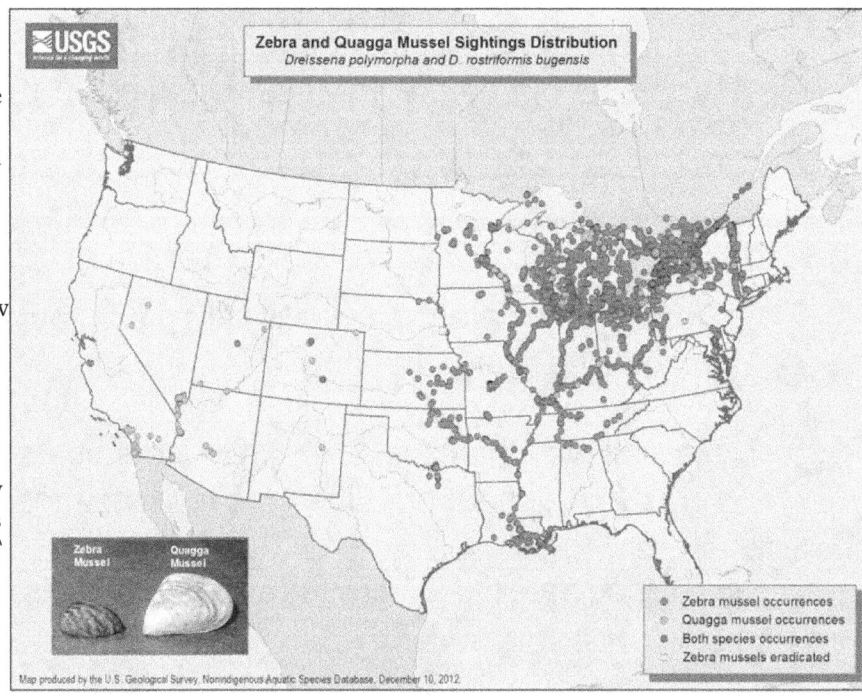

Don't Forget the Docks

Photos courtesy of Rick Petry, Windsor Wood Care, www.WindorWoodCare.com

Just as all exterior wood needs to be protected, wood docks perhaps need even higher levels of protection. "Docks receive weathering from all points of the compass. They erode quicker due to constant moist conditions," explained Adrian Carrier of ABC Pressure Washing & Deck Rescue in Houston, Texas. "Wind, harsh weather, traffic in high density – all of these contribute to erosion. Sealing slows that rapid erosion and adds longevity to the wood."

Again, being on the water brings with it an array of unique challenges: marine traffic, wildlife, high winds, drought conditions, and of course, contaminants.

"Environmental challenges all depend on the authorities," said Doug Rucker of Clean and Green Solutions in Houston. Rucker stressed that he only cleans the boat docks – usually with water only – and he doesn't restore them. "We try to have the customer contact the local authorities to find out what the regulations are and get something in writing. Some have strict guidelines; some do not."

"Check with your local water authorities to see if your current BMPs (Best Management Practices) coincide with locals laws for cleaning and sealing over water," said Carrier. "Make sure you have enough insurance. Ask the pros in your area questions about compliance."

Another concern is physically getting out to the boat dock. "Having our water dragon skid unit from PowerWashStore.com on our truck has helped us tremendously on the last two we've done. We were able to pull right up to the dock and only needed a 150 foot hose run," Rucker added.

However, the dock often cannot be accessed by land only – especially when fascia boards need to be cleaned – in which case a canoe or small boat is necessary. "Many times we have used an inflatable raft to creep around the perimeter of the project," Carrier added.

"During the drought, we were able to clean most of the ones we did by simply walking around the docks as the water had receded past the ends of the docks," Rucker added.

Docks generally take extra work and material, and that needs to be taken into account when pricing the job. "Docks are not average restorations," stressed Carrier. "Each has a different set of conditions. Material costs are much higher due to what is required in oils socks and tarping alone."

Finally, Rucker gives a few words of advice before cleaning your first dock: "Be careful if you use anything other than water to clean with. Make sure that you don't use anything that could harm the water or its inhabitants. I love fishing and love anything that has to do on the water, so I am very careful to protect it and the wildlife."

eClean Magazine

Cleaning Products as Add-Ons

Tom Sickel of Knight Norros Explains Why It's a Smart Idea

by Allison Hester

You have just washed a homeowner's roof, or squeegeed a store's windows, or cleaned a restaurant's exhaust system. That means their cleaning needs are satisfied until your next visit, right? Of course not.

Think about it. *Every* customer – whether residential, commercial or industrial – is going to have something that needs to be cleaned on a daily, weekly or monthly basis. They are going to need to purchase cleaning products from *somewhere*. Rather than having them buy the products from their local Wal-Mart, why not have them purchase it from you?

That's the question recently posed to me by Tom Sickel of Knight Norros Specialty Chemical Solutions, which has been serving national and international markets since 1968. "You are already there providing a service," he explains. "Why not sell them a product while you're there? You are making their cleaning efforts easier by providing a better quality product than they'll find at their local retail store, and you're building their confidence in you as well."

For instance, Knight Norros – which produces several products for the kitchen exhaust cleaning industry – also sells general purpose cleaners and metal polishers. Restaurants need to keep their kitchens and dining rooms spotless and their metal in tip-top condition, so these are natural add-ons that are meeting the customer's already existing needs.

Selling cleaners as add-ons makes sense for several reasons:

"Clean" is already on the customer's mind. Your client has just hired your company to meet their cleaning needs. They are happy with the results. They are experiencing the value of paying for clean, so it's the perfect time to suggest a product that can help them continue the joy of clean.

"Or you can simply tell the customer, "I have an XYZ product that you might like. Let me plan to bring you a sample he next time I come clean for you," adds Tom. "It's that easy."

You are currently their cleaning expert. If your customers are happy with the work you've done, they realize you are the expert when it comes to clean. If you tell them they can benefit from a particular product, they will listen. They may not purchase, but they will at least likely listen.

They are paying you anyway. There are three ways to make more money in sales: increase the number of people you target, improve your closing ratio, or sell more to your current customers. The method that takes the least amount of time and effort is the third – to upsell. While you may already have developed ways to upsell add-on services, you may not have thought about adding products. But the same principles apply.

Add-Ons build customer satisfaction and trust. The more ways you can meet your customers' needs, the less likely they are to take their business elsewhere.

If you're hesitant to sell cleaning products, think hard about why. Do these apply?

Excuse 1: I don't want to have to carry and store products. Depending on which company you work with, you won't have to. Instead, just bring a brochure with you to each job showing the products you carry and leave it with the customer. If your supplier provides product samples, tell them to let you know if they'd like to try any of the products out and you'll get a sample to them.

Better yet, keep a small personal stash with you so that if you see an area where your customer could use your product, you can demo it there on the spot. "Look for something dirty, then clean just a small part with the product so they can see the difference," says Tom. "Then ask, 'doesn't the clean spot look better?' Of course they're going to agree that it does."

That said, you don't have to keep a large supply on hand, just enough for your own use. If you do choose to carry an inventory, however, you must make sure you provide your customers with the correct product MSDS sheets. In many cases, you can order the product for the customer and have it delivered to their door from your product supplier.

You aren't out any money, and your only inconvenience is filling out some paperwork – oh, and depositing an extra income check!

Excuse 2: If I sell them cleaning products, they won't need my services as often. While this could possibly be true, depending on the particular product, it probably isn't. For instance, if you clean windows and don't want to sell a window-cleaning product, don't. But your customers still have cars, bathrooms, countertops, floors and so on that need to be cleaned. (And I'm willing to bet 99% of your window cleaning customers have a bottle of Windex somewhere in their cabinets!)

Excuse 3: I wouldn't know what products to carry. Then research it. Who do you buy your cleaning products from? Many chemical companies produce products for a variety of markets. Talk to them and see what they offer that you aren't familiar with, and if they offer any kind of incentives for referrals.

Excuse 4: I'm afraid I'll come across as too pushy. This comes down to basic sales practices. Remember to approach the situation as filling a need that the customer has, not trying to make a buck. We'll look at how to upsell in just a moment. Keep in mind, however, that compared to the cost of a roof cleaning, a 5-gallon bucket of an all-purpose cleaner is minimal.

Now that we've covered why adding cleaning products is a smart move, let's look at how to do it. (These principles apply for upselling services too.)

Know your product and what makes it valuable. Why should your customer buy a professional-grade product over the Wal-Mart off brand? You may not know, honestly, but your supplier should be able to tell you. Listen. Study the differences. Practice your explanation.

Sell your cleaning services first and don't start promoting products until you're finished. Don't automatically add the product price into your final bill, or at least separate the costs on your invoice. First and foremost you want customers to return to buy your services next time. They need to remember that the cost of your cleaning services are not necessarily the total cost of the bill. So record the cost of the service(s) so that the customer sees it before you start talking add-on products.

When upselling, provide information on each product individually – but don't overwhelm them with too many products. You don't want to be remembered as the pushy sales guy who wouldn't stop talking! Pick a product or two that you feel might benefit the client most.

Provide a benefit for purchasing while you're already there. This is obvious when upselling cleaning services. You're saving gas by not having to return to the location. Your equipment is already set up. Offering a discount to clean the driveway when you're washing the house makes perfect sense. But what about with products? Perhaps you can offer a 5 to 10 percent discount if they order while you're on the premises. Also, encourage them to purchase additional products or larger quantities at the same time because it saves on shipping.

Finally, -- and this goes for ALL sales of any kind -- reaffirm your customer's decision. Let them know they've make a smart choice. Perhaps even offer a limited money back guarantee (e.g., they have seven days to change their minds), especially if it's a product you can use in your business if they change their minds. Most customers won't take you up on it, but offering such a deal on products helps build trust and remove the barriers that may keep them from buying in the first place.

While you may not get rich from adding cleaning product sales to your repertoire, you will certainly gain more than you'll lose. Added profits. Increased customer loyalty. Year-round income. And all it takes is a little research and the willingness to try. Not bad.

2013 New Products Recap
Stop by your local distributor to give one a try

HYDRO TEK.US

Updates to AZV / RZV recovery & filtration system
- Rustproof, stainless vacuum box with drain
- Lift-out basket stainer replaces bag filter
- New stringwound replaceable filters
- Same small footprint, 5-10gpm process rate

For current Specials, go to www.hydrotek.us click 'what's new'

Redesigned surface cleaners
- Octagon and square decks, giving you an angle over your competition
- Splash reducing brush on rear of deck
- Contractor Twister is now 4-in-1 tool: edger, gum spotter, water broom, surface cleaner
- Hydro Vacuum surface cleaner picks up even better with its new vacuum ring

Two Honda models added to the SS Series product line
Available as a 3500psi @ 5.5gpm or 4000psi @ 4.8gpm
Belt drive pump and PowerLight 12v burner module

All the Best Things You've Come to Expect From Us
- Wash Skids & Trailers
- Electric, Hot Washers
- Wash Accessories

Brilliant Design, Tough on Grime

Manufacturing pressure washers and wash accessories for over 25 years.
Visit website or call for a distributor near you. Distributor inquiries welcome.

www.hydrotek.us   (800) 274-9376

Networking – Why Bother?

by Tony Evans, A New View Window Cleaning, www.windowcleaningschool.blogspot.com

Most business owners have barely enough time in the day as it is without the thought of spending time talking to other cleaners on the Internet or at events. In fact I've talked to a growing number of cleaners who just want to do their own thing and be left alone. Maybe you are feeling the same way – *why bother*? Let's examine some pros and cons to networking and see if you can benefit from it as a cleaner and/or business owner.

Downsides

First we'll start with what might be considered the downsides of networking (either in person or on the net).

Drama – unfortunately with business owners there can often be personality conflicts that can quickly escalate. Add to this that on social networking sites we often form groups of friends and while this can be good it can mean more people involved in a disagreement between two individuals increasing the drama and conflict.

No emotional fonts – It may seem silly but when we type something on the keyboard there is not always a way for the reader to distinguish the emotional content of your words. This can and often does lead to misunderstandings which in turn lead to more drama.

Anonymity – On some social media sites you often don't really know who you are talking to. Are they a real cleaner? Are they located in your service area? This factor can lead to a false bravado encouraging the individual to say things they wouldn't if you were face to face which in turn can add to the existing drama.

Time and expense – If we opt for face to face networking at events then we have the time and expense of travel, hotels, food, and taking a couple days off work. Depending on your business model this may or may not be a large issue.

Benefits

Now let's talk about the benefits networking can offer to those willing to accept its limitations.

Hands on experiences – With all the networking events I've attended there is always a portion set aside for the attendees to get their hands on or at least see in person the tools of the trade. This benefit can't be emphasized enough for those who are contemplating adding an expensive tool to the business.

Clear communication – There is something to be said for the ability to talk face to face with cleaners who are facing the same issues (maybe even tougher ones) as you. At networking events you have the opportunity to get in depth answers to some of those tricky problems you've wanted to ask without having to type out a small novel to get answered.

Global experience – Going back to online networking we get a broader knowledge base to deal with problems or just tweak our business model. For instance not every country has the same standards for cleaning frequencies. Maybe by talking to cleaners in different countries you will try a different approach that could lead to a new market and more money.

Real time answers – One major benefit to online networking has to be the ability to get real time answers. Remember with the advent of smart phones and tablets we have access to our online groups while we are in the field. I know I've been able to email, text, or call (yeah some of us still us phones as phones) when I had a question or problem and I've had many reach out to me as well.

Is It For You?

The answer is – maybe. We all have different goals, family commitments, values, and time constraints. Too, anything we do in life is only as successful or useful as the effort we put into it. To get the full benefit of networking you'd have to get involved and see for yourself the way it can enhance your business. I'm sure that this article won't sway you into jumping online or booking a flight to the next networking event but maybe it's given you pause for thought. And after all that too is a benefit of networking – knowledge.

Tony Evans and his wife own and operate A New View Window Cleaning, which offers window cleaning, house washing, roof cleaning and scratched glass restoration. He will be hosting the 5th Annual Midwest Conference, July 19-20, in Des Moines, Iowa. Read more about this event on page 25.

3 Tips for "Streak-Free" Business Networking

by Larry Miller, owner of Larry Miller, Inc. & IWCA Board Member

Power networking for your business is a lot like professional window cleaning. It's a skill you learn that gives you an advantage to see opportunities clearly. Networking isn't just about business. It's about building relationships. Today, meeting face-to-face is more memorable and a stronger way of getting to know people. Especially in this fast-paced, high tech environment. Here are three tips I suggest that you use in your strategy to help sustain and grow your window cleaning business.

1) Join your local chamber of commerce and become an active member. Participate at networking events where you can meet members, exchange business cards and get to know each other. Find out more about people you connect with and help them find leads for what they're looking for. The more you help them, the more they'll remember you.
2) Many chambers also have "leadshare" groups. Find out if your chamber does and go visit one or two leadshare groups. When you find a group that feels friendlier and more comfortable for you, join and start building relationships.
3) Get to know more about non-profit charities that have activities going on in your local community. Help sponsor an event that shows you care about a cause and support it. For instance, my company (Larry Miller, Inc.) supports The Daffodil Ball (http://www.thedaffodilball.com/) and Habitat for Humanity (www.loudounhabitat.org/).

PWNA Vendor Profile

Seal 'n Lock

by Allison Hester

In 1989, when pavers were just becoming popular, Rich Colletti owned a small landscaping supply and paver installation business in the Northeast.

Pavers – a.k.a. interlocking concrete pavements – are a "special dry mix, pre-cast piece of concrete commonly used in exterior hardscaping pavement applications" (Wikipedia). Pavers are used in patios, walkways, driveways and other outdoor hard services. Pavers "are installed over a compacted stone sub-base and a leveling bed of sand." The sand particles are used instead of grout to stabilize the pavers, which allows for a little breathing room so the pavers do not crack, break or buckle as easily as poured concrete.

That's not to say pavers are without problems!

When Rich and his family moved to Florida in 2003, he was introduced to paver sealing, which provides a barrier to protect the paver from wearing down to the aggregate. Some sealers also stabilize the joint sand, which tends to dissipate with time, causing the pavers to move.

However, in those days, paver sealing was causing huge problems. "There had been nothing but complaints and lawsuits from pavers turning white, and probably a 95 percent failure rate in the sealing industry," he explained.

Because Rich had spent several years as a contractor and was very familiar with the use of pavers, he was asked by a Florida-based paver manufacturer to see if he could correct the sealing-related problems. That's when Rich entered into the sealing industry.

After studying what was available on the market, he realized that "with all the products available, there was no way contractors could be successful in sealing." Instead, he took a differnt approach altogether, creating a new type of sealing system now known as Seal 'n Lock.

The Introduction of Seal 'n Lock

For the past nine years, Rich has focused on creating products that are different from those one the market. He worked with three different chemists to create the Seal 'n Lock "All in One Day Process," which made it possible for contractors to pressure wash, re-sand, and apply two coats of sealer within one day.

Additionally, Seal 'n Lock products:

Are non-toxic. Whereas a solvent-based

sealer has 600 grams per liter of volatile organic compounds (VOCs), Seal 'n Lock's Super Wet 2-Part Urethane has 31 grams.

Eliminate the downtime between cleaning and sealing. Most products on the market require the contractor to pressure wash one day, then wait to allow plenty of drying time, then return to seal. This, in turn, leads to the next advantage.

Abolish the problems with pavers turning white from moisture. As Rich explained, the long wait time between cleaning and sealing leads to other issues. "The problem is that the moisture and/or upcoming rains will turn pavers white." The Seal 'n Lock product removes the need to wait and prevents the pavers from turning white due to trapped moisture.

Stabilize the sand joints. If the sand joints are not stabilized, the pavers start to move and fail. "The sand is the final interlock," Rich explained. Standard acrylic-based solvent products seal but don't stabilize. Water-based joint-stabiliation sealers do not provide the sealing enhancement that customers desire. Seal 'n Lock does both – seal and stabilize. Additionally, Seal 'n Lock's "ultra low water base system" enhances the longevity of the paver protection, leading to happier customers.

Working with Pressure Washing Contractors

For the past seven years, Seal 'n Lock has worked with pressure washing contractors and organizations such as the PWNA. (They are also members of the UAMCC, International Concrete Paver Institute, the Southern Society for Coatings Technology, and the Florida Paint & Coatings Association.)

"The pressure washing contractors have been the best market for us. They already have the equipment, they know how to clean properly, and many of their customers already have concrete and pavers," said Rick. "Adding our sealing system as an add-on to their business has been a great match, and makes us both successful."

When Rich entered the paver sealing industry 10 years ago, there was no training

available from any company – "and that has been the biggest part of the failure rate.," he explained. "I realized that as easy as our products are to use, education and training still play a big part in success. So, our policy is not to hand a pail of sealer to a contractor without training and technical support." And Seal 'n Lock offers technical support 24/7.

Seal 'n Lock provides free training seminars around the country, and will be leading part of the PWNA's Flatwork certification course during this Fall's Annual Conference and Trade Show, October 17 through 19 in Orlando. "I always believed in education as the key answer for anyone's success. The PWNA provides strong educational offerings and I want us to be part of it," he stressed.

More on the Horizon

Seal 'n Lock recently added a research and development chemical engineer from Europe – "probably one of the best chemists in the world" – and built a new blending facility earlier this year. As such, the company has never been stronger or had more to offer.

"Now we are producing photocatalytic coatings, anti-graffiti coatings, our bio-Stripper, degreasers – and have much more to come," Rich explained. "We have always taken pride in building a product as a contractor for a contractor, and not just a bucket of 'marketing margins' or 'stuff on the shelf.'"

To learn more about Seal 'n Lock's company and products, visit their website at www.SealNLock.com. To register for the PWNA's Flatwork/Paver Sealing certification course in October, visit www.PWNA.org.

eClean Magazine

PWNA Flat Work Certification

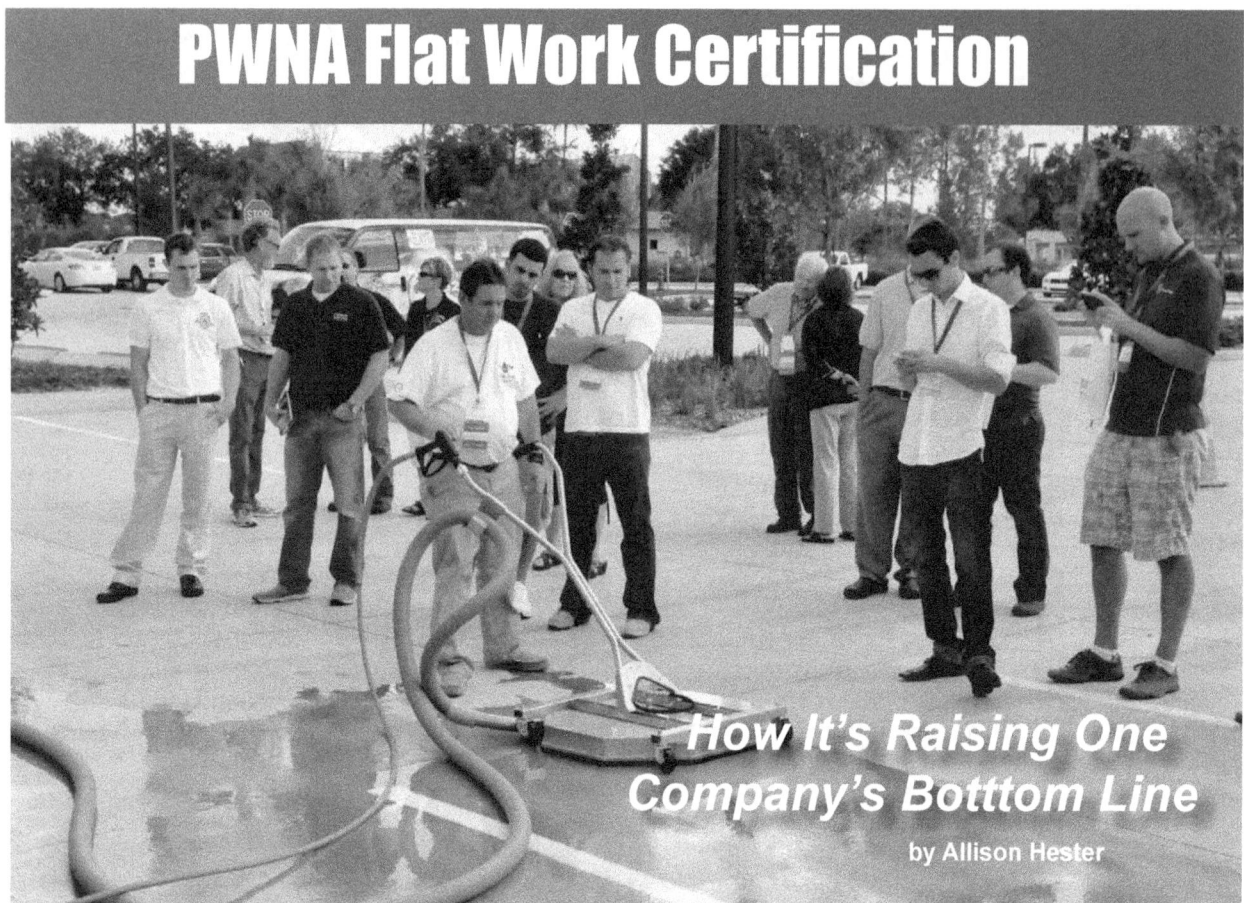

How It's Raising One Company's Botttom Line
by Allison Hester

Do PWNA Certifications really add to your bottom line? They do if you're Perfect Power Wash in Akron, Ohio.

Last Fall, Aaron Carter – the company's sales manager – took the Seal 'n Lock Authorized Technician & PWNA Certification Course during the Power Washers of North America's Annual Convention in Orlando. As a result, flatwork calls and sales have increased by 30 percent.

"Perfect Power Wash has always done a lot of flatwork, but before taking the certification course, we didn't know many of the technical aspects of flatwork cleaning," Carter explained. "We didn't know the ins and outs of rust stains. We weren't clear on the drying time for sealers. And so on."

Carter, who is in charge of the company's sales, has been able to take what he learned and turn it into literal dollars by being able to better educate customers, and in turn, close the deal. Also, he has passed on his PWNA training to the company's local technicians which helps them better communicate with customers while on the job. "Now we can really educate our customers on why what we do works, or when something isn't going to work, we can let them know why. It's given us a huge advantage over our competition."

The Value of Flat Work Certification

In late May, Fox News in McAllen, Texas ran an article entitled "How to Get Grease off of a Driveway." One of the author's main tips was to "NEVER" use a pressure washer on a driveway. (He also said the best way to remove grease was with dish soap and a brush.)

A day or so later, a radio program in Las

Vegas interviewed a pressure washing company live on the air. The first words out of the contractor's mouth were spent explaining how a pressure washer has the power to completely destroy a driveway.

These are two examples of what appears to be a growing trend in publicizing the hazards of using a pressure washer on concrete. And there are legitimate reasons for it. In untrained hands, a pressure washer can damage concrete – leaving pits, stripes, discoloration…or worse.

However, when handled correctly, a pressure washer is the most efficient way for cleaning flat concrete surfaces. And yet these scare tactics about the hazards of pressure washing concrete may understandably leave customers confused. "But I read that power washers destroy concrete."

If the power washing contractor tells the customer his practices are safe, it's one thing. If, however, the contractor can educate his customer on why the practices are safe, then show the customer that he has been trained specifically in flatwork cleaning and has been certified by the nation's premier national pressure washing association, then that puts the contractor in much more trustworthy position. That's the power of certification.

The PWNA Certification Course

Each of the PWNA certification courses follows a similar outline, covering these topics as related to the specific type of cleaning:
1. Background of service
2. Economic Opportunity of service
3. Chemicals, detergents and cleaners
4. Equipment
5. Cleaning Process
6. Water Reclamation
7. Safety
8. Pricing
9. Advertising
10. Available add on service

In addition to cleaning flatwork, the PWNA course also delves into sealing concrete. This is an add-on service that has grown exponentially over the past few years, and a natural add-on for pressure washing contractors.

Because paver sealing is a related market that is a real money maker for some contractors, and because Seal 'n Lock already had a quality technician training program in place (See the Seal 'n Lock vendor profile article on page 16), the Seal 'n Lock Technician Training Course has been added to the PWNA Flat Work Certification program.

"I always believed in education as the key answer for anyone's success," explained Seal 'n Lock founder Rich Colletti. "Because PWNA is offering quality education, I want us to be part of it."

Is the PWNA Flat Work Certification for everyone? "It's for everyone – newcomers and veterans alike – who do flatwork cleaning and want to separate themselves from the competition," explained Charlie Arnold of Arnold's Powerwash in Lewes, Delaware, who helped create and teach the course. "No matter how long you've been cleaning, you can always find a new nugget or two of information that you can apply to your business, as long as you're willing to listen for it."

Carter agreed. "None of the competition around here is certified. They just are spraying off the concrete, applying sealer, but not able to explain why. Certification has placed Perfect Power Wash in a league of its own."

> The Seal 'n Lock Authorized Technician & PWNA Flat Work Certification Course will be offered during the PWNA's annual convention, October 17 through 19, in Orlando, Florida. To learn more or to register, go to www.PWNA.org, email info@pwna.org or call 800-393-7962.

The following PWNA members have received PWNA certification since October 2012:

Aaron Carter
Perfect Power Wash, Akron, OH
Fleet Washing; House Washing; Flatwork

Alvin E. Figueroa
A & M Fire and Safety Equipment, Apopka, FL
House Washing; Roof Cleaning; Flatwork; Environmental

Barry Marno
New Finish Power Washing, Calgary, AB
Fleet Washing

Ben Enneking
Enneking Pressure Cleaning, Inc., Batesville, IN
Wood Restoration

Charles Puglisi
Absolute Fleet Wash,Riverhead, NY
Fleet Washing; House Washing; Flatwork

Clint Reynolds
HydroTech Solutions, Lake Mary, FL
Environmental; House Washing; Roof Cleaning

Curtis Hunsinger
Klean King Services, Inc., The Woodlands, TX
Environmental; House Washing

Dan Galvin
East Coast Power Washing, Buzzards Bay, MA
Fleet Washing

Doug Alderink
Cleaner Imagem, Irving, TX
Environmental

Drew Johnson
Klean King Services, Inc., The Woodlands, TX
Roof Cleaning

Frank DiBenedetto
Mr. Grime, Mt. Sinai, NY
Environmental; Roof Cleaning

Glenn McFarland
Maddie & Daddie Pressure Washing, Winter Garden,FL
Roof Cleaning

Gus Mejia
Mr. Grime, Mt. Sinai, NY
Fleet Washing; House Washing

Guy Triger
Puma Power Washing, Day City, CA
Environmental; Fleet Washing; House Washing

Jean-Blaise Kiza
Lakeland Professional Services Ltd.,Cold Lake, AB
Environmental; House Washing; Wood Restoration

Jerome Khan
Clean Image Limited, St. James, Port of Spain
House Washing; Roof Cleaning

Jesse (Shay) Juban
Juban's Pressure Washing LLC, Walker, LA
Fleet Washing; House Washing; Roof Cleaning; Flatwork

John Tornabene
Clean County Powerwashing, Kings Park, NY
Environmental

Joseph Luck
Absolute Fleet Wash, Riverhead, NY
Environmental; Fleet Washing; House Washing

Josh Born
Oberlin, OH
Environmental; Fleet Washing; House Washing; Roof Cleaning

Kamren Kaloi
Oahu Power Wash, Honolulu, HI
Environmental

Kyle Nebeker
Riverbend, Lindon , UT
Environmental; House Washing; Wood Restoration

Michael Krakower
Quality Pressure Cleaning Solutions, Sunrise, FL
House Washing; Roof Cleaning; Flatwork

Michael Palubiak
Perfect Power Wash, Akron, OH
Environmental; Roof Cleaning; Wood Restoration

Mike Westerfield
The Gutter Boys, Berea, OH
House Washing; Roof Cleaning; Wood Restoration

Neil Matheson
Sparkleen, Toronto, ON
Wood Restoration

Nevin Mast
Holmes Siding Contractors, Millersburg, OH
House Washing; Roof Cleaning

Paul Laramee
Exquisite Finishes, Warwick, RI
Fleet Washing; House Washing

Rob Alderink
Cleaner Image, Irving, TX
Environmental

Rudy Palmer
Optimal Powerwashing LLC, Philadelphia, PA
Flatwork

Scott Klein
Riverbend, Lindon, UT
Fleet Washing; Roof Cleaning; Flatwork

Shaun Downham
Oahu Power Wash, Honolulu, HI
Environmental

Stewart Esposito
Absolutely Clean, Raleigh,NC
House Washing; Wood Restoration; Flatwork

Thomas Heasley
Cleaner Image LLC, Roanoke, VA
House Washing; Wood Restoration

Ty Eubanks
South Shore Building Services Inc., Anaheim, CA
Fleet Washing; Flatwork

Wilfredo Gutierrez
C&W Cleaning Service Inc., Arlington, TX
Fleet Washing; House Washing; Roof Cleaning; Wood Restoration

Commercial Power Washing Equipment: Types of Trigger Guns

by Paul Horsley, Editor

It may surprise you to learn that the earliest power washers did not have trigger guns at all. The original commercial pressure washer was very simple: It was composed of a hose connected to a nozzle. That's it. There was no way to stop the spray, other than turning off the water flow. How challenging it must have been back then to prevent the high-power spray from going berserk while you went to turn off the hose!

Today's commercial power washing equipment is significantly more sophisticated. Even so, the technology behind pressure washer triggers is pretty simple. A spring inside the trigger holds a ball in place, blocking the flow of water. When the trigger handle is compressed, the spring is released and the water is able to push the obstructive ball out of the way.

With this design, it is guaranteed that a pressure washer will turn off if the trigger is dropped. This is very important because power washing equipment is extremely strong – some models can emit in excess of 30,000 pounds of pressure per square inch. Without a spring-loaded trigger, an unmanned power washer would flip-flop around like a fish out of water and could easily hurt nearby people or cause serious damage to property. This is why some states have statutes banning the taping or tying of power washer triggers in the open position.

There are several trigger options for your commercial pressure washer, as explained below. We've also included a few tips on how to choose the best commercial power washing equipment for your needs.

Commercial Pressure Washer Options: Types of Trigger Guns

Front-entry guns: The hose enters the gun just before the trigger, underneath the wand mounting. These are usually best for at-home use, as they're inexpensive but of too low quality for commercial applications.

Pistol-style guns: This is the most common type of commercial trigger. If you buy commercial power washing equipment off the shelf at home improvement stores, you will almost certainly end up with this type of trigger. If you want a versatile gun for many different angles and applications, this trigger offers the most comfortable arrangement for the wrist. Walls, fences, equipment and some overhead work can be done with this trigger.

Straight-through guns: This trigger does not change the angle of the flow, as is the case with a pistol gun; rather, the water goes straight through the trigger. If you do lots of overhead and wall work, choose a straight-through trigger, which offers the best angle for these jobs.

Weep guns: This trigger type allows a little water to flow through the pressure washer even when the trigger is released. It's a good choice if you don't want an unloader valve, as the minimal water flow even when the trigger is not activated removes the need for one.

Open guns: Some steam-based commercial pressure washers do not have a trigger, as shutting off the steam flow can cause dangerous levels of heat and pressure to build up. The only way to shut them down is to turn the machine off at the source.

As with most power washing equipment, triggers must be replaced from time to time. Many commercial pressure washer manufacturers offer trigger replacement kits.

Lessons from the Sales Rack

by Allison Hester

Have you ever made a mistake?

Of course you have, and fortunately, so have your customers. That's good news because it means your customers can empathize with you when you mess up – not that they always will. But how you respond to your mistakes can play a big role in how your customers respond to you.

Perhaps no one knows this more right now than JCPenney. The 100-year-old department store implemented a number of changes last year, and they weren't well received – causing a $4 billion loss for the company. Ouch! While analysts are still delving into the exact reasons for the loss, the primary problem was that in their attempt to reach a younger, hipper audience, they neglected their core clientele, and the customers quit buying.

In early May, Penney's launched an online ad campaign where they did the unthinkable – they apologized! Whether it will be enough to save the company is yet to be seen, but early indications are positive.

So how can this apply to you (and me)? I believe there are several lessons here.

Customers don't really care WHY you mess up; they just want you to make it right.

And making it right begins with admitting when you were wrong.

This often goes agains human nature, where we naturally want to make excuses, point fingers and place blame. "My technician called in sick." "My equipment gave out on me." "We ran out of time." And so on. That's not to say these things don't happen, but it still doesn't right the wrong of not fulfilling your end of the bargain. So start with an apology, then figure out how to fix the situation as best as possible.

The following are two true stories.

First, on our "Cleaning in the News Page," we recently mentioned a newspaper "consumer watchdog" columnist who took on a complaint about a local roof cleaning contractor. The customer was very happy with the way his roof came out, but claimed that the roof cleaning chemicals used killed $600 in plants. The roof cleaner, in turn, said he had verbally explained to the homeowner when to water the plants and what to do if it rained versus didn't rain. (The instructions apparently were somewhat complicated.) Verbal instructions or not, the plants died. The unhappy customer took the matter to the newspaper, and the watchdog columnist sided with the homeowner. Now the roof cleaner's reputation has been soiled publically in his local community and across the Internet... over $600.

Now for the second example. In his book *The Pressure Cleaning Marketing Bible*, Steve Stephens talks about an EXPENSIVE mistake that still pains him to think about today.

His technicians were washing an expensive-neighborhood's houses for an upcoming parade of homes. One of the houses had sandy-faced brick. While Stephens had trained his technicians on how to clean this delicate surface, one of his technicians apparently spaced off and before he realized what he had done, he had removed the sand from the lovely pink-colored brick, changing the house's color to red! What did Stephens do? He spent over $25,000 out of his pocket (it was not covered by insurance) to have the messed up bricks corrected. Ouch!

Expensive mistake? Absolutely. BUT, as word traveled about the way Stephens handled the situation, he ended up gaining several new homeowner's associations and new construction companies as clients.

Customers want you to listen to what they say!

This is perhaps the most powerful line from the JCP commercial: "We learned a very simple thing: to listen to you, to hear what you need, to make your life beautiful."

As contract cleaners, your job is to make your customers' lives beautiful! Whether that's by giving them a gorgeously cleaned and sealed deck, or by attracting customers to their businesses because the sidewalks are washed, you are making their lives better. But are you listening to what the customers have to say? Perhaps an even better question is whether you are even asking?

I know of at least one window cleaning that bases their technicians' promotions and raises, in part, not only on what kind of survey responses they get back, but how many they get back. It's that important. So, are you asking – *really* asking – your customers for feedback? If not, why not? Is it because you just haven't taken the time to implement this essential practice, or are you perhaps afraid of what you'll find out?

Customers want to feel valued.

The JCPenney commercial concluded with these words: "Come back to J.C. Penney. We heard you. Now we'd love to see you." It is clear throughout the video that Penney's realized they cannot exist without their customers. Do your customers feel this way? Do you follow up after your services to see if they have any questions or problems? Do you send thank you cards? Do you extend special offers to your best customers?

All of these things increase intimacy and connection with your customers. In turn, they also make your customers more apt to forgive you if and when problems do arise.

eClean Magazine

5th Annual Midwest Cleaning Event

July 19-20, Des Moines, Iowa

Tony Evans of A New View Window Cleaning is joining forces this year with the National Cleaning Expo (NCE) to host the 5th Annual Midwest Cleaning Event, July 19 through 20 in Des Moines, Iowa.

Developed for pressure washing, window cleaning, roof cleaning and soft washing professionals, this FREE two-day event is designed to provide attendees with plenty of educational and networking opportunities.

"My biggest goal is always education," explained Evans, who decided a few years ago there needed to be some sort of event held in his area of the country. "At this year's event, attendees will be overwhelmed with opportunities to gain knowledge on tools, techniques, and business – no matter what field of cleaning they are in."

Specifically, this year's event will include the following presentations:
- Networking Your Way to the Top, Jason Evers,
- Facebook is for Kids, Jason Evers
- How to Write a Winning Commercial Proposal, AC Lockyer
- Commercial Sales: 500 Companies and Property Management, by Ron Musgraves
- Window Cleaning for Pressure Washers, Tony Evans
- Pressure Washing for Window Cleaners, Randy Borio
- Pure Water System Maintenance
- Pressure Washer Pump Maintenance, Paul Kassander
- Proper Chemical Storage
- Work Truck Safety and Compliance
- Ladder, Harness and Rappelling Safety and Compliance
- Extension Ladders vs. Sectional Ladders
...and more

The event will also include a number of how-to and product comparisons such as:
- Window Cleaning
- Pressure Washing
- Using the IPC Screen Cleaner
- Properly Setting Up a Water Fed Pole

"This event is a must attend for anyone that is serious about growing their business," said Randio Borio of Panther Outdoor Maintenance Services, Inc., Granville, Illinois, who first attended the Midwest conference last year. "As business owners, we often talk about how important it is to educate our customers, but we often forget that we need to educate ourselves first. Top quality speakers and true industry leaders will be at this event to share what they know to help others get better faster."

While Evans says he sees value in all networking opportunities, he believes "that we will hold what will prove to be the preeminent educational event of the summer, maybe even the year. The level of speakers and variety of demos we will have has truly amazed me. I'm so grateful for the Industry leaders who have volunteered time - and expense -- to speak. The real winners here will be the attendees."

To learn more about the upcoming event, visit their Facebook page: https://www.facebook.com/events/136091109900754/?fref=ts

eClean Magazine

Marine Cleaning Requires Smart Equipment Choices

by Steel Eagle, www.SteelEagle.com

Marine cleaning may very well be one of the most diverse areas of the contract cleaning business. Cruise ships pretty much have all the needs of a small city, with cleaning jobs ranging from waste disposal to maintaining heavy equipment, food service cleaning, and surface cleaning. Maintaining docks and port areas, and many other specialty jobs are also needed. After thinking about all these things, don't forget to factor in that these jobs will be complicated by some of the most difficult environmental obstacles – salt, humidity, access/portability and EPA regulations.

Having the equipment and know-how to offer many different kinds of services will place you above your competition. You also want to promote efficiency – both for your customers' satisfaction and your labor costs.

So what do you need to be prepared to say "YES" to any request made by these customers? Have the specialty tools needed to do the job.

Where should you start?

Self-contained Vacuum and Pressure Washing Systems. With marine cleaning, portability is key. Being able to trailer mount or boat mount your cleaning system is a must. You also need your system to be both durable and powerful.

Another consideration is the need to capture wastewater. Many circumstances demand (either by law or location) capturing and removing wastewater created by the cleaning process. These washing systems do just that.

There are oher things to think about, and they are things we considered when developing our Fury System. Some things you may want to consider is choosing a system, such as Fury, that has the following features:

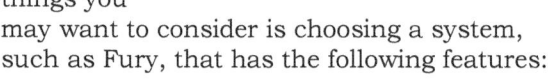

• Powder coated steel frames and cabinets to protect from the harshest conditions.

• A range of top quality powerful engines (gas or diesel) by Honda, Kohler and Isuzu.

• Large capacity fuel tanks for longer run jobs that are further out.

- Belt driven vacuum blowers.

- The capability of capture tools up to 24".

- Capture hose lengths up to 600' for even the most access challenging jobs.

- Quality hose reels.

- Vacuum tools, for both horizontal and vertical cleaning.

The most imporan thing is to make sure the system you choose is the system and accessories that will fit you best. Give us a call and explain your particular set of needs and we will build you a system that is suited just for you.

We understand your time is important and you need the correct product for your application. Take a minute to discuss your particular cleaning situations with your Steel Eagle salesperson. They can recommend the perfect system utilizing the correct accessories for the job. No matter what you are cleaning, Steel Eagle has a system that will do the job with ease and speed.

eClean Magazine

Classifieds: Products & Services

www.ArmClark.com
Armstrong Clark Quality Wood Stains. Specializing in wood restoration, oil-based coatings for wood & non-toxic wood stains of all kinds for your wood shake restoration & water repellant needs. 800-916-8211

www.PowerWash.com
Mobile power wash equipment, schools, training, videos, environmental supplies & maintenance services. Call for a free catalog, 800-433-2113.

www.PowerWashStore.com
Bigger Selection - Better Quality - Amazing Customer Service. Serving the professional cleaning community for more than 25 years. Call 855-351-9274.

www.PWNA.org
Power Washers of North America. For certification or membership information, visit our website, email info@pwna.org, or call 800-393-7962. Annual Trade Show and Convention, Oct. 17-19, Orlando, Fla.

www.SteelEagle.com
Mfr. of World Class Industrial & Commercial Cleaning & Storage Products, including surface spinners, vacuum systems, undercarriage cleaners, hose reels & more. Custom designs available. 800-447-3924

www.PressureWasherKy.com
Southside Equipment multi-line power equipment distributor. Pressure cleaning equipment, waste water recovery & recycling, generators & cleaning chemicals. Quality products & impeccable service. 888-243-6506

To Advertise in our New Classifieds Section
Contact Kelly Jacobsen

kelly@ecleanmag.com

Bring in the Bounty:
Spring Cleaning Exposed

by Rick Meehan
Vice President of Marko Janitorial Supply, www.MarkoInc.com

Okay, so you've got some steady clientele and your cleaning business is on a roll. That's great, wonderful, and superb! But, are you milking those clients for all they are worth? Git it whilst the git'ins good – as long as it is mutually beneficial. That's my motto. Well? They don't call it "spring cleaning" for nothing! Now is the time to ask for extra work from those steady accounts, not to lay back and soak up the sunshine while your competitor garners your business.

For those of you who mainly contract for outside cleaning, get some inside jobs. Likewise, you domestic folks need to pull some extra profits from outside scrub-ups. This is called "adding on." Like, duh. The fact is, add-on services are the most overlooked profit centers for any type of business. You've already done the tough part by garnering customers from a fickle marketplace, so why haven't you continued to sell them on new stuff that you can do? Every season offers a different set of opportunities for adding on new cleaning jobs, but springtime beats them all!

Learning to ask for more business from existing customers is perhaps the most important aspect of keeping them. A contracting firm's public representative, whether it's the owner or a hired salesperson, is responsible for bringing in the bounty. So why is it that asking for more business is so difficult? It's not really, just overlooked. In the hustle and bustle of daily servicing, we forget that customers have to be engaged or else they get bored with us. To prevent a good customer from looking elsewhere for excitement, it is our representative's job to keep them busy – by stimulating them with new opportunities for cleanliness – especially in the spring/early summer.

Spring weather is good in several ways: the outside temperature is comfortable, the inside climate is looking outward at the return of greenery; people get the urge to make things happen; excitement fills the air. Remember how it was sitting in that classroom on a brilliant spring day, watching the rustling of the new leaves filled with chirping birds, feeling the sunshine through the window, while trying to concentrate on the latest algebra problem in a stuffy classroom with a stuffy teacher? (My

wife is a teacher, so she won't let me get away with this one.) Antsy! And, this is how your customers feel right now!

Take advantage of Spring Fever by offering up some extras to keep your customers focused on what you do for them; otherwise, your competitor might just sneak a foot in the door by offering to do these things in your stead. Don't forget that as add-on services, this means add-on charges too. Price and bill these things separately. Here's a short list of ideas:

- Window washing, both inside and out
- Concrete and sidewalk cleaning
- Extract winter mud from the carpets and entry mats
- Shine up the floors after a long winter's abuse
- Polish old brass door knobs
- Scrub ceramic tile and stone to remove wet weather grime
- Pressure clean the outside of the building
- Detail interior walls, especially around ductwork and doors
- Wash the outbuildings
- Minor to major landscaping projects
- Clients hate to deal with many different contractors
- If you don't handle yard maintenance, consider subcontracting
- Sweep the garage
- Box possessions for clients that may be moving
- Minor to major painting projects
- See above reasoning and partnering
- Minor building repair projects
- See above reasoning and partnering

A really wise thing to do would be to create a spring add-on flyer listing your extra services. Don't put prices on these handouts, though. Always create a special contract for special services, priced by the job.

Extra work during the spring is available right now, so once your list is complete, put it in the hands of your regulars pronto. When it comes to labor for the new work, pay overtime or hire more people. After all, spring only comes once a year. Besides, if your company can handle all of the spring cleaning needs of your clients, there is less of a chance that one of your competitors will be able to plunk a foot in your door. Of course, it is always best to stick with what you know. That's why I'm a proponent of continual education. If I don't know how to do it, I learn. Think of self-education as self-preservation.

Speaking of preservation, if your competitor isn't offering spring cleaning add-ons, you've been handed the Golden Opportunity to inch your foot in their door. As U.S. Attorney General Erik Holder once said, "You never want a serious crisis go to waste." That's exactly what it is when a competitor misses out on your Spring Cleaning Extravaganza – a crisis for them – so git it whilst the git'ins good!

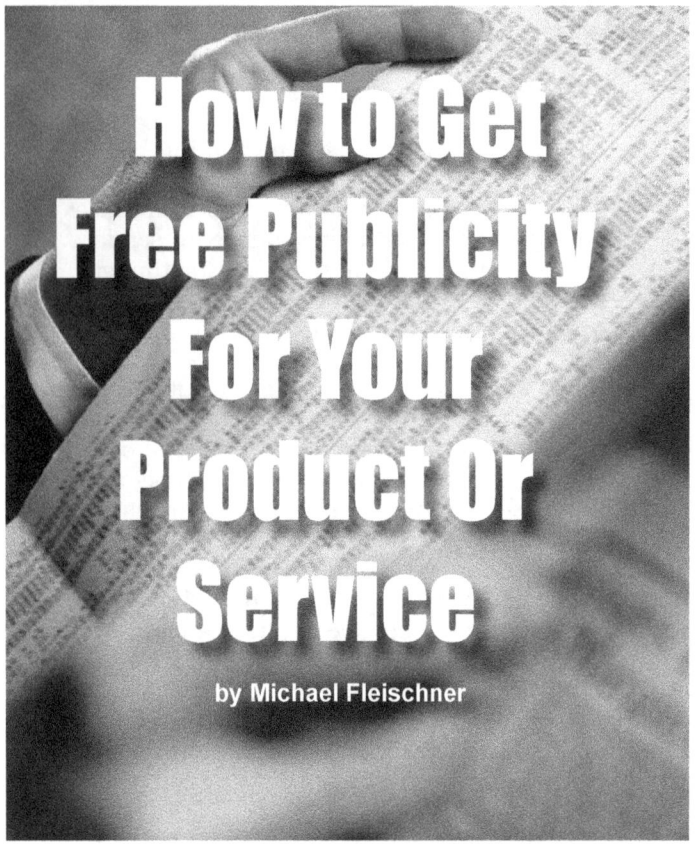

How to Get Free Publicity For Your Product Or Service

by Michael Fleischner

Have you ever wondered how some companies always seem to obtain good placement in print publications, online, and even on TV? What's even more impressive is that many of these companies don't even spend a single cent on advertising. Why would they? They're getting all of the media coverage they need simply by following a few basic public relations principles.

Position yourself as an expert.

The media relies on experts for their information. The news that gets printed is only as credible as the source from which it comes. Begin by selecting a news related story to comment on. It should be a story that you are qualified to speak about, aligned with your area of expertise.

If your background is in engineering, and a building falls down, you are qualified to speak about the structure and answer possible engineering related questions. Being an expert simply means that you have a background in a specific area and can lend your expertise.

Do your homework.

To get coverage, find the reporter who is covering the news you wish to comment on. For example, if the news is about a specific current event, then Google the current event name followed by the name of a popular newspaper like the Wall Street Journal or USA Today. You'll quickly find the reporters who have written on the subject. Call the newspaper (contact information available on their website) and ask for the reporter by name. If the operation asks what your call is in reference to, simply state that you have information related to a specific news item.

Compliment the reporter.

When you locate the reporter, and contact him, start with a compliment. Reporters take great pride in their work. Be sure to compliment their position on a given topic or their previous work. After complimenting them, you're ready for the pitch.

Talk to them about your position on the given news story and what you have to offer.

Again, referring back to our earlier example of the building, mention that you have an engineering background and have a position on the story. For example, you might be able to comment on why buildings collapse and the structural aspects that could be the cause. Let the reporter ask questions but have a point of view. After the dialogue, the reporter will verify your information such as name and company.

Leave a compelling yet non-descript message.

If you're unable to get in touch with the

eClean Magazine

reporter directly, leave a message – but be discreet. You don't want to show all of your cards before speaking to him directly. However, if you leave enough information to get them to return your call, they will call you. Reporters follow up with any leads they consider opportunistic.

When leaving a message, simple say, "I have something you need to hear about (fill in name of story here)." Be specific with regard to the story the reporter is covering. You want them to consider your possible information valuable.

State your expertise.

After complimenting the reporter about their coverage on a specific article or issue, let them know your position on a given topic and why you are qualified to comment on it. Give them your pitch and be confident that your opinion matters base on the experience you have to offer.

In today's environment, it's difficult to attract the media's attention. The best way to get PR for your product or service is by commenting on current stories being covered by the media. The process is simple. When you hear a news story that you can comment on, find the reporter using Google and the name of a major publication.

Read a few of the reporter's previous articles for background and then contact him directly.

Let him know that you have some information that he may find valuable or a comment relevant to the story. Be sure to provide him with your credentials. After just a few calls, you'll be quoted in some of today's leading media.

Michael Fleischner is an Internet marketing expert with more than 12 years of marketing experience. To discover how to improve search engine rankings on Google and other major search engines, visit http://goodmarketingtips.blogspot.com

Correct, Don't Break: Improving Your Skills

By Bill Kinnard

Why can't they just do what you asked them to? It's not that hard. You spent the time thinking through the processes you want them to use. Every time they pull up to a customer's home, they will park on the street, be prepared, know the customer's name, use it within the first 30 seconds of the conversation, wear shoe covers, etc., etc., etc. They just don't seem to get it. You asked them to do something – they work for you - they should just do it! Right? You have sat down with them a few times now and asked them to change but they still don't seem to get it. Can they be fixed?

Course Corrections Are a Part of the Job

As the leader of your company, you need to define the culture in your company. If your vision of what your company culture should look like differs from what it is, you will have some corrections to make in your team members. Correcting others is a critical skill that leaders need to develop. There are occasions where you need to be objective and non-emotional during difficult discussions. It's even harder to address performance issues or disciplinary matters.

A person who has not yet developed skills in correcting others could either tend to be too insensitive or harsh in correcting others. If you find yourself doing this, you likely also notice that you tend to view your employees or direct reports as simply "units of work." How they feel is irrelevant. On the other hand, you could be too sensitive and not willing to provide the constructive criticism or positive discipline required to develop and employee. If this is you, chances are you place too much emphasis on empathy and may be so sensitive to the feelings of others and put their emotions over the needs of correcting a problem. Either way, it's a problem.

On the other hand, a person who has developed his capacity in correcting others can usually provide constructive criticism to others in such a way that it is not received as insulting or degrading. The balance he exhibits in weighing the needs of the situation versus the needs of the people involved allows him to address both adequately.

This Is the Real Deal

Good skills in correcting others are directly related to your skills in other related areas. For example, if you have not established Key Results Areas or Key Performance Indicators for your employees, they have no clear job performance goals and therefore you have no good framework for discussing performance issues. Similarly, if you are not a motivator for your troops every day – a positive role model and coach – you will be much less successful at managing the same people during difficult times that require conflict management or disciplinary action.

Correcting others is not just about the "here and now" of a difficult situation. You can only be skilled at correcting others – and your corrections will be accepted by your employees – if you have their respect and trust at other times.

What Are the Skills Associated with Correcting Others?

Someone who has mastered the skills associates with correcting others:

- Remains calm and in control in an emotionally charged environment.

- Does not verbally or non-verbally confront others when the environment is different, demanding or emotional.

- Is able to resolve an issue and move past it unemotionally.

- Has the ability to confront controversial or difficult people or issues in an objective manner.

- Is able to identify alternative solutions and select the best option in the face of conflict.

- Is aware of, but not slave to, the feeling of disputing parties

- Can divorce personal allegiances and come to the best solution for all concerned.

- Is receptive to hearing both sides and all facts before jumping to any conclusions.

Managing employees can be a challenge. You need to be able to lead them, guide them and discipline them when necessary. At the same time, you don't want to end up running an adult daycare. You know what I'm talking about. Joe can't get along with Ben so you can't have them working together on a job. Lisa is having problems with her boyfriend and drags it into work every other day. It's during these times that you wish you are still a one man shop. At least then you didn't have to deal with this "Relational Garbage". At the same time, your employees can make your company what it is. They can help you create a culture that they all want to be a part of but you have to lead the way.

Listening Skills

Active listening is a key element in order to correct others objectively. I teach a program called "Providing Great Customer Service…In the Trenches" where I go through an exercise with the class on listening. I play one audio clip at the standard speaking rate, and a different clip at the standard listening rate. I ask the class to tell me specific information about each message. I have a bunch of service techs giving me specific information about a wine tasting event from a message that they just listened to at a rate of 350 words per minute. They do it with remarkable ease. The question I have is that if people speak at a rate of approximately 150 words per minute and they listen at a rate of 350 words per minute, what are they doing for the remaining 200 words per minute?

When involved in a difficult situation, many times you are preparing your rebuttal or thinking about your own viewpoint instead of what the other person is saying. Resist this urge. Focus on what the person is saying without immediately becoming defensive or judgmental.

Remember – You're All Involved

When dealing with employees who are in disagreement with others on your team, keep in mind that your goal is to help others work through difficult situations themselves in a calm and dignified manner. Help those involved define the problem issues. If tensions get high, suggest that you meet at a later time when everyone has "cooled off" a little. When you do get down to discussing the issue, have them search for a common goal on which they agree and define that goal clearly so both know what the outcome of the conversation is.

Handle conflict as an opportunity for collaborative resolution. If all parties are involved in the resolution, they will all have a vested interest in carrying it out – they all have buy-in. Don't try to WIN the argument. Try to see each disagreement as an opportunity to attain mutual satisfaction – even if it is in a slightly different way than what you had imagined. Unless the issue you are dealing with is in regard to a performance issue, remember to focus on that common goal and try to design an outcome that includes some things you want and some things the other person wants. If the issue is a disagreement between multiple people, make sure all parties are heard and ultimately get that buy-in from everyone involved.

Disciplinary Actions

The first thing to have in place when dealing with disciplinary actions of your team members is having Key Results Areas, or KRAs. What does success in this job look like? Every employee on your team should have their KRAs and they need to understand that this is what you expect from them. If they are not hitting their KRAs, they are falling short of your expectations. If your team members don't know what you expect from them, they don't know if they are missing the mark. Develop KRAs for each position in your company. From here, handling disciplinary actions become much easier. Think of yourself as a mentor or coach to your employees.

Here are a few points to keep in mind when dealing with a disciplinary issue:

Timeliness – Give regular feedback to your employees and team members. If you wait until the end of the year to do an annual performance evaluation, know that you are really missing the mark. If I did something wrong a year ago, and you are just now getting around to talking to me about it, you have allowed me to only further entrench that bad habit into my routine. What did that cost you? Give daily, positive feedback to employees and team members. Be specific and personal in your praise. This allows you to have the credibility to address problem areas when then arise. When they do, address issues immediately. Express criticisms in terms of specific job requirements and required behaviors.

Never Attack the Person – The problem is not the person, it's the behavior. If the problem is the person, they need to be invited to work somewhere else. If it's the behavior, look at performance issues as an opportunity to discuss job functions and make cooperative, beneficial improvements.

Make Recommendations for Corrective Action – Once you have allowed the employee to explain their perspective, discuss the job functions. Make recommendations for corrective action based on the discussion. Maybe you will find that the process needs to be modified. Both parties can suggest improvements to the process. If an improvement plan for the employee is needed, it is important to allow the employee to take part in developing the plan. They are more likely to implement the correction action if they were involved in creating it in the first place.

Action Steps – Once attainable action steps are determined, assign each of these steps to a person. Be sure to put each step in writing and assign a completion date. Having the "who," "what" and "when" in writing is important to correcting the performance issue. Everyone will know what is expected of them. Lastly, follow up on the action steps once they have been completed.

Correct the problem traits of your employees in a way that won't break their spirit. Part of this means you have to possess or develop the skills required to do this. You also need to know the communication strengths and weaknesses of your employees.

At Grandy & Associates, we can help you with this through our TEAM Solutions assessments. Know exactly how your employees' communicate, what gets them out of bed in the morning and what skills they possess that you can grow. We have redesigned our TEAM Solutions website. Now you can find short training videos and actual benchmarks and report samples that you can use and learn from. Contact us today to start using TEAM Solutions assessments with your team.

Play Business Like Golf
by George Hedley, Hard Hat Presentations

One of my dreams is to play the top 100 rated golf courses in the world. Often these courses are private country clubs that hold professional golf tournaments. To date, I have been fortunate to play over 30 of them. Every year, I look forward to "Golf Digest" magazine's new rankings to look for new courses I may be able to play.

No Targets?

Imagine getting invited to play golf at a brand new top golf course. You plan your trip for months and finally arrive excited. On the first tee you hit your first shot right down the middle around 240 yards. Not able to see the green yet, you hit a three wood down the left side of the fairway 215 yards. The green should be close now. As you approach your ball, you still can't see the green so you ask your playing partner for directions. He then informs you this course is unique as there are no greens, pins, or holes to aim at. Only a long fairway meandering through the beautiful countryside. The object of this four hour round is to enjoy the scenery and try your best. No score will be kept. Just golf all day until time to quit.

Can you imagine wanting to play golf without greens, targets, pins, or holes. Just hit the ball down the continuous fairway. Seems absurd doesn't it? Look at your business. Is it like this game of golf? Are there clear targets for everyone to shoot at?

Why Golf?

Think about the game of golf. It takes four plus hours to play in the hot sun fighting the elements. You hit a little white ball into the rough, lakes, traps, and out of bounds. You miss shots and look for lost balls. Every once in a while you hit a good shot, but you can always do better. What makes the game of golf so attractive or appealing to millions of crazy people?

Golf is a competitive and challenging game. There are lots of different shots, club selection is a personal choice, and the game is enjoyed with friends working towards a common goal. No matter what you shoot, you can always improve. The targets are clear and the greens are easy to see. Everyone knows exactly what they're shooting for. Par is a good score and everyone knows the rules and what's at stake.

Make Business Like Golf!

Do you play the game of business like golf? Do all of your employees, project managers, supervisors, foreman, field crews, business teams, departments and divisions know the rules? Do they have clear targets and know where the pin is placed every week? Is their game competitive and fun? Do they know when they make a par, birdie or bogey? Is there a reward for hitting a good shot or being successful? Most employees don't have clear targets. Without a scorecard or targets, there is no competition, no game or incentives to work harder, improve, or do more than the minimum. Work becomes the same old thing, month after month, year after year. No new terrain, targets, holes to play, or anything different.

To make your business more like the game of golf, give everyone clear targets to hit. Try one of these ideas: Weekly targets for most work installed, most product produced or shipped, most customer sales calls, most invoices processed, most bills paid, or most contracts let under budget. Monthly contests can include: most referrals, fewest service call-backs, fastest schedule, fewest crew days on a project, largest invoice, best new idea implemented, or most new sales leads. Quarterly achievements can include: most cost estimates, largest proposal, best customer service action, fewest accidents, most job profit, most man-hours saved versus the estimate, most new employees recruited, or accurate on-time job cost reports.

Add A Wager!

As a golfer, I always play better when there is a small wager on the game. The stakes don't have to be very high to keep my mind on the game. A $5.00 bet keeps me focused, improves my concentration, and lowers my score every time. Try adding small prizes to your business targets to get the team excited about winning the game. Simple and fun incentives work as well or often better than cash.

The list of ideas to target can be endless. The key to a good game of business is to shoot for something! Any target is better than no target. Keep them simple and clear. Align them towards your top business priorities. Involve everyone and have fun. To get your copy of a 'Business Targets & Goals' template, send an email to gh@hardhatpresentations.com. Playing business like golf is the perfect shot towards shooting par. Keep your head down, tee it high and watch them fly!

George Hedley works with contractors to build profitable growing companies. He is a professional business coach, popular speaker and best-selling author of "Get Your Business To Work!" available online at www.HardhatPresentations.com. To sign-up for his free e-newsletter, join his next webinar, be part of a BIZCOACH program, or get a $100 discount coupon for online classes at www.HardhatBizSchool.com, e-mail GH@HardhatPresentations.com

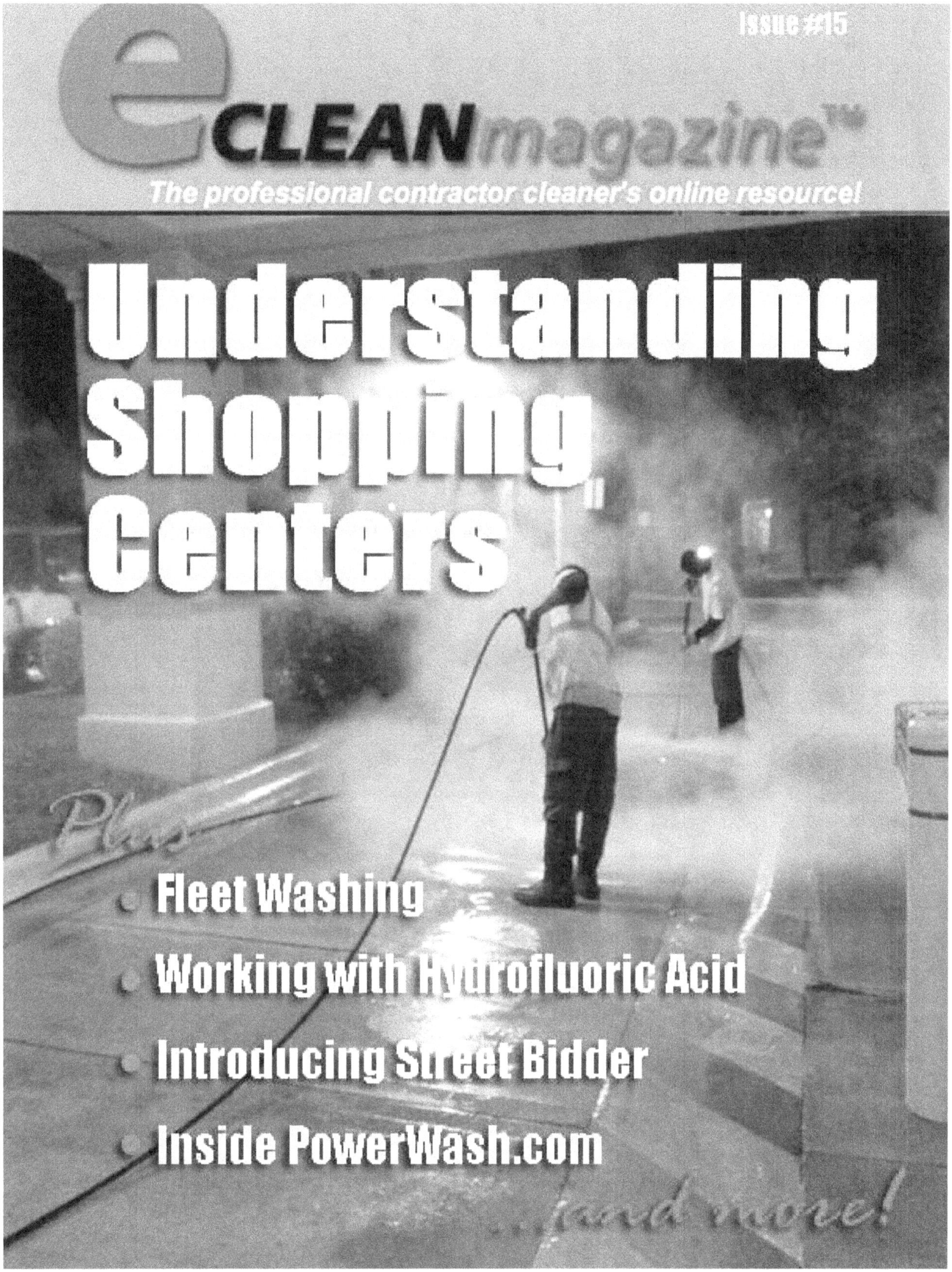

eCLEANmagazine™

The professional contractor cleaner's online resource!

Issue #15

Understanding Shopping Centers

Plus

- Fleet Washing
- Working with Hydrofluoric Acid
- Introducing Street Bidder
- Inside PowerWash.com

...and more!

POWERWASH.COM
SUPPLIES   CHEMICALS   TRAINING
1.800.433.2113
2513 Warfield St. Fort Worth, TX 76106

Click any item for more details

Pressure Washers

Surface Cleaners

Chemicals & Detergents

Cleaning Supplies

Parts & Accessories

Pumps & Unloaders

Training Materials

SPRAY TIPS Newsletter
Our SprayTips newsletter is packed with tips to help you build your business. Topics include tips for business management, marketing, equipment selection and best practices for increased efficiency.
Sign up at: www.PowerWash.com

V-502-C Grease and Grime Remover for Concrete(*)
New

A perfect choice for when you need to penetrate and route out heavy grease, soil and grime on parking lots, dumpster pads, drive thrus, and other high traffic concrete areas.

"V-502 is a really great cleaner to have in your arsenal. We have used it with pretty great success on oil stains and tire marks and have found it to not only clean, but also brighten significantly!"
Curt Kempton - 5StarWindowCare.com

DNB-1430 Degreaser (*)
A liquid cleaner formulated to penetrate and route out heavy grease, soil and grime on houses, concrete and masonry surfaces. Can be set at (100 to 1) to (50 to 1) depending on soil and grease conditions.

R-202 Concrete Cleaner
Cleans heavy grease, oil and scuff marks from unpainted concrete, brick, stone and other alkaline water safe surfaces. USDA authorized for use in meat, egg, dairy, food packing and processing plants. One 50 pound box makes 200 gal. of solution

Rust Remover Plus™
Rust Remover Plus™ is a perfect choice for removing tough oil and rust stains from concrete and exposed aggregate surfaces. Just spray it onto the concrete with a pump up garden or chemical sprayer and watch the rust and oil stains disappear. After a a 5 to 10 minute dwell time you can pressure wash the area with a 40 degree tip. Rust Remover Plus™ will brighten the concrete as it dries.

(*) Denotes $27.00 shipping surcharge by UPS.

Chapin Degreaser Sprayer
This poly sprayer features an auto/manual high pressure relief valve, SealTite acid and chemical-resistant gaskets and a wide opening for easy filling and cleaning. An adjustable polycone nozzle allows a range of spraying from fine mist to a coarse stream.

Chapin Degreaser Sprayer
- Built-in relief valve pressure gauge for added safety
- The container and discharge assembly have no fiberglass additives, only pure virgin grade material which stands up to acidic cleaners
- Available in ½ or 1 gallon sizes

Industrial Concrete Sprayer
- TriPoxy coated Sprayer with Viton Seals for the Concrete Professional (Chapin's Most Popular Industrial Sprayer)
- Large Tri-Lock opening
- Brass Spray handle and wand bottle
- Brass Pump

Steel Eagle Surface Cleaners
Use the force generated by your pressure washer to spin two spray nozzles at high speeds, which maximizes cleaning on flat surfaces. It produces consistent quality and cuts cleaning time by as much as 66%. It also decreases operator fatigue.
There are two models available.
- B models have a brass swivel, Max PSI-4,000, Max Temp-200°F, Max Flow-5.5GPM
- D models have a stainless steel swivel, Max PSI-4,000, Max Speed-2000RPM, Max Temp-200°F, Max Flow-6 GPM

Specify GPM, and Pressure when ordering

Deublin Swivel
- NPT Hose Connection
- 3/4-16 UNF Rotor Thread Size
- Union Size
- Standard Seal Connection
- Max Temperature: 200 F
- Max Speed: 2000 RPM
- Max PSI: 4000 PSI
- Maximum Flow: 4 GPM

Whisper Pro Big Guy Platinum Series Surface Cleaner with FREE! Cleaner Pack

The Whisper Wash Big Guy Surface Cleaner incorporates a signature balance and machine spray bar with a wide surface coverage area. The Big Guy's pivoting wheel design and a heavy-duty nylon brush provide for easy navigation through large areas while still containing the pressurized spray. The Platinum Series of Whisper Pro Surface Cleaners offers:
- A One-Piece Unitized Swivel Cartridge
- A One-Year Full Coverage Warranty
- 5000 PSI Max Working Pressure
- 212° F Max Working Temperature
- BONUS! This PowerWash.com EXCLUSIVE Bundle Pack also includes a FREE 5 lb. Sample Pack of R-202 Cleaner. This powerful sudsing alkaline powdered detergent is designed to clean heavy grease, oil and scuff marks from unpainted concrete and other alkaline water safe hard surfaces.

Big Guy Surface Cleaner Specifications:
- Nylon Brush
- One Caster
- Two (2) 10" Pneumatic Tires
- Oversized self-lubricating thin thrust bearings
- 2000-5000 PSI Pressure Range
- Max Temperature: 212° F
- Max Flow: 4-10 GPM
- Housing Size
- Two 40-Degree Size
- Spray Tips

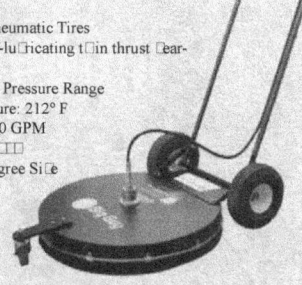

In This Issue:

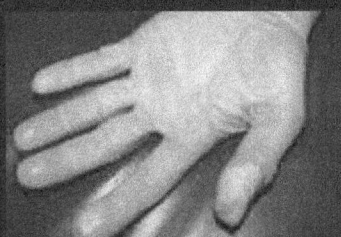

207 Understanding Shopping Center Power Washing, by Steven Button, Clean Fast USA

212 Introducing Street Bidder: A New Mobile App that May Put an End to the Flyer

216 PWNA Fleet Washing Certification: Landing More Customers, Making More Money

220 PWNA Vendor Profile: PowerWash.com

222 Working with Hydrofluoric Acid, by Linda Chambers, Soap Warehouse

226 The PWRA: Closing in on 200 Members...Fast

229 Build a Win-Win Relationship with Your Distributor, by Tom Grandy, Grandy & Associates

232 Surviving the Storm: One UAMCC Member's Personal Experience with the Moore, Oklahoma Tornado

235 Focus on Neutral Cleaners, by Rick Meehan, Marko Janitorial

238 Commercial Pressure Washing: Essential Elements of an Employee Training Program, by Paul Horsley

240 Look for Cost-Saviing Options When Choosing a Pressure Washer for Fleets, by Aaladin Industries & Steel Eagle

241 Classifieds: Products and Services

Cover Photo
Courtesy of Steven Button, Clean Fast USA, Orlando, Florida, www.CleanFastUSA.com

eClean Magazine is published monthly.

Box 262, 16 Midlake Blvd S.E.
Calgary, Alberta
Canada T2X2X7
www.eCleanMag.com

Publisher: Paul Horsley, paul@ecleanmag.com
Editor: Allison Hester, allison@ecleanmag.com
Sales: Kelly Jacobsen, kelly@ecleanmag.com

eClean Magazine

Understanding Shopping Center Pressure Washing

by Steven Button, Cleast Fast USA, www.CleanFastUSA.com

What did you think the last time you drove by THAT shopping center in town?

You know, the one with the gum-riddled sidewalks, stained walls, dirty windows and mildewed curbs. Yes, the one with the property manager who, when you call, is offended by your offer to help get the place clean, then says they already have 'a guy' that takes care of it and that they will keep your information on file.

Don't fret... there can be a number of reasons why the property looks the way it does and why the property manager is indifferent to your services. Furthermore, for every 'dirty' shopping center, there are probably an equal number or more that are kept clean, inviting and in good repair.

Photo courtesy of Clean Fast USA, www.CleanFastUSA.com

The reasons for either scenario could be related to vacancy rates, types of lease in place, ownership type/directives, trade area demographics and the level of understanding related to the value of a clean center or of hiring a professional pressure washing service.

As mobile cleaning contractors, we all know that a clean property is more inviting and more attractive to prospective customers and tenants. In fact, it is our job to make conscious associations with cleanliness such as professionalism, trustworthiness, attention to detail and success. However, the ability to effectively communicate this to shopping center owners and managers can often stem from a better understanding of their business.

We cannot just look at a shopping center and make all of our assumptions based off of whether it is 'clean' or 'dirty', and then try to sell based off of these assumptions.

Firstly, it is useful to understand the many different types of shopping centers, their makeup, typical size, number and type of tenants and trade area served.

Shopping Center Basics

In the broad sense, the name shopping center covers many categories of commercial retail type properties; however, they generally fall under the three configurations as defined by the International Council of Shopping Centers (ICSC):
- General-Purpose Centers (Strip/Convenience, Neighborhood, Community, Regional and Super-Regional)
- Specialized-Purpose Centers (Power Center, Lifestyle, Factory Outlet and Theme/Festival)
- Limited-Purpose Property (Airport Retail)

These are typically defined by size, layout and tenant type. The trade area demographics and market characteristics play a huge part in center location and success.

A comprehensive list of US Shopping Center Classifications and Characteristics can be found on the ICSC website (http://www.icsc.org/uploads/research/general/US_CENTER_CLASSIFICATION.pdf).

Pricing

Understanding the different types of centers can help us focus our service delivery to shopping center owners and managers. It also acts as a starting point in recognizing that each center has specific characteristics that will affect our service price and actual service provision.

For example, a Neighborhood Center anchored by a grocery store typically has a Gross Leasable Area (GLA) of 30,000 to 125,000 square feet and a tenant mix that feeds off of the 'traffic' generated by the grocery store anchor tenant. The sidewalk layout is generally straightforward, usually no more than 20' wide. There may also be a variance in tenant operating hours and a disproportionate buildup of sidewalk dirt depending on tenant and customer type - different food service and retail stores can greatly affect the amount of gum and grease needing cleaned.

In terms of service provision, this type of center has key issues in regard to pricing and performing service. Consideration will have to be given to shopping carts, vending machines and tenant merchandise displays placed on sidewalks. A further consideration would have to be operating hours, often it is a contract stipulation that equipment cannot be operating during tenant hours.

As always, a comprehensive scope of work should be sought to ensure that the service is priced correctly. Of equal importance is our ability to communicate what we need to the property manager in order to complete the scope of work and minimize any potential issues for them, us and the tenants.

Contrast this with a Power Center with a typical GLA of 250,000 to 600,000 square feet. The tenant mix at these centers is usually more complex with discount department stores, home improvement stores, electronics and office supply stores. There can often be 3+ 'anchor' type stores with their own buildings and lease agreements in place with different requirements related to Common Area Maintenance (CAM).

The service provision at this type of center, although it is bigger, can often be easier for the contractor - provided they have obtained a clear scope of work. With the exception of home improvement stores, there are usually not many items on sidewalks surfaces that would impede a smooth service call. With wider, open sidewalks the mobile cleaning contractor may have a larger area to clean but fewer issue with hose management and truck parking.

Other Considerations

In terms of the vacancy rate of a shopping center, more unoccupied space generally means less income for property ownership. It is important to recognize that depending on tenants' lease arrangements within the center that this may also have a negative effect on CAM budgets - which ultimately affects whether our service is affordable or a priority for the property manager.

Obviously changes in the economy have an effect on vacancy rates - a good point to note is that Regional Malls are generally not affected as quickly as Convenience or Neighborhood Centers because of a stronger tenant mix, presence of better-capitalized national retailers and longer leases.

Furthermore, the type of leases in place can have an effect on whether a center is 'clean' or 'dirty'. The lease will define who is responsible for what as it relates to common area maintenance, insurance, taxes and janitorial service. Some common lease types are:

• Gross Lease (Property owner responsible for all operating expenses)

• Net Lease (Tenant pays pro rated share of operating expenses)

• Triple Net Lease (Tenant responsible for all operating expenses and repairs. Often found in single-tenant properties)

• Percentage Lease (Usually only found in large malls, where tenants pays a percentage of sales over a specified amount in addition to base rent. Landlord has a financial stake in tenants success)

The ownership type can have a significant effect on the importance placed on property maintenance, presentation and cleanliness. Ultimately, the property owner is looking for a return on their investment and for the property to generate income. Often, the owners are shareholders in the form of Real Estate

Photo courtesy of Clean Fast USA, www.CleanFastUSA.com

Investment Trusts (REITs) who have a stake in portfolio of properties - generally, these properties will have budgeted for exterior cleaning and common area maintenance services.

The owner may be a development company whose purpose is to sell the property they built for a profit. This profit may be realized immediately following construction, or they may hire the services of a competent management and/or leasing team to add value to the asset by building a strong tenant mix. Again, with the ultimate goal being disposition at maximal value, there will normally be a budget for our services in order to keep the asset looking great for potential buyers.

Other types of owners may be private investors, joint ventures, institutional investors, banks and smaller scale property developers. Each of these will have their own priorities as related to income generation and importance placed on common area maintenance. Sometimes our service is not a priority because the tenant mix or trade area demographics are not affected by cleanliness or property presentation.

It is pretty clear that there are contributing factors to the physical condition and cleanliness of shopping center properties, many of which have not been covered in this article. They should not be considered barriers to selling our service, as mobile cleaning contractors, we know that a clean shopping center can be the start of a more financially profitable chain for all stakeholders (tenants, customers, owners, property managers, leasing agents, local community). When prospecting potential new business with shopping center property managers, having knowledge of their industry can be beneficial to focus your sales approach.

Steven Button is the owner of Clean Fast USA in Orlando, Florida. CleanFast focuses on providing commercial cleaning services, while providing safety and sanitation. To learn more about Clean Fast USA, visit their website at www.CleanFastUSA.com.

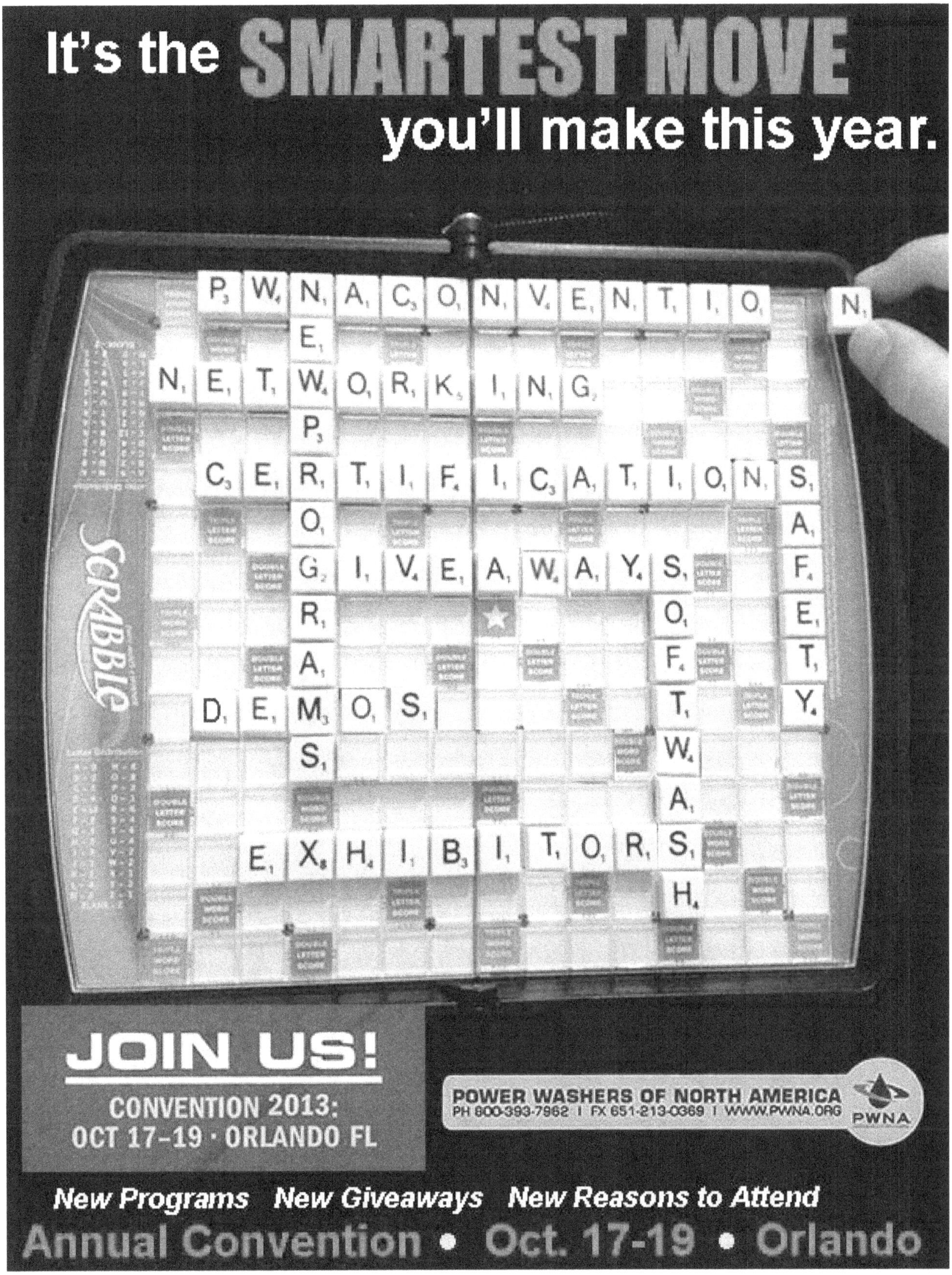
It's the SMARTEST MOVE you'll make this year.
PWNACONVENTION
NEWPROGRAMS
NETWORKING
CERTIFICATIONS
SAFETY
GIVEAWAYS
SOFTWASH
DEMOS
EXHIBITORS
SCRABBLE
JOIN US!
CONVENTION 2013:
OCT 17–19 · ORLANDO FL
POWER WASHERS OF NORTH AMERICA
PH 800-393-7962 | FX 651-213-0369 | WWW.PWNA.ORG
PWNA
New Programs New Giveaways New Reasons to Attend
Annual Convention • Oct. 17-19 • Orlando

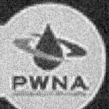

Introducing Street Bidder

A New Mobile App That May Put an End to the Flyer

by Allison Hester, eClean Editor

Window cleaner turned entrepreneur, Josh Latimer, stresses that he is just an ordinary guy. "I enjoy being a husband. Playing with my kids. I love God. I like my work. I try to do my best at whatever I do, but I am not obsessed with power or money. I just want to be able to spend more time with my family."

"When I started using pictures of peoples' houses on our estimates, something **MAGICAL** *happened!"*
– Josh Latimer
Founder of Street Bidder &
Owner of Birds Beware Window Cleaning

Six years ago, Josh made a bold career move, leaving the security of his job as a banker to start a window-cleaning business in an economically struggling area in Michigan. "My wife was pregnant with our first child, and I wanted to be able to take the winters off to be home with my family," he explained. "Window cleaning seemed like it could make that happen… and it has. But that first year about killed us financially."

Today, however, Birds Beware Window Cleaning has grown significantly, due largely to the dedication and hard work of the company's 13 full-time staff members, as well as the implementation of several unique marketing approaches that have paid off – big time.

Their most successful marketing idea to date began with a simple concept – putting photos of people's houses on the front of his company's estimates. "When homeowners saw pictures of their homes, something magical happened. Suddenly we had much higher closing rates. We made more dollars per job. It was a simple, special touch – and homeowners loved it."

That got Latimer thinking: rather than distributing generic flyers around

This will change your business forever.
Street Bidder
Where is Your Business Going?

Visit www.FlyersAreDead.com
Learn More >>

neighborhoods – you know, the ones that often end up in trash cans or littering the streets – he could create custom postcards for potential customers featuring their house and an estimate.

"It's a tool we used in our own business," Latimer explained. "We were trying to figure out a really awesome way to control our growth. We wanted a predictable, measurable system in place to drive phone calls. That's when we came up with Street Bidder."

Initially, Latimer only planned to use Street Bidder for his own window cleaning/pressure washing company. However, "as we started implementing the process and we saw our profits begin to significantly rise, we realized this was a tool that a lot of companies could benefit from."

And so Street Bidder was born.

This past week, after more than nine months of development, Latimer introduced the new Street Bidder mobile app to a select mobile cleaning market – members of the Window Cleaning Resource Association (WCRA) and the Pressure Washing Resource Association (PWRA). In July, the app will be available for all.

How it Works

To use Street Bidder, contractors first download the app on their mobile device, such as an iPad. Next they take pictures of houses in a neighborhood that they want to target. (Note that this is perfectly legal as long as photos are taken from the public street.) "You go capture Street Bidder files. You go take a picture, load the address, add a price. The process literally takes about six seconds per house," Latimer explained. "The Street Bidder app remembers which road you're on so you don't have to fill in the full address each time. Just take the picture, add the house number, and move on to the next one."

At any point after the photos are taken, contractors can order individualized postcards

An example of one of many roof cleaning cards available.

by choosing from the pre-designed cards and adding the home's customized information. The map overlay feature places pins on a map for each home that you enter. To send to a specific neighborhood, simply circle the pinned area on the map with your finger, hit send, and you're done.

With the simple click of a button, postcards are ordered, printed, stamped and mailed within 48 hours, and should arrive at the potential customers' house three to eight days later. "The response rate we are getting from our

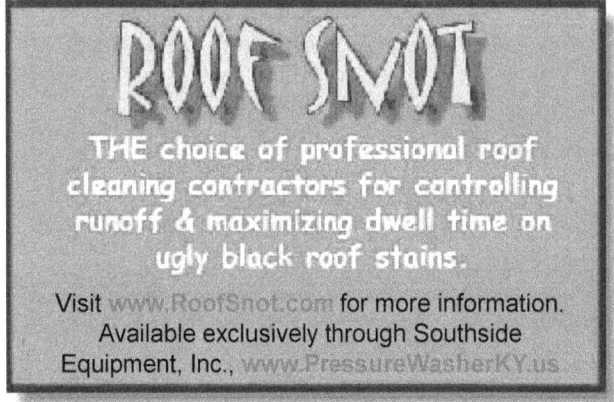

ROOF SNOT
THE choice of professional roof cleaning contractors for controlling runoff & maximizing dwell time on ugly black roof stains.
Visit www.RoofSnot.com for more information. Available exclusively through Southside Equipment, Inc., www.PressureWasherKY.us

eClean Magazine   213

postcards is amazing. They really do work!"

When Will It Be Available?

As mentioned, Street Bidder was exclusively introduced to WCRA and PWRA members this past week. The app will be available to all sometime in July.

"We're excited to work with the WCRA and PWRA so that we can have a small initial adopting group. This will allow us to work through the unforeseen details that arise, and help ensure we are equipped to provide quality customer support. I don't want to have 10,000 people buy the app all at once, then struggle to keep up with our customers' needs. Starting with a small group is going to make Street Bidder even better for everyone."

How Much Will It Cost?

The Street Bidder app itself can be downloaded for free. To send postcards, you have two options.

First there's the free plan, which allows you to send Street Bidder postcards for as low as $.79 each – depending on the number of credits purchased. Street Bidder data is stored on their servers for 90 days.

Then there's the Platinum Plan. This one lets you send postcards for as low as $ .47 each – depending on the number of credits purchased. There is also a monthly charge of $39.95 ($29.95 for WCRA and PWRA members), and the Street Bidder data is stored on their servers forever. This plan also allows access to the map overlay feature.

"You need to assess how many cards you expect to send out, then figure out which plan makes more sense," said Latimer. "There is no minimum quantity, so you can send as few – or as many – postcards as you want. If you only anticipate sending a handful of cards, then the free plan would be the right choice. If you're going to send out a lot of cards, then Platinum makes more sense."

But What About _____?

Since word of Street Bidder has hit the online mobile cleaning communities, the overwhelming response has been extremely positive. However, some contractors have voiced a few concerns. I asked Latimer to tackle these:

I don't have time to take all those pictures. Sounds like a lot of work.

"The Street Bidder app doesn't take any longer than it would to distribute flyers throughout a neighborhood, and the good news is once you've walked a neighborhood, you never have to do it again. The files are saved and you can mail to those potential customers any time you want."

Additionally, Latimer has found in his company's experience that the read/response rate for the postcards has been significantly higher from the individualized postcards than from generic flyers. "If they see a picture of

Joseph D. Walters
POWERWASH INSURANCE OPTIONS

America's #1 Insurer of Power Wash Contractors

WOW!
Get a **fast quote** for **Power Wash Insurance!**

For a FAST telephone quote:
1-800-878-3808
Get proof of coverage **TODAY**

I called and got quoted instantly. The prices were very good & it was easy! – Charlie Arnold, Lewes, DE

Walters even has a Saisfaction Guarantee Policy. If you're not 100% satisfied for any reason, they will return your money. No questions asked. They're good to work with. – Mike Strejeck, Monroeville, PA

www.JosephDWalters.com

their house on a postcard in the mail, they *will* look at it rather than just throw it away."

Finally, there are other types of personalized cards that can be sent using Street Bidder – including thank you cards. "After you finish a job, you can take a quick snapshot of yourself standing in front of your customer's shiny clean house, hit a button, and you've got a customized thank you card on its way. The card not only builds goodwill with your customer, it reminds them how nice their house looked when it was cleaned, and most importantly, that you are the one to call when it's time to clean it again."

I'm afraid potential customers will be mad when they see I've photographed their home.

This can happen, but it doesn't happen very often. Latimer adds that if an unhappy homeowner does call and complain, Street Bidder has an option to permanently remove that address from its files so that you can never add it again. Apologize to the homeowner. Tell them you intended no harm and assure them you will permanently remove their photo from your files.

As a sidenote, one of the early testers of Street Bidder had an upset customer call about the photo on the postcard. Guess what? After talking to the contractor on the phone, the homeowner ended up hiring the window cleaner.

Soon, there will be another solution available as well. For those who prefer not to take photos of houses, Street Bidder will allow you to instead take a photo of a street sign, or a development entry sign, or whatever landmark you select that is easily identifiable by your target neighborhood. "That way you are still sending them a customized card, but one that's less intrusive."

I can't afford to spend several thousands of dollars on postcards.

You don't have to. As mentioned before, you can purchase a single postcard if you want. "We designed Street Bidder to give the little guy an affordable option to help professionalize his image without costing a fortune."

A Few Final Words from a "Nerd in Training"

"I'm just a window cleaner. A colleague," Latimer stressed. "This is all new to me, and this is the hardest thing I've ever done." Latimer said he had no idea when he started developing Street Bidder how to go about creating an app, but he worked with a variety of designers and developers and is slowly become a "tech nerd." He adds, "It's taken a massive amount of time and effort to create a tool that I believe will truly benefit a wide variety of markets. We're starting close to home, with the mobile cleaning contractor, and we hope customers can be a little patient as we get started and work through a few growing pains."

Latimer also stressed that as the product is introduced and tested this month, Street Bidder will get better and better. "As we hear back on what you want, I'm certain we'll come with ideas to make it faster. Cooler. Everything you need it do to help your business grow."

Where can I Learn More?

You can read more about Street Bidder on the company's website, *www.flyersaredead.com*. Additionally, there is a new Facebook group page located at *https://www.facebook.com/Streetbidder?fref=ts*. Finally, Latimer will also be talking more about the product as a presenter and an exhibitor at the upcoming PWRA National Convention, August 23 and 24 in Nashville, Tennessee. Read more about the PWRA and the National Convention on page 24.

PWNA Fleet Washing Certification

PWNA Certified Contractors are Landing More Customers, Making More Money

by Allison Hester

Truck fleets are constantly exposed to the elements and every extreme condition imaginable. Keeping a fleet looking clean and professional is hard work, and many fleet owners turn to outside contractors to handle the washing. This is good news for contract cleaners.

However, fleet washing is different from a lot of pressure washing markets. It's volume, not details: get them in and get them out. It's usually performed late at night or on weekends, and you only have a short window of time to do the task. It's carefully regulated environmentally, as the contaminants being removed from the trucks have come from off-property sources. The chemicals used can be very dangerous. It's performed year-round, even in cold weather. And it's hard, physical work.

On the positive side, unlike many other cleaning markets, fleet washing is consistent and repeat. Clients typically need their fleets washed anywhere from weekly to monthly. Gain a few regular clients, keep them satisfied, and you don't have to keep looking for more work.

It's also a competitive market, with lots of lowballers who win accounts based on low prices. They show up a couple of times, then the next thing you know their quality of work starts to go down. They show up late. Their equipment stops working. And eventually they just quit showing up at all.

The best way to distinguish yourself from the rest of the crowd of fleet washers is to exude professionalism. And one of the best ways to exude professionalism is to become PWNA Fleet Washing Certified.

"Being a certified contractor is a nice feather in your cap. It's one of the things that will help you get more accounts," explained Dan Galvin of East Coast Power Washing, who took the course last Fall. "Managers of trucking companies have enough problems to deal with already.

When they see that you are certified and can be trusted, it takes one problem off their plate."

The PWNA Fleet Washing Certification Course

Because of the tight regulations involved with fleet washing, as well as the various cleaning methods and equipment options on the market, the PWNA Fleet Washing Certification Course is one of the association's more intensive certification programs.

"This was a no nonsense course that was laced with many 'nuggets,' or takeaways," said Ty Eubanks of South Shore Building Services, who took the course at last October's annual PWNA convention. "Even though I've since decided not to incorporate fleet washing into my business, I still learned skills that will help me better perform flatwork and the other types of cleaning that we offer."

The course is currently being taught by Paul Horsley – Publisher of *eClean Magazine* – who owns Scotts Pressure Wash in Alberta, Canada. Horsley has been in the pressure washing industry for over 35 years, and has over 40 staff members and 23 vehicles. Scotts Pressure Wash specializes in fleet washing, commercial cleaning, flat surface cleaning and rail car cleaning.

"It is a great course to take and Paul is a very informative business owner," said Barry Marno of New Finish Power Washing who took the course with Paul in Calgary, Alberta. "For anyone who is starting a power washing company or adding a new area of business to their company, this is a great source of knowledge."

"Paul is an excellent instructor," Eubanks agreed. "I appreciated that he demonstrated an expert knowledge in the course curriculum. He knows his customers and understands how to meet their expectations."

Galvin, who has been washing fleets for 10 years said he still learned several things that have helped him in his business and in growing his bottome line. "I learned several tips and techniques that have saved me time and money. People need to understand that if you can save a few dollars per truck, that

> **"I have made THOUSANDS upon THOUSANDS of dollars on the information I have received from the PWNA certification courses."**

could add up to thousands of dollars a year."

As with all PWNA certification courses, the fleet washing course follows a specific outline, covering each of these topics: background of service; economic opportunity of service; chemicals, detergents and cleaners; equipment; leaning process; water reclamation; safety; pricing; advertising; available add on services.

This is important because becoming a successful fleet washing company requires more than just knowing how to wash a truck. "Over the years, I've found that a lot of contractors get into fleet washing without understanding the management side of the business," said PWNA Board Member Michael Hinderliter, owner of Steamaway, who has been washing fleets for around 30 years. "They don't know how to price the job. They don't know how to market. They don't know what it takes to stay in business."

PWNA certification not only provides a jumpstart to better understanding the business aspects of fleet washing, but PWNA membership also provides a network of successful fleet washers and business owners to call upon with questions and ideas.

And apparenttly fleet washing certification works.

Increasing Bottom Lines

"I just landed a new contract with 500 vehicles, trucks and forklifts, and I used my certification to help me land the job," Galvin explained. "I have made thousands upon thousands of dollars on the information I received from the PWNA certification courses. Think about it, you add just one new fleet washing client at $1000 per week, that's $52,000 per year. It's not that hard to do when you have the knowledge to do it and that's what you will get when you attend the PWNA convention."

Guy Triger, owner of Puma Power Wash in San Francisco, took the Fleet Washing Certification Course at last year's PWNA convention. "By implementing the strategies I was taught, I was able to build a steady customer base in a very short time," he said. "When prospective customers call me for an estimate, I always show them my certifications from PWNA, Their next question is the same: 'When can you start?'"

"If you're reading this wondering if you should take the (fleet washing) course, just do it!," agreed Ross Wilhelms of West Coast Fleet Wash. "The value I got out of this program is easily worth 10 times the amount it cost. Five stars."

Whether it's fleet washing or one of the many other PWNA certification classes, Eubanks said he strongly encourages contractors to take advantage of the educational opportunities that PWNA will offer at October's annual convention. "The cost of the PWNA certification courses pales in comparison to the cost of the learning curve in the school of hard knocks," he explained. "I have started every one of my service lines – window washing, steam cleaning, waterproofing, bird abatement, metal restoration – from scratch with huge learning curves… . Wish I had taken certification courses to learn from the experts and hit the ground running."

> The Fleet Washing Certification Course, along with several other certifications programs, will be offered at the PWNA Annual Convention, October 17-19 in Orlando. To learn more or to register, go to www.PWNA.org.

Welcome New PWNA Members!

Mike Tricarico and Pat Steffen
Clear Choice Pressure Washing

Rachel Rich
The Pool Supply Company, Inc.

Freddie B Smith and Levi Easley
A&M Stripping - Powerwashing

Keith Quinn
Wood Re New/Renew Crew

Tina Kitts
T.A.S.K.

Jon Welker
Clean-Tech

Jean-Paul Guzllemette and Hossein Naghidzadeh
To be determined

Jamie Stallworth
To be determined

Nigel Griffith
Griffs Services

Herman Brown
Service Alliance LLC

Irtan Mutle
Beluga Cleaning, LLC

Mark Maierdan
Mr. Super Clean Power Wash, Inc.

Ben Enneking
Enneking Pressure Cleaning Inc.

Eric Dyer
Industrial Steam Cleaning

Feberico Perez
Porpillo & Perez Power Wash Industries Inc.

Carrie Dubbie
New Finish Power Washing

Dave Warren
TWS Facility Services

Greg Reveles
Renorr Dynamics, Inc.

Ray Daniels
Superclean Service Co. Inc.

Matthew E. Smith
Twin Lakes Commercial Cleaning

Mike Pruitt
Gale Force Cleaning & Restoration

Kulwinder Nahal
Janico Cleaning Solutions

Ben Shelton
Dirtzero, LLC

Jefferson Leroy Lehman
Steel Eagle, Inc.

Robert C. Strong
Strongs Painting & Pressure Washing

Thomas Martin
Araya Clean Property Services

Meg and Bo Josetti
All Clean Power Washing, LLC

Hyon J. Ouh
Pro-Duct Cleaning

Sean Hartigan
Dr Cleanhood

Stanley Viverette
Stanz Integrated Cleaning Solutions

Andrew S Reinsel
A2Z Pressure Washing LLC

Brooks Peacock
Wash Worx LLC

Eric McCullough
Sunrise Power Wash

John K. Collins
Facilitec East

Mike Coleman
CCI

Richard H. Redfern
Groundscape Maintenance, LLC

Bernard Eisenbeck
Bernard Eisenback

Justin Brown
To be determined

Eric Chavez & Ricky Wycliff
Steam Kitchen

Jennifer and Matt Doty
Super Hoods, Inc.

Robert Figueroa
High Tech Detail Cleaning Inc.

Ian Bresnahan
Dr. Clean Hood

Garland Smith Jr.
Precision Service Co.

Aaron Bohnert
Pressure Force

Adam Smith
PressurePro Cleaning

Make Plans NOW to Attend the PWNA National Convention, October 17-19 in Orlando, Florida. To learn more, www.PWNA.org

PWNA Vendor Profile

Although Michael Hinderliter grew up around his father Robert's power washer distributorship, Michael was busy running two successful contract cleaning operations of his own. So when he took over his father's distributorship on March 1, 2010, it was not a seamless transition.

"I had only spent about five percent of my time in the distributorship business. There was a huge learning curve for me," Michael explained. "I knew we would make some mistakes, and it took us awhile to find our way."

Changing to PowerWash.com

One of the first things Michael implemented was changing the company's name.

Under his father Robert's leadership, Rahsco Mfg. Co. Inc. DBA Delco Cleaning Systems of Fort Worth, had been known for its many innovations. For one, it was one of the only distributorships early on that focused primarily on the contract cleaner. It was also one of the only early distributorships that sold nationwide.

The advent of the Internet, however, changed all that. Suddenly, the concept of selling outside your local territory stopped being an industry no-no and became an acceptable marketing model.

By the time Michael took over the busines, the Internet was a daily way of life. Keeping up with how the Internet changed business only made sense. So he immediately changed the company's name to PowerWash.com.

"I knew we needed a stronger Internet presence, and the PowerWash.com name was a no brainer," he explained. "It's simple. It tells what we do, and it tells people how to quickly find us."

Changing the company's name was fairly easy. Changing the company's website was much more difficult."I made repeated changes to the website layout, ever increasing the amount of information we provided online," he explained. He has also since added the Powerwash Community Bulletin Board, where his goal is to keep the focus on education. "That's what's most important."

And PowerWash.com is all about providing education. Michael also created Power Wash University, which regularly offers classes on a variety of pressure washing related topics, including marketing, awning cleaning, kitchen exhaust cleaning, an introduction to power washing and more.

Changing the Company's Focus

Michael says his biggest mistake since taking over was placing too much focus on price. "If you make your prices to low, there's no way you can afford to provide quality service," he said. "Low prices may bring in first-time buyers, but they don't bring repeat business. That's not the direction I wanted to go.

So his business model changed. He looked for high quality products and hired expert

Michael recognizing industry pioneer Larry Hinckley at his retirement.

support staff – including contract cleaners – who understood the equipment inside and out, who were well spoken and who could educate and troubleshoot over the phone. He hired in-house designers to ensure the website was up-to-date, top-of-the-line and running smoothly.

"We really stress customer service," he said. "We understand the contract cleaning side of the business, and so we are able to empathize, troubleshoot and brainstorm with our customers. We also work with distributors around the country to help them fix your equipment if you have a problem. We can often help you fix the equipment over the phone as well."

These are things that PowerWash.com can offer over many local distributors who may not be as familiar with contractor needs. Because they are selling nationwide, they are also able to get a better price break from suppliers to help keep costs down as well.

Another cost-saving program PowerWash.com just began is paying the shipping for any power washer that costs $200 or more.

And additional new changes are on the way.

Involvement with the PWNA

Michael has been around the Power Washers of North America since its inception; his father was the founder. However, historically Michael's involvement was exclusively as a contract cleaner, and he credits the PWNA as being a great benefit to his contractor businesses.

"For me personally, the biggest benefit of being involved in the PWNA is the open exchange of ideas and being able to share experiences with others who do the same thing that I do. You can't put a price tag on that."

While this kind of networking often begins at the annual convention – which will take place October 17 through 19 in Orlando – it certainly doesn't end there. "I've always been amazed by the willingness and desires of the members to reach out and help each other," he explained. "You don't necessarily see it online – on the bulletin boards and such – because most PWNA members prefer to avoid the online drama. But the support is certainly there. I've found PWNA members to be a group that is more focused on

PowerWash University student receive hands-on and classroom training.

the things that really make a difference when it comes to building a successful business, and in turn, that's why many are very successful."

Not an Easy Transition, but a Good One

Running PowerWash.com has been much more challenging than running his two contracting businesses. "You have to keep up with more than 3,000 products so that you can ensure you're giving customers the best product for their needs. That's a lot."

Running PowerWash.com has been a lot of work, but it is finally becoming enjoyable. "It took us awhile to get our footing and find our direction. Today we have a stronger focus on the needs and wants of our customers. We aim to provide positive customer experiences, and ask for and apply our customer feedback. At the end of the day, satisfied customers are what really matters.

To learn more about the company, Powerwash Community or Powerwash University, go to www.PowerWash.com. To learn more about the Power Washers of North America, visit www.PWNA.org.

Michael surprising GM Trey Posey for his birthday

Working with Hydrofluoric Acid

By Linda Chambers, Soap Warehouse,
www.SoapWarehouse.biz

Hydrofluoric Acid is the most hazardous chemical you can deal with as a pressure washer. If you have crews working for you, a regular "how to handle chemicals class" with your technicians is required to be OSHA compliant. Additionally, you need to do extra training with those employees who may work around or with Hydrofluoric Acid chemical solutions such as our Aluma Brite, Aluma Brite super concentrate, H.D.A.B., Bay Wash, No.1 Truck Wash and Concrete Truck Cleaner. These are all fantastic cleaners for the jobs they are for and two step washing is the most effective method out there for many fleets, but these jobs must be done correctly and with the proper caution.

You should keep extra MSDS (Material Safety Data Sheet) copies attached to the containers of HF solutions besides in the normal MSDS binders that should already be on your rigs, in your trucks and at your office location. We also supply our customers with an additional sheet "First Aid for Hydrofluoric Acid Exposure" I would also have a copy of this attached with the MSDS. It would also be wise to place tubes of Calcium Gluconate Gel to be used as a first aid measure close to all HF solution storage and use locations. Bottles of Calgonate 1% calcium eye wash or similar is also a recommended first aid kit supply for any business using HF chemical solutions. If you can afford it the best option would be a complete HF first aid kit, that are commercially available as well as HF spill kits.

Employees should be trained in the use of protective equipment for their eyes and body, such as goggles and a face shield, full chemical suit or splash apron, along with heavy long sleeve shirt, gloves approved to be used with HF – neoprene, not latex – and closed-toed, heavy leather or rubber shoes.

Mixing or pouring of HF chemical solutions should be done only be in well-ventilated areas wearing appropriate safety gear. Storage should only be in properly labeled HF compatible containers – no metal, ceramic or glass. Containers should be stored on or low to the ground to reduce the chance of drops and spills. HF containers should not be stored on an open trailer rig where an unknowing passerby can reach and touch the outside of HF

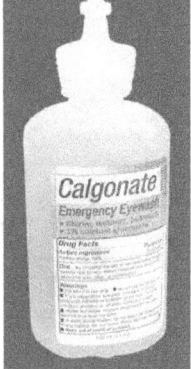
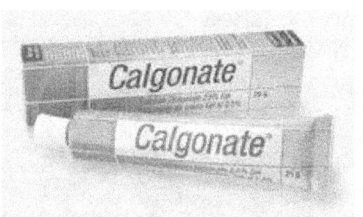

solution containers.

HF solutions should be applied to create the least amount of spray as possible. Lowpressure, pump up, directed application is much better than high pressure, wide pattern application. Be mindful of spray blow back off of surfaces and in wind, using during windy conditions should be avoided. If clothing or foot wear becomes damp from spray, application should be stopped and items removed while wearing gloves and placed into plastic bags or bins labeled hazardous. DO NOT continue to work in items like a shirt or shoes that have become soaked and allowed to sit on your arms or feet until you are finished washing.

This is what can happen... and these are low exposure results.

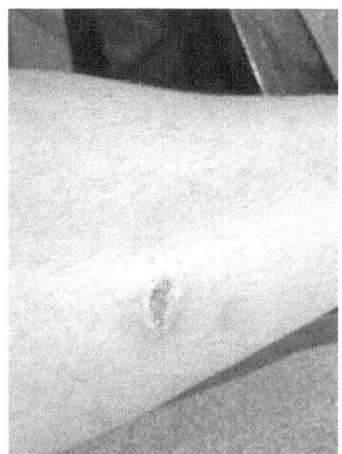

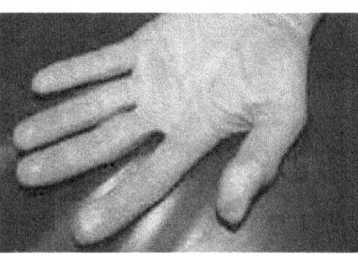

Safety First

Employees should never be allowed to work with HF solutions if alone or while tired. They should not eat, drink or smoke while handling HF chemical solutions. As soon as the employee has finished handling any HF solution, they should be sure no liquid residue is left on the out side of the containers; that any materials that came in contact with any solution – such as a rag or towel – has been properly stored and labeled as hazardous; and that they have washed their hands with soap and water to reduce the chance of improper contact to their skin or to others. All equipment that came in contact with the solutions should be rinsed to be sure no raw solution is on them to be touched. Protective gear and equipment should also be rinsed and properly stored after being removed or used by employee.

If you go to aid a person you know has been handling solutions containing HF follow, the same protective and safety procedures as if you would be handling HF directly yourself.

First Aid

Hydrofluoric acid exposure is very hazardous and the full extent of injuries from contact may not be obvious for some hours. Urgent first aid is very important, even for minor exposure. Contact with lower dilutions of HF can be overlooked and the severity misleading at first. Workers may even get home and not begin to experience irritation and pain from a burn until several hours later. Even a slight skin irritation should be treated immediately. HF acid is rapidly absorbed through the skin and can produce deep and extremely painful burns, along with the destruction of underlying tissue. Untreated absorption of any kind can decalcify bone, cause a systemic toxic effect of a calcium and magnesium imbalance, which can lead to heart and organ damage and or failure. Be sure anyone who will be washing clothes or towels with HF contamination knows they could be contaminated and not to touch them barehanded. You would hate to harm a family member by accidental exposure.

If HF solutions are ever splashed into the eyes, immediate action needs to be taken.

1-800-762-7911   www.soapwarehouse.biz

With this ad buy 2-6, 5 gallons of any of our Hydrofluoric Acid cleaners in July and we will pay $50 on the shipping on that order. *Aluma Brite, H.D.A.B., Triple Duty, No. 1, Bay Wash, Nutra Salt Concrete Truck or Concrete Residue remover.*

Rinse with strong streams of water forcing the eye lids open for at least 15-20 minutes. Remove contacts if present while rinsing. Follow water with Calgonate or similar eye wash if available, and of course, seek immediate medical attention. I have heard a wives tail of pouring milk into the eyes but this should not be done and will not be effective, as milk does not have enough free calcium to give aid and might even lead to an additional infection in the eye.

As soon as irritation is seen or burning felt, flush area with copious amounts of water. Remove any clothing or items that could have come in contact with the area since exposure, including hats, watches and jewelry. Rinse for five minutes if Calcium Gel is available, or at least 15 minutes or until medical help arrives if not. Additional scrubbing will be required if HF has gotten under the fingernails as retention under the nails can extend absorption into the body and lead to possible nail loss. As soon as flushing has finished, while wearing neoprene (not latex) gloves, apply calcium gel to the effected area, gently rubbing it into the skin and burns. Continue reapplying as the gel is absorbed for at least 15 minutes after any pain has stopped. Seek urgent medical attention for possible further treatment of IV calcium fluids and injections that may be needed. Deaths have been reported from concentrated acid burns involving as little as 2.5 percent of body surface area and with as little as a one percent solution when little pain was felt and skin irritation was ignored over a long time.

If getting to medical treatment will be delayed due to distance, travel time, or time of day to find help, have the victim eat up to 30 regular Tums or Caltrate calcium tablets, or drink several glasses of whole milk for calcium, or several ounces of Milk of Magnesia, Mylanta, Maalox or similar magnesium product. Using the calcium products first would be the most helpful but if not available the magnesium ones will still help. They may aid as an antidote and help to get needed calcium into the victims system and slow down ill effects of a calcium magnesium imbalance. Just be sure to advise medical staff of when, how much and which products were consumed for accurate calcium and magnesium ingestion calculations. And never give anything by mouth to an unconscious person.

Cleaning with products that contain HF can be a very powerful addition to your cleaning arsenal, but you must treat them like a loaded gun – with respect and care. If you do, you will get the results you want, but if you don't, it can kill.

Linda Chambers is the Brand and Sales Manager for Soap Warehouse, where she has worked since 2007. She enjoys writing blogs and social media. She also travels for the company, exhibiting at trade shows and events. Visit their website to learn more at www.SoapWarehouse.biz.

Literature references
Source: Segal, Eileen, B "First Aid for a Unique Acid, HF: A Sequel" Chemical Health and Safety, Jan/Feb 2000 vol. 7, #1, p18.
Bronstein, A. C. and Currance, P. L. "Emergency Care for Hazardous Materials Exposures" Mosby Company 1988.

Web sites references:
http: www.calgonate.com/safety_info.php www.tums.com
web.utk.edu/~ehss/training/has.pdf

2013 New Products Recap
Stop by your local distributor to give one a try

Updates to AZV / RZV recovery & filtration system
- Rustproof, stainless vacuum box with drain
- Lift-out basket stainer replaces bag filter
- New stringwound replaceable filters
- Same small footprint, 5-10gpm process rate

For current Specials, go to www.hydrotek.us click 'what's new'

Redesigned surface cleaners
- Octagon and square decks, giving you an angle over your competition
- Splash reducing brush on rear of deck
- Contractor Twister is now 4-in-1 tool: edger, gum spotter, water broom, surface cleaner
- Hydro Vacuum surface cleaner picks up even better with its new vacuum ring

Two Honda models added to the SS Series product line
Available as a 3500psi @ 5.5gpm or 4000psi @ 4.8gpm
Belt drive pump and PowerLight 12v burner module

All the Best Things You've Come to Expect From Us
- Wash Skids & Trailers
- Electric, Hot Washers
- Wash Accessories

Brilliant Design, Tough on Grime

Manufacturing pressure washers and wash accessories for over 25 years.
Visit website or call for a distributor near you. Distributor inquiries welcome.

www.hydrotek.us   (800) 274-9376

The PWRA
Closing in on 200 Members

Photo courtesy of Laurie Benjamin, All Aspects Maintenance, Trinidad & Tobago

by Allison Hester

"I've got something REALLY EXCITING to tell you about!"

That was the start of a phone call I received from Thad Eckhoff one evening in late April, 2012. For the next hour or so, I listened as Thad explained how the Pressure Washing Resource Association (PWRA) was about to become a reality. "The PWRA is going to be about helping honest, hardworking individual contractors make money so they can support their families...period. And the benefits begin as soon as they sign up," he explained.

At that time, the benefits primarily consisted of members having immediate access to over 60 tested and proven marketing materials, including postcards, door hangers, proposal packets, email templates, mailings, business forms, and more. Members also received a 5% discount off of purchases from PowerWash.com. Oh, and a ginormous PWRA sticker.

Just a little over a year later, the benefits have grown significantly, with new programs being added almost monthly. New marketing templates. New business forms. Exclusive networking opportunities. Plus discount programs that run the gamut. In fact, the most recent benefit – a 25% discount on Street Bidder (see article on page 10) – was introduced just this past week.

"A lot of our discounts will more than cover the cost of PWRA membership. The at-cost printing program alone has saved people thousands of dollars," Thad explained. "The Ambidexrous Services web design discount is huge. It's at least $300 off, and some members have saved up to $800 with the service. Responsibid is another big one. Members get $350 off. That's your membership fee right there."

Now, to top it all off, PWRA is hosting its first National Convention and Trade Show, August 23-24 at the Opryland Hotel in Nashville. "This is much more than a regional round table. It's 22,000-square-feet of meeting and trade show space at a world renowned hotel, plus key industry speakers, three seminar tracks, a large trade show floor and national networking opportunities," said Thad. "And we're talking *pressure washing*-related topics only."

Just as the benefits have grown, so has the PWRA's membership. In late March, membership was at 120. Three months later, they've added another 50+ members...and it just keeps growing.

So what is it about PWRA that members like so much? To find out, I decided to interview three of its members:

Tim Fields, Complete Power Wash, LLC, Hagerstown, Maryland; Josh Dodson, Greasepro, LLC, Boiling Springs, SC; and Alex Curry, ARC Powerwashing, Raleigh NC. Here's what they had to say:

Q. Why did you join the PWRA?

TIM: I had heard good things about Thad's annual NOLA event, and had seen some of Chris Lambridines' (co-founder of PWRA) business successes, so it was an easy decision to sign up for the PWRA.

JOSH: Being associated with awesome business people was my main reason for joining. I appreciated the honesty and concept of the PWRA, and I love my big PWRA sticker!

ALEX: When I found out about the PWRA, I was impressed with the benefits they were offering at the time. I waited though, thought about it some more, then went back to look at the site again. That's when I saw they had already added more benefits that would save my company money.

Q. Which Benefits Have Helped You Most?

TIM: We send a lot of postcards. I've paid for my membership fees several times over just in the savings from the at-cost printing program alone.

Another benefit I receive from the PWRA is being able to feel like I can help the new guys when they ask questions. It really is just squirting soap at stuff and spraying water on it after you've waited a few minutes, but there are a million ways to mess it up. And old guys have a responsibility to teach the young.

JOSH: I just signed up for the PWRA payroll and will be saving about $80 a month compared to my previous payroll processor. That's $960 a year I'll save from that one benefit alone.

The best benefit for me, however, is the networking. The ideas and input I get from fellow members and presenters at the networking events is priceless.

ALEX: I've really taken advantage of the at cost printing. The discount that they offer on printing is enough for anyone to join the PWRA. I don't know how much I've saved, but it's well above the price to join.

I've also used the discounts from Powerwash.com as well as Pressuretek.com. Using Street Bidder is going to be awesome, as well as Responsibid to sell when I'm not even at home. The PWRA offers so many tools and systems to help companies like mine grow.

Q. Will You Be Attending the PWRA National Convention, August 23 and 24 in Nashville?

TIM: We have our rooms reserved already and we are looking forward to attending it as a family trip and business builder. We have not studied which classes to take, but I am encouraged that there will be something for my wife Sandy, the operational brains; my son Zach, the wash tech; and myself, the sales dude.

JOSH: ill e atten ing the ashville event here ill e hea ing up a rea out session for Kitchen haust Cleaning m reall loo ing for ar to the entire event There is a great line up of presenters m sure ill learn a lot a out ho to ma e m usiness or etter

ALEX: Yes I will be at the Nashville event. The reason I'm attending is to hear all the different ways to grow my business, as well as new cleaning techniques to add or learn to do things a new way. The part I'm looking

The first National PWRA Convention and Trade Show takes place Augustt 23-24 at the Opryland Hotel in Nashville. As an *eClean* reader, you can save $50 off your PWRA membership and attend the convention for FREE! Click here to join!

ALEX: Yes I will be at the Nashville event. The reason I'm attending is to hear all the different ways to grow my business, as well as new cleaning techniques to add or learn to do things a new way. The part I'm looking forward to the most is networking with other contractors, which is critical now in our industry.

Q. Do you recommend joining PWRA?

TIM: I recommend the PWRA for people who are looking to grow their business and don't have a lot of extra time for nonsense.

JOSH: The PWRA is the best association for pressure washers – for the networking and the member benefits. If you buy things for your pressure washing business, then you will spend less if you are a member. It pays for itself in no time.

ALEX: YES! I would definitely recommend that other companies join the PWRA. If you want to take your business to the next level then this is the place to be. The PWRA and all its members will help you grow, give you tips, and help with any problems that arise. PWRA is where it's at. Sign up and find out for yourself.

Not a member yet? Join today & save $50 for reading this article AND get a *free ticket* to the exciting new PWRA National Convention & Trade Show, August 23-24 in Nashville!

BLENDING OUT THE COMPETITION

KNIGHT HD 26-P
HEAVY-DUTY POWDER CLEANER DE-GREASES AND DE-SCALES EXHAUST HOODS AND DUCTS FOUND IN RESTAURANTS. STATE OF THE ART DETERGENT SYSTEM WITH A COMPLEX EMULSIFIER PACKAGE TO EASE THE REMOVAL OF HEAVY GREASE/SOILS FROM THE SURFACE.

DUCT SHINE
DUCT SHINE LEAVES SUBSTRATES WITH A SHINE THAT RESISTS FINGERPRINTS AND STREAKS. WILL PRESERVE STAINLESS STEEL, FORMICA, PORCELAIN, FIBERGLASS, ENAMEL, PLASTIC AND STEEL SURFACES AGAINST DETERIORATION.

128 W. LAKE STREET
NORTHLAKE IL 60164
(708) 531-1234 (708) 531-0010
www.knightnorros.com

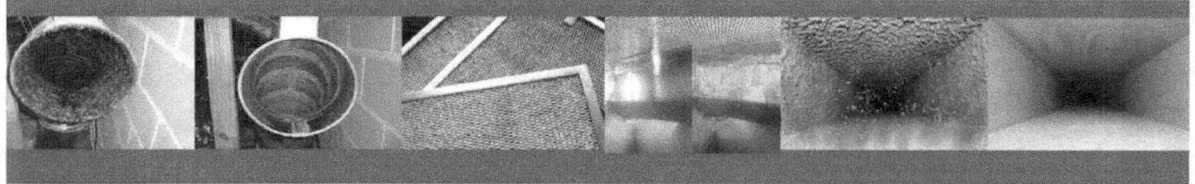

Build a Win-Win Relationship with Your Distributor

by Tom Grandy, Grandy & Associates,
www.GrandyAssociates.com

The art of building a relationship with someone is really pretty straightforward. Step one is finding out as much as you can about the other person: What are their likes and dislikes? What makes them happy? How do they like to spend their free time? If it's a marriage, your goal is to make the other person as happy by spending time with them and doing things you both like to do. As you talk and share, you learn more about the other person and you invest time, energy and money trying to make the relationship a win-win for both of you.

When it comes to building a win-win relationship with your distributor, the first step is still the same; find out what the other person (the distributor in this case) wants out of the relationship. The obvious answer is sales – they want to sell you as much product as possible. But it goes a bit beyond that. A distributor wants three basic things from the contractors they serve: cash flow, communication, and commitment.

Cash Flow

The name of the game, if you are a distributor, is cash flow. The more dollars they can collect, the more parts and equipment they can stock. Over the past 25 years, I have continued to ask distributors what percentage of their contractors consistently pay their bills within

30 days. Most tell me about 10-15% of their entire customer base routinely pays their bills on time. When asked what percentage pay within the 10-day period (and therefore take the discounts), most say about 10-15% of those that pay on time.

Translated, about 2-3% of their entire customer base pays within 10 days and takes their discount. Now if the name of the game is cash flow, and your company pays on time and takes the discounts, where do you suppose that puts you in the pecking order? Right, you are right at the top of the list of "very important, and appreciated, contractors."

I want to encourage you to pay your distributors on time in order to take your discounts. Yes I know, many reading this article struggle with paying their rent and utilities on time, which means the distributor often becomes your banker. By the way, that is NOT the way to build relationships with your distributor. Next month we will talk about how to pay your distributor on time. Suffice it to say the first building block of a win-win relationship with your distributor is paying your bills on time!

Communication

Personal relationships are built on communication. You talk to one another on a regular basis. The communication isn't just about sharing the good stuff. A true relationship is built on being totally honest with each other. The same principles apply when it comes to the contractor/distributor relationship. Talk to each other. Even great companies, that normally pay their bills on time, have occasional situations where cash flow problems arise and they can't pay their bill on time. When that happens (and it does to every contractor), pick up the phone and talk to your distributor. Look at it this way: a spouse normally understands when things change. If you told your wife you would be home for dinner at 5:30 she is planning on your being there close to 5:30. Now something comes up at the office, and you realize you won't be home till 7:00. What do you do if you are a wise husband and you want to keep the relationship intact? You call home and tell her you are going to be late. A little communication goes a long way.

Now it's the first of the month and time to pay your distributor. However, that $35,000 check that was due a week ago has not come in yet, and you are unable to pay your bill on time. If you want to maintain your relationship with your distributor, the wise thing to do, like the wise husband above, is to communicate. Call your distributor and tell them your situation. Make them aware your bill may be a week or two late, and tell them why.

If our earlier husband failed to call his wife, knowing he was going to be 90 minutes late, what kind of response do you think he will receive when he finally does get home? There would probably be a cold shoulder to go along with the cold dinner! Likewise, communicating with your distributor builds the relationship, it doesn't tear it down. However, if you have not paid your bill and you are always "busy" when your distributor calls, the relationship will soon break down. Rule number two, communicate with your distributor.

Commitment

Most distributors work really hard to fill your orders in a timely manner at a consistent fair price. Many also invest huge amounts of money training you in the areas of sales and/or business training. That cost is part of the price you pay for the part or equipment, just like rent and utilities are part of your hourly rate. These types of training programs are part of their investment in helping you grow and prosper. Wise distributors realize they will grow and prosper if your company grows and prospers.

Your part of the relationship is to be committed to the distributor that provides outstanding service and consistently fair pricing, and that helps you become more profitable. You will always be able to shop around and find a better price on a specific part or piece of equipment but realize the distributor has to turn a profit too. That means they will not be able to provide the cheapest price on every item if they are going to stay in business and continue to serve you. If you, as a contractor, are always the lowest price in town chances are pretty good that it's only a matter of time before YOU go out of business. Another building block, when it comes to strengthening your relationship with your distributor, is being committed. Translated, that means buying the majority of your equipment and parts from the distributor that supports you and helps you grow.

Personal, and business, relationships will grow and prosper when both sides are fully committed to each other. If you want to build a lasting, and committed, relationship with your distributor remember the three C's; Cash Flow, Communication and Commitment.

This article was brought to you by Grandy & Associates. If you are seriosu about running a profitable business, go to www.Grandy Associates.com or contact them by phone at 800-432-7963.

Photo: on the site where they daycare once stood.

Surviving the Storm

One UAMCC Member's Personal Experience with the Moore, Oklahoma Tornado

by Allison Hester, Editor

On May 20, shortly after Oklahoma City-residents Bryan Henson and wife Jami Sobkowiak, owners of Xstream Pressure Washing, heard that a tornado had hit their neighboring community of Moore, they loaded their dog into their work truck and headed to the area. "Honestly, the reason we went there in the first place was to assess what types of cleaning services we might be able to sell."

Never did they anticipate what they would find.

Bryan and Jami were two of the first people to arrive on the scene, even before most first responders, and before news stories of the severity of the damage had hit the air. "It looked like a war zone," he said. "Total devastation."

Bryan found he could not turn left because of all the destruction and debris on the road. To his right, where a neighborhood once stood, a single church, covered in mud remained. Jami could only mutter, "Oh my God. I don't understand."

Then they pulled over next to a police officer on the side of the road. "I remembered I had a brand new pack of work gloves in the back of the truck, so I grabbed them and started passing them out to the officers who were standing among the debris. That's all I could think to do."

When Bryan asked how they could help, the officer asked him to help clear the area because they were trying to get to the elementary school that had been hit.

Once the path was cleared, Bryan and Jami headed to the school where the young children were trapped in the debris. "We were there for the search and rescue, and people were everywhere trying to help however they could. I wasn't really even sure where to begin."

Someone told Brian to look for hard, flat surfaces that could be used for triage. They ran to the cafeteria where they scrounged up tables, then kicked doors off of hinges. Anything that could be used to carry out the injured.

Then news of the first child fatality hit. Around that same time, the responders ordered everyone out because there were gas leaks all around. "A neighboring house caught on fire because of the gas leak, but there was nothing that could be done. They just let it burn."

Returning to their truck, they saw a young lady on the side of the road crying uncontrollably, so they asked if they could help. She explained she needed to get to the school. Her kindergarten-aged was missing.

Bryan knew the children had been taken to "the church on the hill with a steeple" and so the young lady piled into the back of their truck, bawling, while they began their way toward the church – a mile and a half journey that took over 3 hours to reach.

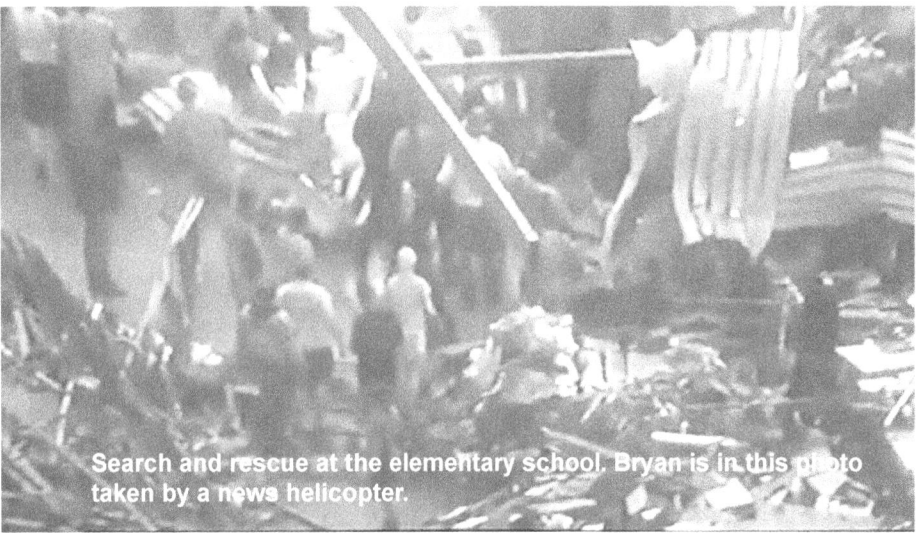
Search and rescue at the elementary school. Bryan is in this photo taken by a news helicopter.

When they finally arrived, the young lady ran into the church, but there were no children there. Then they received good news. The young woman's boyfriend had picked up her son about 45 minutes prior. He had a few scrapes, but he was fine.

A Concerned Community

As Brian and Jami were experiencing the tornado's devastation first hand, industry friends from the UAMCC (United Association

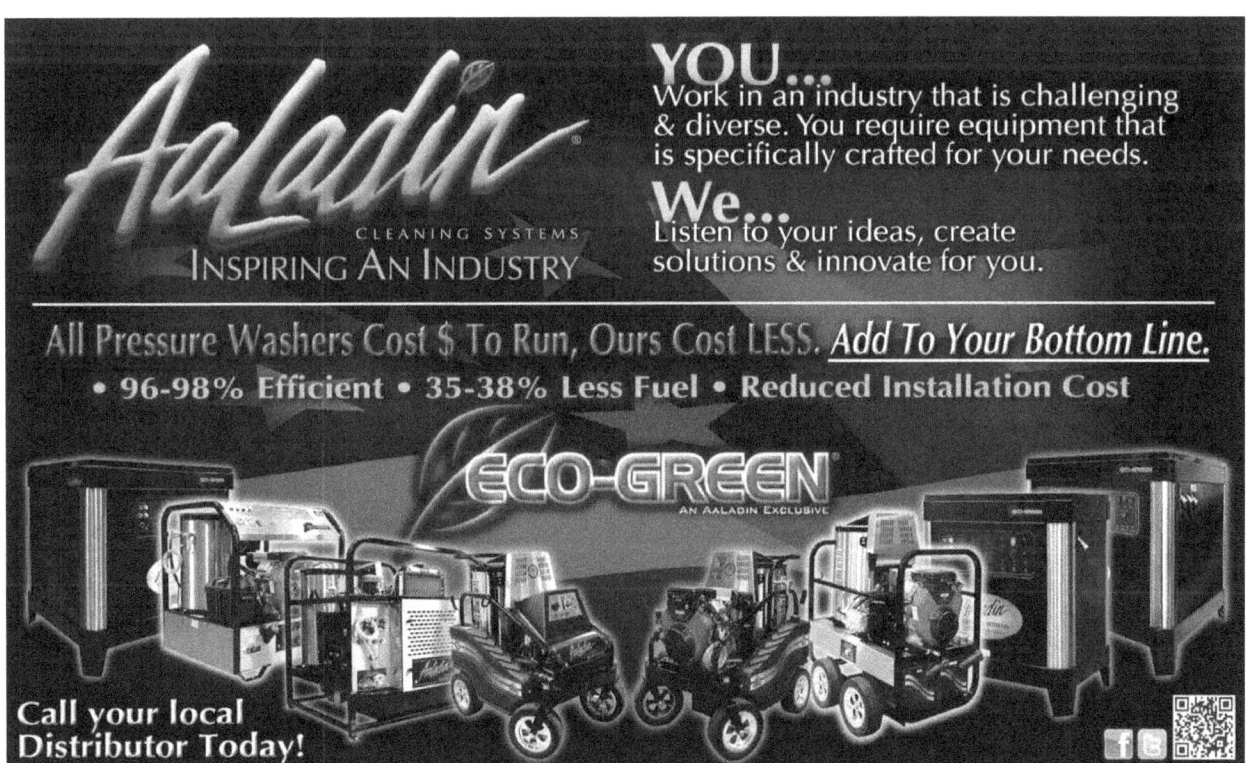

of Mobile Cleaning Contractors) – to which Bryan belongs – were frantically trying to check in on the couple. Calls. Texts. Posts on the Pressure Washing Insitute (PWI) bulletin board including one entitled, "Bryan Henson, are you ok?" But he had no way to contact anyone.

Several hours later, Bryan and Jami made it home. Bryan was able to let his industry friends know he was indeed ok, and that they would be delivering water to the area the next day if anyone wanted to contribute. "The water treatment plant was down and there was no clean water." The calls and donations from fellow UAMCC members began pouring in. "And these weren't nickel and dime donations," Bryan said. "These guys were donating hundreds of dollars."

That next day, the couple headed back to Moore with their vehicles loaded down with as much water as they could carry – around $300 worth. They could not get into the heart of the devastated area, but they found a small tent three women had set up outside of a church. The ladies had brought a kiddie pool full of ice, some water and Gatorade, and sandwiches they had made for the victims. Bryan asked if they needed some water, and they said they'd take all he had. "They were shocked to find how much we'd brought!"

More Donations

Additional UAMCC members began sending Bryan money to donate at his discretion. Additionally, Russ Johnson of Southside Equipment not only donated money out of his own pocket, he also donated Pressure Pro EB4035 – a 4 gpm, 3,500 psi belt driven pressure washer that retails for $1650 – to auction off on PWI for the cause. It sold for $1400 with shipping included.

"Bryan is a good customer, and I thought it admirable that he was willing to help others in his community rather than looking out for only himself. I wanted to help him," Russ Johnson explained. "I know the money was used to benefit the people who were affected by the storm. How exactly, I left to Bryan's discretion. I feel sure the money went where it was needed most."

Next, UAMCC Vice President Doug Rucker donated a flat surface cleaner he had recently purchased but decided he really didn't need. It was bought by UAMCC member Tony Shelton for $500, who turned around and auctioned it off again so more money could go to the victims.

Bryan chose to give the money to a preschool teacher who had lain on top of several young children when the eye of the storm passed over them. At that time, a little blonde girl, probably no more than 30 pounds, started to get sucked in by the tornado. The girl looked at her teacher, "I guess I'm flying!" The teacher grabbed the little girl's leg and cried, "If you go, I go." The little girl was saved. The teacher lost everything – her job, her car and her home.

"Don't Call Me A Hero"

Since the tornado hit, Bryan has voluntarily cleaned several of Moore's churches and homes, something he says he couldn't have cone a few years ago. "If it weren't for the members of the UAMCC, I wouldn't have learned how to be successful enough that I could afford to take off of work and help these people who've lost everything."

Several industry members have referred to Bryan and Jami as heroes, a label Bryan is not comfortable wearing. "I'm not a hero. I'm just a vessel who was put in the right place to be able to help give back to my community that has suffered such great loss," he explained. "Those UAMCC members who donated their resources for strangers are the real heroes. I wouldn't have been able to help those people without their selfless generosity."

To learn more about the UAMCC, go to www.UAMCC.org.

FOCUS ON "NEUTRAL" CLEANERS

by Rick Meehan
Vice President of Marko Janitorial Supply, www.MarkoInc.com

To tackle the frothy subject of so-called "neutral" cleaners, we have to do a little review on the purpose of detergents. You may recall from one of my prior articles, "Soap Is Not An Opera," that surface tension affects your bottom line. By adding a detergent to water, surface tension is reduced, thus increasing the "wettability" of the surface to be cleaned.

Profits are directly affected by the ability of a detergent to do its job – clean the surface. Therefore, the wettability factor of a detergent determines whether it will aid in cleaning that surface. Notice that I said "aid." Wettability is not the only determining factor in how well a detergent works for you. Yet, a detergent should work for you, reducing your overall labor and chemical costs.

Neutral Cleaner, also known as the Pink Soap (sometimes other colors), the Foamy Junk, the All-Purpose Detergent, the General Sanitation Cleaner, the General Purpose Grime Remover, or in the case of my own company, Marko SC-100 All Purpose Cleaner (part of our Super CareTM floor maintenance line), is the most common type of detergent used by cleaning contractors. Naturally this means they carry the biggest load of dirt, pun intended. For this reason a thorough understanding of their capabilities means monetary savings.

Wettability

Now, let's review surface tension (wettability).

Every surface has tiny pores and blemishes that harbor dirt and germs. The surface tension of water covers over those blemishes much like a skin, which in turn traps the debris in those near-microscopic pockets.

See how the paper clip floats on that "skin?" Adding a detergent to water reduces the surface tension so that the mixture will penetrate into those small pockets, thus allowing the detergent to surround and breakdown the grime. The detergent then buoys the grime so it can't sink back to the surface as easily.

It is also important to remember what the word "neutral" means as pertaining to cleaning chemicals. Ideally, a neutral cleaner should have a pH that runs between 6.9 and 7.3, about the same as tap water. The closer the pH is to 7.0 on the scale, the more neutral the detergent. Here's the pH Scale for reference:

Why should a neutral cleaner have this

Battery Acid	Vinegar	Tallow	Milk	Water	Baking Soda	Ammonia	Lye
0 1 2	3 4	5	6 7	8 9	10	11 12	13 14
ACIDIC			NEUTRAL				BASIC

narrow pH range? The strict definition of "neutral" according to Merriam-Webster is "not helping or supporting either of two opposing sides; impartial." In our case, the opposing sides are acidic and basic. When combined, chemicals from the opposite ends of the scale cancel each other out to become "neutral," neither acid nor base.

Think of it this way. Drinking water does no harm to your body, but battery acid or lye will eat your guts out. That's pretty graphic, but essentially what would happen to an acrylic floor finish if a harsher chemical like bleach were used in the mop water. In medical vernacular, a neutral detergent is designed to "do no harm." In fact, the way I always explain neutral cleaners without this background information is to say, "If tap water won't harm the surface, then a neutral cleaner won't either." It is therefore reasonable to assume that a neutral cleaner is designed to clean most surfaces not harmed by plain water.

The traits of a quality, all-purpose neutral cleaner are:

- Color is usually light, ranging from pink to sky blue, sometimes clear to translucent.
- 100% biodegradable, meaning it will not harm the environment if poured on the ground. (All bets are off after the cleaner is contaminated with grime.)
- Concentrated, highly dilutable with water.
- pH very close to 7.0 – neutral.
- Good stability when the ambient temperature is very cold or very hot. In other words, the product doesn't separate while sitting on the shelf.
- Not flammable or combustible.
- Free of harsh solvents (No Volatile Organic Compounds, or V.O.Cs)
- Water soluble and free rinsing, leaving no residue.
- Good wettability, meaning it loosens soil from microscopic surface pockets and keeps debris buoyed and surrounded while rinsing.
- Does not create harsh fumes under any circumstances.
- Will not harm multiple surface types.

Quality neutral cleaners tend to be pricey. However, if you are purchasing your product from a reputable dealer, the extra money saves the most dollars in the long run. Don't be fooled into purchasing a special "Green Cleaning" product at a higher price. The fact is, unless some harsher chemical such as a petroleum based solvent has been added, or the detergent is significantly higher or lower than 7.0 on the pH scale, the very act of manufacturing a neutral cleaner makes it a "green" cleaner. It always has. Besides, once any cleaner is used for its intended purpose, it becomes contaminated with whatever type of grime it was used to remove. Sometimes that grime is not environmentally friendly when disposed of improperly. Know your cleaning chemicals so you don't spend extra money based on "green cleaning" pseudo-science.

Since neutral cleaners are the most popular detergents on the market, choosing good ones from the thousands out there can be challenging. Besides the list of traits to look for, there are other ways to determine the best soap for your company. It is important to understand that household cleaners are NOT the same as industrial/commercial cleaners. In general they are weaker, less dilutable with water, safer to use and store. They are designed for laymen, not professionals. Under no circumstances should a commercial cleaning outfit be using household chemicals if they are serious about saving money.

Let's take an example (without naming names, but using real prices):

XYZ Fresh 'n Clean All Purpose Detergent (household national brand) is used straight from the 32 ounce trigger spray bottle, one quart, that it comes in. Sure, it works fine, and is fairly cheap at only $3.49 per bottle. Let's divide that out: $3.39/32 = $0.10, or a dime per ounce. The job is large enough to require the use of a full 32 ounce bottle every day.

ABC Commercial Cleaner (national brand) is diluted at the rate of 1 part cleaner to 128 parts water to achieve the same results as XYZ Fresh 'n Clean, but it doesn't come in a convenient trigger spray bottle. It comes in gallon jugs instead. The cost per gallon is $14.99. A gallon equals 128 ounces, so let's divide that out: $14.99/128 = $0.12, or 12 cents per ounce. Why, that's more costly by two whole pennies!

Or is it? Don't forget to factor in the dilutability – one ounce of ABC per gallon of water. What? Why that's really a cost of only 12 cents per gallon! With a bit more math we find that by dividing 12/4 (4 quarts in a gallon, remember), the cost of ABC is really only three cents per quart versus XYZ at a whopping $3.39! Since the job requires a quart of cleaner per day, we save $3.36 EVERY DAY!

What about the cost of the trigger sprayer and the labor involved with diluting the product before use? These are valid questions.

A trigger sprayer can be used many times and the spray nozzles can be replaced without having to buy the bottle too. The average cost of a good quality trigger sprayer is $2.29. Spread that out over the course of a month or so until the trigger wears out – add seven cents per day to your chemical cost to be safe. If labor costs $11 per hour and it takes 10 minutes each day to prepare a properly diluted quart, add another $1.83 in labor costs. Let's see, that's 1.83 plus .03 plus .07, which equals $1.93 per day. That's still a savings of $1.46 per day.

Keep in mind that there are dilution methods and dispensing options that will reduce the costs of this process drastically too.

Now, let's get down to the brass tacks, or in other words, the basics of finding the right neutral cleaner which will save a commercial cleaning company the most money in the long run. Claims on labels are sometimes misleading, especially when you consider that every cleaning job is different.

General purpose cleaners are generally labeled with general instructions that cover general cleaning jobs. The key here is the word "general." Generally speaking, it's always a good plan to run tests on various brands of neutral cleaners, following instructions exactly, to determine which particular cleaner works best for most general cleaning purposes. General cleaning purposes include projects such as mopping waxed floors, wiping countertops and fixtures, washing painted or vinyl-covered walls, exterior window cleaning, light degreasing of surfaces, etc. By diluting a target product according to the label and testing it on these various general surfaces, using the same janitorial staff person, with the same cleaning equipment if possible, a fair determination can be achieved.

My personal favorite way to pick the best neutral cleaner is to actually test products side by side so results can be seen immediately. When it becomes apparent which of the test products works best for your particular situation, nail it down in writing and train all of your personnel in its proper uses.

Keep in mind that the biggest drain on chemical dollars comes from untrained personnel either overusing or underusing said product. Overuse is waste; underuse means harder labor; both situations mean a poorer job. Poor jobs cost customers.

Test, test, and retest. Save a bunch of headaches and get yourself a quality all-purpose neutral cleaner for your company.

Just as having the right tool for the job saves labor, increases safety, and gets the work done, so does using the right cleaner. Neutral cleaners are staple tools of our trade.

If the soap performs poorly, a variety of problems will occur. Wet shoes may slip on soapy film, windows may look greasy, floor finishes may become dull or yellowed, other surfaces may feel dirty, odors may exude from dirt and germs that remained behind to fester, among a myriad other problems.

In short, an incorrect choice of detergents will not have the characteristics needed to perform well. So make your all-purpose neutral cleaner carry the dirty load to leave a sparkling facility behind that would make any client ecstatic!

eClean Magazine

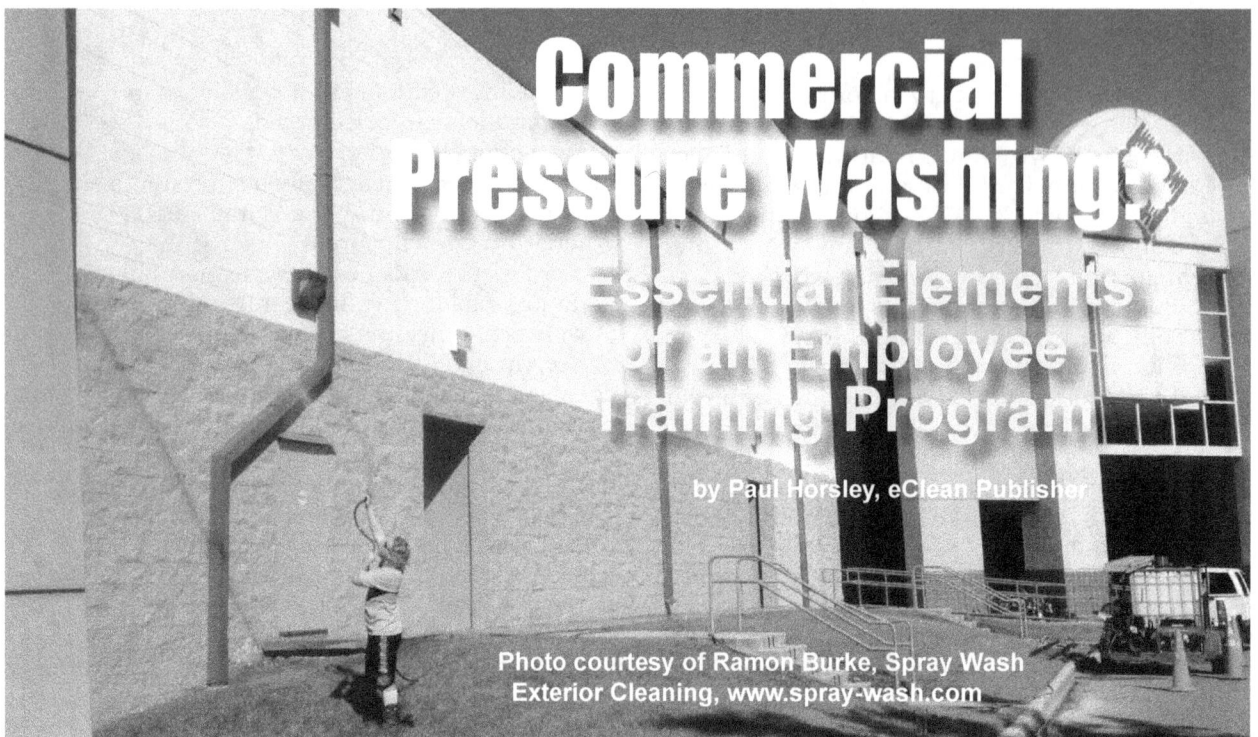

Commercial Pressure Washing:
Essential Elements of an Employee Training Program

by Paul Horsley, eClean Publisher

Photo courtesy of Ramon Burke, Spray Wash Exterior Cleaning, www.spray-wash.com

As any experienced commercial pressure washer knows, pressure washing equipment is anything but intuitive. For those of us who are not commercial pressure washers, this may come as a surprise. After all, how hard can it be? Just point and shoot, right? Not quite. To become successful professional power washers, employees must receive training in how to properly use pressure washing equipment.

Below, we outline the essential elements of a pressure washing employee training program. Whether you are planning on starting a pressure washing business or simply using pressure washing equipment in-house, use these tips to ensure your workers are well prepared. And if you're hiring a commercial pressure washer, this framework can help you assess the professionalism of power washing companies.

Avoiding Commercial Pressure Washing Injuries

Pressure washing equipment is extremely powerful. Commercial pressure washers can emit water at 4,000 pounds per square inch. That level of pressure will certainly blast away grime, but if used improperly it can also cause serious injury. A few of those injuries are listed below:

Abrasions. Just as with guns, pressure washing equipment should never be aimed at people or pets. Should a person be hit with a commercial pressure washer, painful skin abrasions can occur. A power washer is strong enough to sweep away entire layers of skin. And if such injuries are not properly treated, they can become infected. Commercial pressure washers are also strong enough to lift and throw objects, which can be dangerous if they strike others.

Electric shock. Some commercial pressure washers are powered by electricity. If safety precautions are not followed, electric shock can occur while using these machines. Workers must understand the importance of wearing rubber-soled shoes, which will not conduct as much electricity if an accident does occur. They should also be taught to avoid dragging power cords into puddles and to use GFCI (Ground Fault Circuit Interrupter) plugs.

Monoxide poisoning. Other power washers are gas powered. If they are used in confined spaces, monoxide poisoning can ensue.

Preventing Property Damage while Pressure Washing

Employees must also be trained in how to apply the proper pressure levels, cleaning solutions and techniques for various materials. If too much pressure is applied, or the wrong tip is used, softer materials such as wood can sustain serious pressure washing damage.

Choosing the correct cleaning solution for the job is also crucial. Some pressure washing equipment is outfitted to spray chemical cleaning solutions as well as water. This comes in handy when extremely greasy or oily stains must be removed. However, if the wrong kind of cleaning solution is applied, a commercial pressure washer might also eat away at underlying material, causing permanent damage. Commercial pressure washers must train their employees in how to safely remove all kinds of grime from all kinds of materials – as well as how to safely handle commercial cleaning products.

Maintaining Commercial Pressure Washing Equipment

Today's commercial pressure washers can clean with cold water, hot water or steam. As mentioned above, they may also be able to shoot special cleaning solutions. In other words, these are complex machines that require regular maintenance. Employees must be trained in how to use power washing machines properly. As workers become more experienced, they may also be trained in how conduct maintenance by changing a machine's oil, repairing faulty pumps, refueling or any number of other tasks.

Protecting the Environment

Wastewater from power washing operations can harm downstream life forms. Heavy metals and other toxins are removed during pressure washing; these chemicals can be deadly to flora and fauna. Environmentally aware power washers prevent ecological damage by collecting their wastewater and transporting it to the proper disposal facilities. Eco-friendly cleaning solutions also help prevent environmental damage.

In certain parts of the country, such as Colorado and California, these green power washing techniques are required by law. In these locations, employees must receive training in green power washing. In other areas, a commercial pressure washer may choose to educate employees on green techniques as a way of protecting the earth and garnering new business.

Pressure washing employees should be trained to avoid injury, prevent damage and maintain equipment. Depending on commercial pressure washers' locations, local laws may also require environmental cleanup. If you operate a power washing business, make sure to provide comprehensive training to protect your employees and your brand. You will also want to carry three types of power washing insurance: workers' compensation (in case your employee is injured), liability insurance (in case your clients' property is damaged) and equipment insurance (to protect your investment in your pressure washing equipment).

Let us put our expert knowledge of **legendary Landa equipment** to work for your cleaning needs.

Specializing in Power washing equipment sales, service and custom manufacturing

(403) 771-7774

www.HydraEquipment.com

HYDRA

eClean

Look for Cost-Saving Options When Choosing a Commercial Pressure Washer

by Aaladin Industries and Steel Eagle

Maintenance costs, downtime, rising fuel prices…all of these impact your efficiency and your profitability. Your choice in pressure washers directly impacts your bottom line.

When selecting a pressure washing system, look for a solution that minimizes operation costs. All pressure washers cost money to operate, and fleet washing cleaning projects often require their washers work longer and harder than most. Choosing a washer that conserves fuel as well as minimizes time to refuel and maintain will help protect your bottom line – and your customer's.

A good example, AaLadin holds an exclusive patent on technology that will essentially pay for your washer over a short period of time. The more hours used per week, of course, the faster you rack up the savings. Our units save up to 38 percent on fuel over any other pressure washers. We call this innovation our Exclusive Exchange Technology.

Other advantages to this technology are being 98% efficient as compared to other equipment lines that grasp for just up to 75%. Stack temps are as low as 85° as opposed to 650°, which allow our units to be vented with CPVC straight out of the wall, saving hundreds or thousands of dollars in traditional stacking. For your industries' heavy usage, it's really a "no brainer." For example, if you were to use one of our LP machines an average of just 20 hours/week at the national average of $2.87/gallon you would save $6,208.38 in just a year's time. As you can see, it doesn't take long to enjoy using a free pressure washer.

Another cost-saving item is our clutch system. With many systems, if a technician forgets to shut down your washer when they set down the gun for awhile, the pump goes into bypass and heats the water, which speeds wear and results in the need for costly premature pump replacements. With our clutches, as soon as you let go of the trigger, the pump is shut down preventing the previously mentioned damage. Smart right?

The second thing to look at when choosing the most cost-effective system is the tools you attach to your washer. Steel Eagle has a tool that is a necessity for fleet washers. Most of the time fleet washing services do a great job with the outside of the vehicle, but what about the underside where grease, salt and corrosive road debris collect? Traditional wands just don't reach up under the vehicle well enough to remove those damaging materials. That's why we created the Bottom Feeder Undercarriage Cleaner. No product on the market deals with tough jobs like it can. The spray pattern is the product of four nozzles, two of which are 0° nozzles that cut through the toughest dirt, and two of which are 15° nozzles that fan out to sweep away the debris. The alternating combination of this nozzle pair makes the perfect one-two cleaning punch! The Bottom Feeder was one

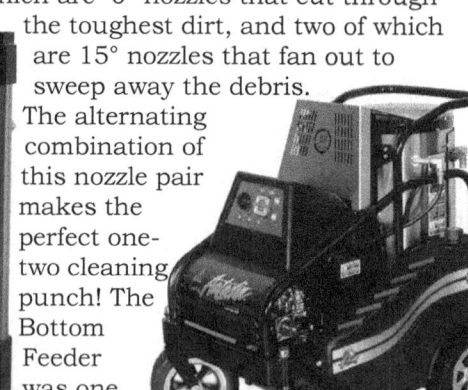

of the first of its kind and top of the line quality, with features including:
• Only 5.5" of clearance needed allowing for low profile vehicles
• Powder coat paint
• Adjustable handle with adjustment for operator comfort
• Tilt handle for further reach under vehicles
• Guard for spray bar protection
• High quality low profile swivel
• 4000 psi rated
• 24" cleaning area
• 250° F max.

Keep your customers' fleets free from salt, grease and other debris. Protect their vehicles' resale value and have a professional looking fleet. Clean difficult to reach areas without the use of a hoist, and decrease the man hours needed to protect their vehicle investment. See the Bottom Feeder in action at www.steeleagle.com.

We understand your time is important and you need the correct product for your application. Take a minute to discuss your particular cleaning situations with your Steel Eagle sales person. They can recommend the perfect system utilizing the correct accessories for the job. No matter what you are cleaning, Steel Eagle has a system that will do the job with ease and speed.

AaLadin Cleaning Systems offers pressure washers to fit any situation. We do this because we understand you aren't the same as every other fleet out there. We pride ourselves on being the innovator of many pressure washer features. We also are proud to be offering our exclusive Eco-Green High Efficiency Line of Equipment. Please go to www.aaladin.com or visit your local AaLadin distributor to learn how our products can save you time and money.

Classifieds: Products & Services

www.ArmClark.com
Armstrong Clark Quality Wood Stains. Specializing in wood restoration, oil-based coatings for wood & non-toxic wood stains of all kinds for your wood shake restoration & water repellent needs. 800-916-8211

www.PowerWash.com
Mobile power wash equipment, schools, training, videos, environmental supplies & maintenance services. Call for a free catalog, 800-433-2113.

www.PowerWashStore.com
Bigger Selection - Better Quality - Amazing Customer Service. Serving the professional cleaning community for more than 25 years. Call 855-351-9274.

www.PWNA.org
Power Washers of North America. For certification or membership information, visit our website, email info@pwna.org, or call 800-393-7962. Annual Trade Show and Convention, Oct. 17-19, Orlando, Fla.

www.SteelEagle.com
Mfr. of World Class Industrial & Commercial Cleaning & Storage Products, including surface spinners, vacuum systems, undercarriage cleaners, hose reels & more. Custom designs available. 800-447-3924

www.PressureWasherKy.us
Southside Equipment multi-line power equipment distributor. Pressure cleaning equipment, waste water recovery & recycling, generators & cleaning chemicals. Quality products & impeccable service. 888-243-6506

To Advertise in our New Classifieds Section
Contact Kelly Jacobsen
kelly@ecleanmag.com

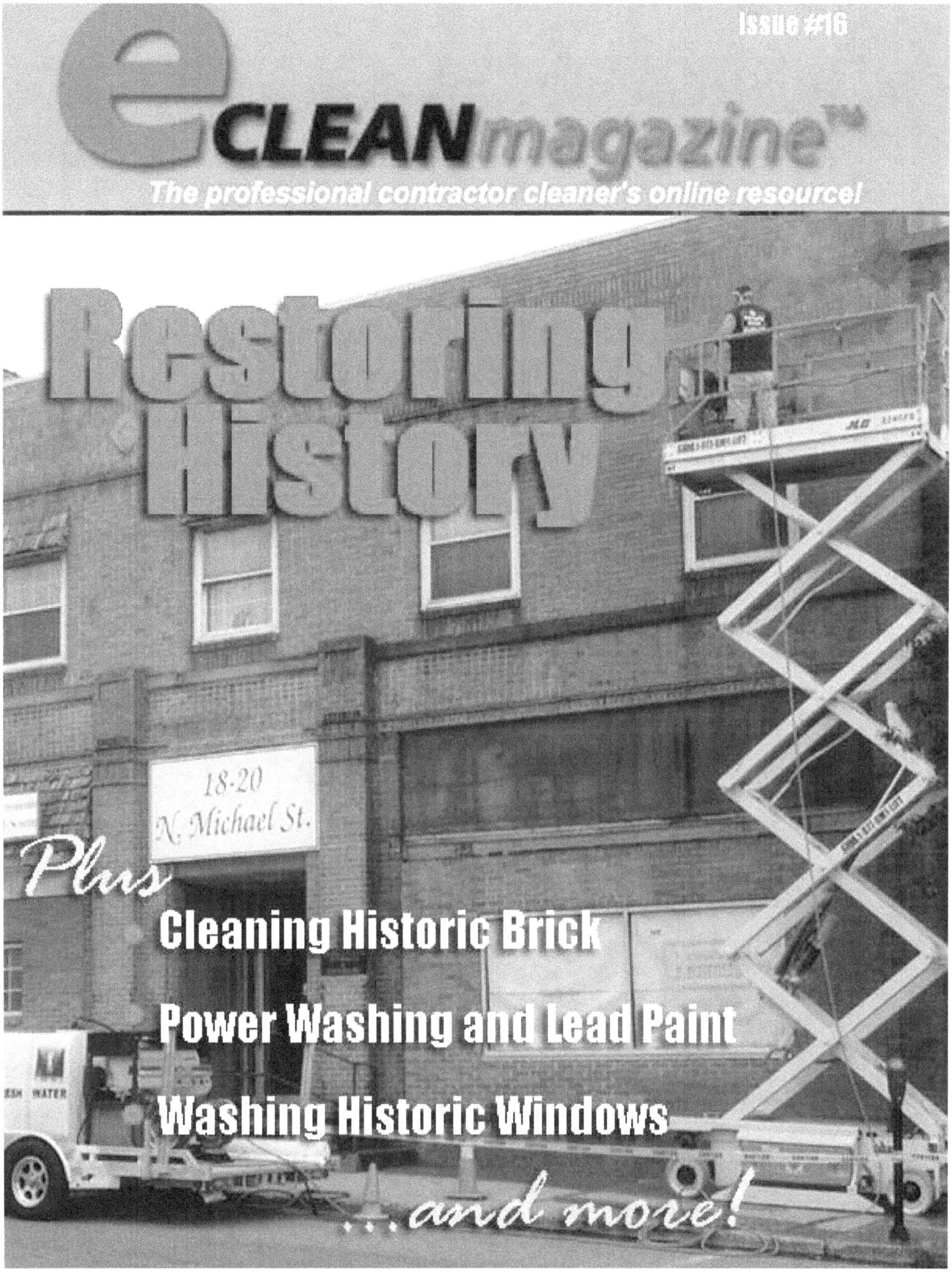
Issue #16
eCLEANmagazine™
The professional contractor cleaner's online resource!
Restoring History
18-20
N. Michael St.
Plus
Cleaning Historic Brick
Power Washing and Lead Paint
Washing Historic Windows
...and more!

POWERWASH.COM ™ **1.800.433.2113**
SUPPLIES CHEMICALS TRAINING
2513 Warfield St. Fort Worth, TX 76106

Click any item for more details

Pressure Washers

Surface Cleaners

Chemicals & Detergents

Cleaning Supplies

Parts & Accessories

Pumps & Unloaders

Training Materials

V-502-C Grease and Grime Remover for Concrete(*)
A perfect choice for when you need to penetrate and route out heavy grease, soil and grime on parking lots, dumpster pads, drive thrus, and other high traffic concrete areas.

"V-502 is a really great cleaner to have in your arsenal. We have used it with pretty great success on oil stains and tire marks and have found it to not only clean, but also brighten significantly!"

Curt Kempton - 5StarWindowCare.com

New

Elite Graffiti Remover (1 Gal)
Penetrates and loosens spray paint graffiti and allows for easy removal of the graffiti from masonry, brick, concrete, stone, mild steel, stainless steel, painted surfaces, and wood surfaces.

R-202 Concrete Cleaner
Cleans heavy grease, oil and scuff marks from unpainted concrete, brick, stone, and other alkaline water safe hard surfaces. USDA authorized for use in meat, egg, dairy food packing and processing plants. One 50 pound box makes 200 gal. of solution

Rust Remover Plus™
Rust Remover Plus™ is a perfect choice for removing tough oil and rust stains from concrete and exposed aggregate surfaces. Just spray it onto dry concrete with a pump up garden or chemical sprayer and watch the rust and oil stains disappear. After a a 5 to 10 minute dwell time, you can pressure wash the area with a 40 degree tip. Rust Remover Plus™ will brighten the concrete as it dries.

(*) Denotes $27.00 shipping surcharge by UPS.

Our Soft Wash Machines are Contractor TESTED & Contractor APPROVED!™

Soft Wash in a Box™ Complete System
The Soft Wash in a Box is built in a heavy duty locking aluminum box for protection against the weather and theft. The unit uses a powerful 12 volt Flojet Pentaflex pump that will pump up to 7 GPM at 80 PSI, a heavy duty corrosion resistant on/off switch, and a breaker to protect electrical components. A chemical resistant three way polypropylene flow valve is used to control flow through your system. The system can be ordered with one or two tanks.

A single tank system allows the user to pump concentrated cleaning agents from their original containers directly to the systems blending tank, and redirect flow from the hose reel back to the blending tank to agitate the mix.

A double tank system allows the user to pump concentrated cleaning agents from the original container directly to one of the two tanks. Then redirect the flow from the tank containing the concentrate to the mixing tank. This eliminates the need to make multiple trips back to the shop to get a blend for each job. It also reduces the amount of liquid on the truck, so that blends can be made at the job site by just adding water.

Mustang
- 12 volt, 7 GPM, 80 PSI, Flojet diaphragm pump with a maximum temperature of 160º F.
- Water tight battery box
- 10"x16" aircraft grade aluminum frame
- ½" x 24" PVC Wand
- VJ-0080B Brass Nozzle
- ¾" x 225' Rubber Hose
- Clear Vinyl Tubing with a mesh filter screen.

Colt
- 12 volt, 100 PSI diaphragm pump with a max temp of 140°F.
- JA-8000 Soft Wash Gun
- 1/2'" x 24" PVC Wand
- 1/4" stainless steel quick coupler socket
- 4 1/4" stainless steel quick coupler plugs
- Four V-Jet Nozzles 0º, 15º, 25º, 40º
- 200' of 5/8" poly braid hose
- 50 mesh filter screen

New Products at PowerWash.com

Hudson Float Valve
This valve is ideal for any application where it is necessary to control the level of fluid.
- No exterior moving parts
- Resistant to freezing
- Installs in seconds
- No float ball
- High volume
- Rust-proof

FLOJET Accumulator Tank
The FLOJET Accumulator Tank gives you the best of both worlds! High flow when you need it and the ability to restrict the flow for sensitive situations.
When the pump starts, liquid enters the reservoir compressing the bladder until the maximum pressure for the pressure switch is reached then the pump shuts off. Pump stays off until the minimum pressure is reached. Then pump turns on, reducing cycling leading to longer switch and pump life.

SPRAY TIPS™ Newsletter
Our Spray Tips Newsletter is packed with tips to help you build your business. Topics include tips for business management, marketing, equipment selection, and best practices for increased efficiency.
Sign up at: www.PowerWash.com

In This Issue:

247 Cleaning Historic Brick, by Larry Kotke, Dietrich Technologies

247

252 Lead Paint and Pressure Washing

254 Insurance for Power Washers: Understanding What You Need

256 "Live the Dream" – The PWNA Annual Convention & Technical Seminar, October 17-19 in Orlando

260 PWNA Vendor Profile: Timber Ox Green

262 Cleaning Historic Windows

262

264 No Job Is Too Big or Too Small, by Rick Meehan, Marko Janitorial

267 How to Pay Your Distributor on Time, by Tom Grandy, Grandy & Associates

270 History of the Modern Squeegee

272 Helping Resurrect Classic Cars, by Aaladin Industries

273 Classifieds

274 Pressure Washing Guidance for Cleaning Stains from Concrete, by Paul Horsley

Cover Photo
Courtesy of Ryan Wehler, PA PowerWashing, St. Marys, Pennsylvania

---

eClean Magazine is published monthly

Publisher: Paul Horsley, paul@ecleanmag.com
Editor: Allison Hester, allison@ecleanmag.com

Box 262, 16 Midlake Blvd S.E.
Calgary, Alberta
Canada T2X2X7
www.eCleanMag.com

eClean Magazine

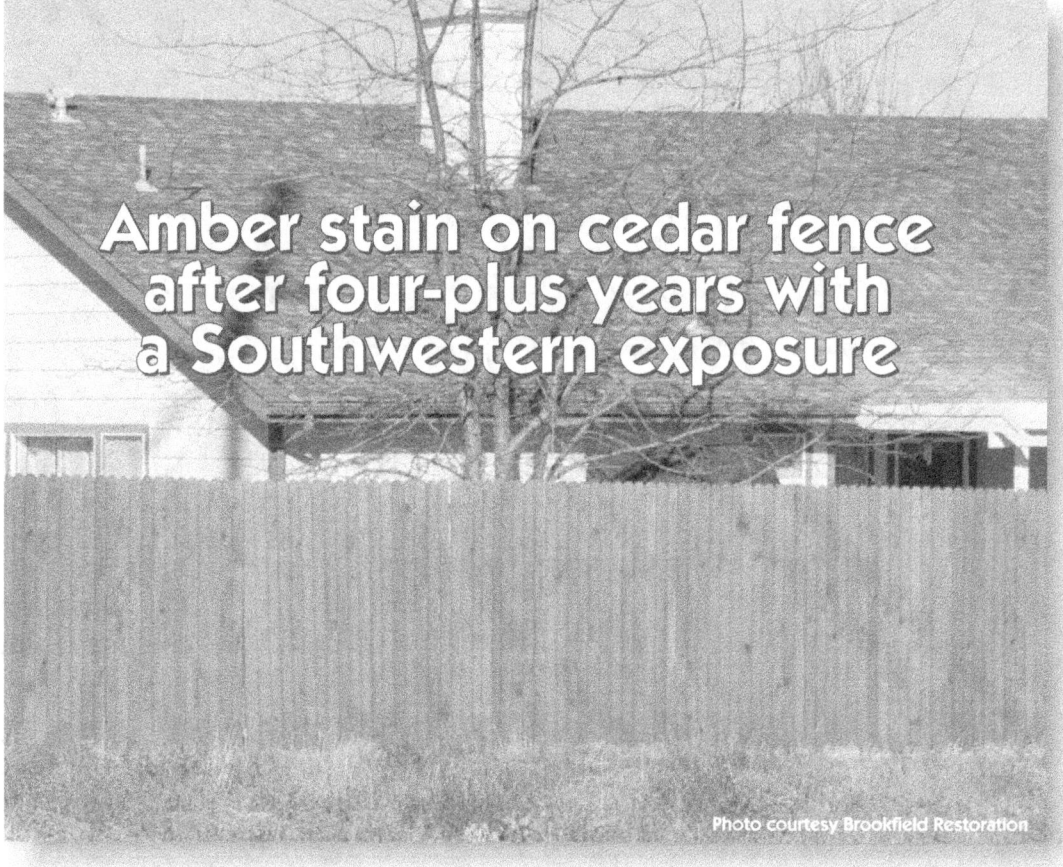

Cleaning Historic Brick

by Larry Kotke, Technical Sales Director for Diedrich Technologies, www.DiedrichTechnologies.com

Photo courtesy of Diedrich Technologies, www.DiedrichTechnologies.com

Why clean old dirty brick, be it a historic building or not?

It is not unusual to hear preservationists say not to clean because it removes "character" or "venerable patina" from the structure. But, in fact, the dirt is hiding the design features, colors, and textures the original architect selected to make his creation unique. Plus, the fact is that these dirt deposits on exposed surfaces aid in moisture retention. This retention can lead to both chemical and mechanical deterioration of the substrate.

Some of these – such as freeze-thaw damage – can be increased by the proportion of retained water. Acid rain deterioration and spauling can be accelerated by the quantity of acid held on the surface for extended time by the dirt/grime crusts. And then there is biological action (chemical deterioration and stains) that result from trapped water, resulting in the growth of micro-vegetation, i.e. mold, mildew, and moss.

So, how does one go about cleaning old dirty brick? If it is a building listed on the National Register of Historic places, the main guideline to go by is the "gentlest means possible." This should apply whether it is historic or not. In other words, do not sandblast or use any other abrasive method such as corncobs, walnut shells, baking soda, or dry ice, to name a few.

Chemical cleaning with a proprietary cleaner formulated for the specific type of surface will render the best results without damaging the surface. Beware of the "one product will clean everything" claims. Or the old just-hit-it-with-muriatic-acid to clean it. This couldn't be further from the truth.

While muriatic acid – or for that matter, hydrochloric acid – are effective for cleaning new construction mortar smears and residue, they will not clean old dirty brick. They could cause irreparable damage to the brick and historic mortar.

At Diedrich Technologies, we've developed cleaners to address the type of surface to be cleaned as well as the level of soiling. As in,

Photo courtesy of Ray Burke, Spray Wash Exterior Cleaning, www.spray-wash.com

"why use an elephant gun for rabbit hunting?"

Our main brick masonry cleaner is the Diedrich 101 Masonry Restorer. This would be considered our heavy duty brick restoration cleaner to address the soiling conditions one might run into in what were some of the heavy industrial areas of the country, such as Pittsburgh, Cleveland, Milwaukee, or Chicago, for example. For other areas of the country where you didn't have the heavy coal-fired industries, the Diedrich Envirestore 100 might be a better choice. Again, this goes back to the "gentlest means possible" mantra.

Ok, let's get down to the nitty gritty. The most effective cleaners for old dirty brick are hydrofluoric acid based products. Don't run out and buy hydrofluoric, dilute it with water and start cleaning. This is dangerous and you can cause major damage to yourself and the building. Plus, these bathtub/moonshine mixes are not accepted for cleaning historic buildings.

The Historic Trust and State Historic Preservation Offices only accept proprietary cleaners that have over time proven safe and effective. As I said earlier, the Diedrich 101 Masonry Restorer is our heavy duty cleaner for the most difficult brick cleaning situations. It is hydrofluoric acid based, but also incorporates wetting agents and surfactants that allow cleaning with less actual acid than if you used hydrofluoric and water.

The Diedrich 101 Masonry Restorer is a concentrate that is meant to be diluted to address jobsite conditions. Test samples must be conducted to determine the most effective dilution rate. Always use the highest effective dilution rate. If, for example, five parts water to one part cleaner is effective, going to a lower, say three to one, won't clean any faster. You will just be wasting money on unnecessary cleaner and subjecting the building to additional unneeded acid. Again, gentlest means possible.

However, should you be in an area where there was not a lot of coal-fired industries like steel mills and foundries, etc., you may not need the strength of the Diedrich 101. An alternative might be the Diedrich Envirestore 100. This product is a citric, phosphoric acid based cleaner and will clean effectively on light to moderate atmospheric soiling and removal of biological growths.

Before You Bid

If you as a contractor haven't done much – if any – restoration cleaning and want to get into it, here are some things to do before bidding on a project:

Always do test samples. It is not a bad idea to a sample each elevation. Pick areas that are indicative of soiling conditions throughout the building. Get a feel for the surrounding area. Was it an industrial area? Residential? What contributed to the soiling/pollution?

As an example, I had a contractor call who was working on an old mill. Three sides cleaned quickly and easily. The fourth side was giving him fits. As this was an old mill, I asked him if there were railroad tracks adjacent to that side. He said there weren't; however, he checked further and it turns out there had been tracks there for years but they had been removed. Because of this, he had to do a pre-treat of the brick with the Diedrich 808X Black Encrustation Remover (sodium hydroxide based) and then follow with the Diedrich 101 he had been using.

In another case, a contractor was cleaning a church and one side just wasn't cleaning even after he had tried different dilution rates. It turned out there had been trees along that side of the church that had been removed a while before and sap had sealed the dirt in so the cleaner couldn't get at the dirt. From some old photos, we were able to determine what the problem was and suggest a remedy, but it cost him some extra time and money to get that side clean.

Do some investigating before bidding. See if there are old pictures. These steps can save you time and money. Also, see if you can determine what type of businesses had been in the building, especially if it was industrial at one time.

What different building materials were used? It's not uncommon to have a combination of brick, limestone, sandstone, or granite on a building. These may require a combination of cleaners because one product may not be suitable or effective on all.

Some newcomers may have difficulty in determining what type of stone might be involved. I get calls all the time asking "how do I tell limestone from sandstone?" Do not be afraid to ask for help. Talk to your local stone or brick supplier, or give us a call. A few minutes of time can save you a lot of headaches.

Different types of brick will also clean differently, as in an old common brick will not clean as quickly or easily as a brick that has a harder burned face. This is something you will have to learn over time. In Diedrich's case, we will have a product for your needs, be it the 101 for brick, 101G for granite, terra cotta and glazed brick, Envirestore 100, 707X Limestone Cleaner and 707N Limestone Neutralizer or the 808X Black Encrustation Remover.

Don't get in over your head. Start small on, say, an old store front. This will give you experience and can generate additional business for you. One cleaned building can lead to other customers who want to improve the appearance of their business. We have seen this many times in downtown redevelopment initiatives. Later you can move on to bigger projects.

Equipment can make or break you. Invest in good quality equipment. Cold water pressure washers will work well; however, hot water machines can give you an advantage in that the hot water will enhance your cleaning capabilities. Hot water can make a big difference, especially on heavily-carboned surfaces, be they brick or stone, and also early or late in the season when surface and air temperatures can reduce product performance.

Application equipment for the cleaners can be a huge benefit. When you compare application rates and time for the acid cleaners using pump-up sprays to that of some of the powered sprayers, the labor savings can be significant. In some cases they will pay for themselves in one or two jobs.

As I said before, do not be afraid to ask for help. We at Diedrich Technologies take pride in our technical support. A few minutes on the phone can get you a lot of good product and procedure information. It is also possible for you to email pictures of projects you may be looking at. From those we can give you a lot of guidance. It is almost like being on the jobsite. You don't have to worry about information on a project you are looking at getting spread around. If you come to us for assistance, that information stays in-house. We also have sales people around the country that might be available for jobsite visits and assistance. We are here to help you.

Larry Kotke is the Technical Sales Director for Diedrich Technologies, where he has worked for over 29 years. Larry handles technical support for Diedrich's products, and has been involved in product development and testing over the years. Part of his duties involve training sales people, distributors and contractors, and leading cleaning seminars for architects and others. www.DiedrichTechnologies.com.

BLENDING OUT THE COMPETITION

KNIGHT HD 26-P
HEAVY-DUTY POWDER CLEANER DE-GREASES AND DE-SCALES EXHAUST HOODS AND DUCTS FOUND IN RESTAURANTS. STATE OF THE ART DETERGENT SYSTEM WITH A COMPLEX EMULSIFIER PACKAGE TO EASE THE REMOVAL OF HEAVY GREASE/SOILS FROM THE SURFACE.

DUCT SHINE
DUCT SHINE LEAVES SUBSTRATES WITH A SHINE THAT RESISTS FINGERPRINTS AND STREAKS. WILL PRESERVE STAINLESS STEEL, FORMICA, PORCELAIN, FIBERGLASS, ENAMEL, PLASTIC AND STEEL SURFACES AGAINST DETERIORATION.

128 W. LAKE STREET
NORTHLAKE IL 60164
(708) 531-1234 (708) 531-0010
www.knightnorros.com

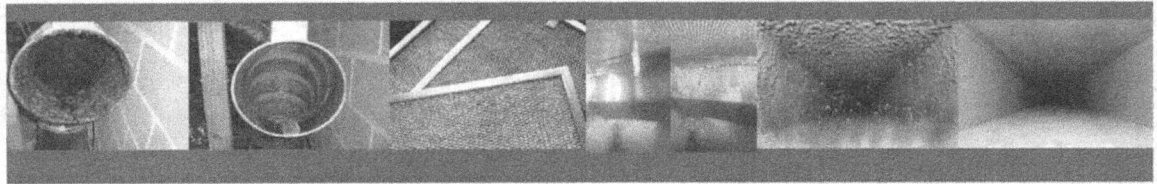

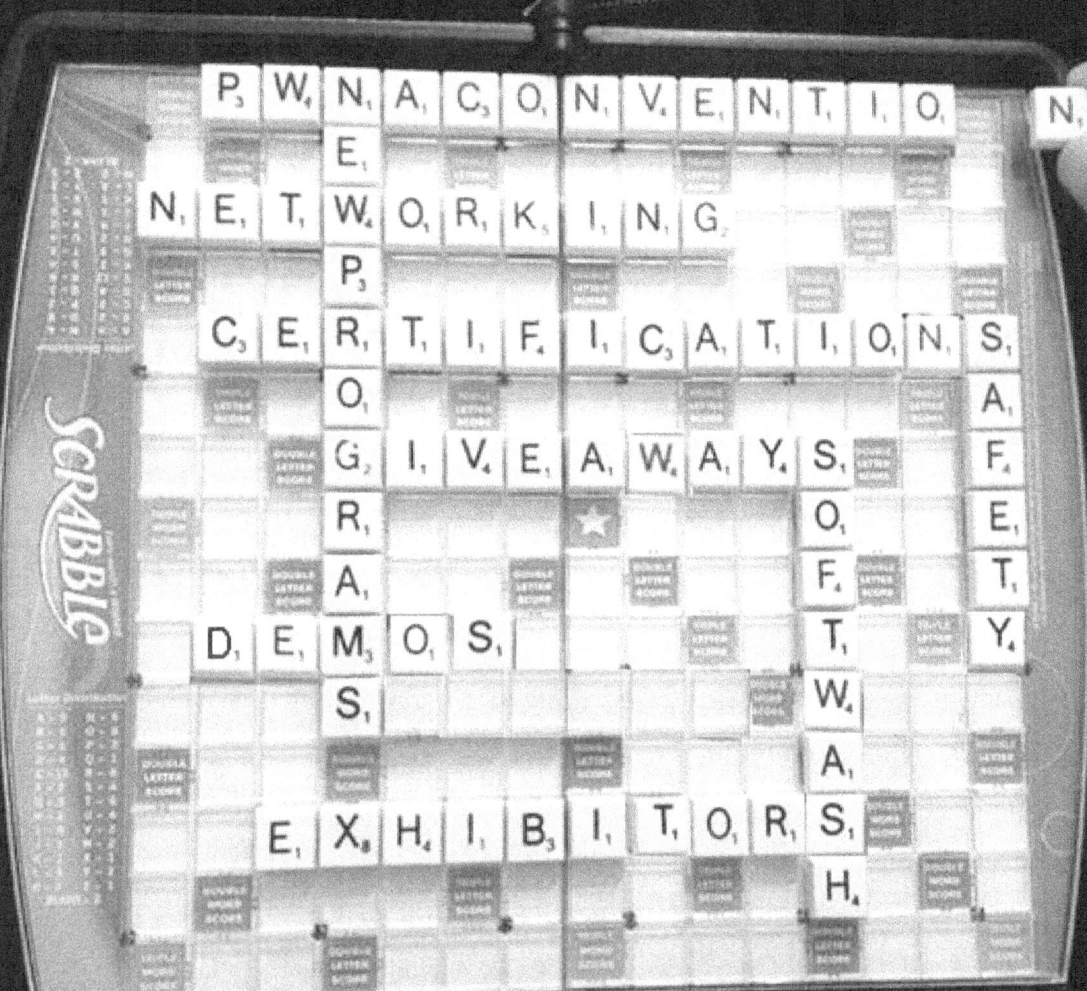

Lead Paint and Pressure Washing

by Allison Hester

If you clean a house that was built prior to 1978, there's a possibility you may be dealing with lead-based paint, which is subject to a host of EPA regulations.

The EPA's Lead Renovation, Repair and Painting Rule (RRP Rule), which went into effect in January 2011, was created to help protect children from lead poisoning. The rule requires that residential renovations, repairs and painting projects where lead paint is found must have a "certified renovator" assigned to each job. Additionally, all individuals on the job must be trained in the use of lead-safe work practices. But what exactly is a "renovation" contractor and do pressure washing contractors fall under this category?

A Little Background

In 1977, the U.S. Consumer Product Safety Commission banned lead in paint "to reduce the risk of lead poisoning in children who may ingest paint chips or peelings." Lead paint tastes sweet, so children who find the paint chips often like to ingest them. Lead can cause nervous system damage, stunted growth, kidney damage and delayed development.

The RRP Rule was created to keep children safe, and therefore the law only applies to residences and "child occupied dwellings" such as schools, day cares, or churches where children could potentially get their little hands on lead paint chips. The law also only applies if lead paint is found in more than a six-by-six area of the residence or building.

The federal law also does not apply to several states – Alabama, Georgia, Iowa, Kansas, Massachusetts, Mississippi, North Carolina, Oklahoma, Oregon, Rhode Island, Utah, Washington, and Wisconsin – which have enforced their own training and certification requirements. So if you are located in one of these states, you'll need to check with your area's regulations. The information in this article may not pertain to you.

But how does this apply to the pressure washing industry?

That's the question, and it's kind of a confusing one. To help me figure this out, I contacted Randy Fornoff of MTS Painting in Phoenix, Arizona. MTS is not only an EPA certified lead safe firm, Fornoff is also an approved instructor for RRP training.

Before looking deeper into the pressure washing issue, it's important to say that your safest, smartest route is to go through the EPA certification training, especially if you're going to be cleaning a number of pre-1978 homes. This is an eight-hour course that runs around $200. Upon completion, you can become an EPA lead-safe certified contractor, which will lessen your liability as well as give you a marketing edge. But is certification really necessary? It depends.

When bidding a house wash in a neighborhood built around or before 1978, one of the first things you want to ask is when the house was built. If the homeowner isn't sure, you can look it up on the house's deed, which is public information. The older the house, the more likely lead paint was originally used.

Start by inspecting the house like a painter would do. Watch for chipping or peeling paint. If there is none, chances are you're safe. More than likely, any home built prior to 1978 has been repainted since 1978, so if there is still lead-based paint on the structure, it has been covered up by EPA-approved latex paint. As a pressure washing contractor, you are simply washing the grime off the latex paint layer, and as long as you don't REMOVE paint, you're technically ok. "Keep in mind, however, that every job has a risk," Fornoff warns.

If the house was built prior to 1978 and there is peeling paint, the smart bet is to test for lead. While this is something any contractor can do, if you are not an RRP certified contractor, your test results will not be accepted by the EPA if a problem arises. "If you follow the EPA rules and go through the training and certification process, you are lessening your liability in the eyes of the law," Fornoff explained.

If, however, the lead paint test comes up positive, the price and the liability of the project just went up. DO NOT continue unless you are certified. This type of project will require following the RRP guidelines, which requires certification, extensive tarping, proper personal protective equipment (PPE), wastewater recovery, and so on.

Finally, if you are being brought in as a subcontractor on a paint prep job, the liability for the project should fall on the painting contractor, not you. However, an EPA certified painting contractor will likely prefer to work with an EPA certified power washing contractor, which again leads to the benefits of becoming certified.

"If in doubt, the best option is just to treat it like it has lead-based paint. Otherwise you're opening yourself up to all kinds of liability," Fornoff added.

Future Legislation

While the RRP rule currently only applies to residential and "child occupied dwellings," potential changes may be on the not-too-distant horizon. The EPA is looking to expand the rule to cover pre-1978 commercial properties as well, an issue that does not make a lot of sense to some members of the painting industry.

Fornoff is a member of the Painting and Decorating Contractors of America (PDCA), a group that is fighting against this change. The PDCA is asking the EPA to stop the expansion of the RRP Rule until "current, accurate studies are performed to assess need for public and commercial regulations." "The rule was created to protect children, who aren't going to be exposed to lead paint chips on an office building," Fornoff added.

In the meantime, the PDCA is asking industry members to share this web page with other industry members who may be impacted: www.pdcarrp.org/. There is also a letter that can be downloaded and sent to your local legislators about this issue.

To learn more about the RRP Rule and how to become certified, visit www2.epa.gov/lead/renovation-repair-and-painting-program-contractors.

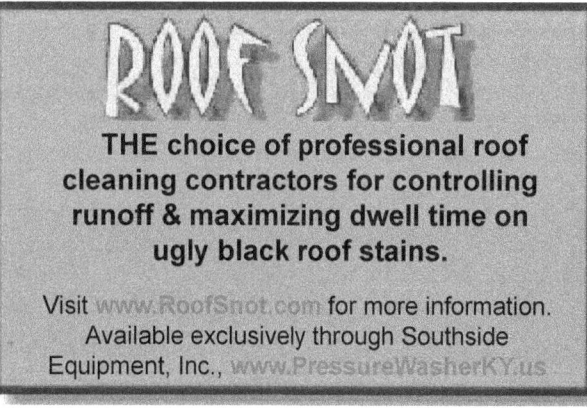

eClean Magazine

Insurance for Power Washers: Understanding What You Need

by Allison Hester

One of the first things new pressure washing contractors hear is that they need to get insurance. Sounds simple enough, right?

But what kinds of insurance? What coverages do they need? Will traditional insurance protect their specific liabilities? Does their agent understand their unique business?

In truth, most insurance companies actually don't provide the types of insurance that a power washing contractor needs. And, unfortunately, most contractors don't know what types of insurance they need either. It's only after a claim is filed that they realize they've been wasting their money on inadequate coverage.

"As a power washing contractor, you need insurance that can cover anything that can hamper your business and endanger your revenue stream. Anything less than that is inadequate," said Tom Svrcek of the Joseph D. Walters Insurance Agency, which has been serving the power washing community for over 20 years.

This past May, Svrcek's firm, CSC Insurance Options, acquired the Joseph D. Walters Agency, allowing the two firms (and long-time friends) to join forces and become a larger, stronger agency with more negotiating power. The agencies' personnel remained the same. "Joe Walters, who has helped thousands of pressure washing contractors over the years, is still a very active part of the agency, as is his staff," Svrcek explained.

However, the merger of the two agencies has made the company an "insurance powerhouse," allowing them to have more pull when it comes to negotiating with major insurance carriers. "That means we've been able to obtain new and better overages for power washing contractors at new, lower rates," Svrcek said.

"The newly merged agency makes us stronger, and that will help our clients in regards to coverage and pricing with the leading companies," added Lynn Rauch, the agency's Vice President.

Additionally, the agency now is able to carry new coverage, including commercial automotive, worker's compensation and umbrella policies. "That means now you can get all the insurance coverage your company needs all in one place and all on one bill," Svrcek added.

So what coverage does a pressure washing contractor need?

Many different kinds of contractors fall under the broad definition of "Artisan Contractors" – plumbers, cabinet makers, electricians and even power wash contractors. They need property coverage for their building and business contents too, as well as general liability, Workers Compensation, Business Auto and a Commercial Umbrella policy. However, very few agents know how to order proper coverage for their Artisan contractor clients, especially the Power/Pressure washer contractors.

One of the most important coverages for power washing contractors is Care, Custody and Control, but it is sometimes hard to obtain.

"Accidents do happen. This 'good will" coverage protects you for customer's property that you are working on," Svrcek explained. "Sometimes referred to as the 'faulty workmanship coverage,' we protect you for mistakes you make."

Most general liability policies have an exclusion that takes the "accidents happen" or "faulty workmanship" out of their policy. So if you are cleaning a deck and damage the deck, the deck is not covered by the policy.

Overspray from the deck that lands on the car and damages would be covered, but not the deck itself.

"If you're not dealing with a specialist in the Power wash business, you're probably not going to get the coverage you need at a price that's affordable," Svrcek added. "With our new power wash liability program, this coverage is automatically included for free."

Here are a few additional enhancements provided by the Joseph Walters' new power wash liability program:

• Blanket additional insured endorsement — FREE. Property owners require you to name them as additional insured. Most carriers charge up to $100 per job. This important coverage will save time and money.

• Blanket Waiver of Subrogation — FREE. This coverage is for jobs where the property owner requires you to waive the right of recovery for losses you may have with the owner.

• Identity Theft — $25,000 FREE.

• General Liability Limits up to $5,000,000 if necessary and from a AAA+ national carrier.

• Broadened Equipment Coverage

• Rented Equipment — FREE

• Guaranteed Pricing with No Audits. The problem with an auditable policy is that if your business does well, you give your insurance company the right to increase your premium and more.

• Employee Practices Liability: Harassment, discrimination, wrongful termination, etc.

"We also know that you sometimes need proof of insurance quickly, which is why we get it to you the same day you ask for it," Svrcek added.

Where to Begin

Whether you are just getting into the business or whether you've been power washing for years, it's a smart idea to determine if you have the insurance protection your business needs. To get started, Svrcek suggests the following steps:

Have a business insurance specialist conduct a risk analysis of your company and its operations. No two companies are the same, even two that are in the same business. No contractor does exactly what you do or how you do it. You need an expert to assess your company and the specific risk it faces—and put together a comprehensive insurance plan to protect you.

Use an Independent Insurance Agent. As a business owner, you want options. As such, don't call on an agent who is an employee of an insurance company. You want someone who will work for you. Someone who has access to a variety of insurance carriers. You want an agent that specializes in what you do.

Don't Trust Your Business to an Insurance Agent who does not know the Power Wash Business. You don't want to use an agent that does not have a comprehensive understanding of the special problems contractors like you face every day. You want and need a specialist.

"We have one niche market that we serve – the power washer – and we serve thousands of contractors across the country," Svrcek added. "We know how to protect their businesses. And we know which insurers provide the best rates and have the best claim service."

Joseph D. Walters
POWERWASH INSURANCE OPTIONS

America's #1 Insurer of Power Wash Contractors

WOW!
Get a **fast quote** for **Power Wash Insurance!**

For a FAST telephone quote:
1-800-878-3808
Get proof of coverage **TODAY**

I called and got quoted instantly. The prices were very good & it was easy! – Charlie Arnold, Lewes, DE

Walters even has a Saisfaction Guarantee Policy. If you're not 100% satisfied for any reason, they will return your money. No questions asked. They're good to work with. – Mike Strejeck, Monroeville, PA

www.JosephDWalters.com

Annual Convention & Technical Seminar
"Live the Dream"
October 17-19
Orlando, Florida

PWNA. POWER WASHERS OF NORTH AMERICA

For over 20 years, the PWNA Annual Convention has helped companies grow their businesses and gain success. It's why so many successful business owners continue to take part in the PWNA annual convention year after year after year. The education, networking, certifications, mentoring and product knowledge gained at the PWNA Annual Convention is what keeps many new pressure washing contractors from failing, and many established companies growing.

And this October's event looks to be the biggest and best in PWNA history – with tons of new offerings, along with several tried and true favorites. So if you've ever thought about attending a PWNA event, there's no better time sign up than today.

A New Vision for a Proven Event

This year, the PWNA is changing things up a bit, implementing a new vision entitled "Live the Dream."

"As pressure washing business owners, we all have dreams: whether it's to become an industry leader, to be a million dollar company, or something else. Whatever your dream is, the PWNA has members who have done all these things and more," explained PWNA Board member Ty Eubanks of South Shore Building Services in Southern California. "Best of all, they're willing to share how they did it, to answer all your questions and to help you achieve your goals. That's what the PWNA convention is all about."

With this theme in mind, this year's convention will be adding a variety of unique programs, fresh classes, new vendors and additional giveaways to help attendees "live the dream."

"We want every moment of the PWNA convention to be valuable in helping our attendees reach their goals," said Eubanks. "So we're making some changes, not only to give attendees more opportunities during the day, but to keep the camaraderie and networking building well into the evenings."

Education

The changes begin with educational classes, with several new courses and new instructors being added this year, along with some tried and true favorites. This year's courses include:

Fall Protection, presented by Charlie Arnold,
Water Remediation, presented by Jefferson Lehman of Steel Eagle
Scaffolding, presented by Charlie Arnold
Soft Washing, by Micah Kommers
Parking Garage Cleaning – John Tornabene and Paul Laramee
9 Tips to Manage the Growth of Your Business – Michael Hinderliter
Insurance for Power Washers – by Tom Svrcek, Joe Walters Insurance
Power Washing 101 – Tracy Handl, PressureWashOutlet.com
Kitchen Exhaust Cleaning, Daryl Mirza
Window Cleaning with Pure Water, by Steve Blythe, J. Racenstein

In addition to the new classes, this year's event will also include the return of a favorite, the "Taking Your Business into the Millions" panel discussion, led by several PWNA members whose company's bring in $1 million or more a year. "We have always received great feedback from the panel discussion, as attendees can get all their questions answered candidly by some of the industry's most successful contractors," added PWNA Executive Director Jackie Gavett.

Of course, PWNA also will be offering certification classes in a variety of fields. These include Wood Restoration, House Washing, Fleet Washing, Roof Cleaning, Flatwork (which includes the Seal 'N Lock Authorized Technician Training), and Environmental Certification Courses. Additionally, $99 of your registration fee can be applied toward the certification program of your choice.

"I've personally found that taking certification classes has not only helped me in the markets we currently serve, they also helped me decided whether or not to venture into some new fields," Eubanks added. "I realized after taking a couple of certification classes that those were not the right markets for me. That realization alone saved me thousands of dollars in mistakes."

Finally, even lunchtime will be educational, as the PWNA again offers "Snack 'N Chat" roundtables. Attendees will not only fill up on a delicious meal, they will gain new insights on the roundtable topic of their choice.

Networking and Team Building

An exciting new program being implemented this year is a team-building exercise that will take place throughout the convention. Each attendee will be placed on team, along with one PWNA board member and one exhibitor. "Whichever table you decide to sit at during the opening ceremonies will be your 'team' for the rest of the event," Eubanks explained.

Each team will be taken to tour two locations where they will look for various cleaning opportunities, then put together a proposal – complete with a Power Point presentation. "This way participants get to practice putting an actual bid together and develop their marketing skills," explained

Eubanks. "It will also help ensure that attendees get to know exhibitors, board members and other attendees better, because they'll be working together throughout the event." Additionally, he members of the winning team – which will be named after the convention is over – will be given free admission to next year's convention.

Even the socials – which last year took place in the hotel lounge – will be moved into the meeting space (a.k.a., "The Dream Room"), and after hours activities are being organized to help ensure that everyone connects throughout the day as well as the evenings.

Exhibits and Demonstrations

This year's event is providing extended opportunities to not only talk with vendors on the trade show floor, but to get to know them on a deeper level. Several new vendors have already signed up to take part in this year's event, and the list keeps growing.

The trade show will be open throughout the day on Friday and Saturday, and equipment demonstrations will take place on Saturday, allowing participants to see the products in action. "We are very excited by the growing list of exhibitors at this year's event, many of whom will be leading classes as well as exhibiting,"

added Gavett. "Attendees are going to get more one-on-one time with exhibitors this year, and exhibitors are going to have more time to meet face-to-face with both current – and future – customers."

New Prizes

One of the most exciting opportunities for attendees is the chance to go home with not only new knowledge and contacts, but also with physical prizes.

This year, the PWNA has added a new grand prize, which is part of the association's mentoring program. One lucky winner will be given an all-expense paid trip to Alberta, Canada, to train with Paul Horsley of Scotts Pressure Wash (and publisher of eClean Magazine), one of North America's largest pressure washing companies. Paul has been in the pressure washing industry for more than 35 years and has trained contractors around the world through his consulting services. He has also been on the PWNA board of directors since 2006.

While with Paul, the lucky winner will gain new insight on a wide variety of business and pressure washing related topics, which may include business operations; marketing and advertising; pricing; upselling customers; human resources; tracking results; setting up chemicals and detergents; equipment maintenance; setting up a mobile unit; reclamation; safety and much more.

"I really enjoy teaching and mentoring contractors, and am excited to be a part of this unique new opportunity that PWNA is offering," Paul explained. "It's the type of program that really represents what the PWNA is all about."

To learn more about the Power Washers of North America, visit their website at www.PWNA.org. To register for the PWNA Convention, go to www.pwna.org.

No Water Wasted Promo

Hydro Tek National Special — July 2013

$12,495
save $4700

save the drain for the rain

FREE freight*

Want a larger trailer? Upgrade to a 400 gallon, dual axle trailer with electric brakes for only $2500 more

Mobile Wash Skid
Gas Powered, Diesel Heated – 110v burner
3500psi, 5gpm, Belt drive pump
570cc Vanguard twin cylinder engine
On-board 3000w generator

Trailer
200 gallon ProTowWash® trailer with rear storage tray and high pressure hose reel

Vacuum Recovery/Filtration System
Recover and filter your washwater for reuse or disposal. No external power needed, runs off pressure washer generator.
<u>Package also includes</u> containment berms, scupper & vacuum hose

NO WATER WASTED Recycle Trailer
model# SC35005VS/T2NWA/AZV55

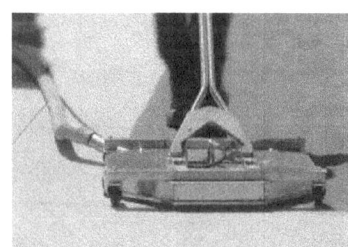

Add a Twister Vac recovery surface cleaner for $1500

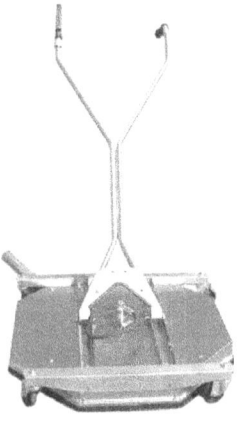

AUTHORIZED LOCAL DISTRIBUTOR:

Limited time offer starts July 15, 2013. Price does not include sales tax or battery, if needed. *Free freight to distributor location within the continental US. Ask your distributor for the *No Water Wasted* Special. Not to be combined with any other offers, programs, or discounts. Available through a participating distributor, call for a local distributor. 400 gallon trailer upgrade model# SC35005VS/T4NWA/AZV55

Brilliant Design, Tough on Grime
2353 Almond Avenue • Redlands, CA 92374 • (P) 800-274-9376 • (F) 909-799-9888 • www.hydrotek.us

PWNA Vendor Profile

by Allison Hester

John Nearon spent 18 years in the coatings industry, developing, marketing and implementing application specific Coatings Process Solutions to manufacturers throughout North America, Western Europe and Mexico. He had consulted and provided sales engineering to a wide variety of clients including ABB, Amcast Automotive, American Woodmark, Chrysler, The Ford Motor Company and General Motors among others.

Then he learned about wood restoration. His neighbor, Todd Forth, owned a wood restoration company and John not only liked the restoration process, he saw potential in the industry. In 2004, John decided to join forces with Todd as Exterior Wood Restorations, Inc., but under one condition: John insisted they develop their own wood preservation products.

Specifically, John wanted to come up with a wood preservative that was durable, effective, easy to apply, and environmentally friendly. "We needed to create a product that would represent the warranty that we were offering our customers," he explained. "We also needed a product that would not only last a long time, but look beautiful in the process."

It took around three years of trial and error in the laboratory, but they eventually developed a product that did everything they wanted it to do. It became exclusive product line for Exterior Wood Restoration's projects throughout Indiana, Illinois, Kentucky and Ohio.

"We designed the product for our wood restoration business – period. We never intended to sell our products to anyone else," John explained.

But people started asking for it. "At that point, we were faced with a dilemma. Do we tell them they have to use our services if they wanted their new fence to match the deck we sealed last year, or do we provide them with the product?" John and Todd decided to sell them the product, and that's how Timber Ox Green was introduced onto the market.

About Timber Ox Green

Timber Ox Green is unique in that it is castor-oil based, rather than mineral oil based, meaning it is an agriculturally renewable oil-based stain. This allows it to deeply penetrate the wood, provide exceptional UV protection, and have a three year guarantee on horizontal surfaces and a five year warranty on vertical surfaces. It also exceeds all state and federal VOC EPA standards, which allows it to be sold in all 50 states.

Timber Ox Green can be used as both an interior and exterior stain that beautifies and protects wood surfaces. "We also formulated so that it's easy to apply and inhibits lap marks," John added. "It enhances the natural grain of the wood and restores life to old damaged wood."

While the Timber Ox Green line began with a wood restoration product line, they have also introduced a line of concrete and masonry sealers. The design of the Timber Ox Green Timber Ox® Green Concrete and Masonry Sealer applies the same principles as the wood sealer, providing a bio-based, deep penetrating, film forming wet look or satin finished sealer. These products can be used on concrete, brick, tile, stucco, pavers, flagstone, driveways, garage floors, granite, marble, travertine and cementaceous materials.

Joining the PWNA

With the Timber Ox Green product line on

Timber Ox Green has several unique traits:
- BIO-BASED Formulation
- Unique Nano Particle UV Sunscreen which contains nano-sized, transparent, titanium dioxide as a sunscreen to prevent ultraviolet light damage to the wood.
- Exclusive Triple Polymer Protection - Unique to Timber Ox® Green acrylic, urethane and polyester formula: Three resins in one extend the product life and are non-yellowing and fade resistant with exceptional water resistance and weatherability.
- Powerful anti-oxidant formula: Protects against oxidation and resultant cracking and degradation of base resins.
- High performance anti-mold, mildew & algae formulation: Exceptional mold, mildew and algae resistance.
- Transparent iron oxide pigments: Highlight and protect the natural warmth and beauty of wood.
- Castor bean, citrus, soy, and corn oil formula: Castor bean, citrus, soy, and corn oils are wood loving, natural, renewable, agricultural carrier oils with exceptional heat resistance and durability which protects wood fibers creating a water resistant barrier.
- Non-ozone producing & non-ozone depleting formulation: Timber OX does not create ozone (smog) or deplete upper atmosphere ozone.

Timber Ox® Green's environmental performance has been measured to be 0.0067 (using the BEES life cycle assessmen testing sytem), which is extremely low for an oil-based stain.

the market, John read about the Power Washer of North America's Annual Convention and decided to take part – both as an exhibitor and a contractor. He attended his first meeting in 2008 in Chicago, where he not only made new contacts for his product line, he gained valuable knowledge for his wood restoration business as well.

John joined the PWNA Board of Directors in 2010, where he currently serves as Vice President. He also teaches the PWNA's Wood Restoration Certification Course.

"It's a pretty intensive, detailed course, and I enjoy not only teaching others about wood restoration, but also keeping myself sharp on the topic by going over the ins and outs again, and again, and again," John added. "That has also helped me be better in my own wood restoration company."

From John's unique perspective, joining the PWNA has definitely been a beneficial move for him personally. "Joining the PWNA has opened many new doors for Exterior Wood Restorations," John explained. "I've developed a number of strong friendships, gotten ideas for new ways to grow my contracting business, and had a network of peers to call on when something unusual came up and I needed some help. It's been a wonderful resource for me personally in both my contractor and distributor business."

To learn more about Timber Ox Green, visit their website: www.TimberOxGreen.com.

Cleaning Historic Windows
by Allison Hester

Photo courtesy of Mark Munro of Burton Bradstock, England

In my years as editor for Little Rock's local historic preservation association's newspaper, I realized that there are many homeowners who are "die hard" preservationists. Not only do they live in historic homes, they want to maintain as much of the original architectural integrity as possible – including the window glass.

In my community – and I'm guessing in others as well – these preservationists are a tight-knit group. When they find a contractor who knows about their community's specific needs and who does a good job, word spreads quickly. So, for instance, understanding historic window glass can help set your company apart from other window cleaners, even though the work is not much different from most other residential cleaning jobs.

A Brief History of Window Glass

Before 1900, window glass was hand blown and expensive, especially large pieces, primarily because it was not readily available. So most windows contained small, individual glass panes that let in light and helped keep out the elements. But the glass was far from even and clear, making outside images blurry.

Then in 1900, machine-drawn glass was created, which significantly improved the clarity of glass. Larger panels became available (but nothing today's options). The quality and consistency of window glass we see today did not come about until 1959, however.

Many historic homes have replaced their window glass with modern glass, but many preservationists still prefer the look and feel of historic glass.

"Pre-1959 glass is typically thinner and more brittle," explained Scott Austin Sidler, owner of Austin Home Restorations in Orlando, Florida, and author of TheCraftsmanBlog.com. "The older the glass, the more imperfections it will have, such as waviness, fish-eyes, etc."

Cleaning Historic Windows

Cleaning historic windows is not a lot different from cleaning modern windows, except that you may need to avoid using a waterfed pole, depending on how long ago the windows were sealed. Historic window are sealed with a putty glaze – not caulking – and it works wonderfully…when it works. However, it does need to be replaced at times, and those windows are going to be prone to leaking from a waterfed pole. The last thing you want to do is get water on the home's restored historic hardwood floors!

Also, extra care needs to be taken to keep the glass from breaking. "The brittleness makes it prone to breakage," Sidler explains. "And since it is not tempered, it breaks into long sharp shards that can be very dangerous."

The following window cleaning tips are from Jen Miret, Director of Marketing for Bendheim Restoration Glass:

1. Know the right cleaners. Just like regular window glass, mouth-blown glass can be cleaned with non-abrasive, ammonia-free commercial cleaners, household vinegar and water solutions, or mild dish soap solutions. Using warm (not hot) water will ensure dirt is loosened without damaging the caulk and wood frames, and the cleaning solution will not evaporate too quickly.

2. Know the right tools. While commercial window washers typically use a 14" or wider squeegee to clean modern windows, the relatively small size of antique window panes and the waviness of the glass make lint-free (terry) cloths a more convenient and efficient tool way to wipe cleaning solutions off the glass and framing. For small, stubborn spots (not stains), a new razor blade can be used to carefully scrape them off. The blade should be moved in the same direction, not back-and-forth, to avoid dragging dirt particles across the glass surface, causing scratching. Also, special care should be given not to confuse small air bubbles and imperfections – a unique characteristic of mouth-blown window glass – with dirt.

3. Know your limitations. Finally, not all deterioration can be cleaned or removed from glass, and may require replacing the affected panes. Etching, for example, can occur on windows that have been exposed to wind-blown grit over long periods of time, left unprotected during sandblasting of masonry facades, or exposed to masonry cleaners containing hydrofluoric acid.

Getting into the Market

If this is a market that you really want to get into, it's important to get to know the community – and be known by the community. If there is a local preservationist organization in your area, join it and get involved. These groups regularly have fundraisers, so donating your window cleaning services as an auction item is another good way to become recognized. As with any organization, the more you put in, the more you'll benefit yourself.

Historic Window Glazing – A Potential Niche Service

Many historic windows were glazed with a linseed oil putty to make the panes air tight. Replacing window glass and putty is a niche market that can be a nice addition for window cleaners in communities with lots of historic residences, but it takes knowledge, skill and practice.

Like most things on an old house, the putty glazing has a specific lifespan - about 30-40 years," explained Scott Austin Sidler, owner of Austin Home Restorations in Orlando, Florida, and author of TheCraftsmanBlog.com. "As it ages it becomes more brittle and eventually loses the elasticity that allows it to seal the window. The glazing putty is an integral part of the window and should be replaced when it is worn out."

Removing the putty is a somewhat delicate process because, again, the window glass is brittle and can break fairly easily. Additionally, it requires removing paint from around the windows first to expose the putty. The paint around the window may contain lead and lead paint removal is regulated by the EPA.

Rather than try to explain the details of removing the putty, I found a video located that shows the process. Click on the photo to go to the video.

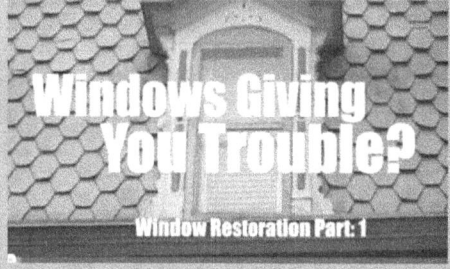

Next you will need to apply new putty. Sidler has put together a nice video on how to do this. Click photo below.

Finally, Sidler also offers a "Working With Old Windows" workshop a couple times a year where students learn how to maintain and repair old windows. To learn more about the class and when it will next be offered, email Sidler at austinhomerestorations@gmail.com.

No Job is Too Big or Too Small

by Rick Meehan
Vice President of Marko Janitorial Supply, www.MarkoInc.com

I've got a pet peeve. Yes, and when someone strokes it without permission, I have to say something about it. My pet's name is "No Job Too Big or Too Small," or "Nojob" for short.

Someone petted Nojob just the other day by mentioning how tough it is to get new business in this economy. After a few qualifying questions, I discovered that this particular small business person was going after mega-corps for cleaning jobs – exclusively. While this is a noble goal, most mega-corps have layers upon layers of red tape to cut through for one to finally get an opportunity even to be considered for making a quotation to possibly handle some of the cleaning business somewhere in the system, maybe. Put on your gloves boys and girls, because Nojob's getting ready to bite!

Unless your cleaning company is a national chain with mega-resources to match the needs of mega-corps, you need to take a step back and think:

Layer Number One: if you don't have the ability to handle a particular type of client, don't take them on! This does not mean that at some point your company can't take the job, only that you take the job when you know beyond doubt that you can do a good one. Otherwise, you'll end up losing the new business. Not only that, but you'll damage your company's reputation. Building a good reputation in this industry, where word-of-mouth advertising can make or break a cleaning company, should be your biggest concern. Do a fabulous job within your capabilities. Guard your reputation like an armored knight!

Layer Number Two: involves product knowledge. You've heard me harp on this before. To quote from Sarris, the bad alien in the sci-fi spoof Galaxy Quest, "You think that I am a fool – that the Commander does not know every bolt, every weld, of his ship?" A cleaning contractor's product, or "ship," contains many facets, from accounting and inventory, to material safety, to proper cleaning methods, to human resources, to taxation, to sales techniques – it's all in the boat and much more. The trick is to continue to increase your knowledge of all areas in your vessel.

With growth in your knowledge comes the possibility of growth in your business. Skills must be acquired, especially those pertaining to sales and presentation. Either you do it yourself, or you hire a professional salesperson to do it for you. However, if you hire a

representative, make absolutely sure they understand not to oversell your company's abilities. (See Layer Number One.)

Layer Number Three is the avoidance of delusions of grandeur. We all start getting the "swelled head" after we've been stroked for doing a good job. Confidence builds, so we jump out to top the last good job with something even better. But, as Nojob can tell you from experience, this is a fleeting sensation that evaporates at the first sign of inability to complete a task. Not only do we lose our confidence, we start the mouths a'wagging about the poor performance we provided. For a salesperson, I would term this "salesperson slump." It is the downside of the bell curve, or the slippery slope of decreasing business.

Stretching our muscles is fine; overstretching causes pain and injuries. Grow a business of course; only make sure to build in a controlled fashion.

The idea that "no job is too big" is ludicrous, as I've just pointed out. What about small jobs though?

Layer Number Four, or "no job is too small," has detrimental effects on our business too. This concerns the concept of costing, or pricing our products and services. Let's take an example. The factors involved are thus:

My company has three employees including me, myself, and I.

I have one pickup truck loaded with sundry cleaning tools and products.

Five small offices, each with less than 20 employees, are the perfect size for me to handle.

I just obtained a new customer through word-of-mouth – a small church. I hated to turn them down because I could use the extra money.

Now, I'm heading out to go clean the church. It's about an hour's drive from my furthest small office, well outside of my normal route between jobs. The question: is it worth it? Well, maybe, maybe not. It depends on the costs involved.

Churches have lots of nooks and crannies, especially under pews and chairs. They take a lot of extra time and labor that normal office cleaning does not. Plus, there's the cost of travel and maintenance on the old truck to think about. Uh oh, and small churches normally don't have a lot of money to spend on cleaning maintenance, so the pay is low compared to the other business I already have. Hummmm, I don't want to upset anyone though, so I continue on my way to handle the job. With some newly acquired knowledge about costing my jobs, I still wonder if this is the right way to grow my business. Figures like these start rumbling through my head:

My hourly rate is based upon X dollars invested in cleaning chemicals, truck, gas, storage space rental, office equipment, cleaning equipment, bonded insurance, taxes, in short, the factors that detract money from my profits, termed "overhead." After I've tallied all that, I have to make at least $36.85 per hour to cover the overhead, fund my wage, and make a small profit to reinvest. I can handle cleaning each of these small offices in just under an hour per unit. The office units fall within the size range

of about 500 square feet each. So, five hours times $36.85 divided by 2500 total square feet, means billing of about 7 cents per square foot. The jobs are simple and fairly easy on my back too.

I find that cleaning the church takes a full eight hours every week after 5:00 PM on Friday. Things have to be nice and tidy when the church opens for Sunday morning service, so this is the best time for my cleaning to occur. By multiplying my necessary hourly rate of $36.85 by 8, this totals $294.80 billed to the church. They are a little slow to pay, relying on donations as they do, but usually the check comes within thirty days. The church is actually 6200 square feet too, much bigger than the other jobs combined. Eight hours

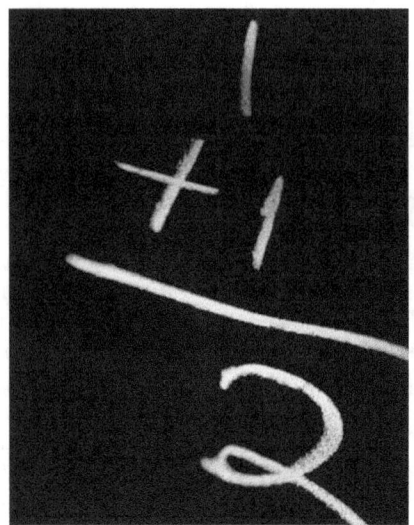

times $36.85 divided by 6200 square feet, means a billed rate of about 4.75 cents per square foot – that's 2.25 cents per square foot less money than the offices, and my back aches something fierce the rest of the weekend. Not only am I working longer and harder, but I'm actually taking half the pay, well below my threshold for making my wage after overhead. After careful consideration, I find that handling the church business is costing me money!

Sometimes it is necessary to walk away from prospective business to preserve the bottom line. These instances will become less frequent if you do the math up front before taking on more work. While the above example is fairly simplistic, peeling back the layers to get to the nitty-gritty is important. This is called qualifying the prospect, a staple philosophy in Selling.

Still think no job is too big or too small? No matter what mathematical formula you use to arrive at your bottom line, facts are facts. Some jobs are definitely too small and some jobs are ludicrously large. It is all based on your individual contracting company's costs of doing business.

Everyone's company may be different, but the math works for all – even the one-horse operation. Do your best with what you have, but increase profits by increasing your knowledge. Ensure that your reputation is paramount and secure all along the way by learning to screen jobs with grace; otherwise, they will cut into your profits.

Grow into larger jobs as you obtain the necessary tools of education and equipment. Don't end up like Nojob – dejected, neglected, angry...and out of business. Muzzle the beast by doing the diligence of qualifying your prospective customers before taking on the extra work!

How to Pay Your Distributor on Time

by Tom Grandy, Grandy & Associates,
www.GrandyAssociates.com

You will remember from our last month's article that we talked about how to build a win-win relationship with your distributor. One of the things that really helps strengthen and build that relationship is paying your invoices on time. You may also recall that only 10 to 15 percent of the distributor's customer base routinely pays their bill on time and only 1 to 2 percent pay within 10 days and take advantage of the terms discount. This month we are going to address how to pay your distributor on time.

Paying your distributor on time involves three key factors: properly set hourly pricing, collect a deposit on all major residential installations, and manage the deposit dollars properly.

Establishing Proper Pricing
The foundation of every successful company is establishing and executing proper pricing. If your hourly rates are not set properly, nothing else matters. You can be the best marketer in the area, perform top quality work, provide outstanding customer service, and be growing at 20 percentt a year; but if you are not priced properly, you are still going to go out of business! Proper job cost pricing is essential! If you haven't gone through the process of properly establishing your labor pricing STOP EVERYTHING else you are doing and find out what those numbers are!

Check out our website where you will find a robust variety of tools and programs to help you set appropriate and profitable hourly rates that are based on your costs of doing business. You may even be interested in purchasing our Business Boot Camp Materials Packet which includes our Labor Pricing software.

Collect A Deposit on Big Jobs
Cash flow will improve substantially if you are priced accurately. However, it won't solve all your cash flow issues and it won't necessarily allow you to pay your distributors on time. The next critical step is requiring customers to pay a deposit if the job is going to take several days.

I ask contractors in every boot camp class that I teach who gets a deposit. On average, about 20% of the class collects a deposit upon signing the contract. Those who do receive the deposit routinely average between 25%-50% down. I then ask the rest of the class why they don't get a deposit and the standard answer is…"Because we don't ask!"

We want to get a deposit on each time-consuming job for two primary reasons:

If the deposit money is handled properly, you will be able to pay your distributors on time and hopefully take your discounts. We will cover how to do that later in this article.

You could lose the customer. Consider the scenario. It's your busy season and the customer has just agreed to use your services

and they have signed your contract. Then you share the bad news..."Mr. and Mrs. Jones, I know you would like the job done tomorrow, but this is our busy season. It could be a week or more before we can complete the job. Is that a problem?" The customer says okay with a less than totally positive attitude. Now you're caught up and you call to tell them you will be able to start their project in the morning. Mr. Jones informs you they have decided not to wait and another contractor has already done he job. Yes, you have a signed contract ... but so what?? Are you going to sue them? I doubt it. However, I can promise you if you had the 25%-50% down payment in your pocket, the Jones' would not have had anyone else do the job.

So yes, request a deposit. It will allow you to pay your distributor on time and it will keep you from losing that occasional job where the customer really doesn't want to wait.

Handling the Deposit Money Properly

There is this thing called The Law of Money. Simply stated, The Law of Money says any significantly sized budget (personal or business) will tend to absorb every dollar that is deposited in it. If you had a great month, all the money seems to disappear. If you had a slow month, somehow you made it. We tend to spend whatever is in the checkbook. So, factor number three is being disciplined not to spend the deposit money.

Now, if we do a great job of collecting the deposit on the job, and we leave it in the checkbook, what is going to happen to it? Correct. It's going to be spent, resulting in being in worse shape than before. When the invoice arrives from your distributor, you don't have any money to pay it. What is the answer? Set up a liability account within QuickBooks, or whatever accounting system you use.

Step one is to go to your bank and set up a new savings account. While there, also set up all your business bank accounts so you can access them online. This will allow you to transfer money from one account to another in a matter of minutes, without having to make a trip to the bank. Your new savings account will be the place where you will "hold" your deposit money until your distributor's invoice arrives. Out of sight, out of mind! It's really hard to spend money that is not in your checkbook - although some people do. It's called a bounced check!

Now when you collect your job deposit, put it in your checkbook along with your other deposits. However, after depositing the money in your basic checkbook, transfer the down payment money into your new liability account. The deposit money no longer shows up in your checkbook balance ... but it will still

eClean Magazine

be available in your liability account.

Step two is establishing the habit (at the end of each day) of moving the money out of your business checkbook and into your new savings or liability account. This can be done within QuickBooks through "Transfer." Once you have transferred the money within your QuickBooks account, you will then go online with your bank and transfer the money from your business account into your alternative liability account.

When the distributor's bill arrives, you simply transfer the money from your liability account back into your business account. Bingo, you have the money to pay your distributor on time, and better yet, you can take the discount!

Yes, I hear you! "Tom, I can't do that; we need that money to operate on." If that's the case, go back to the original discussion in this article. If you can't live without spending your deposit money that was intended to pay your supplier, then take that as a big red flag. You are not priced for profit! Return to step one and determine your profitable hourly rates, in each department. Proper pricing will allow you to use your deposit money for its intended purpose, which is to pay your supplier......on time!

Your customers want three things: 1) do what you said you were going to do, 2) do it when you said you were going to and 3) do quality work. If you are doing these things consistently, you can increase your price. Get feedback from your customers on a regular basis. After all, what they are telling other people is the marketing message that is being spread about your company. Take advantage of this month's online special and get easy to use Customer Response Cards that you can start using immediately. Have your techs hand these out to customers after the job is done and ask them to mail it back. You will start getting good solid feedback that you can use to improve the services you are providing within days.

This article was brought to you by Grandy & Associates. If you are seriosu about running a profitable business, go to www.Grandy Associates.com or contact them by phone at 800-432-7963.

History of the Modern Squeegee

by Allison Hester

Editor's Note: This past February, I had the pleasure of sharing a table with Diane Smahlik, Chairman of Ettore Products Company, at the International Window Cleaning Association's Women's Luncheon. During the event, she told the story of how her father invented the modern-day window cleaning squeegee. It's a story I've been wanting to share, and since this issue is focused on historic restoration, it seemed like the perfect opportunity. So the following information was gathered in a recent interview with Diane. Enjoy!

In 1922, after the end of World War I, Ettore Steccone traveled from Italy to America, where his brother had settled down in Oakland, California. Ettore started out working with his brother in the produce industry, but quickly realized it was too confining and not enjoyable. He returned to Italy where he married, then came back to the U.S. with his bride and the newlyweds started a window cleaning business in 1932.

Ettore became known for traveling around town on his Indian motorcycle, ladder on his shoulders and a bucket dangling from the end. He reveled in the newfound freedom his window cleaning business presented, but was unhappy with the available window cleaning tools of the day.

At that time, the tool of the trade was the Chicago Squeegee, which was made of steel and very heavy and bulky. The Chicago Squeegee used two heavy red rubber blades, and changing them out required loosening 12 separate screws.

Ettore felt there had to be a better option, and so he began "tinkering" with ideas in the garage behind his home. Eventually he created the modern T-type squeegee that is still used today. It was made from brass, and used a single precision rubber blade. "He really researched the best choice of rubber, which is key to the squeegee's success," Diane explained. In 1936, he patented his squeegee as "the New Deal."

Ettore knew he had something big, and he knew that if other window cleaners had access to his squeegee, it would become their tool of choice as well. However, convincing the window cleaning world of this was no so easy.

After approaching – and being turned down by several window cleaning supply companies, Ettore headed to New York City to see the biggest supplier of them all – George Racenstein of the J. Racenstein Company. Racenstein had been selling window cleaning products since 1909.

Like the others, George Racenstein was not convinced there was a need to change. The New Deal was too small. Too light. But Ettore had a plan. He offered a proposal that Racenstein could not pass up. Ettore bet "the finest hat in New York" that George Racenstein would call Ettore within 30 days, asking to put the new squeegee in his catalog. Racenstein took the bet.

Ettore, however, had a secret strategy. He determined that the only way to get people to try his new squeegee was to actually give them away. So he shared them with his window cleaning friends, but only if they would call George Racenstein and ask him to put the new squeegees in his catalog.

Did it work? Let's just say the "finest hat in New York" still graces the foyer of the Ettore plant today.

A True American Success Story

Ettore Steccone won in the long run, but that's not to say he didn't face numerous trials along the way.

For one, he went into business with a building owner who "helped" him get the Steccone squeegee copyrighted. In truth, his partner actually stole the Steccone name. He also lost his patent after it was challenged in Chicago court.

That's when he changed the company name to Ettore, which, of course, is now one of the world's leading window cleaning equipment manufacturers. The logo – a set of wings – represented the idea of the Ettore squeegee "flying across glass."

Another challenge came along during WWII, when brass availability became limited and the government planned to prohibit Ettore from using the metal in his business. Fortunately, one of Ettore's customers had some pull, and was able to get Ettore an exemption for the use of brass.

In the 1950s, Ettore and his employees moved from his home's garage to an actual factory. That's where his wife, and eventually his daughter Diane, helped in the nuts and bolts of the business. Diane, who is now Chairman of the company, grew up putting squeegees together and getting paid 10 cents per box of completed products. "That was until I negotiated my way up to a quarter a box," she added.

Ettore Steccone died in 1984 at the age of 87. Ettore is remembered for his hard work and his dry wit. He was often seen leaving his desk as company president to sweep the floors outside. Unsuspecting visitors would stop and ask him if Ettore was available. "What do you want him for?" he'd ask. If it was someone he was interested in talking with, he'd let him know his little secret. Otherwise, he'd tell them Ettore could not be reached.

Ettore Steccone is a true example of someone living out the American Dream, and a real game changer for the window cleaning industry.

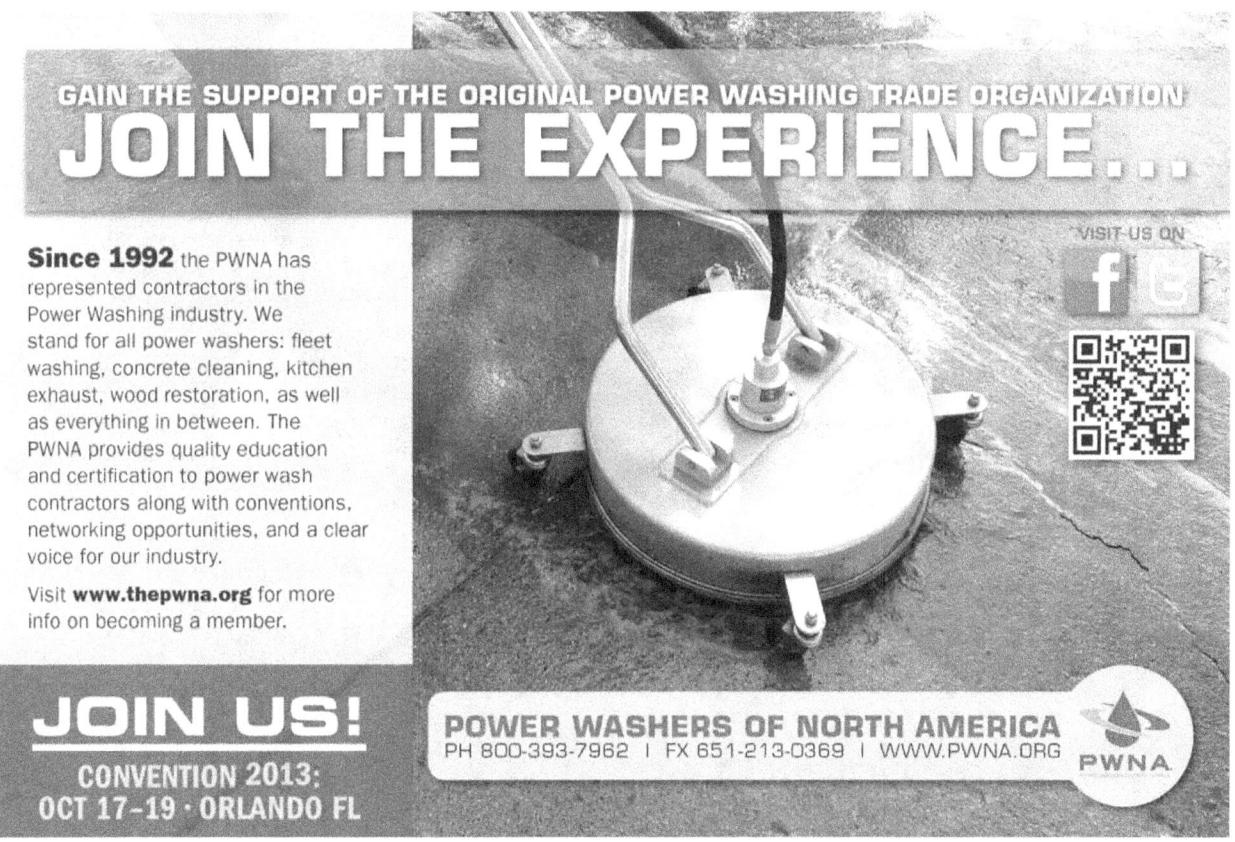

Helping "Resurrect" Classic Cars
by Aaladin Industries

AaLadin is proud to be a sponsor of the Discovery Velocity show Graveyard Carz. Soon in its third season, Graveyard Carz is a show that centers around the restoration and "resurrection" of various classic MOPAR vehicles. They begin with cars that have been exposed to the worst conditions imaginable for many, many years. Due to this they need cleaning solutions that are powerful and dependable. AaLadin stepped up to the plate and supplied them with one of our portable units - specifically the 14-423SC.

Our 14-Series pressure washer was the perfect fit for GYC. The 14 filled their specific needs of power and portability. Other features that the 14 boasts are too many to completely list but some of the highlights are:

Swivel Flat-Free Wheels: Ease of maneuverability saves your energy for the task at hand! Swivel wheels also help diminish the possibility of falls with heavy equipment. Most pressure washers with fixed wheels require the operator to lift one set of wheels to make a turn increasing the probability of slipping and falling. Flat free tires save time and money. Flat tires tend to take the portability out of a portable unit and cause expensive downtime.

Clutch Drive: When the gun is not engaged there will be no wear to the pump, allowing it to perform longer under the toughest conditions. This

> "I have used about every other brand of pressure washer on the market over the past 30 years and nothing performs like an AaLadin. Power, durability and mobility...you can have my AaLadin when you pry it from my cold dead hands"
> – Mark Worman, Graveyard Carz

effectively extends the life of your washer resulting in less downtime and increased profits.

Heavy Duty Welded Powder Coated Steel Frame: The 14-Series is built to last. We use the highest quality automotive powder coating and weld (not bolt) our heavy gauge steel frames together. We also use Stainless steel heat chamber wraps for longevity and the best looking machine on the market!

The unit supplied to Graveyard Carz runs at four gallons per minute at pressures of up to 2300PSI. It is capable of 210° but we also carry combination steam units with temps up to 300°.

Watch for the 14-Series on the upcoming season of Graveyard Carz on Discovery Velocity. You can keep an eye out for the schedule at: www.graveyardcarz.com https://www.facebook.com/graveyardcarz?fref=tsthe 14-Series will be shown in use on many of the episodes! Check out some behind the scenes and featurettes in the mean time at: http://velocity.discovery.com/tv-shows/velocity-presents/videos/mopar-tricks.htm

AaLadin Cleaning Systems offers pressure washers to fit any situation. We do this because we understand you aren't the same as every other customer out there. You have created a place in your market that demands specific solutions. We pride ourselves on being the innovator of numerous pressure washer features.

We are also proud to be the ONLY pressure washer manufacturer to offer a High Efficiency Line of equipment. Our Eco-Green Line is available in several different models to fit your needs. Please go to www.aaladin.com or visit your local AaLadin distributor to learn how our products can save you time and money.

Classifieds: Products & Services

www.ArmClark.com
Armstrong Clark Quality Wood Stains. Specializing in wood restoration, oil-based coatings for wood & non-toxic wood stains of all kinds for your wood shake restoration & water repellent needs. 800-916-8211

www.PowerWash.com
Mobile power wash equipment, schools, training, videos, environmental supplies & maintenance services. Call for a free catalog, 800-433-2113.

www.PowerWashStore.com
Bigger Selection - Better Quality - Amazing Customer Service. Serving the professional cleaning community for more than 25 years. Call 855-351-9274.

www.PWNA.org
Power Washers of North America. For certification or membership information, visit our website, email info@pwna.org, or call 800-393-7962. Annual Trade Show and Convention, Oct. 17-19, Orlando, Fla.

www.SteelEagle.com
Mfr. of World Class Industrial & Commercial Cleaning & Storage Products, including surface spinners, vacuum systems, undercarriage cleaners, hose reels & more. Custom designs available. 800-447-3924

www.PressureWasherKy.us
Southside Equipment multi-line power equipment distributor. Pressure cleaning equipment, waste water recovery & recycling, generators & cleaning chemicals. Quality products & impeccable service. 888-243-6506

To Advertise in our New Classifieds Section
Contact Allison Hester

allison@ecleanmag.com

Pressure Washers' Guidelines for Cleaning Stains from Concrete

by Paul Horsley, eClean Publisher

Cleaning concrete is one of the most common requests fielded by power washers, for several reasons:

First, business owners recognize that customers appreciate clean storefronts. Unsightly concrete stains in front of a store may send customers elsewhere. Clean concrete can also boost employee engagement. After all, who wants to work in a dirty workplace, with oil stains on the floor? Clearly, removing stains from concrete is an important role for power washers. Business owners and pressure washers can also vouch for the fact that this task isn't always easy.

Below, we've gathered a few tips on how to remove various stains from concrete.

Clean up spills ASAP. Whenever possible, clean up spills right away, before contaminants have a chance to sink deeper into the concrete. Soak up the spill with patting movements; don't push down or rub hard, which will only drive the stain deeper into the concrete.

Use absorbent material to soak up oil and grease stains. You can't scrub away oil or grease stains; instead, you'll need to mix a cleanser, such as trisodium phosphate, with an absorbent powder, such as powdered talc, to create a paste. Spread this paste over the stain to a depth of 3/8 inch. Let the paste sit for 24 hours, or until it is dry, and then scrape it up and clean the spot with a nylon bristle brush. You might need to repeat this process several times for old, set-in stains. (Or you could just hire a crew of Canada power washers instead.)

For paint stains, mix an absorbent powder with paint stripper. Then follow the procedure described above. Beware that many paint strippers contain hazardous materials such as methylene chloride; make sure your work area is well ventilated.

Rust stains may be removed with diluted muriatic acid. However, this process will leave a rough, sandpaper-like surface on concrete. When working with muriatic acid, be sure to protect nearby areas where acid could splash up. Wear gloves, sturdy rubber boots and a breathing mask rated for acid vapor. Pour 2 cups of water into a tub, and add ¼ cup of muriatic acid. Always add acid to water, not water to acid. Use a long handled nylon bristle brush to apply a light layer of acid solution to the rust-stained area. Let the mixture sit for 5 minutes while the acid dissolves the cement in the surface layer of concrete. Once the mixture stops bubbling, use plenty of water and your long-handled brush to flush away residue. If you are not experienced at working with acid, we recommend instead hiring power washer. Business owners will find it much easier to entrust this stain removal process to the pros, rather than risk harming themselves or their property.

eCLEANmagazine™

Issue #17

The professional contractor cleaner's online resource!

How Chemicals Clean

Plus

- Snapshots from the PWRA Convention
- Alkota Asks: How Messy Can You Get?
- Inside J Racenstein
- When to Fire Your Customers

...and more!

POWERWASH.COM™
SUPPLIES CHEMICALS TRAINING
1.800.433.2113
2513 Warfield St. Fort Worth, TX 76106

Pressure Washers □Surface Cleaners □Chemicals □Cleaning Supplies □Parts □Pumps & Unloaders □Training Materials

Rust Remover Plus™

Rust Remover Plus™ is a perfect choice for removing tough oil and rust stains from concrete and exposed aggregate surfaces. Just spray it onto dry concrete with a pump up garden or chemical sprayer and watch the rust and oil stains disappear. After a 5 to 10 minute dwell time, you can pressure wash the area with a 40 degree tip. Rust Remover Plus™ will brighten the concrete as it dries.

#1 Choice for Removing Fertilizer Stains!

V-502-C Grease and Grime Remover for Concrete(*)

A perfect choice for when you need to penetrate and route out heavy grease, soil and grime on parking lots, dumpster pads, drive thrus, and other high traffic concrete areas.

"V-502 is a really great cleaner to have in your arsenal. We have used it with pretty great success on oil stains and tire marks and have found it to not only clean, but also brighten significantly!"

Curt Kempton - 5StarWindowCare.com

R-202 Concrete Cleaner

Cleans heavy grease, oil and scuff marks from unpainted concrete, brick, stone, and other alkaline water safe hard surfaces. USDA authorized for use in meat, egg, dairy food packing and processing plants. One 50 pound box makes 200 gal. of solution

(*) Denotes $27.00 shipping surcharge by UPS.

Chapin Degreaser Sprayer

- Built-in relief valve pressure gauge for added safety
- The container and discharge assembly have no fiberglass additives making this sprayer a perfect choice for acidic cleaners
- Available in 2 or 3 gallon sizes

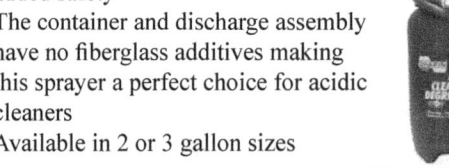

www.eCleanMag.com   Issue #17

IN THIS ISSUE:

288

293

7   How Chemicals Clean, by Linda Chambers, Soap Warehouse

288 Snapshots from the First PWRA National Convention

293 Alkota Wants to Know: How Bad Can it Get? (Your Answer Could be Worth $500)

295 Window Cleaner, 32, Dies in Tragic Accident: Cleaning Community Reaches Out to Support Grieving Family

296 Unprecedented Giveaways Planned for the 2013 PWNA Convention, October 17 - 19 in Orlando

298 PWNA Vendor Profile: J. Racenstein

300 Rules of Removal: Chemical Paint Strippers and Historic Masonry, by Courtney Murdock, AMT Labs

304 Take That to the Bank! By Rick Meehan, Marko Janitorial

306 Classifieds

307 When to Fire Your Customers

309 Industry Happenings

310 Power Washing Do's and Don'ts, by Paul Horsley

COVER PHOTO
Courtesy of Jud West, WashRite Pressure Washing, Valdosta, Georgia, washritepressurewashing.com

---

eClean Magazine is published monthly

Publisher: Paul Horsley, paul@ecleanmag.com
Editor: Allison Hester, allison@ecleanmag.com

Box 262, 16 Midlake Blvd S.E.
Calgary, Alberta
Canada T2X2X7
www.eCleanMag.com

eClean Magazine

Do you make money washing houses? Boost your income by also *protecting* houses.

PlexMaster

from EnviroSpec is the amazing invisible shield you can easily apply to your customer's homes after washing. It helps guard surfaces from mildew, mold, oxidation, acid rain and general 'fall-out' pollutants. Which means the house you just washed will retain that 'fresh' look for up to a year.

Regular applications of PlexMaster are a smart investment for the homeowner, and a new source of revenue for the contractor. Isn't that what they call a win-win?

PlexMaster preserves surfaces by sealing them, so pollutants "can't get a grip." It also acts as a gloss enhancer, which returns siding, shutters, trim and doors to a like-new appearance.

That's not all. Since a PlexMaster treatment also cleans, coats and protects the windows, the homeowner only needs to quickly rinse them occasionally with a garden hose to keep them crystal clear. It's an added plus, since nobody enjoys cleaning their windows regularly *or* paying someone else to do it. A great selling point!

Annual PlexMaster protection agreements can be sold to the customer as an add-on, for a fraction of what they're paying to have their homes professionally cleaned. People generally tend to be open to a solution that effectively protects their biggest asset (especially when you point out all the surface mold before you start washing). And of course after many years, a home that's been protected retains a better appearance, enhancing resale value.

How to apply it, and what to charge.

Mix 5 gallons of PlexMaster with 55 gallons of water. Washing the average house will require about 5 gallons of that mix.

Applying PlexMaster after washing is typically about a 20 minute process for a 2,000 square foot house. Just apply it through your down-stream injector, thruster nozzle or X-Jet, but be sure to rinse it off before the product dries.

Though you'll find that PlexMaster rinses off easily, it's best to apply it, then rinse it off, in sections.

Naturally, you may experiment a bit for the washing sequence and exact concentration that works for you.

Many contractors charge about $150 for that 20 minutes of work. Then they make a note to contact the buyer the following year to re-do the treatment.

Yet each application of this chemical only costs you pennies.

PlexMaster works great on vinyl and aluminum siding, painted wood, and metal surfaces, leaving no discoloration. The protective blend of silicone and polymer is combined with a powerful mildew retardant, giving the whole house, in effect, a clear plastic coating.

Of course, any mildew that does

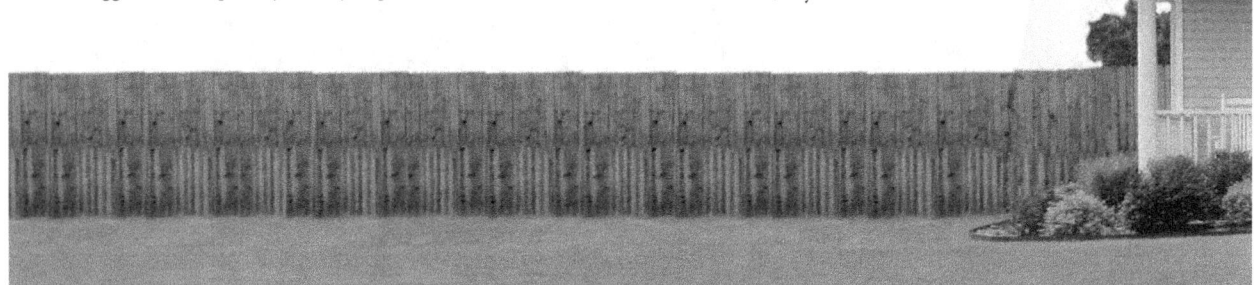

"The one product that EnviroSpec introduced me to that has made me hundreds of thousands of dollars, and has put my company in the top 10% of power washers in the country, is PlexMaster."
– Dan Galvin, PWNA's House Wash Certification Instructor

form on a PlexMaster-treated house after a year will be much easier to remove.

PlexMaster is smart business.

If you're looking for a competitive advantage among house cleaners in your area, you've just found it. Not only does this premium service it separate you from the "splash-n-dash" amateur cleaners, but offering PlexMaster shows homeowners that you care about their house as much as they do. The first time they see the brighter shine of their homes,
they'll be
sold.

Order PlexMaster online at
EnviroSpec.com/Chem_PlexMaster.htm
or call 1-800-346-4876

For the very best results, use PlexMaster with the **Allison Super Suds Sucker,** also available online from EnviroSpec.

EnviroSpec.com

Your Authority for High
Performance Cleaning

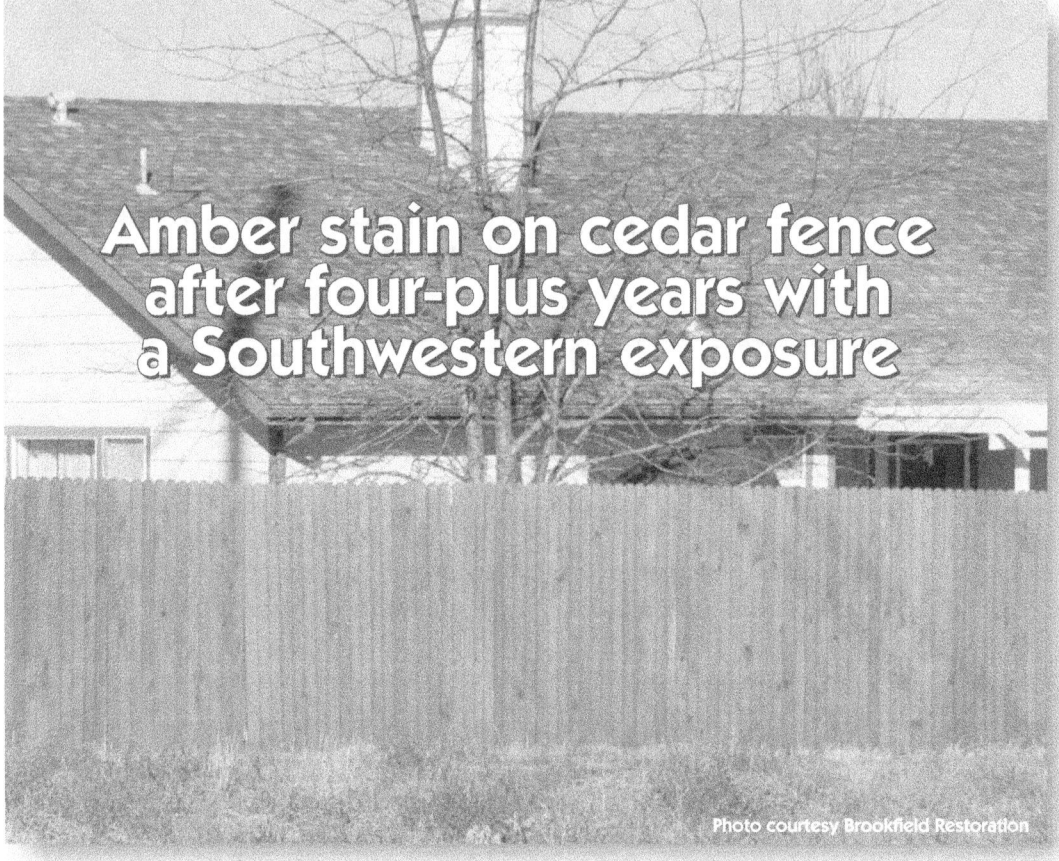

ARMSTRONG'S WOOD STAINS

Amber stain on cedar fence after four-plus years with a Southwestern exposure

Photo courtesy Brookfield Restoration

Armstrong Wood Stains are available in twelve attractive colors

Long Lasting, Easy to Apply and a Breeze to Maintain

For FREE sample cans,
call or email us now at info@armclark.com

Manufacturers of VOC-Compliant, Oil-Based Wood Finishes Since 1989

(800) 916-8211 • www.armclark.com

PLEASE VISIT THE WEB'S PREMIERE SITES FOR OUTDOOR WOOD RESTORATION TOPICS AND DISCUSSIONS,
www.thegrimescene.com/forums   www.thewoodpros.com

How Chemicals Clean

by Linda Chambers, Brand & Sales Manager, Soap Warehouse, www.SoapWarehouse.net

We all know when a cleaner is or is not working, but we do not always know why. Unfortunately for most, learning why becomes a lesson of trial and error. But understanding the basic science of elements and the pH scale can help you safely figure out what should work before you choose a chemical.

Also the ability to explain to a customer what you are using and why separates you from the competition as a true professional with specialized knowledge and training.

The Periodic Table of Elements

Most of the products you use will only come from a small portion of these elements. For example, two similar elements that are used in cleaning chemicals every day are Sodium and Potassium. Both are basic alkaline metal elements and are so close to each other they are like cousins. That is why chemical compounds made with the exact same other elements make almost similar chemicals such

by Allison Hester

as Sodium Hydroxide, NaOH (also known as Caustic soda) and Potassium Hydroxide, KOH, also called pot ash.

Due to Potassium Hydroxide's properties being highly soluble in water and highly reactive to acids, its ability to molecularly infiltrate, (that is break apart acids) and its corrosive nature, it works faster than Sodium Hydroxide when used at the same percentage in a mixture.

To give you an example of the solubility difference, **approximately 121 g of KOH will dissolve into 100 ml of water at room temperature, compared with only 100 g of NaOH in the same 100 ml volume, a 20 percent increase. That is why KOH makes a better cleaner – you can get more of a faster-acting chemical in the same volume.** But because Potassium Hydroxide is harder to produce, it costs more. That's why each year in the US, approximately 100 times more Sodium Hydroxide is made over Potassium Hydroxide.

pH Scale

Now let's do a quick review of the pH scale, which ranges from zero to 14, with a pH of seven considered neutral, like plain pure water.

An acid all of you deal with every day that you may not have even thought about is acid rain and its aftermath. Normal clean rain has a pH of between 5.0 and 5.5, which is slightly acidic, like a cup of coffee. However, when rain combines with sulfur dioxide or nitrogen oxides — produced from power plants and automobiles— the rain in the atmosphere becomes much more acidic. Typical acid rain has a pH value of 4. Depending on the part of the country you work in, the time of year, and other weather conditions, you may be getting an even lower pH.

Acid rain can also have a damaging effect on many objects, including buildings of all types of materials, roofs, decks, concrete, stone, statues and monuments, and vehicles. The chemicals found in acid rain can cause paint to peel and stone to begin wear down, years ahead of its time.

It is more important than ever to have regular washings of outside structures to diminish the effect of acid rain on them. Increasing routine exterior cleaning will help your customers keep their property in good condition for a longer amount of time. This could be a major selling point in your area so please check it out.

eClean Magazine

The pH scale is a logarithmic scale, meaning each point on the scale is based on a multiplier of 10. Moving either direction from neutral (pH 7) means every number on the pH scale is ten times stronger than the previous number unit. Thus, the strength of the acids and bases increase significantly as you move to the extreme ends of the scale. So when you have two cleaners that are only one unit apart, know that the higher one is not just a little stronger, but 10 times stronger. For instance if the pH of 7 equals one inch then a pH of 3 or 11, just four units in either direction of neutral, would be equal to 278 yards. And the difference of 7, out to 0 or 14 from neutral would equal 158 miles or 10,000,000 inches! Differencesof only 4 pH are a million times different in strength.

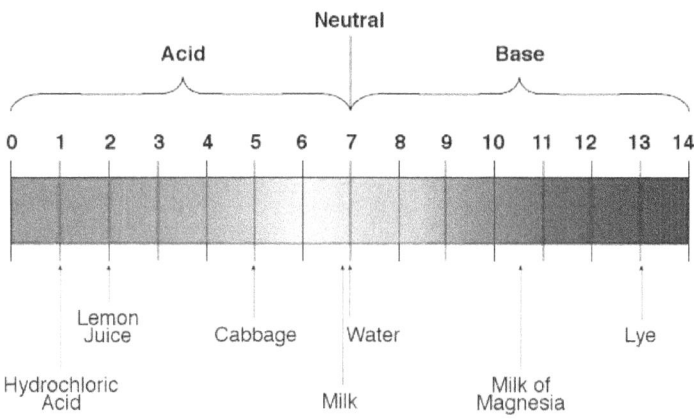

The pH Scale

Bases

Bases are often used in degreasers and caustic cleaners like concrete, truck wash and drain cleaners, which work great in these products for two reasons. First, strong bases break down organic matter such as proteins and greases. Second, when a strong base (alkaline) is mixed with a fat, it turns the fat into soap through a process called saponification. This means it literally turns the thing we are trying to get rid of into a new agent – soap – that helps us clean.

Sounds great, right? Hang on. You first need to be aware of what you are cleaning to be sure it can handle the pH of the cleaner. For instance, bases of high pH are

not recommended when cleaning soft stone surfaces like marble or limestone. You also have to be very careful when working with bases, because they breakdown organic matter – which includes skin, muscle and even bone!

Acids

On the lower side of the pH scale are acids, which are used for some very specific cleaning jobs: removing rust stains, calcium deposits, and efflorescence on brick; to etch concrete; to dissolve salts and mineral scale created by hard water; to clean coils; and to clean metal surfaces, such as removing tarnish and cleaning polished aluminum. But they also eat, pit and dissolve some soft metals like chrome, and soft stone like limestone and marble. Strong acids can be the deadliest chemicals you may ever have to deal with and must be treated accordingly.

What's in Your Water?

Checking for the hardness and the pH of the water you are using to mix your chemicals and rinsing can make a big difference in cleaning results. Every decrease in the pH of the water you are using to make your chemical solutions is also reducing the pH of your mix.

You can easily measure pH with a strip of litmus paper that is easy to buy. When you touch a strip of litmus paper to something, the paper changes color depending on whether the substance is acidic or basic. If the paper turns red, the substance is acidic, and if it turns blue, the substance is basic. There will be a color chart that you use to judge the pH level.

We have had customers call to say that a product is not working or is harming a surface. We have usually been able to track it back to improper dilution rates or the water source that customer is using. If the pH is higher than it should be, it usually turns out to be an increase due to salts and other minerals in the water, or water hardness that is increasing the pH. Adding water softeners can help, but most municipalities are already doing this.

Hardness is hard to measure out in the field. You should be getting a water report mailed

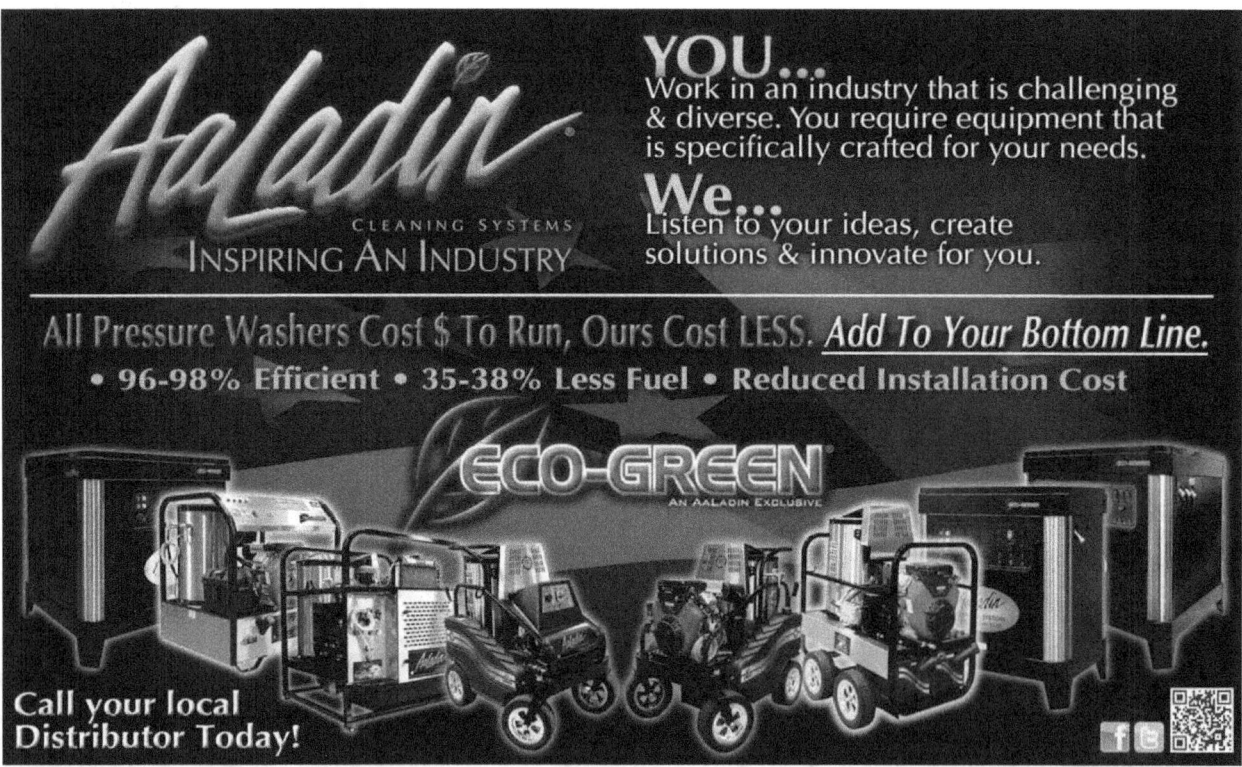

to you from your local water agency each year that tells you about your water, the hardness and pH. If not, or if you work in other areas, you can request copies. If you use well water, you especially should test it your self a few times a year.

Hardness is associated with the ability of the water to work with soap. As hardness increases, more soap is needed to achieve the same level of cleaning due to the hardness positive ions, most commonly calcium and magnesium.

Undisclosed Products

If you read the box of a yellow cake mix, you may see a lot of the same things in each one, but some may need you to add eggs, oil and water while others only need water. Unfortunately, with chemical products, the only things that must be listed on a label or a Safety Data Sheet are the hazardous parts. Companies are not required to say what else is in them or how available those ingredients are to the product as a whole. Some percentage of ingredients you think would be working for cleaning may be tied up or neutralized by some other non disclosed ingredient. So you have a lot less to go on then when shopping for a cake mix in the grocery store. And with some product categories like window cleaners (until the new SDS laws come into effect in 2016), you may never know what is in them since these products usually contain all non-hazardous ingredients.

Now if you are really understood chemistry, you might be able to figure out some items with clues from the specific gravity, odor, or other physical characteristics of the product then deduce what else could be in it. But as of

Linda Chambers at the 2013 PWRA Convention in Nashville, Tennessee. This article is a condensed version of the presentation she gave during the August event.

today, here in the US there is no way for you to know. It is all a guessing game. You must go with results you can see to compare them.

It is almost like having to judge a cake by its looks, not by it's taste. Even if you knew every ingredient in each similar product you may not have all the information you need.

As of today there are manufactures and vendors that are getting around things with

Glass widows are made of silica and other alkaline things like soda ash and lime. Depending on the percentage of silica used and the exact process of how it was made, glass will constantly be in a slow chemical reaction with water (slightly acidic) or acid rain (more acidic), that will leach alkali ions out on to its surface that will stain or spot it.

Sprinklers using hard water will add to the problem. If cleaned with a good chemical cleaner but rinsed with hard water, alkaline deposits can form after cleaning, leaving spots or streaks. Therefore, instead of using cleaners at all, what many are now doing is using a De-ionized water system to remove the minerals from the glass while leaving a near pH neutral surface to help inhibit new spots and help keep the glass cleaner longer.

Now this is not to say cleaners do not work, but you need to use water as free of minerals as possible. Water softeners can help cleaning chemicals do a great job as well.

the current MSDS laws and they know it. Many companies use statements on their MSDS like "The information contained herein is believed to be accurate," or "Vendor assumes no responsibility for injury with use." In others words, buyer and user BEWARE.

I am not saying that companies that use these phrases have something to hide, just that they only know as much as their manufacturer is telling them, which may not be everything, so be careful and hopefully in a few year with new SDS regulations it will get better for the contractor.

Which is best?

A question I am asked a lot is "Which brand product (that contain the same ingredients) will work better?" That can be very hard to say. The reason is the same ingredients can have a vast difference in quality, which can make a big difference in results. That will usually show up in the price – but not always.

Take white rice for instance. Do you ever notice that the there can be a wide range in price for plain white rice? There isn't anything else in that bag, so why the difference between the store value brand, Mahatma or Uncle Ben's? Price may judge some types of quality – whole grain kernels instead of broken pieces, the cost of proper bleaching methods, a better genetic strain of rice.

So too with chemical ingredients. Was it made in a clean facility, not cut with fillers, is the ingredient 100 percent chemically available? So do not always think the cheapest product will still be able to do the job, and don't think the highest priced product must work the best. You must do your own evaluation of products. Just be sure you are comparing apples to apples. You must get them to the same level to be able to judge them head to head.

Linda Chambers is the Brand and Sales Manager for Soap Warehouse, where she has worked since 2007. She enjoys writing blogs and social media. She also travels for the company, exhibiting at trade shows and events. For more information, visit their website at www.SoapWarehouse.biz.

No Water Wasted Promo

Hydro Tek National Special

$12,495
save $4700

save the drain for the rain

FREE freight*

Want a larger trailer? Upgrade to a 400 gallon, dual axle trailer with electric brakes for only $2500 more

Mobile Wash Skid
Gas Powered, Diesel Heated – 110v burner
3500psi, 5gpm, Belt drive pump
570cc Vanguard twin cylinder engine
On-board 3000w generator

Trailer
200 gallon ProTowWash® trailer with rear storage tray and high pressure hose reel

Vacuum Recovery/Filtration System
Recover and filter your washwater for reuse or disposal. No external power needed, runs off pressure washer generator.
Package also includes containment berms, scupper & vacuum hose

NO WATER WASTED Recycle Trailer
model# SC35005VS/T2NWA/AZV55

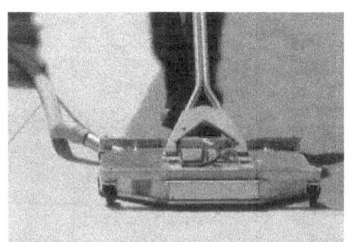
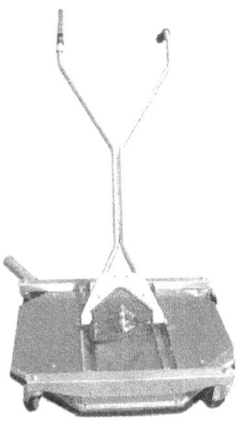

Add a Twister Vac recovery surface cleaner for $1500

AUTHORIZED LOCAL DISTRIBUTOR:

Limited time offer starts July 15, 2013. Price does not include sales tax or battery, if needed. *Free freight to distributor location within the continental US. Ask your distributor for the *No Water Wasted* Special. Not to be combined with any other offers, programs, or discounts. Available through a participating distributor, call for a local distributor. 400 gallon trailer upgrade model# SC35005VS/T4NWA/AZV55

Brilliant Design, Tough on Grime
2353 Almond Avenue • Redlands, CA 92374 • (P) 800- 274-9376 • (F) 909-799-9888 • www.hydrotek.us

SNAPSHOTS from the PWRA First National Convention

by Allison Hester

On August 23 and 24, Thad Eckhoff and Chris Lambridines of the Pressure Washing Resource Associaton (PWRA) made industry history as hosts of the 2013 National PWRA Convention. The first-time event, which took place in Nashville, Tennessee, had an amazing turnout and has gotten phenomenal reviews.

Attendees traveled from around the country (and beyond), and represented a mixture of cleaning specialties, years in service, and number of prior conferences attended. One thing was certain, the vast majority were blown away by the number of vendors, the assortment and quality of presentations, and the overall atmosphere of comraderie, all of which took place in the spectacular Opryland resort.

"I found the attendees receptive and eager to learn. The agenda for the show was fully packed and had something for every part of the pressure washing industry. I will not only be back next year, but I will also be a driving force promoting the show for everyone to attend. Great people and a great time!" – Jason Wellman, KitchenExhuastSupply.com

"Being in such a classy venue made us feel as though our business matters. Being in a place like Opryland brought a legitimate feel to the whole cleaning industry." – Steve Stevens, Son Light Window Cleaning, Murray, Kentucky

In all, the two-day convention welcomed 224 contractors representing 132 companies, held two keynote sessions, 27 breakout sessions, and hosted vendors from 22 companies, including:
- Advanced Chemical
- Ambidextrous Services
- Bidslot
- eClean Magazine
- EZ Finishes
- F9
- Glass Renu
- HydroTek
- IPC Eagle
- KichenExhaustSupply.com
- Mobile Systems, Inc.
- Mosmatic
- PowerWash.com
- Pressure Tek
- PWRA
- Saint Gobain
- Soap Warehouse
- Southern Stain & Seal
- Southside Equipment
- Street Bidder
- Symphosize
- WCR.

"The highlight of the event for me was running into Guy Blackmon in the hallway late Thursday night. I really look up to him as a mentor.... We talked until almost 2:30 in the morning and I learned so much."
– Sean Kilgore, Hampton Roads Powerwashing LLC

The event kicked off early Friday morning, with a keynote presenation entitled "Money is Not the Motivator" by Curt Kempton of 5-Star Window Care. Curt is known for his humor and enthusiasm, along with success in keeping his employees motivated.

"For us, Curt's address was more than worth the time and money needed to travel to and participate in the PWRA 2013 Convention! Sheila and I took years off trial and error experimenting on business practices, best techniques, products, and equipment by attending the PWRA Convention in Nashville 2013. Thanks Thad for making this happen!" – Steve LeBold, SSR Pure Clean, Ontario, Canada

"Nobody was trying to jam sales pitches on top of me which is nice. It had a 'one for all' feeling and really made me proud to be a member of the PWRA. It also made me excited to make it to this convention yearly." - Brian Sauls, Sunco Exterior Solution, Bluffton, SC

For the remainder of the convention, attendees studied the vendors and

'The Vendors were very generous with time spent with the attendees and the give aways. I will benefit most from the relationships that were made between vendors and the industry giants that were there to learn and give back as well." - Jeff Byrne, Roof Renew of Michigan

products on the trade show floor – which remained busy from the time the doors opened until they closed 10 to 12 hours later. Breakout sessions – all 27 of them – were well attended and received, and several were standing room only.

"Thad knocked it out of the park by including spouses at no charge. It was so cool to see my wife, Jodi's, excitement when she came out of the breakout sessions. We also had a good time having lunches, dinners and evening entertainment with so many that attended the event. Way to Go PWRA for getting this convention done right. We Loved IT!" – Jeff Byrne, Roof Renew of Michigan

The overall consensus was the same. The First National PWRA Convention was a slam dunk, and one of the biggest and best events the pressure washing industry has ever experienced. And the best part is it's only going to get better. Plans are already being made for next year's event, which will likely be held again a the Opryland Hotel in Nashville.

"I was blown away. The convention was 110 percent worth every nickel, and then some. There are a lot of guys spraying water; this was for the business guys. The guys who are really building companies, not just working for a check. Vendors had great deals and my wife even had a blast." – Brian Sauls, Sunco Exterior Solutions Bluffton, SC

To learn more about the Pressure Washing Resource Assocation (PWRA) and its many member benefits, visit their website at www.PressureWashingResource.com. As an eClean reader, you can SAVE $50 when you join by simply clicking here.

Joseph D. Walters
POWERWASH INSURANCE OPTIONS

America's #1 Insurer of Power Wash Contractors

Get proof of coverage TODAY
www.JosephDWalters.com

WOW!
Get a **fast quote** for Power Wash Insurance!

For a FAST telephone quote:
1-800-878-3808

Download Your FREE GUIDE to Power Washing Insurance Today!

NEW INSURANCE BENEFIT!
Joseph D. Walters
POWERWASH INSURANCE OPTIONS

- 25% discount on your premiums
- Plus you will get the first $2500 of equipment coverage included at no charge

And much more!

Join the Standard PWRA today
FOR ONLY $349!
AND GET ACCESS TO THIS AWESOME NEW BENEFIT

$299 for eClean Readers!

Join Now

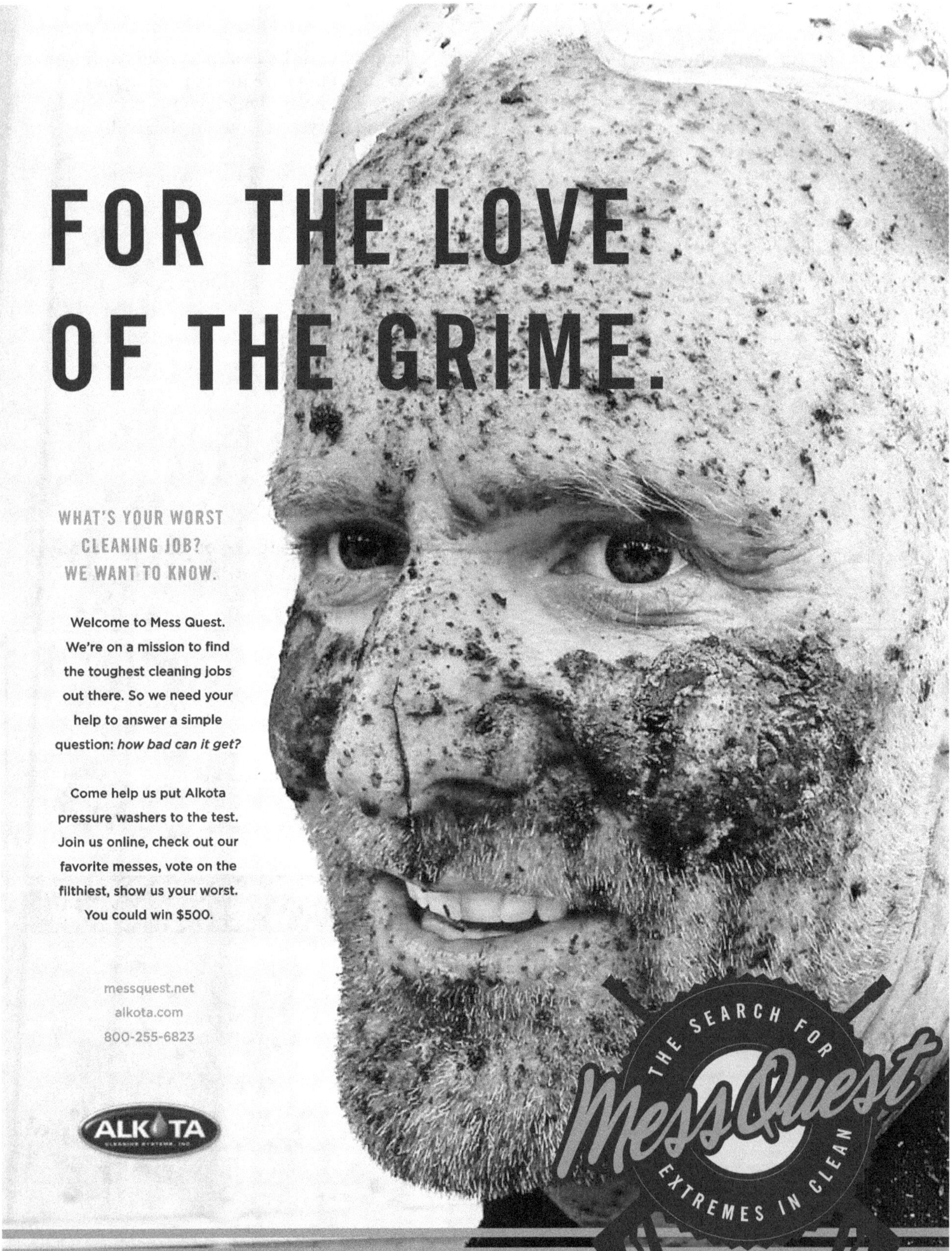

FOR THE LOVE OF THE GRIME.

WHAT'S YOUR WORST CLEANING JOB? WE WANT TO KNOW.

Welcome to Mess Quest. We're on a mission to find the toughest cleaning jobs out there. So we need your help to answer a simple question: *how bad can it get?*

Come help us put Alkota pressure washers to the test. Join us online, check out our favorite messes, vote on the filthiest, show us your worst. You could win $500.

messquest.net
alkota.com
800-255-6823

MessQuest — THE SEARCH FOR EXTREMES IN CLEAN

by Allison Hester

Alkota Wants to Know:

HOW BAD CAN IT GET?
(Your Answer Could be Worth $500)

If you are one of the millions of fans who enjoyed the TV show "Dirty Jobs," you're going to love "Mess Quest," a new YouTube show developed by Alkota Cleaning Systems in its search for the messiest cleaning jobs around. The videos are short, entertaining, and best of all, they're all about power washing.

"Let's be honest: some of the messes our customers have to deal with every day are more than just demanding, they're interesting," said Alkota President Gary Scott. "We're in a great industry that doesn't get the attention that we believe it deserves. But the job of cleaning up big messes is something that gets people's attention."

As Scott explained, most people never think about or let alone experience the extreme messes that are a normal part of manufacturing, livestock production, agriculture, natural resource extraction, food production, and so forth. But one thing we can all relate to, "When confronted with a frightful, filthy mess, there's something extremely satisfying about cleaning it up." That's what Mess Quest is about. "We wanted to celebrate the experiences our customers have every day on the job and show how much fun you can have obliterating the grime with a piece of Alkota equipment."

How the "Mess" Began, and How You Could Win $500

Alkota's staff began putting together the idea for the Mess Quest challenge late last year, then launched the campaign with several high-quality episodes. "Everything we do or show is a reflection of what we represent as a company. We felt it was critical that the campaign be built to standards as high as we keep for our equipment," Scott explained. "Even though Mess Quest is fun, we're serious about our work and we hope everyone sees a little of both in these shows."

Possibly the biggest reason for Mess Quest's "fun" is because of its host, J.B., a "regular working guy" that Alkota recruited to find

Three Episodes of Mess Quest can be found online at www.Alkota.com/Mess-Quest

Hog Heaven

Spread the Love

Big Red

tough messes and put Alkota to the test. J.B. is quick-witted, smart, and definitely not afraid to get messy.

"The fun part is that J.B. had to learn about Alkota at the same time he was learning about the kinds of messes our customers deal with every day," said Scott. "In that sense, he's a true rookie, but he's also a true soldier. He really threw himself into the job we gave him. But that's exactly what we try to do for the people who trust us."

Now Alkota is searching for the next big mess. "We hope to receive many photos and videos of a lot of tough messes," Scott added. "What challenges do people face? How bad can it get? That's the fundamental question we're asking."

The messes will be reviewed by three expert judges who will decide what they believe is the toughest mess. "But to be fair, we're encouraging those that submit a mess to generate their own support through votes," Scott explained. "We are using a 50/50 process in which our judges have half the vote and online users have the other half. Long story short, when people submit, they should get their friends, family and colleagues to vote. It could tip everything in their favor."

Based off these submissions, there will be more Mess Quest shows, but the schedule is not set in stone. "Our commitment is that we will continue to make sure the videos are kept fresh."

Over its 50 years in business, Alkota has always taken pride in being a pressure washer and cleaning equipment manufacturer that "designs and builds the perfect fit to handle any mess in any and every industry — inside, outside or underground," Scott concluded. "We wanted a campaign that would offer a challenge to demonstrate our commitment. At the end of the day, we want our customers to know that we understand them, we're interested in their world and we're committed to putting them first."

To learn more about Mess Quest, to view the current videos, or to enter your photos for a chance of winning $500, visit their web site: www.Alkota.com/Mess-Quest/Introduction

Window Cleaner, 32, Dies in Tragic Accident
Cleaning Community Reaches Out to Support Grieving Family
by Allison Hester

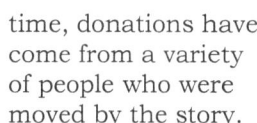

On August 19, 32-year-old window cleaner Justin Bass was cleaning the windows of a new home in the Knoxville, Tennessee area when the unthinkable happened.

Justin was working from an aerial lift at about 60 feet high when the brakes gave out and the lift began to roll. The lift operator, Ian Zapower, told police investigators that despite pushing the brake button "to no avail," the lift continued to roll until it fell over a retaining wall and landed at the edge of Douglas Lake, approximately 50 yards from where Bass had been cleaning.

After being flipped onto the rocks, Justin suffered from multiple fractures and severe head injuries. Justin died the following day, leaving behind his wife, Season, four-year-old son Parks, and one-year-old daughter Aspen.

Justin did not have life insurance.

www.ForJustin.com

Brennon Williams, owner of New Albany Window Cleaning in Ohio, had first met Justin at a friend's wedding several years ago. While they did not know each other well, Justin and Brennon were planning to attend the PWRA National Convention together on August 23.

"This tragedy really hit home," Brennon explained. "We were both around 32, both had been married eight years, both had a four year old and a one year old, and we were both professional window cleaners. We lived parallel lives, and just like that, Justin was gone."

To help raise money for Justin's grieving family, Brennon founded a website – www.ForJustin.com – and began contacting the cleaning community. Since that time, donations have come from a variety of people who were moved by the story.

Brennon was also allowed to speak about the fundraiser during the opening session of the PWRA National Convention, and several donations were received afterward, including a few large ones from attending vendors.

While in Tennessee for the convention, Brennon drove to Knoxville where he had dinner with Justin's wife, Season, and her family. "It was really good to meet them," he added.

On August 22, Justin's wife, Season, wrote the following note : *"I want to personally thank each and every one for their donation. I am literally in tears over the loving support from friends, family, acquaintances, and those whom I have never met. It is a tremendous blessing from Jehovah... .Thank you for helping me to continue to provide for the needs of my little ones. Each and every donation is amazing to me and very special. And I thank everyone from the depths of my heart."*

To date, Brennon's efforts have raised over $35,000, but there's still plenty of need for the family. To learn more, or to make a donation, please visit www.ForJustin.com.

> *"Justin Bass loved his family, his relationship with God and working hard to provide for his wife (Season), their 4 year old son (Parks) and their 1.5 year old daughter (Aspen). Due to a very unfortunate equipment failure, Justin suffered a fatal fall from a lift while cleaning windows in Knoxville on Saturday. If you're a window cleaner that's thankful for your safety, you're a friend of Justin's that will miss his smile or if this story touches you in any other way, please help his family with their expenses by donating whatever your situation allows."*
> – Brennon Williams, New Albany Window Cleaning

Unprecedented Giveaways Planned for the 2013 PWNA Convention
October 17-19 in Orlando
by Allison Hester

This year's PWNA Convention and Trade Show, October 17 through 19 in Orlando, will have more of everything – more vendor support, more educational seminars, more networking with highly successful company owners, and more fantastic giveaways.

While education is the top priority for any PWNA event, prizes are a big bonus – and this year they've got some BIG prizes. In addition to smaller giveaways from various vendors, attendees will also have the opportunity to potentially take home the following confirmed giveaways.

Hydro Tek Skid

Once again, Hydro Tek is donating a complete skid unit to be given away. This year it's a Hydro Tek SC Series (Model SC35006KG) 3500psi, 5.5gpm, skid with an adjustable thermostat that goes up to 250°. The unit's list price is $10,295.

"We continue to support the contract cleaning industry through associations like PWNA. It is impossible to place a dollar value on the knowledge attendees get by going to conventions and not only browsing products at the trade show but taking the time to attend the educational seminars," explained Denise Tyo of Hydro Tek. "The more information contract cleaners learn from each other, the more the industry will continue to grow as more efficient cleaning accessories or cleaning processes are created. Being involved in these associations gives us an open door to suggestions of the members to make needed changes to our equipment."

Hydro Tek's donation could not have been made possible without the generous donations and support of Kohler Engines, General Pump and Beckett Burners. "Suppliers like General Pump, Beckett Burners, and Kohler Engines continue to make quality components used on many pressure washers. Their generous donations make this skid giveaway possible," Tyo added.

The pump is the heart of any pressure washer, and this unit features one from the General Pump/Interpump 47 series family. The 47 series line of pumps are the work horses of the industrial power washer market and have been recognized as the leader in the market for decades.

"General Pump believes the PWNA is a great organization for the continuous training for power wash contractors and contributes to the professionalism of the industry," explained Troy Benike, Director of Marketing for General Pump, when asked why they made the donation.

Kohler Engines, which has been a leader

in the small engine market since its founding in 1920, graciously donated the power needed to run the unit. Kohler Engines manufactures a wide range of gas and diesel engines for the lawn and garden, commercial and industrial, agricultural and construction markets.

Finally, the unit's burner came from RW Beckett, which was founded in 1937 and has built the reputation of being a leading burner supplier for the pressure washing industry. "Hydro Tek is an important customer of ours, and we fully support them in their relationship with the PWNA," said Charles Tibboles, Beckett Product Manager.

Pressure Pro, 18-inch Hammerhead Surface Cleaner

The Hammerhead Surface Cleaner, which generally sells for around $350, is a durable, professional grade product. The Hammerhead actually hovers over the surface, and features composite housing and a hearty handle, and is a well-receive product by professional contract cleaners.

"We are very excited and appreciative to Pressure Pro for donating this popular item," added PWNA Board Member Shaun Downham of Oahu Power Washing.

The PWNA Mentoring Program

Finally, perhaps the most valuable of all the prizes awarded will be a new offering for a new program that kicking off this October. One winner will be this year's recipient of the PWNA's mentoring program, and will receive an all-expense paid trip to Calgary, Alberta. There, the winner will spend two full days under the tutelage of industry veteran and professional consultant Paul Horsley, who has owned Scott's Pressure Wash for over 30 years.

Paul, who also happens to be *eClean Magazine's* Publisher, has consulted and trained individuals around the world in not only cleaning techniques, but also how to build and sustain a successful business. "Cleaning is cleaning, and while it's important to learn the proper techniques and procedures, being able to clean correctly is not going to guarantee success," Paul explained.

Through his consulting services, Paul provides companies with guidance in growing their pressure washing business and improving their bottom line. Paul caters his programs to each particular client's needs. Some topics Paul has helped clients with include business operations; marketing and advertising; up-selling customers; chemicals, detergents, and cleaners; equipment maintenance; setting up a mobile unit; hot water / cold water; 1-step and 2-step cleaning processes; water reclamation; safety; pricing; human resources; available add-on services; tracking results; and more.

Generally, Paul's consulting fee is $1800 per day, but one lucky winner will receive two-full days worth of consulting for free, as well as continued phone support throughout the year. PWNA will also cover the cost of the winner's travel, hotel, and food.

"I enjoy mentoring people in the pressure washing business, and am honored to be a part of this new program," Paul explained. "It's programs like these – and the professionalism and success of our many veteran members – that separates the PWNA from the rest of the organizations out there."

Three fantastic prizes, plus invaluable networking and educational opportunities await those attending this year's PWNA Convention and Trade Show.

But, as they say, you can't win if you don't enter. Or in this case, if you don't attend. And you must be present to win, so make plans to stay through the end of the end of the day Saturday!

To learn more about PWNA National Convention or to register, visit www.PWNA.org and sign up today.

eClean Magazine

PWNA Vendor Profile

J. Racenstein
Window Cleaning Supply

by Allison Hester

J. Racenstein has been a leading supplier of window cleaning equipment for over 100 years. The industry has significantly grown and evolved since the company began in 1909, and so has J. Racenstein. No longer just a window cleaning equipment supplier, today's J. Racenstein provides not only a huge variety of window cleaning supplies, but also a wide assortment of cleaning chemicals, soft washing equipment, pressure washing accessories and safety equipment.

"Today there is a very large cross section in the cleaning industries. We're finding that at least 50 percent of window cleaners have also done some pressure washing, and 50 percent of pressure washing contractors have also done some window cleaning," said Steve Blyth. "It makes sense. The more services the mobile contractor can offer the same customer, the less time you have to spend traveling and looking for additional work."

About J. Racenstein

Steve Blyth and Cameron Riddell purchased J. Racenstein in April 2005. The company has two physical offices: a corporate headquarters and warehouse in Carson, California, and another warehouse in Secaucus, New Jersey. However, the company's staff is spread out across the country.

"We have a virtual workforce that work from various parts of the country," Blyth explained, adding that their sales staff includes long-time window cleaners. "So when you call with questions, we have knowledgeable, helpful people on staff who understand how to help you."

J. Racenstein's expert, highly-trained staff is one factor that Blyth says separates their company from its competitors. Some other advantages include their:

- Variety of products from more than 35 top brands
- Deep inventory – products are in-stock and ship the same day
- Widespread industry support, meaning the company regularly attends a number of educational venues as well as hosting their own educational events for the industry; and
- Deep selection of water-fed poles and pure water systems.

It's these last two points that led J. Racenstein to recently join the PWNA.

J. Racenstein at PWNA Convention

J. Racenstein's staff strongly believes in supporting and educating the industry, which is why any time there is an educational event where a dozen or more people are coming to learn, J. Racenstein will do its best to show up.

"We believe in really supporting our

J. Racenstein at the 2013 Pressure Washing Seminar in Albany, New York

customers, and we go where they ask us to go," Blyth added. Last March, the company participated in the 2013 Pressure Washing Seminar in Albany, New York, and at that time several customers asked if they would come to the 2013 PWNA Conference and Technical Seminar in Orlando. "We wanted to support those who have supported us, and so we have joined the PWNA and are looking forward to attending their upcoming event."

On Friday, October 18, Blyth will be speaking on "The Power of Pure Water."

As he explained, power washing companies often come in to clean a building or home, leaving the building itself looking beautiful, but the windows are spotty and unattractive. Contractors may have no interest in going back with a squeegee to clean the windows, but they no longer have to. "Power washing contractors can now easily add window cleaning services using pure water technology – which means more money in their pockets and happier customers at the same time," Blyth explained.

Specifically, Blyth's presentation will focus on how the technology works, how to choose equipment, and how to use it to increase your bottom line. "Most contractors carry two sizes of poles – a 12-foot pole for reaching ground-level floors, and a 31-foot pole for higher buildings. We will also have these in the exhibit hall for people to see first-hand and ask questions."

Meeting with the "Boss"

As the "New Kids on the Block," Blyth added that he's very much looking forward to meeting new power washing contractors, as well as talking with his current customers who attend the PWNA event. "We want to evolve our understanding of the power washing industry, as well as help more contractors gain new understanding power of pure water. They are very compatible. It's definitely a win-win."

Finally, Blyth added that he is very interested in learning what J. Racenstein can do to better serve PWNA members. "My boss is my customer. We're always open to finding any need we can help fill."

To learn more about J. Racenstein or to order a catalog, visit their website at **www.JRacenstein.com**.

eClean Magazine

New PWNA Members

JP Genovasi of Sundance Pressure Cleaning Solutions located in Ontario, Canada

Sherry Brewer of All American Cleaning Company located in Portland, Tennessee

Steve Blyth of J Racenstein Company located in Carson, CA

Bob Judge of Judge Mobile Wash located in West Chester, PA

Robert Norwood of East Coast Window Cleaning located in Lewes, DE

Rogelio Marquez Jr. of Bay Power Wash, located in Morgan Hill, CA

Jeffrey Burros of Alkota Cleaning Systems located in Alcester, SD

Barbi Brumback of Tricon Group located in Skokie, IL

Christopher Kooker of SurfaceLogix located in Pompano Beach, FL

AC Lockyer of Softwash located in Winter Springs, FL

Carol Lippstreu of Cal Exhaust & Steam Clean located in Auburn, CA

Miguel Perez of Valley Vent A Hood Cleaning Service located in Olmito, TX

Paulo Teixeira of HoHe - Hoods Quebec located in Montreal, Quebec

Jud West of WashRite Services located in Valdosta, GA

rules of Removal:
chemical paint stripping and historic masonry

By Courtney Murdock, Project Testing Director, AMT Labs

In restoration cleaning of historic masonry, you usually know based on contaminants and building fabric what kind of cleaner will be effective on a dirty building.

You'll use one type of restoration cleaner for atmospheric staining, and another for biological soiling. You'll have an idea, going in, what kind of restoration cleaner to at least try.

Not having that kind of information, in my experience,

Dwell – When you don't have any other information, you must rely on testing to discover what will best remove coatings applied long ago. This test panel shows good results after a second application of an alkaline paint stripper.

Rinse – An effective rinse with freshwater at low pressure and high volume, ideally 6- 8 gpm, is important for the test panel and the overall paint removal.

Inspect – With the experience gained from this test panel, contractors and conservators can proceed with confidence to remove paint from the entire building. Note the deteriorated state of the mortar joints revealed by the paint removal.

(Above) US Capitol – Two hundred-year-old sandstone emerges as layers of paint come off the U.S. Capitol Building. The paint stripping took place during renovations in preparation for the 1988 inauguration of President George H. Bush.

(Left) Knoxville City Hall – A technician rinses away spent paint stripper & dissolved paint at 300 psi. It took two applications of an alkaline paste paint stripper with organic solvents & an overnight dwell to break the grip of this 50-year-old coating on the old city hall, Knoxville, Tenn.

is what makes paint removal from historic – or just old – masonry the most challenging branch of restoration cleaning.

On most paint-removal projects you go in knowing something about the building. You usually know how old it is. You often know the substrate.

And that's about it.

What's the condition of the masonry under the coating? Usually you won't know. So that's my first rule for historic masonry coating-removal:

Assume the masonry beneath the coating is sensitive. It's likely been there since before your parents were born. Vigorous cleaning could cause damage.

The most valuable piece of information and the one you will almost never have is what kind of paint is on the building.

For instance, if it's an oil-based paint, then you know an alkaline product will probably remove it. Latex or epoxy paint – a solvent or solvent-substitute paint should do the trick.

You likely won't know that. The people who could tell you are probably long buried. The issue is complicated by the fact that old buildings often have multiple paint layers.

During paint-stripping at the U.S. Capitol in the 1980s, conservators discovered about 40 layers on the Aquia Creek sandstone masonry. In some places, paint was all that held the masonry units together. See rule number one.

There is only one way to discover what kind of paint you're facing. That's rule number two.

Test. My first test is invariably for lead-based paint. I don't find it that often – maybe 25 percent of

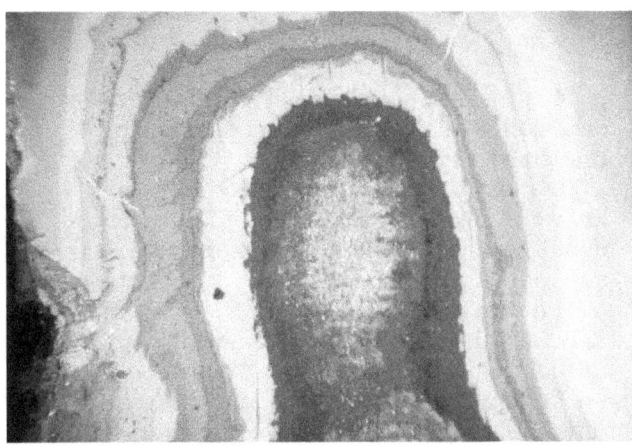

PaintCrater – While it won't tell you what kind of paint was used it's possible to expose original paint colors by using a small sanding device to produce a paint "crater." This image is from the General Electric Building, a 1920 skyscraper in New York. Here the original primer on the metal substrate and green finish coat are revealed below several layers of subsequently applied beige paint.

---

the time. But effluent from lead-based paint removal is hazardous waste. Precautions must be taken.

The test isn't hard. I use an EPA-approved swab kit, where I dab on a chemical. If the swab turns red, it's lead.

Unfortunately, that doesn't help determine what kind of paint stripper to use. Test panels are the only way to discover that.

How do you know which of the available paint-stripping products to test? Look for products made specifically for removing paint from masonry. Most will work on other surfaces as well, but be sure masonry is included.

Local environmental and historical office regulations will also help you know what's appropriate. For instance, you wouldn't use a methylene chloride paint stripper on an historic building.

Make a test panel for every type of appropriate paint stripper to which you've got access.

There have been many cases where I was sure I knew what would remove the coating. But due diligence dictated I test the spectrum, and to this date testing has nearly always proved me wrong.

I always start with test panels about a half-square-foot each on a representative area of the coating. I let the products work over night, about 16 hours or more.

On my return, I almost always find one or two that worked well, several that worked to some degree, and others that did little.

Sometimes I find the surface coating removed, only to see where another layer of some other paint stopped the paint stripper cold. Then I have to start over again. I create new test panels using the stripper that worked, to give my other products a chance to tackle the underneath coating.

As you can see, testing is a systematic narrowing down of what works.

Once I've settled on an effective paint stripper or strippers, I test to determine dwell time, number of applications and other procedures as specified in the product literature.

I follow the instructions closely, especially the safety instructions. That's rule number 3:

Follow all safety instructions, and use the product only as specified. Results may be unpredictable if you use the paint stripper in any other way. Unpredictability is the last thing you want when working on historic masonry.

Once I've verified dwells and other procedures, I make my recommendation, and my job is mostly over.

From there, the work goes to the contractor. I get called only if there's a glitch.

The following rules speak to avoiding glitches.

Use coating removers from manufacturers who back up their products with literature, technical customer service and job-site and spec-writing assistance.

The most important ingredient isn't in the paint stripper. It's the technical support that comes with it. A reputable company wants to do more than just sell you a product. A reputable company wants you to succeed. They'll make sure you have the right products and information to do so.

A reputable manufacturer can assist with testing as well as identifying applicable environmental rules and regulations.

Distributors, architects and contractors are all good sources for identifying such companies.

Use the proper equipment. For most paint strippers this means applying with brushes and rollers. For peels, trowels are included. Since paint removers are often alkaline or solvent-based, it's important to make sure your tools are resistant.

Once the paint stripper has debonded the old coating, you'll generally use a pressure washer to rinse the coating and spent cleaner from the surface. Remember rule number one!

The secret to a successful rinse is low pressure, not above 800 psi; and high gallons per minute. Six to 8 gpm is ideal. It's the amount of water, more than the pressure that governs rinse effectiveness.

Protect everyone and everything not set for paint stripping from contact with the stripper, wind-drift, fumes, residue and rinse water.

Simple plastic sheeting is a good way to protect grass, plantings and nearby surfaces from spray- and wind-drift during rinsing. Don't clean in windy conditions.

I use special impermeable paper made for the purpose to protect curious fingers from my paste or gel test panels while they work overnight. You can also use plastic warning tape to rope off the area where tests or paint stripping operations are ongoing.

You can protect yourself and your project by consulting the local regulatory agency, usually under the jurisdiction of the federal or state EPA, before beginning paint-stripping operations. The National Park Service's Preservation Brief 1 – Assessing Cleaning and Water Repellent Treatments for Historic Masonry Buildings is required reading.

Begin paint removal slowly and cautiously. Again, recall rule number one. Blasting away with a pressure washer, even at relatively low psi, can harm deteriorated masonry.

Never assume the coating you're removing is the only one you'll see. If a new coating shows up, against which your current cleaner is ineffective, test.

Reputable manufacturers of paint-stripping products will be glad to help, usually at no cost.

And that brings up my most important rule: **Never go it alone.** Never try to guess your way through problems or questions. The product distributor, field representative or manufacturer's technical customer service specialists are always happy to help.

The right answer is usually just a phone call away.

As Project Testing Director for AMT Laboratories, Lawrence, Kan., Courtney Murdock's work includes laboratory and field testing on new and existing buildings. She has given presentations to masonry professionals around the country on various subjects including the importance of laboratory testing, aspects of building cleaning, and substrate identification. Courtney has a Bachelor of Science from Texas A&M University at Galveston where she did extensive field work and laboratory testing.

For more information, contact Gary Henry at 785-830-7343 or e-mail gary.henry@prosoco.com.

Take That to the Bank!

by Rick Meehan
Vice President of Marko Janitorial Supply, www.MarkoInc.com

Those of you who have been reading my articles for a while know that I harp on acquiring more knowledge to increase profits in our contract cleaning companies. Although it has a wonderful sound – p…r…o…f…i…t…s – many of you simply do not understand what I'm driving at.

Let's face it, the cleaning industry as a whole has a reputation for employing educationally challenged personnel. Many owners barely made it through high school, much less college. Few janitors and maids reached beyond high school. None of this really matters in the world of cleaning, especially if you understand that this industry is as much a trade as bricklaying or carpentry. A good cleaning person learns tricks of the trade from someone with more experience. It may not take a lot of studying to sling a mop or scrub with a brush, but a true professional can make a facility look so good that it sings without a diploma.

Unfortunately, to run a cleaning business it takes far more than manual labor done properly. Although no one can really get enough schooling, knowledge is not simply about books. Knowledge is about information and wisdom. You can take that to the bank!

Of course, what any good business owner wants is take more money to the bank. If some of that money gets to stay there instead of being spent on the costs of doing business, that's really great. This excess is called profit.

Since the contract cleaning trade is a hands-on field, anything that makes it more rewarding is a good thing. Obviously, moneymaking is what the trade is all about. So how do you turn a higher profit? Are you afraid I'm getting ready to say "crack the books?" Well, actually I am – you can take that to the bank too.

To soften the blow, let me tell a personal story. My son, age 21, joined the U.S. Army this past May. His reasoning, "I don't like college and I don't want to waste any more of your money, Daddy."

Well, I appreciate saving some money, for sure. However, I know enough about the U.S. Army from friends and family that have served to know that training never stops. Some of that training is done in the classroom. My son picked a field that requires tremendous volumes of book-learning, testing, field training, and more testing. All this is to keep him as safe as possible, and I am truly thankful for that. His last phone call was, "I'm learning a lot, especially since I have spent eight hours a day for the last five weeks in the classroom." If I can't lead a horse to water and make him drink, the U.S. Army surely can... and you can take that to the bank!

Now, I can't force-feed knowledge and wisdom into you, but I surely can lead you to the trough. Resources for the cleaning industry are boundless these days.

When I first started in the trade, virtually nothing was available except a couple of magazines and maybe a book or two at the public library. Since the advent of the World Wide Web, every form of media has hopped on board to educate the cleaning industry. People like me are flooding the system daily with tips and tricks, how-to manuals, videos, books, e-zines (like this one), websites – you name it. The trade is inundated with a smorgasbord of information.

Big words for an unlearned occupation. However, like my son, I implore you to educate yourself in whatever fashion works best for you. Along with your education level, your profits will rise, and you can take that to the bank.

Here is a list of my top ten favorite resources to help increase my product knowledge:

1. **Trade magazines,** both printed and on the web: www.ecleanmag.com, this very e-zine; www.cleanlink.com, run by Trade Press, publisher of Sanitary Maintenance; www.maintenancesalesnews.com, by Rankin Publishing, publisher of Maintenance Sales News.

2. **Your local public library** in the "building maintenance" section.

3. **YouTube (www.youtube.com)** where you can search for videos on virtually every cleaning machine and procedure.

4. **Manufacturers' websites** list resource materials on their products – how to, specification sheets, material safety data, sales flyers, seminars, training sessions.

5. *Secrets of Closing the Sale,* by Zig Ziglar, world famous sales trainer and motivational speaker, now deceased. His sales methods are timeless, however.

6. **Cleaning associations** offer resources and training events. The largest of these is the International Sanitary Supply Association, or ISSA (www.issa.com).

7. **Your local janitorial supply house** is the place to get one-on-one instruction, mostly for free.

8. **Janitorial and cleaning staff working in the trenches every day.** Some of them are masters willing to train apprentices. Learn from them.

9. **Government agencies** like OSHA, EPA, DOT, and USDA contain the rules and regulations governing occupational, environmental, transportation, and food safety. Cleaning procedures and materials handling

Classifieds: Products & Services

www.ArmClark.com
Armstrong Clark Quality Wood Stains. Specializing in wood restoration, oil-based coatings for wood & non-toxic wood stains of all kinds for your wood shake restoration & water repellent needs. 800-916-8211

www.PowerWash.com
Mobile power wash equipment, schools, training, videos, environmental supplies & maintenance services. Call for a free catalog, 800-433-2113.

www.PowerWashStore.com
Bigger Selection - Better Quality - Amazing Customer Service. Serving the professional cleaning community for more than 25 years. Call 855-351-9274.

www.PWNA.org
Power Washers of North America. For certification or membership information, visit our website, email info@pwna.org, or call 800-393-7962. Annual Trade Show and Convention, Oct. 17-19, Orlando, Fla.

www.SteelEagle.com
Mfr. of World Class Industrial & Commercial Cleaning & Storage Products, including surface spinners, vacuum systems, undercarriage cleaners, hose reels & more. Custom designs available. 800-447-3924

www.PressureWasherKy.us
Southside Equipment multi-line power equipment distributor. Pressure cleaning equipment, waste water recovery & recycling, generators & cleaning chemicals. Quality products & impeccable service. 888-243-6506

To Advertise in our New Classifieds Section
Contact Allison Hester at allison@ecleanmag.com

---

ignore them get put out of business.

10. Use the Federal Register, www.federalregister.gov, to study up on changes in the laws governing business operations.

No one ever said it would be easy to run a cleaning business. In addition to the resources above, it is wise to have local investment advisors, bankers, lawyers, accountants, insurance agents, and even other cleaning company professionals in your repertoire of consultants. I have been told by many cleaning pros who started off as apprentices and worked their way into becoming masters that they never had a clue about the level of expertise it takes to run a cleaning business until they tried it for themselves. The story is one about the School of Hard Knocks, so you can take that to the bank.

Now that we've about reached the fall of the year, many of us are evaluating where our profits stand so far. Are we better off than last year to date? How are we going to improve our profits in the years to come?

One of my favorite old television shows was a police drama called *Baretta*, which aired from 1975 to 1978. The main character, a New Jersey plainclothes detective named Tony Baretta, held the answer to staying in business: "surviving in a tough world." He was pragmatic; hence, his favorite phrase, "You can take that to the bank!" He meant what he said and backed it up using whatever ethical force necessary to bring a successful outcome to the situation. It was the force of willpower, just the same as the power needed to buckle down to study.

Studying is the path to knowledge; Wisdom comes from experience on the streets. So, starting right now, this fall, hit the Information Highway to discover what it will take to increase your profits and stay in business. Otherwise, like so many undereducated cleaning contractors, this fall may be your last – and you can take that to the bank!

eClean Magazine

When to fire your customer

Everyone knows it's important to retain customers. Good customers are hard to find and worth keeping. It's almost always more profitable to keep existing customers than to replace them with new ones.

But what about that problem customer? You know, the one that everyone wishes secretly (or not so secretly) would just disappear?

Sometimes it's best to just let that problem customer go. Not only can this save you and your team some grief—it might actually save the company money. Let's take a look at some of the common types of problem customers:

• **The Check is in the Mail.** Customers who pay late cost you money. If it's habitual and you're in a tight margin or credit intensive business, it may be time to cut them loose.

• **I'm Outta Here Unless You...** This customer continually threatens to pull his/her account unless you give something extra. This reduces margins. If it happens once, it might be a genuine threat and worth handling. If it happens often, it's probably just a negotiation technique. Stop giving in, and don't worry if the customer actually follows through.

• **The Chronic Complainer.** This customer constantly speaks negatively about your product, prices, or service, but still buys from you. Address the complaints, but don't let it continue. If someone is complaining to you, s/he is probably complaining about you to others, hurting your brand.

• **Captain Rude.** No one should have to endure verbal abuse. Don't be afraid to set clear boundaries with this customer. Communicate your expectations about rudeness, and if this customer breaks the rules, say goodbye

• **The Other Guy Does It Better.** Some customers constantly talk about your competition. The really brazen ones may even tell the competitor they're playing a back-and-forth game with you. If this happens once, it may be worth working through, but again, if it's happening often, this customer may not be worth the trouble.

Check the Math

When you're dealing with a problem customer, take a look at the math to determine that customer's monetary value. It may seem a bit uncaring, but math is cut and dried and makes decision-making far easier.

- **Determine the customer lifetime value.** Look at the customer segment and the average lifetime value of a customer in that segment. If a problem customer is in a low value segment, it's an easy decision to let them go.

- **Estimate the replacement cost.** Losing an easy-to-replace customer isn't necessarily a loss. Don't keep a customer if retention costs more than securing a new one in the same segment.

- **If the math doesn't provide a clear answer, consider the qualitative.** Think about how the customer makes you or your employees feel or how hard you must work to keep them happy.

- **Has this customer always been challenging/ dissatisfied?** Chronically unhappy people usually don't become satisfied after sufficient wooing. It's pointless exhausting yourself to please others.

- **Can they be converted?** Say a customer is giving off a "maybe I'll change my mind" vibe. If you sense a potential behavior change, retention efforts may be wise even if the math doesn't say so up front.

- **Does this customer mistreat your employees?** This must be a consideration – always. If a customer is verbally abusive or harassing one of your employees, let them go in a hurry.

Firing a customer is not an easy decision. After you work hard to earn their business, the idea of cutting them loose may seem counter-intuitive. Check the math and consider the ramifications of keeping them around. Sometimes a fond farewell is the wisest investment.

Read more: http://www.marketingmo.com/how-to-articles/customer-service/when-to-fire-your-customer/#ixzz2dqxYWPWR

Since 1992 the PWNA has represented contractors in the Power Washing industry. We stand for all power washers: fleet washing, concrete cleaning, kitchen exhaust, wood restoration, as well as everything in between. The PWNA provides quality education and certification to power wash contractors along with conventions, networking opportunities, and a clear voice for our industry.

Visit **www.thepwna.org** for more info on becoming a member.

CONVENTION 2013:
OCT 17-19 · ORLANDO FL

POWER WASHERS OF NORTH AMERICA
PH 800-393-7962 | FX 651-213-0369 | WWW.PWNA.ORG

Industry Happenings

MWCoA Regional Seminar

The Master Window Cleaners of America (MWCoA) is conducting a Fall Regional Educational Seminar, Sept. 20 & 21 in Louisville, Kentucky.

Friday's seminar sessions will include: High Rise 101; our own Scraper "less" education course development; making route effective and profitable and closing the evening a keynote session Business Structures 101 with Christopher Stephen, Esq. A catered meal will be served.

Saturday's classes includes representatives from Kentucky's OSHA department giving instruction on Hazmat and the new GHS system that goes into effect later this year, as well as ladder safety and fall restraint/protection; Social Media Law 101; Screen Repair; and Phone and Instant Online Quotes. Product demos and vendor displays as well as drawing for door prizes rounds out the seminar.

Other speakers spotlighted are Jeff Scott of Green Window Cleaning Services; John Martin of Waukesha Window Cleaning; Drew McClevelry of Magnolia Metal and Plastic Products and Josh Lawlor of QuoteFlare.

All window cleaners and window cleaning business owners are invited and encouraged to attend. You do not have to be a MWCoA member.

For more information, schedule details, and to sign up, go to www.mwcoa.com

---

Recap: Pacific Northwest Networking Event, Sponsored by Windows 101

Over 120 window cleaners from around the Pacific Northwest joined Windows101 at their Seattle-based shop for their 1st Annual Networking Event & Dinner in late July. Attendees were treated to a free barbeque and seminar, which featured several speakers representing Titan Cleaning Solutions and Unger, plus talks on Growing a Successful Window Cleaning Business, Ryan Tolmich, Ryco Window Cleaning, and Bidding and Winning Big Contracts, by Ron Musgraves

The evening event – which was attended by around 70 people and featured a prime rib and salmon dinner – was held a few miles north at the Country Village in Bothel. The dinner allowed attendees to network with fellow window cleaners.

Dinner was followed by an Awards Ceremony, as the Lifetime Achievement Award was presented to 81-year old Ralph Swalwell, whose Seattle-based company, Lift Off, has been cleaning windows for over 50 years. "It seems he was also a comedian," said Yvette of Windows 101. "He had everyone laughing as he accepted the award."

The photo contest winner was Matt Fleming of Cascade Window Cleaning, who submitted a photo of his daughter, Ivy, cleaning windows.

eClean Magazine

Power Washing Do's & Dont's

by Paul Horsley, eClean Publisher

Power washing is an incredible thing. With only a few blasts from your power washer, years of grime can be swept away. However, it's important to understand how to properly use such a powerful tool in order to avoid causing damage to your business or personal property. The power washing dos and don'ts listed below will help you understand how to best use your pressure washer. We'll also discuss when it's smart to contact a power washing company for professional help.

POWER WASHING DOS:

Do protect yourself and others. Remember, this machine is exuding water at 1,500 to 3,000 PSI. When you're dealing with such high water pressures, it's not unusual for sharp particles to fly off the surface being cleaned. Don't risk permanent eye damage – wear protective eye goggles when using a power washer. For especially hazardous jobs, power washing company managers often require employees to wear full face masks. It's also smart to wear long-sleeve clothing, just as you would when using a weed whacker.

A little more safety advice: Be sure family members and pets stay far away from the spray of your pressure washer. Finally, avoid accidents by engaging the safety lock whenever you're not in the middle of power washing.

Do check oil levels before turning on your power washer. Running any engine without oil will cause lasting damage. Be sure to check oil levels in your machine before power washing. Your owner's manual should have additional maintenance instructions.

Do notice the distance between the surface you're cleaning and the tip of the power washing nozzle. Different cleaning surfaces will require more or less space. When blasting built-up BBQ gunk off of your grill, you can hold the nozzle as close as three inches away. The highly pressured water emitted from a power washer won't damage a metal grill. However, other surfaces will require more space. When cleaning the exterior of a home, for instance, you should keep the nozzle at least six inches away from the surface being cleaned. In general, it's best to be cautious – start farther away, and move closer once you see that no damage is occurring.

Do conduct power washing tests first. If used incorrectly, a power washer can cause permanent damage to your home or business. Therefore, if you're unsure about the correct pressure setting, cleaning agents, nozzle type, water temperature or nozzle distance for any job, you should test a small, inconspicuous area first. Alternatively, you can call in a power washing company to show you how to properly clean a particular surface.

Do store your power washer in a climate-controlled area with good ventilation. If your machine will be kept in an unheated room, conduct winterization to avoid damage caused by freezing temperatures.

Do clean out your chemical injector after every use. Built-up chemicals will only cause problems down the road, so be sure to flush out your machine after using the chemical injector.

POWER WASHER DON'TS

Don't power wash windows. You're asking for trouble if you try power washing windows. They can crack or break, and weather seals can be destroyed. Moreover, manufacturer warranties are typically voided if the owner uses a pressure washer to clean windows.

Don't add fuel while the machine is running. Just as you turn your car engine off before adding gas, you should turn off your power washer before refueling.

Don't leave your pressure washer running unattended. If your machine is on, you should be right next to it.

Don't point your power washer at animals or people. Basic safety protocols advise against aiming any powerful tool at fellow living beings, even in play.

Don't use acid-based products or bleach with your chemical injector. This is both to protect your machine (which can be irreparably damaged by such liquids) and to protect people and pets (who could be seriously hurt by these chemicals). If your machine isn't powerful enough, call a power washing company instead of tinkering around with dangerous chemicals.

Don't use hot water unless it's approved in product specifications. Some pressure washer pumps are rated for hot water, and others aren't. Don't use hot water unless you're certain your pump is made for it. If not, a power washing company will have the tools needed to clean the surface in question.

Don't leave your pressure washer running for more than two minutes without pulling the trigger.

Photo courtesy of Mike Hockman, Gutter Dogs, www.GutterDogs.com

Issue #18

eCLEANmagazine™
The professional contractor cleaner's online resource!

The Gutter Cleaning Issue

Why It's Needed & How to Do It

Plus

- Laurie Benjamin: Professionalizing Trinidad & Tobago
- Inside GCA Largo
- Sales: Persistence Pays Off

...and more!

powerwash.com™
SUPPLIES CHEMICALS TRAINING

1.800.433.2113
2513 Warfield St. Fort Worth, TX 76106

Pressure Washers | Surface Cleaners | Chemicals | Cleaning Supplies | Parts | Pumps & Unloaders | Training Materials

Order Today & Pay Later! NET 30
Shop Online 24 Hours a Day
Get Approved Today!

MarXoff Gutter Cleaning Applicator

The MarXoff Gutter Cleaning Applicator is the new and affordable way to clean stained gutters without having to climb up and down a ladder, while standing safely on the ground. Simply attach a MarXoff Gutter Cleaning Applicator to the Mr. LongArm Telescoping Brush Handle (sold separately -- or any extendable painter's pole), dip into a bucket of Gutter Zap, apply and rinse. That's it! You're done!

MarXoff turns an all day job into one that just last minutes. The cleaning pad is made of soft, synthetic lambs wool and is safe to the gutter finish.

Super Concentrate Gutter Zap

Zap those gutters clean with Super Concentrate Gutter Zap. It cleans black streaks off gutters caused by electrostatic bonding. Simply wet down the gutter, spray on Gutter Zap, and rinse off with garden hose pressure. It's that easy! Light brushing is required on heavily soiled areas.
One bottle makes 3-5 gal. of ready-to-use-mix.

Gutter Cleaner Attachment

The unique angle of the Gutter Cleaner attachment makes cleaning leaves and dirt out of gutters a breeze.
Approximately 14" Long
135 degree bend.
1/4" Quick connectors on each end
Max Pressure: 3,000 PSI
Max Flow: 8 GPM

4035HG Belt Drive Power Washer

We take care of our customers before, during, and after a sale! Equipment that is standard to us is considered to be add-ons by others. Use this checklist to make sure you know what we offer with the purchase of a power washer that others don't!

PowerWash.com Standard Equipment

PW Others
- ✓ ☐ 50' High Pressure Hose
- ✓ ☐ 36" Insulated Wand w/QC
- ✓ ☐ Trigger Gun
- ✓ ☐ 4 Color Coded, quick coupled nozzles
- ✓ ☐ Extra 1/4" & 3/8" O-Rings
- ✓ ☐ Down Stream Injector

Features
Aircraft grade aluminum frame
50 mesh inlet filter
Low oil shutdown
2 Models Available, Electric Start (4035HGES) & Pull Start (4035HGPS) Both models can be equiped with hot pack seals for hot water operation.

Specifications
3,500 PSI at 4 GPM
Honda, 13 HP, 4 Stroke Motor, Gas Tank Size: 1.75 Gal, General TSS 1511, Belt Drive Pump
Dimensions: 47"L X 27"W X 29.5"H
Weight: 230lbs.

www.eCleanMag.com　　　　　　　　　　　　　　　　　　Issue #18

IN THIS ISSUE:

The Gutter Cleaning Issue:

317　Why Clean Gutters Matter

320　Gutter Cleaning: The In's & Out's of Rims & Spouts

326　Tiger Stripes: Safely Gettiing Rid of Those Ugly Black Streaks on Gutters

328　20 Tips from Mike Hockman of Gutter Dogs

330　The 2013 PWNA Convention & Trade Show: New Classes Galore

332　PWNA Vendor Profile: GCA Largo

334　Laurie Benjamin, All Aspects Maintenance Ltd., Bringing Professional Cleaning to Trinidad & Tobago

338　Getting in the Biz, by Rick Meehan, Marko Janiorial

341　Classifieds

342　Persistence Pays Off, by Tom Grandy, Grandy & Associates

344　Leadership Means High Ethical Standards, by Joe Scarlett

346　Building Your Sales Foundation, by April Dodson, Bidslot Marketing

326

334

COVER PHOTO
Courtesy of Tim Fields, Complete Power Wash, Hagerstown, Maryland, www.CPSoftwash.com

---

eClean Magazine is published monthly

Publisher: Paul Horsley, paul@ecleanmag.com
Editor: Allison Hester, allison@ecleanmag.com

Box 262, 16 Midlake Blvd S.E.
Calgary, Alberta
Canada T2X2X7
www.eCleanMag.com

eClean Magazine

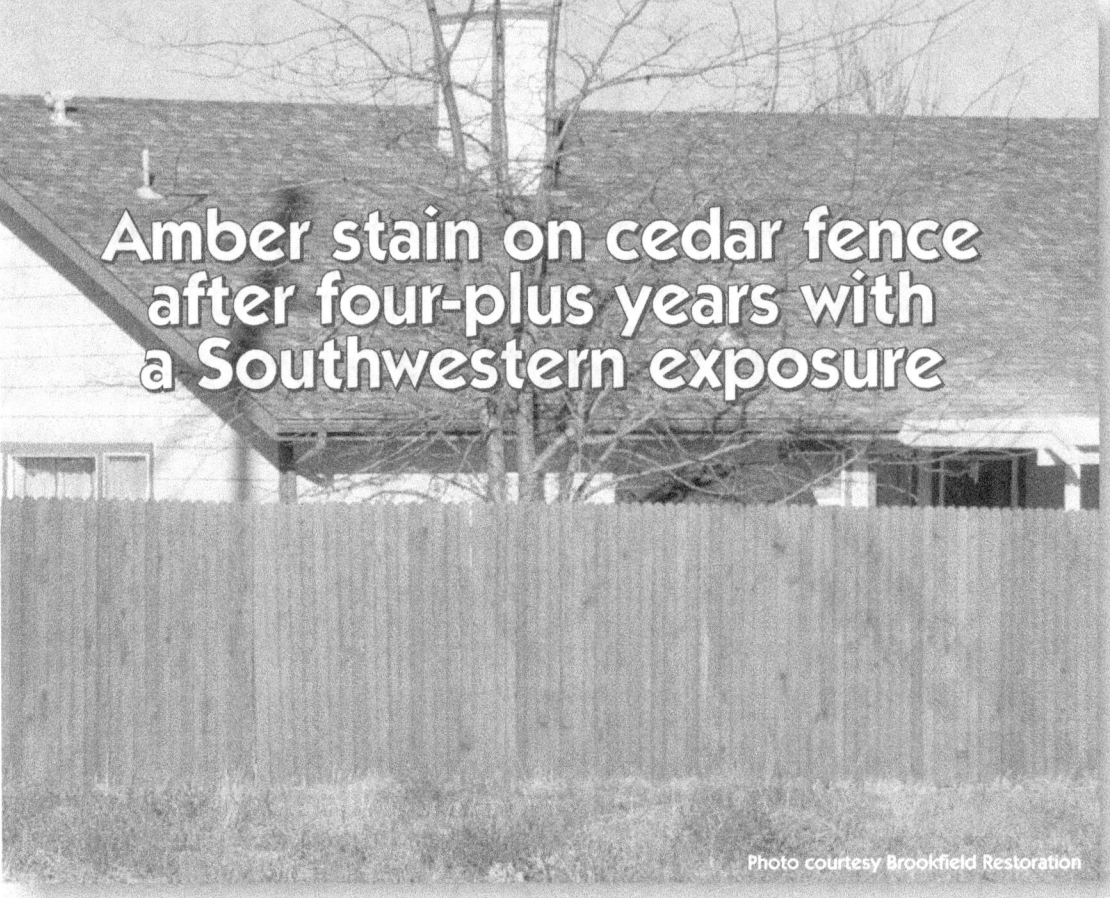

Photo courtesy of Curtis Lambert, Lambert/Martin Power Washing & Glass, Cranton, RI

Why Clean Gutters Matter

Gutters are one of the most valuable and affordable methods for homeowners to protect their homes from the elements. By channeling water off the roof and directing it to a location away from the home, properly working gutters help protect the home's shingles, wood under the eaves, siding, flooring and landscaping from a whole host of problems and expensive repairs. These include:

- Flooding
- Stained walls, siding, floors, etc.
- Rotting doors and wood elements
- Cracking walls and foundations
- Warping or bowing floors

Not only do these cost money to fix, they also devalue the home itself.

However, if gutters are clogged and not working properly, homeowners may find themselves facing the same above problems that gutters are designed to prevent, but a whole host of new ones. These include:

- Infestation of mosquitoes and other pests
- Damage caused from gutters ripping down after becoming too clogged and heavy.
- Frozen gutters (i.e., ice dams)
- Added mold and mildew from the backed up, decomposed leaves and other organic materials

Keeping gutters clean is not a fun job. For the average homeowner, it's also not an easy one. Worst of all, it's a job that is often made to be more costly than necessary due to neglect.

When and How Often Should Gutters be Cleaned?

While there is no set answer to these

Photo courtesy of It's Gutter be Clean, www.ItsGutterBeClean.co.UK

Questions, the general rule of thumb is that most gutters should be cleaned twice a year. Fall and Spring are usually the months of choice because that is when they gutters become the most clogged due to falling leaves, pine needles, blooms, seed pods, and so on.

Homes surrounded by a lot of foliage need to have their gutters cleaned more often than those without. Also, houses in areas with four distinct seasons may need to have gutters cleaned more often than those with mild weather year round.

Proper maintenance is less expensive in the long run than catastrophic failure. Maintaining gutters throughout the year not only will help prevent clogged gutter-related damage, it often costs less to have them cleaned should the homeowner hire a professional to do it.

Are Gutter Protection Systems Worth It?

One "solution" to the gutter cleaning problem has been the growing market of gutter guards, inserts and screens. These are supposedly designed to prevent large items from entering the gutters that create clogs and help the water flow freely.

However, despite what a lot of homeowners believe, none of these products are perfect. Many of these items will keep large items like leaves, bird nests, and rodents out of the gutters, but they can't keep the small items out. Things like pine needles, flower buds, dirt or sand, and roof granules still get past the protection systems and cause problems. Gutters may not have to be cleaned as often – depending on how well the product works – but when they do have to be cleaned, they are generally more expensive because it's harder to access them.

Plus, gutter guards, inserts and screens can be expensive – ranging anywhere from around $1 to $10 a linear foot for the average home, depending on the type installed. Some of the professionally installed versions do cover any future maintenance or cleanings, but these are the systems that cost around $10,000 or more on the average sized home. Considering an average gutter cleaning job costs a few hundred dollars, homeowners need to figure out if it's really worth it.

According to a 2010 *Consumer Reports* study, many of the "do it yourself" versions of gutter protection systems work as well the high-end versions and cost significantly less – if they are installed properly. But again, they will almost certainly have to be cleaned in time, and those cleanings will cost more.

Why Hire a Professional?

A lot of DIY homeowners decide to tackle gutter cleaning themselves. But is this really smart?

Most gutter cleaning requires working from either the roof or a ladder. Yes, there are some garden hose, vacuum and pressure washer attachments that allow some levels of cleaning to be done from the ground. However, when working from the ground, there's no way to see how dirty the gutter really is or how clean it's getting. Plus some of those systems are hard to control if you're not used to it. It's easy to cause accidental damage.

Right: Ladder Accidents by Gender & Age. This 2012 graphic is based on figured in the U.K, but the numbers are still very telling for North American homeowners. Note that the majority of injuries happened to men ages 15 to 64 who were in the middle of a home maintenance project (like cleaning their gutters.)

Ladder work is dangerous. (See the graphic to the right.) And the more you have to move the ladder, the more dangerous it becomes. The higher you up you have to go on the ladder, the more dangerous it is as well.

When a homeowner cleans out a gutter, they're not just climbing a ladder. They're climbing a ladder and carrying tools – like a scoop or a vacuum or a blower. They are climbing a ladder and trying to remove a gutter protection system. They are on top of a ladder reaching out to grab that leaf that's a little too far away, and with each reach they are increasing their risk of injury.

Additionally, professionals can also check a homeowners' gutter system to look for, and correct, problems. They know how to ensure that downspouts are not clogged to keep the gutter system flowing properly.

The Smartest Solution

Homeowners need to look at their gutter systems as an investment in their home's value and their family's well-being. Cleaned gutters not only help prevent problems with the home, they help promote a healthier home environment. And along those same lines, hiring a professional rather than doing it themselves is an investment in their family's well being. One slip from a ladder or roof could result in expensive medical bills, weeks off of work – or much worse.

Again, gutter protection systems are an option, but they are not an all-out solution. Gutters will still need to be cleaned periodically to ensure they are working properly. Homeowners need to evaluate whether the expense of the system will pay out in the long run, and even all installation systems should ideally be put in by a professional. Again, it keeps the homeowner safely on the ground, and helps ensure the system is installed and working correctly.

Most importantly, homeowners should not wait until after a problem arises to have their gutters cleaned. It's better to get on a maintenance program with a reputable, professional cleaning contractor and determine how many cleanings that particular homeowner really needs. Regularly scheduled maintenance gutter cleanings can save significant money in the long run.

eClean Magazine

Ladder Injury Statistics

Accidents by Ladder Type

Accidents by Gender and Age

MEN X2 AS LIKELY

32,821 | 14,514

3,362 — 0-14 Years
33,866 — 15-64 Years
9,964 — 65+ Years

Type of Injury

- Head: 8,795 (16.3%)
- Neck: 882 (1.6%)
- Chest: 5,638 (10.4%)
- Arms: 17,630 (32.7%)
- Legs: 15,047 (27.9%)

Activity Undertaking when Injured

- DIY Maintenance Repairs Gardening: 18,594
- Household Activity Cooking Washing: 7,503
- Hobby Or Leisure: 2,030

RoSPA | HSE
Statistics from www.rospa.com
www.hse.gov.uk/statistics

Gutter Cleaning:
The In's and Out's of Rims & Spouts

by Allison Hester

Photo courtesy of Mark Cave, Mr. Clever Clean, www.MrCleverClean.co.uk

As this month's cover article already explained, gutter cleaning is a necessity for homeowners who want to protect their property. Again, the best option for homeowners is to hire a professional. (See "Why Clean Gutters Matter" on page ? for more on this.)

But, what are the best gutter cleaning options for professional contractors?

To help us figure this out, I developed a 10-question survey for industry members, then followed up with a few interviews. Within a couple of days of the survey being announced, I received more than enough responses to help me gain a better understanding of the gutter cleaning market. Thanks to all of you who participated. The following is based off of these findings, along with some additional research.

When to Clean

Fall tends to be the primary season for gutter cleaning, with Spring coming in a close second, which corresponds with the times that the majority of leaves, seedlings, buds, pine needles, and acorns fall, clogging the gutters. These are the primary types of items – although generally decaying and sloppy – that need to be removed. However, contractors have seen it all – trees, ferns, cacti, golf balls, bird nests, dead birds, dead rats, live snakes, fire ants, bee hives, and the list goes on and on.

Roof granules are another problem, and one that can be a pain to remove. While mud and decay can be scooped out and disposed of, granules have to be gathered together then scooped (depending on the amount) or flushed out with water for smaller quantities.

As mentioned in the cover article, getting a maintenance contract is the best option for professional cleaners and homeowners alike. This helps keep the gutters working properly, and makes the gutter cleaning job easier. Providing a discount for regular maintenance may be something worth considering.

For example, Mike Bingler of Firehouse Power Washing in Senoia, Georgia, estimated a gutter cleaning job for $125, but the customer asked Bingler if would discount it to $100 if he agreed to have his gutters cleaned regularly. Bingler agreed and has been cleaning the customer's gutters almost monthly for the past two years. "The only months he does not want them done is in June and July, which is when I wash his house and driveway for more money," he added. "It just goes to show you that occasionally a 'one time' gutter cleaning can turn into a $1,000 a year account."

How to Price

While around 75 percent of those who responded will offer gutter cleaning services alone, one-fourth only provide gutter cleaning in conjunction with other cleaning services. Part of this is because gutter cleaning can a make a mess of the house and windows. Another aspect is that some people just don't like doing it. A few also mentioned they will throw in gutter cleaning for free to residential customers who buy larger cleaning packages from them.

"Gutters that are clogged and packed with mud and mold are very hard to clean while keeping the rest of the property spotless," explained Tyr Fenlinger of Pacific Window Cleaning Company in Wailuku, Hawaii. "If I can't negotiate a fair price on other types of cleaning with this type of customer, I'm sometimes better off just passing on the job."

While most contractors agree that you never know what you're going to find in a gutter, not everyone figures in how dirty the gutters are when giving a price. In fact, almost half of those who answered do not include this in their estimates.

Pricing is figured several ways. Most start with the linear footage, then also factor in how many stories high the gutters are. Some stop there. Others will look at the pitch of the roof to see if roof access is possible. Still others try to figure out how dirty the gutters are, either through a customer questionnaire, by examining the property (and how much foliage surrounds the house) or by actually visually inspecting the gutters. This last option is the exception, not the norm.

"I have a webpage dedicated to gutter cleaning, so customers can familiarize themselves with us and the process before they call. I ask several questions about the height of the house, the size of the house, the type and pitch of the roof, maintenance history of gutters, travel distance to the site, and so on. I occasionally ask for photos emailed or texted to me, then I quote over the phone nine out of 10 times," explained Bill Neil of GutterX in St. Charles, Missouri. "Some projects require a visit to examine the site before a firm price is possible."

"It's also important to look at the condition of the gutters and downspouts," stressed Bill Schoenherr of B Home Services in Rochester, New York. "Are they pitched properly? Are the hangers all secure?"

This is a really important point, and one that Frank Francoi of Hydroclean in Brighton, Michigan, learned the hard way. While cleaning the front of a home, I was midway through when the whole section collapsed and fell to the ground. The homeowner was aware of this and expected it, but I still fixed the situation even while the homeowner was raving mad and threatening to sue. They have not called nor have I heard from an attorney. I guess being nice paid off in the long run."

Another reason to inspect the gutters is because you never know you're going to have to remove.

Matt Schaltenbrand of Advanced Pressure and Gutter Cleaning, Inc., in Marietta, Georgia,

THE choice of professional roof cleaning contractors for controlling runoff & maximizing dwell time on ugly black roof stains.

Visit www.RoofSnot.com for more information. Available exclusively through Southside Equipment, Inc., www.PressureWasherKY.us

Photo courtesy of Curtis Lambert, Lambert/Martin Power Washing & Glass, Cranton, RI

obtained a contract through a third party that included cleaning the gutters of २० buildings. When we got there, it was all trash on the roof, not organic debris. We had to bag and haul thousands of pounds to dumpsters over about four days. To top it off, we never got paid as the middle subcontractor took the money and ran."

Almost everyone (around ९० percent) agreed that they charged more for cleanings when gutter protection systems were in place.

"I do one each year that has covers that don't work well," said Dan Wagner of Dan Wagner Window Cleaning in Honesville, Penn. "Each section has several screws holding them in place. They are very hard to remove and get worse each year."

"One of our first jobs was a single level home that had mesh gutter guards that were not working to well," said Curtis Lambert of Lambert/Martin Window Cleaning in Cranston, RI. "The gutter beds were full of bird poop, mud, twigs, leaves— you name it. We got through it, but learned just how to let our customers know what to do to fix their problem." In his case, Lambert upsells and installs the Rain Flow Gutter Protection System.

Ironically, one of the biggest complaints by contractors about gutter cleaning is that they have undercharged for jobs. That's why some prefer to charge an hourly rate. That way if there are surprises, at least they are getting paid to deal with them.

The Cleaning Process

Note: this article focus on the interior of cleaning gutters only. For external cleaning, and the removal of zebra stripes, see the article on page १०.

One of the primary things contractors wanted to know was if there was a good way to clean the interior of gutters from the ground. Unfortunately, if there is, I didn't learn about it, especially on multi-story homes. A few people have come up with ways to clean first-story gutters from the ground by using vacuums or pressure washers and special gutter attachments.

Two specific products were mentioned. First, a couple of contractors liked the GutterBall – a special gutter cleaning nozzle that attaches to a pressure washer. The only complaint was that the Gutter Ball created a mess on the ground. We posted an article about the Gutter Ball back in January 2012 that you can **read on our website**.

Another item that was mentioned was the Gutter Blaster, which is a special bent wand

and nozzle that attaches to a garden hose. There are other similar products on the market.

However, in most cases, cleaning from the ground simply doesn't do as good a job as cleaning from a ladder or rooftop. In fact, in many cases, scooping the gutters out by hand is simply the professional method of choice.

When not working from the ground, most contractors do the majority of their gutter cleaning work from a ladder. Because ladder safety is such a huge issue, we are going to produce a separate resource (due out later this month) dedicated to this topic. However, it is imperative to say that a ladder standoff stabilizer attachment needs to put in place any time ladder work is being done. LadderMax was the brand mentioned by a few.

"Using the LadderMax standoff attached to the top of the ladder means that you are letting the feet of the standoff rest on the shingles and stabilizing the ladder. It is a lot safer than just leaning an extension ladder against a gutter, in which case the ladder could travel and one could fall to the ground," explained Chris Thompson of Attention to Detail Window Cleaning Bottineau, ND. "The other benefit is that it prevents you from scratching the face of the gutter, which happens when leaning the ladder against the gutter." Thompson also pointed out the need for using leg levelers at the base of any extension ladder.

Another ladder tip is one that Glenn Igler of Enviroclean Pressure Washing in Atlanta learned the hard way. "If you leave the ladder to work on the roof, make sure the ladder is secure. On several occasions when I first started, I was on the roof with the wand and hose, and the hose caught the ladder and knocked it down. Fortunately, there were some nice folks nearby that put it back up for me so I could get down."

While most work is done from ladders, roof work is generally preferred to ladder work when possible. "I like to stay safe, and as ironic as it sounds, the roof is a lot safer than a ladder, especially when using tools like a pressure washer to clean gutters," explained Igler. "Back pressure is created when you pull the trigger, and it can slide the ladder down the gutter and result in a fall."

Walking the roof allows for the use of additional tools, like a leaf blower. You'll want

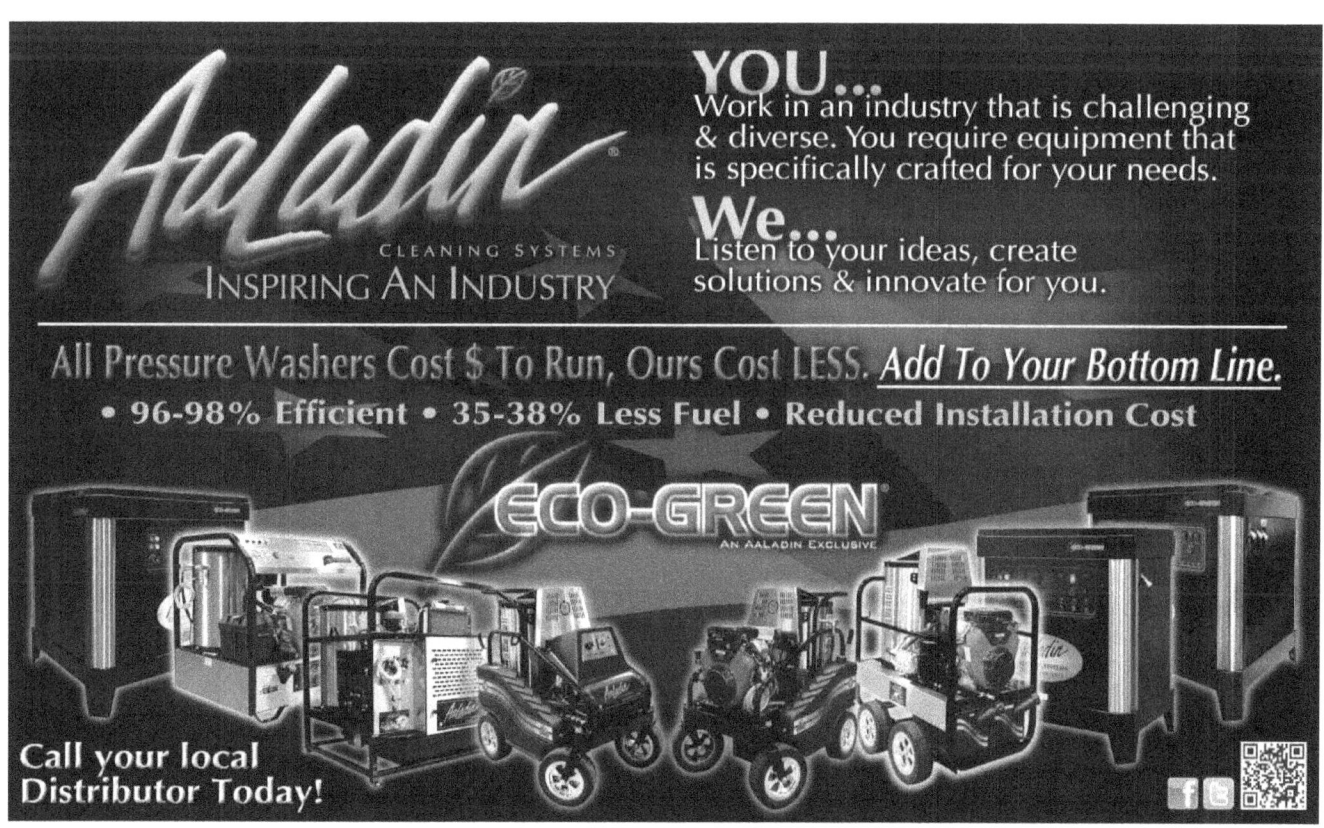

Bucket of gutter debris. Courtesy of Tim Fields, Complete Power Wash, Hagerstown, Maryland, www.CPSoftwash.com

something that is gas powered and commercial grade. "I have an ECHO, but STIHL makes a good product as well," said Thompson. "You want a backpack blower because it is safer and they have more power than a handheld. A gas powered is also safer than an electric, since there is not a chance of tripping over the electrical cord while walking on the roof."

Beyond these items, there are no real magical tools of choice either. Buckets. Brushes. Extension poles. Scoops. Those were the most common tools mentioned. But a lot of cleaning is done by hand.

"Most gutters that my son Zach cleans contain wet contents, so the cleaning is done by hand and the contents are placed in a bucket," explained Tim Fields, owner of Complete Power Wash in Clear Spring, Maryland. "On walkable ranchers, he scoots along the roof's lower edge on his hands and knees, hand scooping the contents into buckets."

A couple of bucket related tips. First, several recommended using some sort of hook so the bucket can hang safely and free up the technician's hands. Thompson also suggested attaching a rope to the bucket using a dog leash clip so you can lower the bucket down safely to the ground from the roof or ladder.

Marc Cournover of Comes a Time Powerwashing in Canton, Ohio, averages 10 houses a day doing everything by hand. "We call it a 'white glove service' and we actually wear white Atlas gloves." All collected debris goes into five gallon buckets and is dumped either in the woods or in the back of the truck.

Extension poles with scoops or tools such as the Gutter Grabber were particularly popular choices when doing ladder work. "On two story homes, Zach will set the ladder at the downspout end to make sure that it is clear and then move the ladder 10 or 12 feet down the gutter," said Fields. "After resetting the ladder, he uses an eight-to-16-foot extended pole with a WCR (Window Cleaning Resource) gutter tool on the end, pulling from about 12 feet in each direction, placing the contents in the bucket. This allows them to clean as much as 20 feet of gutter with only one ladder set up. When Zach reaches the far end of the gutter, he uses a pressure hose with a ball valve attached and flushes the gutter and downspout with water.

Wes Buckner of MidOhio Window Cleaning in Galion, Ohio, uses gutter scoops, but also has created some homemade tools to assist in gutter cleaning. "I have a tool to help drag or push debris from under one section of gutter cover so I only have to remove every other section to clean the gutter. However, there is no 'golden ticket' when it comes to gutter cleaning tools. I haven't really found that one tool works better than the other because you have so many different circumstances that come into play. You have to diversify. What works for one job may not work for the next."

Cleaning the Downspout

Perhaps the most important aspect is ensuring the downspout is working properly. Some prefer to get the downspout flowing first thing, while others tackle that feat last.

Generally, contractors will use a water hose to determine how well the downspout is flowing, then remove any clogs. Contractors usually begin by attempting to push any debris inside the downspout downward – using a hose and nozzle, a pressure washer, a sewer snake, or a leaf blower – until it all comes out the other end.

"I unclog downspouts two different ways – either with a long snake-like metal device that goes down the downspout to push leaves and debris out," said Jeff Stinnell of J's Window Cleaning in Green Lane, Penn. "Or, if the clog is really bad, I disassemble the downspout, remove the clog and reassemble everything.

"That's why it's important to always carry a cordless drill with a ¼ inch hex driver," said Billy Gallagher of Jm Gallagher Gutter & Window Cleaning Inc., in Fort Washington, Penn. Next, disassemble the elbows because this is usually where the clogs are."

Another tip from Keith Ayotte, Top Notch Soft Wash LLC, West Brookfield, Massachusetts: "Always have tools with you—you never know when something might happen that you weren't planning on, like a down spout falling or gutter caps coming off."

Gutter Cleaning Wisdom

Gutter cleaning gets easier with time and experience, but you always have to expect the unexpected. "I've had tough ones have been frozen. Downspouts packed solid that you had to take apart. Underground drains that are plugged. Some installed so tight to the roof that you can't get your hands into them. Some with bee and wasp nests, and probably about 20 other things," said Rick Swope of Grime Busters LLC in Cement City, Michigan. "But it all goes with the job."

"We all can share an experience of gallons of smelly gutter water gushing on top of us after taking a drain assembly apart," added Don Perks of Perks Window Cleaning Ltd. in West Vancouver, BC. "The busy season is coming up. It's best not to think of it."

Gutter cleaning, unfortunately, is one of those markets that is filled with lowballers. As with other cleaning services, the key is to differentiate your company through professionalism – maintaining liability and workers comp insurance, ensuring downspouts are working properly, not leaving a mess on the yard, and showing up when scheduled.

And again, experience is going to become more valuable than any gutter cleaning gadget on the market. "Just like pressure washing, with proper training, a good crew can handle many jobs easily in one day," added Schaltenbrand. "Some specific tools can be used, but it's more about the skill of the tech."

Tiger Stripes
Safely Getting Rid of Those Ugly Black Streaks on Gutters

by Allison Hester

Photo courtesy of Jon Gutowski, Total Pressure Washing, www.totalpressurewashing.com

Ever wonder what causes those ugly black streaks on the outsides of gutters and why they are so hard to remove?

Those streaks, often referred to by industry members as "tiger stripes," are actually caused by a chemical reaction that occurs between the asphalt from roof shingles and the aluminum in the gutters. "The gutter manufacturer anodizes the aluminum to get paint to stick," explained Mike Taylor, owner of Absolute Chemical in Nashville, Tennessee, which manufactures a number of house wash, gutter cleaning and wood staining products. "Not only are different brands of gutters anodized differently, the same gutter manufacturer's process may vary from batch to batch. Depending on the process, the paint may easily come off when cleaning gutters if the wrong product or wrong mixing ratio is used. In other words, there is no magic mixing ratio when it comes to gutter cleaning chemicals—each job is unique.

The black streaks are not simply stains, and therefore can't be removed with traditional housewashing chemicals that remove mold or mildew. The asphalt actually creates an electrostatic bond with the aluminum – much the same way that road film sticks to fleets – and the bond must be broken in order for the stains to be removed.

A lot of contractors use various forms of butyl-based products, which basically means various degreasers. When these butyl-based products are diluted with water, they lose their strength rapidly. In other words, these products have to be mixed pretty hot to work

correctly, and the hotter the mixture, the more likely to remove paint from the gutters, and the more dangerous it is for workers.

While butyl-based products work, it's also easy for contractors to accidentally take the paint off of gutters while removing the black streaks. "I've had to send my technicians back to a customer's home with a can of spray paint," admitted Mike Hockman of Gutter Dogs in Maryland. "Those Home Depot gutters are the worst for this."

A few companies have successfully come up with alternatives to butyl-based products. One item that is quite popular (according to our industry survey) and has gained a strong reputation for working is Gutter Grenade (F13) by Pressure Tek. (See the ad on this page for more information on how to purchase this product.) A mild potassium hydroxide-based solution that was developed almost 10 years ago, Gutter Grenade removes the oxidation layer of the paint where the streaks are trapped through electrostatic bonding. However, Gutter Grenade will not remove the paint on gutters unless the paint has completely failed, meaning it has oxidized through the whole paint layer – which is rare.

When working with Gutter Grenade, contractors should keep the siding under the gutters wet with water and avoid dripping Gutter Grenade on the siding without rinsing it off relatively quickly. Otherwise, Gutter Grenade will create clean streaks on the siding where it dripped. The average mix strength is 1:1, but can be effective with as little as a 2:1 mix. The strongest it needs to be is 1:1. Contractors should also wear safety glasses and gloves when working with the product. F13 is safe for plants, although they should be pre-wet for protection. You may want to cover flowering plants.

Another product that is really just being introduced to the general cleaning market (although it's been available to their local customers for a few years) is Absolute Chemical's Citrus Gutter Cleaning and Housewash. (See the ad on page 1 to learn more about where to get this product.) "We've sold Gutter Shock (our butyl based product) for years, but I wanted to take a step back and see if we could come up with a safer solution that would remove gutter striping without messing up the paint and without all the dangerous chemicals that are in traditional cleaners," explained Taylor. "We've come up with a solution that really works – and it's safe."

The Chemical's Citrus Gutter Cleaning and Housewash contains d-limeonene, which not only is a good cleaner, but also leaves behind a pleasant odor for the customer. The product can also be diluted and used as a housewash.

The good news about tiger stripes is that they can be removed, and they can be removed without destroying paint or putting workers at risk.

"It's important to understand, however, that these are not just like every other stain you find on a home," Taylor concluded. "You have to attack them in a different manner, and being able to educate your customer about this will help set you apart from your competition as well."

20 Tips from MICHAEL HOCKMAN
GUTTER DOGS
DIRT AND MOLD HAVE A WORST ENEMY

When I called Mike Hockman of Gutter Dogs at our scheduled interview time, he answered elated. "Hey Allison. Guess what? I just got off the phone with a customer. I took what was going to be a $125 gutter cleaning job and added a $500 housewash. Plus, now my schedule's full for the week."

I share this because it reiterates Guttter Dogs' philosophy: don't be afraid of the small jobs. They can help fill in the gaps in your schedule, and often turn into bigger jobs.

This is a lesson Hockman has learned since starting his own business in 2000. Early on, this Maryland-based contractor worked as a painter/lawnmower/gutter cleaner. While mowing lawns was his favorite task, cleaning gutters was the one that seemed to stick.

Since that time, Hockman – whose business has been 100 percent residential until recently – has added a number of other services, including house washing and roof cleaning. Yet, gutters remain Hockman's bread and butter service, and it's a skill that he and his Gutter Dog crew have mastered. The following tips have resuled from cleaning hundreds and hundreds of gutters over the years.

1. If you don't want gutters to be your primary source of business, don't use the word "gutter" in your name! Despite attempts to promote and advertise other cleaning services, Gutter Dogs still gets more gutter-related calls than anything else.

2. You owe it to your customer to inform them about other services you offer. "It took me awhile to practice this, but I now realize that I'm actually doing my customer a disservice if I don't offer add-ons," he explained. "They already know me. It makes sense to offer other services, then perform them at a discount since I'm already on the property."

3. Never give away work. This was a hard lesson Hockman learned a couple of years ago when he referred a number of gutter cleaning clients to a competitor during his busiest season. "By fall, I was wishing I still had those customers," he said. "I should have found a way to get their cleanings done, even if it meant buying another vehicle and hiring more workers."

4. Ask for customer testimonials. Hockman supplied his technicians with a video camera and trained them to ask for video customer testimonials before leaving the site. "We've collected 16 so far."

5. When it comes to cleaning gutters, get in, get up and get out. "Unless there's a real problem with the downspouts, you should be able to get the gutters cleaned in 10 minutes."

6. Check the roof while you're up there. As a courtesy, let your customers know if you find soft spots or damaged shingles.

7. Use a blower. If the roof is walkable and the gutters are dry, Gutter Dogs does the majority of the cleaning with a blower. This even works in cases with mesh-type gutter protection systems in place.

8. If the gutters are wet – and there hasn't been a recent rain – it means the downspouts are clogged somewhere.

9. If the downspouts appear to be clogged, clean them first then drain the water.

10. When the downspouts are clogged, check the elbows first. "Ninety percent of the time, that's where the clog is going to be."

11. Use a penny to tell you if the downspout is clean. Hockman has crew members carry a pocket full of pennies with them, then drop them into the downspout and listen. "If you hear metal all the way down — ding, ding, ding, ding — then you know it's clear. But if you hear ding, ding, THUD, ding — there's still a clog. And by using this method you can tell where the clog is.

12 Never skip downspouts, thinking you'll return to them later. The Gutter Dogs team stops at every downspout and gets them cleaned before moving on to the next batch of gutters. Otherwise, you'll inevitably skip one by accident. We've found it's better to just do them as you come to them."

13 Clean the highest gutters first. "It seems like common sense, but some guys don't catch this," said Hockman. "If you clean the lower gutters first, you're going to get them dirty again when you clean the higher gutters. Work your way down."

14 For exterior gutter cleaning, use a pole and work from the ground. Hockman has two 24-foot poles from Home Depot that he uses, and his product of choice for gutter whitening is #1 Gutter Grenade from Pressure Tek. (See ad on page 1__.) "Working those poles is kind of tricky until you get them figured out," he said.

15 Tie a t-shirt or towel about two feet above where you grip the pole. "This will significantly help reduce the amount of solution dripping down your arms."

16 Don't leave a mess. Clean up whatever you blow to the ground, either by mixing it with the landscaping or bagging it.

17 Stay away from frozen gutters. "Those are bad news and not worth it."

18 Don't be greedy. "I don't believe in charging $300 for a $100 job. I don't lowball, but I also don't overcharge. If I can do the job for $60, then I'll do it for $60. That way, the customer is happy, they've gotten a fair deal, and they'll come back for more. Plus, sometimes that $60 gutter job will turn into a $400 house washing job."

19 Don't be afraid to take on the small jobs. Again, Hockman has built his business off of the small jobs. While he would love to bring in more high-dollar historic roof restoration projects, the small jobs are fast and often bring repeat business as well as add-on services.

20 Learn from others. Hockman is a big participant in the industry's social media groups and has also participated in a number of industry-related events.

Along those lines, Hockman asked me to be sure to include the following point in this article. "I really need to thank Chris Tucker of RCIA (Roof Cleaning Institute of America). My roof cleaning business has more than doubled because of Chris and the help he's given me."

With that said, Hockman was also more than thrilled to be able to share his gutter cleaning knowledge with *eClean* and our readers. "I've gained so much knowledge from others giving back to this industry. I'm happy to finally be able to do the same for someone else."

To learn more about Mike Hockman and Gutter Dogs, visit their website: www.GutterDogs.com

Click on the image to see one of Gutter Dog's cleaning videos

Oct. 17-19, Orlando, Florida REGISTER TODAY

The 2013 PWNA Convention & Trade Show
New Classes Galore!

The PWNA Annual Convention and Trade Show is less than two weeks away October 17 through 19, but there is still plenty of time to participate. And this one is going to be spectacular, filled with brand new seminars as well as several returning favorites. The seminars begin on Friday, October 18, and attendees have a host of NEW choices, including:

- **Window Cleaning with Pure Water,** by Steve Blyth of R. Lacenstein. "Today there is a very large cross section in the cleaning industries. We're finding that at least 60 percent of window cleaners have also done some pressure washing, and 40 percent of pressure washing contractors have also done some window cleaning," said Steve Blyth. "It makes sense. The more services the mobile contractor can offer the same customer, the less time you have to spend traveling and looking for additional work."

- **9 Tips to Help Manage the Growth of Your Business,** by Michael Hinderliter. This presentation highlights one of the PWNA's unique strengths: successful industry veterans openly sharing their wisdom to fellow PWNA participants. Michael Hinderliters – who owns both a successful fleet washing and kitchen exhaust cleaning company, as well as PowerWash.com – delves into nine essential keys he's learned through experience on how to successfully grow and manage your business.

- **Parking Garage Cleaning & Water Recvoer Practices,** by Jim Gamble. As the owner of Crystal Cleaning Company, Gamble has been cleaning parking garages in California for 20 years. This presentation is designed for anyone who wants to move forward in the garage cleaning business. It is designed for those who want to see, learn, and experience what it will take to make $10k in a weekend.

- **Insurance for Power Washers,** by Joe Walters of Joe Walters Insurace. Pressure washing is a unique industry, and one that many insurance companies don't really understand. Too many contractors pay high insurance premiums each year for insurance, only to find out that their policies don't actually cover what is needed when a claim arises. Joe Walters Insurance has one specialty market – power washers – and they know what contractors need to cover their liabilities and losses.

- **Soft Washing,** by Micah Sommers, EcoClean Upsate. More power washing contractors are implementing this technique for cleaning roofs...and beyond. In this presentation, Micah will focus on basic and intermediate Soft Washing techniques and equipment. Rather then simply stating facts, such as what's making the house dirty or what kind of equipment is used, the presentation will focus on methods that participants can immediately take back to their service area and implement.

- **Fall Protection and Scaffolding** (two separate courses), presented by Charlie Arnold. As more power washing and softwashing services are reaching new heights – literally – proper safety training is imperative. That is why two separate presenations are being dedicated this year to safety – both of which will be led by Charlie Arnold of Arnold's Power Wash.

For these classes and more, plus certifications, round tables, exhibits, demos and other networking opportunities, register today :

www.PWNA.org.

October 17-19
2013 PWNA ANNUAL CONVENTION & TRADE SHOW
Embassy Suites - Lake Buena Vista South in Orlando, Florida

October 17th

A.M. Schedule - See Class for start time and fee

Wood Restoration Certification
8:00am to 2:00pm - $395 member - John Nearon

House Washing Certification
9:00 am to noon - $99 for course plus $50 for certifcation testing - Dan Galvin

Seal'N Lock Authorized Technician & PWNA Flatwork Certification
9:00 am to noon - $99 for course plus $50 for certification testing - Rich Colletti

P.M. Schedule - See Class for start time and fee

Roof Cleaning Certification
2:00-5:30 pm - $99 for course plus $50 for certification testing - Charlie Arnold

Kitchen Exhaust Cleaning
Not a Certification - 2:00 pm to 5:30 pm - $69 for members; $99 for non-members - Daryl Mirza

Fleet Washing Certification
2:00pm to 5:30pm - $249 member - Paul Horsley

5:30-7:30 PM
Cocktail Reception in Hotel put on by hotel

October 18th

8:00-9:00 AM
Convention Kick Off - Welcomes and Intros - John Nearon as Master of Ceremonies

9:00-9:15 AM - Break

9:15-10:45 AM
Environmental Certification Part I of II - ($99 for two part course plus $50 forcertifcation testing) - Robert Hinderliter
Fall Protection - Charlie Arnold
Window Cleaning with Pure Water - Steve Blyth
Power Washing 101 (Part I of II) - Tracy Handl

10:45-11:00 AM Break

11:00-12:15 PM
Environmental Certification Part II of II - ($99 for two part course plus $50 forcertifcation testing) - Robert Hinderliter
9 Tips to help Manage the Growth of your Business - Michael Hinderliter
Scaffolding - Charlie Arnold
Power Washing 101 (Part II of II) - Tracy Handl

12:15-1:30 PM
Snack and Chat Roundtable - $20.00/person in advance, $25.00 at the door

1:30-2:45 PM
Roof Cleaning Certification Part I of II - $99 for two part course plus $50 for certifcation testing - Charlie Arnold
House Washing Certification Part I of II - ($99 for two part course plus $50 for certifcation testing) - Dan Galvin
Parking Garage Cleaning & Water Recovery Practices (Part I of II) - Jim Gamble
Softwash - Micah Kommers

2:45-3:00 PM - Break

3:00-4:30 PM
Roof Cleaning Certification Part II of II - ($99 for two part course plus $50 for certifcation testing) - Charlie Arnold
House Washing Certification Part II of II - ($99 for two part course plus $50 for certifcation testing) - Dan Galvin
Parking Garage Cleaning & Water Recovery Practices (Part II of II) - Jim Gamble
Insurance for Power Washers - Joe Walters

1:30-5:00 PM
Exhibit Hall Open

5:30-7:30 PM
Cocktail Reception in Hotel put on by hotel

October 19th

8:00-12:15 PM
Exhibit Hall Open

9:00-10:15 AM
Taking Your Business into the Millions - Panel

12:15-1:30 PM
Snack and Chat Roundtable - $20.00/person in advance, $25.00 at the door

1:30-2:45 PM
Vendor Auction

2:45-5:00 PM
Exhibit Hall Open

3:30-4:45 PM
Outdoor Demonstrations by Vendors

4:45-5:30 PM
Skid Giveaway and General Membership Meeting

5:30-7:30 PM
Cocktail Reception in Hotel put on by hotel

PLEASE NOTE THAT ALL CERTIFICATION COURSES ARE AN ADDITIONAL FEE (FEE VARIES BY COURSE) - YOU MUST BE A PWNA MEMBER IN ORDER TO TAKE A CERTIFICATION TEST

Gain your Competitive Advantage through PWNA Education

info@pwna.org | 1-800-393-7962
www.pwna.org/annualconvention2013.php

PWNA Vendor Profile

LARGO CLEANING SYSTEMS

GCA Largo Cold Water 2-Step Skid Unit

Combining Military Training with Pressure Washing

Largo and the PWNA

New PWNA Members

George Aguilar
Empire Highrise USA

Dustin Anderson
Steamericas, Inc.

Richard Bond
Affordable Home Solutions

Bob Jacobs
Safetytec Industries

Sean James Mullane
Housewash New Zealand, Ltd.

Todd Steadman
Great Southwestern Fire & Safety

Michael Tucker
Window Cleaning of Augusta, Inc.

Steve Whetzel II
EcoChoice, Inc.

eClean Magazine

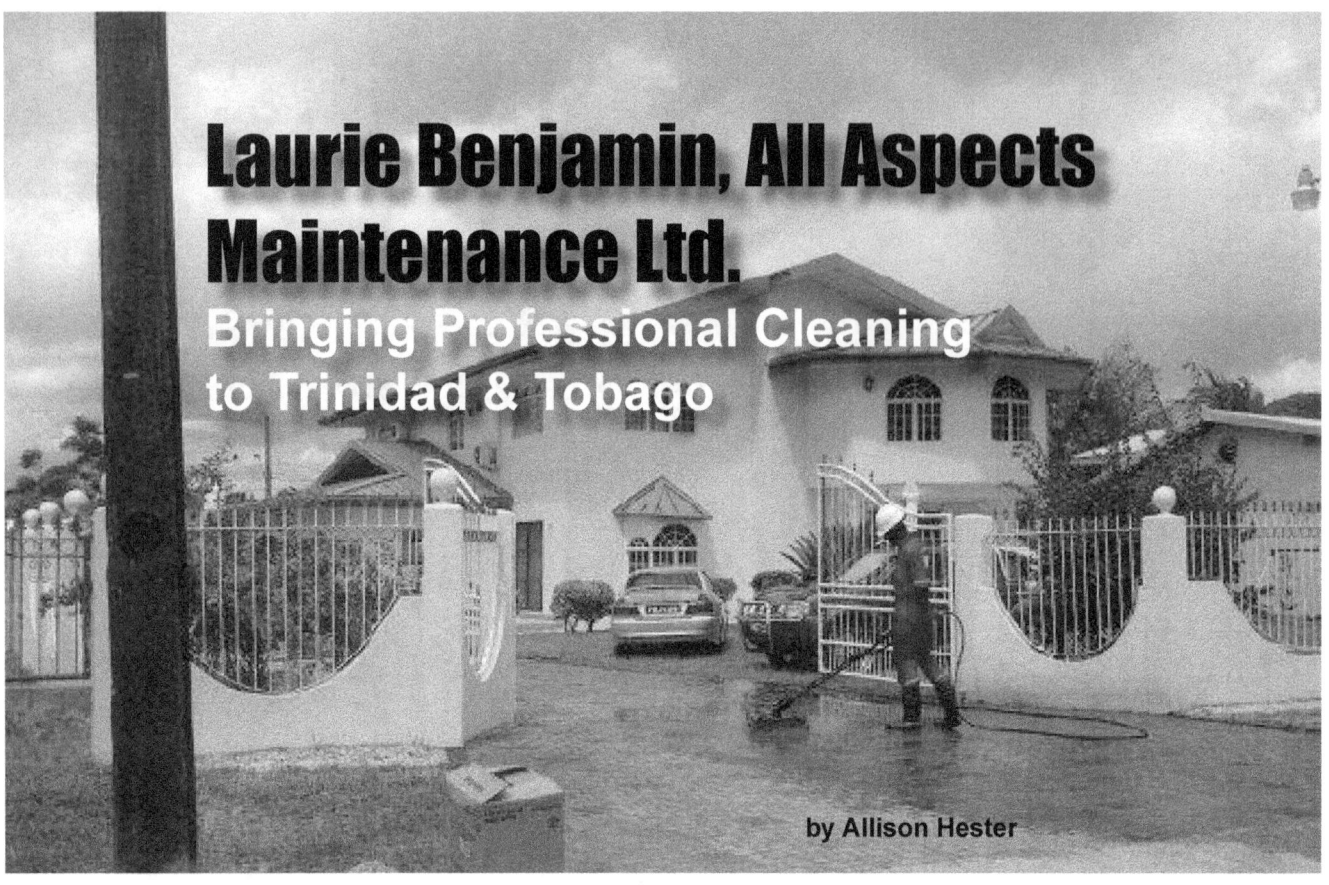

Laurie Benjamin, All Aspects Maintenance Ltd.
Bringing Professional Cleaning to Trinidad & Tobago

by Allison Hester

In the Carribean Islands of Trinidad and Tobago, the material signs of success used to include owning a big, foreign used car, a thin cell phone, and a plane ticket to Miami, according to area resident Laurie Benjamin, owner of All Aspects Maintenance (T). Today, however, island contractors have invested in another prized possession: a pressure washer.

Moss is a serious problem on the islands, and pressure washers are the accepted method for keeping the average home (a three bedroom flat, made of concrete and different substrates) clean. Same goes for the roofs, which are generally made of new-wave metal, (although the upscale sections may have tile, shingle, slate and other roofs.) The building materials are diverse — you name it. Once they can afford it, they bring it onto the island — but the cleaning tools and methods are not.

As the number of pressure washers has grown, so has the number of contractors. Only in Trinidad and Tobago, pressure washing is seen as an add-on service that anyone can do, requiring no training or education. "When contractors get together, the conversations always start with 'What job are you doing now?' but end up discussing whether their pressure washer is gas or electric and how much PSI they get," explained Benjamin. "No regard is given to gpm or temperature."

Benjamin himself entered into the maintenance industry over three years ago much the same way as all of his area competitors. He saw it as a way to leave his full-time job and work for himself. However, what started out as a painting, lawn care and other general services business has evolved into something much different.

"After months of toiling at what seem to be the bottom of the barrel, I joined different industry forums in search for an avenue to quickly rise to the top." What he discovered was that his country's accepted pressure washing practices were incorrect. "Pressure washing was always viewed as a secondary service, and anyone owning a pressure washrer can offer these services. For example, zebra striping is considered normal after a cleaning."

This fact, combined with the severity of moss growth on area homes, gave Benjamin the idea to set All Aspects Maintenance apart from his competition. Benjamin instead adopted North American cleaning methods and rather than diversify like everyone else, he honed in his skills.

All Aspects Maintenance now specializes in "organic stain removal"—i.e., anything that is not man-made, including mold, moss, mildew, algae, mineral (hard water) stains, mud, nests, cobwebs, etc. "Good old mother nature is the one who creates jobs for us," he explained.

And slowly, Benjamin is finding success.

Separation by Specialization

Connecting with North American contractors has helped Benjamin "in way words cannot explain: standards, procedures, do's and don'ts. The only thing I did not get help with was pricing my jobs—that I had to figure out on my own."

He also joined the PWRA (Pressure Washing Resource Association) early on after the association was first introduced. "I have recently started purchasing from one of the PWRA's distributors for an in-house discount," he explained. "I am not able to take advantage of all the PWRA's wonderful benefits because of my location, but I am still glad to be part of a growing organization. I hope that one day my region will be ready to accept the PWRA's standards of professionalism and invite other local contractors to join."

Additionally, all of Benjamin's equipment and chemicals are imported from North America. "I sometimes joke with my clients and say 'the only local thing we use is water.'" All Apects hosts a trailer-mounted Pressure Pro Series, with a 12v roof cleaning system. "I wanted something larger but it cost almost half the price of the unit just to get it here," he explained. "However, I know that in order to be the best, you have to use the best. I continue to deal with quite a few distributors in North America."

"Owning equipment that is not readily available in Trinidad has really helped set All Aspects Maintance apart. I knew that if I used equipment that was not readily available here, it would only be a matter of time before we stood out from our competitors as the number one cleaning company in Trinidad," he explained.

Changing His Focus, Changing the Market

At first, Benjamin was targeting everyone and accepted any and all jobs. Now he's learned to pick and choose his customers. "This takes the hassle out of driving all over the country for on-site visits that never materialize into actual jobs."

Because soft washing is a new concept in Trinidad, most homeowners still believe the

best — and only — way to clean anything is with a pressure washer. "With residential, there's a lot of time spent trying to convince homeowners that they need our services for just one job — and that's not even considering whether or not they can afford the service."

For that reason, Benjamin has shifted his attention to commercial markets. "With commercial clients, we explain less and do more," he adds. "We talk to property managers about our new services. Once they are convinced, we are given a few properties that are under their care. Additionally, government contracts have become the 'biggest piece of the pie.'"

"Whether or not Benjamin can successfully maintain an 'organic stain removal' specialty company in such a small country has yet to be seen, but Benjamin is feeling optimistic. "My operating costs are high due to duty and import taxes and I know that only those who appreciate this new service will go that extra distance to cover their cost," he explained. "However, in this industry, the right equipment and training used correctly does the work of two or three average workers."

And Benjamin has an even greater reason for wanting All Aspects Mainenance to succeed.

Earlier this year, he became he father to a beautiful baby boy — his first. "To be honest, I can't wait for him to take over the company. My son has given me the extra motivation to make All Aspects Maintenance a success," perhaps changing an entire nation's viewpoint on pressure washing in the process.

To learn more about Laurie Benjamin and All Aspects Maintenance Ltd., visit their website at www.AllAspectsLtd.com

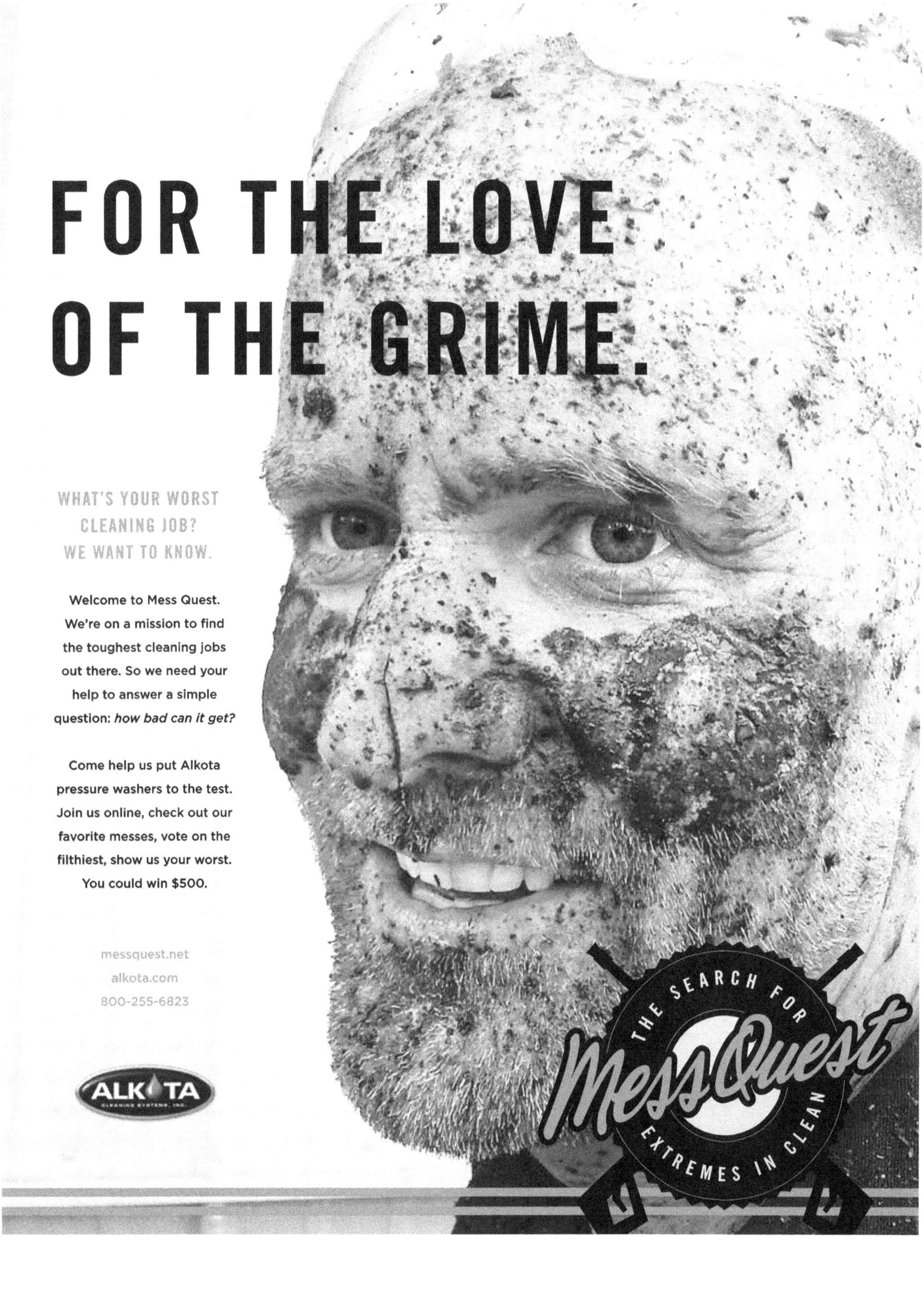
FOR THE LOVE
OF THE GRIME.
WHAT'S YOUR WORST
CLEANING JOB?
WE WANT TO KNOW.
Welcome to Mess Quest. We're on a mission to find the toughest cleaning jobs out there. So we need your help to answer a simple question: *how bad can it get?*
Come help us put Alkota pressure washers to the test. Join us online, check out our favorite messes, vote on the filthiest, show us your worst. You could win $500.
messquest.net
alkota.com
800-255-6823
ALKOTA
THE SEARCH FOR
MessQuest
EXTREMES IN CLEAN

Getting in the Biz

by Rick Meehan
Vice President of Marko Janitorial Supply, www.MarkoInc.com

A few days ago I spoke with a husband and wife about going into the cleaning business. This is a common occurrence in our showroom.

Excited, the prospective new team asked the number one question within moments of arrival: "What will it cost us?" It seems logical to get an idea of how much money it might take to get started. However, there are more costs involved with the cleaning industry, – potentially business-busting costs – than just money spent on equipment and supplies.

Money should not be the biggest concern. Anyone with a few bucks can "get in the business." Since I am a supplier to the cleaning world, you might think all I care about is selling as much equipment and detergent as possible. Not so. In fact, I try to educate my customers to make sure they completely understand what they are getting into – if they allow me the opportunity to present my case.

I'm in the cleaning supply biz for the long haul. It's in my best interest to help my customers stay in business too so they can keep coming back for more of my products.

To meet this goal, I gently try to ensure that the entire question of costs is answered without dampening enthusiasm over starting a new venture. Unfortunately, many in the cleaning trade have an attitude. They've been there, done that, and know how to do it better than me, although I've been doing it since I was eight years old. Marko Janitorial Supply (and at one time Briter Business service division) is my family business, remember?

If a monetary investment is not the major cost of starting a cleaning company, what is? Good question. Glad I asked it for you. The major cost of any cleaning business is *time*; the next major cost is *effort*. The old adage "time is money" applies doubly to effort-intensive janitorial work. Efficiency cuts the cost of labor, saving real dollars that can be reinvested in the company, or taken out as wages. Thus, time is directly related to effort: the less time and effort required doing the job, the more money can be made – time really is money.

The Tailoring Approach

Although my husband/wife cleaning team understood about applying effort to get the job done, it came as a surprise when I began to ask seemingly unimportant questions revolving around how they spend their time on the job. I call it the "Tailoring Approach."

Every cleaning company is different right down to the amount of elbow grease used to achieve results. For instance, I would never hand a 6′ long mop handle with a 32 oz. industrial cotton mop head to a lady that is only 5′2″ tall and weighs less than a squirrel.

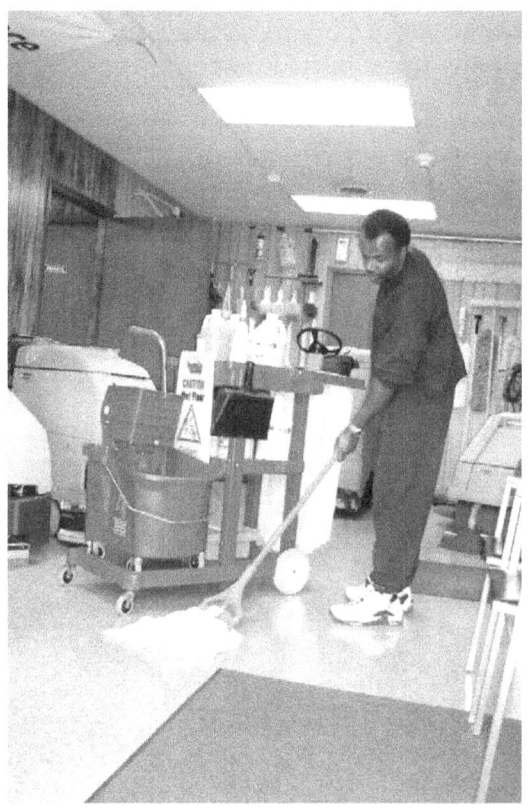

Once the mop absorbs over six pounds of liquid, it would work her near to death. She might injure her back and be unable to work at all. A wrong choice in a simple mop setup could actually cause this business to close.

I've seen this happen. Just as everyone has a unique fingerprint, so cleaning contractors have different equipment needs. Therefore, effort can become a major cost of doing business if the wrong cleaning equipment and supplies are chosen.

A few weeks ago one of my local churches hired a contractor to strip and wax a 7200 square foot gym. This was the contractor's first job. He offered the lowest price over others. Although he had years of experience with a local school district, he owned no equipment. So, the church let him use their 20 inch rotary floor machine, wet vacuum and mopping equipment. The church purchased the materials - over $100 worth of stripper, gym floor finish, stripping pads, and mops. In other words, the church was only paying labor costs to the contractor.

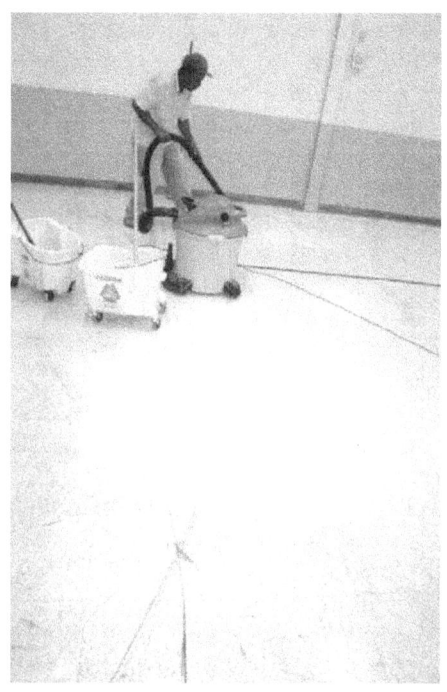

Witnesses claim that the job was a fiasco from the start. The contractor brought in three helpers who worked like gangbusters. Despite their best efforts it seemed that they simply could not get all the old finish off the floor. After a marathon 12 hours, day and night, the contractor and his helpers disappeared, leaving behind an unfinished mess. They had not been paid a bit of more than they could chew evidently. The church had to hire another contractor to do it all over again.

This scenario could have been a success except for a misunderstanding on the part of the new contractor concerning the amount of time and effort it would take to do the job with the equipment at hand. With a bit of equipment tailoring and a better stripper, this contractor could have been successful.

I hear about situations like this several times each year. Time and Effort are costs not to be sneezed at, and completely beyond mere money. The fact is anyone with a few bucks, a rag, soap, and a trigger sprayer can get started in the cleaning biz, but the hard part is keeping the company going.

Matching products to the crew and the job type is paramount. Rather than searching for the cheapest products, an adjustment in buying habits needs to be considered. Since the real savings comes from reducing the amount of time and effort used to complete a cleaning job, picking equipment and materials to suit the situation would be the wise move. Sure, supply costs are important, but not nearly to the same extent.

Using the gym scenario as an example, we can easily determine how best to handle the account:

FACTS: We know the size of the gym is 7200 square feet. Our proven floor stripper covers 600 square feet per gallon diluted according to directions. The floor finish itself covers 1200 square feet per gallon. A 175 RPM rotary scrubbing machine covers about 1000 square feet per hour when used for stripping. The church agreed to pay for the chemicals and allow the use of church-owned equipment. Cost of materials: about $100.

ORIGINAL ISSUE: Four men using church equipment spent a total of 32 hours stripping the 7200-square-foot gym. During this stretch one man ran the 175 RPM rotary machine while the other three used mops to sop up old wax, stripper, and water. This meant a whole lot of shuffling of fresh water. Because the procedure was unsatisfactorily slow, the contractor began to rush. Conservatively speaking, the contractor went in the hole just over $120 after labor costs were tallied. Remember, he was not paid in advance.

TWO-MAN SOLUTION: Since two working days were available, or 16 normal work hours, the stripping and waxing procedure needed to be expedited. The only way to have done this would have been to rent or purchase equipment designed to handle the 7200 square foot size. Since this contractor was brand new, I suspect rental would have been the proper route to consider.

PERSON #1: This person runs a rented 20" 175 RPM Automatic Walk-Behind Scrubber (about $100 per day). This machine will apply the stripper solution, scrub the floor, and vacuum up the liquid. A typical gym usually takes about five hours to strip this way. The machine will then be cleaned thoroughly and refilled with clear water. It can be used to rinse the floor prior to applying floor finish. This takes about two hours. I always recommend doubling the expected time in this case unforeseen issues occur. Here a two-day rental would have been appropriate. Cost: $200.

PERSON #2: This person uses the church's smaller side-to-side machine for stripping tight areas. He also mops up wherever the larger auto-scrubber cannot fit. Many areas require more scrubbing time, he can concentrate on those areas while Person #1 continues to work the rest of the floor. For the most part, the auto-scrubber handles the major floor area.

BOTH PEOPLE: Visual inspections must be performed to insure that all old floor finish and stripping solution are completely removed from the floor. Person #1 then uses a rented Finish Applicator machine (about $80 per day) made for large floor areas. These machines can usually lay a coat of finish in about 20 minutes on a 7200 square foot floor. The labor time to lay finish on the gym would be about an hour, although drying time must be included.

Most finishes will dry in ?? minutes, so that's another 1.? hours. So, total labor time for applying finish is about 2.? hours. Person #2 acts as a spotter in case streaks or missed spots occur. He or she also uses smaller tools like a mop or 1?? wax applicator to catch tight areas or minor misses. Cost: ??? rental.

TOTAL JOB COST: Assuming a high labor salary of ??1?.6?/hour for both workers, and a total number of hours in this scenario of ?.? hours, that's ?26?.71. Add in the cost of rental machines and you get ??1?.71, the contractor's cost of labor and equipment. ? always add in 1?? overage just in case of unforeseen material usage, so the final job cost of labor and equipment would be about ??67.2?. Add in the church's material purchase of about ?1??? and you get ?1?67.2?. Divide ?1?67.2? by the square footage of ?72?? and the cost per square foot to totally strip and refinish the gym is just under 22 cents. Research shows that this type of job brings between 1? and 26 cents per square foot, so this would have been a good estimate.

Creating a job cost analysis like this one is perhaps the most important way a cleaning contractor has of predicting what should be quoted for a job. Note that it is imperative to match the equipment to the job. The job includes the labor force. In the above scenario, we cut two laborers, paid a high hourly rate, and brought in the completed job in less time that allotted. Of course, all this may seem like fiction; therefore, ? challenge you to do the figures yourself. You'll find that Time really is Money – and you can make more of both.

One more thing to consider when it comes to cutting time and effort is that a good janitorial supply company can be your greatest ally. Folks like me that back our products with our reputation are good resources on time studies, especially concerning machinery, equipment, and detergents. ? leave the labor to you, since that's a personal question. When you walk in the door, refrain from asking how much it will cost to get in the bid. Instead, prepare the details of your envisioned company by creating a business plan so when you do visit your janitorial supply company you may ask, "How can ? reduce my costs of cleaning?"

eClean Magazine

Classifieds: Products ? Services

www.ArmClark.com
Armstrong Clark Quality Wood Stains. Specializing in wood restoration, oil-based coatings for wood ? non-toxic wood stains of all kinds for your wood shake restoration ? water repellent needs. ????16?211

www.Power?ash.com
Mobile power wash equipment, schools, training, videos, environmental supplies ? maintenance services. Call for a free catalog, ???????211?.

www.Power?ashStore.com
Bigger Selection ?Better Quality ? Amazing Customer Service. Serving the professional cleaning community for more than 2? years. Call ?????1?27?.

www.P??A.org
Power ?ashers of ?orth America. For certification or membership information, visit our website, email info@pwna.org, or call ???????7?62. Annual Trade Show and Convention, ?ct. 17?1?, ?rlando, ?la.

www.SteelEagle.com
M?r. of ?orld Class ?ndustrial ? Commercial Cleaning ? Storage Products, including surface spinners, vacuum systems, undercarriage cleaners, hose reels ? more. Custom designs available. ?????7??2?

www.Pressure?asher?y.us
Southside Equipment multi-line power equipment distributor. Pressure cleaning equipment, waste water recovery ? recycling, generators ? cleaning chemicals. Quality products ? impeccable service. ???2??6?6

To Advertise in our New Classifieds Section
Contact Allison Hester at allison@ecleanmag.com

Persistence Pays Off

by Tom Grandy, Grandy & Associates

Many years ago I worked for a boss who would occasionally ask me questions that he already knew the answers to. Why? He wanted to know if I knew the answer. A couple years ago I started asking contractors in my seminars a question. Like my old boss, I thought I knew the answer to the question before I asked it. I was wrong!

The simple question involved how many times the contractor called back after providing the customer with a written quote for replacing their equipment. The first year or two I would ask, "How many in the class contact the customer five or more times after providing the quote?" Very few hands went up. "How about four times?" Another hand or two went up. Today I frame the question a bit differently. Today I ask, "How many of you make one or more follow up contacts with the customer after having provided them with a written quote?" To my continued surprise, less than 2% of the class calls back … even once! Now, that's scary.

I recently read that 48% of all salespeople NEVER call back after having provided the customer with a written quote. That, at least to me, is an amazing statistic. Please write this down, put a sticky note on your sales pad, and stencil this on the back of your wrist: Persistence = Sales

Persistence is the key to sales. Want to hear another statistic from the same source? Seventy percent (yes 70%) of all sales are made after the fifth contact with the customer. To be honest, the statistics I am quoting apply to all sales people in all professions. Our profession is a bit different. The average salesperson closes 20% of their sales at the conclusion of the initial presentation, so in that area we are a bit better that all salespeople. However, based on my class question, and 26 years of working with contractors, we are not all that different than others when it comes to follow up.

You have all attended marketing classes, so you know the cost of creating a lead is very expensive. Some contractors' only marketing investment is the yellow pages. If that is you, sign up for a marketing class ASAP.

On the other end of the spectrum, I just completed a Company Overview with a contractor who had "budgeted" a bit more than $700,000 over the coming 12 months for marketing. He does about $11,000,000 in gross sales, so that means 6.6% of his gross income is budgeted for marketing. Notice I said he "budgeted" those dollars. Translated, that means he had solid plans concerning how he was going to market his company over the coming months AND those dollars were part of his budget. Therefore, it was included in part of his hourly rate. Remember, the customer pays for everything – it's all ground into (or should be) the hourly rate you end up charging the customer.

Yes, I am a bit off topic here, but the point is easily made. A well-run company spends a lot of money generating a lead. You made the investment, you have the lead, and the presentation has been made. Doesn't it make sense to follow up with the customer? Just closing one or two more leads per month can make a huge difference in the company's overall gross sales. Do the math for your company, the numbers may surprise you.

More than 26 years ago, before I founded Grandy & Associates, I was the general manager of a service company. I cannot tell you how many salespeople spent anywhere from 15 minutes to an hour or more in my office telling me about the product and/or service they offered. The irony is this: I actually would have purchased many of the products and services they offered but ... they NEVER called back. Did you hear what I said? I would have purchased their product or service, but they never called back.

Your potential customer is about to hundreds or thousands of dollars for cleaning services. Sure, 25% will decide on the spot. But what about the other 75%? They need time to think about it, discuss it with their spouse, or perhaps look around a bit more before they make their final decision. What if the customer was you? You just had presentations from three contractors. Two contractors never called back while the third called back routinely (in a gentle, friendly, non-pressure way). What are each telling you, without saying it?

As a consumer the two that don't call back are either telling me they are not really interested in my business and/or they are saying they are too busy to do my work. Besides that, I am thinking to myself, "If they won't take the time to call back, what's the probability they will show up if they did get the job?" Bottom line, you think they don't care about having my business. The third contractor "must" want my business because he or she continues to follow up. Assuming the customer really wants the work done, which contractor do you think the customer will choose? Which would you choose?

We have an unwritten rule in our company when it comes to following up on leads. We call back, call back and then call back again.

Eventually one of two things will happen. The contractor and/or organization will either schedule a seminar and/or consulting project, or they will tell us they are not interested. Either answer is fine. The amazing thing, in our case, is that 90 percent of our work is actually scheduled when we call back. Less than 1 percent actually call back to say they want to schedule a program. By the way, it is typically six months to two years before the decision to use us is made. Get the point?

Keep one simple fact in mind. Neither our company, nor yours, is usually the number one priority in the customer's life. If the customer is not called back (your initiative) they will soon forget about you. The key to sales is persistence.

This article was brought to you by Grandy & Associates. If you are seriosu about runninga profitable business, go to www.Gr andy Associates.com or contact them by phone at 800-432-7963.

eClean Magazine

Leadership Means High Ethical Standards

by Joe Scarlett, Founder of the Scarlett Leadership

Pressures to excel in business come from everywhere and from time to time, some of our business leaders find it expedient to take shortcuts that are unethical –and potentially even illegal. Moving down this path inevitably leads to disaster. They all get caught sooner or later –usually sooner.

Business leaders are frequently critical of the media for focusing on negative news that so often makes us look so bad in the eyes of the public. We should come to the reality that without the media putting the bad news in our face so frequently, we sure would not be as focused today on raising the bar on business ethics. Negative publicity has a way of inspiring us to strive for improvements that will keep us off the front pages. Hence, I have a feeling there is a growing movement among business leaders to achieve higher levels of integrity.

Good leaders embrace the highest level of ethical behavior.

First rate leaders do not bend in the face of temptation to take shortcuts. In my 40 plus years in business –including more than a decade as the CEO of a public company –it has never been clearer that ethical leadership is the only path to long-term success.

Pressures to excel in business come from many sources – from bosses, stockholders, competitors and even from competitive peers inside the organization.

It is easy to be pushed or push yourself into making a "panic decision."

It is easy to blame someone for dropping the ball and then firing that person without really understanding the facts. My experience is that almost everyone strives to do the job well.

When something goes wrong, our ethical obligation is to understand the facts.

In most cases, a clear understanding of the facts coupled with good coaching by leadership provides the best results. Employees learn every day on the job and leaders are frequently too quick to let that knowledge go elsewhere.

Pressures to take shortcuts are often self initiated in a quest to show results or by an ambition to get ahead. A little shortcut when bending this rule or exaggerating something else or making a small adjustment seems so minor the first time. But over a longer period, the little rule benders grow and before you know it, you are trapped by your own web. You always get caught – by the accountants, the auditors, and the security people or, most likely, you get turned in by your co-worker who has at least a slightly higher sense of integrity.

Some of our leaders can become overconfident to the point that they begin to believe that they "know it all."

They begin to see in their own results a sense of infallibility and then make decisions on that basis. Over time, they become more and more isolated because they don't listen. Separated from reality, these leaders have it all come falling down when they are forced to face reality – a reality that usually results in a personal crisis.

Business leaders have an obligation to their constituents to operate in a way that is right and just for all.

If behavior is unethical, business relationships deteriorate and in the long term all will go bad. It is incumbent on our business leaders to act in an ethical way and continually talk about the importance of ethics in the business world.

We – i.e., our community and our nation – need a passionate drive to rebuild the ethical leadership skills of our managers and executives. We need a drive to raise the ethical bar for business leaders. The United States sets the world standard for ethical business leadership. It is time for reawakening. Or, more likely, we are in the midst of that reawakening.

First-rate business leaders set the direction, set the moral compass and do everything possible to assure the success of the leadership team and the entire organization.

The really good business leaders act personally and professionally with the highest degree of integrity because they know that is the only path to long term success.

It is very simple. Violate the basic rules of business integrity and conduct and you lose. There is absolutely no room for a lack of ethics among any of our leaders.

Joe Scarlett is the retired chairman of Tractor Supply Company and the founder of the Scarlett Leadership Institute. He can be reached at joe@scarlettleadership.com.

Building Your Sales Foundation

by April Dodson, Bidslot Marketing & Answerworx

Have you ever had someone convince you to buy something you knew you'd never use? ...E T *How do they do that?* Did you want to buy anything else from them? Did you have a good relationship with them? These are some questions that come up when you think about what techniques your sales team should use.

The foundations of most modern sales techniques lie in five stages of action:

Attention: You have to get the attention of your prospect through some advertising or prospecting method.

Interest: Build their interest by using an emotional appeal such as how good they will look to their boss when they make this deal that will save the company thousands of dollars.

Desire: Build their desire for your service/product by showing them its features and letting them sample or test drive it. A demo.

Conviction: Increase their desire for your product by statistically proving the worth of your product. Compare it to its competitors. Use testimonials from happy customers.

Action: Encourage the prospect to act. This is your closing. Ask for the order. If they object, address their objections. Always think of rebuttals and know your rebuttals before you ask for the sale.

If you're in a consulting or service-oriented business, you know that it's going to require a relationship building process, but a service/product sales environment may require the same thing. The art of selling is not as straight forward as you may think. If you haven't been out there and sold before (as many new business owners haven't), then you need to mimic what has been proven to work.

My best advice to you – if you really want to get good at selling – is to "shadow" somebody who is good at closing. Watch. Listen. Sense what's going on. Then afterwards, ask what was going through that person's mind when they moved to each stage of the sale.

Then, when you're in similar situations, think "what would she do?"—you can emulate the thought process, it's easy to emulate the behavior. You'd be surprised how much can be absorbed, and how quickly, using this method.

I have done what I describe above and have proven it successful time and time again.

April Dodson is the entrepreneur, marketer, and inventor who founded BidSlot Marketing, a leader in in bid appoinment setting. Because of BidSlot, April Dodson also partnered in an answering service called Answerworx, where her team is daily relaying accurate messages at an affordable price to service professionals. April also owns a commercial kitchen exhaust cleaning company. To find out more about April Dodson, visit Facebook, Twitter or Linkedin.

BIDSLOT

Let us put our expert knowledge of **legendary Landa equipment** to work for your cleaning needs.

Specializing in Power washing equipment sales, service and custom manufacturing

(403) 771-7774

www.HydraEquipment.com

HYDRA EQUIPMENT LTD

Subscribe to eClean Digital Magazine for FREE:
www.eCleanMag.com

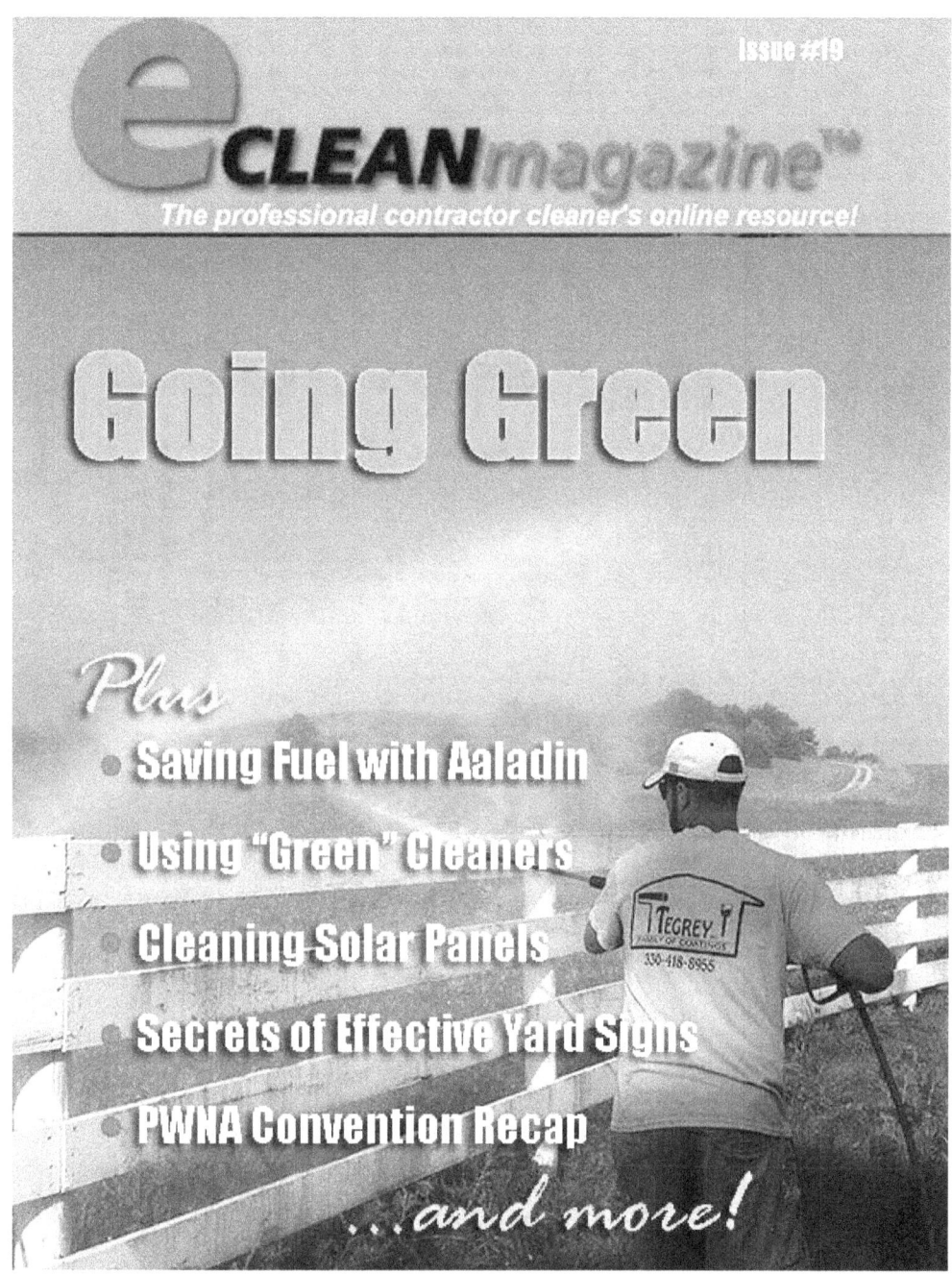

Click for more details!

1.800.433.2113
2513 Warfield St. Fort Worth, TX 76106

Pressure Washers | Surface Cleaners | Chemicals | Cleaning Supplies | Parts | Pumps & Unloaders | Training Materials

Save As Much As $7,072 per Year!

Our High Efficiency Portable Pressure Washers with the new exclusive Exchange Technology are designed to decrease the use of heating fuel required by 30% or more over a standard pressure washer. These revolutionary machines utilize a heat exchanger to capture wasted exhaust heat from the burner chamber and redirect that energy to preheat incoming water before it enters the actual heat chamber. Every Exchange High Efficiency Power Washer also includes a Clutch Drive System that reduces pump wear by as much as 70% - making them the most durable pressure washers available.

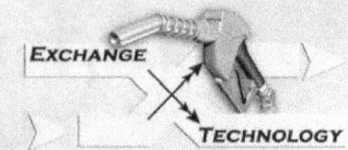

The Exchange High Efficiency Washers will save you money, and also:
- Reduce carbon monoxide exhaust by 47% over the standard models
- Reduce nitrogen monoxide exhaust by 39% over standard models
- Reduce nitrogen oxide exhaust by 39% over the standard models

Savings*	10 hrs / week	20 hrs / week	30 hrs / week	40 hrs / week
Weekly savings	$34	$68	$102	$136
Monthly savings	$136	$272	$408	$544
Yearly savings	$1768	$3536	$5304	$7072

Savings* based on a diesel fuel cost of $4.50 per gallon with a nozzle using 2 gallons of fuel per hour.

RK-53C-HE Hot High Pressure Power Washer with Exchange Technology

PowerWash.com Standard Equipment

PW	Others	
✓	☐	800 CCA Battery
✓	☐	100' High Pressure Hose
✓	☐	36" Insulated Wand w/QC for Nozzles
✓	☐	Trigger Gun
✓	☐	Winterize Kit
✓	☐	4 Color Coded, quick coupled nozzles (5.5)~0°, 15°, 25°, 40°
✓	☐	Pressure Gauge (5,000PSI)
✓	☐	Extra 1/4" & 3/8" O-Rings
✓	☐	Maintenance & Safety DVD
✓	☐	Maintenance & Environmental Class

Clutch Included

Hour Meter with Break-In and Oil Change Alerts
High Limit Temperature Shut off
Low Water Shut Off Protection
Pressure Relief Valve
Low Engine Oil Protection
18 Amp Charging System
Extended Engine Oil Drain

Specifications
3,000 PSI at 5 GPM
Briggs & Stratton 16 HP, 4 Stroke, Electric Start Engine, with a 7 Gal. Unleaded Gas Tank,
General Belt Drive Pump with a Clutch,
12v DC Burner with a 16 Gal. Diesel Fuel Tank, Input BTU's 299,000
Max Output Temperature: 190° F
Schedule 80 Heating Coil
Racor Fuel Water Separator
Enhanced Burner Protection
Hour Meter
Number of Guns: 1
Mobile, Skid Mount design
Dimensions: 43"L X 34" W X 43"H
Weight: 675lbs

Features
Durable Hi-Gloss Powder Coated Automotive Quality Paint Finish
Exchange Technology
Exclusive Highly Efficient Combustion Chamber Design
Stainless Steel Combustion Chamber
Quick Coil Access
Pressure Atomized Burner
Automatic Electric Burner Ignition
Stainless Steel Control Panel

Your #1 resource for power washers, chemicals, supplies, and training!

Hose Reel Hannay
- Comes with a cam-lock drag brake, and a spring actuated pin lock.
- Standard inlet 90° swivel joint 1/2" female NPT threads.
- Standard outlet 1/2" female NPT threads.
- Pressures to 5000 psi
- Temperatures from +20° F to +400° F
- 25"L X 17"W X 18"H

10" BI-Level Brush
The unique angled design of this soft-bristle non-marking wash brush maximizes contact with the surface to be cleaned.

Trigger Gun YG-5000
- Max Fluid Temp: 200°
- Max Discharge: 5000 PSI
- Flow Rate: 10 GPM
- Inlet: 3/8" FNPT
- Outlet: 1/4" FNPT

High Pressure Washer Hose
- 3/8" Hose
- 1 swivel end, 1 solid end
- 3/8" MPT

Get $10 Back!
On Orders of $100 or more!
Use Coupon Code: eClean10
Cannot be combined with any other offer.

In This Issue:

351 How New Pressure Washing Technology Is Conserving Fuel, Saving Money, by Aaladin Industries

354 Proven Secrets of Effective Yard Signs for Professional Cleaning Contractors

358 What Does "Green" Really Mean? by Linda Chambers, Soap Warehouse

360 Building the Dream, Living the Dream: The 2013 PWNA Convention Recap

367 PWNA Vendor Profile: Joseph D. Walters Insurance

371 A Soldier's Story: How Three Days in Orlando Changed One Contract Cleaner's Life

376 Get Sales Mileage from Your Holiday Cards

379 Pink Mohawk: How One Pressure Washing Contractor Is Paying It Forward

380 Solar Panel Cleaning: Good for the Environment and for Your Bottom Line

384 Say "Yes" to Web Presence, by Rick Meehan, Marko Janitorial

386 How I Turned My Business Green, by Todd Turner, ATP Results

387 Classifieds

389 Can a Pressure Washer Damage Your Car or Truck? by Paul Horsley

Cover Photo
Courtesy of Terry Miller, Tegrey Family of Coatings, Canton, Ohio, www.TegreyPainting.com

---

Clean Magazine is published monthly

Publisher: Paul Horsley, paul@ecleanmag.com
Editor: Allison Hester, allison@ecleanmag.com

Box 262, 16 Midlake Blvd S.E.
Calgary, Alberta
Canada T2X2X7
www.eCleanMag.com

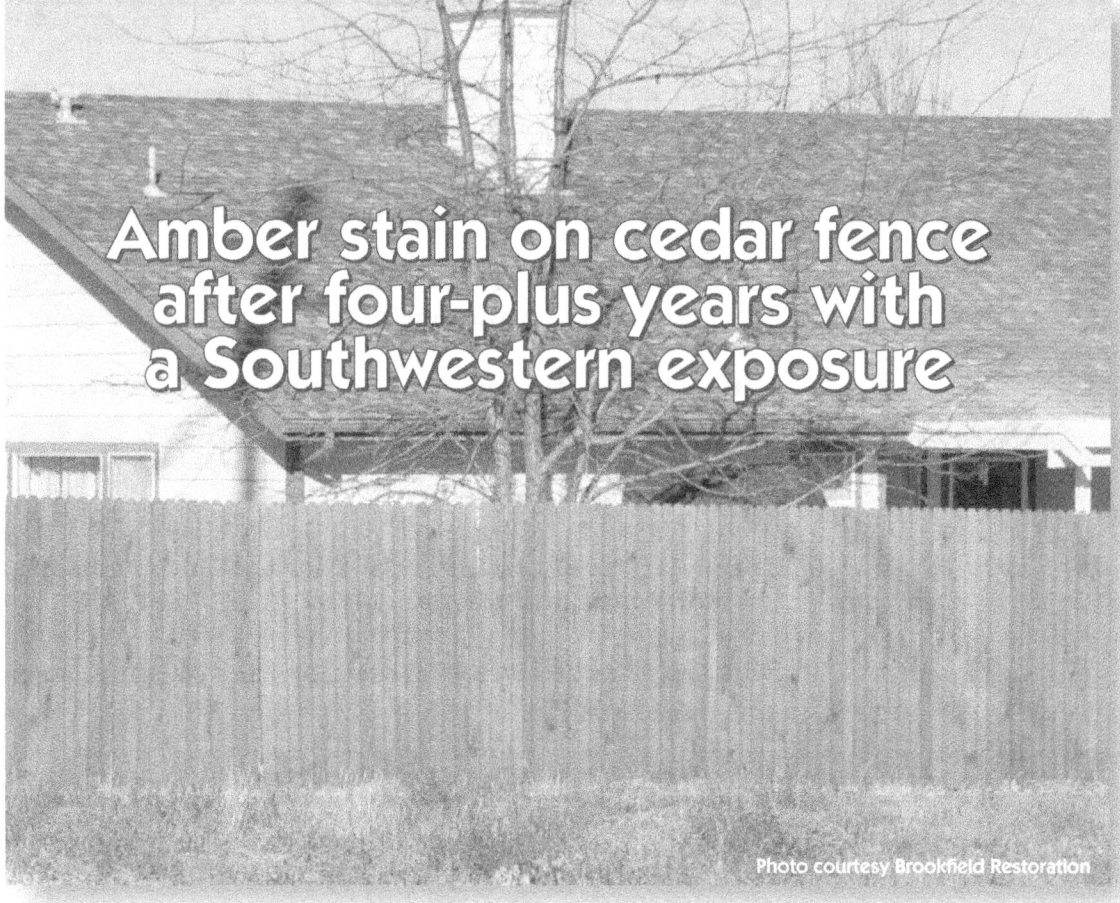

How New Pressure Washing Technology is Conserving Fuel, Saving Money

by Aaladin Industries, www.Aaladin.com

Now more than ever it's important to do whatever we can to conserve energy and fuel. With dwindling supplies of fossil fuels creating higher pricing, and the negative impact we as a population (and an industry) have on the environment, searching for high efficiency solutions and ways in which we can conserve should be paramount. We need to do this not only to increase our profits, but to protect the future of our children and generations to come.

Beyond our ethical need to conserve fuel, there's also a very practical need. How are fuel costs affecting your business? Are you seeing your profits decreasing? Are high fuel costs preventing you from cleaning as much or as well as you feel you should? Are you hearing that your bids are high due to using fuel guzzling equipment? Are you frustrated by the high cost of several feet of insulated exhaust stacks needed to ventilate your pressure washer through the roof? Would you like to have less of an impact on the environment?

What if you could run your pressure washer as much as you want while saving money each and every hour? What if your pressure washer's exhaust venting was as simple as using inexpensive CPVC through the side wall instead of expensive traditional exhaust stacks through the roof? What if you could do your part to preserve our planet for the future?

The Aaladin Answer

Through in-house research as well as constant communication with our distributors and end users, we've identified several issues/concerns that numerous people had in common:

• Reduced profits due to increasing fuel prices.
• Traditional equipment putting excessive toxic NOX emissions into the air, damaging the environment for our future generations.
• Not being able to clean as often due to the need to conserve fuel, causing increased maintenance issues, dingy looking facilities and fewer clients.

Beyond the above, we also wanted to lead the industry in working on ecologically responsible alternatives to traditional equipment that is not so ecologically friendly.

We then began working through the engineering process to address these problems and create technologies that would lessen fuel consumption, and therefore lessen the ecological footprint of the equipment we manufacture. The end result of our research and development was our patented Exchange Technology.

In a nutshell, our patented Exchange Technology recycles the "waste" heat other manufacturers release into the environment, and uses it to preheat the hot water you clean with. Reduced fuel consumption, fewer toxic

> **ec·o·log·i·cal** [ek-uh-loj-i-kuh l]
> *adj.* Relating to the environment and the way that plants, animals, and humans live together and affect each other.
>
> **eco-logical:**
> Producing environmentally responsible results in an economically attractive manner.

emissions, less heat entering the environment, those are good things. How efficient are we? Hold your hand over the escaping air from one of our machines utilizing our Exchange System – the air is just warm. Don't do the same if you are checking out traditional equipment – you'll get burned.

What Does This Mean for You?

Why is our Green Technology important to you? Two reasons – it saves you money and it's good for the environment.

Aaladin models that utilize our Exchange Technology are considered part of our Eco-Green Line of Equipment. This line includes portable 1?HE Series?, self-contained ??HE Series? and stationary ?7? Series? models.

Our Exchange Technology means higher fuel efficiency and savings technologies:

• Machines utilizing Exchange Technology are up to 98 percentt efficient. This reduces the amount of fuel required and ensures you get the most out of every dollar you spend operating your equipment.

• Exchange Technology reduces the amount of fuel required to heat your water by up to ?? percent by using the energy that has traditionally been wasted by other pressure washing equipment, resulting in unmatched performance and fuel efficiency

• Exchange Technology decreases your carbon footprint by reducing the amount of NOX emissions released into the environment through normal machine usage by up to ?7 percent. This means users are creating a smaller negative environmental impact and assuming greater environmental responsibility.

• The equipment's Unique Helical Heating Coil design ? Molded Insulation Bucket allow for the most efficient transfer of heat-to-water in the industry, resulting in higher efficiency & cleaner combustion.

So what this means for you is ?higher profits, more jobs due to being more competitive, and the peace of mind that comes with being ecologically responsible. On top of that, it also means you will enjoy money savings on stacking of stationary models due to the lowered exhaust temps.

Responsible Manufacturing

Aaladin is steadfast in our commitment to preserving the environment through the use and production of high efficiency equipment. From high efficiency factory lighting to recycling wherever possible, Aaladin products are manufactured with the future in mind, reducing environmental impact and conserving our resources.

Most importantly, we constantly innovate ? pioneer new technologies ?like our Exchange Technology?that conserve our resources.

The Aaladin Eco-Green Line of Equipment
For some it's simple ?greener is better.

Savings Illustrated

HOURS OF BURNER OPERATION	STANDARD FUEL USAGE	ECO-GREEN FUEL USAGE	FUEL SAVED PER WEEK	ANNUAL SAVINGS
NATURAL GAS AT $0.96/THERM				
10	44	24	20	$977.60
20	88	48	40	$1,955.20
40	176	96	80	$3,910.40
LIQUEFIED PETROLEUM AT $2.87/GALLON				
10	45.7	24.9	20.8	$3,104.19
20	91.4	49.8	41.6	$6,208.38
40	182.8	99.6	83.2	$12,416.77

14HE-Series

40HE-Series

Without a doubt, AaLadin is your greenest pressure washer option by using less fuel and releasing fewer toxins into the environment. If being environmentally green isn't such a big deal to you, the same Exchange Technology that reduces toxins also reduces the amount of fuel used to heat the water... therefore saving you dollar bills – that's something green that we all care about!

AaLadin Cleaning Systems offers pressure washers to fit any situation. We do this because we understand you aren't the same as every other customer out there. You have created a place in your market that demands specific solutions. We pride ourselves on being the innovator of numerous pressure washer features.

We are proud to be the ONLY pressure washer manufacturer to offer a High Efficiency Line of equipment. Our Eco-Green Line is available in several different models to fit your needs. Please go to www.aaladin.com or visit your local AaLadin distributor to learn how our products can save you time and money.

70-Series

Proven Secrets of Effective Yard Signs for the Professional Cleaning Contractor
An Interview with Tim Fields of Sign2Day.Com

by Allison Hester

Yard signs are a simple yet powerfully effective marketing tool for service industry contractors – when they are correctly designed and utilized. Otherwise, they are simply a waste of money.

For Tim Fields – who has been around the cleaning industry since the ▢▢▢s, and who, along with his son, has owned Complete Power Wash, LLC in Hagerstown, Maryland, since ▢▢▢▢ – yard signs have been an integral part of his business for almost ▢▢ years.

"When I worked in the construction trades, signs were a very real part of my early sales success," Fields explained. "Those signs were ▢▢x▢▢ inches, two color vinyl on a metal sign blank with a ▢ inch metal iron frame. They cost about ▢▢▢ a piece – but they lasted for months – and they worked."

Moving into the pressure washing business, there was no need for that heavy-duty or expensive of a sign, so Fields went the opposite direction – a ▢▢ screen print on coroplast. "We used them for years and tried several different designs. They all performed poorly. As a small business owner married to an accountant, Fields measures everything. He knew he received almost no response from his signs. Sure they were cheap. But what was the point?"

Fields then turned to his local sign guy for full color signs that cost ▢▢▢ a piece, plus stakes, on ▢ mil coroplast. While they did look better, they didn't perform any better. "Almost $250 for 10 signs. They were definitely more attractive, but were still a waste of money."

Early last year, Fields took a different route. He contacted a graphic artist and asked her to come up with new type of design. "I wanted a yard sign that was bold and eye catching, that featured a service, that did not headline the logo, and that could take advantage of the new, lower cost, full color printing systems." He also wanted them to be "Ferrari friendly" – meaning that even a sports car traveling at road speed would be able to see the sign and know what service they were offering. "And just as quickly, I wanted them to know that there was something different about the company behind the sign."

After a little bit of back and forth with the designer, a new sign was developed.

And it worked.

Soon after launching his new signs, Fields was able to track that one of his first signs produced seven separate jobs, totaling almost ▢▢,▢▢▢ so far. "The lifetime value of that one ▢▢▢ sign is likely to exceed ▢▢▢,▢▢▢."

With fall being gutter cleaning season, Fields' gutter cleaning sign has resulted in over ▢▢,▢▢▢ in work – within a two block radius in

the same neighborhood.

Fields shared his signs and his successes on RoofCleaningForums.com. A fellow roof cleaner asked if he could borrow the design and have some of his own signs made. He posted the results a few weeks later and they were lacking in many respects. He had gone local, which in many cases is a wise thing to do, but the signs were a very poorly done copy and were very high priced. I knew that there was something better out there."

Fields and his brother both worked around the sign industry for over 20 years. Using his contacts from many years of exposure to the sign industry, Fields began laying the foundation for a new business venture. "The folks in the service trades that depend on a steady flow of new customers can really benefit from correctly-done yard signs," he explained. "They just needed a reliable and affordable way to do that. It was a need waiting to be filled, and that's why I started Sign2Day.com."

Why Your Signs Matter

Signs, according to Fields, do more than simply tell about your company's basic information. Yard signs actually:

• **Convey a sense of trust** that is especially important in more expensive neighborhoods that frequently use service contractors on a regular basis

• **Catch people where they are, add credibility, and establish your qualifications** – in an instant.

• **Speak on behalf of your customers.** "We all like to think that our customers will rave to their friends what wonderful contractors we are, but the reality is that they don't. At least not as often as we would like. But a yard sign does that for them. It gives us instant third party credibility to everyone that passes by and views the sign."

• •

Why Sign2Day.com is Different

When I asked Fields what makes an effective yard sign, he gave the following real world example:

Tim Wagner of Wagner Window Cleaning in Upton, Mass., had his first yard sign printed by Vistaprint, and it featured his logo, phone number and website. Over the course of six months, Wagner did not receive a single call off that sign. (See before photo below.)

Wagner saw one of Fields' gutter cleaning signs online and it piqued his interest. It was simple yet vibrant, and right to the point.

"So Wagner decided to give Sign2Day.com a chance and ordered 10 yard signs to try out (below right). I got two calls within the first few days, so I immediately ordered 20 more," Wagner explained. "When those came in, I place one in my yard and went inside. Less than an hour later, someone called from that one. I actually had earned my money back from those signs before the charge reached my debit card."

Unlike the many generic sign companies out there, Sign2Day.com is owned by a member of the professional cleaning industry, and their products are designed exclusively for similar service industry markets. That is why Sign2Day has a number of unique things to offer, including:

• **Adaptations of proven designs, created by a service company, for service companies.** Tim Wagner's example above is just one of many stories from contractors who are having tremendous responses – and making sales – because of the products from Sign2Day.com. "I offer a proven design that has generated calls for guys in as little as one hour from the time they receive their signs."

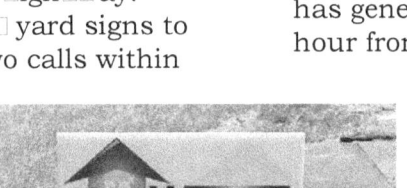

- **"Incredibly fast" turnaround.** "We had one customer who posted pictures of their new signs ?? hours after placing the order," Fields said. "Our turnaround time has been fantastic. We have had many orders on the East coast deliver within two days of placing the order. A recent customer in California approved his artwork on Thursday and had his signs in hand the following Monday."
- **Unique sizes and shapes.** "One recent customer reported that zoning officials did not grant him permission to place his new signs in certain areas because they were greater than one foot square. Three days later, he had a batch of ??x??inch signs arrive at his doorstep. Sure, they were a bit small, but they were still blazingly visible and no one else in his service area advertises in this manner."
- **Additional products, such as decals.** "A cleaning contractor recently asked if he could have some stickers made with his logo. Most sign guys will tell you to buy stickers at Wal-mart and print them off yourself. We, however, set our team into motion and had self-adhesive, custom graphics printed on vinyl with durable plastic laminate over them available on our webstore within three days of his request. The decals are custom produced with the customer's information and are made from the same material used for creating wraps on box trucks or graphics on dirt track race cars. It's pretty tough stuff."
- **Extremely Competitive Prices.** "Many of the guys in the business – myself included – want to sell our time and services for top dollar, but shop for the best prices when it comes to buying products and services," Fields explained. "Our prices are extremely competitive – to the point that they are just plain hard to beat."
- **A commitment to top-quality service.** "I realize the true test of a service provider is not always the initial delivery, but how issues are handled when they arise," Fields explained. "We haven't had any issues arise yet – and I hope that we don't – but we ask our customers to notify us right away of any adjustments needed and we shall do everything reasonably within our power to make it right."
- **Discounts for Pressure Washing Resource Association (PWRA) and Window Cleaning Resource Association (WCRA) members.** "I am a strong believer that being affiliated with the right groups of people – whether it is an online forum or a more formal organization, such as the PWRA and WCRA – can boost your business by helping you learn from those that have gone before you," Fields added. "In addition to the very competitive prices we offer, we also have additional discount codes for some of the major groups. Note: If you are not yet a member of the PWRA, you can save $?? off of your membership when you join through eClean Magazine."
- **Free shipping for eClean readers, through December 21**, when you order from Sign2Day.com and use the promo code "eClean Free Shipping."

To learn more or to place an order, visit www.Sign2Day.com. Remember, mention eClean Magazine and receive free shipping through December 21.

What Does "Green" Really Mean?

by Linda Chambers, Soap Warehouse,
www.SoapWarehouse.biz

These days, every cleaning company is trying to use the word "green" to get in on the marketing/money making bandwagon. But what does it really mean?

Does "green" mean it is 100 percent safe for the environment? Safe for the user? What about "all natural"? Does that equate to being the same as "green"? Does "organic" equal "green"? And once you use a "green product," is the residual wash water still safe and "green"?

Let me try to clear up and answer some of these questions.

A product may like to say it is "green" because the ingredients come from naturally derived plants or naturally occurring minerals, which could have also been man made. "Green" does not mean these ingredients are 100 percent safe and may still need to be listed on a Material Safety Data Sheet (MSDS).

Vinegar can be naturally derived from many different plants, grains and fruits, and vinegar is a favorite ingredient for "green products" as well as for "I make" at home, "eco friendly," "all natural" cleaners. But companies that make vinegar have to have a MSDS for their product. It is an acid (around 3 pH), and is considered a hazardous material by OSHA due to eye, skin and respiratory hazards.

So why are products with these ingredients being approved by companies in the business of certifying "green" products saying they are "green" while not being 100 percent safe? *Because "green" cannot equal safety.*

Today due to the high demand for vinegar, it is not usually produced from organic, natural plants, but rather is man made from Acetic acid, an organic, man made compound. Yet manufacturers will still call the produced vinegar "green" because it is organically based.

Believe it or not, there are no federal rules or guidelines that must be followed saying what constitutes a "green product," even though it may be connected with words such as "non toxic," "biodegradable," or "environmentally friendly" – leading you to believe it is safe for people and the environment. So until we have steadfast requirements, take the word "green" with a grain of salt.

So How Do You Become Green?

To be a "green" chemical product, a manufacturer can follow and pass certification from a number of organizations to try and prove they are indeed "green." These are ones like USDA Biopreferred, Designed for the Environment, Ecologo, and Green Seal. But these certifications take a lot of money to get and still are not federally guided.

There are major companies that instead are making their own specialized product line to try and lead buyers into thinking the products in this category have somehow been certified when they have not. A good example is Clorox Green Works, where they defend every ingredient as to how it really is green to include up to 1 percent of a product's make up.

But until manufactures are given a clear, clean-cut definition of what "green" is, there will be lots of leeway and grey areas for products to be labeled as such.

Another problem with pressure washing chemicals is that contractors not only have to worry about the "greenness" of the initial cleaner, but how not-green or hazardous the residual wash wastewater is after removing contaminates from the surfaces that they are cleaning. You can use the most perfect and effective "green" cleaner and still have to deal with the issues of oil filtration, pH levels, debris particle filtration and EPA approved discharging.

So, all this to say that the concept of "going green" is not as simple as it might seem. While promoting the fact you use green cleaners might help in your marketing, there's actually a lot more to ensuring that you protect the environment than simply choosing a natural or environmentally friendly cleaning product. To truly protect the environment, what you do to dispose of your cleaning waste is more important than which product you use.

Linda Chambers is the Brand and Sales Manager for Soap Warehouse, where she has worked since 2007. She enjoys writing blogs and social media. She also travels for the company, exhibiting at trade shows and events. For more information, visit their website at www.SoapWarehouse.biz.

Building the Dream, Living the Dream
The 2013 PWNA Convention & Trade Show Recap

October's PWNA Convention and Trade Show in Orlando was all about dreams. Building dreams. Living dreams. Sharing dreams. And, in at least one case, making dreams come true.

This year, the PWNA Board of Directors looked hard at what could be done to make this year's convention the very best it could be. They examined ways to play to the organization's strengths – which include quality education and training, as well as the professionalism and successes of many of its long-term members – and they implemented new strategies to support all PWNA members, no matter where they were at in their careers.

And it worked. This year's convention brought with it a renewed level of excitement, camaraderie and vision. "This year's conference was very different from the one I attended before," said Abu Woldeamanuel of Colonial Parking in Washington D.C. "It proved that the PWNA is indeed growing and is becoming a great organization."

October 17 – 19 in Orlando

Over 200 contractors – a mixture of rookies, long-time veterans, and everyone in between – gathered for a weekend filled with education and networking. It was also filled with surprises. Surprise guests. Surprise awards. Surprise winners. But, perhaps the biggest surprise was simply how much the event exceeded expectations.

"Where do we begin?" commented first time attendees Peg and Bo Bosetti of All Clean Power Washing in Selbyville, Delaware. "We both learned more than we had thought possible. It was great to meet so many quality people – from the board members, bigger companies and vendors, to the guys just starting out."

Another first time attendee, Josh Minx of Southern Clean in Knob Noster, Missouri, decided to attend after winning a free PWNA membership through PowerWashCommunity.com, but admits he wasn't anticipating much. "To be honest, I thought it would be closed group where if you didn't know people they wouldn't speak to you. I was *way* wrong. I spoke with other power washers like I'd known them for years. I felt like I was accepted right off the bat. It was a great event."

Even those who had attended PWNA events before were pleasantly surprised. "This year's convention impressed me. It was better organized, the classes were great and the instructors were very good," said Jeff Jacobs of Jacobs Pressure Cleaning in Melbourne, Florida.

Another PWNA event veteran, John McIntyre of John McIntyre Maintenance, Inc., attended this year but actually made other business appointments late Friday and Saturday night, so he had to leave early. "I did not expect for the show to be as good as it was," he explained. "That won't happen again. This show far exceeded the one I attended before. I will definitely be willing to travel for future events."

Certifications and Education

One of the PWNA's strengths has always been the quality of educational programs and certifications offered. This year, around 50 individuals gained PWNA certifications in wood restoration, house washing, flatwork cleaning, fleet washing, roof cleaning, and environmental cleaning.

For Meg and Bo Josetti, the certification courses were their main reason for attending. "We thought it was very important to provide our customers with the best services possible. Certification through the PWNA would both confirm what we were already doing and also teach us some new things. Certifications set us apart from the many companies that are popping up all over our area."

McIntyre had his general manager take the flatwork/Seal N Lock certification course while he participated in the House Washing course. "Both exceeded our expectations." He added, "I will be reviewing the class I attended with my staff tomorrow night. I feel totally prepared thanks to Dan Galvin's instruction in the House Washing Certification Course."

Jorge Aguilar of Empire Highrise USA came to the convention to meet pressure washing professionals around the country who might be interested in offering window cleaning through his company. "I also wanted to get certified in roof cleaning and house washing for the knowledge in washing highrise buildings," he explained. "I was very impressed with the knowledge, along with the written information given. I learned a lot!"

"The conference was very inspiring. I learned a great deal from the classes and even more from the people I met while attending the conference," added Jessica Norwood of East Coast Window

cleaning. I came back from this event with an extremely long list of things I wanted to put into place in my company."

Jared Greene of ??? in Fayetteville, in North Carolina, said he knew that he could learn more in a few hours through PWNA's certification classes than he could in years on his own. "And boy was I right. The amount of knowledge I gained throughout the entire convention was unbelievable. To read more of Jared' story, see the article on page ??."

Networking

While this year's event offered a variety of formal educational opportunities, much of the learning continued outside the classroom. "By far the best thing about this year's convention was the participation by the members," said Jacobs. "The snack and chats and cocktail hours are invaluable."

First time attendee Greg Loucks of Poseiden Power Wash in Venice, Florida, attended, in part, "to get definitive answers about power washing techniques, skills, knowledge, and equipment, that my online research and own experience had yet to settle." What he found was that "not only did I get to learn something from every single attendee, instructor, presenter, and exhibitor I talked with, but so many people were just really cool people."

That was one of the goals of the ??? for this year's convention – to create an atmosphere that fostered networking from the moment attendees entered the convention. And by attendee feedback, it worked.

"From the moment I walked in and started networking with guys from around the world, I knew I had made the right decision by attending," said Jinx.

The night before the event began, Aguilar said he met some "very nice people" who invited him to join them for dinner. Little did

"I couldn't believe it. It was very cool. Adriana my daughter and I are planning a trip for my birthday to visit some special people who live by the beach. She and I are very excited. It's her second time to the ocean."

– Jorge Aguilar (second from left) of Empire Window Cleaning, winner of over $2500 in the 50/50 raffle.

Contractors were not the only ones who benefited from networking. This was the first PWNA convention for exhibitor Jefferson Lehman of Steel Eagle, and he assured me he'd be back again. "The feedback we got from end users was invaluable," he said. "It was extremely beneficial to hear from them what we were doing right as well as some suggestions on what might make their jobs easier."

"One of our suppliers took us to dinner Friday night," added McIntyre. "It was awesome to be able to meet with them and discuss the various business challenges that we all face."

Many agreed that the networking did far more than simply introduce industry members to one another. It created relationships that participants are looking forward to continuing well beyond this year's event.

"It was a great event and I walked away with not only learning some things, but also with some new friendships," said Linx.

Aguilar agreed. "The networking I was able to gain by attending was the best thing about the event. It's priceless to have friendships with pressure washers whom I can reach out to if I need anything."

"Being able to spend time with people in the industry was refreshing. It gave us a new outlook on what we wanted to do to grow our business," answered the Rosettis. "We hope to stay in contact with all the new friends we met and look forward to seeing everyone next year."

Loucks added, "I look forward to seeing new friends again, finding out how their businesses are going and sharing how mine is progressing."

Next Year's Event

"In addition to getting to meet a bunch of great people, one of the best things about the convention was the venue," Loucks added. "The

I was extremely excited about winning the mentoring program. Paul Horsley was the leader of my group project at the event and I heard so many great things from other people who have worked with him. I would really value his opinion on questions I have pertaining to my own company as well as information about what he has done to make his own business successful. I think I will benefit from this and gain invaluable insight beyond my own education and experience to apply at East Coast."

- Jessica Norwood, winner of the PWNA mentoring program's all-expense paid trip to Calgary, Alberta, to be mentored by Paul Horsley of Scotts Pressure Wash

Next Year's Event

"In addition to getting to meet a bunch of great people, one of the best things about the convention was the venue," Loucks added. "The Embassy Suites in Orlando was a beautiful site and the staff was great."

While the dates for the 2014 PWNA Convention are still being worked out, the location has been confirmed. Due to the support and customer service that the Embassy Suites has shown the PWNA for the past two years, next year's convention will again return to Orlando, Florida.

When asked if they were planning to attend next year, here are the responses I received:

"This year I saw that PWNA is attracting many new participants who believe in the organization and are willing to join," said Woldeamanuel. "I will be back."

"First impressions are everything. Well, the PWNA made a great one – above and beyond what I imagined," said Linx. "Yes, I'll be there."

"I sure will be," added Aguilar. "I'm a proud member."

"After this year's event, most definitely," said McIntyre. "And I'd be willing to travel for future events."

A Few Final Words

When asked if there was anything else they wanted to share, a few participants expressed their gratitude. "Thanks to so many people who were there to help and share experiences. It was a great help," said McIntyre.

Aguilar concurred. "I want to thank the people who were responsible of putting it together. It was a very nice experience from beginning to end. I look forward to next year."

Norwood took the sentiment a little further. "I learned so much from the people I met and appreciate the organization for providing this program. I think the PWNA is a great benefit to pressure washers. The people I met at the event were awesome and even though it was my first event, I felt at home."

Linx said he wanted to encourage others to take part in next year's convention. "One of the best things you can do for yourself is go and see for yourself. You will love every part of it."

Loucks – who admitted he was leery about whether the cost of joining the PWNA and attending the event would be worth it – had this to add: "After attending the convention, I appreciate the huge value that comes wih being part of PWNA."

Finally, Greene – whose story can be seen on page 25 – asked the share the following: "Joining the PWNA and becoming a part of this family will be the *best* decision you make for yourself, your family, and your business. I will happily tell anyone how the PWNA has changed my life. The education, the certifications, the networking, but above all, becoming part of this tight-knit family, is the most amazing thing you could do for yourself."

To learn more about the PWNA or to join the PWNA, visit www.PWNA.org.

Special thanks to Dan and Heather Galvin for supplying us with all the wonderful photos. For more highlights from the 2013 PWNA convention, visit our website: www.eCleanMag.com/blog

To learn who won the amazing Hydro Tek Self-Contained Hot/Cold/Steam, High Pressure Washer Skid, worth $10,295, read the amazing story starting on page 25.

PWNA 2013 Conference Certifications:

Jorge Aguilar, Empire Highrise USA
House Washing, Roof Cleaning

Megan Babcock, Pro-Jet Services
House Washing

Ray Bailey Sr., Asteroid Cleaning Solutions, Inc.
House Washing, Roof Cleaning, Flatwork

Shaun Barnard, EcoChoice, Inc.
House Washing, Fleet Washing, Wood Restoration, Environmental

Richard Bond, Affordable Home Solutions
House Washing, Roof Cleaning, Environmental

Butch Chapman, Jenkintown Building Services
Roof Cleaning

Stephen Cowley, Weekend Mobile Wash
House Washing, Fleet Washing

Michael Craver, Compass Building Solutions
House Washing, Fleet Washing, Environmental

Randy Duchesne, Randy's Handyman Service
House Washing, Roof Cleaning, Flatwork, Environmental

Ryan Edrington, Excellent Xteriors
House Washing

Stewart Esposito, Absolutely Clean
Fleet Washing, Roof Cleaning, Environmental

David Fahari, Super Dave's Pressure Cleaning
Environmental

John Fister, Affordable Home Solutions
Wood Restoration, Roof Cleaning

Jared Greene, DCS of Fayetteville
House Washing, Roof Cleaning

Kyle Hecimovich, Northern Tool & Equipment
House Washing, Environmental

Dave Irons, Sunrise Power Wash
House Washing, Flatwork

Bob Jacobs, Safetytec Industries
Fleet Washing

Jeff Johnson, Shine Time Services LLC
House Washing, Wood Restoration, Roof Cleaning

Larry Johnson, John McIntyre Maintenance Inc
Flatwork

Bo Josetti, All Clean Power Washing
House Washing, Roof Cleaning

Alexis Kruayai, The Pressure Kru, Inc.
House Washing, Roof Cleaning

Chris Kruayai, The Pressure Kru, Inc.
House Washing, Roof Cleaning

Nicholas Lacorte, Fairway Window & Pressure Cleaning
House Washing, Wood Restoration, Roof Cleaning

Nick LoGrasso, SNL Painting, Inc.
House Washing, Wood Restoration, Roof Cleaning

Greg Loucks, Poseidon Power Wash
House Washing, Roof Cleaning

Trey Mathias, Trey Mathias Pressure Washing
House Washing, Roof Cleaning

Eric McCullough, Sunrise Power Wash
Roof Cleaning, Environmental

John McIntyre, John McIntyre Maintenance Inc
House Washing, Flatwork

Robert Norwood, East Coast Window Cleaning
Fleet Washing, Flatwork

Mike Pasiuk, Northern Tool & Equipment
House Washing, Roof Cleaning, Flatwork, Environmental

Jim Pasternak, Northeast Power Washing
Wood Restoration

Bob Popenhagen, Sunshine Cleaning Systems
Fleet Washing, Wood Restoration

Nathan Pierce, Fish Window Cleaning
House Washing, Roof Cleaning

Tim Rancourt, Northern Tool & Equipment
House Washing, Roof Cleaning, Flatwork, Environmental

Andrew Reinsel, A2Z Pressure Washing LLC
House Washing, Roof Cleaning, Environmental

Mike Reome, Pro-Jet Services
Wood Restoration

Clint Reynolds, HydroTech Solutions
Fleet Washing

Michael Rucker, Window Cleaning of Augusta, Inc. Dba Fish Window Cleaning
House Washing, Roof Cleaning

Don Sanderson, Atlantic Pressure Cleaning and Services
House Washing, Roof Cleaning

Ben Shelton, Dirtzero, LLC
House Washing, Fleet Washing, Flatwork

Adam Smith, Pressure Pro Cleaning
House Washing, Roof Cleaning

Garland Smith, Precision Service Co.
Environmental

Paul Stringer, Jenkintown Building Services
Roof Cleaning

Greg Swinea, Sunshine Cleaning Systems
Environmental

Mike Thomas, Mikes Exterior Home Care
House Washing

Dale Toomey, J and J Powerwashing
Roof Cleaning

Clayton Townsend, Townsend Power Washing
House Washing, Wood Restoration, Roof Cleaning, Environmental

Guy Triger, Puma Power Washing
Wood Restoration, Roof Cleaning

Abu Woldeamanuel, Colonial Parking
Environmental

Patrick Wooten, Mikes Exterior Home Care
House Washing

New PWNA Members

Jorge Aguilar, Empire Highrise USA

John Allison, EnviroSpec

Justin Anderson, Steamericas Inc

Richard Bond, Affordable Home Solutions

Stephen Cowley, Weekend Mobile Wash

Miguel Diaz, Doing Green Maintenance Services, LLC

Annette Donahue, DCI Services, Inc.

Randolph Duchesne, Randy's Handyman Service

Ryan Edrington, Excellent Exteriors

David Fahari, Super Dave's Pressure Cleaning

Devon Fox, Foxx Mobile Pressure Washing

Gilbert Gentry, Strategic Filtration

James Gillespie, Sam Spray

Jerry Green, J and J Powerwashing

Jared Chandler Greene, JCG of Fayetteville

Rich Honahan, Crockett Services

Bob Jacobs, Safetytec Industries

Jeff Johnson, Shine Time Services LLC

Christopher K. Kruayai, The Pressure Kru, Inc.

Nicholas LaPorte Fairway, Window & Pressure Cleaning

Brian Lipker, Under Pressure Washing LLC

Greg Loucks, Gosideon Power Wash

Trey Mathias, Trey Mathias Pressure Washing

Josh Minx, Southern Clean

Sean James Mullane Housewash New Zealand Limited

James Pasternak, Northeast Power Washing

Matt Pierce, Pierce Property Services, LLC

Tom Raba, R/T Heating & Air Conditioning Ltd.

James Robinson, Premier Window Cleaning

Robert S. Rodgers Jr., Clean n Clear

Michael Rucker, Window Cleaning of Augusta, Inc. Dba Fish Window Cleaning

Steve Tolley, USA Largo Industries, Inc.

Clayton Townsend, Townsend Power Washing

PWNA Vendor Profile

For over 30 years, Joseph D. Walters Insurance Agency has had one specialty niche – the pressure washing industry. That's what has made them the number one insurer of pressure washers in the nation, serving thousands of pressure washing contractors across 48 states. In recent months, the agency has undergone a few changes and expansions. This, in turn, has strengthened the service, programs and commitment to pressure washing contractors, and have allowed them to expand to now serve window cleaning contractors as well.

The Joseph D. Walters Agency was founded in Pittsburgh, Pennsylvania, by Joe Walters back in 1978. Walters was first introduced to the power washing industry by his good friend, Steve Wiley, who at the time was the vice president and sales manager for Wash on Wheels in Gettysburg, Pennsylvania. "Power washing insurance was virtually unheard of, and it was hard to convince our agency's insurance carriers to take a chance and cover the equipment," Walters said. In those days, the use of propane caused several accidental explosions, and insurance carriers did not want to take the risk. However, after spending weeks conducting some tough negotiations, Walters came up with a special insurance program for pressure washing contractors.

From there, Walters decided to start promoting his pressure washing insurance nationally. He began by advertising in the newly created *Cleaner Times* magazine. He also connected with Robert Hinderliter, who asked Walters to join him in Fort Worth for what would become the very first Power Washers of North America (PWNA) convention. (Wiley actually served as the first keynote speaker at the first PWNA event.) "And I've never missed a PWNA convention since in 30 years."

Joseph D Walters and the PWNA

The PWNA has been an integral part of the Joseph D. Walters Agency's growth, as has the support of Walters' good friend Robert Hinderliter. Years later, Joe and Robert started another organization – the United Association of Mobile Cleaning Contractors (UAMCC). Through both of these groups, Joe said he has met and worked with numerous industry leaders, including Robert and Michael Hinderliter, Eric Clark, Daryl Pirla, Carlos Gonzales, John Tornabene, Paul Horsley, John Allison and many, many others. "Our industry has had some outstanding leaders, and I've been fortunate to get to know and support these and other professionals over the years," he explained.

For years, Walters has also served as the PWNA convention's chairman and emcee because of his excitement and enthusiasm for this industry and organization. The PWNA also honors Walters' contributions each year by giving out a special honor – the Joseph D. Walters Award – to the association's most valuable vendor.

The Acquisition

Last year, Walters announced that his agency was joining forces with longtime family friend Tom Svrcek. This resulted in the acquisition of the Joseph D. Walters Insurance Agency by JDW Insurance Options, which is one of the largest family-owned independent agencies in Western Pennsylvania. While the agency has changed physical locations, the top-quality staff and customer service has remained the same.

"If there was ever a natural business move, this is it. Joseph D. Walters Insurance will continue to operate for the exclusive power wash program, and I will continue to work with the power washers and with JDW as a consultant," Joe explained. "For nearly 30 years I have pioneered and enjoyed servicing and working with all of my friends and clients to become America's number one power wash insurer."

Increased Services

The joining of the two agencies gave Joseph D. Walters Insurance added influence and power for negotiating better customer coverages and rates. Specifically, Tom Svrcek worked hard to develop a program, underwritten by Liberty Mutual, designed specifically for pressure washing contractors. The package provides a number of important, often hard-to-find coverages that many insurance agencies simply don't offer, and at a rate that is much less than if you were to purchase each coverage individually.

Here are some highlights of the new power insurance washing program:

- **Care custody and control** including broad form property damage. Accidents happen. This exclusive "good will" coverage protects you for customer's property that you work on. We provide coverage without regard to legal liability. And there is also coverage to real property including building.

- **General liability** limits $300,000. To $2,000,000.

- **Blanket additional insured by written contract.** This coverage saves you times on jobs where the property owner requires you to name them as additional insured. This important coverage is Included at no additional costs.

- **Blanket waiver of subrogation as required by contractor.** This coverage is for jobs where the property owner requires you to waive of right of recovery for loss that we may have with that owner. One-half of all commercial owners require this coverage and usually cost $250 per job.

- **Identity theft coverage $25,000.00.**

- **Garage keepers insurance** for coverage on vehicles that you wash without regard to liability.

- **Broad inland marine equipment coverage** including rented equipment to protect your pressure washing equipment and tools.

- **No premium audit.** Insurance cost is known upfront. Guaranteed for the term of the policy.

- **Employment practices liability.** Discrimination, harassment, wrongful termination.

- **Important optional policies and coverage.** Business automobile, Umbrella Liability, Equipment Coverage, Workers compensation, Limited Pollution, Employment practices, Property insurance, Garage Keeper Liability.

The Joseph D. Walters Agency serves contractors in 48 states, and insurance claims can be taken care of quickly and locally.

Another hugely popular offering by the Joseph D. Walters Agency is the ability to provide contractors with proof of insurance very quickly. "We've had customers call needing proof of insurance sent to a customer, only to find it waiting for them when they arrived on the jobsite," said Vrcek.

"In addition to offering the power wash program, we can bundle your auto, worker's compensation, equipment, and umbrella coverage and help you save even more," Vrcek added.

Finally, just as it's been a natural move for many pressure washing contractors to add window cleaning services – and vice versa – it also has been a natural addition for the Joseph D. Walters Agency. The agency now offers a plan designed specifically for window cleaning contractors as well.

Through its experience with the PWNA, the Joseph D. Walters Agency has learned the value of belonging to and working with industry trade associations. Today, the agency remains a strong supporter of the PWNA, but has also spread its support to other groups including the Pressure Washing Resource Assiocation (PWRA), Window Cleaning Resource Association (WCRA), and the IACSM.

"We prefer to market through associations because we believe those who are involved are better trained on how to properly clean and run their businesses," said Vrcek. "We are proud to be involved with several groups, including the PWNA."

To learn more about Joseph D. Walters Insurance and its unique programs for cleaning contractors, visit www.JOSEPHDWALTERS.com.

SMART SOLUTIONS FROM **ENVIROSPEC**.COM

PowerWashAcademy

FEBRUARY 2014 Jekyll Island, Georgia

Since 1985 we have been The Industry's #1
EDUCATIONAL RESOURCE

become a
BURNER EXPERT

Diagnose and repair ANY AND ALL
EQUIPMENT PROBLEMS

REBUILD PUMPS
and save
HUNDREDS

Entry Level and ADVANCED
HOUSE WASH MARKETING

We have KEPT more contractors in business than any other company in the industry.

http://www.envirospec.com/academy2014.htm

A Soldier's Story
How Three Days in Orlando Changed One Contract Cleaner's Life

by Allison Hester

Jared Greene of Fayetteville, North Carolina, first joined the military in 1998 with plans to serve as a career infantryman. However, in 2011, while serving with one of the last groups remaining in Iraq, Jared's unit was attacked with an IED. He lost two very close friends in the incident, and was later diagnosed with an injury that would prevent from continuing with the infantry. Jared left the Army in March 2012 and began pursuing military disability.

With a wife to support and no clear career plans, a friend offered to pay Jared to power wash one of his rental properties. Jared had a small Craftsman electric pressure washer he had received as a gift. "I spent the better part of six hours 'pressure washing' the single-wide mobile home," he explained. "Although I realized that I was going WAY too slow because of my equipment limitations, I figured out that I absolutely loved pressure washing."

Jared researched residential power washing and purchased a 3.5 gpm, 3000 psi machine from Craigslist. "I started advertising on Craigslist and landed some jobs. Even early on, I never had a bad review or an unhappy client. I made sure the job was done to the best of my ability no matter how long it took me."

He also researched industry schools and certifications. That's how he found the Power Washers of North America. "I immediately reached out to them to ask how I could become a member and grow in my chosen career," Jared explained. "I had NO idea exactly how much they would end up doing for me."

An Unexpected Offer

"I knew it would cost me something to become part of the organization and receive formal training. However, after leaving the Army, I had gone through all of my savings while simply trying to pay the bills. So I offered to make payments for my membership fees every month until I was able to pay it off."

Jared said the response he received was "WAY unexpected. PWNA's Jackie Lavett reached out to the Board of Directors, who agreed to cover one year of Jared's membership. They also allowed him to pay for certifications when he could afford to do so. "I couldn't believe it. I was part of an organization that I knew would help me tremendously. I could receive the education that could help propel my company to the next level."

In the meantime, Jared worked hard to try to save up money to attend the PWNA Conference in Orlando. However, business tapered off. Feeling desperate, Jared began offering "crazy discounts, printing flyers at home and going door-to-door passing them out whenever I had the time. But the money for the trip to Orlando just wasn't there.

"Of course I wanted to go, but I had no idea how I could afford to attend. If I went, things would be extremely tight," he explained. "On the other hand, if I attended the certification courses, I knew I'd learn more in a few days than I could learn in a few years on my own."

John and Shelley Allison of Envirospec heard that Jared was struggling to make

An Even Bigger Surprise

Envirospec owners John and Shelly Allison – both Vietnam Veterans – founded the Washin' Warriors program in ☐☐☐ as a means to help qualified veterans in need of help start a new career in the pressure washing industry. A PWNA member who learned about Jared's situation contacted John Allison, and literally within a matter of minutes, John wanted to help.

John and Shelly Allison, along with Tim McCoppin and Naomi Parker of Envirospec, traveled from Somerville, Georgia, to the PWNA convention. And they brought some very special surprises with them.

On Friday night, the group from Envirospec – along with Steve and Lisa Tolley of GCA Largo, Greg Dupree of Kohler Engines, and Dan and Heather Galvin of East Coast Power Washing – went to dinner with Jared. In the car, Dan and Jared talked business and marketing strategies. Throughout dinner, John and Jared talked equipment. Still, Jared had no idea of what was going on.

During Saturday morning's meeting, Dan Galvin called up Naomi Parker to make an announcement. They began by acknowledging a veteran at the show. Then Naomi read off a list of awards and medals this veteran had received. "It took me a moment to figure out how he had even gotten that information because it's very personal and I don't exactly hand it out. Then he remembered that John Allison had requested a copy of his ☐☐☐☐☐ military record and he put two and two together.

Next, Dan asked Jared to come to the front – which he admitted made him very nervous. "Then again, I will do anything that A☐☐ member at the convention asked me to do because of how grateful I was for everything

The Washin' Warriors program, sponsored by Envirospec, could not have been made possible without the support of all involved. (From left to right) Dan Galvin, East Coast Power Washing; Greg and Deborah Dupree, Kohler Engines; Steve Tolley (back), GCA Largo; John Allison, Naomi Parker, and Shelley Allison (Envirospec); Lisa Tolley, GCA Largo; Tim McCoppin, Envirospec; and Recipient Jared Greene.

the event, so they paid for Jared's hotel and travel, and gave him ☐☐☐☐ to cover additional expenses. So, of course, I made the necessary preparations and drove to Orlando."

While at the PWNA Convention, Jared talked to "every single person he possibly could about the industry, asking for advice on how to overcome problems he was currently facing. In particular, and he asked about "methods of approaching problems, necessary steps to be taken, what solutions to use, how to market my company, and pricing. That was huge – knowing how much my time is worth."

everyone had taught me.

At that time, Dan announced that Staff Sergeant Jared Greene had been chosen as Envirospec's first ever "Washin' Warrior" Project Recipient.

That's when a Largo 5.6 gpm @ 3500 psi, 200° hot water skid unit with a 26 hp Kohler engine was rolled in, a $16,000 value. In addition to Envirospec's contribution, the machine was donated in part by Steve Tolley of SKA Largo (one-half the cost of the machine) and Greg Dupree, who donated the Kohler Engine filtering package. Dan Galvin also contributed to the package by agreeing to serve as Jared's mentor, and donating access to a variety of marketing materials and marketing schools.

In addition to the machine, Envirospec's Washin' Warriors package also includes:
• $5,000 worth of Envirospec Chemicals
• A One-Year Local Area Marketing Program (valued at $10,000)
• The opportunity to attend all Envirospec Systems Certifications Schools and Power Wash Academy's Marketing School free for life.
• A 10% Veteran's Discount which is available to all Vets for life

"The appreciation I had for that machine – and all the things that Envirospec was donating – was immense," Jared said. "I knew what it meant for me and my business. I couldn't believe I was just given something that would guarantee my company's success."

Jared added that the entire presentation was overwhelming. "I was SO humbled that I was being recognized for things that I did months and even years before, in places on the opposite side of the Earth, from people I have never met before. I became very emotional. It took every bit of strength that I had to not allow my knees to buckle and just fall to the floor crying. The love and sincere appreciation that I was given was so overwhelming. I've never experienced anything like that in my life, and I venture to

A note from Jared:
I would like to thank the following people for making this possible for me.
Jackie Gavett - Thank you for seeing something in me that sparked ALL of this to happen. You have changed my life, and I will always be indebted to you and strive to give back what you have given me.

Dan and Heather Galvin – You offered to be my mentors. I could not think of a better couple to strive to be like. If I can attain half the success and happiness that you both have, I will consider myself a VERY lucky man and husband. Dan, you called me before ever meeting me, while my wife was hospitalized, and said some very kind things. You have NO idea how much that meant to both of us. We will never forget your kindness and generosity.

John and Shelley Allison – I didn't have a clue why this guy named "John Allison" wanted a copy of my military records, and I was VERY skeptical to send them. Hahaha. Now I understand. You have given me something that will stay with me for life, John…you gave me hope and have made my dreams possible when I began to question them. I will always be in your debt.

Steve & Lisa Tolley, Greg & Deborah Dupree - Although I wasn't able to speak to you much, you were an integral factor in everything. So that you both realize the impact of what you've done for me, my wife and I will never worry about our next meal again because of YOUR generosity.

Hydro Tek – for your generous donation that I somehow amazingly won. You will never know how much your contribution means to me and my family.

And to the countless people who showed me the respect and kindness that you did (and the patience that some of you showed 'the new guy'), I will never forget it. I can promise you that. Each one of you, from Clemson fans, to a Missouri painter, to my long-haired buddy that struggles in FL with the same things that I do, to the millionaires, and the little guys, and that guy that heard my story in passing and gave me a $200 handshake on my way out to come home to my wife. I sincerely thank all of you for everything you have done for me, what you represent, and allowing me to become a member of your family. I couldn't ask for more.

say that I probably never will again – and that is ok with me. This was more than enough to last a lifetime."

NO ONE suspected what happened next...

The Drawing

Each year, Hydro Tek – along with the support of General Pump, Beckett Burners and Kohler Engines – gives away a skid unit in a drawing at the end of the PWNA convention.

While some people purchased hundreds of dollars in tickets, Jared bought a mere five. "I had jokingly told some guys there was no way I would make it out of that building alive if I was lucky enough to win the giveaway skid."

As they announced the other PWNA drawing winners, Jared clapped and was excited for each one, and was looking forward to seeing who won the skid giveaway. "I figured I would take a couple of pictures with them and then get on the road to head home. I couldn't wait to see my wife and talk about all the wonderful experiences I had and things I had learned."

When the ticket was drawn, Marv from Hydro Tek asked, "Is there a Jared here? Jared C. Greene?" Jared thought he was joking.

But it was no joke. Jared had just won the Hydro Tek skid giveaway!

"If you consider the odds of this happening, they are surreal," said Jared. "It's just insane."

Jared walked to the podium, shaking hands with people along the way, then "managed to mutter something that I can barely remember." Someone asked if he would be back next year, and Jared just smiled. "Definitely."

He immediately left the stage and called his wife, who literally screamed on the phone when she heard the news. She was crying, and he knew exactly why.

"This could not be mistaken by anyone. This WAS a sign from God. You don't have to share my Christian beliefs to realize that all of these events are impossible to label as coincidence," he said. "Never in my life has something been SO clear for me. This was the path I was meant to travel down. The kindness of strangers – who became mentors, shoulders to lean on, business advisors, and honestly, like loved family – combined with the will of God, laid out my entire life before me."

Later that night, on the drive home, Jared said he could not stop crying. "That's right, the big, tough, tattooed Infantryman cried his eyes out for almost the entire 10-hour drive home. To not have to worry about how I will support my family is such a relief. To know that I won't have to worry about where to get food or how to pay for it is simply the most amazing feeling. And lastly, to know that I AM walking the path I am meant to, and doing the ONE thing that I have found that I LOVE to do, with the support of everyone, is the most fulfilling thing on Earth."

As he drove home, Jared said he vowed he would give back to the PWNA every single thing that he could for the rest of my life. "Even if you take away the very generous gifts that have been donated to my family from EnviroSpec, Largo Industries, and Kohler Engines, take away the generous donations from Dan and Heather Galvin, and if you take away the amazing Hydro Tek machine that I unbelievably won, I was STILL given everything that I needed from the members of the PWNA to succeed in this industry," he concludes.

"I have never felt so genuinely cared for in my entire life, and this was given to my family and me from people that we have never even met before. The PWNA has LITERALLY changed my life."

No Water Wasted Promo

Hydro Tek National Special — July 2013

$12,495
save $4700

save the drain for the rain

FREE freight*

Want a larger trailer? Upgrade to a 400 gallon, dual axle trailer with electric brakes for only **$2500** more

Mobile Wash Skid
Gas Powered, Diesel Heated – 110v burner
3500psi, 5gpm, Belt drive pump
570cc Vanguard twin cylinder engine
On-board 3000w generator

Trailer
200 gallon ProTowWash® trailer with rear storage tray and high pressure hose reel

Vacuum Recovery/Filtration System
Recover and filter your washwater for reuse or disposal. No external power needed, runs off pressure washer generator.
<u>Package also includes</u> containment berms, scupper & vacuum hose

NO WATER WASTED Recycle Trailer
model# SC35005VS/T2NWA/AZV55

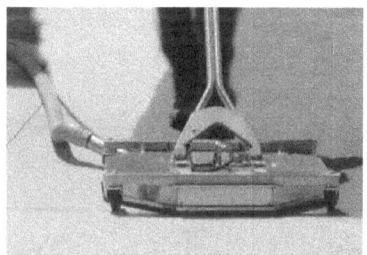

Add a Twister Vac recovery surface cleaner for $1500

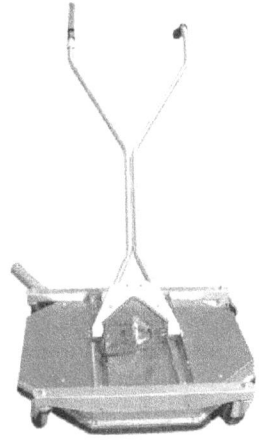

AUTHORIZED LOCAL DISTRIBUTOR:

Limited time offer starts July 15, 2013. Price does not include sales tax or battery, if needed. *Free freight to distributor location within the continental US. Ask your distributor for the *No Water Wasted* Special. Not to be combined with any other offers, programs, or discounts. Available through a participating distributor, call for a local distributor. 400 gallon trailer upgrade model# SC35005VS/T4NWA/AZV55

Brilliant Design, Tough on Grime
2353 Almond Avenue • Redlands, CA 92374 • (P) 800-274-9376 • (F) 909-799-9888 • www.hydrotek.us

SALES

Get Sales Mileage from Your Holiday Cards

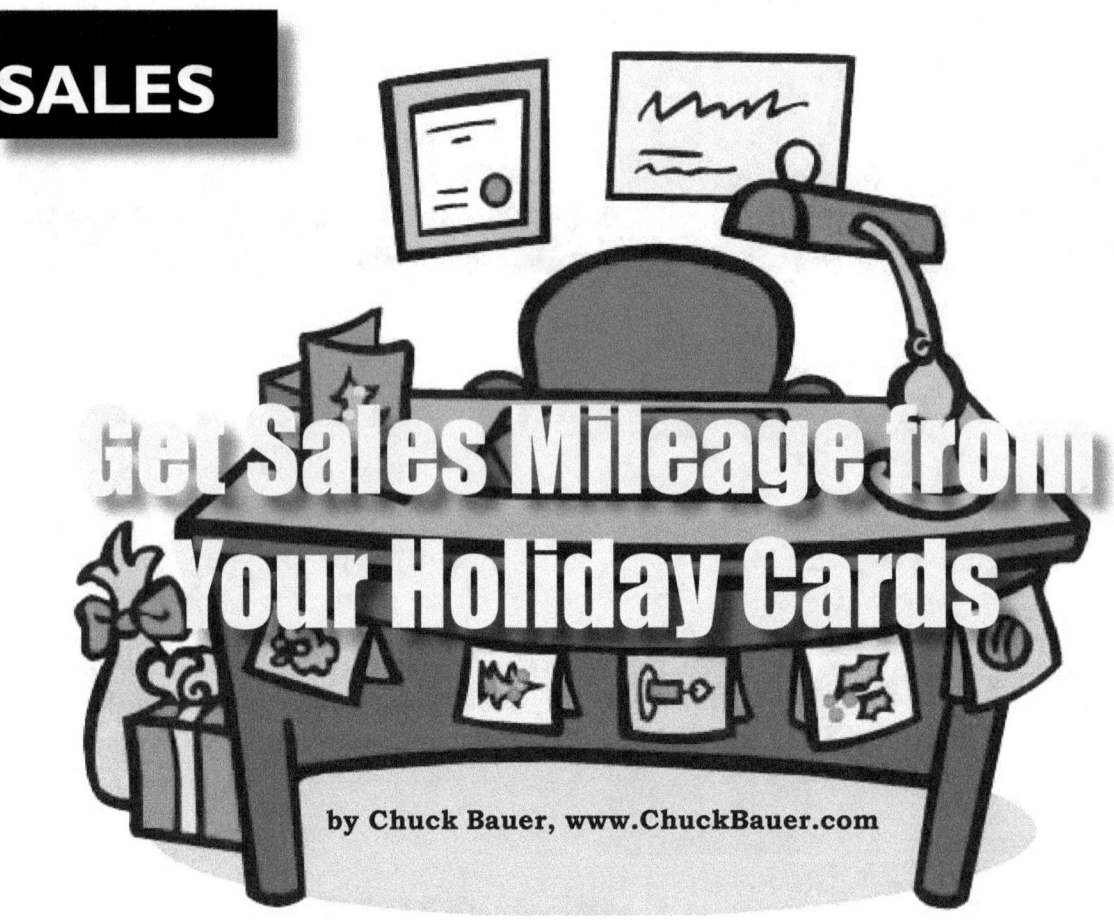

by Chuck Bauer, www.ChuckBauer.com

As fall arrives, most (not ALL) salespeople, companies, and entrepreneurs *dread* the thought of *having* to send holiday cards to their clients. Those who dread this task are often consumed by the daily grind of business. Yet you can implement some simple and practical ideas, starting today, so you can have the best holiday season ever.

But first, let's put some STOPS in place!

- **STOP** using holiday cards that have your name or company name pre-printed on them.
- **STOP** placing business cards or marketing material in your holiday cards.
- **STOP** using the boring white mailing labels.
- **STOP** using a metered mailing machine for postage.
- **STOP** waiting until the last minute to send your holiday cards.
- **STOP** using United States flag stamps for your holiday cards.

Before We Begin

As we supercharge our Holiday Touches, I want to bring to your attention some major philosophies that I need you to understand and embrace.

1. Understand the game you are in. When sending holiday cards, you are up against the busiest time in the world for mail. The more holiday cards that are sent, the less effective they become. You, just like everybody else, are competing for your clients' attention. If you want to win their attention, start sending them 4th of July cards (in July, of course!) instead.

2. Stop treating all your clients the same way. Some of you have client database numbers that vary from just a few to thousands. Your challenge is to stop treating the entire database the same way. Regardless of your database numbers, treating them all the same way is highly ineffective. Nor is it a way to utilize proper time management skills.

To work smarter, apply this rule to your database numbers.

3. Take the top 10% of your client base . . . you know, the 10% that really means the most to your revenue. That is the group of clients you want to target with *personalized* holiday cards! So if you have 100 clients, you'll send 10 holiday cards out. If you have 1000 clients, then you'll send 100 holiday cards.

If the 10% figure doesn't work for your circumstances, then figure out the percentage that does work.

Personalized Holiday Cards – One Size DOES NOT Fit All!

You keep hearing me state, "personalized holiday cards." That's correct – they must be personalized. If you don't personalize them, then don't send them. It is that simple. Why would you send a very impersonal card to a client when it has no TOMA (Top Of Mind Awareness)? Hint: You *guilt* yourself into sending the cards because it is the holidays. STOP the guilt. Stop sending lousy, one-size-fits-all holiday cards!

Supercharge An Effective Holiday Card Campaign

• START your Holiday Card Campaign in EARLY November.

• START identifying your Top 10% (or your Top Clients) who you will be sending cards to.

• START using a different type of pen or marker that will make the client notice your written message.

• START buying significant Assorted Holiday Cards. I found a great assorted holiday card collection – 50 handcrafted cards – for less than $15 a box.

• START buying your Holiday Stamps from usps.com. Save time, buy online!

• START becoming aware that some cards might take two 44-cent stamps.

• START conducting a Google Images search for "Holiday Stickers." This will yield a variety of ideas for cool holiday stickers you can use on envelopes and even inside the card.

• START mailing your cards so they will hit mid-week, not on a Monday. If you mail on the first Tuesday in December, your cards should arrive by the end of the week. If that date is too early, mail on the second Tuesday. If you mail any time after that, you had better plan on a minimum of seven days for delivery.

• START remembering that you are competing with the rest of the world's holiday cards.

• START demonstrating courage to not use a return address on the card. The curiosity of no return address will entice your client to open the card first before any other mail.

• START being authentic when writing your notes. You could start your note by writing "Just a short holiday note to say it has been a pleasure having you as a . . . "

• START your one-card-a-day campaign.

The One-Card-A-Day Campaign

Daily, starting in early November, handwrite

a short and personalized note inside the holiday card to that client. Your note might be just a couple of sentences or as much as a paragraph or two. The main idea is that you handwrite it and personalize it.

After finishing your note on the inside of the card, seal it and handwrite the client's name and address on the outside of the envelope. Add your holiday stamp and your cool holiday sticker. Place in a secure area or box.

Repeat all these steps the next day. PRESTO – after 0 days, you will have 0 Holiday Cards *personalized*!

If you need more time to complete your list, continue this pattern through the first half of December, and that will give you about personalized cards.

The Remaining 90%

Now, what to do with the other 0 in your database? That's simple Send them a nice holiday electronic Card via e-mail, one that you can send to all of them with one click of the mouse.

Remember, these are the clients who are important to you, but are just not as significant as the other 10%.

Get Creative

You can certainly modify these ideas. One of my students who is a successful financial planner modified her program with this method Her top clients received a huge block of Hershey's chocolate with a personalized Holiday Message. Her secondary clients received a smaller Hershey's Kiss with a personalized Holiday Message. The rest of her database received a special holiday electronic card.

A few years ago, another client personally delivered customized calendars to his Top 0 clients – unannounced. He took the time to just show up in the late afternoon, and many of his clients were pleasantly surprised.

This techni ue he attributed to a best ever December business because the law of reciprocation took over – with the result that many of those who received the customized calendar freely gave him more business or referral business.

The biggest payoff rests with the fact that you went the extra mile to reach out to your special clients. Your thoughtfulness was distinctive. You took the time to do something special for them.

Believe me, among the onslaught of non-distinctive holiday cards your clients receive, your personalized – and thus distinctive holiday card will stand out!

urthermore, when they read your handwritten comments, they will certainly notice your effort and their esteem for you will rise to higher levels of trust and appreciation. Better yet, when that client is ready to enter into your market or they hear of someone who is they will automatically think of you.

Get Personalized. Get Remembered!

Pink Mohawk

How One Pressure Washing Contractor is Paying It Forward

When I met Richard Velazquez of Southeast Mobile Pressure Cleaning LLC at the PWNA Convention in Orlando, I admit my eyes were immediately drawn to his hair – completely shaved on both sides of his head, highlighting a pink mohawk down the center. Figuring it was just a form of self expression, I pretended I didn't even notice. However, that was not the response he was looking for.

"I want people to say something," he explained. "That's the whole point."

Being impacted by movies such as "Pay It Forward," and the idea of doing a random act of kindness, Velazquez decided to do something to support breast cancer awareness. So he had a professional stylist give him a pink Mohawk – which he plans to keep until he's raised □□00 for his local Susan G. Komen Lowcounty Chapter in Charleston, South Carolina. "I really like that □□ percent of our chapter's funds stay in Charleston to help women in our community who are impacted by the disease."

To help promote his cause, Velazquez has appeared on several podcast programs, including "It's Your Business," and "My Positive Perspective," both of which are on kinetichifi.com. He has also attended various events, including the local Susan G. Komen race, sporting his "Pink Mohawk" awareness signs.

Velazquez's customers have been very supportive of his efforts and his cause as well. "Once they learn why I look like this, they love it and are excited about helping."

Velazquez has had family members and friends alike who have been impacted by breast cancer. More than that, however, he just saw this as a way to give back and help others. "I truly believe that when we give, it will come back to us. This is simply my way of paying it forward."

To learn more about Velazquez's efforts or to make a contribution, visit his Facebook page: www.Facebook.com/PinkMohawkSC.

Solar Panel Cleaning:
Good for the Environment and for *Your* Bottom Line

by Allison Hester

*T*he solar energy market has seen significant growth over the past decade, and shows no signs of slowing down. This is good news not only for the environment, but also for the solar panel cleaning industry.

For a solar panel to work properly, it must be subjected to sunlight. That's why most industrial solar panel fields are located in sunny locations, such as the Southwest U.S., where the weather is fairly constant with many hours of sunshine.

Just as solar panels lose efficiency on cloudy days, they also don't work as well when they are dirty. In fact, the solar panel owner can actually monitor and measure how much efficiency is being lost due to dirty panels. However, unless they are properly educated on the need for cleaning, they may not recognize why their efficiency is going down. It's up to the professional cleaning industry to inform customers about the need for cleaning because, unfortunately, the panel manufacturers traditionally have told them otherwise.

Solar panel manufacturers generally say that rainfall should be enough to clean a solar panel. However, that's similar to an automobile manufacturer saying that rain is enough to keep your car clean. And it's not even considering that many solar panels are in locations where rain rarely falls.

More significant, however, is the fact that the contaminants in rain and tap water can actually damage the panel's glass. Again, this is good news for you as a professional cleaning contractor, but you must educate customers on the need for proper cleaning.

How to Clean Solar Panels

The traditional method for cleaning solar panels is using a brush and deionized (DI) water, washing each panel individually by spraying on the water, brushing, and rinsing. DI or purified water removes the solids from tap water so that it does not damage the surface and dries spot free. For those who already own the equipment, this is a good option. However, it will require either hauling in DI water to the site, and making sure you have enough on hand to do the job, or creating your own DI water on site, which takes time and money.

An innovative new cleaning technique developed by Saint Gobain Corporation simplifies the cleaning process. This new eco-friendly cleaning product, AmberClean Solar GS-1 from Saint Gobain-Innovative Organics, is designed to allow for solar panel cleaning using regular tap water. Saint Gobain – Innovative Organics AmberClean Solar GS-1 added to tap water can be easily applied using a downstream injector and a pressure washer, brushed, then rinsed. "Our chemicals bind up the calcium and minerals from tap water, lkeeping them from depositing on the panels," explained Dennis Cook, Solar Products Sales Manager. Another important fact is that solar panels are wired in series. The same principle applies to solar panels that does to the old-fashioned Christmas lights – if one is not working efficiently, it affects the whole strand. So cleaning one panel that appears dirty is not going to do much good they all need to be cleaned to maximize efficiency.

AmberClean Solar GS-1 is a corrosion inhibitor, so unlike deionized water, it is safe to run through the pressure washing system's pump without causing damage. DI water can corrode pump parts depending on which type of material they are made from. The costs of the two cleaning materials are about the same, depending on which equipment you already own. The DI system takes longer to set up, however, and generally requires more planning and takes longer to complete the task due to logistics issues, according to

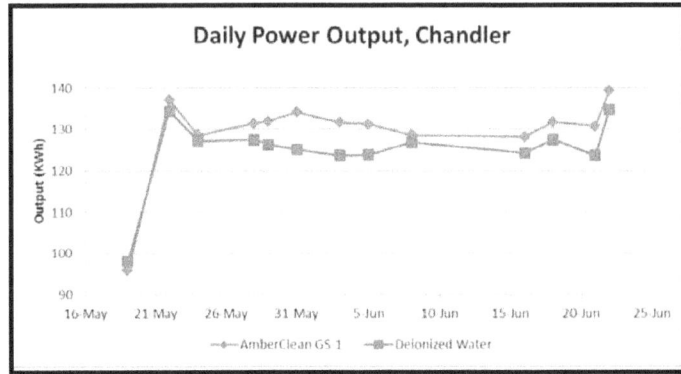

Graph shows solar panel output efficiency improves significantly after cleaning. Both AmberClean GS-1 and Deionized Water Cleaning are fairly comparable.

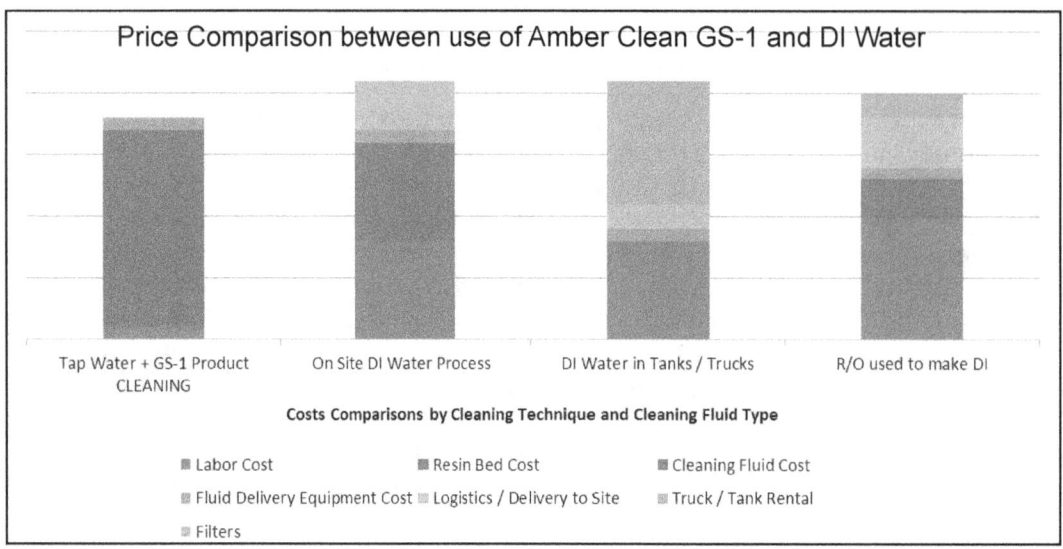

Cook. So that's something to keep in mind as well.

The Solar Panel Market

There are three general types of customers in need of solar panel cleaning. First is the residential customer, which is potentially the easiest sell – especially if you're already there cleaning something else. Or, sell the homeowner on solar panel cleaning, then get them to buy a house wash or window cleaning in the process.

Commercial customers are likely where most of the work will come from, and again, solar panels can be a good add-on service, or a smart way to get a new commercial client. These customers most likely monitor their efficiency more closely than homeowners, and will notice when their panels are not working properly and need to be cleaned.

The third market – which is probably the hardest to break into, is the large industrial power producing fields of solar panels. These groups generally have an annual budget and contract with a maintenance company. To land this type of client, you will most likely need to find out who the maintenance contract is with and then subcontract for that company.

In the final analysis, the product Saint Gobain is producing cuts labor costs, increases daily cleaning potential (we are now aiming for 1,500 panels per person per day), simplifies the water delivery process and all the while improves the productivity of the solar panels. This means we can do a better job with lower operational expense (financial and other), and make more money with less headache. I would recommend the product to anyone looking to get into the solar panel cleaning world!

– Curt Kempton, 5-Star Window Care

As far as how much to charge, it depends on the type of client and the amount of cleaning required. Residential customers may be willing to pay more per panel, but there are fewer panels so the overall sum is less than commercial or industrial customers.

"It also has to be cost effective for the customer," Cook stressed. "The amount of savings from having clean panels has to be more than the cost of the cleaning."

The frequency of cleaning will also vary. For instance, if an area has a number of dry, windy days, the panels may need to be cleaned much sooner than if there were many rainy or calm days. Generally, customers will notice when their panel efficiency is dropping and, if properly educated on the reason, contact someone for a cleaning.

While solar panel cleaning may not become a full-time job for most contractors, it certainly can be an easy and profitable add-on service for pressure washing and window cleaning companies alike. Customers have already invested in solar panels they simply need to be made aware of how get the greatest return on their investment. That means keeping those panels clean using proper techniques. Best of all, it's with equipment that you most likely already own.

IWCA

The International Window Cleaning Association
Annual Convention & Trade Show
February 12-15, 2014 • The Peabody Hotel • Memphis, TN

celebrating 25 years

The Annual Convention & Trade Show brings together more than 400 professional window cleaning companies from around the globe. Learn from colleagues how to grow your business! Attend the educational seminars, hands-on demonstrations and hands-on safety training to keep you and your employees current with OSHA regulations and American National Standards. Equipment vendors, manufacturers of products and suppliers in the window cleaning industry will be on hand and demonstrating the latest tools for window cleaners.

Visit www.IWCA.org for more information.

If you are interested in exhibiting, complete the exhibitor prospectus and return it to IWCA at Info@IWCA.org. Questions can be directed to the IWCA Business Office at 800-845-4922, ext. 3351.

Say "YES" to a Web Presence

by Rick Meehan
Vice President of Marko Janitorial Supply, www.MarkoInc.com

"Should we get a website?" Cleaning contractors ask me this question often. In the past I would simply have replied in the negative as this industry's main form of advertising is WOM, word-of-mouth (referrals from other satisfied customers) – but times change. Now, a cleaning firm without a website is like a fish without a tail. It can't swim—it can't even tread water. In addition to all the other challenges that we face in the cleaning industry we must tackle the issue of web advertising or drown in the rising sea of Social Media.

Everyone has a website these days, so what's the big deal? Websites are nothing special anymore. Very true—however, it's not about being special. Instead, it's about being found and "social." With the advent of "smart" phones and other mobile devices, practically everyone can quickly search the Internet for local cleaning services, instantly and accurately. This is fast replacing the traditional Yellow Pages (YP) and other forms of paper listings. AT&T recognizes this switch in the way people find contact information. That's why they now offer Internet listings. Unless an electromagnetic pulse of massive proportions engulfs the entire Earth at one time, all these new electronic gizmos with their high-powered search features are not going away anytime soon. As businesses we're stuck with figuring out how to keep our contact information in front of individuals so our services can be discovered. Websites can be the new word-of-mouth advertising for cleaning contractors. In the vernacular of text messaging, ALW, ain't life wonderful?

If you have been reading my stuff for long you've probably gathered that I am not a big fan of all this invasive social technology that keeps us instantly in touch, and even located on the GPS (global positioning system) map, every moment of every day. I think it's a GWOT, glorified waste of time. Although I am forced to use this technology constantly, I refuse to let it take over my life like so many others. Personal opinions aside, I do recognize the need for businesses to utilize ST, smart technology, if they wish to compete in today's world. Every day I witness an almost addicted attitude among users of smart devices. All ages are affected, and the best way I can describe them is "plugged in."

So, how do you reach a person who is tied to a device in his or her ear or palm – someone who is fast becoming oblivious to face-to-face social interaction, someone who can instantly find almost any type of information without having to work for it, someone who is losing the ability to let their "fingers do the walking" as the AT&T Yellow Pages have purported everyone should do to find local businesses? You have to reach out using the

same technology of course – FFWF, fight fire with fire so to speak.

Don't believe me? Let's do a simple test. Open your Internet browser, the Google search engine, and then type these words cleaning insert the name of your nearest city or town. In my case, I typed in "cleaning Spartanburg." Instantly I got ,00 results for cleaning companies of all types in my area of Spartanburg, South Carolina. I can narrow the focus of the search with terms like "janitorial Spartanburg," "pressure washing Spartanburg," or "maid service Spartanburg." One of the top hits for my terms includes "Top 11 Pressure Washing Services in Spartanburg, SC." Wow! So now I don't even need to look for someone to give me a referral. I can find happy customers and testimonials on the Web and not have to face anyone personally!

With this kind of power in the hands of nearly everyone, to ignore the Information Highway is suicide. Already my own company is vetted on the web before we can even send a sales representative to make a presentation. It is becoming more difficult to get face-to-face meetings for the purposes of selling our supplies and services. Years ago I wrote an article entitled, "The Personal Touch Will Never Be Replaced," concerning direct selling to end users. Boy, I may have to eat those words. What I didn't count on was the ability of the individual to tune out the world around him or her simply to yak and play on a mobile device. SMM – shut my mouth!

Just last night, at my 0-instrument community symphonic band practice, I witnessed a dozen people texting or playing games on smart phones when they didn't have their horns to their lips. Traditionally during a practice folks would actually listen to the conductor and pay attention to what's going on around them. Speaking with the conductor about this afterward, he told me that he was considering banning the use of mobile devices during practice because the distraction was detrimental to the uality of the rehearsal. That's it in a nutshell use of mobile devices, for good or ill, is destroying the uality of our social interaction.

There's too much blabbing and gaming and not enough substance. Words are cheap acronyms are cheaper. This is the ocean that we as cleaning companies must learn to sail.

The long and short of it is GET A WEBSITE before your vessel sinks for lack of providing enough information! sing the conventions of email and SMS texting eti uette, I just yelled at you. Text messaging uses tremendous volumes of shorthand to keep the number of words to a minimum, STS so to speak . It's like another language, the language of the rising tide of social media. SOW, or speaking of which, this new language will re uire an investment beyond simply throwing a page up on the Web. Anyone can do that. The trick is to make sure that page gets found and viewed.

A good website with integrated social networking can be had fairly cheaply these days – under 1000 – but ongoing maintenance must be considered too. or DIYS, do-it-yourself-ers, check out WordPress wordpress.com . Someone has to put the reviews, comments, successful cleaning stories, testimonies, photos of great contracting jobs, etc., on the Web so your company can be found. Think of the extra work and advertising investment as ADAD, another day another dollar. So STPPYNO GTW, stop picking your nose, get to work, integrating the social media into your overall advertising campaign if you want to stay afloat! I truly hate to be saying all this, but I'm just TILII, telling it like it is.

How I Turned My Business Green

by Todd Turner, ATP Results, El Dorado, Arkansas

I love the look on peoples faces when I tell them I own an industrial cleaning company and run it entirely on renewable energy. When I go on to tell them I design all of my chemicals to be readily biodegradable using renewable and sustainable ingredients, they really give me a puzzled look. Some think I'm a treehugger. Maybe so. But I think trees are a great crop for lumber and making paper, which is the industry I've served for many years. I just tell them I'm a "compassionate capitalist."

"Green" and Safety Go Together

Actually, my move toward being "green" started with safety. I'm a second generation chemical guy. My father got into the business a year before I was born and I was raised around mixing vats and 55 gallon drums. I joined my father in the business in 1981 after graduating college. Most of his work back then involved providing the chemicals, equipment and supervision to help plant workers clean equipment. Naturally, these workers were leery of spraying a bunch of chemicals because they weren't used to working around chemicals. My father would tell them he was exposed to these chemicals more than anyone else in the world. Pointing to me, he would go on to say he wouldn't design a chemical that would be dangerous for his own son, much less for them to use.

My father passed away in '88 but not before getting me into the lab and introducing me to formulating. I didn't understand a lot of what he was talking about but it gave me a start. Those were tough times to be in the chemical business. OSHA and EPA were churning out lots of new regulations. Few people really understood what most of it meant.

Not long before he died, my father asked if it was time for us to find some other way to make a living. I told him I wanted to keep going. Rather than run from the rules, I wanted to learn how to operate within them.

Working in large industrial facilities, my chemicals have to be approved by their safety and environmental departments in order for me to get the sale. In time, I learned how to replace certain ingredients to make my products safer. I also found that designing a chemical to be safe for people almost always makes it safer for the environment as well.

For years, I've designed all of my chemicals and cleaning processes to be safe enough to allow down my customer's sewer or to pick up and recycle and burn as a fuel.

I'm proud to say my name is not on any hazardous waste manifest anywhere. I either design a non-hazardous alternative or pass on the project.

Changing My Ford's Fuel

In 2002, I bought a Ford pickup with a diesel engine. Soon afterward, I started hearing about using waste vegetable oil as a fuel. Thanks to the Internet, I learned lots on the various online forums. When my truck had used up 75,000 of its 100,000 mile warranty, I took the plunge and started running my truck on used cooking oil from my favorite restaurants. The learning curve back then was pretty steep. And I'm still learning.

My regular industrial cleaning work involves lots of process engineering. I have applied that same detail to collecting and filtering the oil as well as modifying my truck. That truck now has over 300,000 miles on the odometer, still smelling like French fries as I drive by. I've used heated vegetable oil, biodiesel and vegetable oil blended with other ingredients.

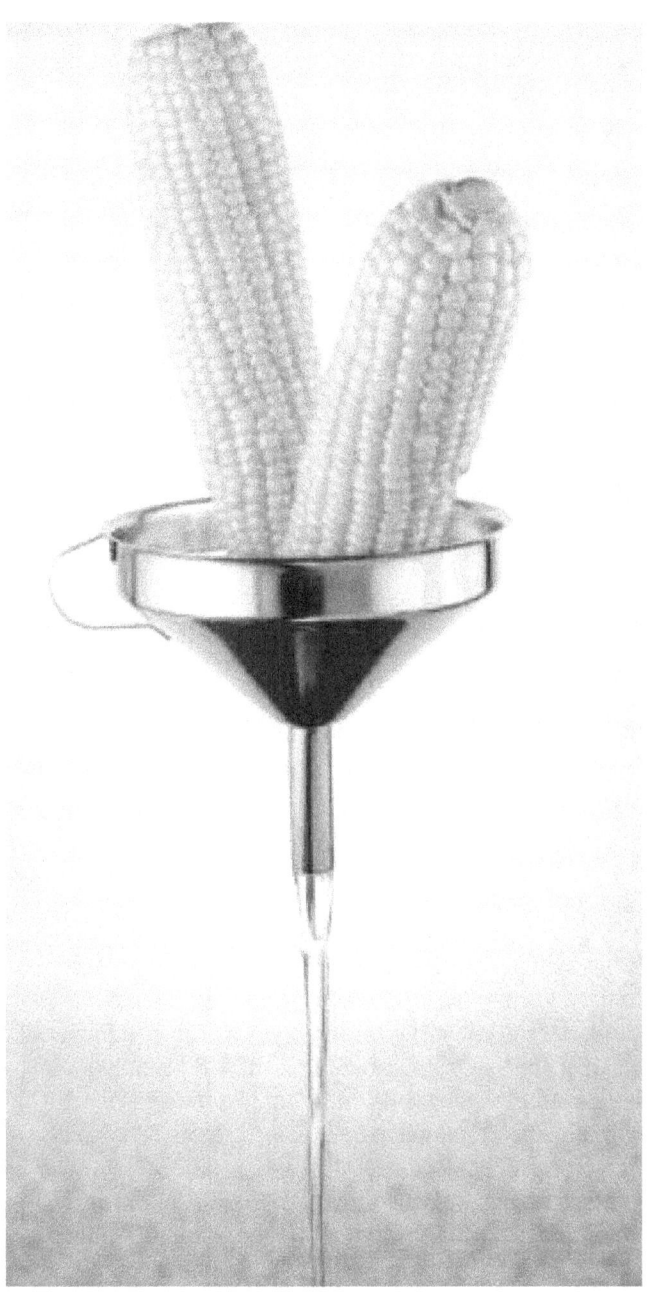

Recycling My Recycled Oil

Working with used cooking oil only helped fuel my interest in recycling. I even recycle my recycled oil. The hydrogenated cooking oil that is bad for our hearts is bad for my truck as well. Plus there's always a lot of other stuff that ends up being tossed out.

When I generated a drum or two of what I simply called "veggie glop," I had to find a way to get rid of it. Being environmentally responsible, I couldn't just toss it out. So, I got wood chips from a friend's sawmill, plus some heavy cardboard tubes from a carpet dealer, and started making "glop logs". Mix the veg oil goo in with

Classifieds: Products ▢ Services

www.ArmClark.com
Armstrong Clark ▢uality Wood Stains. Specializing in wood restoration, oil-based coatings for wood ▢ non-toxic wood stains of all kinds for your wood shake restoration ▢ water repellent needs. ▢00-▢1▢-▢▢11

www.PowerWash.com
Mobile power wash e▢uipment, schools, training, videos, environmental supplies ▢ maintenance services. Call for a free catalog, ▢00-▢▢▢-▢11▢.

www.PowerWashStore.com
Bigger Selection - Better ▢uality - Amazing Customer Service. Serving the professional cleaning community for more than ▢▢ years. Call ▢▢▢-▢▢1-▢▢▢▢.

www.PWNA.org
Power Washers of North America. ▢or certification or membership information, visit our website, email info▢pwna.org, or call ▢00-▢▢▢-▢▢▢▢.

www.SteelEagle.com
Mfr. of World Class Industrial ▢ Commercial Cleaning ▢ Storage Products, including surface spinners, vacuum systems, undercarriage cleaners, hose reels ▢ more. Custom designs available. ▢00-▢▢▢-▢▢▢▢

www.PressureWasherKy.us
Southside E▢uipment multi-line power e▢uipment distributor. Pressure cleaning e▢uipment, waste water recovery ▢ recycling, generators ▢ cleaning chemicals. ▢uality products ▢ impeccable service. ▢▢▢-▢▢▢-▢▢0▢

To Advertise in our New Classifieds Section
Contact Allison Hester at allison▢ecleanmag.com

the wood, pack it into sections of the heavy cardboard tubes and now I have 18" logs that burn great in a barrel heater. And of course, that heater was made from a couple of recycled metal drums. Free heat!

Cleaning with Bugs

About six years ago, a friend heard about a new company developing technology to convert wood chips into diesel. "You need to meet my friend Todd!" I ended up doing some work for that company and even though they folded after a couple of years, by that time I had become fully immersed in the world of "green energy." It also introduced me to chemists and other specialists who turned me on to all sorts of alternative energy as well as "green" waste disposal – using bugs and worms to clean up waste. All of this was right up my alley.

One of my chemist friends developed a method of using bugs to convert the same hazardous waste as in the movie *Erin Brockovich* from being a cancer-causing heavy metal into a soil amendment. He used waste from a sawmill, chicken farm and sugar cane production to feed the bugs while they did what is known as "bioremediation." Rather than bury or burn our hazardous waste, bioremediation involves using nature to break down waste.

Creating Power Through Gasification

These days, I run my company "off the grid." That means I make my own electricity, not even connected to the power company. For me, that means a diesel generator running on biofuels. I have a small amount of solar equipment but that technology is still too expensive. In my world, something has to pay for itself within three years to be justifiable. Solar doesn't work for my budget and we don't have enough wind around here. Biomass is what I have so that's what I use. Ultimately, I want to run my generator with a gasifier using wood.

Essentially, gasification involves burning wood (or any biomass) in an oxygen-deprived environment. Instead of just burning it all up, a gasifier operates under a slight vacuum converting the fuel into a combustible gas. Think of it as a low grade natural gas made up mostly of carbon monoxide and hydrogen. Done right, the only byproduct is a type of carbon called biochar. Talk about a soil amendment! It can be better than chemical fertilizers and puts beneficial carbon back into the environment.

Gasification is actually old technology. Most vehicles in Europe during WWII ran on charcoal or coal using gasifiers on the bumper.

A couple of years ago I bought an older Ford pickup truck with a gasoline engine to use as my "green test mule." Using plans from a guy who has driven over a quarter million miles on scrap wood, I'm building a gasifier for that truck. Running right, I'll get 5,000 miles on a cord of wood while polluting less than gasoline. The equipment will take up about half the truck's bed and the power won't be as good as on gasoline, but running on free fuel makes it worthwhile. Engine modifications to optimize running woodgas are the same for running 100% ethanol (no gasoline at all). I bought another truck for spare parts including an engine which I'll rebuild specifically for the application.

Being a process guy, I'm always working on ways to capture the waste heat from a gasifier or generator to provide building heat and/or heat for making my biodiesel. I'm also using an old coil from a hot water pressure washer and a radiator from my "spare" Ford truck to generate heat for my shop. Eventually, I'll have one for burning biomass and another for burning waste motor oil.

Being a Good Steward

More than anything, I want to be a good steward

Let us put our expert knowledge of **legendary Landa equipment** to work for your cleaning needs.

Specializing in Power washing equipment sales, service and custom manufacturing

(403) 771-7774

www.HydraEquipment.com

HYDRA EQUIPMENT LTD.

of all that God has provided. For me, it goes beyond just designing non-hazardous chemicals and avoiding hazardous waste. It means taking care of the environment as well as the people living here. Our culture of "buy it, use it and toss it in the trash" is just plain dumb, not to mention being unsustainable.

For example, everything coming out of the typical garbage truck can be recycled one way or another. Separate out the metal, glass and plastic which are all recyclable and the remaining 80% is cellulosic in nature. That means it can be used as a fuel. Even better would be to separate out our trash first, including kitchen scraps and trash that can be used in compost. Throw in some worms and you have some really good soil amendment.

I joke about what I call the AVD... Arab Venezuelan Disconnect. I didn't want to buy any fuel from a country that hates me. I'm all for American oil & gas. But, I want to learn how to make fuel apart from that industry. I don't want to be held hostage by price fluctuations so heavily based on politics. That means pressing sunflowers into oil to convert to biodiesel to run a farm. I'm also playing with making ethanol though not from corn. A couple of years ago I went down to Florida to spend a few days with a customer who had gotten in trouble for having a moonshine still. "Come on down, Todd. I can teach you how to make that smooth sippin' whiskey." I told my friend that I didn't want to drink the stuff. I want to run it in my car!

I find it fascinating how renewable energy, waste disposal and sustainable agriculture are all tied together. For example, you can grow wood and corn to make ethanol. The solid byproduct of the fermentation serves to feed fish grown in tanks which in turn provides nutrient rich water to grow vegetables. Meanwhile, the carbon dioxide generated by the process can be pumped into a greenhouse to increase the crop yield. And, the greenhouse can be heated by a compost pile that generates heat naturally while converting yesterday's trash into great soil for tomorrow. It is all inter-related and nothing goes to waste. Essentially, it is going back to how our ancestors ran their farms a hundred years ago. Farmers joke that they knew how to use everything from the pig but the squeal.

My drive to learn about alternative energy is twofold. As an American, I'm concerned about where our country seems to be heading. If gas and diesel prices jump to ten dollars a gallon, I want to have Plan B operational, not just some ideas on paper. I also have a strong passion for missions in developing nations. I'm actively equipping myself to be able to go pretty much anywhere in the world to help people use locally available resources to make their fuel and energy. Whether it is biodiesel, ethanol or biomass gasification, one way or another we can make our own fuel while actually helping the environment.

I have found that my real world experience in the industrial cleaning business can help in missions as well. Beyond just making energy, I've found developing countries are hurting for clean water and effective waste disposal. I deal with that stuff every day! It makes more sense for me to work out the details of water filtration than having some missionary take the time to learn all about it. Let me handle the technical details so they can get back to their core work.

Everything I do in my own operation is small scale – just right for use in a small village or farm. But, there's a catch. The people I want to help don't have much money. Therefore, I must pay my own way to help them become more self-sustaining. These days, what drives my work is a passion to make lots of money specifically to turn around and invest it in projects to help others.

Plus, it's just plain neat to smell my truck running on cooking oil.

Todd Turner, owner of ATP Results in El Dorado, AR., provides specialty cleaning chemicals and process design consulting for heavy industry. He joined his father in the family business in 1981 and has served as president since 1988. Todd has been involved in projects throughout the United States and Canada as well as Europe, Australia and the Far East. Having worked so often through interpreters, Todd jokes ,"I can point in six languages!"

eCLEAN magazine™
The professional contractor cleaner's online resource!

Issue #20

Featuring Car Dealerships

Plus

- The "Mole & Jersey Show"
- Building Your Company's Facebook Page
- ICE Expo in Las Vegas
- Inside Dultmeier Sales
- Sales 101 for Cleaning Companies

...and more!

POWERWASH.COM
SUPPLIES CHEMICALS TRAINING

1.800.433.2113
2513 Warfield St. Fort Worth, TX 76106

Pressure Washers | Surface Cleaners | Chemicals | Cleaning Supplies | Parts | Pumps & Unloaders | Training Materials

The best investment you can make for your business is an investment in yourself! — POWERWASH UNIVERSITY — 2013 Class Schedules

RP-1020 Armour Coat
Guard sun sensitive surfaces against attack from ozone, ultra violet light and oxygen which crack, fade, dull and harden materials like rubber, vinyl, leather and plastic. Surfaces stay cleaner longer with its special antistatic formula. Safe and easy to use, this product is non-flammable, non-toxic, non-corrosive, and odorless.

R-109 Truck Detergent Concentrate
Quickly remove diesel smoke from tractor cabs and trailers. Clean grease and grime from engine blocks. Also good for airplanes, fiberglass, boats and many other difficult surfaces. Put 25 Lbs in 55 Gallons of water to make a concentrated solution tank mix.

W-200 Spray Wax
A lemon fragrance wax designed to give a bright, waxed appearance to all painted metal and vinyl surfaces. Once applied, it causes immediate beading of water. It reduces water spotting on glass, metal trim and slows the bonding of dirt and road film on surfaces to be cleaned. The ideal using concentration range for W-200 can be achieved by making a mix consisting of 8oz. of W-200 to 5 gallons of water and meter through metering valve at 20 to 1.

RP-9019 Orange Peel Concentrate
Orange Peel quickly penetrates tough soils like inks, mastics, tar and heavy oil deposits on a variety of surfaces. It is intended for use in industrial, commercial and intuitional cleaning. Good for cleaning greasy spots on carpeting, removal of black heel marks on flooring, cleaning white side-wall tires, vinyl upholstery, or as a pre-spotter for heavy soiled laundry. One gallon of this concentrate make 15 gallons of cleaner.

R-430 Presoak (*)
Used to penetrate and route out heavy grease, soil and grime on tractor trailer rigs, and heavy equipment.. Excellent on diesel smoke.

Window Cleaner Concentrate
This non-streaking cleaner leaves glass with reflective finishes and a film-free sparkling appearance. 1 gallon of concentrate makes 10 gallons of cleaner.

R-111 Classic Brown Vehicle Detergent
This fluffy free-flowing detergent is a popular favorite with self-service car wash operators, trucking firms and detail shops looking for a great powdered detergent. This compound leaves cars with a wax like sheen and will not streak vehicle finishes.

R-1400 Super Foaming Booster
Designed for enhancing detergent performance by increasing dwell time on vertical surfaces. This fantastic surfactant system boosts the cleaning performance of acid or alkaline based cleaning compounds in foamers.

A-400 Hydroflouric Acid (**)
Banishes white oxides, and road film from aluminum surfaces and leaves dull, dingy aluminum sparkling clean. No scrubbing, buffing or polishing.

RA-130 Rinse Aid
Designed to cause water to "sheet off", reduce spotting in hard water and help lubricate the brushes in brush type automatic car wash systems.

(*) Denotes $27.00 shipping surcharge by UPS. (**) Indicates that this item must ship by motor freight.

www.eCleanMag.com   Issue #20

IN THIS ISSUE:

- 395 Auto Dealerships: Because "a Clean Car is a Sold Car"
- 397 5 Keys to a Successful Carwashing Business, by Bryan Henson, Xstream Pressure Washing
- 398 Choosing the Right Undercarriage Cleaner, by Steel Eagle
- 400 What TO Do (and NOT to Do) with Your Facebook Business Page, by Anya Curry, Ambidextrous Services
- 402 Introducing the Mole & Jersey Show
- 404 PWNA Announces 2014 Vision
- 406 PWNA Vendor Profile: Dultmeier Sales
- 409 ICE Expo: The Coolest Show in Town, January 30-31, Las Vegas, Nevada
- 412 What Are You REALLY Going to Do in 2014? by Tom Grandy, Grandy and Associates
- 414 Sales 101 for Cleaning Firms, by Rick Meehan, Marko Janitorial Supply
- 417 WJTA-IMCA Announces New Strategic Plan
- 417 Classifieds
- 418 How to Write a Fabulous Vision Statement, by Susan L. Reid
- 421 IWCA Announces 25th Annual Convention & Trade Show Schedule
- 422 Business Owners Will Take on New Roles in 2014, by Peter Williamson
- 424 Pressure Washing Services: A Fresh, Clean Start to the New Year, by Paul Horsley

eClean Magazine is published monthly

Publisher Paul Horsley, paul ecleanmag.com
Editor Allison Hester, allison ecleanmag.com

Box ☐☐☐, 1☐ Midlake Blvd S.E.
Calgary, Alberta
Canada T☐☐☐☐☐
www.eCleanMag.com

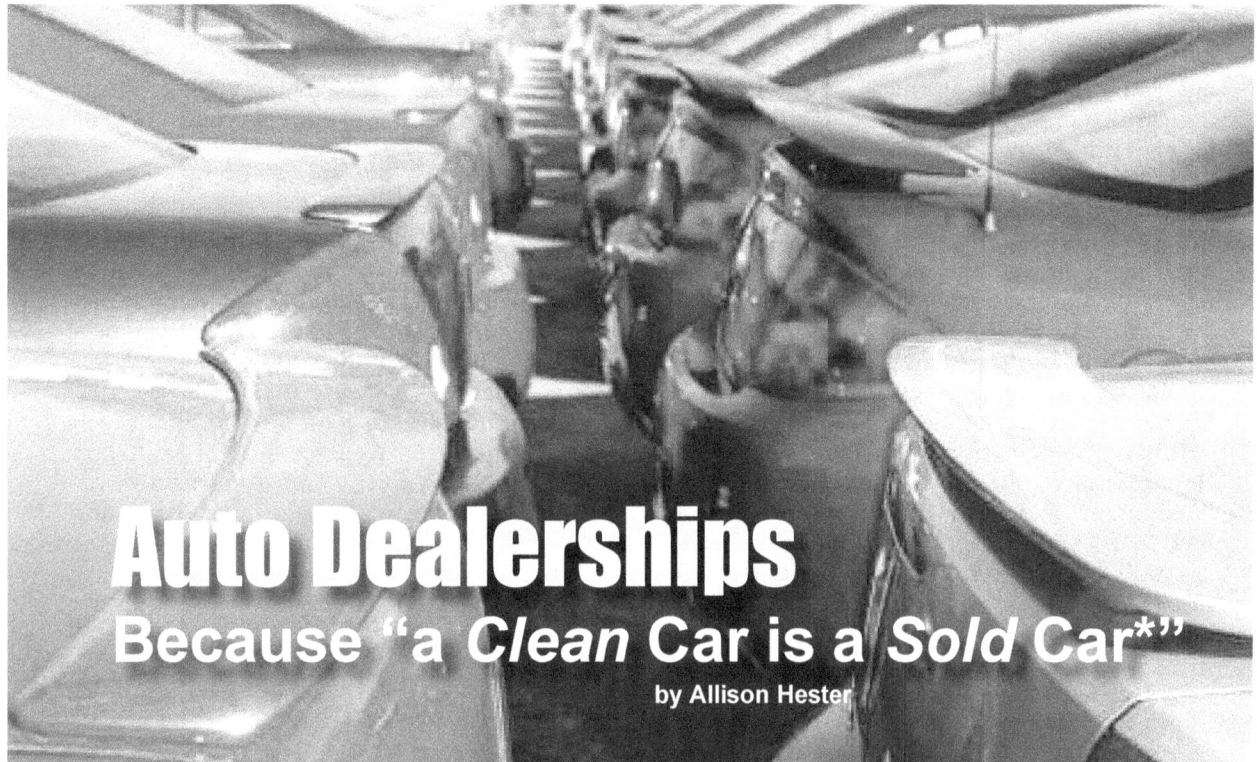

Auto Dealerships
Because "a *Clean* Car is a *Sold* Car*"
by Allison Hester

Automotive dealerships are a market that most contract cleaners don't necessarily enjoy. The work is hard, monotonous, and very competitive. More and more dealers are taking the work in-house. Others are outsourcing to companies that charge ridiculously low rates.

Despite the downsides, however, cleaning automotive dealerships has its benefits. The work is generally pretty fast – a simple rinse taking about a minute or less per vehicle. The work is also regular, as the dealers need their vehicles cleaned on a scheduled basis. The work is repetitive – i.e., the same thing over and over and over – which can be nice at times in that it becomes second nature. Finally, at least in some markets, there's good money to be made.

That's why Chris Dubbs of The Wash Wizards in Indianapolis – who stopped cleaning dealerships in ☐00☐ – said he is planning to get back into the dealership business. In ☐00☐, he was getting ☐1.☐0 per car, which e☐uated to around ☐☐☐00 a week for a three-person crew. Each crew consisted of a manager who drove the truck and soaped the cars, then two technicians who rinsed with RO (reverse osmosis☐ water for a spot-free shine. No drying was necessary in his case. "We averaged about ☐000 cars a week, and could wash one every ☐0 to ☐0 seconds," he explained. "We have ☐☐☐ dealerships in Indianapolis and it only takes five big ones to keep a crew busy for the year."

Tim Nunez, owner of Tim's Auto Detailing and Pressure Washing in Virginia, began in the automotive detailing industry 10 years ago, starting his own company in ☐010. His customer base included several car dealerships. In Nunez's case, his crews performed what they referred to as a "lot wash" – i.e., rinsing off the vehicles, drying them by hand or with a blower, touching up tires and shining the windows. His dealerships were small – such as one account that re☐uired cleaning about ☐0 cars two times per month – and he was charging ☐uite a bit more per vehicle.

"I would send a two-man crew out to lot wash – one to rinse cars and one to start the drying process. To fully soap, wash and dry a car might take around eight minutes ☐less than a minute for a simple rinse☐," Nunez explained. ☐or a lot wash, Nunez got around ☐☐.☐0 per car, charging more if there was salt or other extra contaminants that had to be removed,

*Quote from Bryan Henson, Xstream Pressure Washing

such as from a snow storm. For actual individual car washing, he would charge $?0 for cars and $?0 for trucks.

However, Nunez has decided to get out of the car cleaning business completely to focus one-hundred percent on his residential pressure washing business. "It's hard to make good money cleaning a house, then only make $?0 for cleaning a truck," he explained. "When I started in the auto detailing business people would pay more to get their cars cleaned. Now it's not a good market to me."

It has been a great market, however, for Bryan Henson, owner of Xstream Pressure Washing in Oklahoma City. Currently, Henson has ?? weekly accounts, washing an average of ?,000 to ?,?00 vehicles per week at a rate of $1.?? to $?.?0 per car. Soaping cars earns between $? and $10 per vehicle. "It all depends on number of cars and frequency of cleaning."

For rinsing, Henson's team – which ranges from a three- to five-man crew depending on the season – takes about ?0 seconds per car. He does, however, dry the cars by hand, which averages an additional ?? seconds. Soaping vehicles takes between four and seven minutes. "We have it down to a science."

Equipment

When washing car lots, be careful not to damage the cars. "We used a ?000 psi, ? gpm hot water skid, but the pressure was always set to low to prevent damage to the paint and clear coat," explained Nunez.

When it comes to gpm, ?000 is about the maximum you'll need. Otherwise, you'll just

5 Keys to a Successful Carwashing Business
by Bryan Henson, Xstream Pressure Washing, Oklahoma City, OK

Washing cars is not for everyone. You need to be focused. Sure, anyone can wash a car but there are only a select few that can wash ?00 in a day. Becoming successful in car lots took some time, but the systems we now have in place came from these five key elements:

1. Show up: I know it sounds simple, but that what makes us stand out from the other companies. Do what you say your going to do. If you tell them Mondays, be there on Monday. If you tell them every two weeks, don't show up every three. Being reliable and dependable is what they expect. We show up to every lot, every week. We call the lot before we show up just to let them know we are on our way. It also works the other way. If you're not going to be able to make it, you need to call them and let them know. It says a lot about your company.

2. Routing: You can't make it in this business by driving ?0 miles to one lot then ?0 miles to the next. Your drive time needs to be minimal. The closer your lots, the more cars you can wash in a day, putting more money in the bank.

3. Vehicle Placement: You need to be able to wash as many cars as possible without moving. You cannot afford to stop, turn off the machine, move the rig, start the machine and continue to wash. When you do this, you just lost five to seven minutes. By the end of the day, you lost a lot you could have washed, costing you money.

4. DI Tank or RO Water: DI stands for deionized water and RO stands for reverse osmosis. These systems convert regular tap water to spot-free water. Either one of these systems is a must to do car lots. Washing with regular tap water will hurt you in the long run, either by slowing you down or by damaging the car windows and paint.

5. Dryer: Saved the best for last. The person/persons you have drying the cars is what keeps the lot managers happy. They expect no spots or streaks on the car. It's about the appearance when it's dry. You need to take the time to find the right people to dry the cars. They need to be very picky. If they tell you need to rewash the car then do it. Without them there is no way you will make it in the car lot side of the pressure washing industry. In my opinion, they need to be the highest paid employees. The dryers are the ones who keep the accounts on the books. This one key alone is what builds the loyalty between you and the lot.

waste water. "Use wide fan nozzles to cover faster and idle your machines on low," Dubbs added. "This eats less gas and water but effectively cleans the car."

Dubbs cautioned about watching out for chipped paint on used cars. "You could blow off damaged paint pretty easily. But we've never had issues with a customer. I think the people who damage things are the guys that wipe down vehicles with dirty rags and put swirl marks in the paint."

Keeping cars spot-free is imperative, so most contractors use either RO or DI water. Henson says he rents his DI tanks, and exchanges them out for new ones when needed.

Another tip: "Try and keep your hoses short. Fifty to 00 feet is nice to get in and out between cars faster. Move your truck often to keep up," added Dubbs. "We also liked to use different color hoses to keep tangles down to a minimum among the three guys."

When selecting soap, it's important not to skimp on quality. "Use the best soap for the job. A good soap will lift dirt off the surface and give the car a shine," said Dubbs. He also pointed out that you should go back and check after every 10 cars or so to make sure the rinse is not missing soap and leaving streaks.

Work Smart

One of the things Dubbs did not like about cleaning car dealerships was that it gets really hot on the asphalt during the summer. "I recommend rotating one guy out every hour for a break to keep the guys fresh and hydrated. The other two guys can keep working so you don't have downtime."

If done correctly, Dubbs said you should be able to make about 00 percent profit. "And finally, it's not a glamorous job, but have fun and stay professional. Remember you are on a multi- million dollar lot in most cases so wear uniforms and don't let the guys play around."

Henson agreed. "Don't make it a job. Have fun with it. Keep an open mind and watch what other services they outsource. Detail, window tint, PDR, etc. You can open these doors and make more profits."

by Steel Eagle, www.SteelEagle.com

Prevent and identify possible damage before it happens! Save man hours and employee strain when detailing...

Hard to reach or see areas of vehicles are often overlooked and or neglected when washing them. The "out of site – out of mind" proverb comes into play. But what is the ultimate cost of this neglect? First, increased repair costs, and second, premature oxidation, rust and wear to the vehicle.

How does this relate to auto detailers and dealerships?

Detailers: Servicing your customers better than your competition is what will keep them coming back. Having the tools that will demonstrate you have an edge and can clean their vehicle better will also allow charging a premium due to the extra value you bring to them.

Dealerships: When taking in a trade in, removing the built-up debris on the undercarriage is necessary to assess the value and mechanical soundness of the vehicle. That way the dealership can repair any hidden damage before selling the vehicle and chancing their reputation with an immediate breakdown. It will also make the vehicle that much more attractive to prospective buyers and increase the perceived value.

So how do you do the job?

An undercarriage cleaner is the tool that will most effectively do the job. They are designed with spinners and arms with nozzles that point upwards to spray debris from underneath a vehicle when it is on the ground.

What should you look for in an undercarriage cleaner?

Different undercarriage cleaners have different features. Some of the most important to look for are

• **Spray Bars and Nozzles** – The most effective undercarriage cleaners have four spray bars with two different types of nozzles two 0 and two 1 . The reason you want to look for this nozzle combination is that it is designed to both cut caked on debris (with the 0°) and then sweep it away (with the 15°).

• **Low Profile** – Make sure the undercarriage cleaner you are looking at has the lowest possible minimum clearance so you are able to fit it under the lowest vehicles you can. There are models that are capable of down to 5½".

• **Adjustability and Flexibility** – You want a unit that can be adjusted to fit the operator and is effectively hinged to reach far under the vehicle. Specifically, check for handle height adjustability and a lower pivot point that allows the handle to drop all the way to the ground. Having a tool fitted to you will increase efficiency and reduce operator fatigue.

• **Cleaning Power** – Insist on an undercarriage capable of no less than 4000PSI max. pressure and water temperature ratings of 250°.

• **Cleaning path** – The larger the cleaning path the faster you will get the job done. Don't compromise for under 20".

• **Durability** – Keep an eye out for a quality build. Look for things like heavy-duty swivels, steel construction, powder coat finishes, stainless steel spray bars and nozzles and finally made in the USA attention to detail.

Steel Eagle continues to build the best undercarriage cleaner on the market. In addition to our standard model we have options for all kinds of under cleaning applications. See our undercarriage cleaner in action at www.steeleagle.com/index.cfm?page=ptype_results&category_id=&home_id=&mode=cat&cat=.htm

We understand your time is important and you need the correct product for your application. Take a minute to discuss your particular cleaning situations with your Steel Eagle sales person. They can recommend the perfect tools utilizing the correct accessories for the job. No matter what you are cleaning, Steel Eagle has a system that will do the job with ease and speed.

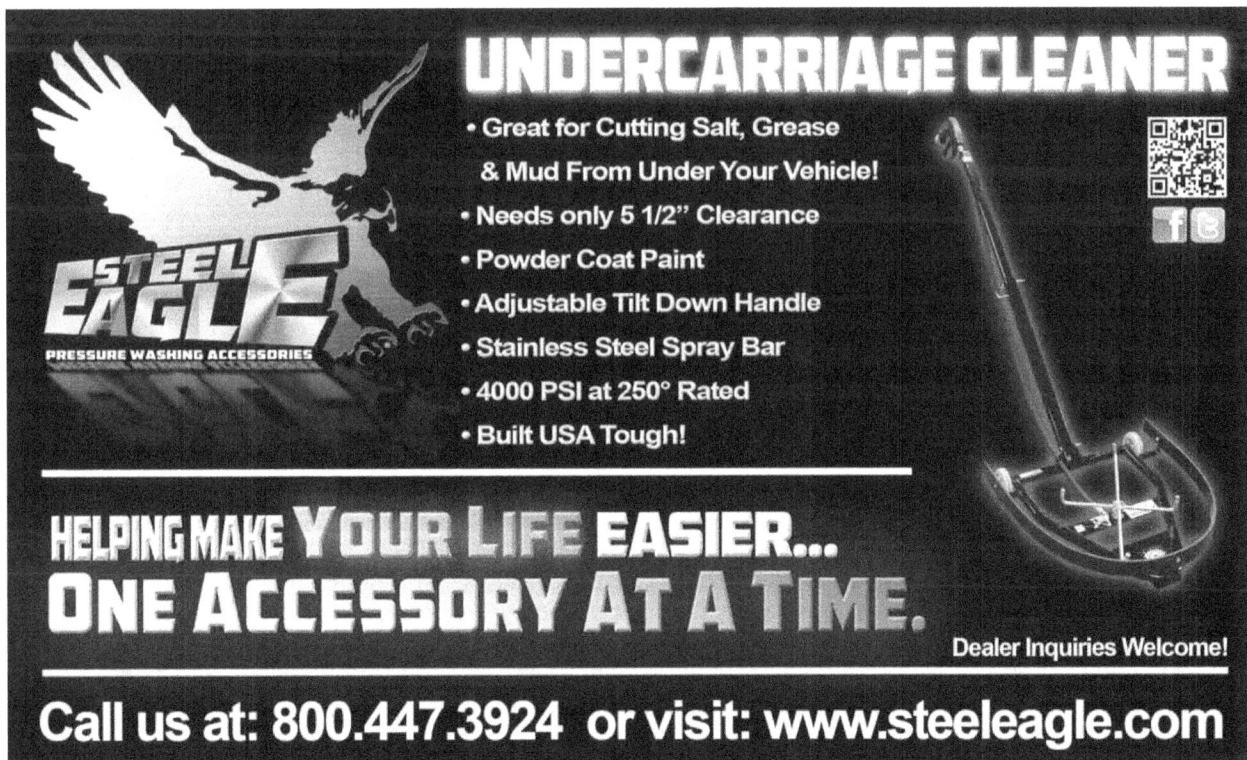

What TO Do (and NOT to Do) with Your Facebook Business Page

by Anya Curry, Ambidextrous Services, www.UniqueAmb.com

It may have come up once or twice. Or a hundred times. We all know you HAVE to have a Facebook page for your cleaning business, but does anyone actually get any business from it? Does the number of fans make a difference? Does it really help if half of those fans – or more, let's be honest – are really just other cleaners across the country?

It's okay to admit you have no idea what you're doing. The fact is, most businesses on Facebook don't! Which is the main reason why there have been some changes. Let's start with a few "Don'ts", a few "Do's" and a few tricks that don't cost much.

Don't Do It!

You should, by now, know who your target audience is. You should also know, by now, how to conduct yourself professionally in front of that said audience. So why the heck would you behave differently on your business Facebook page??!?

DON'T:

1. Post inappropriate content. Seems obvious, but...not so much.

2. Post meme's. If there were a rating for lowest quality photos, these would score a zero. Save them for your personal account.

3. Make a "Person" out of your business. Take the next step and make an actual business page.

4. Post negative comments about a customer, job, or employee.

5. Post rebuttals to any negative reviews or customer comments.

To some of you, the above may be obvious and basic. However, one or more of the above happens EVERY DAY on Facebook. There are personal and business page separations for a reason.

Do It, Do It, Do It

Positive interactions are what we are all hoping for on a Facebook page. Here are a few items you should check off your social media to-do list.

DO:

1. Add a profile picture and cover photo. These do not need to be professional graphics. A great before and after photo, or a shot of your crew doing a great job will suffice.

2. Completely and accurately fill out your business information. Utilize the "About" section for short and long descriptions to get more targeted and in depth.

3. Add a Like or link from your website to your Facebook page.

4. Search for and "Like" other industry websites or Facebook pages.

5. Organize your photos into galleries. Add descriptions and links to these galleries as well.

6. Add descriptions or captions to your photos.

7. Invite customers, friends, family AND business associates to like your page.

Organizing your content and filling in all the gaps will not only make your page more complete, it will start affecting search. If you could get your website AND your facebook page ranking in your town, how much would that be worth?

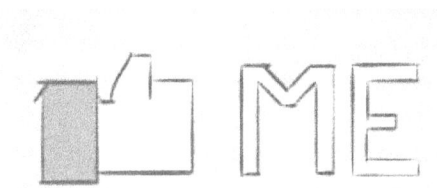

Facebook Page Fans

Does having your uncle Stevie in Michigan, which happens to be states away, really help with your facebook page? How about the 10 guys who are in the same association as you that own pressure washing businesses? These aren't your customers, but you were thinking the more likes the better. Is that really a good thing?

The short answer is *yes*. I'm sure you've noticed that everything you post doesn't reach your entire fan base. In fact, you may see that pesky little notice under your posts that says "__ reached" when you actually have 1__ fans. WHAT?? That's because facebook has decided that they are not only the god of social media, but they will also decide what content to show, and to whom. This is based roughly on a few items:

1. The number of fans you have.
2. The amount of times your posts have been "hidden" in the past.
3. How many times your posts have "engaged" users.
4. The relevance of your post to your fans interactions.

In other words, you have to be interesting. Not only that, you have to show facebook that you have something interesting in the first place, in order for your fans to find it interesting.

Dizzy yet? Don't despair! This is where you can leverage the fan base you have built, even if it is mostly other cleaning professionals.

• **Post photos.** Before and afters are very effective. Photos of your crew working or your rig at a job are great!

• **When you post a photo, write some text about it in the post.** Tell your users what's happening, and where. Tag people, places, and locations.

• **Use hashtags.** I know, I know. Just do it! It makes your posts searchable.

• **Tell your customers that you are posting their before & afters on your Facebook page.** People inevitably want to see it. If you do email follow ups, send them the link.

The more interactions you get, the higher your relevancy. The higher your relevancy, the more people your posts go out to. There is a snowball effect. But it can go backwards too, so consistency is key.

Turn Interactions Into $$$

By establishing your facebook page, you brand your business. Social media is the most used medium IN THE WORLD. Think of it as your outlet to speak to the masses. We've covered a lot, so stay tuned for our next article about advertising on facebook:

1. Create News Feed Advertisements
2. Create & Track Facebook Promotions
3. Use Your Customer Email List to "Clone" Your Customers on Facebook

Anya Curry is the owner of Ambidextrous Services, which specializes in designing websites for the mobile cleaning industry. She is the wife of Alex Curry, a second generation power washer and owner of ARC Powerwashing in Raleigh, NC. Visit wwww.UniqueAmb.com to learn more.

Introducing THE MOLE & JERSEY SHOW

by Allison Hester

The Mole and Jersey Show is a new online talk show gaining momentum among cleaning industry members. The show is produced by two professional window cleaners, Michael Mole ("Mole" of Mole Cleaning Services and Josh Cronin ("Jersey") of SI Window Washing. "Mole and Jersey." Each 0(ish)-minute episode includes a few regular segments—a product review (i.e., "Jersey's Junk"), a Top list, and a "fail of the week," plus a lot of banter. Mole and Jersey is fun, informative and worth giving a watch.

I recently interviewed both Mole and Jersey, separately, about their new endeavor. Here's what they had to say:

Q. How did you guys meet?
Mole: Jersey Josh and I met in NOLA in January 01. I had viewed some previous videos he'd made, so Jersey was a bit of a star to me. I asked for his autograph, and it was B‿‿s from then.
Jersey It was fate, really. We have talked almost daily since that NOLA.

Q. I get the "Mole" part of the title, but Josh, you're from Wisconsin. So what's with "Jersey?" Is that where you're originally from?
Jersey: No, not from Jersey. I just have super gelled hair so some friends of mine call me "Jersey." Plus "The Mole and Wisconsin Show" sounds terrible.

Q. Why did you decide to make the show?
Mole: I love sports talk radio, and can watch/listen to it for hours. I have always wished for something similar that touched on the industry that I obviously care a lot about. Josh and I had kicked an idea around over a year ago. Then, a few months ago he had a dream about the show, fully formulated. He called and pitched it to me, and I was sold.
Jersey: The industry is lacking an awesomely amazing life changing show. Someone had to fill the void.

Q. Do either of you have a background in making videos?
Jersey: I made a series for one of the window cleaning forums before, but neither of us have any REAL video talent.

Q. Does anyone pay you to produce the show?
Mole: We own the show 100 percent, and we have several sponsors for the show. Shout out to Glass Renu, Responsibid and WCR! We want to be able to be 100 percent honest, so having

(the annual New Orleans networking event put on by Thad Eckhoff of the PWRA.)

100 percent control is important to us.

Q. *How do you pick which products to feature?*

Jersey: We pick because we use or love the product. We try to do "different" products, not your run-of-the-mill kind of stuff.

Q. *Do you ever anticipate reviewing a product you don't like?*

Mole: Yep. I have one on my desk to cover at some point very soon.

Jersey: That's probably something we will do. We want to be fair to everyone, however, and almost everything has something positive that can be said about it.

Q. *Do you spend much time planning the show, or do you mostly just wing it?*

Mole: Plan it.
Jersey: Wing it.

Q. *How do you pick the weekly Top 5?*

Jersey: The University of Wisconsin has authorized us to use their highly advanced super computer which comprises the awesomeness of owning a business and prints the lists out for us.

Mole: We stare at each other and say, "Well, what do you think? Well no, I think this is ▢▢ and that's ▢▢."

Q. *How do you get your fails of the week?*

Mole: Our viewers submit them to us on Facebook or through email at theguys@moleandjersey.com

Jersey: They are easy...With so many stupid people in this world, they find us.

Q. *I know your fans send you swag items to wear/show off during the show. What's the favorite item you've received so far?*

Jersey: The hats from Dave Carroll. They have our persona stitched into them. But we are always open to someone else taking best swag!

Q. *Michael, I've tried and tried to figure it out.... .What do the decorative letters on the wall behind you spell?*

Mole: The Internet at my office isn't high quality enough to shoot the show, so I record in my son's room at home. It spells Zeke.

Q. *OK, let's talk about the dancing "mole"... is it even a mole? Really?*

Mole: The dancing mole is something that we can't talk about much. We tried to get the Geico gecko, but it turns out he doesn't do dancing videos, and we knew that's what we wanted. Gecko's agent put us in touch with our dancing rodent.

Jersey: This is our little secret, but it's not really a mole. It's actually a guinea pig. Either way it shows that we're not real serious...and we lie.

Q. *How do you find time to run a cleaning business and still produce a 30-minute show regularly?*

Jersey: Well that's the difficult part. It's hard, but a lot of fun. Being that I don't do field work, it's easier for me than Michael, but we make it happen.

Mole: It's a lot of fun, so we make time for it. You will always accomplish the things that are important to you.

Q. *Finally, are you just doing this for fun or is it something you hope will make you rich and famous?*

Jersey: Well, we definitely like the chase of making a buck, but as cheesy as it sounds, helping someone is pretty cool also. That is how Michael and I met after all.

To check out the online Mole and Jersey online, visit their website at www.MoleandJersey.com.

*NOLA is the annual New Orleans Contractor Networking Event.

eClean Magazine

PWNA Announces 2014 Vision

One of the biggest surprises for October's PWNA Annual Convention attendees was the genuine willingness of its members – particularly, its board members – to openly share their knowledge and experiences in order to help others "build the dream."

"People are often amazed that we really hold no secrets," explained PWNA President John Nearon. "That's because we honestly want to see our members succeed in this industry,"

In the coming year, the PWNA Board of Directors (BOD) plans to build on the excitement and positive energy generated during the 201 annual convention. The BOD's vision is to expand member benefits in ways that build on the organization's primary strengths providing education, training, certification and networking opportunities to help member build strong foundations for their companies.

Specifically, the PWNA is planning to implement several new benefits for its members, which will include

- **Online Certifications:** While the BOD believes that initial certifications need to be completed in a classroom setting, certified members can now gain their PWNA recertification online. "That way, members can keep their certifications without having the expenses of traveling to the PWNA Annual Convention, if their schedule or circumstances prohibit them from doing so," said Nearon.

And online re-certifications are already a hit among the PWNA membership. "It's really starting to happen," Nearon added. "or example, we've had five people complete their online recertifications over the past two weeks."

Enhanced Website – The PWNA website will be getting a facelift this year as new resources are implemented to make www.PWNA.org more interactive and beneficial for members.

- **Online Product Purchases** – As part of the new website, the PWNA will begin selling a variety of materials and items online.
- **Regional Training Sessions** – "We plan to conduct some regional training, like the round tables we used to do, so that we can get out and be closer to our membership," Nearon explained. "We will be working with our vendors and membership to determine where and when those events should take place."
- **Membership Newsletter** – "We want to keep members informed of changes in business practices, technical innovations, networking opportunities, and other information that is important to them," Nearon explained. "The uarterly newsletter is just another method for us to share in our general desire to bring value to our members through networking."
- **Environmental Advocacy** – The PWNA is planning to bring on board an environmental consultant position to help answer member uestions as well as keep the BOD abreast of changing policies.

"It truly is the intention of the PWNA to provide its members with essential tools that will help them responsibly build their businesses and turn their dreams into a reality," Nearon concluded. "We are excited to see where the BOD's vision leads us in the coming year."

To learn more about the PWNA visit their website www.PWNA.org.

NEW – Gas Powered Water Recovery System

Become EPA compliant and responsibly recover your wash water as you clean.
Automatic pump out…no need to stop and dump the collection tanks or worry about the tanks overfilling.
It is ideal for facilities maintenance contractors who need to collect wash water or for restoration contractors who need to pick up water after a fire or flood and need to have their rig parked far away. The vacuum system is gas powered, requiring only electricity for the transfer pumps. Unique to this RGV is the ability to have a self contained system, just plug the transfer pumps into your Hydro Tek SC or SCU Series skid generator.

- Recovers up to 25gpm at 350'
- Debris filter and air filter for protection of pumps and blower motor
- Light, non-corrosive vacuum separation tanks
- Small footprint with large fuel tank integrated into frame base
- 50 state CARB and EPA emissions certified

Watch the video: http://www.hydrotek.us/rec-hydrovac-gasvac.htm

For current Specials go to www.hydrotek.us click 'What's new'

Stop by your local distributor and ask to try the NEW RGV40 Gas Vacuum

Brilliant Design, Tough on Grime

Manufacturing pressure washers and wash accessories for over 25 years.
Visit website or call for a distributor near you. Distributor inquiries welcome.

www.hydrotek.us   (800) 274-9376

PWNA Vendor Profile

by Allison Hester

Dultmeier Sales is not your average cleaning equipment distributor or manufacturer. With two facilities, three divisions, □□0 vendors lines, and a □□0□ page catalog, Dultmeier truly is a one-stop shop for customers from a broad range of industries.

Dultmeier was founded as an agricultural equipment manufacturing company in the 1□□0s in Manning, Iowa, by John R. Hansen, and has remained a family-owned business for nearly a century. In the 1□□0s, Dultmeier Sales was opened in Omaha, Nebraska. At that point, the company began carrying other agricultural lines and eventually the manufacturing arm of the company went away.

In 1□□0, Mike Hansen – the grandson of founder John Hansen – joined the company, opening a new washing division, which focuses on three primary markets□ carwash, truck wash and pressure washing. "A recession hit in the early □0s, and we decided to diversify," he explained.

Dultmeier is defined as a "fluid handling house," and high pressure equipment fit into the company's structure. "We handle pumps, valves, hose, nozzles – anything that is used with fluids. We already knew these products for the agricultural sector. We took the same concepts and put it into the high pressure side."

As time passed and the wash division grew, Dultmeier began assembling pressure washers and taking on new lines. "Soon we built a completely different catalog with high pressure components," Hansen explained.

The Best Catalog in the Industry
Today, Dultmeier Sales has three specific divisions□the wash division, which makes up about □0 percent of sales□the agricultural divison, which accounts for around □0□ in sales□and the industrial□government division, which makes up the remaining □0 percent. They employ □0 staff members at their two facilities – their Omaha, Nebraska headquarters, and their second sales center in Davenport, Iowa.

The Dultmeier catalog was the brainchild of Walter Hansen in the 1□□0s – "back when very few companies even had catalogs." Now Dultmeier publishes three full catalogs, one for each division. The □01□ wash catalog is about □□0 pages□the agricultural catalog is over □00. Each year, Dultmeier sends out about □0,000 catalogs around the world. "We have an employee whose sole job is working on the catalogs all year long," Hansen added. "The □01□ catalogs are at the printer and he is already working on □01□."

In addition to the mere size of the catalogs, Dultmeier prides itself on the thoroughness of the information each catalog contains. "We try to provide complete information on product specifications and aim to answer any questions a customer may have right there in the catalog itself. We also work to ensure that we have very clear pictures of each item as well."

These days, all the information in the catalogs can also be found on Dultmeier's website, www.Dultmeier.com. "Customer can easily order online, check pricing, check out specifications and so on," Hansen explained.

eClean Magazine

Dultmeier's Corporate Headquarters in Omaha, Nebraska

around ☐0 to ☐0 truck shipments a day. "Around ☐☐ percent of our orders ship the same day," he adds. ☐inally, the wash division accounts for about ☐1☐ million in sales each year.

Additionally, "any updates to our catalog go live to our website very ☐uickly."

A Manufacturing Distributor

Dultmeier began as a manufacturing company, and while its focus is primarily on distribution these days, the company has not completely abandoned those early roots. "We're a distributor first, but we also build our own power wash e☐uipment, pumping stations, RO units, and so on," Hansen explained.

Additionally, Dultmeier regularly custom builds e☐uipment for customers. "Someone may call and say they want this pump instead of that one, or a different engine than what comes with the unit. We can do that."

☐inally, the custom-design also extends into markets with niche needs. ☐or example, Dultmeier has built a number of specially-designed systems for animal shelters. "It started when a local humane society here in Omaha called us about helping them design a washing system for their new building," Hansen said. "Now we've built them for shelters all around the country. We've never marketed to that industry☐they just came to us through word of mouth. But we have a lot of niche markets like that."

A One-Stop Shop

One reason customers keep coming back to Dultmeier is that they do carry so many different types of products. "Whereas other companies are primarily selling high pressure e☐uipment, we carry it all. We have such a broad range of products that we can handle pretty much anything customers bring our way, from start to finish."

To give you an idea of Dultmeier's volume, the company keeps about ☐ million items in inventory this time of year, including around ☐0,000 line items. During their busiest season, Dultmeier sends about ☐00 ☐PS packages and

End User Support

While Dultmeier does have customers who are distributors, the biggest percentage of its wash customers are the end users – be it an animal shelter, a carwash owner, or a power washing contractor.

As mentioned, in addition to its catalog listings, Dultmeier will does a lot of custom building for its customers. That also includes private labeling or generic labeling when re☐uested. They also have a full service department to work on downed e☐uipment.

Because the end user is Dultmeier's target audience, they support a number of contractor organizations, including the Power Washers of North America ☐PWNA☐. "We believe in supporting our customers, and that includes the members of the PWNA," Hansen concluded.

To learn more about Dultmeier or to order a copy of their catalog, visit their website: www.Dultmeier.com.

New PWNA Members

Marshall ☐rance, Hogwash

Kenneth Webb, West Texas Hoods

Trevor Smith, BGE Service ☐ Supply

Eduardo Garcia, Blue Shark Power Washer

Paul Worthington, Paramount Cleaning Pty Ltd.

Johathan Thiessen, Jet Pressure Wash, LLC

Blane Odom, OLO Clean

Kyle Pect, ERMC

Patric LeLievre, BluByopowerwashing LLC

JANUARY 30 & 31, 2014 • SOUTH POINT HOTEL • LAS VEGAS, NV
Register now for FREE at www.iceexpo.org

What's So Cool About ICE?

FREE SEMINARS — $2,500 worth of seminars for **FREE!** Gain the knowledge necessary to expand and market your detailing business without the cost.

DEMOS — See live demos of the newest products and techniques by industry experts.

PRODUCT GIVEAWAYS — Pre-register NOW for your chance to win great prizes donated by some of the best manufacturers in the industry. Visit www.iceexpo.org/giveaways for more info.

What Are The FREE Seminars?

Thursday

More Money. More Time. (Part 1) – Lisa Wagner & Mark Kennedy
Cypress Room

Cleaning For Health – John Sales
Cypress Room

Advanced Spot & Stain Class – Taf Baig
Cypress Room

Are You Ready For Rug Cleaning? – Aaron Groseclose
Show Floor Stage

Establishing a Stronghold in the Industry – Paul Brown
Cypress Room

Spot Dyeing (with contest) – Melody David
Show Floor Stage

Live Music Featuring: *The Day Trippers*
Show Floor Stage

Friday

Sharpening the Impact of your Website – Jeff Cross
Cypress Room

How to Make Big Money Cleaning Little Apartments – Jerry Valentine
Cypress Room

Friday (cont.)

How To Build Your Auto Detailing Business Brand – Nick Vacco
Cypress Room

Truckmount Maintenance 101 – Les Jones
Show Floor Stage

Benefits of the IICRC – Craig Jasper
Cypress Room

Detailing Made Simple – Tony Goren
Cypress Room

Natural Stone Services Will Instantly Increase Your Revenue – Rob Fairfield
Show Floor Stage

Getting Into Restoration- The High Profit Side of Cleaning – Annissa Coy
Cypress Room

Trivia
Show Floor Stage

Grand Prize & Exhibitor Awards Announced
Show Floor Stage

More Money. More Time. (Part 2) – Lisa Wagner & Mark Kennedy
Cypress Room

LIVE MUSIC FEATURING:

THE DAY TRIPPERS — a Beatles tribute band

Who Will Be There?

& more joining constantly!

ICE EXPO: The Coolest Trade Show in the Industry

January 30-31, Las Vegas, Nevada

by Allison Hester

This January, there's a cool new cleaning show coming to Las Vegas – the ICE Expo – and it's a different kind of show all around.

ICE – which stands for International Cleaning Experts – is being developed by cleaning industry members, for cleaning industry members. Specifically, due to the growing crossover in cleaning specialties, the ICE Expo is targeting four major cleaning fields—auto detailing, carpet cleaning, janitorial, and restoration services.

"Industry feedback has shown that a lot of companies are either crossing over into these multiple markets, or are wanting to cross over, but having to attend several events each year is expensive, time consuming, and frustrating," explained Gianna Hammer. "We believe the ICE Expo is the solution."

Specifically, ICE has tackled several common problems with other events:

1. Cost – again, rather than having to attend several separate events around the country and throughout the year, attendees will be able to learn about these four industries under one roof – and they can do it free of charge. Participants who register by December 1 can attend for free. Also, the hotel fees are minimal – averaging per night.

But contractors aren't the only ones who will be saving money. ICE Expo exhibitors can participate for a "fraction of the cost" of other events, according to Hammer. "That allows for companies that might not otherwise be able to afford to exhibit to participate and network in the ICE Expo trade show."

2. Hours – "A lot of trade shows host odd hours, making it hard to participate," said Hammer. The ICE Expo will neither begin too early nor run too late, allowing participants time to enjoy Vegas and still attend every aspect of the Expo. Seminars start at 0 both days, and end at on Thursday and 0 on riday. The trade show floor will be open from 10 to both days.

3. Time of Year – the winter is a slower season for most contract cleaners, making January "the perfect time for an event like this one," Hammer explained. Additionally, the Expo will finish up just prior to Super Bowl weekend. "With our great hotel rates, attendees can plan to stay in town and experience the Super Bowl in Vegas."

The Seminars

ICE attendees can participate in all of the educational seminars free of charge, and the show will offer a full schedule of programs covering a variety of topics. "There should be something for everyone," Hammer explained.

Thursday, February 12

8:30 – 10 a.m., More Money, More Time (Part One) – Lisa Wagner, owner of one of the nation's top rug wash and repair facilities, and Mark Kennedy, business consultant and author of "Secrets of the Carpet Cleaning Super Giants," will show attendees how to get your cleaning business into the ultimate position in the market – i.e., how to be the higher priced company that is in highest demand because you are known as the best in your field. Part two will continue riday afternoon from - 0.

10:00 – 10:30 am, Cleaning for Health – John Sales of the National Institute of Professional Carpet Cleaners will teach how to maximize profits by cleaning for health, giving insight into the latest technology and chemicals that help you clean wall to wall like never before. Learn how to remove environmental, biological, dry, and grimy soil and how to protect against spills and stains.

10:30 am - 1:30 pm, Advanced Spot & Stain Class: IICRC instructor Taf Baig shows you everything you ever wanted to know about how chemistry applies to carpet cleaning. Learn how to take out any stain you will ever encounter. Walk away with an understanding of the chemistry and advanced techniues in order to remove spots using only four products.

1:00 – 2:00 pm., Aaron Groseclose

1:30 - 2:30 pm, Establishing a Stronghold in the Industry, presented by Paul Brown

2:00 – 3:00 p.m., Spot Dyeing (with Contest), presented by Melody Davis

At p.m., the Expo will conclude for the day with live music featuring Beatles' tribute band, The Day Trippers. Hammer explained, "The day Trippers will be a fun way to end the first day on a high note. We are really excited about them playing."

Friday, January 31

8:30 – 10 a.m.: Sharpen the Impact of Your Website: In this fast-paced, one-hour session by Cleanfax Senior Editor Jeff Cross, you will learn specific website and search engine optimization strategies that will help you build a more successful business. Get ready to look "under the hood" of what really runs a website and to get the attention of the search engines – especially Google. A bonus section on smart social media practices is included in this presentation. Everyone goes home with ideas they can easily implement for immediate results.

10:00 – 11:00 a.m.: Make Big Money Cleaning Little Apartments – Discover how to consistently and predictably add an extra $100,000 per van to your annual income by cleaning apartment carpets. Jerry Valentine, owner of Tri-County Carpet Care and Tri-County Carpet Supply will teach you how to pick profitable properties, how to get the contracts, and how to develop the skills necessary to maximize your income from apartments by doing repairs and restoration services. Many cleaners think that apartments aren't worth the effort due to low prices. Jerry will teach you how to successfully grow your business and reduce your cash flow worries by adding apartments to your client list.

11:00 a.m. – Noon: How to Build Your Auto Detailing Brand, presented by Nick Vacco

11:00 a.m. – Noon: Truckmount Maintenance 101, presented by Les Jones

Noon – 1:00 p.m.: Benefits of the IIRC, presented by Craig Jasper

1:00 p.m. – 2:00 p.m.: Detailing Made Simple, presented by Tony Green

1:00 — 3:00 pm. Natural Stone Services Will Instantly Increase Your Revenue – You have no idea the lost opportunities and revenue you pass by or walk over when natural stone is not part of your repertoire. Come learn from Rob Fairchild of Stone Pro several add-on services that natural stone can offer your business. All services have a very small learning curve, take little to no capital, and pay good money.

2:00 – 3:00 p.m.: Getting Into Restoration, the High Profit Side of Cleaning, presented by Annissa Coy

Trade Show, Demos and Giveaways

While the seminars are taking place, the trade show floor will also be open featuring a variety of products and services from the industry's leading providers.

Additionally, the ICE Expo has set up another cool offering – the demo pavilion – which will be located in the center of the trade show floor. "This is where attendees can actually test out equipment and do side-by-side comparisons," said Hammer.

Each attendee will automatically be entered into a drawing for a number of giveaways. However, there will also be three grand prize packages—one for detailing, one for carpet cleaning, and one for janitorial services. The Expo will conclude —minus the second half of the More Money, More Time presentation—with drawings for the prizes.

"Currently. we've received over $0,000 in giveaways," said Hammer. "These are huge giveaways too. Companies have been really gracious with their donations."

To learn more about the ICE Expo, or to register, visit the event website: www.ICEExpo.org. Register by December 31 to attend for free.

What are you REALLY going to do in 2014?

by Tom Grandy, Grandy & Associates, www.GrandyAssociates.com

So how was 2013 for you? Sales up? Sales down? Profits up? Profits down? What were your expectations for 2013, and were they met? We have all heard the definition of insanity – doing the same thing over and over again while expecting different results. Does that sound like you? Sure, you worked really hard in 2013, but what did you do "differently" that would have achieved different results?

Chances are good that you attended a seminar or two last year or maybe attended a national and/or state convention. Many others participated in online training or webinars. Some of us even invested in new software that, for whatever reason, never got installed, much less used. That's right, you invested significant amounts of time and money last year in education, but the bottom line was the same as the year before – nothing really changed. So what's going to make 2014 different?

Create The Plan

If things are truly going to be different this year the first step is to have a plan. What do you want to be different by this time next year? Do you want to increase profits by $20,000? If so, what's your plan to make that happen? Maybe you want customer service to improve. What specifically needs to change and what will you do differently to make that happen? Perhaps you want to start a maintenance agreement program or significantly increase the number of maintenance-agreement customers you currently have. What steps will need to be taken for that to happen?

Nothing will happen until you create specific goals and then document the steps to the plan – on paper. My suggestion would be to list three or four specific things you want to accomplish for the year. Then do the following:

1. **Write down your specific overall goal or goals.** Determine a date that you want the goal completed.

2. **Detail the specific steps.** Map out what has to happen first, second, third, etc. and put a time table on each step. For example, step one will take three weeks, step two five days, step three will

take a month, etc.

. Once all the steps are detailed, look at your desired completion date and then look at your total timeline. This will tell you what your "Start Date" needs to be in order to stay on task.

Ok, your plan is in place. Now it's time to work the plan. Does someone need to be called? Do you need input from employees? Perhaps something needs to be purchased. What is the next step in your plan and what needs to happen to be sure you stay on schedule? You have the detailed plan in front of you, so follow it! Remember if nothing changes chances are your will be in the same position next year.

Accountability is the Key

Unless you are a person of tremendous discipline, I doubt much happens "differently" in your life without some kind of accountability. If you told little Johnny to make his bed each day, but you never went to his room to see if he made it, I suspect before long the bed would be left unmade.

Nearly all of us need some sort of accountability for real change to take place in our lives. That is why people pay personal trainers and join Weight Watchers. With accountability comes change – real change. If someone isn't watching over your shoulder to be sure things get done, the daily fires consume our time and no real change takes place. I would suggest you select someone inside your company to hold you accountable. Meet with that person for 1 minutes each week at a specific time, on a specific day. During the short meeting, review your specific progress against stated goals. If there is no one in the office to meet with, then accountability might mean meeting with a fellow contractor for lunch each week for fellowship, networking together and, yes, to review your progress. Without being accountable to someone, little gets accomplished.

Celebrate the Victories

Now for the fun part. Celebrate your victories! Everyone likes to be rewarded for doing a good job. You are no different. If you have someone outside your company that you are accountable to and you meet your goal, take them to dinner, with their spouse. If it's a company goal, like selling 00 more maintenance agreements, than take the whole company to dinner, a show or a ball game. Celebrating victories is much like the carrot held in front of the donkey. You will keep moving towards the incentive until the goal is accomplished.

Do yourself a favor. Pick at least one goal, one thing you want to accomplish this year. Design the plan to reach that goal and be ready to celebrate by this time next year.

Need some help setting goals? One solution might be for Grandy & Associates to perform a two-day Company Overview. We will model your company, set specific goals and if you wish, will hold you accountable for meeting those goals. If you just need a kick start to get you moving then you might want to consider attending one of our three-day Basic Business Boot Camps! Go to www.GrandyAssociates.com to learn more.

Sales 101 for Cleaning Firms

by Rick Meehan
Vice President of Marko Janitorial Supply, www.MarkoInc.com

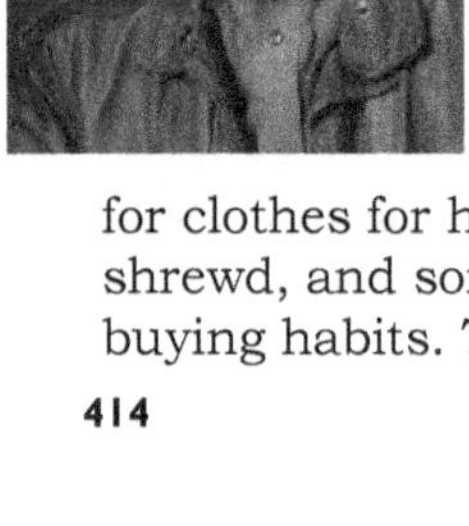

To talk about selling in the Industry of Clean, first we must understand the act of purchasing. We all buy things in order to survive, especially clothes and food. That's why we're labeled consumers. Even the most stalwart purchasing agent cannot make better decisions than a mom on a tight budget shopping for clothes for her kids. Both are tough, shrewd, and sometimes even logical in their buying habits. Their decisions are based on series of complex emotional stimuli. Sounds forbidding, doesn't it?

Let's put it another way—my wife is cagey when it comes to spending money. She shops for the best price, haggles if possible to get the price down, but she doesn't buy junk no matter what the price.

There is nothing simplistic about the act of purchasing, yet most cleaning contractors take a simplistic approach to representing themselves. If we rely solely on low prices to sell our services, not only do we lose profits, we lose sales. Pricing is not the primary factor in the purchasing thought process – emotions are.

What does all this sales mumbo jumbo have to do with cleaning? Not one single thing unless you consider that without sales there is no cleaning to be done. All businesses must sell products and services to survive, even non-profits – all except government agencies. They get propped up by everyone's taxes no matter how bad their service. The rest of us have to do what we can to stay in business. No one props us up artificially. We make sales, provide good service, or we fail, unless we are deemed "too big to fail" by the government, which then pumps us up with taxpayer money. I'd like to shake the hand of the owner of that cleaning business! Therefore understanding the dynamics of making a new customer is the most important thing any cleaning business can do.

Shopping and haggling are emotional actions, which means our five senses must come into play every time we buy something. Our intangible six sense of intuition may play a large role too. Think about the last time you purchased a really great steak at the grocery store. You looked for the best color on the meat, tested the air around the meat counter for freshness with your nose, felt the package for softness, and listened to the crinkle of the wrapping. The only thing you couldn't do was taste the meat, yet I expect your mouth watered at the thought of doing so! Your intuition even told you the meat would be moist and tender after cooking, although you couldn't know that for fact. You convinced yourself based on the emotional responses from all these sensations that you needed to buy that meat. Only then did logic take a stand.

At last, it gets down to reasoning. Can you afford it? Should you afford it? After all, a good porterhouse steak is rather expensive. Is it worth the price for that moment of palatability? You savor the taste in your mind again to make sure you really want it. Sometimes you do, sometimes you don't. I'll bet it's really hard to put that package back in the meat counter, though. Logic must take over in order to refuse a purchase that in every other way has been decided upon. You must tell yourself firmly, "I can't afford it. I don't really need this. I need something else instead." A good salesperson can identify this final moment of indecision.

Let's continue with the porterhouse steak example. A good butcher would be watching for signs that a customer might be hesitant. "Putting together a special meal tonight? Ah, going for a treat are you? It sure would be good with a baked potato, wouldn't it?" Questions like these, empathetic in nature, are designed to keep the customer on track in the final stage of purchasing making the decision to buy. In this case, the butcher knows the customer wants a very good steak because the butcher noticed signs of interest (visual scrutiny, fiddling with the package, a furrowed brow). The questions are couched to remind the customer of why he or she wants the steak. This kind of query must come at that moment of hesitancy, when logic has nearly toppled the idea of making the purchase. Otherwise, it is best to keep quiet!

A person's body language can be most telling, like reading a book. Salespeople should watch their clients with an eye toward recognizing signs of stress. Everyone goes through moments of hesitancy when it comes to spending money. Buying can be stressful, especially when the purchase represents a sizable amount of the family budget like buying a car, house, or even a porterhouse steak! The cost of an item versus

eClean Magazine

the affordability of that item can be painful. Salespeople should offer relief. Relief takes the form of justification—if the customer needs the item, help them justify the purchase.

I can feel your question on the back of my neck. What does porterhouse steak have to do with cleaning? Selling is all the same, my friends, whether it's a porterhouse steak or the chance to pressure wash five thousand square feet of concrete. A cleaning company must depict itself professionally just as any other business. I

contend that every person involved is a salesperson, the face of the company. Not only do the janitors and maids need to look and act professionally on the job, but the management must learn to be good representatives. The fuel

of Sales drives the motor of every company except those businesses run by the government. Government agencies don't need sales to stay in business, only taxpayers. Meanwhile, the rest of us must make sales— and pay the taxes!

Selling is a combination of art, science, and religion. Good salespeople are moral in their dealings with others, so they don't take advantage of client's indecisions to push products or services that aren't really needed. Salespeople should know their offerings thoroughly, like medical doctors who understand details of anatomy necessary to triage, diagnose, a prescribe remedies for physical maladies. Finally, a product demonstration or display should have the qualities of a masterpiece—understandable theme, emotional evocation, and satisfaction through purchase. What? You mean you've never cleaned a trial area to prove the capabilities of your company? Samples are a sales tool. Give them out!

Never let price be the overriding factor in selling products and services. Allow the benefits to be shown to a potential buyer in a manner that brings out the emotions necessary to make the decision to purchase. Be attentive for a client's stressful moment of indecision and help channel that stress into a buying decision using empathetic questions. "Wow! That floor shined right up, didn't it? That section of brick we cleaned sure does pop, doesn't it?" Know when to shut up. Too much input at that final indecisive moment can cause the loss of the sale. The salesperson who talks too much is usually labeled "pushy." Be helpful instead.

Selling is far more than a simple job. It's a profession – one that every cleaning agency must tackle to stay in business. Whoever represents your company in terms of garnering more business is the salesperson, whether the owner, manager, or janitor. Most salespeople do not approach their jobs as professionals, though. Like all professionals, salespeople must study and become experts on their products and services, bone up on sales techniques, become better observers, and listen carefully. When a purchaser has greater skills in these areas, it is far easier for the "no" word to slip out. "The price is too high," is rarely the true reason for not buying. Instead, it should be considered a question as to what value you offer against the price you ask. Buyers must justify the price they pay— otherwise, money could get wasted, jobs lost, heads rolled.

Negative responses should always be viewed as a desire for more information rather than a brick wall. If a customer truly wants something, can afford it, and turns it down, shame on the salesperson that didn't learn enough to close the sale! It doesn't really matter who in your company asks a potential client for business. What does matter is that person must understand the dynamics of making the sale. There's a world of information out there available on the subject of Selling. Start studying if you wish to survive and thrive in the World of Clean!

WJTA-IMCA Announces New Strategic Plan

The WaterJet Technology Association-Industrial & Municipal Cleaning Association (WJTA-IMCA) announces details of its new strategic plan. "As the largest association dedicated to waterjet technology, industrial cleaning and industrial vacuuming, we take our commitment to developing and improving the industry very seriously," says association Chairman Bill Gaff.

"While the mission, vision and core values of the association remain much the same as when WJTA was founded," says founding member and association President George A. Savanick, Ph.D., "they have been updated to reflect WJTA-IMCA's growing global presence, the continuing evolution of the waterjet industry, today's technology-driven communications, and the new and dynamic ways WJTA-IMCA will interact with its members."

WJTA-IMCA's goals include:

Safety – Providing and promoting best practices in health and safety for the waterjetting and industrial vacuuming industries.

Membership Growth – Growing and sustaining our membership in the primary industries and sector targets of our stakeholder audience.

Conference & Expo – Designing and offering our Conference and Expo in a format and with content that drives high participation from our industries and sector targets.

Financial Stability – Responsibly managing the finances of our association, ensuring our valued contribution to our members.

Information Delivery – Ensuring accessibility to our resources and content to our members.

Technology Development – Disseminating new technology and automation and supporting academic focus on the areas of interest and benefit to our members.

Training – Providing high quality and relevant training and documentation to our membership.

Networking – Fostering trade and promoting learning and engagement within our industry sectors.

"This new strategic plan sets the vision for the organization and will help keep us focused on the future for the benefit of our members and for the betterment of the industry," ays Savanick.

Classifieds

www.ArmClark.com
Armstrong Clark Quality Wood Stains. Specializing in wood restoration, oil-based coatings for wood & non-toxic wood stains of all kinds for your wood shake restoration & water repellent needs. □00-□1□-□□11

www.PowerWash.com
Mobile power wash equipment, schools, training, videos, environmental supplies & maintenance services. Call for a free catalog, □00-□□□-□11□.

www.PowerWashStore.com
Bigger Selection - Better Quality - Amazing Customer Service. Serving the professional cleaning community for more than □□ years. Call □□□-□□1-□□□□.

www.PWNA.org
Power Washers of North America. For certification or membership information, visit our website, email info□pwna.org, or call □00-□□□-□□□□.

www.SteelEagle.com
Mfr. of World Class Industrial & Commercial Cleaning & Storage Products, including surface spinners, vacuum systems, undercarriage cleaners, hose reels & more. Custom designs available. □00-□□□-□□□□

www.PressureWasherKy.us
Southside Equipment multi-line power equipment distributor. Pressure cleaning equipment, waste water recovery & recycling, generators & cleaning chemicals. Quality products & impeccable service. □□□-□□□-□□0

To Advertise in our New Classifieds Section
Contact Allison Hester at allison□ecleanmag.com

How to Write a Fabulous Vision Statement

by Susan L. Reid

Many people mistakenly think vision statements and mission statements are one and the same. They haven't really stopped to consider what the purpose of a vision statement is or why having one could be an asset.

Vision statements are meant to be big and bold. They're meant to inspire, energize, and create a captivating picture of where you see your business going in the future.

If you don't write a vision statement, your business will be without direction. When you complete one, your vision statement will then supply the inspiration for the daily operations of your business and motivation for its strategic decisions.

Every business needs a vision statement. Want to make sure you've written a great one? Just follow these guidelines, fill out the vision statement formula at the end of this article, and you will have created a vision statement that clearly articulates the future of your business and paints a vivid picture for its success!

What's the difference between a vision statement and a mission statement?

Top Five Things to Keep in Mind When Writing Your Vision Statement

1. **Describe outcomes that are five to ten years out.**

2. **Dream big and focus on success.**

3. **Write your vision statement in the present tense, as if it has already happened.**

4. **Infuse your vision statement with passion.**

5. **Paint a graphic mental picture of the business you want.**

There is no space limit when writing a vision statement. They often contain one or more paragraphs. Write as much as you need to in order to create a dynamic mental picture of your business that will serve to energize and inspire you and your team.

Vision and mission statements are two separate entities that answer two different questions about your business. Questions that are complementary in nature.

Simply put, your vision statement answers the question, "Where do I see my business going?" Your mission statement answers the question, "Why does my business exist?"

From the start, vision statements are future-focused and written with the end result in mind. Mission statements are focused in the present and state the fundamental purpose of your business.

Which comes first—the vision or the mission?

If you are a new business just starting up, a larger company getting ready to add a new program, or an existing organization planning to overhaul your current services, then write your vision statement first.

If you are an established business with a mission statement already in place, then let your mission guide the writing of your vision statement.

Two Vision Statement Formulas for Success

Here are two basic vision statement formulas. The first one is for any business starting up without a mission statement. The second is for businesses that already have a mission statement in place.

1. Five years from now, _____ (name of your business) will become a successful _____ (type or description of business including whether it will be local, regional, national, or international in its scope) by providing _____ (description of your products and/or services) to _____ (your customers).

2. Within the next _____ (add a number) years, grow _____ (name of your business) into a successful _____ (type or description of business including whether it will be local, regional, national, or international in its scope), increasing revenues to _____ (amount) by _____ (date) providing _____ (description of your products and/or services) to _____ (your customers).

Your vision statement sets the tone for your business. It defines its future. It inspires, energizes, motivates, and, above all else, describes what will be achieved if your business is successful. It is nearly impossible to plan the direction of your business without one. Follow these guidelines, and use the vision statement formula to perfectly articulate your dream, your passion, and the direction you envision for your business.

Dr. Susan L. Reid is a business coach and consultant for entrepreneurial women starting up businesses. She is the author of "Discovering Your Inner Samurai: The Entrepreneurial Woman's Journey to Business Success."

The International Window Cleaning Association
Annual Convention & Trade Show
February 12-15, 2014 • The Peabody Hotel • Memphis, TN

celebrating 25 years

The Annual Convention & Trade Show brings together more than 400 professional window cleaning companies from around the globe. Learn from colleagues how to grow your business! Attend the educational seminars, hands-on demonstrations and hands-on safety training to keep you and your employees current with OSHA regulations and American National Standards. Equipment vendors, manufacturers of products and suppliers in the window cleaning industry will be on hand and demonstrating the latest tools for window cleaners.

Visit www.IWCA.org for more information.

If you are interested in exhibiting, complete the exhibitor prospectus and return it to IWCA at Info@IWCA.org. Questions can be directed to the IWCA Business Office at 800-845-4922, ext. 3351.

IWCA Announces 25th Annual Convention & Trade Show Schedule

The International Window Cleaning Association (IWCA) is hard at work planning an amazing 25th Anniversary Convention, February 12-15 in Memphis, Tennessee. Next month, we will a take an in-depth look at the convention and the association. For now, however, readers can get a glimpse of what to expect by reviewing the convention's (tentative) schedule.

Wednesday, February 12, 2014
?:?0 - ?:00 am — First Time Attendee Coffee

?:00 - 10:?0 am — Breakfast with Keynote Speaker Andres Gutierrez

11:00 am - Noon
- Understanding the Dynamics of Your Team
- Water?ed Pole Safety
- Don Chute's Tips and Tricks

1:?00 - ?:00 pm — Women in Industry Luncheon

1:?1? - ?:1? pm
- ADP
- Highrise Panel ? ? A
- Professional Image Competition

?:?0 - ?:?0 pm
- Successor Plan for Your Business
- Highrise Panel ? ? A continues
- Window Restoration — Mineral Deposits

?:?? - ?:00 pm — Outdoor demonstrations

?:00 - 11:00 pm — Welcome "Jam" Reception

Thursday, February 13, 2014
?:00 - ?:00 am — Breakfast Roundtables

?:1? - 10:?1? a.m.
- Sunbelt Rentals Permit ? Lift Training (Classroom)
- Hiring?iring Practices
- Multiply Your Profits with Power Washing ? Roof Cleaning
- Highrise Safety - Tips Tiebacks and Knots

10:?1? am - 11:?1? am
- Ronald McDonald House Cleaning
- Insurance — What You Need and Should Know
- Residential ?? A Session

11:?0 am - ?:?0 pm — Tradeshow Opens

1:00 - ?:00 pm — Sunbelt Rentals Permit ? Lift Training (Outdoors)

?:?0 – ?:?0 pm — Equipment Showcase

?:00 - ?:00 pm — Happy Hour with Exhibitors

?:?0 - ?:?0 pm — Speed and Medley Contest

Friday, February 14, 2014
?:00 - ?:00 am — Breakfast Roundtables

?:?0 am - 1:00 pm — Tradeshow Opens

1:?0 - 1:?0 pm
- Getting the Most out of Quickbooks
- Residential Safety Do's ? Don'ts
- Marketing — What Works ?or ?s

1:?? - ?:?? pm
- Best Business Apps

1:?? - ?:00 pm
- How Your Business can Benefit from OSHA
- The Science of Glass

?:00 - ?:00 pm — Sunbelt Lift Certification"

?:00 - ?:00 pm — Past President's Reception ? Cocktail Reception
?:00 - ?:00 pm — Auction ? Awards Reception
?:00 - 11:00 pm — President's Party

Saturday, February 15, 2014
?:00 am - ?:00 pm — Safety Training

1:00 pm - ?:00 pm — Certification Exam

1:00 - ?:00 pm — Outdoor Training

Business Owners Will Take on New Roles in 2014

by Peter Williamson

Many business owners haven't even begun to think about the new year. They're too busy trying to get through this one. How to reach customers in the most effective manner is a significant challenge of all business owners and their marketing teams.

Being Top Dog affords business owners a certain status and independence, but the irony is that the effectiveness of their interdependence plays a huge role in whether a business owner will succeed or fail.

Where once the business owner had control, now the customer is in the driver's seat, but all that means is that business owners must stand back, look at what their new roles are, and adapt.

Four new roles business owners will find themselves in include:

As **balancer**, business owners focused much of their efforts on the internal workings of their company, including:

• Balancing budgets
• Balancing time
• Balancing family with business

The new role of business managers involves balancing a whole new entity—customers. What does this entail? A consistent, unified, and appealing message, that's what. While business is quite a juggling act, owners must be aware of the new role of the customer. They (the customer) have more power now than ever before in history to determine the direction and success of your business. Balancing your needs with your customer wants and desires is a must.

The Internet certainly has opened avenues of communication to literally millions. Just as the role of balancer has required business owners to be more actively involved with both the internal and external functions of business, as **navigators**, they must be able to help departments communicate interdependently with each other, and they must help customers navigate through their "systems" effectively and efficiently to make getting information and ordering products or services as easy as humanly possible.

Business owner must put tools in place to *educate* the customer to trends, processes, services, and products that can make their lives better in some way. By the same token, they must put employee handbooks, training guides, and educational workshops, seminars, and training in place for their employees.

Many business owners are in a "learn as I go" existence. They had a great idea for a product or service, did not want to be someone's employee, and "took hold of the reins" in starting their own business. The problem is, most found themselves tethered to their businesses □□□, ironically becoming the employee to their own company! So, again, this role is twofold□The successful business owner must always read and keep up on new processes, theories, developments, and innovations to keep his or her mind sharp. They must keep an open mind to new ideas and let go of age-old practices of "my way or the highway" thinking.

Running a business need not involve running out of steam. The best way to prevent that from happening is to prepare. Start the New Year with a new attitude, beginning with a mantra□Seeking Help is Not A Sign of Weakness.

Key areas most business owners need help with include□

Lead generation

Effective advertising

Phone scripts that are natural and lead-generating

Developing a "Rave □an" referral system

Improving sales

Developing more effective strategies to get back former customers

Increasing Average Dollar Sale and Margins

Creating a step-by-step development plan with clear-cut goals

Developing a stronger and more efficient "team"

Time management

Automation of systems for efficiency

It may seem like the New Year is way in the future, but it's almost upon us, and it's time to start laying the groundwork now for success around the corner.

Why not start a □0-day plan NOW. Then, on March 1, □01□ you will already be off to a roaring start. You can then review your plan. How'd you do? What worked? What needs revising?

Once that process starts, you've begun your next □0-day plan. Talk about getting a head of the game.

The bottom line□Play like the pros. Anticipate. □se Effective Strategies. And take Action.

Peter Williamson, Business Coach and Master Licensee, helps you find instant and lasting solutions to boost your profits by 61% or more - guaranteed. Email peterwilliamson@actioncoach.comnn For advice and access to proven systems that will advance your business, visit hwww.actioncoachcalteam.com/ and www.

eClean Magazine

Pressure Washing Services: A Fresh, Clean Start To The Year

by Paul Horsley, Publisher

If your New Year's resolution is to enhance your company's image, the simplest technique, and one with an instant payoff, is often the most overlooked—pressure washing. Whether you own a retail business, head a trucking company, work in the construction industry or run with the rail industry, there are many reasons to take advantage of what power washing can do for your business.

Pressure Washing for Commercial Buildings and Properties

Appearance is everything. A clean environment possesses an air of safety and value, whereas a dirty warehouse or a building coated with grime suggests an air of neglect – as if the business owners do not take pride in how they appear to the public.

Pressure washing for commercial buildings and warehouses is a fast and reliable way to enhance your company's reputation. Because pressure washing can clean surfaces like brick, wood, metal and concrete much more easily and thoroughly than other methods, it's one of the most cost-effective ways to spruce up a storefront or other commercial building. Pressure washing for commercial buildings not only makes your facility more attractive to customers, but it improves the environment for employees or tenants, as well.

Pressure Washing for Construction Sites

There are few vehicles that attract as much dirt, rocks, muck and grunge as the heavy equipment at a construction site. Within a matter of days – and even, in some cases, a matter of hours – construction equipment can get all gunked up. If there is excessive rubbish on the equipment, it might compromise the machine's capacity to function properly, and that can pose several risks such as employee injuries, machine malfunctions and the delay of necessary work.

Regularly pressure washing these large, heavy and necessary machines can minimize some of these safety and efficiency issues on the work site and will keep your crew working like clockwork. Pressure washing for heavy machinery may also lengthen the working life of your equipment, as it will help mechanics more easily spot any number of malfunctions, leaks or issues the machine may have.

Pressure Washing for Trains

Rail cars pick up a lot of dust and dirt while barreling along the tracks. Unfortunately, cleaning a 100-car metal serpent is no simple task without a pressure washer. Pressure washing for trains can save a huge amount of cleaning time by getting rail cars back on track in a matter of one or two days.

Trains are also graffiti magnets. As they coast alongside the highway, they can expose passersby to a whole host of gang tags, vulgarities and other messages from vandals. Fortunately, pressure washing for trains is effective at removing even the nastiest graffiti marks—the right power washing company can even apply an anti-graffiti coat, which makes future cleanup twice as easy.

Pressure Washing for Trucks and Fleets

Trucks are moving advertisements for your company. If they're thick with dirt, grey from exhaust and coated with flaky bug bodies, your business will project an image of sloppiness. Pressure washing for trucks is a safety issue, as well. Clean trucks are more visible to other cars, and they're also much easier to maintain properly, as grime can often conceal leaks or other mechanical problems until it's too late.

Pressure washing for commercial buildings, trucks, rail cars and construction equipment can benefit your company in various ways. Most notably, it can boost the image of your business by giving you a good, clean leg to stand on. So in the coming New Year, when you're planning a strategy for improving your company's position within the economy, make a resolution that is easy to achieve, environmentally friendly, and reliable—regular power washing.

www.ingramcontent.com/pod-product-compliance
Lightning Source LLC
Chambersburg PA
CBHW080232180526
45167CB00006B/2252